The Growing Child

The Growing Child

Helen Bee

HarperCollinsCollegePublishers

Acquisitions Editor: *Jill Lectka*
Developmental Editor: *Becky Kohn*
Cover Illustration/Photograph: *Kotoh/Zefa/H. Armstrong Roberts*
Photo Researcher: *Rosemary Hunter*
Electronic Production Manager: *Eric Jorgensen*
Project Coordination, Text and Cover Design: *Thompson Steele Production Services*
Electronic Page Makeup: *Thompson Steele Production Services*
Printer and Binder: *RR Donnelley & Sons Company*
Cover Printer: *The Lehigh Press, Inc.*

For permission to use copyrighted material, grateful acknowledgment is made to the copyright holders on pp. 485, which are hereby made part of this copyright page.

The Growing Child

Library of Congress Cataloging-in-Publication Data
Bee, Helen L., 1939–
    The growing child/Helen Bee.
    p.   cm.
    Includes index.
    ISBN 0-673-99359-0
    1. Child development.   I. Title.
HQ767.9.B43   1995
305.23'1—dc20   94-37748
                                                      CIP

94 95 96 97 9 8 7 6 5 4 3 2 1   3/94

To Anne, whose idea this was,

and to Becky, who made it possible.

Brief Contents

Contents

Chapter 4

Physical Development in Infancy   97

Chapter 5

Perceptual and Cognitive Development in Infancy   121

Chapter 6

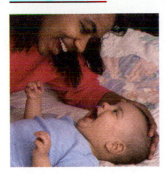

Social and Personality Development in Infancy   153

Interlude 1: Summing Up Infant Development   184

Chapter 7   Physical and Cognitive Development from 2 to 6   189

Chapter 8

Social and Personality Development from 2 to 6

223

Chapter 9

Chapter 10

Social and Personality Development from 6 to 12

295

Chapter 11

Physical Development in Adolescence   325

Chapter 12

Cognitive Development in Adolescence   351

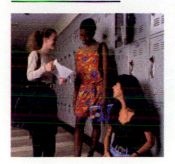

To the Student

Hello and welcome. Let me invite you into the study of a fascinating subject—children and their development. This is a bit like inviting you into my own home, since I have lived in the world of the study of children for a great many years. Unfortunately, I cannot know each of you individually, but by writing this book as if it were a conversation between you and me, I hope I can make the reading, and the studying of this subject, as personal a process as possible.

Because such personal involvement is one of my goals, you will find that I often write in the first person and that I have included a number of anecdotes about my own life. (One of the amusing side effects of this style of writing is that I often meet students from around the country who, having read this book, know all kinds of personal things about me and feel that they know me well, even though we have never met.)

Welcome, too, to the adventure of science. From the very first text I wrote, over 20 years ago, one of my goals has been to try to convey a sense of excitement about scientific inquiry. I want each of you to take away some feeling for the way psychologists think, the kinds of questions we ask, and the ways we go about trying to answer those questions. I also want you to take away with you some sense of the theoretical and intellectual ferment that is part of any science. Think of psychology as a kind of detective story. We discover clues after hard, often painstaking work; we make new guesses or hypotheses; and then we search for new clues to check on those hypotheses.

Of course, I also want you to come away from reading this book with a firm grounding of knowledge about child development. There is much that we do not yet know or understand. But a great many facts and observations have accumulated. These facts and observations will be of help to you professionally if you are planning (or are already in) a career with children—such as teaching, nursing, social work, medicine, or psychology; the information will also be useful to you as parents, now or in the future. There is much to be learned. In the midst of all that learning, though, I hope you enjoy the reading as much as I have enjoyed the writing.

Helen Bee

To the Instructor

For many years I have heard from instructors who tell me they would like to use my book, *The Developing Child*, but that they teach their courses chronologically and can't adapt to the topical format of that text. This first edition of *The Growing Child* is for them. It has the same personal voice, clear writing style, and basic content, but it follows a chronological oganization. Reorganizing the material in this way has been fascinating and challenging for me. I have learned a good deal in the process, and I hope that fascination is evident in this text.

Basic Goals

In this book, as in all the texts I have written, I have several basic goals:

1. To find that difficult but essential balance between theory, research, and practical application;
2. To make the study of child development relevant not just for psychologists but also for students in the many other fields in which this information is needed: nursing, medicine, social work, education, home economics;
3. To keep all discussions as current as humanly possible, so that students can encounter the very latest thinking, the most recent research;
4. To write to the student in as direct a way as possible, so that the book is more like a conversation than a traditional text. Such a personal style need not clash with either theoretical clarity or research rigor, both of which I continue to work hard to achieve.

In this text, as in the 7th edition of the topical text, *The Developing Child*, two additional goals have guided my work.

A Cultural Perspective. First and most important, I wanted to enrich the book throughout with discussions of the impact of culture on development. In the past, I think many of us have operated with the implicit assumption that we were studying or searching for basic developmental processes that would be the same for all children in all cultures. In such a search, it doesn't matter which specific children you study. There may well be some such basic processes, and certainly we will go on attempting to uncover them. But it has become more and more evident that we will understand development fully only when we also understand the immensely complex way in which the basic biological and psychological processes are embedded in the family, the neighborhood, an ethnic group, and the larger culture. Thus one of my key goals has been to infuse the entire book with this perspective. I've done this in several ways.

- There are several subtypes of boxes, including one group called *Cultures and Contexts*, which quite explicitly focus on cross-cultural research or on studies of ethnic subcultures.
- Throughout the text, I have drawn examples from research in countries other than the United States and have repeatedly raised the question of cross-cultural validity.
- I have added a discussion of cross-cultural research in the methods section of Chapter 1.

Controlling the Length. A second specific goal in this text has been, perhaps paradoxically, to keep the overall length of the book under some kind of control. With such a flood of new research and commentary each year, so many new research areas and topics under study, it is too easy just to keep adding and adding and adding. But students do not need an encyclopedic text; they need a text that lays out the issues clearly. I think I have done that.

Other Special Features

Critical Thinking Questions. Each chapter in the text contains 6 to 10 critical thinking questions, which appear in the margins at strategic points. Some ask the students to pause and consider a point before going on, or they ask the reader to consider how the material may apply to his or her own life. In other cases, they ask the student to think about how one could design a piece of research to answer a particular question. In still other instances they ask theoretical questions or ask the student to consider her or his own point of view on the subject at issue. These questions may be useful for provoking class discussion; it is also my hope that they will make the reading process more active and thus provide for deeper learning.

Student Projects. Another important feature is the set of student projects, although for this text (as for the 7th edition of the topical version) they appear in the Instructor's Manual rather than in the text itself. This change was suggested by a number of instructors who felt they could maintain far better control over the process of obtaining informed consent for the projects if they were in the IM, rather than in the text itself. The Instructor's Manual includes 3 types of projects:

- Fourteen *Research Projects*, each of which involves students' observing or testing one or more individual subjects of some age, such as listening to the language of a 2-year-old, or observing on a playground, or testing 5- or 6-year-olds with conservation problems.

- Four *At Home Projects*, each of which involves some analysis that students can do at home, without having to locate individual subjects or obtain any informed consent, such as analyzing aggression or sex roles on TV programs.
- Five *Investigative Projects*, each of which is designed for a single student or a small group of students to determine the availability of certain kinds of services within your own community, such as day-care options, birth options, or the like.

In order to make it possible for each instructor to select appropriate projects and to tailor the projects or the project instructions to his or her own needs, HarperCollins will also provide a computer disk containing all the projects.

Boxes. This text, like the new 7th edition of *The Developing Child*, contains many more boxes than I have used in previous texts. They are of several types:

- **Cultures and Contexts boxes** (N = 16) focus on two aspects of cross-cultural or cross-ethnic group research: evidence showing that basic developmental processes are the same in children or adults of every culture, and research cataloging the variations in life experience or developmental patterns as a function of culture or subcultural differences. An example of the first type is a box on common patterns of early language development around the world in Chapter 5; an example of the second type would be a box on ethnic identity in adolescence in Chapter 13.
- **Research Reports** (N = 19) are more detailed descriptions of individual research projects or highly specific research areas, such as Anne Streissguth's studies of fetal alcohol exposure (Chapter 3), or an analysis of recent evidence on the child as witness (Chapter 9), or an Australian study of sex differences in body image among adolescence (Chapter 11).
- **The Real World boxes** (N = 17) all explore some practical application of research or theory, such as a discussion of postpartum depression (Chapter 6), or the use of performance tests to assess school achievement (Chapter 9), or the application of Kohlberg's theory to education (Chapter 12).
- **Soap boxes** are the last and least common type. There are only three, one on the need for a family policy in the United States (Chapter 6), one on whether one ought to spank children (Chapter 8), and one on children living in inner-city poverty (Chapter 10). In each, I have expressed my own views.

Supplements

Naturally there are a variety of supplements available to the Instructor and the Student.

Instructor's Manual. The IM for this text is a variation of the one I prepared for the 7th edition of *The Developing Child*, rearranged and revised (ISBN 0-67-355783-9). It suggests a plan for an entire course using this text, including the preplanning, a sample syllabus, the organization of lectures, and lecture material for each chapter. For those of you who have taught this course many times, the planning detail will of course be unneeded, though I hope you may still find the lecture suggestions helpful. For those of you approaching the teaching of this course for the first time, the manual may be a timely form of assistance.

Included with the Instructor's Manual is also a set of transparency masters, some of which duplicate figures that appear in the text—to make it easier to review some figures in class. Many of the transparencies provide new data, designed to illustrate particular points you may cover in lecture.

Finally, there is a new film/video guide included in the Manual.

Test Bank. Written by Sharon Hawkins of the University of Southern Colorado, the test bank contains approximately 2,000 questions. Each of these multiple-choice and essay questions is referenced to page number, topic, and skill. Some also appear in the student study guide or SuperShell II software tutorial and are referenced as such.

Study Guide (ISBN 0-67-399361-2). Bill Cunningham of Thomas Nelson's Community College has written a comprehensive study guide. Each chapter contains a brief chapter outline, learning objectives, a definition of key terms, lists of key concepts and individuals, and three practice tests containing multiple-choice, matching, and fill-in-the-blank questions with their answers.

SuperShell II Student Tutorial (ISBN 0-67-397158-9). Supershell is an interactive computerized tutorial for IBM and IBM-compatible computers. In addition to chapter outlines and glossary terms, it provides immediate correct answers to multiple-choice, true-false and short answer questions. All of the material is referenced to the text page. It contains material not found in the study guide and provides a running score for students.

Software. Two forms of software are available with the test bank. TestMaster Computerized Testing System is a flexible, easy-to-master computerized test bank that includes all the test items in the printed test bank. The TestMaster software allows instructors to edit existing questions and add their own items. It is available in IBM or Macintosh formats.

QuizMaster is a new software program, available to instructors, that allows students to take TestMaster-generated tests on computer. QuizMaster gives the students their scores right away as well as a diagnostic report at the end of the test. This report lets the students know what topics or objectives they may need to study to improve their scores. Test scroes can be saved on disk, allowing instructors to keep track of scores for individual students, class sections, or whole courses.

Some Bouquets

In planning this chronological text, I was aided by the suggestions and comments of a number of reviewers who looked over the organizational plan ahead of time and pointed out problems or omissions. My thanks, as always, for their careful work:

S. A. Fenwick, *Augustana College*
Sharon Antonelli, *San Jose City College*
Jo Kuykendall, *University of Alaska*
Mick Coleman, *University of Georgia*
Patricia Stanley, *Louisiana State University, Shreveport*
Ellis Gesten, *University of South Florida*
Brad Caskey, *University of Wisconsin, River Falls*
Helen Swanson, *University of Wisconsin, Stout*
Bob Keller, *Kishwaukee College*
Olivia Eisenhauer, *Palo Alto College*
Pamela C. Griesler, *Rutgers University*
Lauren Shapiro, *University of North Carolina, Chapel Hill*

Special bouquets, also, to the HarperCollins staff, who have made this as easy as possible. Both Meg Holden and Jill Lectka have been very supportive and helpful in the role of acquisitions editor; Rosemary Hunter, the photo researcher, has once again done stellar work, on a tight schedule; and Becky Kohn, developmental editor extrordinaire, has taken on far more than her usual role with this book so that we could meet a speeded-up schedule without a hitch. She is a wonder, and I don't think I could survive without her.

Finally, to all the friends who bring laughter into my life, my profound thanks. The older I get, the more I realize how important those giggles and guffaws are in keeping me sane and eager to face each new day's writing.

Helen Bee

Chapter One

Basic Questions

Each summer, I spend several months at an unusual camp in the state of Washington, where adults of all ages as well as families with young children come each year to live for a short time in a kind of temporary community. Because many of the same people come back year after year, bringing their children (and often later their grandchildren), I see these growing children in once-a-year snapshots. When a family arrives, I am quite naturally struck by how much the children have changed, and I find myself saying to the kids, "Good grief, you've grown a foot," or "Last time I saw you, you were only this big." (I say these things, even remembering full well how much I hated it when people said these things to me at the same age. Of *course* I had grown. And because I was always taller than anyone my age, I didn't like to be reminded of this peculiarity.)

At the same time, I am also struck by the consistency in these kids from year to year. Sweet-tempered young Malcolm and ebullient Crystal always give me many hugs; Malcolm's older brother Elliot, far shyer, always begins by gazing at me silently from some measured distance. He warms up as the days go by, but his behavior is quite different from his brother's and remains noticeably constant from year to year, just as 13-year-old Stacey remains dreamy and a little slow-moving. Each of these children has a particular style, a particular set of skills, a particular personality, and these qualities appear to be at least somewhat consistent from year to year, perhaps even into adult life.

These simple examples illustrate one of the key points about human development: it involves both change and continuity. To understand development, we will need to look at both. Equally important, we need to understand which developmental changes and which types of consistency or continuity, are shared by individuals in all cultures, and which are unique to a given culture, to a group within a culture, or to a particular individual. For example, you probably know that in the first weeks after they are born, babies do not sleep through the night; they wake every two hours or so to be fed. But by about 6 weeks of age, most babies are able to string several two-hour stretches together and begin to show something approximating a day/night sleeping pattern (Bamford et al., 1990). That certainly sounds like a basic biological change, one that would occur in pretty much the same way regardless of the child's environment. But according to one study (Super & Harkness, 1982), babies in rural Kenya who are carried about by their mothers in a sling all day and fed on demand at night do not show any shift toward a nighttime sleep pattern over the first 8 months of life. So what seems like a universal, biological process turns out not to be universal at all. It is affected by culture—by attitudes and values expressed through variations in care and handling. This issue of what is universal and what is not will be a persistent theme.

This example also illustrates the point that to understand how development works, we will need to explore both *nature* and *nurture*, both biology and culture, and how they interact to explain both consistency and change. Throughout these chapters, I will be trying to sort out the relative impact of nature and nurture in each domain of development and at each age. That task will be a great deal easier if you have at least a grounding in some of the basic concepts and theories that form the framework for such an analysis. So let me take you on a quick tour of current ideas about nature and nurture.

In many parts of Kenya, babies are carried in slings all day, and allowed to nurse on demand at night. This cultural pattern, quite different from what we see in most western societies, seems to have an effect on the baby's sleep/wake cycle.

Nature and Nurture: An Ancient Debate

The argument about nature versus nurture, also referred to as heredity versus environment or nativism versus empiricism, is one of the oldest and most central theoretical issues within philosophy as well as psychology. When asked by developmental psychologists, the question is basically whether a child's development is governed by a pattern built in at birth, or whether it is shaped by experiences after birth. Historically, the nativist/nature side of the controversy was represented principally by Plato and (in the more modern era) René Descartes, both of whom believed that at least some ideas were innate. On the other side of the philosophical argument was found a group of British philosophers called "empiricists," such as John Locke, who insisted that at birth the mind is a blank slate, in Latin a *tabula rasa*. All knowledge, they argued, is created by experience.

No developmental psychologist today would cast this issue in such black-and-white terms. We agree that a child's development is a product of some interaction of nature and nurture. In every culture, puberty occurs sometime between roughly age 9 and age 16, but the timing is affected by such environmental factors as diet. Similarly, some temperamental patterns may be inherited, but they can be and are modified by the parents' style of caregiving. And so on. *No* aspect of development is entirely one or the other. Nonetheless, there is still a good deal of disagreement about the relative importance of these two factors.

Because of this disagreement, and because it is easier to introduce the various concepts separately, I'll begin by talking about each of the two halves of this dichotomy, saving for later the question of how nature and nurture interact.

> Think about your own patterns of behavior for a moment. Which ones do you think are the *most* governed by basic human biology (nature)? Which ones seem to be most a product of your environment, including your upbringing?

The Nature Side of the Equation

Inborn Biases and Constraints

Descartes' notion of inborn ideas has not totally disappeared from our thinking. The most modern version of it is the concept of "inborn biases," what psychologists sometimes call "constraints" on development. The argument is not that infants are born knowing many things, or that they have built-in concepts, but rather that the baby is "programmed" in some fashion to pay more attention to certain kinds of information or to respond in particular ways to objects. For example, Dan Slobin (Slobin, 1985b), who studies early language learning, proposes that children are born with certain "operating principles" that govern the way they listen to and try to make sense out of the flow of sounds coming at them. One such principle, according to Slobin, is the tendency to pay special attention to the beginnings and ends of strings of sounds. Similarly, in the study of infants' perceptual skills a number of researchers and theorists have emphasized built-in "rules babies look by" (Haith, 1980), such as paying attention to movement or to shifts between dark and light. Unlike Descartes, current theorists do not propose that these built-in response patterns are the end of the story; rather they are seen as the starting point. What then develops is a result of experience filtered through these initial biases. But those biases *constrain* the number of developmental pathways that are possible (Campbell & Bickhard, 1992).

Maturation

Nature can shape processes after birth in other ways as well; we see it most clearly through genetic programming that may determine whole sequences of later development. Arnold Gesell (Gesell, 1925; Thelen & Adolph, 1992) used the term **maturation** to describe such genetically programmed sequential patterns of change; and this term is still uniformly used today. Changes in body size and shape, in hormones at puberty, in muscles and bones, and in the nervous system all may be programmed in this way. You can probably remember your own physical changes during adolescence. The timing of these pubertal changes differs from one teenager to the next, but the basic sequence is essentially the same for all children. Such sequences, which begin at conception and continue until death, are shared by all members of our species. The instructions for these sequences are part of the specific hereditary information passed on at the moment of conception.

In its pure form, as Gesell described it, maturationally determined development occurs regardless of practice or training. You don't have to practice growing pubic hair; you don't have to be taught how to walk. In fact, it would take almost herculean efforts to *prevent* such sequences from unfolding. But even confirmed maturational theorists agree that experience has some effect. At a minimum, the powerful, apparently automatic, maturational patterns require at least some minimal environmental support, such as adequate diet and opportunity for movement and experimentation.

Specific experience may also interact with maturational patterns in intricate ways. For example, Greenough (Greenough, 1991) points to the fact that one of the proteins required for the development of the visual system is controlled by a gene whose action is only triggered by visual experience. In other words, the child needs *some* visual experience for the genetic program to operate. In normal development, of course, every (nonblind) child will have some such experience. But examples like this one tell us that maturational sequences do not simply "unfold" automatically. The system appears to be "ready" to develop along particular pathways, but it requires experience to trigger the movement.

I should point out that the term *maturation* does not mean quite the same thing as *growth*, although the two terms are sometimes used as if they were synonyms. *Growth* refers to some kind of step-by-step change in quantity, as in size, and it can occur either with or without an underlying maturational process. A child's body could grow because her diet has significantly improved, or it could grow because she is getting older. The first of these has no maturational component, while the second does. To put it another way, the term growth is a *description* of change, while the concept of maturation is one *explanation* of change.

Behavior Genetics

Both of the "nature" concepts I have described so far (inborn biases and maturation) are designed to account for patterns and sequences of development that are the *same* for all children. But nature also contributes to variations from one individual to the next, since genetic inheritance is individual as well as collective. The study of genetic contributions to individual behavior, **behavior genetics,** has become a particularly vibrant and influential research area in recent years. Behavior geneticists have shown that specific heredity affects a remarkably broad range of behaviors, including physical characteristics such as height or body shape, cognitive abilities like IQ, personality characteristics, and even pathological behavior—all of which I'll talk more about in the next chapter. For now, the crucial point is that this new behavior genetic research leaves no doubt about the pivotal importance of inherited tendencies or characteristics in explaining individual differences among children and adults. Each of us is clearly born with certain built-in tendencies and characteristics that will affect our behavior, the choices we will make, and the way others will respond to us.

The Nurture Side of the Equation

Models of Environmental Influence

Concepts on the nurture side of this ancient dispute have also become considerably more subtle and complex. One particularly helpful analysis of the potential impact of environment has come from Richard Aslin (1981a), who suggests five models of influence, shown schematically in Figure 1.1. In each drawing the dashed line represents the path of development of some skill or behavior that would occur without a particular experience; the solid line represents the path of development if the experience were added.

For comparison purposes, the first of the five models actually shows a maturational pattern with *no* environmental effect. The second model, which Aslin calls *maintenance*, describes a pattern in which some environmental input is necessary to sustain a skill or behavior that has already developed maturationally. For example, kittens are born with full binocular vision, but if you cover one eye for a period of time, binocular skill declines. Similarly, muscles will atrophy if not used.

The third model shows a *facilitation* effect of the environment in which a skill or behavior develops earlier than it normally would because of some experience. For example, children whose parents talk to them more often, using more complex sentences, in the first 18–24 months of life appear to develop two-word sentences and other early grammatical forms somewhat earlier than do children talked to less. But less-talked-to children catch up shortly thereafter, so there is no permanent gain.

When a particular experience does lead to a permanent gain or to a higher level of performance, Aslin would call it *attunement*, which is his fourth model. For example, children born to poverty-level families who attend special enriched day care in infancy and early childhood have consistently higher IQs throughout childhood than do children from the same kinds of families who do not have such enriched experience.

Aslin's final model, *induction*, describes a pure environmental effect; without some experience a particular behavior would not develop at all. Giving a child tennis lessons or exposing him to a second language would fall into this category.

These five models illustrate the greater complexity of current thinking about nature/nurture issues. But they still do not take us far enough. At least

The preschool program Head Start was designed, several decades ago, to improve the school preparation of children growing up in poor families. Which of Aslin's models do you think best describes what the designers of Head Start thought (or hoped) would be the result of the program?

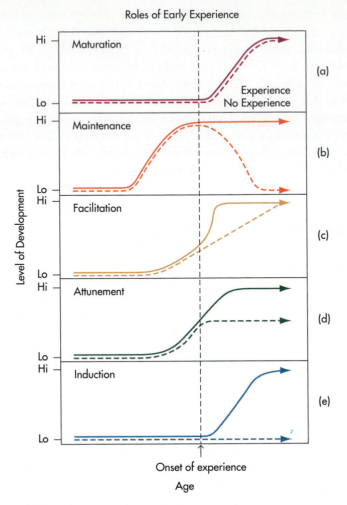

FIGURE 1.1

Five models of possible relationships between maturation and environment, as proposed by Aslin. The top model shows a purely maturational effect; the bottom model (induction) shows a purely environmental effect. The other three show interactive combinations: **maintenance,** in which experience prevents the deterioration of a maturationally developed skill; **facilitation,** in which experience speeds up the development of some maturational process; and **attunement,** in which experience increases the ultimate level of some skill or behavior above the "normal" maturational level. (Source: Aslin, 1981, p. 50.)

three other aspects of the environmental side of the equation are also significant in current thinking about development: the timing of experience, the child's own interpretation of experience, and the total ecological/cultural system in which experiences occur.

The Timing of Experience

Just as the importance of nature may vary from one time in development to another, so the timing of specific experiences may matter as well. The impact of day care on an infant may be quite different when he is 6 months old than when he is 16 months old; moving from one school to another may have a different effect if it coincides with puberty than if it does not, and so forth.

Our thinking about the importance of timing was stimulated, in part, by research on other species that showed specific experiences had different, or stronger effects, at some points in development than at others. The most famous example is that baby ducks will become *imprinted* (become attached to and follow) any duck or any other quacking, moving object that happens to be around them 15 hours after they hatch. If nothing is moving or quacking at that critical point, they don't become imprinted at all (Hess, 1972). So the period just around 15 hours after hatching is a **critical period** for the duck's development of a proper following response.

We can see similar critical periods in the action of various **teratogens** in prenatal development. A teratogen is some outside agent, such as a disease organism or chemical, which if present during prenatal development, adversely affects the process of that development. While some teratogens can have negative consequences at any time in gestation, most have effects only during some critical period. For example, if a mother contracts the disease rubella (commonly called German measles) during a narrow range of days in the first 3 months of pregnancy, some damage or deformity occurs in the fetus. Infection with the same virus after the third month of pregnancy has no such effect.

In the months after birth, too, there seem to be critical periods in brain development—specific weeks or months during which the child needs to encounter certain types of stimulation or experience for the nervous system to develop normally and fully (Hirsch & Tieman, 1987).

Psychologists also widely use the broader and somewhat looser concept of a **sensitive period.** A sensitive period is a span of months or years during which a child may be particularly responsive to specific forms of experience, or particularly influenced by their absence. For example, the period from 6 to 12 months of age may be a sensitive period for the formation of a core attachment to the parents. Other periods may be particularly significant for intellectual development or language (Tamis-LeMonda & Bornstein, 1987).

If the first year of life is a sensitive period for the establishment of a secure attachment (as some contend), then is it risky for a child of this age to be separated from her parents every day in day care? There is a hot debate among psychologists on this point.

Internal Models of Experience

Another concept appearing more and more prominently in our theoretical reper-toire is that of an internal model of experience. The key idea is that the effect of some experience lies in an individual's *interpretation* of it, the *meaning* the individual attaches to it, rather than any objective properties of the experience. You can easily come up with every-day examples from your own life. For instance, if a friend says something to you that he thinks is innocuous but that you take as a criticism, what matters for your experience is how you interpreted the comment, not how he meant it. If you regularly hear criticism in other people's comments, we would say that you have an internal model of yourself and others that includes a basic expectation that might be something like this: "I usually do things wrong so other people criticize me," or "No matter how hard I try, people are always critical of me."

Theorists who emphasize the importance of such meaning systems argue that each child creates a set of internal models—a set of assumptions or conclu-sions about the world, about himself, and about relationships with others—through which all subsequent experience is filtered (Epstein, 1991). John Bowlby (Bowlby, 1969; Bowlby, 1980) expressed this idea when he talked about the child's "internal working model" of attachment. A child with a secure model of attachment may assume that someone will come when he cries, and that affec-tion and attention are reliably available. A child with a less-secure model may assume that if a grown-up frowns it probably means she will be yelled at. These expectations are based on actual experiences, to be sure, but once formed into an internal model, they generalize beyond the original experience and affect the way the child interprets future experiences. A child who expects adults to be reliable and affectionate will be more likely to interpret the behavior of new adults in this way and will re-create friendly and affectionate relationships with others outside the family; a child who expects hostility will read hostility into otherwise fairly neutral encounters.

Such a view of the pathway or mechanism of environmental effects is not yet dominant in developmental psychology, but has gained importance in recent years.

The Ecological Perspective

A third facet of current thinking about environmental effects is a growing emphasis on casting a wider environmental net. Until quite recently, most research on environmental influences focused on a child's family (frequently only the child's mother), perhaps on playmates or on some proximate inanimate stim-ulation such as toys. If we looked at a larger family context at all it was usually in terms of the general wealth or poverty of the family.

In the past 10 or 15 years, however, there has been a strong push to widen our scope, to consider the *ecology* or *context* in which each child develops. Urie Bronfenbrenner, one of the key figures in this area (1979; 1989), emphasizes that each child grows up in a complex social environment (a social ecology) with a distinct cast of characters: brothers, sisters, one or both parents, grandparents, baby-sitters, pets, schoolteachers, and friends. And this cast is itself embedded within a larger social system; the parents have jobs that they may like or dislike;

they may have close and supportive friends or they may be quite isolated; they may be living in a safe neighborhood or one full of dangers; the local school may be excellent or poor; and the parents may have good or poor relationships with the school. Bronfenbrenner's argument is that we must not only include descriptions of these more extended aspects of the environment in our research, we must also understand the ways in which all the components of this complex system interact with one another.

A particularly nice example of research that examines such a larger system of influences is Gerald Patterson's work on the origins of antisocial behavior in children (Patterson, DeBarsyshe, & Ramsey, 1989a). His studies show that parents who use poor discipline techniques and poor monitoring of the child are more likely to have noncompliant or antisocial children. Once the child has established an antisocial behavior pattern, this pattern has repercussions in other areas of his life, leading to both peer rejection and academic difficulty. These problems, in turn, are likely to push the young person toward a deviant peer group and still further delinquency (Dishion et al., 1991; Vuchinich, Bank, & Patterson, 1992). So a pattern that began in the family is maintained and exacerbated by interactions with peers and with the school system.

But it is not enough even to look at these settings. We also have to understand which parents are likely to use poor disciplinary techniques, and why. Patterson finds that those parents who were themselves raised using poor disciplinary practices are more likely to use those same poor strategies with their children. But even parents who possess good basic child-management skills may fall into poor patterns when the stresses in their own lives increase. A recent divorce or period of unemployment increases the likelihood that parents will use poor disciplinary practices and thus increases the likelihood that the child will develop a pattern of antisocial behavior. Figure 1.2 shows Patterson's conception

How would you describe the ecology of your own childhood? What sort of family? What sort of neighborhood and school? What other significant people were in your life? What significant events affected your parents' lives?

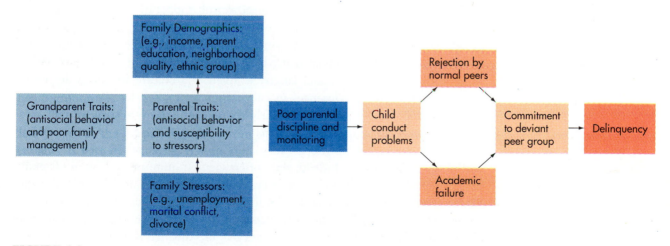

FIGURE 1.2

Patterson's model describes the many factors that influence the development of delinquency. The core of the process, in this model, is the interaction between the child and the parent. One might argue that the origin of delinquency lies in that relationship. But Patterson argues that there are larger ecological or contextual forces that are also "causes" of the delinquency. (Source: Patterson, 1989, Figures 1 and 2, pp. 331, 333.)

of how these various components fit together. Clearly, by taking into account the larger social ecological system in which the family is embedded, our understanding of the process is greatly enhanced.

Cultural Influences.   What is missing from Bronfenbrenner's and Patterson's formulations is any mention of the still-broader concept of **culture.** There is no commonly agreed-upon definition for this term, but in essence it describes some *system of meanings and customs,* including values, attitudes, goals, laws, beliefs, and morals, as well as physical artifacts of various kinds—tools and forms of dwellings, for example. Furthermore, this system of meanings and customs must be *shared by some identifiable group,* whether that group is a subsection of some population or a larger unit, and *transmitted from one generation of that group to the next* (Betancourt & Lopez, 1993; Cole, 1992). Families and children are clearly embedded in culture, just as they are located within an ecological niche in the culture—a set of relationships depicted in simplified form in Figure 1.3.

The figure also suggests that within a broad culture there may be subcultures of various types, often linked to membership in one or another **ethnic group,** defined as "a subgroup whose members are perceived by themselves and others to have a common origin and culture, and shared activities in which the common origin or culture is an essential ingredient. (Porter & Washington, 1993, p. 140). In the United States, there are myriad such subgroups and subcultures; in the school systems in Los Angeles, New York, and Chicago, for example, there are more than 100 separate languages spoken.

Note, by the way, that *race* and *ethnicity* are not the same. Ethnicity refers primarily to social and cultural characteristics, while race normally designates a group with specific physical characteristics. Thus we may view Hispanic-, African-, and Asian-Americans as both ethnic and racial categories, while we would consider Polish-Americans or Italian-Americans only as ethnic groups.

Most of us are only aware of the powerful impact of culture or subculture when we find ourselves outside our own cultural milieu. My own awareness was greatly enhanced by a year spent living in Germany in 1992–1993. My goal had been to learn German, which is my husband's native tongue, but I learned a lot more about culture than about language. Even in a culture so outwardly similar to U.S. culture, small differences in cultural patterns often left me feeling dislocated and uncertain. Consider one fairly trivial example. As an American, I quite naturally smiled at strangers I might pass while out walking on one of the many special paths crisscrossing the country. Yet those I met rarely made eye contact and never smiled at me. Indeed, they often seemed quite put off by my friendliness. I experienced their behavior as coldness and felt quite isolated by the experience, even when my logical mind told me that it was merely a different cultural pattern. Experiences like this convinced me that Sapir was right when he said: "The worlds in which different societies live are distinct worlds, not merely the same world with different words attached" (Sapir, 1929, p. 209).

Studying culture and subculture is important for our understanding of child development for a whole host of reasons, but two are particularly clear. First, if we are going to uncover those developmental patterns or processes that are truly universal, it is not enough to study white American middle-class children and

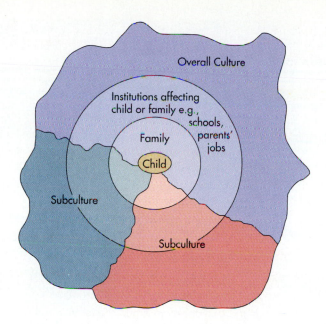

Overall Culture

Institutions affecting
child or family e.g.,
schools,
parents'
jobs

Family

Child

Subculture

Subculture

FIGURE 1.3

An ecological perspective in schematic form. Bronfenbrenner emphasizes the central three
rings; in recent years psychologists have also begun to look more specifically at culture and
subculture as elements in the equation.

assume that what we see in their development is true for all children. If we think
we have uncovered some basic sequence or process, we need to observe or test
children from a variety of subcultural or cultural groups, from as wide an array of
cultures as possible, to check on the universality of the developmental pattern.
Researchers have done this in some areas already, such as cross-cultural studies of
language development, moral development, and attachment. But such work is
only beginning in most other areas.

As part of this first task, we also need to discover whether the *relationship*
between some environmental event and the outcome for the child is the same in
all cultures. For example, in a recent study in Egypt, Ted Wachs and his colleagues (Wachs et al., 1993) found that in those families in which the parents
talked a lot to their babies, the children were later rated as more competent—a
result that closely parallels the relationship between these two variables found in
studies in the United States.

But in other cases, the same relationships may *not* hold across cultures or
subcultures. For example, an African-American pediatrician, Ronald David, has
recently pointed out (Lambert, 1993) that the relationship between the availability of prenatal care and the rate of infant mortality is not the same in the
Mexican-American subculture as in the African-American subculture. Among
Mexican-Americans, he reports, poverty is *not* associated with high infant mortality, while among African-Americans it is. Such a difference obviously has
implications not only for our understanding of culture, but also at a practical
level for any attempt to design an appropriate intervention to reduce infant
mortality.

CULTURES & CONTEXTS

Basic Values of Major Ethnic Groups in the United States

Figure 1.3 suggests that subcultures as well as overall cultural values may be significant for any given child's development. As an illustration, consider the different sets of values that characterize several minority ethnic cultures in the United States, as summarized recently by the American Psychological Association Commission on Violence and Youth (1993, p. 38–40):

African Americans

- Harmony and interrelatedness with nature
- Spirituality and strong religious orientation
- Communalism rather than individualism
- Child-centeredness, emphasizing the importance of the child to ensure the continuity of the family
- Flexibility of roles

Hispanics

- Preference for participating in groups (allocentrism)
- Strong adherence to family (familism)
- Avoidance of interpersonal conflict (simpatia)
- Deference and respect for authority systems

Asian and Pacific Island Americans

- Pacifism, self-control, and self-discipline linked to Confucianism, especially among Chinese, Korean, Vietnamese, and Japanese cultural groups

- A social order in which there is a hierarchy of interpersonal relations (i.e., parents are superior to children, men to women, and ruler to subject) and in which respect and "saving face" are highly valued
- Strong family ties, a link to ancestors, and expected obedience of the young to their elders
- Internal locus of control, with symbolism as a major cultural mechanism of control
- Strong cultural affiliation and bonding
- A strong work ethic and achievement motivation

Native Americans

- Harmony with and respect for nature
- Emphasis on family and tradition
- Emphasis on group cooperation rather than on individual achievement

If you were to make an equivalent list to describe the Anglo or majority American culture, what items would you list? What effects do you think these different sets of cultural values are likely to have on children growing up in a given subcultural group? How would a Hispanic child's experience differ from that of an Asian child, for example? We understand these effects only imperfectly as yet. But psychologists have increasingly realized that cultural variations such as these form significant backdrop for all of development.

A second reason to study culture is that if we are to understand "nurture," surely we must understand culture as part of the environment in which the child is growing up. How is children's development changed by cultural variations, as in the example of "sleeping through the night" I already mentioned? How do different cultural values affect the way children experience their childhood and adolescence? For instance, one feature of the majority American culture is a powerful emphasis on individual freedom, independence, and achievement. Some have argued that one consequence of this value is a much higher level of tolerance of aggression and violence than is true in other cultures (Lore & Schultz, 1993). Such tolerance, in turn, may well be one factor in creating the "war zones" we see in many of our inner cities.

To achieve understanding of cultural variations it will not be enough simply to catalog a whole series of cultural patterns and describe the children in each setting—although that may be one place to begin. Ultimately, we will need to develop theories about the *ways* cultural variations affect children.

As yet we have relatively little cross–cultural research to draw on, so most of what I will say in this book will be based entirely on studies done in the United

In the Hispanic-American subculture, families like the Limons, shown here at their annual reunion, are tightly knit, with frequent contact and support. Such a cultural pattern may have wide repercussions.

States, mostly on middle-class white children. But the cross-cultural database is growing, and I will bring it in whenever I can.

Interactions of Nature and Nurture

The ecological/cultural approach underlines the importance of understanding the interactions among many different environmental influences. Equally, we need to understand the interactions among various internal and external influences, between nature and nurture.

There are at several ways we could look at this interaction. One possibility is to look for the common or normative patterns of interaction between nature and nurture. What skills is every child born with, how is the basic system "wired," and how does it mature? And how are those skills altered or shaped by specific experience? This is basically the approach taken by most of those who have studied perceptual development and language development, and by many who have studied cognitive development. I'll be describing the current conclusions drawn from this work in later chapters.

Alternatively, we might look for ways in which nature/nurture interactions *vary* from one child to another. The basic idea is that the same environment may have quite different effects on children who are born with different characteristics. One influential approach of this type is the study of *vulnerable* and *resilient* children.

Vulnerability and Resilience

A baby born weighing only 2 pounds, a child born into a highly impoverished family, a baby who has an unusually cranky or difficult temperament, all seem to start life with several strikes against them, while a child with a particularly sunny disposition begins the developmental journey with certain advantages. In recent years, theorists and researchers such as Norman Garmezy and Michael Rutter (Garmezy, 1993; Garmezy & Rutter, 1983; Rutter, 1987) have argued that such variations in children's qualities or assets are highly important, making some children highly vulnerable to the stresses of childhood, while others are buffered from the worst consequences.

In their writings, Garmezy and Rutter have largely emphasized social origins of vulnerability, such as inadequately loving relationships with parents. Frances Horowitz uses the term "vulnerability" primarily to describe inborn problems, for instance, premature birth or a "difficult" temperament. In Horowitz's model, shown in Figure 1.4, the child's inborn vulnerability or resilience interacts in a particular way with the "facilitativeness" of the environment (Horowitz, 1987; 1990). A highly facilitative environment is one in which

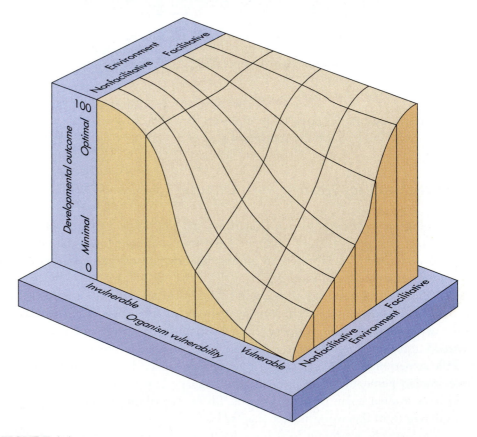

FIGURE 1.4
Horowitz's model describes one possible type of interaction between the vulnerability of the child and the quality of the environment. The height of the surface is the goodness of the developmental outcome (such as IQ or skill in social relationships). In this model, only the combination of a vulnerable infant and a nonfacilitative environment will result in really poor outcomes. (Source: Horowitz, 1987, p. 23, Figure 1.1.)

the child has loving and responsive parents and is provided with a rich array of stimulation. If the relationship between vulnerability and facilitativeness were merely additive, we would find that the best outcomes occurred for resilient infants reared in optimum environments, the worst outcomes for vulnerable infants in poor environments, and the other combinations would lie somewhere in between. But that is not what Horowitz proposes. Instead she is suggesting that a resilient child in a poor environment may do quite well, since such a child can take advantage of all the stimulation and opportunities available; similarly, she suggests that a vulnerable child may do quite well in a highly facilitative environment. According to this model it is only the double whammy—the vulnerable child in a poor environment—that leads to really poor outcomes for the child.

A growing body of research shows precisely this pattern, as you will see throughout the book. For example, very low IQ scores are most common among children who were low birth-weight *and* reared in poverty-level families, while low-birth-weight children reared in middle-class families have essentially normal IQs, as do normal-weight infants reared in poverty-level families (Werner, 1986). We are beginning to understand that the same environment can have very different effects, depending on the qualities or capacities the child brings to the equation.

Consider another possible variation of this same idea: do you think it is possible that girls and boys, beginning in infancy, respond differently to the *same* environments? If true, what would be the ramifications of such a pattern?

The Nature of Developmental Change

The nature/nurture controversy is not the only "big question" in developmental psychology. An equally central dispute concerns the nature of developmental change itself: is a child's expanding ability just "more of the same?" Does a child simply get better and better at things like walking or running or reading? That is, are the *processes* the same and only the efficiency or the speed different? Or alternatively, are there different processes at different ages, different kinds of skills, different strategies, or different types of relationships?

For example, a 2-year-old is likely to have no individual friends among her playmates, while an 8-year-old is likely to have several. We could think of this as a *quantitative* change (a change in amount) from zero friends to some friends. Or we could think of it as a *qualitative* change (a change in kind or type) from disinterest in peers to interest, or from one *sort* of peer relationship to another. Where a given researcher or theorist stands on this question of qualititive versus quantititive change has a profound effect on the way he or she perceives children and their behavior.

Stages and Sequences

A very important related question concerns the existence of *stages* in the course of development. If development consists only of additions (quantitative change), then the concept of stages is not needed. But if development involves reorganization or the emergence of wholly new strategies, skills, or behaviors (qualitative change), then the concept of stages may become attractive. Certainly we hear a lot of "stagelike" language in everyday conversation about children: "He's just in the terrible twos," or, "It's only a stage she's going through." Although there is

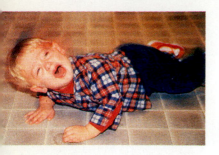

Is this boy behaving like this because he is in a "stage" (the so-called terrible twos) in which tantrums are common? What other explanations can you come up with?

not always agreement on just what would constitute evidence for the existence of discrete stages, the usual description is that a stage shift involves not only a change in skills but some discontinuous change in underlying *structure* (McHale & Lerner, 1990). The child in a new stage approaches tasks differently, sees the world differently, is preoccupied with different issues.

As we move through the following chapters, you will see that stage theories are common in studies of development, although the concept has come under considerable recent attack. John Flavell, a major thinker in the area of cognitive development, points out that research on children's thinking in the past several decades has yielded only limited evidence of stages. What one does see are *sequences* of development in each of a large number of content areas. There are sequences in the development of concepts of gender, sequences in the development of memory strategies, sequences in the acquisition of language skills. Each of these sequences appears to be common across children and to reflect qualitative as well as quantitative changes, but they do not seem to be organized into cohesive wholes that we might think of as broad stages (Flavell, 1982; 1985; 1992). A child might be very advanced in one sequence, and only average in several others, for example, rather than being equally fast or slow in all areas. Thus the idea of stages of development, which seems at first blush to be a tidy way of organizing information, a simple way of describing changes with age, has turned out to be slippery and difficult to sustain. You should keep that in mind as you encounter the various stage theories that are still part of our theoretical language. You should also keep in mind, however, that it is not necessary to assume stages in order to argue that the nature of developmental change is qualitative as well as (or instead of) quantitative. Qualitative change may be gradual as well as abrupt, sequential rather than stagelike.

Finding the Answers: Research on Development

I've asked an enormous number of questions already in this chapter. But before you can understand the answers—before I can get to the really interesting stuff you are probably most curious about—you need one more tool, namely at least a modicum of familiarity with the methods researchers use when they explore questions about development. Let me walk you through the various alternative methods, using a concrete example with clear practical ramifications.

Imagine that you are a social scientist. One day you get a call from your local state representative. She has become seriously concerned about rising levels of crime and lawlessness among teenagers and wants to propose new legislation to respond to this problem. First, though, she wants to have some answers to a series of basic questions:

- Does the same problem exist everywhere in the world or only in the United States? If the latter, then what is it about our culture that promotes or supports such behavior?
- At what age does the problem begin to be visible?
- Which kids are most at risk for such delinquent behavior, and why?

How would you, could you, go about designing one or more studies that might answer such questions? You would face a number of decisions:

- In order to answer the question about the age at which delinquent acts begin to occur, should you compare groups of children and teenagers of different age or should you select a group of younger children and follow them over time, as they move into adolescence? And should you study young people in many settings or cultures, or in only one setting, such as inner city youth in the U.S.? These are questions of *research design*.
- How will you measure delinquent behavior? Can you observe it? Can you ask about it? Can you rely on official records? What other things about each young person might you want to know in order to begin to answer the "why" question? Family history and relationships? Peer contacts and relationships? Self-esteem? These are questions of *research methodology*.
- How will you analyze the data you collect and how will you interpret your findings? Suppose you find that young people whose families live in poverty are considerably more likely to be delinquent. Would you be satisfied to stop there, or would you want to analyze the results separately for each of several ethnic groups, or for children growing up with single mothers, or in other ways that might clarify the meaning of your results? These are questions of *research analysis*.

Research Design

Choosing a research design is crucial for any research, but especially so when the subject matter you are trying to study is change (or continuity) with age. You have basically three choices: (1) You can study different groups of people of different ages; this is a **cross-sectional** design. (2) You can study the *same* people over a period of time; this is a **longitudinal** design. (3) You can combine the two in some fashion, using a **sequential** design (Schaie, 1983a). And if you want to know whether the same patterns hold across different cultures or contexts, you will need to do some kind of **cross-cultural** research, in which you use equivalent or parallel methods in more than one context.

Cross-Sectional Designs

The key feature of a cross-sectional design is that researchers assess separate age groups, testing each subject only once. To study delinquency cross-sectionally you might select groups of subjects at each of a series of ages, such as, 8, 10, 12, 14, and 16. You would then assess each child or teen's delinquent behavior, along with measuring whatever other characteristics you had decided were important. To get some feeling for what the results from such a study might look like, take a look at Figure 1.5, which shows the rate of "conduct disorders" in a large random sample of all children between the ages of 4 and 16 in the province of Ontario, Canada (Offord, Boyle, & Racine, 1991). (A conduct disorder is akin to what is often called delinquency in everyday language, although it also includes excessive aggressiveness, bullying, and the like.) It is clear that conduct disorders

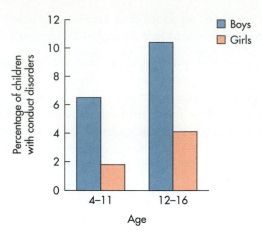

FIGURE 1.5
In this cross-sectional comparison from the Ontario study of conduct disorders, boys and teenagers showed higher rates of problem behavior. (Source: Offord, Boyle, & Racine, 1991, from Table I 2.4, p. 40.)

in this sample were far more common in adolescents and in boys, results that are typical—at least in Western cultures, in which this research has been done.

Cross-sectional research is often enormously useful. It is relatively quick to do, and when age differences are indeed found, it may suggest new hypotheses about developmental processes. And when the investigators collect a rich array of additional information about each subject, it can yield highly interesting results. In the Ontario study, for example, Offord and his colleagues found that the probability of a conduct disorder was four times as high in low-income families, nearly three times as high in "dysfunctional" families, three times as high in families with domestic violence, and so forth. Thus a research design of this type can begin to tell us *which* children are at risk and give us some hints about whys.

At the same time, there are three major problems or limitations with any cross-sectional design. First of all, there is the "cohort problem."

The Cohort Problem.   Social scientists use the word **cohort** to describe groups of individuals born within some fairly narrow band of years, who share the same cultural/historical experiences at the same times in their lives. Within any given culture, successive cohorts may have quite different life experiences. Children growing up in the U.S. in the 1970s and 1980s, for example, were much more likely to experience a divorce between their parents than were kids growing up in the 1950s and 1960s. When we compare different age groups in a single study, as we do in any cross-sectional design, we are also inevitably comparing cohorts to some degree. Thus *cohort* and *age* are totally confounded, and we cannot tell whether some apparent age difference is really attributable to age, or only to cohort differences. When the age groups we are comparing are close in age, as is true in most studies of children, this is not usually a major problem since we can assume roughly similar life circumstances. But over age ranges of as much as ten years, the cohort differences may be significant.

The Time of Measurement Problem.   A related difficulty is that any study is done at some specific historical time, and the results may simply not generalize to other time periods. The Ontario study was done in 1982 and 1983; would we find the same results if we were to repeat the study today? Might all the problem rates be higher? Would the same family characteristics predict conduct disorders now as predicted them then? This problem of generalizing across time periods is especially acute in any society or culture undergoing rapid change, as is the case in many Western cultures today.

Origins, Sequences, and Consistency.   Finally and perhaps most importantly, cross-sectional research cannot tell us much about *sequences* of development or about the cumulative development of some pattern over time. The Ontario study doesn't tell us what happens—in children or in families—to lead to increased rates of conduct disorders in adolescence. It also doesn't tell us if there is some typical sequence through which a child passes, from minor misbehavior to more serious lawlessness. To give you another example, a cross-sectional study of children's gender concepts might show that 2-year-olds have a different idea of gender than 4-year-olds. But this won't tell us whether there are steps in between or whether every child acquires this concept in the same sequence. Similarly, cross-sectional studies will not tell us anything about the consistency of individual behavior over time. For example, it won't tell us if the children who show conduct disorders at 6 or 7 or 8 are likely to show the same kind of problem in adolescence.

Longitudinal Designs

Longitudinal designs can address two of these three problems. Longitudinal designs, in which the *same* individuals are studied over a period of time, allow us to look at sequences of change and individual consistency or inconsistency over time. And because they compare performances by the same people at different ages, they get around the cohort problem. Because of these advantages, they have become extremely common in developmental research.

One example in the same research area as the Ontario study comes from Patterson's longitudinal studies of boys at high risk for later delinquency—research that was designed to test the model you have already seen in Figure 1.2. For instance, in one study, Patterson found that boys who had been rated as high in antisocial behavior by their teachers in fourth grade had a significantly higher incidence of court-recorded delinquency in seventh and eighth grade (Patterson, Capaldi, & Bank, 1991). Boys who were rejected or unpopular with peers in fourth grade were also more likely to be delinquent at adolescence. Both these results are consistent with Patterson's overall model and illustrate some of the questions you can answer with a longitudinal study that researchers simply cannot address any other way.

But longitudinal designs are not a panacea. Because they are time con-suming and expensive, researchers often study quite small samples, so that it is hard to generalize the findings to broader groups. This design also does not solve the time of measurement problem, because each study involves only one group, growing up in a particular historical context.

Only by studying the same children over time, such as this boy at three ages, can we identify consistencies (or changes) in behavior across age.

One solution to this problem is to repeat a longitudinal study several times, each time with a new cohort. This particular strategy, called a *cohort-sequential design*, is one of a family of research designs called sequential designs, which involve either combinations of cross-sectional, or combinations of longitudinal designs, or both. I know of no large cohort-sequential studies in which researchers have followed cohorts as widely apart as ten or more years through childhood, but shorter-term versions of this design are becoming much more common. Patterson's study, for example, involves two adjacent cohorts of fourth graders, one year apart. This makes it possible to check results found on the first group and increases our confidence that a given pattern is not unique to some special set of children.

Cross-Cultural or Cross-Context Designs

Finally, to address the questions of universality or cultural specificity, we would need to compare across cultures. Researchers can do several varieties of cross-cultural studies.

One variety is what anthropologists call an **ethnography**—a detailed description of a single culture or context, based on extensive observation. Often the observer lives within the culture for a period of time, perhaps as long as several years. Information from several different ethnographies may then be compared, to see if similar developmental patterns exist in varying cultures (Whiting & Edwards, 1988). For example, we might ask whether girls and boys are always given different tasks, and if those gender assignments are similar from one context, one culture, to the next.

Alternatively, researchers can use standardized assessment instruments or methods to study some aspect of children's development or behavior in other cultural settings, and then compare their results to existing U.S. or Western data. This is precisely what Wachs and his colleagues did in the Egyptian study I mentioned earlier. As such a body of research in any one area accumulates, it is possible to compare results across many cultures.

Finally, there are studies in which the same investigator compares two or more samples of children or families, each from a different culture or context, using the same instruments or measures or direct translations of those measures. Such comparative research has become quite common within the United States, as we begin to explore the impact of ethnic variations and neighborhood effects on children's development. But of course we can and eventually must reach beyond borders to compare children in quite different cultural milieus. Such studies are growing in number as well (Bornstein, 1991).

This is immensely difficult research to do well. Among the many difficulties, perhaps the most troublesome is the problem of equivalence of measurement (Helms, 1992). Is it enough just to translate some test into another language? Will the same measure or assessment technique be equally valid in all cultures? Do behaviors have the same *meaning* in other contexts, other cultures? I'll come back to this set of issues often as I talk about various facets of development, so I will not belabor the point here. For the moment, it is enough to point out that the amount of cross-cultural and cross-context research is still small, but growing.

What other problems can you think of that would make it hard to do good cross-cultural research?

An Example of A Cross-Cultural Comparison Study

Mark Bornstein and his colleagues (Bornstein, Tal, & Tamis-LeMonda, 1991; Bornstein et al.,1992) video-taped 24 mothers in each of three different cultures, Japan, France, and the United States, interacting in their homes with their 5-month-old infants. They noted that the *babies* behaved very similarly, which suggests that any differences in the mothers' behavior can't be attributed to varying signals or responses from the babies. And in some ways, the mothers responded similarly, too. In particular, they all showed similar rates of nurturance toward their infants and similar levels of imitation. Nonetheless, there were some intriguing differences.

First of all, American mothers simply provided much more stimulation to their babies than did either Japanese or French mothers. They pointed, named, described, touched, and positioned their babies more. Furthermore, there were differences in the relative weight mothers in these three cultures gave to various types of stimulation.

American mothers and French mothers were both more likely to focus efforts on getting their babies to interact with objects, and less on getting their babies to interact with Mom. For Japanese mothers, the two were nearly in balance. A third difference was that American mothers were a lot more likely to use a special, high-pitched sort of speech toward their infants—a form of speech sometimes called "motherese." Both the French and Japanese mothers used motherese occasionally, but much less often than the American mothers. They were more likely to talk to their baby using ordinary adult conversational tones. Such a finding does not—or does not necessarily—mean that the *process* of development is different in these different cultures. Babies in every culture may respond similarly to motherese, for example. Rather, these results suggest some of the subtle but significant ways that babies may be shaped into the cultural pattern in which they are growing.

Experimental Designs

Most of the research designs I have described so far are alternative ways to look at changes with age. But if we are interested in examining a basic process—such as learning or memory—or in *explaining* any observed phenomena, we may do **experiments.**

An experiment is normally designed to test a specific hypothesis, a particular causal explanation. For example, Patterson hypothesized that the beginning of the chain of causal events implicated in aggressive and delinquent behavior lies in the family discipline patterns. To test this, he could devise an intervention experiment in which some families of aggressive children were given training in better discipline techniques, and other families, with similar children, were given no training. He could then check at the end of the training, and perhaps some months or years later, to see if the children whose families had had the training were less likely to show aggression or delinquency.

A key feature of an experiment is that subjects are assigned *randomly* to participate in one of several groups. Subjects in the **experimental group** receive the treatment the experimenter thinks will produce an identified effect (such as training in disciplinary strategies), while those in the **control group** receive either no special treatment or a neutral treatment. The presumed causal element in the experiment is the **independent variable** (in this case the training), and any behavior on which the independent variable is expected to have an effect is a **dependent variable** (in this case aggression or delinquency).

Problems with Experiments in Studying Development.   Experiments like this are essential for our understanding of many aspects of development. But two special problems in studying child or adult development limit the use of experimental designs.

First, many of the questions we want to answer have to do with the effects of particular unpleasant or stressful experiences on individuals—abuse, prenatal influences such as the mother's drinking, family poverty, or parental unemployment. For obvious ethical reasons, we cannot manipulate these variables. We cannot ask one set of pregnant women to have two alcoholic drinks a day and others to have none; we cannot randomly assign adults to become unemployed. So, to study the effects of such experiences we must rely on nonexperimental designs, including longitudinal and sequential studies.

Second, the independent variable in which we are often most interested is age itself, and *we cannot assign subjects randomly to age groups.* We can compare 4-year-olds and 6-year-olds in their approach to some particular task, such as searching for a lost object, but the children differ in a host of ways in addition to their ages. Older children have had more and different experiences. Thus, unlike psychologists studying other aspects of behavior, developmental psychologists *cannot* systematically manipulate many of the variables we are most interested in.

To get around this problem, we can use any one of a series of strategies that are sometimes called *quasi experiments*, in which we compare groups without assigning the subjects randomly. Cross-sectional comparisons are a form of quasi experiment. So are studies in which we select naturally occurring groups that differ in some dimension of interest, such as children whose parents choose to place them in day-care programs compared to children whose parents rear them at home, or children in single-parent families versus those in two-parent families.

Such comparisons have built-in problems, because groups that differ in one way are likely to be different in other ways as well. Families who place their children in day care, compared to those who rear them at home, are also likely to be poorer, may more often be single-parent families, and may have different values or religious backgrounds. If we find that the two groups of children differ in some fashion, is it because they have spent their daytime hours in different places or because of these other differences in their families? We can make such comparisons a bit cleaner if we select our comparison groups initially so that they are matched on those variables we think might matter, such as income or marital status or religion. But quasi experiments, by their very nature, will always yield more ambiguous results than will a fully controlled experiment.

Research Methods

Choosing a research design is only the first crucial decision an investigator must make. Equally important is to decide what subjects to study, and how one will study them.

Choosing the Subjects.   Because we would like to uncover basic developmental patterns that are true for all children, all adolescents, or all adults, the ideal strategy would be to select a random sample of all people in the world to study. Clearly, this is impractical. Instead, borrowing techniques from sociologists and epidemiologists, more and more developmental psychologists are selecting large samples that are representative of some subgroup or population—such as the Ontario study I've already described.

More commonly, psychologists choose to study much smaller groups in greater depth and detail, in an attempt to uncover very basic processes. For instance, Alan Sroufe and his colleagues (Sroufe, 1989; Sroufe, Egeland, & Kreutzer, 1990) have studied a group of 267 children and families, beginning before the birth of the child. The researchers deliberately chose families thought to be at high risk for later caregiving problems, such as low-education, single mothers with unplanned pregnancies. The children have now been repeatedly studied, each time in considerable detail. The sample is not representative of the population as a whole, but the study is enormously informative nonetheless, and may tell us more about the process of emotional and social development than we could possibly glean from larger samples studied more broadly. Neither strategy is better than the other; both are useful. In either case, we need to remember that the conclusions we can draw will be limited by the sample we studied.

Collecting the Information From Your Subjects.   Having chosen your basic design and the subjects you wish to study, you then need to decide how to assess them—how to *describe* their behavior, attitudes, or values in some way. How does a 2-year-old or a 4-year-old react to the presence of a strange adult? How often does a teenager show delinquent behavior? The two time-honored ways of trying to answer questions like this are observing people and asking them questions. Because infants and young children are not particularly good at answering questions, observation has been an especially prominent research strategy among developmental psychologists.

Observation.   Any researcher planning to use observation to collect information about children or their environments will have to make at least three further decisions: What shall I observe? Where shall I observe? How shall I record the observations?

We can divide the decision about what to observe still further: Should I try to observe everything a child does or focus only on selected behaviors? Should I observe only the child or also the immediate environment, such as the responses of the people around the child or the quality of the home? Which I choose will depend largely on the basic question I am trying to address. If I am interested in the child's first words, I would not need to pay much attention to how close the child was sitting to an adult or whether the child exchanged mutual gazes with the adults in his vicinity. But I might want to make note of what the child was playing with, whether other people were present, and what they said to the child. On the other hand, if I were interested in the development of attachment, I would want to make note of mutual gazes as well as how close or far away from the parent the child might be standing or sitting.

It is also no simple matter to decide *where* we will observe. We can observe in a natural setting—a child's home or school—in which case we are introducing

Careful observation of children in both natural and experimentally-created settings has formed the backbone of our knowledge about early development.

an enormous amount of variability into the system and increasing the complexity of the observation immensely. Or we can choose a controlled setting, keeping it the same for each child we observe. For example, the most commonly used measure of the security of a child's attachment to an adult is obtained in what is called the Strange Situation: the child is observed in a series of episodes in a laboratory setting, including periods with the mother, with the mother and a stranger, alone with a stranger, and reunited with the mother. By standardizing the situation, we gain the enormous advantage of having comparable information for each child, but we may lose some ecological validity. We cannot be sure that what we observe in this strange laboratory is representative of the child's behavior in more accustomed settings.

Questionnaires and Interviews.   For researchers studying older children, questionnaires and interviews provide an excellent alternative to observation, such as in studies of children's moral development (which you'll read about in

RESEARCH   REPORT

Ethical Issues in Research on Development

Anytime we try to understand human behavior by observing, testing, or asking questions, we are probing into personal lives. If we go into homes to observe the way parents interact with their children, we are invading their privacy. We may even inadvertently give the impression that there must be something wrong with the way they are raising their family. If we give adults or children laboratory tests, some subjects will do very well, others will not. How will the less-successful subject interpret this experience? What is the risk that some subject will become depressed over what he perceives as a poor performance?

Any research on human behavior involves some risks and raises some ethical questions. Because of this, psychologists and other social and biological scientists have established clear procedures and guidelines that researchers must follow before they can undertake any observation or give any test. In every school or college— the settings in which most such research is done—there is a committee of peers who must approve any research plan involving human subjects. The most basic guideline is that subjects must always be protected from any potential mental or physical harm. More specific principles include:

Informed Consent. Each adult subject must give written consent to participate. In the case of research on children the parent or guardian must give informed consent. In every case, researchers must explain in detail the procedure and its possible consequences. If there are

potential risks, these must be described. For example, if you were studying patterns of communication between teenagers and their parents, you might want to observe each family while they talked about some unresolved issue between them. As part of your informed consent request, you would have to explain to each family that while such discussions often lead to greater clarity, they also occasionally increase tension. And you would need to provide support and debriefing at the end of the procedure, to assist any family who found the task stressful or destabilizing.

Right of Privacy. Researchers must assure subjects that highly personal information they may provide will be kept entirely private—including information about income, or attitudes, or illegal behavior like drugtaking. Researchers can use the information *collectively*, but they cannot report it individually in any way that will associate a subject's name with some piece of data—unless the subject has specifically given permission for such use.

In virtually all cases, it is unethical to observe through a one-way mirror without the subject's knowledge or to secretly record behavior.

Testing Children. These principles are important for any research, but particularly so for research on children. Any child who balks at being tested or observed must not be tested or observed; any child who becomes distressed must be comforted; any risk to the child's self-esteem must be avoided.

Chapter 12), or studies of peer relationships among elementary school- and high school-age children. Assessments of parent–child relationships are also often done with questionnaires.

Each of these alternatives has costs and benefits. Structured laboratory tests give the experimenter excellent control over the situation so that each subject is confronted with the same task, the same stimuli. But because they are artificial, such tests may not give us an accurate portrayal of how individuals behave in the more complex natural environment. Interviews, especially very open-ended ones in which the subject is only guided toward general topics, may give a rich picture of an individual's thoughts and feelings, but how do you reduce the answers to a set of scores that would allow you to compare groups or individuals with one another? Questionnaires solve some of this problem, but the trade-off may be the richness and individuality of replies. Often the best strategy—although one not always possible because of cost in time or money—is to collect many different kinds of information from or about each subject.

Research Analysis

Finally, you need to analyze the results of your research. In studies of development, there are two broad forms of analysis. First, we can compare different age groups by simply calculating the average score of each group on some measure, just as the Ontario researchers did in comparing rates of conduct disorders for each age or gender group in Figure 1.5. You will see *many* examples of exactly this kind of analysis as you go through the book.

A second strategy allows us to look at relationships between two separate variables, most often using a statistic called a **correlation.** A correlation is simply a number ranging from −1.00 to +1.00, that describes the strength of a relationship between two variables. A zero correlation indicates that there is no linear relationship between those variables. For instance, you might expect to find a zero or near-zero correlation between the length of big toes and IQ. People with toes of all sizes have high IQs, and those with toes of all sizes have low IQs. The closer a correlation comes to −1.00 or +1.00, the stronger the relationship between the two variables. If the correlation is positive, it indicates that high scores on the two dimensions tend to go together, and low scores tend to go together, such as length of big toes and shoe size, for example. Height and weight are also strongly positively correlated.

If the correlation is negative, it describes a relationship in which high scores on one variable are associated with low scores on the other. There is a negative correlation between the amount of disorder and chaos in a family and the child's later IQ (high chaos is associated with lower IQ, and low chaos with higher IQ).

Perfect correlations (−1.00 or +1.00) do not happen in the real world, but correlations of .80 or .70 do occur and correlations of .50 are common in psychological research, indicating a relationship of moderate strength. For instance, in the Patterson study I have mentioned several times, the correlation between fourth grade ratings of antisocial behavior and eighth grade delinquency was

.46—a moderate relationship, well above chance but still with a fair amount of variation.

Correlations are an enormously useful descriptive tool. They can tell us about consistency over time, or about links between two environmental variables, or between the child's behavior and some experience he may have had. Useful as they are, though, correlations have a major limitation: they do not tell us about *causal* relationships. For example, several researchers have found a moderate positive correlation between the "difficultness" of a child's temperament and the amount of punishment the child receives from his parents: the more difficult the temperament the more punishment the child experiences. But which way does the causality run? Do difficult children *elicit* more punishment? Or does a greater rate of punishment lead to a more difficult temperament? Or is there some third factor that may cause both, such as perhaps some genetic contribution both to the child's difficultness and to the parent's personality? The correlation alone does not allow us to choose among these alternatives. Stating the point more generally: no correlation, standing alone, can prove causality. A correlation may point in a particular direction, or suggest possible causal links, but to discover the causes, we must then explore such possibilities with other techniques, including experiments.

A Final Word

It may seem to you that these details about research design are of interest and value only to professional researchers. But that is not true. There are many practical, daily applications for knowledge of this kind, even if you never take another course in psychology. Consider the following example.

An issue of *Time* magazine I read recently included an article about a new system for providing stimulation for the unborn baby. The pregnant woman apparently wears a belt full of audio equipment, on which is played tapes of various complex patterns of heartbeat sounds. The article reported that the maker of this gadget had done some "research" to demonstrate that this procedure produces smarter, faster-developing babies. To quote *Time*: "Last year 50 of the youngsters (whose mothers had worn the belt), ranging in age from six months to 34 months, were given standardized language, social and motor-skills tests. Their overall score was 25% above the national norm." (September 30, 1991, p. 76).

I hope you would not go out and buy this apparatus on the basis of that finding! After reading what I've said about research design, you should to be able to see immediately that self-selection is a major problem here. What kind of mothers will buy such a gadget? In fact this reported "research" tells us nothing. It isn't even a quasi experiment because there is no comparison group. There are equivalent reports of research on children, on adolescents, on adults in the newspapers and popular magazines every day. Obviously I want you to be critical analysts of the research I'll talk about in this book. But if nothing else, I want you to become very critical consumers of popularly presented research information. Some of it is very good. A lot of it is bunk or, at the very least, inconclusive. I hope you are now in a better position to tell the difference.

See if you can design a really good study to test the manufacturer's claim that this gadget will make babies smarter.

S U M M A R Y

1. To understand children's development, we must understand both change and consistency, both universality and individuality.

2. Both nature and nurture, biology and culture, are involved in all aspects of development, although there has been long-standing disagreement on the relative importance of these factors.

3. Current thinking about the nature side of the equation emphasizes not only the role of maturation but also points to potential inborn strategies of perceiving or responding to the environment.

4. Modern behavior genetics research has also shown clearly that there is some genetic component in nearly every dimension of behavior and development, including cognitive skills, physical characteristics, personality patterns, and deviant behaviors.

5. Current thinking about the nurture side of the equation emphasizes not only the potential importance of the timing of some experience and the significance of a child's interpretation of some experience, but also the importance of examining the entire ecological system in which development occurs, including culture.

6. We need to understand those aspects of development that are the same across cultures, as well as the ways in which cultural variations shape children's development in distinct ways.

7. Nature and nurture may not interact in precisely the same way for each child. Children with different inborn qualities (such as vulnerability or resilience) may be affected differently by the same environment.

8. Another key question concerns the nature of developmental change itself, whether it is qualitative or quantitative, continuous or stagelike.

9. A first major question in planning research is the basic research design. Cross-sectional studies compare different children of different ages; longitudinal studies observe the same children as they develop over time; sequential studies combine some of these features; and cross-cultural studies compare children, their rearing, or nature/nurture relationships in differing cultures or subcultures.

10. Each of these designs has particular strengths and drawbacks.

11. To study causal connections, researchers normally use experimental designs. In an experiment, the researcher controls (manipulates) one or more relevant variables and assigns subjects randomly to different treatment and control groups.

12. In a quasi experiment, researchers don't randomly assign subjects to separate groups; rather, they compare existing groups. Researchers need quasi experiments in developmental research because they cannot randomly assign subjects either to age groups or to experience such negative treatments as poverty or abuse or poor attachment.

13. Decisions about research methods include: what subjects to study, and what methods to observe or assess subjects.

14. When analyzing research results, the two most common methods are comparing average scores between groups and describing relationships among variables with the statistic called a correlation. It can range from $+1.00$ to -1.00, and describes the strength of relationship.

15. You need some knowledge of research strategies and design to become an informed consumer of research information contained in the popular press. You should not believe everything you read!

KEY TERMS

behavior genetics	culture	longitudinal study
cohort	dependent variable	maturation
control group	ethnic group	sensitive period
correlation	ethnography	sequential designs
critical period	experiment	teratogen
cross-cultural research	experimental group	
cross-sectional study	independent variable	

SUGGESTED READINGS

Bornstein, M. H. (Ed.). (1987). *Sensitive periods in development. Interdisciplinary perspectives*. Hillsdale, NJ: Lawrence Erlbaum Associates. Bornstein's own paper in this collection of reports is an excellent introduction to the concept of sensitive periods, but the book also contains a number of reports of research exploring potential sensitive periods both in humans and in other animals.

Cole, M. (1992). Culture in development. In M. H. Bornstein & M. E. Lamb (Eds.), *Developmental psychology: An advanced textbook* (3rd ed.) (pp. 731–789). Hillsdale, NJ: Lawrence Erlbaum Associates. Not at all easy reading, but the best analysis I have yet seen on this very complicated subject.

Rowe, D. C. (1994). *The limits of experience*: *Genes, experience, and behavior.* New York: Guilford Press. A clear, well-reasoned book arguing that developmental psychologists have greatly exaggerated the effects of "nurture" on variations in personality, intelligence, and other characteristics and greatly underestimated the effects of heredity. This is a good introduction to some current thinking on the nature/nurture controversy.

Seitz, V. (1988). Methodology. In M. H. Bornstein & M. E. Lamb (Eds.) *Developmental psychology: an advanced textbook* (2nd ed.) (pp. 51–84). Hillsdale, NJ: Lawrence Erlbaum Associates. A very good source for a further exploration of various methods of research. This is a well-organized and clearly written paper.

Chapter Two

Theories of Development

Students often tell me that they hate reading about theories. What they want are the facts. But it is a fallacy to assume that facts can simply stand alone, without any explanation or framework. Even in your everyday interactions with friends, family, and acquaintances, you *always* interpret, try to make sense out of what others do or say. If a friend frowns when you had expected a smile, you try to *explain* his behavior to yourself. You have developed a kind of mini-theory about this friend, based on his past behavior, so you interpret his current frown in light of that theory. Social psychologists call this process *attribution*; you attribute the other person's behavior to a specific cause, either some internal property of the individual, or some outside force. The internal models of relationships or of the self that I talked about briefly in Chapter 1 are also a kind of theory: a set of propositions or assumptions about the way the world is organized that help you to organize and interpret experiences.

The same is true of research facts. For example, here is a fact: In a series of recent studies in the United States, researchers have found that a slightly higher percentage of infants in day care have an "insecure" attachment to their mothers than is true of infants reared at home (Lamb, Sternberg, & Prodromidis, 1992). The difference is small (35 percent versus 29 percent) but it's one that researchers have found quite consistently in a number of studies. What does this fact mean?

There are many possible meanings. Because we know that parents who place their children in day care differ in a variety of ways from those who do not, there could be some self-selection involved; it may not be day care at all that is producing this effect. But let's assume for the moment that we have ruled out all explanations of this type and that there is still a difference to be explained. Why might such a difference occur? Does it mean that day care is damaging to children? If so, what (if anything) might we do to alter the pattern? Only theory can help us here—theories about how attachments are formed in the early months of life and about the importance of such attachments.

Here's another fact: Boys are more likely to be negatively affected by their parents' divorce than are girls. Virtually all children show some negative effects of divorce, but the likelihood and severity of problems is greater for boys (Hetherington, 1989; Kline et al., 1989). In particular, boys show a greater increase in aggression and other behavior problems, and their school performance deteriorates more.

This fact is extremely interesting in and of itself, but again we have to ask *why*. Do mothers treat their sons and daughters differently after a divorce? Do boys suffer more from the absence of the father? Or perhaps boys are somehow inherently less able to handle stress of any kind. Each of these alternative explanations is derived from a different theory, and each suggests further research we might do to check on the validity of the explanation. If differential treatment of sons and daughters is the answer, then we ought to study family interactions in recently divorced families in some detail. If the absence of the father in the son's life is the crucial factor, then we ought to study boys and girls living with their fathers after divorce. If response to stress is involved, we would want to look at other stressful occurrences in family life, such as unexpected unemployment, or the death of a family member, or a major move, and see whether in these cases,

When parents divorce, boys are more likely to show disturbed behavior or poorer school performance than are girls. But why? We need theories to help us explain facts like this.

too, boys show more extreme responses. The point is that scientific progress comes not merely by collecting lots of facts. To understand the facts we need theories or models, and these theories then point us toward the next empirical investigation.

A theory need not offer a grand scheme to be classed as a theory. Mini-theories that account for a narrow range of empirical observations are much more common than are grand schemes. I'll be describing many such mini-theories as we go along. But what I need to do in this chapter is to introduce you to the four major families of theories that have been centrally influential in the study of children's development: biological theories, learning theories, psychoanalytic theories, and cognitive-developmental theories. Each offers a different set of assumptions, a different set of emphases, a different vocabulary.

Biological Theories

You have already encountered many of the key concepts of biological theories of development in Chapter 1. The most basic proposition of such theories is that both our common patterns of development and our unique individual behavioral tendencies are at least partially determined by basic physiological processes, including genetic programming or sequences of hormone changes. Biologically oriented theorists do not argue that environment has no effect—no one takes such an extreme position. But increasing numbers of developmental psychologists are persuaded that genetic programming is a powerful framework upon which all of development is built. Gesell's maturational theory, which you met briefly in the last chapter, is certainly one variation of this view. But in recent years, it has been the behavior geneticists who have most profoundly influenced our thinking. Let me give you some examples of their work to flesh out what I have already said about this approach.

How do Behavior Geneticists Identify Genetic Effects?

The first question is a methodological one: just how do we know whether any given behavior has been influenced by heredity? There are two basic strategies: you can study identical and fraternal twins or you can study adopted children.

Identical twins develop from the same fertilized ovum, so they share exactly the same genetic patterning. Fraternal twins each develop from a separate ovum, separately fertilized. They are therefore no more alike than are any other pair of siblings, except that they have shared the same prenatal environment and grow up in the same sequential niche within the family. If identical twins turn out to be more like one another on any given trait than fraternal twins, that would be evidence for the influence of heredity on that trait.

A particularly useful version of the twin study is to compare identical and fraternal twins who have been reared apart from one another. If identical twins are still more like one another on some dimension, despite having grown up in different environments, we have even clearer evidence of a genetic contribution for that trait.

The major alternative is to study adopted children. The basic strategy is to compare the degree of similarity between the adopted child and his birth parent (with whom he shares genes but not environment) and between the adopted child and his adoptive parents (with whom he shares environment but not genes). If the child should turn out to be more similar to, or his behavior or skill better predicted by the characteristics of his *birth* parents than by characteristics of his adoptive parents, that would again demonstrate the influence of heredity.

A new type of approach that combines some of the features of both twin and adoption studies is to compare, in the same study, not only identical and fraternal twins, but also full siblings, half-siblings, and unrelated sibling pairs growing up in step families. A major national study using this design, involving over 700 families, has recently been begun and promises to yield a very rich vein of new information (Plomin et al., 1994; Reiss et al., 1994).

To make all this clearer, let me give you examples of results from both twin and adoption studies, drawn from the extensive research on the heritability of intelligence. In the twin studies the general strategy is to give IQ tests to each member of many pairs of identical and fraternal twins, and then compare the pairs of scores using a *correlation*—a statistic I described in Chapter 1. When Bouchard and McGue (1981; McGue et al., 1993) combined the results of dozens of such studies, they find the following correlations:

Identical twins reared together	.86
Identical twins reared apart	.72
Fraternal twins reared together	.60
Siblings (including fraternal twins) reared apart	.24

Recall that the closer a correlation is to 1.00, the more similar the two sets of scores must be. You can see that identical twins reared together have IQs that are highly similar, more similar than what occurs for fraternal twins reared together. You can also see, though, that identical twins reared apart are somewhat less alike than are those reared together, which suggests that heredity is not the only factor involved.

IQ has also been the focus of adoption studies of heritability. Here are some results from a study of roughly 100 adopted children, conducted by Scarr & Weinberg (1983, Table 1 p. 262). The correlations in this case are between the child's IQ and that of each of the four parents involved:

with the natural mother's IQ	.33
with the natural father's IQ	.43
with the adoptive mother's IQ	.21
with the adoptive father's IQ	.27

Because the children's IQs are *more* similar to the IQs of their natural parents than to their adoptive parents, these results, like the results of twin studies of IQ, tell us that there is indeed a substantial genetic component in what we measure with an IQ test.

Other Behaviors and Characteristics Influenced by Heredity

Using these same techniques, behavior geneticists have demonstrated the influence of heredity on a remarkably wide range of behaviors or characteristics. Physical characteristics influenced by heredity include not only the obvious ones such as height or eye color, but also less obvious traits such as overall earliness or lateness of physical development. Some children move through the whole sequence of physical development very early, including early puberty, while others develop more slowly, and these variations seem clearly to be genetically influenced. Body shape and a tendency toward skinniness or fatness are also at least partially inherited.

Many intellectual characteristics other than IQ are also affected by genetic variations, such as verbal skills, spatial visualization ability, reading ability or disability, and learning disabilities in general (Cardon & Fulker, 1993; Plomin & Rende, 1991).

Many aspects of pathological behavior are genetically influenced, including alcoholism, schizophrenia, excessive aggressiveness, even anorexia (Plomin, Rende, & Rutter, 1991). Finally, and importantly, behavior geneticists have found a significant genetic influence on children's personality or temperament—a set of research studies that offers a very nice illustration of a biological model. Because the studies of temperament have been particularly influential in recent years, let me expand a bit on this body of information.

Temperament: An Example of a Biological Theory at Work

It is clear to any observer that babies vary in the way they react to new things, in their typical moods, in their rate of activity, in their preference for social interactions or solitude, in the regularity of their daily rhythms, and in many other ways. These variations in the child's *style* of interacting with those around her, or in the child's level of emotional reactivity, usually go by the name **temperament.**

Psychologists who have been interested in these differences have proposed several different ways of describing the key dimensions of temperament. Jerome Kagan (1990; 1993) has focused on only a single dimension, which he calls *behavioral inhibition*—an aspect of what most people mean by "shyness." Buss and Plomin (1984; 1986) propose three dimensions: emotionality, activity, and sociability. Thomas and Chess (1977) describe nine dimensions, which they organize into three types, the easy child, the difficult child, and the slow-to-warm-up child, described in Table 2.1.

It is not yet clear which of these views, or some other, will eventually carry the theoretical day. But all begin with the assumption that variations in temperament are at least moderately influenced by heredity. And the evidence generally bears this out.

Inheritance of Temperament. The strongest evidence comes from twin studies, which show that identical twins are quite a lot more alike in their temperament than are fraternal twins (Buss & Plomin, 1984; Robinson et al., 1992). This is true in studies of adults, even when the identical twins have been reared

Children rated as having a "difficult" temperament are more often punished by their parents than are those with an "easy" temperament. How many different explanations can you think of for such a pattern?

TABLE 2.1
Chess and Thomas' Typology of Temperament

The Easy Child	The easy child is regular in biological functioning, with good sleeping and eating cycles, is usually happy and adjusts easily to change or new experiences.
The Difficult Child	The difficult child is less regular in body functioning and is slow to develop regular sleeping and eating cycles. He reacts vigorously and negatively to new things, is more irritable, and cries more. His cries also have a more "spoiled," grating sound than do the cries of "easy" babies (Boukydis & Burgess, 1982).
The Slow-to-warm-up Child	The slow-to-warm-up infant shows few intense reactions, either positive or negative. To new experiences, he may show a kind of passive resistance, such as drooling out unwanted new foods rather than spitting them or crying. Once he has adapted to something new, however, his reaction is usually fairly positive.

Sources: Thomas & Chess (1977).

apart, and it is true in studies of children and infants over age 1. One fairly typical set of results, in Table 2.2, comes from a study by Buss and Plomin of a total of 228 pairs of identical twins and 172 pairs of fraternal twins whose temperament was rated on Buss and Plomin's three temperament dimensions when they were 5 years old. You can see that the correlations between temperament scores of identical twins are consistently high, while those for fraternal twins are essentially zero, indicating a strong genetic effect.

Not all the results are quite this clear. Studies of twins under age 1 show much weaker genetic influence on infant temperament (Gunnar, 1990), and among adopted children, the correlations between the temperament of the child and that of the natural parent is not a whole lot higher than the correlation with adoptive parents' temperament (Scarr & Kidd, 1983), which suggests that environment has a considerable role in shaping the child's temperament. Nonetheless, most experts have concluded that there is good evidence for at least some genetic component in our usual measures of temperament.

TABLE 2.2
Similarity of Identical and Fraternal Twins on Buss & Plomin's Temperament Dimensions

	Twin Correlations	
Temperament Scale	Identical	Fraternal
Emotionality	.63	.12
Activity	.62	−.13
Sociability	.53	−.03

Source: Buss & Plomin, 1984, Table 9.2, p. 122.

Even Environment is Affected by Heredity

One of the most remarkable—and difficult—concepts to emerge from recent behavior genetic research is the idea that the child's *environment* is affected by heredity. I know that sounds totally paradoxical, but bear with me.

There are two ways in which heredity could affect the child's environment. First, the child inherits her genes from her parents, and those same parents create the environment in which the child is growing up. For example, parents who themselves have higher IQs are not only likely to pass their "good IQ" genes on to their children, they are also likely to create a richer, more stimulating environment for their child.

A second path of influence is from the child herself. Because children begin life with varying genetically patterned qualities, they *elicit* different behavior from parents and others. Cranky children thus encounter a quite different set of experiences than do sunny-dispositioned children; large and robust children elicit different kinds of caregiving than do frail children.

Furthermore, each child, each adult, *chooses* her own experiences to at least some degree and *interprets* the experiences that she does encounter. Those choices and interpretations are affected by all the individual's inherited tendencies, including not only IQ but temperament or pathologies. For example, in their study of twins and step-children, Plomin and his colleagues (1994) have found that identical twin adolescents describe their parents or friends in more similar terms than is true for fraternal twins. Furthermore, full siblings describe their parents more similarly than do genetically unrelated step-siblings. It appears that identical twins are *experiencing* their parents, and their family environment, in more similar ways. This does *not* mean that there is somehow an "experiencing the environment" gene. Rather, the full genetic pattern of each child or adult affects the way he or she experiences and interprets. Because identical twins have the same genetic make up, they experience and interpret more similarly.

Research of this kind has forced developmental psychologists to rethink some long-held assumptions, including basic assumptions about the importance of environment in shaping not only specific abilities but also personality or temperament (Reiss et al., 1994; Rowe, 1994). For example, we know from many studies of families that children whose parents read to them often learn to read more easily when they get to school. Most of us concluded from this that reading to the child helped to *cause* the later good reading skills. And that may very well be true, at least in part. But it is now clear that at least *part* of the link between reading to the child and the child's later skill is a genetic effect and not environment at all. Parents who themselves have good reading skills are more likely to choose to read to their children, and children with a genetic propensity toward good reading abilities are more likely to *ask* their parents to read to them and to persist with the activity once it has begun.

This does not mean that family environments have no effect. They clearly do. But the paradox is that what turns out to be important about family environments is probably not the overall richness or deprivation they offer, but the specific ways in which individual parents interact with individual children. Thus it appears to be the *unique* environment experienced by each child, not the broad character of the overall family environment, that is most important. This is a somewhat startling conclusion, and not completely shared by all developmental psychologists. But it is an example of the new directions in which behavioral genetics research and thinking has led us.

Consistency over Time.   Temperament theorists also assume that inborn temperamental predispositions will tend to persist through childhood and even into adulthood, although all would quickly agree that the way the parents and others respond to the child can alter the basic tendencies in important ways. Thus temperament does not inevitably determine personality. Rather, temperamental variations are the building blocks of personality. They create a kind of "bias" in the system toward particular patterns. Given such a bias, there should be at least *some* stability of temperament over time. Such stability ought to show itself in the form of at least modest correlations between measures of a given temperamental dimension from one age to another—which is what researchers have usually found.

For example, Australian researchers studying a group of 450 children found that mother's reports of children's irritability, cooperation/manageability, inflexibility, rhythmicity, persistency, and tendency to approach (rather than avoid) contact were all quite consistent from infancy through age 8. Of these, approach and rhythmicity were the most stable (Pedlow et al., 1993). Thus babies who smile more are friendlier later, and cranky babies tend to be more difficult at school age. Kagan has also found considerable consistency over the same age range in his measure of inhibition (Kagan et al., 1993), which is based on direct observation of the child's behavior, rather than on the mother's ratings of the child's temperament. Half of babies in his longitudinal study who had shown high levels of crying and motor activity in response to a novel situation when they were 4 months old were still classified as highly inhibited at age 8, while three-fourths of those rated as uninhibited at 4 months remained in that category eight years later. And a Swedish study, using mothers' ratings of their infants' inhibition, found some consistency in extreme inhibition between infancy and late adolescence—although only for girls, perhaps because inhibition is considered gender-appropriate for girls, but not for boys (Kerr et al., 1994).

Clearly the consistency in temperament over time is not perfect. In particular, there is less consistency from infancy into toddlerhood than between toddlerhood and later childhood. But there is at least some consistency in temperament over time.

If Kagan is right, this little girl's shyness is the result of the way her brain is organized to respond to novel situations.

Physiological Basis of Temperament.   Some temperament theorists have taken the biological argument one step further, suggesting that these behavioral dispositions are rooted in variations in fundamental physiological processes, such as variations in brain organization. For example, Kagan has suggested that differences in behavioral inhibition are based on differing thresholds for arousal of those parts of the brain—the amygdala and the hypothalamus—which control responses to uncertainty (Kagan et al., 1990; Kagan et al., 1993). Arousal of these parts of the brain leads to increases in muscle tension and heart rate. Shy or inhibited children are thought to have a *low* threshold for such a reaction. That is, they more readily become tense and alert in the presence of uncertainty, perhaps even interpreting a wider range of situations as uncertain. What we inherit, then, is not "shyness" or some equivalent, but a tendency for the brain to react in particular ways.

In support of this argument, Kagan reports correlations in the range of .60 between a measure of behavioral inhibition in children aged 2 to 5 and a series of physiological measures, such as muscle tension, heart rate, dilation of the pupil of the eye, and the chemical composition of both urine and saliva; all of which strongly suggests that temperament is not simply a set of learned habits (Kagan et al., 1990).

Critique of Biological Theories

The biological approaches I have been describing here are not really theories in quite the same way as Freud's or Piaget's models are theories. These are not "grand schemes," but are instead a set of models with a shared central explanatory principle: genetics. From my perspective, there are two crucial points to make about the current status of these models.

First, broad–ranging and sophisticated new behavior genetics research has made it clear, beyond any shadow of a doubt, that heredity plays a role in virtually all aspects of behavior and development. Such a statement represents a significant swing of the theoretical pendulum away from the dominance of environmentalism that was a hallmark of developmental psychology in the 1960s, and 1970s.

But the second point is equally important. As Robert Plomin and Richard Rende say in a recent review (Plomin & Rende, 1991):

> The rush of the behavioral sciences away from environmentalism may be going too far, to a view that all behavior is biologically determined. . . . The evidence from behavioral-genetics research indicates that nongenetic factors are at least as important as genetic factors (p. 162).

What we have reached is a deeper awareness of the profound importance of biases and tendencies built into the human system, both shared and individual. But we are still left with the task of understanding the ways in which the environment and heredity interact.

Learning Theories

Learning theories represent the flip side of the theoretical coin. Theorists in this tradition do not deny the existence or even the importance of genetic effects. They see the environment as fundamentally important in shaping behavior. All would agree with Albert Bandura when he says:

> . . . human nature is characterized by a vast potentiality that can be fashioned by direct and vicarious experience into a variety of forms within biological limits (1989, p. 51).

For these theorists, then, it is the plasticity of behavior that is most striking. In their view, this plasticity is shaped by quite specific processes of learning. The most central of these processes are classical conditioning and operant conditioning. If you have encountered these concepts in earlier courses, you can skim the next section. But for those of you who lack such a background, a brief description is needed.

Classical Conditioning

This type of learning, made famous by Pavlov's experiments with his salivating dog, involves the acquisition of new signals for existing responses. If you touch a baby on the cheek, he will turn toward the touch and begin to suck. In the technical terminology of **classical conditioning,** the touch on the cheek is the **unconditioned stimulus;** the turning and sucking are **unconditioned responses.** The baby is already programmed to do all that; these are automatic reflexes. Learning occurs when some *new* stimulus is hooked into the system. The general model is that other stimuli that are present just before or at the same time as the unconditioned stimulus will eventually trigger the same responses. In the typical home situation, for example, a number of stimuli occur at about the same time as the touch on the baby's cheek before feeding. There is the sound of the mother's footsteps approaching, the kinaesthetic cues of being picked up, and the tactile cues of being held in the mother's arms. All of these stimuli may eventually become **conditioned stimuli** and may trigger the infant's response of turning and sucking, even without any touch on the cheek.

Classical conditioning is of special interest in our study of child development because of the role it plays in the development of emotional responses. For example, things or people present when you feel good will become conditioned stimuli for that same sense of goodwill, while those previously associated with some uncomfortable feeling may become conditioned stimuli for a sense of unease or anxiety. This is especially important in infancy, since a child's mother or father is present so often when nice things happen—when the child feels warm, comfortable, and cuddled. In this way mother and father usually come to be a conditioned stimulus for pleasant feelings, a fact that makes it possible for the parent's mere presence to reinforce other behaviors as well. But a tormenting older sibling might come to be a conditioned stimulus for angry feelings, even after the sibling has long since stopped the tormenting. These classically conditioned emotional responses are remarkably powerful. They begin to be formed very early in life, continue to be formed throughout childhood and adulthood, and profoundly affect each individual's emotional experiences.

Operant Conditioning

The second major type of learning is most often called **operant conditioning,** although you will also see it referred to as *instrumental conditioning.* Unlike classical conditioning, which involves attaching an old response to a new stimulus, operant conditioning involves attaching a new response to an old stimulus, achieved by the application of appropriate principles of reinforcement. Any behavior that is reinforced will be more likely to occur again in the same or in a similar situation. There are two types of reinforcements. A **positive reinforcement** is any event which, following some behavior, increases the chances that the behavior will occur again in that situation. There are certain classes of pleasant consequences, such as praise, a smile, food, a hug, or attention, that serve as reinforcers for most people most of the time. But strictly speaking, a reinforcement is defined by its effect; we don't know something is reinforcing unless we see that its presence increases the probability of some behavior.

The second major type is a **negative reinforcement,** which occurs when something an individual finds *unpleasant* is *stopped.* Suppose your little boy is whining and begging you to pick him up. At first you ignore him, but finally you do pick him up. What happens? He stops whining. So your picking-up behavior has been *negatively reinforced* by the cessation of his whining, and you will be *more* likely to pick him up the next time he whines. At the same time, his whining has probably been *positively reinforced* by your attention, so he will be more likely to whine on similar occasions.

Virtually every child finds a hug reinforcing.

Both positive and negative reinforcements strengthen behavior. **Punishment,** in contrast, is intended to weaken some undesired behavior. Sometimes punishments involve eliminating nice things (like "grounding" a child, or taking away TV privileges, or sending her to her room); often they involve administering unpleasant things such as a scolding or a spanking. What is confusing about the idea of punishment is that it doesn't always do what it is intended to do: it does not always suppress the undesired behavior. If your child had thrown his milk glass at you to get your attention, spanking him may be a positive reinforcement instead of the punishment you had intended.

Reinforcements do not strengthen a behavior permanently. The reverse process is **extinction,** which is a decrease in the likelihood of some response after repeated nonreinforcements. If you simply stopped reinforcing whining behavior in your child, eventually the child would stop whining, not only on this occasion but on subsequent occasions.

In laboratory situations, experimenters can be sure to reinforce some behavior every time it occurs or to stop reinforcements completely so as to produce extinction of the response. But in the real world, consistency of reinforcement is the exception rather than the rule. Much more common is a pattern of **partial reinforcement,** in which some behavior is reinforced on some occasions but not others. Studies of partial reinforcement show that children and adults take longer to learn some behavior under partial reinforcement conditions, but once established, such behaviors are much more resistant to extinction. If you only smile at your daughter every fifth or sixth time she brings a picture to show you (and if she finds your smile reinforcing), she'll keep on bringing pictures for a very long stretch, even if you were to quit smiling altogether.

> Can you think of examples in your everyday life in which your behavior is affected by classical or operant conditioning, or in which you use these principles to affect others' behavior?

Subvarieties of Learning Theory

All theorists who emphasize the central role of learning would agree on the importance of these basic processes. But beyond that basic agreement there are significant theoretical variations.

On one end of the theoretical continuum are the *radical behaviorists*. These theorists, strongly influenced by the work of B. F. Skinner, take an extreme environmental position. Donald Baer (1970) refers to this as an "age irrelevant concept of development." That is, theorists of this persuasion assume that the basic principles of learning are the same no matter how old the learner may be.

Few developmental psychologists today would take such an extreme position. More common today is a second subvariety of learning theory normally called *social-learning theory*. The key figure here is Albert Bandura (1977a; 1982b; 1989), a theorist whose views have undergone some interesting changes over the years. Bandura accepts the importance of classical and operant conditioning, but he makes several additional assertions.

First, he argues that learning does not always require direct reinforcement. Learning may also occur merely as a result of watching someone else perform some action. Learning of this type, called **observational learning** or **modeling,** is involved in a wide range of behaviors. Children learn ways of hitting

It is a lot harder than you may think to apply basic learning principles consistently and correctly with children at home or in schools. Virtually all parents do try to reinforce some behaviors in their children by praising them or by giving them attention or treats. And most of us do our best to discourage unpleasant behavior through punishment. But it is easy to misapply the principles or to create unintended consequences because we have not fully understood all the mechanisms involved.

For example, suppose you have a favorite armchair in your living room that is being systematically ruined by the dirt and pressure of little feet climbing up the back of the chair. You want the children to stop climbing up the chair. So you scold them. After a while you may even stoop to nagging. If you are really conscientious and knowledgeable, you may carefully stop your scolding when they stop climbing in an effort to have your scolding operate as a negative reinforcer. But nothing works. They keep on leaving those muddy footprints on your favorite chair. Why? It could be because the children enjoy climbing up the chair. So the climbing is intrinsically reinforcing to the children, and that effect is clearly stronger than your negative reinforcement or punishment. One way to deal with this might be to provide something else for them to climb on.

The Real World
Learning Principles in Real Family Life

Another example: Suppose your 3-year-old son repeatedly demands your attention while you are fixing dinner (a common state of affairs, as any parent of a 3-year-old can tell you). Because you don't want to reinforce this behavior, you ignore him the first six or eight times he says "Mommy" or tugs at your clothes. But after the ninth or tenth repetition, with his voice getting louder and whinier each time, you can't stand it any longer and finally say something like "All right! What do you want?" Since you have ignored most of his demands, you might well be convinced that you have not been reinforcing his demanding behavior. But what you have actually done is to create a partial reinforcement schedule; you have rewarded only every tenth demand or whine. And we know that this pattern of reinforcement helps to create behavior that is very hard to extinguish. So your son may continue to be demanding and whining for a very long time, even if you succeed in ignoring it completely.

If such situations are familiar to you, it may pay to keep careful records for a while, keeping track of each incident and your response, and then see if you can figure out which principles are really at work, and how you might change the pattern.

from watching other people in real life and on TV. They learn generous behaviors by watching others donate money or goods. Adults learn job skills by observing or being shown by others.

Bandura also calls attention to another class of reinforcements called **intrinsic reinforcements** or intrinsic rewards. These are reinforcements internal to the individual, such as the pleasure a child feels when she finally figures out how to draw a star, or the sense of satisfaction you may experience after strenuous exercise. Pride, discovery, that "aha" experience are all powerful intrinsic rewards, and all have the same power to strengthen behavior as do extrinsic reinforcements like praise or attention.

Third, and perhaps most important, Bandura has gone far toward bridging the gap between learning theory and cognitive-developmental theory by emphasizing important *cognitive* elements in learning. Indeed he now even refers to his theory as "social cognitive theory" (Bandura, 1986; 1989). For example, Bandura now stresses the fact that modeling can be the vehicle for the learning of abstract as well as concrete skills or information. In this *abstract modeling*, the observer extracts a rule that may be the basis of the model's behavior, and learns the rule as well as the specific behavior. In this way a child or adult can acquire attitudes,

Learning to use chopsticks is only one of the myriad skills, attitudes, beliefs, and values that are learned through modeling.

values, ways of solving problems, even standards of self-evaluation through modeling. Furthermore, Bandura suggests that what a person learns from observing someone else is a function of four factors: what she pays attention to, what she is able to remember (both *cognitive* processes), what she is physically able to copy, and what she is motivated to imitate. Because attentional abilities, memory, and other cognitive processes change with age through infancy and childhood, what a baby or child can or will learn from any given modeled event will also change through development (Grusec, 1992).

Bandura introduces other cognitive components as well. In learning situations, children and adults *set goals*, *create expectations* about what kinds of consequences are likely, and *judge* their own performances. The addition of concepts like these make Bandura's learning theory an *age-relevant* theory, because children of different ages are highly likely to observe or notice different things and to analyze or process those observations differently. Thus what is learned in any given situation may vary systematically by age.

Think about your own upbringing. What values or attitudes do you think you learned through modeling? How did your parents or others display (model) those values and attitudes?

Some Research Examples

To my thinking, one of the most interesting current applications of learning theory principles is in Gerald Patterson's studies of highly aggressive or noncompliant boys and their families. If you go back and look at Figure 1.2, you can see that the heart of Patterson's model is the assumption that there is a direct causal link between "poor parental discipline" and resultant conduct problems in the child. He is arguing here that both normal personality patterns and deviant forms of behavior have their roots in daily reinforcement exchanges between family members. For example, imagine a child playing in his very messy room. The mother comes into the room and tells the child to clean up his room. The child whines or yells at her that he doesn't want to do it, or won't do it. The mother gives in, and leaves the room, and the child stops whining or shouting. Patterson analyzes this exchange as a pair of negatively reinforced events. When the mother gives in to the child's defiance, her own behavior (giving in) is negatively reinforced by the ending of the child's whining or yelling. This makes it more likely that she will give in the next time. She has *learned* to back down in order to get the child to shut up. The child has been negatively reinforced for yelling or whining, since the unpleasant event for him (being told to clean his room) stopped as soon as he whined. So he has learned to whine or yell. Imagine such exchanges occurring over and over, and you begin to understand how a family can create a reinforcement system in which an imperious, demanding, noncompliant child rules the roost.

Patterson's thinking, as you saw in Chapter 1, has moved beyond the simple propositions I have outlined here and acquired certain ecological elements. Like the current temperament theorists, he emphasizes that what happens in a given family, for a particular child, is a joint product of the child's own temperament or response tendencies, the parent's discipline skills, the parent's personality, and the social context of the parent's lives. But Patterson is still assuming that basic learning principles can both describe and explain the ways in which the child's behavior pattern is initially formed or changed. He has shown that it is possible to *change* the child's typical behavior by helping families learn new and more effective reinforcement and management strategies.

Hundreds of other studies have also demonstrated the impact of observational learning (Bandura, 1973; 1977). One interesting—and very practical—sidelight to the process of modeling has been the repeated finding that modeling works better than preaching. So displaying the desired behavior yourself—such as generosity, or fairness or diligent work—works better than simply telling kids that it is good to be generous or fair or hardworking.

For example, in one study, Joan Grusec and her co-workers (Grusec, Saas-Kortsaak, & Simutis, 1978) had elementary school children play a miniature bowling game, ostensibly to test the game. They first observed an adult "test" the game and saw the adult win 20 marbles. Next to the bowling game was a poster that said: "Help poor children. Marbles buy gifts." Under the poster was a bowl with some marbles in it. Half the time the adult model donated half his newly won marbles to this bowl; the other half of the time he did not. In addition, the model either "preached" about donating marbles or said nothing. To some of the children he preached in specific terms, saying that the child should donate half his marbles when he played the game, since it would be good to make poor children happy by doing that. To other children, he preached in more general terms, saying that the child should donate half his marbles because it is a good thing to make other people happy by helping them any way one can. The adult model then left the room, and the child had an opportunity to play the bowling game and to decide whether to donate any marbles. You can see in Figure 2.1 how many children in each group (out of a maximum of 16) donated marbles. Clearly, modeling worked better than preaching. And when there is a conflict between what the model says and what the model does—such as when parents smoke but tell their kids that they should not smoke—children generally follow

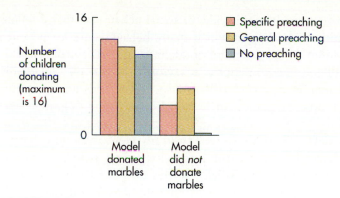

FIGURE 2.1

These results from Grusec's modeling study illustrate the typical finding that modeling is more powerful than preaching in changing children's behavior. (Source: Grusec, Saas-Kortsaak, & Simutis, 1978, from Table 1, p. 922.)

the behavior and not the verbal message. So the old adage "Do what I say and not what I do" doesn't seem to work.

In his explorations of the concept of self-efficacy, Bandura has also shown that changing someone's belief about his ability to do something has a greater impact on his behavior than merely reinforcing him for performing that behavior (Bandura, 1982b). There are a number of ways you can change such beliefs. For example, suppose a child thinks of himself as unable to hit a baseball. We can increase his belief in his *own* ability by simply having him watch other equally inept kids become better hitters. The resulting increase in his own belief (his sense of self-efficacy) will later affect his ability to hit the ball, even without additional practice.

Critique of Learning Theories

Several implications of this theoretical approach are worth emphasizing. First of all, learning theorists can handle either consistency or change in child or adult behavior. If a child is friendly and smiling both at home and at school, this could be explained by saying that the child was being reinforced for that behavior in both settings rather than by assuming that the child had a "gregarious temperament." Or if the child is helpful at school but defiant at home, we need only invoke the principle that there are different reinforcement contingencies in the two settings. To be sure, because individuals tend to choose settings that maintain their accustomed behavior, and because a person's behavior will tend to *elicit* similar responses (reinforcements) from others in many settings, there is a bias toward consistency. But learning theorists have less trouble accounting for normal "situational variability" in behavior than do other theorists.

A related implication is that learning theorists tend to be optimistic about the possibility of change. Children's behavior can change if the reinforcement system, or their beliefs about themselves, change. So "problem behavior" can be modified.

The great strength of this view of social behavior is that it seems to give an accurate picture of the way in which many behaviors are learned. It is perfectly clear that children do learn through modeling; and it is equally clear that children and adults will continue to perform behaviors that "pay off" for them. The addition of the cognitive elements to Bandura's theory adds further strength, since it offers a beginning integration of learning models and cognitive-developmental approaches.

On the debit side of the ledger, from my view, is the fact that this approach is really not developmental. Learning theorists can say how a child might acquire a particular behavior pattern or belief, but they do not take into account the underlying developmental changes that are occurring. Do 3-year-olds and 10-year-olds develop a sense of self-efficacy in the same way? Do they learn the same amount or in the same way from modeling? Given Bandura's emphasis on the cognitive aspects of the modeling process, a genuinely developmental social learning theory could be proposed, although he has not laid out such a model. Still, despite these limitations, all the theories in this group offer useful descriptions of one source of influence on the child's developing pattern of behavior.

Psychoanalytic Theories

There is a whole family of theorists called "psychoanalytic," including Sigmund Freud, Carl Jung (1916; 1939), Alfred Adler (1948), and Erik Erikson (1963; 1964; 1974). All have been interested in explaining human behavior by understanding the underlying processes of the *psyche*, a Greek term meaning soul, spirit or mind. Sigmund Freud (1905; 1920) is usually credited with originating the psychoanalytic approach, and his terminology and many of his concepts have become part of our intellectual culture, even while his explicit influence on developmental psychology has waned.

Freud's Theory

One of Freud's most distinctive theoretical contributions is the idea that behavior is governed not only by conscious but by *unconscious* processes. The most basic of these unconscious processes, according to Freud, is an instinctual sexual drive he called the **libido,** present at birth and forming the motive force behind virtually all our behavior. Further unconscious material is also created over time through the functioning of the various defense mechanisms—those automatic, normal, unconscious strategies for reducing anxiety that we all use on a daily basis, such as repression, denial, or projection.

Freud also argued that personality has a structure, and that such a structure develops over time. Freud proposed three parts, the **id,** in which the libido is centered, the **ego,** a much more conscious element that serves as the executive of the personality, and the **superego,** the center of conscience and morality, incorporating the norms and moral strictures of the family and society. In Freud's theory, these three parts are not all present at birth. The infant and toddler is all id, all instinct, all desire, without the restraining influence of the ego or the

I suspect many of you, hearing the phrase "defense mechanisms," think of some kind of abnormal or deviant behavior. It is important for you to understand, though, that Freud conceived of them not only as unconscious but as entirely normal. Their primary purpose is to help us protect ourselves against anxiety. Since we all feel anxious some of the time, we all use some form of defense.

Suppose I send a paper to a professional journal and it comes back with a rejection letter. To deal with the anxiety I naturally feel after such a rejection, I resort (unconsciously) to some kind of defense mechanism.

All defense mechanisms distort reality to some extent, but they vary in the amount of distortion involved. At one extreme end is denial. I might deny that I had ever submitted the paper, or that it had ever been rejected. Or I could use distortion, such as by persuading myself that the journal really loved the paper but that there hadn't been enough space.

A notch less distorting are mechanisms like projection, in which I push my feelings onto someone else. "Those people who rejected this paper are really stupid! They don't know what they're doing." In this way, I ascribe to others the qualities I fear may be true for me, in this instance stupidity. I might also repress my feelings, insisting that I really don't mind at all that my paper is rejected. Or I could use intellectualization, in which I consider, in emotionally very bland terms, all the reasons why the paper was rejected. Intellectualization sounds quite rational and open, as if there were no defense involved. But what has been pushed away is the emotion.

Another defense that is about equivalently distorting is displacement. If I am upset about the rejection, but cannot direct my distress at the appropriate target (such as the editor of the journal) I might displace my emotion onto someone else. I might find myself being overly critical of a student or pushing the cat off my lap when it bids for some attention.

Among the least distorting defenses is suppression, in which I allow myself to be aware of my distress but still shove it away for a while by saying, a la Scarlet O'Hara, "I'll think about it tomorrow." So I push it away, but not so firmly into the unconscious as is true for repression.

Not long ago I was reminded very forcibly just how powerful these defensive processes can be. I received a phone call at noon one day from a friend, who told me of the death of a mutual friend—a man who was very dear to me. I said all the right things at the time, finished my lunch, and went back to work, pressing to meet a deadline. At dinner that evening, I had this vague feeling that there was some important news I meant to tell my husband, but I couldn't remember what it was. I went to a choir rehearsal that evening and was unbearably grumpy and irritable, but couldn't figure out why. As I got into my car to drive home, the memory of my friend's death suddenly returned, and I burst into tears in the parking lot. This is a perfect example of repression. I couldn't deal with the news when it first arrived, so I pushed it out of my conscious memory long enough to get me through the day.

Can you think of equivalent examples in your own life? When was the last time something uncomfortable happened to you. How did you handle it? Bear in mind that these defenses are entirely normal.

The Real World
We all use Defense Mechanisms Everyday

superego. The ego begins to develop in the years from 2 to about 4 or 5 as the child learns to adapt his instant-gratification strategies. Finally, the superego begins to develop just before school age, as the child incorporates the parents' values and cultural mores.

Freud also proposed a series of five **psychosexual stages,** (summarized in Table 2.3) through which the child moves in a fixed sequence strongly influenced by maturation. In each, the libido is invested in that part of the body that is most sensitive at that age. In a newborn, the mouth is the most sensitive part of the body, so libidinal energy is focused there. The stage is therefore called the *oral* stage. As neurological development progresses, the infant has more sensation in the anus (hence the *anal* stage), and later the genitalia (the *phallic* and eventually the *genital* stages).

TABLE 2.3
Freud's Stages of Psychosexual Development

Stage	Age	Erogenous Zones	Major developmental task (potential source of conflict)	Some adult characteristics of children who have been fixated at this stage, according to Freud
Oral	0–1	Mouth, lips, tongue	Weaning	Oral behavior, such as smoking, overeating; passivity and gullibility.
Anal	2–3	Anus	Toilet training	Orderliness, parsimoniousness, obstinacy, or the opposite.
Phallic	4–5	Genitals	Oedipus complex	Vanity, recklessness, and the opposite.
Latency	6–12	No specific area	Development of defense mechanisms	None: fixation does not normally occur at this stage.
Genital	13–18	Genitals	Mature sexual intimacy	Adults who have successfully integrated earlier stages should emerge with a sincere interest in others and mature sexuality.

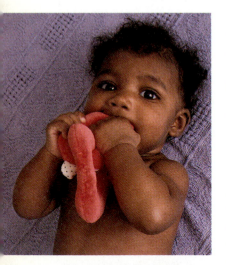

Freud thought that babies put things into their mouths because that is where they have the most pleasurable sensations. If babies don't get enough oral stimulation, he argued, they may become fixated at the oral stage.

The Oral Stage: Birth–1 Year. The mouth, tongue, and lips are the first center of pleasure for the baby and his earliest attachment is to the one who provides pleasure in the mouth, usually his mother. For normal development the infant requires some optimum amount of oral stimulation—not too much and not too little. If the optimum amount of stimulation is not available, then some libidinal energy may remain attached to (*fixated* on, in Freud's terms) the oral mode of gratification. Such an individual, so Freud thought, will continue to have a strong preference for oral pleasures in later life, as you can see in the right hand column in Table 2.3.

The Anal Stage: 1–3 Years. As the trunk matures the baby becomes more and more sensitive in the anal region. At about the same time, her parents begin to place great emphasis on toilet training and show pleasure when she manages to perform in the right place at the right time. These two forces together help to shift the major center of physical/sexual energy from the oral to the anal erogenous zone.

The key to the child's successful completion of this stage (according to Freud) is whether the parents allow the child sufficient anal exploration and pleasure. If toilet training becomes a major battleground, then some fixation of energy at this stage may occur—with the possible adult consequences of excessive orderliness, stinginess, or the opposite.

Phallic Stage: 3–5 Years. At about 3 or 4 years of age the genitals increase in sensitivity, ushering in a new stage. One sign of this new sensitivity is that children of both sexes quite naturally begin to masturbate at about this age.

In Freud's view, the most important event that occurs during the phallic stage is the so-called **Oedipus conflict.** He described the sequence of events more fully (and more believably!) for boys, so let me trace that pattern for you.

The theory suggests that first the boy somehow becomes "intuitively aware of his mother as a sex object" (Rappoport, 1972, p. 74). Precisely how this occurs is not completely spelled out, but the important point is that the boy at about age 4 begins to have a sort of sexual attachment to his mother and to regard his father as a sexual rival. His father sleeps with his mother, holds her, kisses her, and generally has access to her body in a way that the boy does not. The boy also sees his father as a powerful and threatening figure who has the ultimate power—the power to castrate. The boy is caught between desire for his mother and fear of his father's power.

Most of these feelings and the resultant conflict are unconscious. The boy does not have overt sexual feelings or behavior toward his mother. But unconscious or not, the result of this conflict is anxiety. How can the little boy handle this anxiety? In Freud's view, the boy responds with a defensive process called **identification:** The boy "incorporates" his image of his father, and attempts to match his own behavior to that image. By trying to make himself as much like his father as possible, the boy not only reduces the chance of an attack from the father, he also takes on some of the father's power as well. Furthermore, it is the "inner father," with his values and moral judgments, that serves as the core of the child's superego.

A parallel process is supposed to occur in girls. The girl sees her mother as a rival for her father's sexual attentions and also has some fear of her mother (though less than is true for the boy, since the girl may assume she has already been castrated). In this case, too, identification with the mother is thought to be the "solution" to the girl's anxiety.

> Can you think of any kind of study that would tell us whether Freud was right or not about the Oedipal crisis?

The Latency Stage: 5–12 Years. Freud thought that after the phallic stage there is a sort of resting period before the next major change in the child's sexual development. The child has presumably arrived at some preliminary resolution of the Oedipal crisis, so that there is a kind of calm after the storm. One of the obvious characteristics of this stage is that the identification with the same-sex parent that defined the end of the phallic stage is now extended to others of the same sex. So it is during these years that children's peer interactions are almost exclusively with members of the same sex, and children often have "crushes" on same-sex teachers or other adults.

The Genital Stage: 12–18 and Older. The further changes in hormones and the genital organs that take place during puberty reawaken the sexual energy of the child. During this period a more mature form of sexual attachment occurs. From the beginning of this period, the child's sexual objects are people of the opposite sex. Freud placed some emphasis on the fact that not everyone works through this period to a point of mature heterosexual love. Some have not had a satisfactory oral period and thus do not have a foundation of basic love relationships. Some have not resolved the Oedipal crisis with a complete or satisfactory identification with the same-sex parent, a failure that may affect their ability to cope with rearoused sexual energies in adolescence.

Optimum development at each stage, according to Freud, requires an environment that will satisfy the unique needs of each period. The baby needs sufficient oral and anal stimulation; the 4-year-old boy needs a father present with whom to identify and a mother who is not too seductive. An inadequate early environment will leave a residue of unresolved problems and unmet needs, which are then carried forward to subsequent stages.

This emphasis on the formative role of early experience, particularly early family experience, is a hallmark of psychoanalytic theories. In this view, the first five or six years of life are a kind of sensitive period for the creation of the individual personality.

Erikson's Theory

A second enormously influential psychoanalytic theorist has been Erik Erikson. Erikson shares most of Freud's basic assumptions, but there are some crucial differences between the two theories. First, Erikson deemphasizes the centrality of sexual drive and instead focuses on a step-wise emergence of a sense of identity. Second, although he agrees with Freud that the early years are highly important, he argues that identity is not fully formed at the end of adolescence, but continues to move through further developmental stages in adult life. You can see in Table 2.4 that he proposes eight stages, three of which are reached only in adulthood.

In Erikson's view, maturation plays relatively little role in the sequence of stages. Far more important are common cultural demands for children of a particular age, such as the demand that the child become toilet trained at about age 2, that the child learn school skills at age 6 or 7, or that the young adult form an intimate partnership. Each stage, then, centers on a particular dilemma, a particular social task. Thus he calls his stages **psycho**_social_ **stages** rather than psycho-_sexual_ stages. Let me give you a bit more detail on the five stages that Erikson described in childhood.

Basic Trust Versus Basic Mistrust: Birth–1 Year.   The first task (or "dilemma" as Erikson sometimes says) occurs during the first year of life, when the child must develop a sense of basic trust in the predictability of the world and in his ability to affect the events around him. Erikson believes that the behavior of the major caregiver (usually the mother) is critical to the child's successful or unsuccessful resolution of this crisis. Children who emerge from the first year with a firm sense of trust are those whose parents are loving and respond predictably and reliably to the child. A child who has developed a sense of trust will go on to other relationships carrying this sense with him; but those infants whose early care has been erratic or harsh may develop _mis_trust; and they, too, carry this sense with them into later relationships.

Erikson never said, by the way, that the ideal position on any one of the dilemmas is at one extreme pole. In the case of the first stage, for example, there

Does this make sense to you—the idea that one carries unresolved issues forward into adulthood? Can you think of any examples from your own experience?

TABLE 2.4
The Eight Stages of Development Proposed by Erik Erikson

Approximate age	Ego quality to be developed	Some tasks and activities of the stage
0–1	Basic trust versus mistrust	Trust in mother or central caregiver and in one's own ability to make things happen. A key element in an early secure attachment.
2–3	Autonomy versus shame, doubt	New physical skills lead to free choice; toilet training occurs; child learns control but may develop shame if not handled properly.
4–5	Initiative versus guilt	Organize activities around some goal; become more assertive and aggressive; Oedipus conflict with parent of same sex may lead to guilt.
6–12	Industry versus inferiority	Absorb all the basic cultural skills and norms, including school skills and tool use.
13–18	Identity versus role confusion	Adapt sense of self to pubertal changes, make occupational choice, achieve adultlike sexual identity, and search for new values.
19–25	Intimacy versus isolation	Form one or more intimate relationships that go beyond adolescent love; form family groups.
26–40	Generativity versus stagnation	Bear and rear children, focus on occupational achievement or creativity, and train the next generation.
41+	Ego integrity versus despair	Integrate earlier stages and come to terms with basic identity. Accept self.

is some risk in being too trusting. The child also needs to develop some healthy mistrust, such as learning to discriminate between dangerous and safe situations.

Autonomy Versus Shame and Doubt: 2–3 Years. Erikson sees the child's greater mobility during the toddler years as forming the basis for the sense of independence or autonomy. But if the parents don't carefully guide the child's efforts at independence and she experiences repeated failures or ridicule, then the results of all the new opportunities for exploration may be shame and doubt instead of a basic sense of self-control and self-worth. Once again the ideal is not for the child to have *no* shame or doubt; some doubt is needed for the child to understand which behaviors are acceptable and which are not, which are safe and which are dangerous. But the ideal does lie toward the autonomy end of the continuum.

Initiative Versus Guilt: 4–5 Years. This phase, which is roughly equivalent to Freud's phallic stage, is again ushered in by new skills or abilities in the child. The 4-year-old child is able to plan a bit, to take initiative in reaching particular goals. With these new cognitive skills, the child attempts to conquer the world around him. He may try to go out into the street on his own; he may take a toy

If looks could kill! This child is clearly jealous of the new baby and may well be harboring all sorts of angry and aggressive thoughts. A younger child would probably act out those thoughts and feelings directly. But a child of this age, probably in the period Erikson calls *initiative versus guilt*, feels guilty about her feelings and inhibits the angry actions.

apart, then find he can't put it back together and throw it—parts and all—at his mother. It is a time of vigorous action, and of behaviors that parents may see as aggressive. The risk is that the child may go too far in his forcefulness, or that the parents may restrict and punish too much—either of which can produce guilt. Some guilt is needed, since without it there would be no conscience, no self-control. The ideal interaction between parent and child is certainly not total indulgence. On the other hand, too much guilt can inhibit the child's creativity and free interactions with others.

Industry (Competence) Versus Inferiority: 6–12 Years.   The beginning of schooling is a major force in ushering in this stage. The child is now faced with the need to win approval through specific competence—through learning to read, do sums, and other school skills. The task of this period is thus simply to develop the repertoire of abilities society demands of the child. If the child is unable to develop the expected skills, he will develop instead a basic sense of inferiority. Yet, some failure is necessary so that the child can develop some humility; as always, balance is at issue. Ideally, the child must have sufficient success to encourage a sense of competence, but should not place so much emphasis on competence that failure is unacceptable or that she becomes a kind of "workaholic."

Identity Versus Role Confusion: 13–18 Years.   The task occurring during puberty is a major one in which the adolescent reexamines his identity and the roles he must occupy. Erikson suggests that two "identities" are involved—a "sexual identity" and an "occupational identity." What should emerge for the adolescent from this period is a reintegrated sense of self, of what one wants to do and be, and of one's appropriate sexual role. The risk is that of confusion, arising from the profusion of roles opening to the child at this age.

Other Psychoanalytic Views: Bowlby's Model of Attachment

Erikson is not the only influential modern theorist whose thinking has been strongly affected by Freud or psychoanalysis. Among those interested particularly in very early child development, John Bowlby's theory of the development of attachment (1969; 1973; 1980) has had a major impact. He offered an interesting blend of psychoanalytic and biological approaches. Like Freud, Bowlby assumed that the root of human personality lies in the earliest childhood relationships. Significant failure or trauma in those relationships will permanently shape the child's development. Bowlby focused his attention on the child's first attachment to the mother because it is usually the earliest and arguably the most central.

To describe how that attachment comes about, Bowlby introduced several concepts from *ethological theory*, which brings evolutionary concepts to bear on the study of behavior. Human evolution, Bowlby suggested, has resulted in the child being born with a repertoire of built-in, instinctive, behaviors that elicit caregiving from others—behaviors like crying, smiling, or making eye contact. Similarly, the mother (or other adult) is equipped with various instinctive behaviors toward the infant, such as responding to a cry or speaking in a higher voice. Together these instinctive patterns bring mother and infant together in an intricate chain of stimulus and response that causes the child to form a specific attachment to that one adult—a process I'll be talking about in some detail in Chapter 6.

Although Bowlby's theory is not a full-fledged stage theory of development in the manner of Freud or Erikson, it is nonetheless based on many of the underlying psychoanalytic assumptions. It has also stimulated and profoundly influenced the large body of current research on attachment.

Research Examples

Empirical explorations of Freud's or Erikson's theories are relatively rare, largely because both theories are so general that specific tests are very difficult. For example, to test Freud's notion of fixation we would need much more information about how to determine if a given child is fixated at some stage. What is a sign that a child is fixated at the oral or the anal stages? Should we expect some automatic connection between how early a child is weaned and such ostensibly oral adult behavior as smoking or overeating? When researchers have searched for such direct linkages they have not found them. However, this does not rule out the possibility of a process akin to fixation, albeit perhaps at a subtler level.

Despite these difficulties, researchers have managed to devise tests of some of the basic propositions, most notable the Erikson/Bowlby notion of basic trust or security of attachment. Let me give you just a foretaste of the research in this

Research suggests that teens who were securely attached to their mothers as infants form new friendships more easily and quickly than do teens whose earliest attachment was less secure.

area, since it provides a good deal of support for the basic psychoanalytic hypothesis that the quality of the child's earliest relationship affects the whole course of the child's later development. This is particularly clear in the work of Alan Sroufe and his colleagues (Sroufe, Carlson, & Schulman, 1993). In a number of studies, they first rated children at about age 1 on the security of their attachments to their mothers. Later, at preschool, school age, or early adolescence, they observed the same children at school or at special summer camps, where they were dealing with new relationships or strange adults. The consistent finding from these studies is that securely attached infants are later more capable, more friendly, more open to new relationships, more skillful with peers. Thus the relationship formed during the earliest stage of psychosocial development seems to create a prototype for later relationships, as Bowlby and Erikson proposed.

Critique of Psychoanalytic Theories

Psychoanalytic theories like Freud's or Erikson's have several great attractions. Most centrally, they focus our attention on the importance of the child's relationship with the caregivers. Furthermore, both these theories suggest that the child's needs or "tasks" change with age, so that the parents must constantly adapt to the changing child. One of the implications of this is that we should not think of "good parenting" as if it were a global quality. Some of us may be very good at meeting the needs of an infant, but quite awful at dealing with teenagers' identity struggles; others of us may have the opposite pattern. The child's eventual personality, and her overall "health," thus depends on the interaction or transaction that develops in the particular family. This is an extremely attractive element of these theories because more and more of the research within developmental psychology is moving us toward just such a transactional conception of the process.

A second strength is that psychoanalytic theory has offered several helpful concepts, such as defense mechanisms and identification, which have been so widely adopted that they have become a part of everyday language as well as theory. These strengths have led to a resurgence of influence of both Erikson's theory and the several second-order or third-order psychoanalytic approaches such as Bowlby's.

The great weakness of all the psychoanalytic approaches is the fuzziness of many of the concepts (Block, 1987). Identification may be an intriguing theoretical notion, but how are we to measure it? How do we detect the presence of specific defense mechanisms? Without more precise operational definitions, it is impossible to disconfirm the theory. Those areas in which the general concepts of psychoanalytic theory have been fruitfully applied to our understanding of development have nearly always been areas in which other theorists or researchers have offered more precise definitions or clearer methods for measuring some Freudian or Eriksonian construct, such as Bowlby's concept of security of attachment. Psychoanalytic theory may thus sometimes offer a provocative framework for our thinking, but it is not a precise theory of development.

Cognitive-Developmental Theories

The final theory in this quartet of approaches, the cognitive-developmental model, is similar to psychoanalytic theory in that it too emphasizes qualitative changes in stages. Like psychoanalytic theorists, cognitive-developmentalists also strongly emphasize the role of the child as the most active participant in the process of development. But the similarity largely stops there, in part because the two theoretical traditions have turned their attention to very different facets of the child's development. Psychoanalytic theorists have focused almost exclusively on personality development. Cognitive-developmentalists, as the name implies, have attempted to explain the development of the child's thinking and have paid relatively little attention to the specifics of the child's relationship with caregivers.

The central figure in cognitive-developmental theory has been Jean Piaget (1952; 1970; 1977; Piaget & Inhelder, 1969), a Swiss psychologist whose theories have shaped the thinking of several generations of developmental psychologists. Piaget, along with other early cognitive theorists such as Lev Vygotsky (1962) and Heinz Werner (1948), was struck by the great regularities in the development of children's thinking. He noticed that all children seemed to go through the same kinds of sequential discoveries about their world, making the same sorts of mistakes and arriving at the same solutions. For example, if a 2-year-old child loses her shoe, she may look for it briefly and haphazardly, but she is unable to undertake a systematic search. A 10-year-old, in contrast, is likely to use such good strategies as retracing her steps or looking in one room after another.

Piaget's detailed observations of children's thinking led him to several assumptions, the most central of which is that it is the nature of the human organism to *adapt* to its environment. This is an active process. Unlike the learning theorists, Piaget does not think that the environment *shapes* the child but rather that the child (like the adult) actively seeks to understand his environment. In the process, he explores, manipulates, and examines the objects and people in his world.

The Concept of Scheme

A pivotal concept—and one of the hardest to grasp—is that of a **scheme** (sometimes written as *schema*). This term is often used as roughly analogous to *concept*, *mental category*, or *complex of ideas*. But Piaget used it even more broadly than that. He saw knowledge as being more than just passive mental categories, but as *action*s, either mental or physical. Each of these actions is what he means by a scheme. So a scheme is not really a category, but the *action of categorizing* in some particular fashion. Some purely physical or sensory actions are also schemes. If you pick up and look at a ball, you are using your "looking scheme," your "picking up scheme," and your "holding scheme." Piaget proposed that each baby begins life with a small repertoire of such simple sensory or motor schemes, such as looking, tasting, touching, hearing, reaching. For the baby, an object *is* a thing that tastes a certain way, or feels a certain way when it is touched, or has a particular color. Later, the toddler and child develops more clearly mental schemes as well, such as categorizing or comparing one object to another. Over development, the child gradually adds extremely complex mental schemes, such as deductive analysis or systematic reasoning.

But how does the child get from those simple, built-in sensorimotor schemes to the more internalized, increasingly complex mental schemes we see in later childhood? Piaget proposed three basic processes to account for the change: **assimilation, accommodation** and **equilibration.**

Assimilation, Accommodation, and Equilibration

Assimilation.   Assimilation is the process of *taking in*, of absorbing some event or experience to some scheme. When a baby looks at and then reaches for a mobile above his crib, Piaget would say that the baby had assimilated the mobile to his looking and reaching schemes; when an older child sees a dog and labels it "dog," she is assimilating that animal to her dog category or scheme. When you read this paragraph you are assimilating the information, hooking the concept onto whatever other concept (scheme) you have that may be similar.

Using Piaget's language, we would say that 9-month-old Jesse is assimilating this spoon to her grasping scheme.

The key here is that assimilation is an *active* process. For one thing, there is selectivity in the information we assimilate. When I was struggling to learn German last year and listened to my instructor speak, I could only assimilate a portion of what she said—the parts for which I already had schemes—and could only imitate or use the parts that I had assimilated. In addition, the very act of assimilating changes the information that is assimilated, because each assimilated event or experience takes on some of the characteristics of the scheme to which it was assimilated. If I label your new sweater as green (that is, if I assimilate it to my green scheme) even though it is really chartreuse or some other more unusual color, I will remember it as more green and less yellow than it really is.

Accommodation.   The complementary process is accommodation, which involves *changing the scheme* as a result of the new information you have taken in by assimilation. As I assimilated new German words and grammar, I gradually changed (accommodated) my concepts and categories, so that now I had mental categories for several forms of past tense instead of only one, or mental groupings of words with a given prefix. The baby who sees and grasps a square object for the first time will accommodate her grasping scheme, so that next time she reaches for an object of that shape her hand will bend more appropriately to grasp it. Thus in Piaget's theory, the process of accommodation is the key to developmental change. Through accommodation, we reorganize our thoughts, improve our skills, change our strategies.

Think of three or four more examples of assimilation and accommodation in your everyday life.

Equilibration.   The third aspect of adaptation is equilibration. Piaget assumed that in the process of adaptation, the child is always striving for coherence, to stay "in balance," to have an understanding of the world that makes overall sense. This is not unlike what a scientist does when she develops a theory about some body of information (and hence the metaphor of the child as a "little scientist.") The scientist wants to have a theory that will make sense out of every observation, that has internal coherence. When new research findings come along, she assimilates them to the existing theory; if they don't fit perfectly, she might simply set aside the deviant data, or she may make minor modifications in her theory. But if enough non-confirming evidence accumulates, the scientist may have to throw out her theory altogether and start over, or may need to change some basic theoretical assumptions, either of which would be a form of equilibration.

Piaget thought that a child operated in a similar way, creating coherent, more-or-less internally consistent models or theories. But since the infant starts with a very limited repertoire of schemes, the early "theories" or structures the child creates are simply not going to hold up. So Piaget thought the child then made a series of more major substantial changes in the internal structure.

Piaget saw three particularly significant reorganization or equilibration points, each ushering in a new stage of development. The first is at roughly 18 months, when the toddler shifts from the dominance of simple sensory and motor schemes to the use of the first symbols. The second is at roughly age 5 to 7, when the child adds a whole new set of powerful schemes Piaget calls operations. These are far more abstract and general mental actions, such as mental addition or subtraction. The third major equilibration is at adolescence, when the child figures out how to "operate on" ideas as well as events or objects. These three major equilibrations create four stages:

The **sensorimotor stage,** from birth to 18 months
The **preoperational stage,** from 18 months to about age 6
The **concrete operations stage** from 6 years to about 12, and
The **formal operations stage,** from age 12 onward.

Table 2.5 expands somewhat more fully on these stages, each of which I will describe in greater detail in the appropriate age-based chapters. The key for

TABLE 2.5
Piaget's Stages of Cognitive Development

Age	Stage	Description
0–2	Sensorimotor	The baby understands the world in terms of her senses and her motor actions. A mobile is how it feels to grasp, how it looks, how it tastes in the mouth.
2–6	Preoperational	By 18–24 months, the child can use symbols to represent objects to himself internally and begins to be able to take others' perspectives, to classify objects, and to use simple logic.
7–12	Concrete Operations	The child's logic takes a great leap forward with the development of powerful new internal mental operations, such as addition, subtraction, and class inclusion. The child is still tied to specific experience but can do mental manipulations as well as physical ones.
12+	Formal Operations	The child becomes able to manipulate ideas as well as events or objects. She can imagine and think about things she has never seen or that have not yet happened; she can organize ideas or objects systematically and think deductively.

now is to understand that in Piaget's view, each stage grows out of the one that precedes it, and each involves a major restructuring of the child's way of thinking. Piaget did not conceive of progress through all these stages as inevitable. He thought the sequence was fixed, so that if the child made cognitive progress it would be in this order, but not all children would necessarily reach the same end point or move at the same speed. Piaget thought that virtually all children would move to at least preoperational thought, and the vast majority would achieve concrete operations. But not all would necessarily achieve formal operations.

Critique of Cognitive-Developmental Theories

It would be difficult to overstate the impact that Piaget's ideas have had on the study and understanding of children's development. His work has been controversial precisely because it called into question so many earlier, more simplistic views. Piaget also devised a number of remarkably clever techniques for exploring children's thinking—techniques that often showed unexpected and counter-intuitive responses from children, as you can see in the *Research Report* on page 57. So not only did he offer us a theory that forced us to think about children and their development in a new way, he provided a set of empirical facts that were impossible to ignore and difficult to explain.

By being quite explicit about many hypotheses and predictions, Piaget also enabled others to test his theory. Indeed, such tests show that Piaget was often wrong. He was wrong about the specific ages at which children understand certain concepts; researchers have consistently found evidence of complex concepts at much earlier ages than Piaget proposed. More profoundly, it now looks as if he was wrong about the central concept of stages of development. Most 8-year-olds, for example, show "concrete operational" thinking on some tasks but not on others, and they are much more likely to show complex thinking on a task with which they are very familiar than one with which they have little experience. The whole process is a great deal less stagelike than Piaget proposed and more influenced by specific experience than Piaget had thought.

These disconfirmations of Piaget have not meant that Piaget's theory has lost its influence. Many of Piaget's basic concepts have been absorbed into our common base of ideas, (much as Freud's concept of the unconscious has been accepted), and his theory continues to set the agenda for a great deal of the research on children's thinking.

Contrasting and Combining the Theories

I wouldn't be surprised if you are a bit bleary-eyed after reading about all these theories. It's hard to make the theoretical issues real to you before you have delved into the data. And at the same time, it is hard for you to assimilate and integrate the data without having some theoretical models to hook them onto. At the least I hope you can see that there are some real disagreements here, some

Piaget's Clever Research

Piaget had an enormous impact on developmental psychologists not only because he proposed a novel and provocative theory, but because of the cleverness of many of the strategies he devised for testing children's understanding. These strategies often showed children doing or saying very unexpected things—results that other theorists found hard to assimilate into their models.

The most famous of all Piaget's clever techniques is probably his method for studying conservation. Piaget would begin with two equal balls of clay, show them to the child, and let the child hold and manipulate the clay until she agreed that they had the same amount. Then in full view of the child, Piaget would squish one of the balls into a pancake, or roll it into a sausage. Then he'd ask the child whether there was still the same amount of clay in each, or whether the pancake or the ball had more. Children aged 4 and 5 consistently said that the ball had more; children of 6 and 7 consistently said that they were still the same.

Or Piaget would start with two equal water glasses, each containing exactly the same amount of liquid. The child would agree that there was the same amount of water or juice in each one. Then in full view of the child he'd pour the water from one glass into a shorter, fatter glass, so that the water level in the new glass was lower than the water level in the original. Then he'd ask again whether there was the same amount of water in both. Four and 5-year-olds thought the amounts were now different, while 6- and 7-year-olds knew that there was still the same amount no matter what sized glass the liquid was poured into. Thus the older child has acquired the concept of conservation; she understands that the quantity of water or clay is conserved even though it is changed in some other dimension.

In another study, Piaget explored the concept of class inclusion—the understanding that a given object can belong simultaneously to more than one category. Fido is both a dog and an animal; a high-chair is both a chair and furniture. Piaget usually studied this by having children first create their own classes and subclasses, and then asking them questions about them. One 5½-year-old child, for example, had been playing with a set of flowers and had made two heaps, one large group of primroses and a smaller group of other mixed flowers. Piaget then had this conversation with the child:

PIAGET: *"If I make a bouquet of all the primroses and you make one of all the flowers, which will be bigger?"*

CHILD: *"Yours."*

PIAGET: *"If I gather all the primroses in a meadow will any flowers remain?"*

CHILD: *"Yes"*   (Piaget & Inhelder, 1959, p. 108).

The child understood that there are other flowers than primroses, but did *not* yet understand that all primroses are flowers—that the smaller, subordinate class, is *included in* the larger class.

In these conversations with children, Piaget was always trying to understand how the child thought, rather than whether the child could come up with the right answer or not. So he used a "clinical method" in which he followed the child's lead, asking probing questions or creating special exploratory tests to try to discover the child's logic. In the early days of Piaget's work, many American researchers were critical of this method, since Piaget did not ask precisely the same questions of each child. Still, the results were so striking, and often so surprising, that researchers couldn't ignore them. And when researchers devised stricter research techniques, more often than not the investigators discovered that Piaget's observations were accurate.

basic differences in the assumptions theorists make about the very nature of development, or about the proper subject matter for our study.

For example, learning theories, even Bandura's remarkably cognitive version, emphasize the vital role of experience in *shaping* the individual. Piaget, on the other hand, believed that the child uses experience to *construct* her own reality, her own understanding. Psychoanalytically inclined theorists fall somewhere between these two poles. This is not a trivial disagreement. It leads to very different questions, very different kinds of research, very different explana-tions of observed phenomena.

At the same time, you will see as we go along that many current theories involve very interesting mixtures of these four basic approaches. You've already seen this in the cognitive elements now contained in Bandura's theories, and in the ecological concepts added to a basic learning theory approach in Patterson's work. But there are many more examples, such as newer theories of the child's attachment to her parents, which combine basic psychoanalytic concepts with clearly cognitive themes such as the notion of an internal working model. And in virtually every area of study we see a return to an emphasis on biological roots. Having distinctly separate theories may be tidy, but I find the new blends, the new syntheses, far more intriguing.

As we move into the descriptive chapters, I will be coming back again and again to these basic theoretical perspectives, trying to show not only how the data we've collected have been shaped by the theoretical assumptions researchers have made, but also how the different theoretical perspectives can help us to understand the information that has accumulated. So hang in there. These ideas will turn out to be useful, helping you (and me) to create some order out of the vast array of facts.

SUMMARY

1. Facts alone will not add up to an explanation of any phenomenon, including development. Theory is also required.

2. Four families of theories have been especially influential in our thinking about human development: biological, learning, psychoanalytic, and cognitive-developmental theories.

3. Biologically-oriented theorists assume that genetic instructions can explain not only shared developmental patterns (through the mechanism of maturation) but also individual differences.

4. Modern behavior genetic research shows that heredity affects a very wide range of characteristics, including physical characteristics, intellectual skills, per-sonality traits, and psychopathologies.

5. Studies of temperament are a good example of research and theory in a bio-logical framework. There is clear evidence for a genetic contribution to varia-tions in temperament, and at least some indication that temperamental characteristics are moderately stable over the years of childhood.

6. Learning theorists generally place strongest emphasis on environmental influences, which they believe produce largely quantitative changes.

7. Basic learning processes include classical and operant conditioning, with positive, negative, and partial reinforcement principles being especially significant in explaining the acquisition and maintenance of many behaviors.

8. Bandura's influential version of learning theory, called social cognitive theory, includes more cognitive elements and the crucial concept of modeling. It

is clear that children learn not only behaviors, but also attitudes and values through modeling.

9. Psychoanalytic theorists such as Freud and Erikson have primarily studied the development of personality, emphasizing the interaction of internal instincts and environmental influences in producing shared stages of development as well as individual differences in personality.

10. Freud emphasized that behavior is governed by unconscious as well as conscious motives, and that the personality develops in steps; first the id, then the ego, and then the superego.

11. Freud also proposed a set of five psychosexual stages: oral, anal, phallic, latency, and genital. The Oedipal crisis occurs in the phallic stage.

12. Erikson emphasized social forces, more than unconscious drives, as motives for development. The key concept is the development of identity, said to occur in eight psychosocial stages over the course of the life span: trust, autonomy, initiative, industry, identity, intimacy, generativity, and ego integrity.

13. Bowlby's theory of the development of attachment, highly influential in current theorizing, has strong roots in psychoanalytic theory.

14. Cognitive-development theorists such as Piaget and his many followers emphasize the child's own active exploration of the environment as a critical ingredient leading to shared stages of development. They strongly emphasize qualitative change.

15. Piaget focused on the development of thinking, rather than personality. A key concept is that of adaptation, made up of the subprocesses of assimilation, accommodation, and equilibration.

16. The result of several major equilibrations is a set of four cognitive stages, each of which Piaget thought resulted in a coherent cognitive system: sensorimotor, preoperational, concrete operations, and formal operations.

17. No one of these theories can adequately account for all the available evidence on human development, but each offers useful concepts, and each may provide a framework within which we can examine bodies of research data.

KEY TERMS

accommodation
assimilation
classical conditioning
concrete operations stage
conditioned stimulus
ego
equilibration
extinction
formal operations stage
id
identification

intrinsic reinforcements
libido
modeling
negative reinforcement
observational learning
Oedipus conflict
operant conditioning
partial reinforcement
positive reinforcement
preoperational stage
psychosexual stages

psychosocial stages
punishment
scheme
sensorimotor stage
superego
temperament
unconditioned response
unconditioned stimulus

S U G G E S T E D   R E A D I N G S

Lerner, R. M. (1986). *Concepts and theories of human development* (2nd ed.). New York: Random House. A very good discussion of most of the major theoretical approaches I have described here.

Thomas, R. M. (Ed.) (1990). *The encyclopedia of human development and education. Theory, research, and studies.* Oxford: Pergamon Press. This is a very useful volume. It includes brief descriptions of most of the theories I have described in this chapter as well as a helpful chapter on the concept of stages. Each chapter is quite brief but covers many of the critical issues.

Chapter Three

Prenatal Development and Birth

A t a family gathering a decade or so ago, my then four-months-pregnant sister-in-law Nancy complained of a headache. Having heard warnings about the possible ill effects of various kinds of drugs during pregnancy, she was very reluctant to take any aspirin. We tried all the usual home remedies (shoulder rubs, warm baths, herb tea) but the headache persisted. Finally she took a nonaspirin pain medicine, which did the trick.

This incident brought home to me very clearly just how sensitized most women are today to the various hazards (*teratogens*) during pregnancy, including drugs. I was impressed by Nancy's determination to avoid doing anything harmful. Even more, I was struck by how long the list of "don'ts" had become, and how hard it is for a conscientious woman to be sure of what is okay and what is not.

So what do we now know? What does the list of dos and don'ts look like today? It's an important practical question for any of you who plan to be parents, and to answer it I need to explore what we know about the basic processes of development from conception to birth, as well as what we have learned about the things that can interfere with those basic processes. And of course beyond this practical issue, it is also essential for any complete understanding of child development that we begin our search at the beginning—at conception and pregnancy.

Conception

The first step in the development of a single human being is that moment of conception when a single sperm cell from the male pierces the wall of the ovum of the female—a moment captured in the photo in Figure 3.1. Ordinarily, a woman produces one **ovum** (egg cell) per month from one of her two ovaries. This occurs roughly midway between two menstrual periods. If it is not fertilized, the ovum travels from the ovary down the **fallopian tube** toward the **uterus,** where it gradually disintegrates and is expelled as part of the next menstruation.

But if a couple has intercourse during the crucial few days when the ovum is in the fallopian tube, one of the millions of sperm ejaculated as part of each male orgasm may travel the full distance through the woman's vagina, cervix, uterus, and fallopian tube and penetrate the wall of the ovum. A child is conceived. Interestingly (and perhaps surprisingly to you), only about half of such "conceptuses" are likely to survive to birth, (and such survival is rarer for male conceptuses than for female.) About a quarter are lost in the first few days after conception, often because of a flaw in the genetic material. Another quarter are spontaneously aborted ("miscarried") at a later point in the pregnancy (Wilcox et al., 1988).

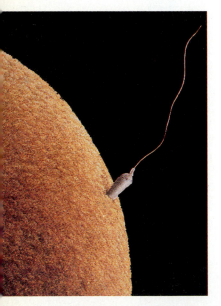

FIGURE 3.1
The moment of conception when a single sperm has pierced the shell of the ovum.

The Basic Genetics of Conception

It is hard to overestimate the importance of the genetic events accompanying conception. The combination of genes from the father in the sperm and from the mother in the ovum create a unique genetic blueprint—the **genotype**—that characterizes that specific individual. To understand how that occurs, I need to back up a few steps.

The nucleus of each cell of our bodies contains a set of 46 **chromosomes,** arranged in 23 pairs. These chromosomes include all the genetic information for that individual, including not only genetic information controlling highly individual characteristics like hair color, height, body shape, temperament, and aspects of intelligence, but also all those characteristics that all members of our species share, such as patterns of physical development or "built-in biases" of various kinds.

The only cells that do *not* contain 46 chromosomes are the sperm and the ovum, collectively called **gametes** or germ cells. In the early stages of development, gametes divide as all other cells do (a process called *mitosis*), with each set of 23 chromosome pairs "unzipping" and duplicating itself. But in gametes there is a final step, called *meiosis*, in which each new cell receives only one chromosome from each original pair. Thus each gamete has only 23 chromosomes, instead of 23 *pairs*. When a child is conceived, the 23 chromosomes in the ovum and the 23 in the sperm combine to form the 23 *pairs* that will be part of each cell in the newly developing body.

The chromosomes, in turn, are composed of long strings of molecules of a chemical called **deoxyribonucleic acid** (DNA). In an insight for which they won the Nobel Prize, James Watson and Francis Crick (1953) deduced that DNA is in the shape of a *double helix*, a kind of twisted ladder. The remarkable feature of this ladder is that the rungs are made up in such a way that the whole thing can "unzip" and then each half can guide the duplication of the missing part, thus allowing multiplication of cells with each new cell containing the full set of genetic information.

The string of DNA that makes up each chromosome can be further subdivided into segments, called **genes,** each of which controls or influences some specific feature or a portion of some developmental pattern. A gene controlling some specific characteristic, such as your blood type or your hair color, always appears in the same place (the *locus*) on the same chromosome in every individual of the same species. The locus of the gene that determines whether you have type A, B, or O blood is on chromosome 9; the locus of the gene that determines whether you have the Rh factor in your blood is on chromosome 1 (Scarr & Kidd, 1983). Geneticists have made remarkable strides in recent years in mapping the loci for a great many features or characteristics—a scientific achievement that has allowed similarly giant strides in our ability to diagnose various genetic defects or inherited diseases before a child is born.

Dominant and Recessive Genes

Because each individual inherits *two* of each chromosome (one from each parent), the genetic instructions at any given locus may be either the same (*homozygous*) or contradictory (*heterozygous*). If you receive a gene for blue eyes from both parents, your inheritance is homozygous and you will have blue eyes. But what if you receive heterozygous information, such as a gene for blue eyes from one parent and a brown-eye gene from the other?

Heterozygosity is resolved in several different ways, depending on the particular genes involved. Sometimes the two signals appear to blend, resulting in some intermediate characteristic. For example, the children of one tall parent and one short parent generally have height that falls in between. Another, rarer, outcome is that the child expresses *both* characteristics. For example, type AB blood results from the inheritance of a type A gene from one parent and a type B gene from the other. The most common outcome is that one of the two genes is *dominant* over the other, and only the dominant gene is actually expressed. The "weaker" gene, called a *recessive* gene, continues to be part of the genotype and can be passed on to offspring through meiosis, but it has no effect on visible characteristics or behavior.

A large number of specific diseases appear to be transmitted through the operation of dominant and recessive genes, such as Tay-Sachs disease, sickle-cell anemia, and cystic fibrosis. Figure 3.2 shows how this might work in the case of sickle-cell anemia, which is caused by a *recessive* gene. For an individual to have this disease, she or he must inherit the disease gene from *both* parents. A "carrier" is someone who inherits the disease gene from only one parent. Such a person does not actually have the disease, but can pass the disease gene on to his or her children. If two carriers have children together (example 3 in the figure), or if a carrier and someone with the disease have children (example 4 in the figure), their offspring may inherit disease genes from both parents and thus have the disease.

Unlike this simple example, most human characteristics are affected by many more than one gene. Temperament, intelligence, rate of growth, even apparently simple characteristics such as eye color, all involve the interaction of multiple genes. Very exciting new genetic research has also pointed toward totally unexpected additional complexities. For example, researchers studying muscular dystrophy, a recessive gene disease, have observed that this disease often becomes more severe from one generation to the next, apparently through some kind of multiplication of the DNA in the section of the chromosome that signals the disease (Fu et al., 1992). Other genetic researchers have discovered that, contrary to the long-accepted theory, the outcome may be different if a particular gene comes from the mother rather than from the father, even though the genes appear to signal precisely the same genotypic characteristic (McBride, 1991; Rogers, 1991). Research like this is beginning to unlock the secrets of genetic transmission, but there is an enormous amount that we still do not know.

> The inheritance pattern for eye color is that brown is dominant over blue. Can you figure out what your parents' genotype for eye color has to be, based on the color of your eyes, your siblings' eyes, and that of your grandparents?

FIGURE 3.2
Some examples of how a recessive gene disease, like sickle cell anemia, is transmitted. In section I, a mother who has the disease passes her sickle cell disease gene to all her children, but since her partner is normal, none of the children actually express the disease. In section II, a normal mother and a carrier father have no children with the disease, but each of their children has a 50/50 chance of carrying the SCA gene. The child can inherit the actual disease either of two ways: with two affected parents (section III) or with one carrier parent and one affected parent (section IV).

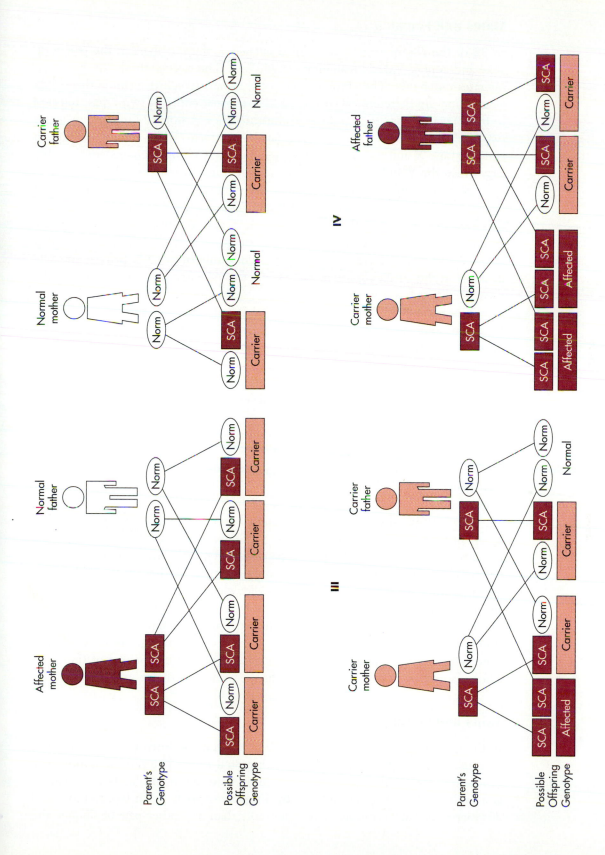

Males and Females

In 22 of the chromosome pairs, called *autosomes*, the members of the pair look alike and contain exactly matching genetic loci. The twenty-third pair, however, operates differently. The chromosomes of this pair, which determine the child's gender and are therefore called the *sex chromosomes*, come in two types, referred to by convention as the *X* and the *Y* chromosomes. A normal human female has two X chromosomes on this 23rd pair (an XX pattern), while the normal human male has one X and one Y (an XY pattern). The X chromosome is considerably larger than the Y and contains many genetic loci not matched on the Y.

Note that the sex of the child is determined by the sex chromosome it receives from the sperm. Because the mother has *only* X chromosomes, every ovum carries an X. But the father has both X and Y chromosomes. When the father's gametes divide, half the sperm will carry an X, half a Y. If the sperm that fertilizes the ovum carries an X, then the child inherits an XX pattern and will be a girl. If the fertilizing sperm carries a Y, then the combination is XY, and the infant will be a boy.

Geneticists have recently discovered that only one very small section of the Y chromosome actually determines maleness—a segment referred to as *TDF, or testis-determining factor* (Page et al., 1987). Fertilized ova that are genetically XY, but that lack the TDF, develop physically as female.

One important consequence of the difference between X and Y chromosomes is that a boy inherits many genes from his mother on his X chromosome that are not matched by, or counteracted by, equivalent genetic material on the smaller Y chromosome. Among other things, this means that recessive diseases or other recessive characteristics that have their loci on the nonmatched parts of the X chromosome may be inherited by a boy directly from his mother, a pattern called *sex-linked* transmission. Figure 3.3 illustrates this with the disease hemophilia.

You can see that for females, sex-linked recessive genes operate just as they do in other recessive diseases; the girl will have the characteristic only if she inherits the recessive gene from both parents. But a male will inherit the characteristic by receiving the recessive gene only from his mother. Since his Y chromosome from his father contains no parallel loci for these characteristics, there are no counteracting instructions and the recessive mother's gene causes the disorder or other characteristic. For sex-linked characteristics like muscular dystrophy or hemophilia, half the sons of women who carry the recessive disease gene will have the disease, and half the daughters will be carriers of the gene. These daughters, in turn, will pass the disease on to half their sons.

Twins and Siblings

In the great majority of cases, babies are conceived and born one at a time. But multiple births occur roughly once in a hundred cases. The most common type of multiple birth is *fraternal twins*, when more than one ovum has been produced and both have been fertilized, each by a separate sperm. Such twins, also called *dizygotic* twins, are no more alike genetically than any other pair of siblings and

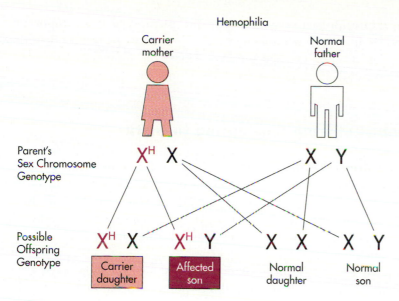

FIGURE 3.3

Compare the pattern of sex-linked transmission of a recessive disease with the patterns already shown in Figure 3.2. In a sex-linked inheritance, like this example with hemophilia, a carrier mother can pass on the disease to half her sons (on average) because there is no offsetting gene on the Y chromosome. But a daughter of a carrier mother will not inherit the disease itself unless her father has the disease.

need not even be of the same sex. In rarer cases, a single fertilized ovum may divide and each half may develop into a separate individual. These are *identical* or *monozygotic* twins. They have identical genetic heritages because they come from precisely the same original fertilized ovum. You'll remember from Chapter 2 that comparisons of the degree of similarity of these two types of twins is one of the major research strategies in the important field of behavior genetics.

Genotypes and Phenotypes

Using such strategies, behavior geneticists have made great strides in identifying those skills, characteristics, or traits that heredity influences. But no geneticist proposes that an inherited combination of genes fully *determines* any outcome for a given individual. Geneticists (and psychologists) make an important distinction between the genotype, which is the specific set of "instructions" contained in a given individual's genes, and the **phenotype,** which is the actual observed characteristics of the individual. The phenotype is a product of three things: the genotype, environmental influences from the time of conception onward, and the interaction between the environment and the genotype. A child might have a genotype associated with high IQ, but if his mother drinks too much alcohol during the pregnancy there may be damage to the fetal nervous system, resulting in mild retardation. Another child might have a genotype for a "difficult" temperament, but have parents who are particularly sensitive and thoughtful, making it possible for the child to learn other ways to handle himself.

Can you think of other examples where the phenotype would be different from the genotype?

The distinction between genotype and phenotype is an important one. Genetic codes are not irrevocable signals for this or that pattern of development, or this or that disease. The specific experiences the individual may have from conception onward affects her eventual developmental outcome.

Development from Conception to Birth

If we assume that conception takes place 2 weeks after a menstrual period, when ovulation normally occurs, then the period of gestation of the human infant is 38 weeks (about 265 days). Most physicians calculate gestation as 40 weeks, counting from the last menstrual period. All the specifications of weeks of gestation I've given here are based on the 38-week calculation, counting from the presumed time of conception.

These 38 weeks have been subdivided in several different ways. Physicians typically talk in terms of three equal three-month periods, or *trimesters*. In contrast, biologists and embryologists divide the weeks of gestation into three subperiods of unequal length. These are the *germinal*, which lasts roughly two weeks; the *embryonic*, which continues until about 8 to 12 weeks after conception; and the *fetal* stage, which makes up the remaining 26 to 30 weeks.

The Germinal Stage: From Conception to Implantation

Some time during the first 24 to 36 hours after conception, cell division begins; within two to three days there are several dozen cells and the whole mass is about the size of a pinhead. This mass of cells is undifferentiated until about four days after conception. At that point the organism, now a *blastocyst*, begins to subdivide. A cavity begins to appear within the ball of cells, and the mass divides into two parts. The outer cells will form the various structures that will support the developing organism, while the inner mass will form the embryo itself. When it touches the wall of the uterus, the outer shell of cells in the blastocyst breaks down at the point of contact. Small tendrils develop and attach the cell mass to the uterine wall, a process called *implantation*. You can see the sequence schematically in Figure 3.4. When implantation occurs, normally 10 days to 2 weeks after conception, there are perhaps 150 cells in the blastocyst (Tanner, 1978).

The Embryonic Stage

The embryonic stage begins when implantation is complete and continues until the various support structures are fully formed and all the major organ systems have been laid down in at least rudimentary form, a process that normally takes another 6 to 10 weeks.

Support Structures. Two of the key support structures that develop out of the outer layer of cells are the **amnion,** which is the sac or bag, filled with liquid, in which the baby floats, and that marvelous organ, the **placenta,** a plate-like mass of cells that lies against the wall of the uterus. The placenta, which is

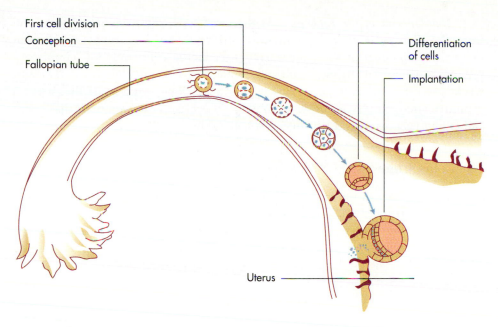

First cell division
Conception
Fallopian tube
Differentiation of cells
Implantation
Uterus

FIGURE 3.4

In this schematic drawing, you can see the sequence of changes during the germinal stage, with the first cell division and the first differentiation of cell function normally occurring in the fallopian tube.

fully developed by about four weeks of gestation, serves as liver, lungs, and kidneys for the embryo and fetus.

Through this large filter, nutrients such as oxygen, proteins, sugars, and vitamins from the maternal blood can pass through to the embryo or fetus, while digestive wastes and carbon dioxide from the infant's blood pass back through to the mother, whose own body can eliminate them (Rosenblith & Sims-Knight, 1989). At the same time, many (but not all) harmful substances, such as viruses, are too large to pass through the various membranes in the placenta and are filtered out, as are most of the mother's hormones. Most drugs and anesthetics, however, do pass through the placental barrier, as do some disease organisms. You can see all these separate structures in Figure 3.5.

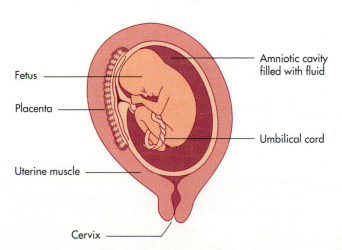

Fetus
Placenta
Uterine muscle
Cervix
Amniotic cavity filled with fluid
Umbilical cord

FIGURE 3.5

You can see here how the various structures are organized during the fetal period. Note especially the placenta and the umbilical cord, and the fact that the fetus floats in the amniotic fluid.

Development of the Embryo. At the same time, the mass of cells that will form the embryo is itself differentiating further into several types of cells that form the rudiments of skin, sense receptors, nerve cells, muscles, circulatory system, and internal organs. Such differentiation is remarkably swift. By eight weeks gestation, the embryo is roughly 1½ inches long, has a heart that beats, a primitive circulatory system, the beginnings of eyes and ears, a mouth that opens and closes, legs, arms, and a primitive spinal cord.

The Fetal Stage

The seven months of the fetal stage involve primarily a process of refining all the primitive organ systems already in place, much like what happens in constructing a house, when the framework is created quickly, but the finishing work is lengthy. You can get a feeling for the rapidity of the changes by looking at Table 3.1, which lists some of the milestones of fetal development.

The point of viability—the weeks of gestation at which a baby born prematurely has a reasonable chance of survival—is about 24 to 25 weeks (Allen, Donohue, & Dusman, 1993). Babies born at 22 and 23 weeks occasionally survive, but that is rare, and most physicians now agree that improved medical technology is unlikely to push this viability limit any further.

Development of the Nervous System. One of the least well-developed elements at the end of the embryonic period is the nervous system, which is composed of two basic types of cells, **neurons** and **glial cells.** The glial cells are the glue that holds the whole nervous system together, providing firmness and structure to the brain (Kandel, 1985). It is the neurons that do the job of receiving

TABLE 3.1
Major Milestones of Fetal Development

Gestational Age	Major New Developments
12 weeks	Sex of child can be determined; muscles develop more extensively; eyelids and lips are present; feet have toes and hands have fingers.
16 weeks	First fetal movement is usually felt by the mother at about this time; bones begin to develop; fairly complete ear formation.
20 weeks	Hair growth begins; child is very human-looking at this age and it's possible to see thumbsucking.
24 weeks	Eyes are completely formed (but closed); fingernails, sweat glands, and taste buds are all formed; there is some fat deposit beneath skin.
28 weeks	Nervous system, blood, and breathing systems are all well enough developed to support life although prematures born at this stage have poor sleep-wake cycles and irregular breathing.
29–40 weeks	Interconnections between individual nerve cells (neurons) develop rapidly; weight is added; general "finishing" of body systems takes place.

and sending messages from one part of the brain to another or from one part of the body to another.

Neurons have four main parts, which are illustrated in Figure 3.6: a cell body; branchlike extensions of the cell body called **dendrites,** which are the major *receptors* of nerve impulses; a tubular extension of the cell body called the **axon,** which can extend as far as 1 meter in length in humans (about 3 feet); and branchlike terminal fibers at the end of the axon, which form the primary *transmitting* apparatus of the nervous system. Because of the branchlike appearance of dendrites, physiologists often use botanical terms to describe them, speaking of the "dendritic arbor" or of "pruning" of the arbor.

The point at which two neurons connect, where the axon's transmitting fibers come into close contact with another neuron's dendrites, is called a **synapse.** The number of such synapses is vast. A single cell in the part of the brain that controls vision, for instance, may have as many as 10,000 to 30,000 synaptic inputs to its dendrites (Greenough, Black, & Wallace, 1987).

Glial cells begin to develop at about 13 weeks after conception and continue to be added until perhaps two years after birth. Neurons begin to appear at about 12 weeks and are virtually all present by 28 weeks. But at this early stage the neurons consist largely of the cell body. Axons are short, and there is little dendritic development. It is in the last two months before birth, and the first few years after birth, that the lengthening of the axons and the major growth of the "dendritic arbor" occurs, making possible the vast numbers of synapses necessary for all aspects of human functioning (Parmelee & Sigman, 1983).

> Can you think of any practical consequences of the fact that all the neurons one is ever going to have are present by about 28 weeks of gestation?

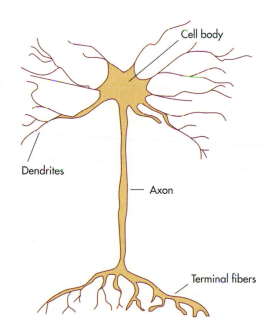

FIGURE 3.6
The structure of a single developed neuron. The cell bodies develop first, primarily between weeks 12 and 24. Axons and dendrites develop later, especially during the final 12 weeks, and continue to increase in size and complexity for several years after birth.

Cell body

Dendrites

Axon

Terminal fibers

Development of Length and Weight. Similarly, the major growth in fetal size occurs late in the fetal period. The fetus is about half her birth length by about 20 weeks gestation, but she does not reach half her birthweight until nearly three months later, at about 32 weeks.

An Overview of Prenatal Development

One of the most important points about the child's prenatal development is how remarkably regular and predictable it is. If the embryo has survived the early, risky period (roughly the first 12 weeks) development usually proceeds smoothly, with the various changes occurring in what is apparently a fixed order, at fixed time intervals, following a clear maturational groundplan.

This sequence of development is not immune to modification or outside influence, as you'll soon see in detail. But before I begin talking about the various things that can go wrong, I want to make sure to state clearly that the maturational system is really quite robust. Normal prenatal development requires an adequate environment, but "adequate" seems to be a fairly broad range. *Most* children are quite normal. The list of things that *can* go wrong is long and getting longer as our knowledge expands. Yet many of these possibilities are quite rare, many are partially or wholly preventable, and many need not have permanent consequences for the child. Keep this in mind as you read through the next few pages.

The potential problems fall into two large classes: genetic errors and those damaging environmental events called *teratogens*. Genetic errors occur at the moment of conception, and there is little that can be done about them. Teratogens may affect development any time from conception onward.

Genetic Errors

Note the distinctive facial characteristics of this Down syndrome child.

In perhaps 3 to 8 percent of all fertilized ova (Kopp, 1983), the genetic material itself contains errors because either the sperm or the ovum has failed to divide correctly, so that there are either too many or too few chromosomes. Current estimates are that perhaps 90 percent of these abnormal conceptuses are spontaneously aborted. Only about 1 percent of live newborns have such abnormalities.

Over 50 different types of chromosomal anomaly have been identified, many of them very rare. The most common is **Down syndrome** (also called *mongolism* and *trisomy 21*), in which the child, because of a failure of proper meiosis in either sperm or ovum, has three copies of chromosome 21 rather than the normal two. Other forms of trisomy also occur, of course, but Down syndrome is by far the most frequent. Estimates of the incidence of this abnormality differ, but all fall in the range of 1 out of 600 and 1 out of 1,000 (Nightingale & Goodman, 1990). These children have distinctive facial features (as you can see in the photo) and are typically retarded.

The risk of bearing a child with this deviant pattern is greatest for mothers over 35. Among women aged 35 to 39, the incidence of Down syndrome is about 1 in 280 births; among 40-year-olds it is roughly 1 in 100, and for mothers aged 45 it is 1 in 30 births (D'Alton & DeCherney, 1993). Recent epidemiological research also reveals a possible link between exposure to environmental toxins of various kinds and the risk of offspring with Down syndrome. For example, one large study in Canada shows that men who work as mechanics, farm laborers, or sawmill workers, who are regularly exposed to solvents, oils, lead, and pesticides, are at higher risk for fathering Down syndrome children than are men who work in cleaner environments (Olshan, Baird, & Teschke, 1989). Findings like this suggest that chromosomal anomalies may not be purely random events, but may themselves be a response to various teratogens.

Sex-Chromosome Anomalies.   A second class of anomalies is associated with an incomplete or incorrect division of either sex chromosome, which occurs in roughly 1 out of every 400 births (Berch & Bender, 1987). The most common is an XXY pattern, or Klinefelter's syndrome, which occurs in roughly 1 or 2 out of every 1,000 males. Affected boys most often look quite normal, although they have underdeveloped testes and, as adults, a sparsity of sperm. Most are not mentally retarded, but language and learning disabilities are common.

Not quite as common is the XYY pattern. These children also develop as boys, are typically unusually tall and have mild retardation. A single-X pattern (XO), or Turner's syndrome, and a triple-X pattern (XXX) may also occur, and in both cases the child develops as a girl. Girls with Turner's syndrome are exceptions to the usual rule that embryos with too few chromosomes do not survive. These girls show stunted growth, are usually sterile, and often perform particularly poorly on tests that measure spatial ability. On tests of verbal skill, however, Turner's syndrome girls are at or above normal levels (Scarr & Kidd, 1983). Girls with an XXX pattern are of normal size but are slower than normal in physical development. They also have markedly poor verbal abilities (Rovet & Netley, 1983). As a general rule, children with sex chromosome anomalies are not as severely affected as what we see in Down syndrome, but they do show unusual physical features and some cognitive deficits.

Fragile-X Syndrome.   A quite different type of genetic anomaly, which has received a good deal of attention lately, involves not an improper amount of chromosomal material, but rather an abnormal section of DNA at a specific location on the X chromosome (Dykens, Hodapp, & Leckman, 1994). This is an inherited disorder, following the sex-linked inheritance illustrated earlier in Figure 3.3. Thus both boys and girls can inherit a fragile X (ordinarily from a carrier mother), but boys are much more susceptible to the negative intellectual or behavioral consequences, because they lack the potentially overriding influence of a normal X. The affected child appears to have a considerably heightened risk of mental retardation; current estimates are that among males, this syndrome causes 5 to 7 percent of all retardation (Zigler & Hodapp, 1991).

Single Gene Defects.   As I have already indicated, a child may also inherit a gene for a specific disease. In a few cases, such diseases may be caused by a dominant gene. The best-known example is Huntington's disease, a severe neurological disorder resulting in rapid loss of both mental and physical functioning, with symptoms usually appearing only at midlife. Dominant gene diseases are relatively rare because the affected parent would almost always know that he or she was

TABLE 3.2
Some Common Inherited Diseases

Phenylketonuria	A metabolic disorder caused by a recessive gene that prevents metabolism of a common amino acid (phenylalanine). Treatment consists of a special phenylalanine-free diet. The child is not allowed many types of food, including milk. If not placed on the special diet shortly after birth, the child usually becomes very retarded (IQs of 30 and below are not uncommon). Affects only 1 in 8,000 children. Cannot be diagnosed prenatally, but can be detected at birth with a test now routinely given.
Tay-Sachs disease	An invariably fatal recessive gene-degenerative disease of the nervous system; virtually all victims die within the first three to four years. The gene is carried primarily by those of Eastern European Jewish ancestry, among whom the risk is roughly 1 in 3,600 births. Can be diagnosed prenatally.
Sickle-cell anemia	A sometimes fatal blood disease, transmitted with a recessive gene, with symptoms including joint pain and increased susceptibility to infection. The gene is carried by an estimated 2 million Americans, primarily Blacks, among whom 1 in 400 infants inherits the disorder. Can be diagnosed prenatally.
Cystic fibrosis	A fatal disease affecting the lungs and intestinal tract. Many children with CF now live into their twenties. This recessive gene is carried by over 10 million Americans, most often whites, among whom 1 in 1,600 infants inherit the disease. Carriers cannot be identified before pregnancy, and affected children cannot be diagnosed prenatally. If a couple has had one CF child, however, they know that each successive child has a 1 in 4 chance of being affected.
Muscular Dystrophy	A fatal muscle-wasting disease, carried on the X chromosome, found almost exclusively among boys. The gene for the most common type of MD, Duchenne's, has now been located, so prenatal diagnosis may soon be available.

Source: Nightingale & Goodman, 1990.

suffering from the disorder and may be unable or unwilling to reproduce. Far more common are recessive-gene diseases, some of which I've listed in Table 3.2. The few examples listed in the table do not begin to convey the diversity of such disorders. Among known causes of mental retardation, there are 141 diseases or disorders with known genetic loci and 361 more whose locus has not yet been identified (Wahlström, 1990).

Geneticists estimate that the average adult carries genes for four different recessive diseases or abnormalities (Scarr & Kidd, 1983), but for any one disease the distribution of genes is not random. For example, sickle-cell genes are more common among Blacks; Tay-Sachs is most common among Jews of Eastern European origin.

Teratogens: Diseases and Drugs

Deviant prenatal development can also result from variations in the environment in which the embryo and fetus are nurtured. I pointed out in Chapter 1 that the effect of most teratogens seems to depend heavily on their *timing* (Vorhees &

Not so many years ago children were born with whatever deformities, diseases, or anomalies happened to come along. The parents had no choices. Today, parents have access to many types of genetic information and tests to detect fetal abnormalities, which increase choice, but may also create difficult decisions.

Prepregnancy Genetic Testing

Prepregnancy blood tests can tell you and your spouse whether you are carriers of genes for those specific diseases for which the loci are known, such as Tay-Sachs or sickle-cell anemia. This may be an important step if you and your spouse belong to a subgroup carrying particular recessive genes.

Prenatal Diagnosis of the Fetus

Four prenatal diagnostic strategies are now available. Two of these, the **alpha-fetoprotein test** (AFP), and ultrasound, are primarily used to detect problems in the formation of the *neural tube*, the structure that becomes the brain and spinal cord. If the tube fails to close at the bottom end, a disability called *spina bifida* occurs. Children with this defect are often partially paralyzed, and many (but not all) are retarded.

Alpha-fetoprotein is a substance produced by the fetus and detectable in the mother's blood. If the blood test, normally done between 16 to 18 weeks of gestation, shows an abnormally high AFP level, it suggests that there may be some problem with spinal cord or brain. It does not mean there is definitely a problem; it means there is a higher *risk* of problems and further tests are indicated.

One such further test is **ultrasound,** which involves the use of sound waves to provide an actual "moving picture" of the fetus. With this method it is frequently possible to detect or rule out neural tube defects or other physical abnormalities. The procedure is not painful and gives parents an often delightful chance to see their unborn child moving, but it cannot provide information about the presence of chromosomal anomalies or inherited diseases.

The Real World
Prenatal Diagnosis of Genetic Errors

If you want the latter information, you have two choices: **amniocentesis,** or **chorionic villus sampling** (CVS). In both cases, a needle is inserted and cells are taken from the developing embryo. In CVS, the sample is taken from what will become the placenta; in amniocentesis, the sample is from the amniotic fluid. Of the two, amniocentesis was developed earlier and is the more widely used. Its major drawback is that because the amniotic sac must be large enough to allow a sample of fluid to be taken with very little danger to the fetus, the test cannot be done until the sixteenth week of gestation and the results are not typically available for several more weeks. If the test reveals an abnormality, and the parents decide to abort, it is quite late for an abortion to be performed. CVS, in contrast, is done between the ninth and eleventh weeks of gestation. Neither of these procedures is without risk. Both procedures sometimes cause miscarriages, and there has been a recent flurry of concern about *possible* links between CVS and slight increases in physical defects in the infant (Report of the National Institute, 1993). Both procedures are recommended only for women known to be at high risk, such as those older than 35, or those who have borne a previous child with defects or chromosomal anomaly.

By the time you are facing this choice, there may be still newer and safer options using maternal blood samples; for example, researchers have just reported that they can identify 89 percent of Down syndrome fetuses with a combination of three blood tests, including an alpha-fetoprotein test (Haddow et al., 1994). But no matter what technique you may select, the moral and ethical choices you may have to make are far from easy.

For example, consider the case of diseases that can occur in mild or moderate as well as severe forms—such as sickle-cell anemia. Prenatal tests can tell you if the child will inherit the disease, but they cannot tell you how severely the child will be affected. Genetic counselors may play a very helpful role, but ultimately each couple has to make its own decisions.

Mollnow, 1987), an example of *critical periods*, or *sensitive periods*. The general rule is that each organ system is most vulnerable to disruption at the time when it is developing most rapidly (Moore, 1988). At that point it is most sensitive to outside interference, whether that be from a disease organism that passes through the placental barrier, inappropriate hormones, drugs, or whatever. Because most organ systems develop most rapidly during the first 12 weeks of gestation, this is the period of greatest risk for most teratogens. Of the many teratogens, the most critical are probably drugs the mother may take and diseases she may have or may contract during the pregnancy.

Diseases of the Mother

There are at least three mechanisms by which a disease in the mother can affect the embryo or fetus. Some diseases, particularly viruses, can attack the placenta, reducing the nutrients available to the embryo. Some others have molecules small enough to pass through the placental filters and attack the embryo or fetus directly. Examples of this type include rubella and rubeola (both forms of measles), cytomegalovirus (CMV), syphilis, diphtheria, influenza, typhoid, serum hepatitis, and chicken pox. Additionally, disease organisms present in the mucus membranes of the birth canal may infect the infant during birth itself. Genital herpes, for example, is transmitted this way. So far as researchers now know, AIDS is transmitted both directly through the placenta and during delivery, as well as through breast milk after birth (Van de Perre et al., 1991). Of all these diseases, probably the riskiest for the child are rubella, AIDS, and CMV.

> Women readers: have you been vaccinated for rubella? If you don't know, find out; if you have not been, arrange for such a vaccination—but only if you are sure you are not pregnant!

Rubella.   Rubella (also called German measles) is most risky during the first month of gestation. Half of infants exposed in this time show abnormalities of the ears, eyes, or heart, while only a quarter show effects if they are exposed in the second month (Berg, 1974; Kopp, 1983). Deafness is the most common outcome.

Fortunately, rubella is preventable. Vaccination is available and all children should receive this vaccine as part of a regular immunization program. Adult women who were not vaccinated as children can receive a vaccination later, but it must be done at least three months before a pregnancy to provide complete immunity.

AIDS.   At present, there are approximately 3,000 infants with AIDS in the United States, a relatively low rate in comparison to many other diseases of childhood. But because the number of infected women of childbearing age continues to grow, the number of infants born infected with the HIV virus will also grow. In areas with a high population of drug users, as many as 3 to 5 percent of all pregnant women are now HIV-infected (Heagarty, 1991). The only good news in all of this is that not all infants born to HIV-infected mothers themselves become infected. Estimates range from 13 percent in a European study (European Collaborative Study, 1991) to 30 percent in U.S. studies (Hutto et al., 1991). Researchers are still searching for good explanations for this pattern of transmission.

CMV.   A much less well known but remarkably widespread and potentially serious disease is cytomegalovirus (CMV), a virus in the herpes group that is the leading cause of congenital infection in the United States. As many as 60 percent of *all* women have antibodies to CMV, but most have no recognized symptoms. One to 2 percent of babies whose mothers have CMV antibodies become infected prenatally. Among those whose disease is in an active phase, the transmission rate is more like 40–50 percent (Blackman, 1990). As with AIDS, researchers have not yet uncovered all the details of the mechanisms of transmission. Nor have they understood why only about 5 to 10 percent of babies infected prenatally show clear symptoms of the disease at birth. But the 2,500 babies born each year in the United States who do display symptoms of the disease have a variety of serious problems, often including deafness and widespread damage to the central nervous system (Hicks et al., 1993). Most are mentally retarded. In fact, CMV is now thought to be the single most important known infectious cause of both congenital mental retardation and deafness.

Drugs Taken by the Mother

Ten or 15 years ago, the average pregnant woman in the U.S. took six to seven prescribed drugs and another three or four over-the-counter drugs (such as aspirin) during the course of her pregnancy (Stewart, Cluff, & Philp, 1977). Today that number is doubtless lower, but it is not zero. What are the effects of any of these drugs on the embryo or fetus?

There is now a huge literature on the effects of prenatal drugs, involving everything from aspirin to antibiotics to alcohol and cocaine. Sorting out their effects has proven to be an immensely challenging task, not only because it is clearly not possible to assign women randomly to various drug groups, but also because in the real world most women take multiple drugs during their pregnancy. Women who drink alcohol are also more likely to smoke; those who use cocaine are also likely to take other illegal drugs, or to smoke or drink to excess. What is more, the effects of drugs may be subtle, visible only many years after birth in the form of minor learning disabilities or increased risk of behavior problems. Still, we are creeping toward some fairly clear conclusions in several areas. Let me give you some examples.

Smoking. One of the most extensive bodies of research is on the effect of smoking. One consistent result stands out: infants of mothers who smoke are *on average* about half a pound lighter at birth than are infants of nonsmoking mothers (Vorhees & Mollnow, 1987) and are twice as likely to be born weighing less than 2,500 grams (5.5 lbs) (Floyd et al., 1993). This does not mean that every mother who smokes has a very small or early baby. It does mean that the risk of such an outcome is higher for mothers who smoke. The causal mechanism seems to work this way: nicotine constricts the blood vessels, which reduces blood flow to the placenta, in turn reducing nutrition to the fetus. In the long term, such nutritional deprivation seems to increase slightly the risk of learning problems or poor attention span at school age (Naeye & Peters, 1984). There are also some signs of higher rates of behavior problems among children whose mothers smoked heavily during pregnancy (Fergusson, Horwood, & Lynskey, 1993).

Although research on the effects of smoking is not always easy to interpret, because women who smoke are likely to differ in other ways from those who do not, the moral seems clear: the safest plan is not to smoke during pregnancy. This

Before you read further, make a list of all the drugs you have taken in the past year, including over-the-counter drugs (for example, aspirin or decongestants) prescription drugs, and such "recreational" drugs as alcohol, nicotine, or cocaine. How many are there? How hard would it be to give them all up if you were pregnant?

Another possible problem, Rh factor incompatibility, is neither a genetic defect nor a teratogenic effect, but an interesting interaction of heredity and environment. One of the many factors in the blood is the presence or absence of a red cell antigen, called the Rh factor because rhesus monkeys have it. Humans who have this factor are called Rh+ (Rh positive), while those who lack it are Rh− (Rh negative). Only about 15 percent of Whites and 5 percent of Blacks in the United States are Rh−; it is quite rare among Asians and Native Americans.

The Real World
Rh Factor.
Another Type
of Genetic Problem

Problems arise if the mother is Rh− and the baby is Rh+. Because Rh+ is dominant, a baby with an Rh+ father could inherit an Rh+ gene from him, even though the mother is Rh−. If the mother's and fetus's blood mix in the uterus, the mother's body considers the baby's Rh+ factor to be a foreign substance, and her immune system tries to fight it off by producing antibodies. These antibodies cross the placenta and attack the baby's blood, producing a chemical substance in the baby called bilirubin. Babies with high levels of bilirubin

look quite yellow; without medical treatment brain damage can occur.

Without treatment, the risk of damage to the fetus increases with each succeeding pregnancy in which an Rh− mother carries an Rh+ baby. Normally, the placenta keeps the two blood systems separate, but during birth some mixing usually occurs. So after the first baby, the mother produces some antibodies. With a second incompatible baby, these antibodies attack the infant's blood, producing negative effects.

This problem used to be treated with rather heroic measures, such as complete exchange of the infant's blood shortly after birth to remove all the antibodies. Fortunately, scientists have now discovered a much simpler and safer treatment. Within three days of the birth of her first child, an Rh− mother with an Rh+ baby can get an injection of rhogam, a substance which prevents the buildup of antibodies, and thus protects subsequent infants, even if they are also Rh+.

research also shows a relationship between the "dose" (the amount of nicotine you are taking in) and the severity of consequences for the child. So if you cannot quit entirely, at least cut back.

Drinking. Recent work on the effects of maternal alcohol ingestion on prenatal and postnatal development also carries a clear message: to be safe, don't drink during pregnancy.

The effects of alcohol on the developing fetus range from mild to severe. At the extreme end of the continuum are children who exhibit a syndrome called **fetal alcohol syndrome** (FAS) (Jones et al., 1973). Their mothers are heavy drinkers or alcoholics, and the infants themselves are generally smaller than normal, with smaller brains. They frequently have heart defects, and their faces are distinctively different (as you can see in Figure 3.7). As children, adolescents, and adults they continue to be shorter than normal, have smaller heads, and IQ scores in the range of mild mental retardation. Indeed, FAS is the leading known cause of retardation in the United States, exceeding even Down syndrome (Streissguth et al., 1991b).

But the effects of alcohol during pregnancy are not confined to cases in which the mother is clearly an alcoholic or a very heavy drinker. Recent evidence also points to milder effects of moderate or "social" drinking. Children of mothers who drank at this level during pregnancy are more likely to have IQs below 85, and show poorer attention span. I've given some details about one of the best studies in the *Research Report* on page 80, so you can get some feeling for how investigators have gone about studying this problem.

We do not yet know if there is any safe level of alcohol consumption during pregnancy, although most of those who work in this field are convinced that there is a linear relationship between the amount of alcohol ingested and the risk for the infant. This means that even at low dosage there is *some* increased risk. Probably it also matters when in the pregnancy the drinking occurs, and it clearly matters how many drinks the mother drinks on any one occasion. Research has shown that binge drinking is significantly riskier than regular smaller doses (Olson et al., 1992; Streissguth, Barr, & Sampson, 1990). In the face of our remaining ignorance, the *safest* course is not to drink at all.

Cocaine. Significant numbers of pregnant women in the United States (and presumably elsewhere in the world) also take various illegal drugs, most notably cocaine, although it is of course difficult to know exactly how prevalent the problem is, because many women are understandably reluctant to reveal such information to researchers or physicians. The best current estimates are that roughly 3 percent of all babies born in the U.S. have been prenatally exposed to cocaine. The risk is far higher among babies born to poor, inner-city mothers. In these groups, by some estimates, as many as 20 or 30 percent of mothers use cocaine (Hawley & Disney, 1992).

Cocaine appears to cross the placental barrier quite readily, but unlike alcohol, it creates no regular or recognizable syndrome of abnormalities. About a third of all cocaine-exposed babies are born prematurely, and among those born after a normal gestation period, many more are lower than normal in birth weight—a pattern that is very similar to what we see with smoking during pregnancy. In addition, they are three times as likely to have very small head circumferences. Some cocaine-exposed babies also show significant withdrawal symptoms after birth, such as irritability, restlessness, shrill crying, and tremors. Whether there are any long-term consequences that can be ascribed clearly to prenatal cocaine exposure, however, is not yet clear. Some studies show long-term effects, while others do not (Griffith, Azuma, & Chasnoff, 1994; Richardson & Day, 1994). My sense is that we will eventually find that, as with alcohol exposure, the effects of cocaine are subtle and long-lasting, but that remains to be shown.

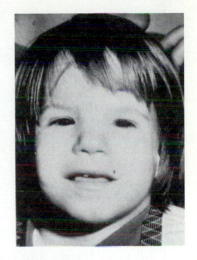

FIGURE 3.7
Fetal alcohol syndrome children, too, have distinctive facial features. (Source: Streissguth et al., *Science, 209* [July 18, 1980]: Figure 2, p. 355. Copyright 1980 by the American Association for the Advancement of Science.)

Other Teratogens

There are a great many other teratogens, including excess amounts of vitamin A, methylmercury, and lead, and many drugs or chemicals suspected of being teratogens about which we have insufficient information. These include anticonvulsant medication taken by epileptics, polychlorinated biphenyls (PCBs, compounds widely used in electrical transformers and paint), radiation at high doses, aspirin, some antidepressants, some artificial hormones, and some pesticides (Vorhees & Mollnow, 1987). There is no room for me to go into detail about what we know (or don't know) in each case, but let me say just a word about several of the more practically significant of the items on this list.

Streissguth's Study of Prenatal Alcohol Exposure

The best single study of the consequences of prenatal alcohol exposure has been done by Ann Streissguth and her colleagues (Olson et al., 1992; 1990; 1989; 1980; 1984; 1981), who followed a group of over 500 women and children beginning in early pregnancy. Since the study was begun before there were widespread warnings about the possible impact of alcohol during pregnancy, the sample includes many well-educated, middle-class women with good diets who did not take many other recreational drugs but who did drink alcohol in moderate or even fairly heavy amounts while pregnant—a set of conditions that would be impossible to duplicate today, at least in the United States or other countries in which the risks are well advertised.

Streissguth tested the children repeatedly, beginning immediately after birth, again later in infancy, at age 4, at school age, and again at age 11. She found that the mother's alcohol consumption in pregnancy was associated with sluggishness and weaker sucking in infancy, lower scores on a test of infant intelligence at 8 months, lower IQ at 4 and 7 years, and problems with attention and vigilance at 4, 7, and 11. Teachers also rated the 11-year-olds on overall school performance and on various behavior problems, and on both measures those whose mothers had consumed the most alcohol during pregnancy were rated significantly lower.

Streissguth also was careful to obtain information about other drug use in pregnancy, including smoking. She also asked mothers about their diet, education, and life habits. She has found that the links between alcohol consumption and poor outcomes for the child hold up even when all these other variables are controlled statistically.

Setting aside those cases in which the child was diagnosed with the full fetal alcohol syndrome, the effects of moderate levels of alcohol use during pregnancy are not large in absolute terms, but they have significant practical consequences. For example, the difference in IQ scores at age 7 between children of abstainers and children of women who drank 1 ounce or more of alcohol per day during their pregnancy was only about 6 points in Streissguth's sample (Streissguth et al., 1990). But this relatively small absolute difference means that three times as many alcohol-exposed children have IQs below 85 than is true among children of abstainers. Alcohol-exposed children are thus greatly overrepresented in special classes in schools and probably also appear in overlarge numbers among high school dropouts and the underemployed in adulthood—although those links remain for longer-term longitudinal studies to confirm.

Diethylstilbestrol (DES). DES is a synthetic estrogen that at one time was commonly given to pregnant woman to prevent miscarriages. The daughters of such women have been found to have higher rates of some kinds of cancers, and as many as 30 percent of the sons have been found to be infertile (Rosenblith & Sims-Knight, 1989).

Aspirin. One of the most widely used drugs, aspirin, is teratogenic in animals when given in high doses. Humans rarely take high enough doses to produce such effects directly, but it turns out that aspirin in moderate amounts can have negative effects on the human fetus if it is ingested along with benzoic acid, a chemical widely used as a food preservative, such as in ketchup. This combination, especially in the first trimester, seems to increase the risk of physical malformations in the embryo/fetus.

Lead. In most industrialized countries, adults are exposed to fairly high dosages of lead, although the introduction of unleaded gasoline has had a significant impact on dosages, as has the elimination of lead-based paint. We have known for some time that high exposure to lead, such as from lead-based paints in old houses, has highly negative consequences, particularly for the child's intellectual development and functioning. But a new set of studies shows that even quite low levels of lead in the blood of newborns or toddlers—levels classified as "safe" by current U.S. federal guidelines and found in children who live in houses without lead-based paint—are associated with slightly lower IQ scores at later ages than we see in children with still lower lead levels (Bellinger et al., 1991; Dietrich et al., 1987). In one longitudinal study, the effects were still detectable at age 10 (Bellinger, Stiles, & Needleman, 1992).

As the study of teratogens expands, psychologists have realized that prenatal development is less insulated, less fully protected than we had first thought. In particular, many chemicals associated with modern industrial societies may have unforeseen effects on the fetus.

Other Influences on Prenatal Development

Diet.   Another risk for the fetus is poor maternal nutrition. In periods of famine, for example, preterm and low-birth-weight births are greatly increased, as is the death rate for infants in the first year of life (Stein et al., 1975). Studies of famine show that the consequences are most detrimental if such acute malnutrition occurred during the last three months of the pregnancy, when neurons are beginning a rapid expansion of dendritic density.

The effects of chronic subnutrition, associated with poverty, are less clear. Most experts have concluded that these milder forms of dietary insufficiency have no *direct* negative effect on the baby's developing brain (Ricciuti, 1993). Instead, what seems to happen is some variation of the interaction pattern I described in Chapter 1 (recall Figure 1.4): malnutrition may make the infant more "vulnerable," perhaps because it makes him less energetic or responsive, or less able to learn from his experiences. In a nonstimulating environment such a vulnerable child is likely to do poorly. But a stimulating environment can overcome the vulnerability (Zeskind & Ramey, 1981).

The Mother's Age.   One of the particularly intriguing trends in modern family life is that more women are postponing their first pregnancy into their late twenties or early thirties. In 1992, 23.5 percent of all first births in the United States were to women over 30, more double the rate in 1970 (Berkowitz et al., 1990; U.S. Bureau of the Census, 1993). Of course there are many reasons for such delayed childbearing, chief among them the increased need for second incomes in families and the desire of young women to complete job training and early career steps before bearing children. For my purposes in this chapter, though, the key question is the impact of maternal age on the mother's experience of pregnancy and on the developing child.

The evidence tells us that for the woman, the optimum time for childbearing is in her early twenties. Mothers over 30 (particularly those over 35), are at increased risk for several kinds of problems, including miscarriage (McFalls, 1990), complications of pregnancy such as high blood pressure or

Until fairly recently, many physicians advised a weight gain of only about 2 pounds per month during pregnancy. The argument was that smaller babies would be easier to deliver, and that the fetus would act as a sort of "parasite" on the mother's body, taking whatever nourishment it needed even if the mother gained little weight. But newer research has shown that the amount of weight the mother gains is directly related to the infant's birthweight and to the risk of a preterm birth (Abrams et al., 1989). And both low birth-weight and preterm births are associated with a whole range of risks for the child.

Because of such evidence, physicians now advise a gain of approximately 25–30 pounds for a woman who is at her normal weight before pregnancy, slightly more for a woman who is underweight before pregnancy

The Real World
How Much Weight Should You Gain in Pregnancy?

(Seidman, Ever-Hadani, & Gale, 1989). Women who gain less than this may have infants who suffer from some fetal malnutrition and who are thus born underweight for their gestational age.

Furthermore, it matters *when* the weight is gained. During the first three months, the woman needs to gain only 2 to 5 pounds. But during the last 6 months of the pregnancy the woman should be gaining at the rate of about 14 ounces (350 to 400 grams) per week in order to support fetal growth (Pitkin, 1977; Winick, 1980). So if you've gained 20 pounds or so during the first four or five months you should *not* cut back in order to hold your weight gain to some magic total number. Restricting caloric intake during those final months is exactly the wrong thing to do.

bleeding (Berkowitz et al., 1990), and death during pregnancy or delivery (Buehler et al., 1986).

For example, in one large study of nearly 4000 women in New York, all of whom had received adequate prenatal care, Gertrud Berkowitz and her colleagues (1990) found that women 35 and older during their first pregnancies were almost twice as likely as women in their twenties to suffer some pregnancy complication. These effects of age are even greater if the mother has not had adequate prenatal care or has poor health habits. For example, the negative effects of maternal smoking on birthweight is considerably *greater* among women over 35 than among young women (Wen et al., 1990).

For infants born to older mothers, the risk of low birth-weight appears to be only slightly higher than for babies born to younger mothers (Berkowitz et al., 1990; Cnattingius, Berendes, & Forman, 1993). And, other than the well-established risk of chromosomal anomalies such as Down syndrome (Baird, Sadovnick, & Yee, 1991), older mothers seem to have no heightened risk for bearing a child with birth defects. However, researchers in Sweden, where mothers of all ages receive remarkably comprehensive and equal prenatal care, have recently reported higher rates of late-pregnancy miscarriage and heightened infant mortality for infants born to older mothers, especially for first births to mothers over 35 (Cnattingius et al., 1993).

For risks among teenage mothers, the data are much less clear. Older data pointed to heightened risk of low birth-weight and other nonoptimal outcomes among very young mothers. But newer studies frequently do not show any such effect. Indeed, one very large study of all the consecutive births at one inner-city hospital in Baltimore over a seven-year period indicated that babies born to mothers younger than 18 were *less* likely to have low birth-weight than those

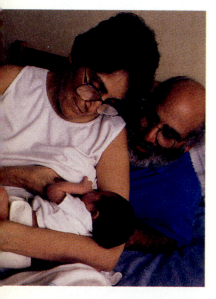

Older mothers, like this one, are becoming much more common in the U.S and in other industrialized countries. Mothers over 30 (especially those over 35) and their infants have *slightly* increased risks of problems during pregnancy and delivery.

born to mothers in their twenties (McCarthy & Hardy, 1993). My best reading of the evidence is that to the extent that adolescent childbearing is associated with higher risks to mother or child, those increased risks are more a consequence of inadequate prenatal care than of age per se. Among those teenagers who have decent diets and adequate prenatal care, problems of pregnancy, preterm delivery, or low birth-weight are *not* increased (Strobino, 1987).

The Mother's Emotional State.   Finally, the mother's state of mind during the pregnancy may be significant, although the research findings are decidedly mixed (Istvan, 1986). Results from infrahuman studies are clear: exposure of the pregnant female to stressors such as heat, light, noise, shock, or crowding significantly increases the risk of low birth-weight as well as later problems in the off-spring (Schneider, 1992). Studies of humans, however, have not pointed to such a clear conclusion, in part because researchers have not agreed on how one ought to measure such potentially relevant maternal states as anxiety or stress. Many investigators have found no link at all between their measures of the mother's overall life stress and either complications of her pregnancy or problems in the infant. Other investigators have found such links for some groups and not others. For example, Emmy Werner (1986) found that among middle-class women in the Kauai, Hawaii, longitudinal study, those who had negative feelings about their pregnancy or were generally anxious or experienced some psychological trauma during the pregnancy had more birth complications and more infants with low birth-weight or poor condition than was true among middle-class women with lower stress or anxiety. But these same patterns did not hold among poor women in this study, many of whom lived in states of chronic stress or disorganization. Thus it may be that long-term, chronic stressors have less impact on a specific pregnancy, while significant *increases* in anxiety or stress during a pregnancy may have more deleterious effects.

Folklore in virtually all cultures certainly points to a causal link between the mother's emotional experiences during her pregnancy and the outcome for the child. But at the moment the best I can do is to say that the hypothesis is still plausible, but not proven. Better epidemiological studies are needed if we are to be able to go further.

Another possible influence on prenatal development is the level of the mother's exercise. What kind of study would you have to do to figure out whether it is all right for pregnant women to maintain high levels of exercise, such as running 30 miles a week?

What three pieces of advice would you want to give a pregnant friend, based on this chapter? Why those three?

Sex Differences in Prenatal Development

Because nearly all prenatal development is controlled by maturational codes that are the same for all members of our species—male and female alike—there aren't very many sex differences in prenatal development. But there are a few, and they set the stage for some of the physical differences we'll see at later ages.

- Sometime between four and eight weeks after conception, the male hormone *testosterone* begins to be secreted by the rudimentary testes in the male embryo. If this hormone is not secreted or is secreted in inadequate amounts, the embryo will be "demasculinized," even to the extent of developing female genitalia. This infusion of testosterone also affects the brain so that the proper male hormones are secreted at the right moments later in life. Girls do not secrete any equivalent hormone prenatally.

- Girls are a bit faster in some aspects of prenatal development, particularly skeletal development. They are about 1–2 weeks ahead in bone development at birth (Tanner, 1978).
- Despite the more rapid development of girls, boys are heavier and longer at birth (Tanner, 1978).
- Boys are considerably more vulnerable to all kinds of prenatal problems. Many more boys than girls are conceived—on the order of about 120 to 150 male embryos to every 100 female—but more of the males are spontaneously aborted. At birth, there are about 105 boys for every 100 girls. Boys are also more likely to experience injuries at birth (perhaps because they are larger), and they have more congenital malformations (Zaslow & Hayes, 1986). Among those infants who experience severe complications during delivery, boys are more likely to die (Werner, 1986).

The striking sex difference in vulnerability is particularly intriguing, especially since it seems to persist. Older boys are more prone to problems as well, as are adult men. Males have shorter life expectancy, higher rates of behavior problems, more learning disabilities, and usually more negative responses to major stresses, such as divorce. One possible explanation for at least some of this sex difference may lie in the basic genetic difference. The XX combination affords the girl more protection against the fragile-X syndrome and against any "bad" genes that may be carried on the X chromosome. For instance, geneticists have found that a gene affecting susceptibility to infectious disease is carried on the X chromosome (Brooks-Gunn & Matthews, 1979). Because boys have only one X chromosome, such a gene is much more likely to be expressed phenotypically in a boy.

Birth

Once the 38 weeks of gestation are over, the fetus must be born into the world—an event that holds some pain as well as a good deal of joy for most parents. In the normal process, labor progresses through three stages of unequal length.

The First Stage of Labor.   Stage 1 covers the period during which two important processes occur: dilation and effacement. The cervix (the opening at the bottom of the uterus) must open up like the lens of a camera (**dilation**) and also flatten out (**effacement**). At the time of actual delivery of the infant, the cervix must normally be dilated to about 10 centimeters (about 4 inches), as you can see in Figure 3.8. This part of labor has been likened to putting on a sweater with a neck that is too tight. You have to pull and stretch the neck of the sweater with your head in order to get it on. Eventually the neck is stretched wide enough so that the widest part of your head can pass through.

Customarily, stage 1 is itself divided into phases. In the *early* (or *latent*) phase, contractions are relatively far apart and are typically not too uncomfortable. In the *late* phase, which begins when the cervix is about halfway dilated and

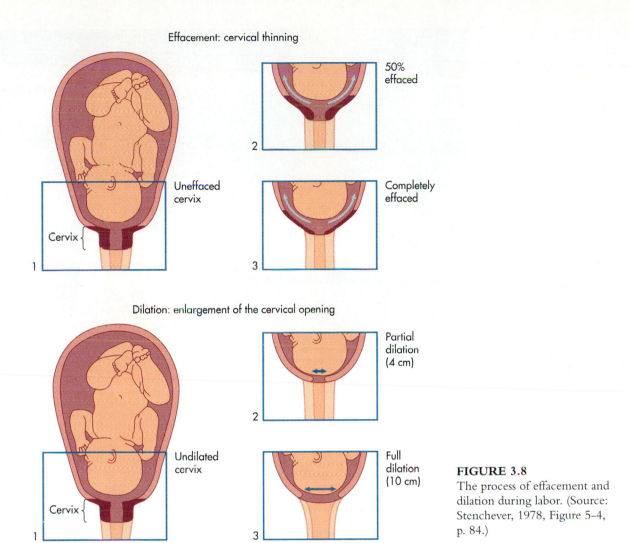

Effacement: cervical thinning

50% effaced

Uneffaced cervix

Completely effaced

Cervix

Dilation: enlargement of the cervical opening

Partial dilation (4 cm)

Undilated cervix

Full dilation (10 cm)

Cervix

FIGURE 3.8
The process of effacement and dilation during labor. (Source: Stenchever, 1978, Figure 5-4, p. 84.)

continues until dilation has reached 8 cm, contractions are closer together and more intense. The last two centimeters of dilation are achieved during a period usually called *transition*. It is this period, when contractions are closely spaced and strong, that women typically find the most painful. Fortunately, transition is also ordinarily the shortest phase.

The length of this first stage of labor varies widely from one woman to the next. The average length of stage 1 is roughly 8 hours for women delivering a first infant without anesthesia, with a range from 3 to 19 hours (Kilpatrick & Laros, 1989). Women delivering second or later children typically have shorter labors, while those with some form of anesthesia typically have slightly longer labors.

Second Stage of Labor. At the end of the transition phase, the mother will normally have the urge to help the infant out by "pushing." When the birth attendant (physician or midwife) is sure the cervix is fully dilated, she or he will encourage this pushing, and the second stage of labor—the actual delivery—begins. The baby's head moves past the stretched cervix, into the birth canal, and

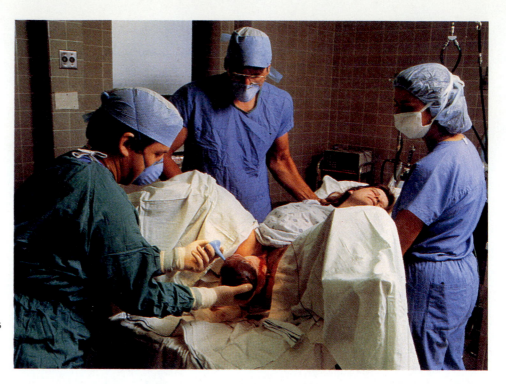

At this point in the delivery, the baby's head is fully out. Notice that the father is present for this delivery (standing on the far side of the table), as is now the norm in the United States.

finally out of the mother's body. Most women find this part of labor markedly less distressing than the transition phase. It typically lasts less than an hour and rarely takes longer than two hours.

Most infants are delivered head first, facing downward toward the mother's spine. Perhaps three percent, however, are oriented differently, either feet first or bottom first (called *breech* presentations). In the United States today, infants in breech positions are nearly all delivered through an abdominal incision (a **cesarean section**) rather than vaginally (Taffel, Placek, & Liss, 1987).

In most delivery situations in the United States, once the baby has emerged he is placed immediately on the mother's abdomen or given to her (and the father) to hold after the cord has been cut and the baby is cleaned up a bit—a matter of a few minutes. For most parents, this first greeting of the baby is a time for remarkable delight, as they stroke the baby's skin, count the fingers, look at the baby's eyes.

The Third Stage of Labor.   The anticlimactic but essential stage 3 is the delivery of the placenta (also called the "afterbirth") and other material from the uterus.

Birth Choices

In the U.S. and in many industrialized countries, mothers (and fathers) can make a variety of choices about the delivery—choices that may affect the psychological or physical comfort the mother may experience. There are decisions about whether to receive pain killing drugs during delivery, whether to deliver in a hospital or at home, or whether the father should be present during the birth. Because many of you will face these choices at some point in the future, let me say just a word about each of them.

Drugs During Delivery.   One key decision concerns the use of drugs during delivery. Three types of drugs are commonly used: (1) *analgesics* (such as the common drug Demerol) which are given during stage 1 of labor to reduce pain; (2) *sedatives* or *tranquilizers* (such as Nembutol, Valium, or Thorazine) given during stage 1 labor to reduce anxiety; and (3) *anesthesia*, given during transition or the second stage of labor to block pain either totally (general anesthesia) or in portions of the body (local anesthesia). Of the three, anesthesia is least often used (at least in the United States currently), but the great majority of women receive at least one of these types of drugs (Brackbill, McManus, & Woodward, 1985).

Studying the causal links between such drug use and the baby's later behavior or development has proven to be monumentally difficult. Controlled experiments are obviously not possible, since women cannot be randomly assigned to specific drug regimens. And drugs are given in myriad different combinations. But there are a few reasonably clear conclusions. First, it's clear that nearly all drugs given during labor pass through the placenta and enter the fetal bloodstream and may remain there for several days. Not surprisingly, then, infants whose mothers have received any type of drug are typically slightly more sluggish, gain a little less weight, and spend more time sleeping in the first few weeks than do infants of non-drugged moms (Maurer & Maurer, 1988). These differences are quite small but have been observed repeatedly.

Beyond these first few days, however, there are no consistently observed effects from analgesics and tranquilizers, and only a few hints of long-term effects of anesthesia (Rosenblith & Sims-Knight, 1989; Sepkoski, 1987). Given such contradictory findings, only one specific piece of advice seems warranted: if you have received medication, you need to bear in mind that your baby is also drugged, and that this will affect her behavior in the first few days. If you allow for this effect, and realize that it will wear off, your long-term relationship with your child is unlikely to be affected.

The Location of Birth.   A second choice parents must make is *where* the baby is to be born. Today there are typically four alternatives: a traditional hospital maternity unit; a hospital-based birth center or birthing room, which is located within a hospital but provides a more homelike setting, with labor and delivery both completed in the same room and family members often present throughout; a free-standing birth center, like a hospital birth center except located apart from the hospital, with a midwife rather than (or in addition to) a physician attending the delivery; and home delivery.

At the turn of the century, only about 5 percent of babies in the United States were born in hospitals; today the figure is 98.8 percent (Declercq, 1993), with 0.7 percent born at home and 0.4 percent born in birthing centers—a choice more common among Mexican-American mothers, particularly in Texas.

Because home deliveries are so uncommon in the U.S., much of what we know about them comes from research in Europe, where such deliveries are thought to be both more natural and less expensive for the medical care system. In countries where this pattern occurs, home deliveries are encouraged only in uncomplicated pregnancies in which the woman has received good prenatal care. In this group, with a trained birth attendant present at delivery, the rate of delivery complications or infant problems is no higher in home or birth center deliveries than in hospital deliveries (Rooks et al., 1989; Tew, 1985). In contrast, infant mortality rates are significantly higher in *unplanned* home deliveries, in those without trained attendants, or those in which the mother had experienced some complication of pregnancy (Schramm, Barnes, & Bakewell, 1987).

Incidentally, there is no evidence that babies born at home or in birthing centers are in any way better off in the long run than are babies born in more traditional hospital settings. Assuming appropriate safety precautions, then, the choice should be based on what is most comfortable for the individual woman or couple.

The Presence of Fathers at Delivery.   A third important decision is whether the father should be present at delivery. In the United States today this hardly seems like a "decision." As recently as 1972 only about a quarter of U.S. hospitals permitted the father to be present in the delivery room; by 1980, four-fifths of them did (Parke & Tinsley, 1984), and today the father's presence has become absolutely the norm.

There have been several compelling arguments offered in favor of such a norm: The father's presence may lessen the mother's anxiety and give her psychological support; by coaching her in breathing and other techniques he may help her control her pain; and he may become more strongly attached to the infant by being present at the birth. There is at least some evidence in support of the first two of these arguments, but—perhaps unexpectedly for some of you—little support for the third.

When fathers are present during labor and delivery, mothers report lower levels of pain and receive less medication (Henneborn & Cogan, 1975). When the mother has a coach (the father or someone else), the incidence of problems of labor and delivery goes down, as does the duration of labor (Sosa et al., 1980). Furthermore, at least one study shows that women are more likely to report that the birth was a "peak" experience if the father was present (Entwisle & Doering, 1981). But presence at the delivery does not seem to have any magical effect on the father's emotional bond to the baby (Palkovitz, 1985). A father who sees his child for the first time in the newborn nursery, or days later at home, may nonetheless become as strongly attached to the infant as are those fathers who were present at the birth.

This statement is not in any way intended as an argument against fathers' participation in the delivery process. The fact that the father's presence seems to help the mother control pain, reduce medication and labor duration, and may enhance the husband-wife relationship all seem to me to be compelling reasons for encouraging continued high levels of paternal participation. In addition, of

After reading this, which birthing location would you choose, and why?

More and more fathers are taking special prenatal classes like this one, so that they can provide support and coaching to their wives during labor.

course, most fathers report powerful feelings of delight at being present at the birth of their children. Reason enough.

Problems at Birth

As with prenatal development, there are some things that can alter the normal pattern I have been describing. One of the most common problems is that the delivery itself may not proceed normally, leading to a surgical delivery through an abdominal incision, called a cesarean section, (usually abbreviated C-section). A second common problem is that the infant may be born too early.

Cesarean-section Delivery.   C-section deliveries occur for a variety of reasons, of which the most common are a breech position of the fetus, an active herpes infection, or a mother who has had a previous C-section. In virtually all industrialized countries, the frequency of C-sections rose rapidly in the 1970s and 1980s. This rise was particularly rapid in the U.S., where the rate more than quadrupled between 1970 and 1988, going from 5.5 to 24.7 percent. The rate has now dropped slightly (to 23.5 percent in 1991), but even this slight drop is widely thought to be substantially higher than medically necessary. The Centers for Disease Control, in fact, lists the reduction of this rate to something closer to 12 to 15 percent as a health objective for the year 2000 (Centers for Disease Control, 1993).

The rise has had many causes, both in the U.S. and in other countries in which similar increases occurred. Fear of malpractice suits may be one element. But much more of the increase appears to be due to changes in standard medical practice, such as requiring any woman who had had one C-section to have all subsequent deliveries in the same fashion, as well as the widespread use of fetal monitors—equipment that allows the physician to hear the fetal heart beat, and thus to detect signs of fetal distress. When such signs of distress occur physicians have increasingly handled them with C-sections, in order to reduce the apparent risk to the infant.

Both these practices have been questioned. For example, there is now good evidence that 50–70 percent of all women who have had one C-section could safely deliver subsequent children vaginally (Levano et al., 1986). The number of such women who are encouraged to do so has been increasing of late, but it is still quite low. Similarly, some physicians (Levano et al., 1986) argue that fetal monitoring has led to many unnecessary C-sections, particularly in otherwise low-risk pregnancies.

I do not want to give you the impression that C-sections are never necessary. They clearly are. But there is now virtually universal agreement that the rate has become too high and that it can be considerably reduced without added risk to mothers or infants.

Low Birth-Weight.   In talking about various teratogens I have often mentioned low birth-weight as one of the clearest negative outcomes. Several different labels are used to describe infants with less than optimal weight. All babies

> Why might the widespread increase in cesarean section deliveries be troubling to psychologists or physicians? How could you decide if this is a negative trend?

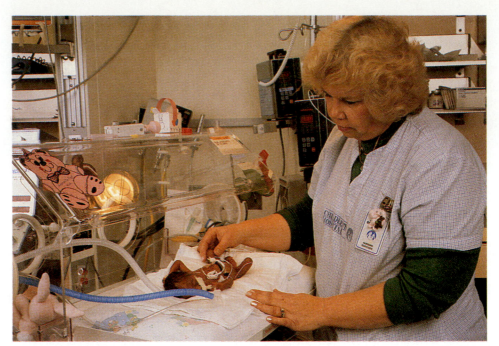

Low-birth-weight infants are kept in special isolettes, like this one, so that the temperature can be controlled. These babies are not only small, they are also more wrinkled and skinny because the layer of fat under the skin has not fully developed.

below 2,500 grams (about 5.5 pounds) are described with the most general term of **low birth-weight (LBW).** Those below 1,500 grams (about 3.3 pounds) are usually called *very low birth-weight*, while those below 1,000 grams are called *extremely low birth-weight*. The incidence of low birth-weight has declined in the U.S. in the past decade, but it is still high: In 1990, 7.0 percent of all newborns were below 2,500 grams—a total of about 45,000 infants each year. Roughly 7,800 of those were below 1,500 grams (U.S. Bureau of the Census, 1993). The risk of such a birth is considerably higher among babies born to poverty-level mothers—a pattern that is found in every country studied (e.g., Reading, Raybould, & Jarvis, 1993). In the United States, the rate is also considerably higher among Blacks than among either Whites or Hispanics, a pattern that will not surprise you, given what I said in Chapter 1. In 1990, the respective rates were 13.3 percent, 5.7 percent, and 6.1 percent.

There are a variety of reasons for low birth-weight, of which the most common is that the infant is born before the full 38 weeks of gestation. Such infants are usually labeled *preterm*. Any birth before 36 weeks of gestation is usually labeled in this way. It is also possible for an infant to have completed the full 38-week gestational period but still weigh less than 2,500 grams or to weigh less than would be expected for the number of weeks of gestation completed, however long that may have been. Such an infant is called *small for date*. Infants in this group appear to have suffered from prenatal malnutrition, such as might occur with constriction of blood flow from the mother's smoking or from other significant problems prenatally. Preterm infants, in contrast, may be early but may have been developing normally in other respects.

All low-birth-weight infants share some characteristics, including markedly lower levels of responsiveness at birth and in the early months of life (Barnard,

Bee, & Hammond, 1984). They also have a higher risk of experiencing respiratory distress in the early weeks, and may be slower in motor development than their normal-weight peers.

Infant mortality is also correlated with birth-weight, as well as weeks of gestation. Babies born at 22 weeks of gestation or earlier rarely survive; about 80 percent of all low-birth-weight infants survive long enough to leave the hospital, but the lower the birth weight the greater the risk of neonatal death. What is surprising is how many of the really tiny babies survive when they have state-of-the-art neonatal care. In hospitals with especially modern and aggressive neonatal intensive care units, as many as half of infants as small as 500 to 1,000 grams at birth (1–2 lbs) may survive (Astbury et al., 1990).

You might think that all babies this small who do survive will have major developmental problems. But that is not the case. The long-term outcomes depend not only on the quality of care available when (and where) the baby was born, but on just how small the baby was and what kind of family he or she grew up in. Because medical advances in the care of LBW infants have been enormous in the past few decades, the more recently such a baby was born, the better the long-term prognosis seems to be (Kitchen et al., 1991).

The great majority of those above 1,500 grams who are not small for date catch up to their normal peers within the first few years of life. But those below 1,500 grams especially those below 1,000—have significantly higher rates of long-term problems, including neurological impairment, lower IQs, smaller size, and greater problems in school (Collin, Halsey, & Anderson, 1991; Hack et al., 1991; Saigal et al., 1991). You can get a better sense of both the type and incidence of such problems from the data in Table 3.3, which lists the results for two recent studies.

Two points are worth making about the findings from follow-up studies like those shown in the Table. First, problems may not show up until school age,

TABLE 3.3
Two Examples of Long-Term Outcomes for Very Low Birth-Weight

	Infants	
	Australian Study[*]	U.S. Study[**]
Number of babies followed	89	249
Weight at birth	500–999 grams	<1,500 grams
Age at testing	8 years	8 years
Percent with severe problems of some type (IQ below 70, deaf, blind, cerebral palsied, etc.)	21.3%	15.7%
Additional percent with significant learning problem or IQ between 70 and 85	19.1%	15.4%

[*] Victorian Infant Collaborative Study Group, 1991. The study included all surviving children of 500–999 grams born in a single state (Victoria) in Australia between 1979 and 1980. A total of 351 infants were born in that weight range, so only a quarter survived.

[**] Hack et al., 1991. The study included originally 490 children below 1,500 grams born in a single Cleveland, Ohio hospital between 1977 and 1979. 64 percent survived to age 8.

when the child is challenged by a new level of cognitive task. Many surviving LBW children who appear to be developing normally at age 2 or 3 later show significant problems in school. Second, even in the extremely low birth-weight group, the majority of children seem to be fine. So it is not the case that *all* LBW children are *somewhat* affected, but rather that *some* LBW children are significantly affected while others develop normally. Unfortunately, physicians and researchers have not yet found reliable ways to predict which babies are likely to have later difficulties, which means that parents of LBW infants may be left in suspense for many years.

One piece of good news is that we do now know something about treatments that seem to improve the long-term chances of good functioning for LBW infants. Babies provided with special kinds of rhythmic stimulation while still in the hospital, such as water beds, rocking beds, heart beat sounds, or body massage, are more alert, gain weight faster, and may even have higher IQs later than preterm babies receiving more typical hospital care (Barnard & Bee, 1983; Scafidi et al., 1990). And when special supports are provided to such infants and their families—helping the mothers to learn better skills for interaction with their babies and providing stimulating day care for the infants directly—the infants have a better chance of developing normally (Brooks-Gunn et al., 1993; Spiker, Ferguson, & Brooks-Gunn, 1993).

A Final Word: A More Optimistic View of Risks and Long-Term Consequences of Prenatal and Birth Problems

As I write this chapter I am aware that the list of things that can go wrong seems to get longer and longer and scarier and scarier. Physicians, biologists, and psychologists keep learning more about prenatal and birth risks, so the number of warnings to pregnant women seems to increase yearly, if not monthly. One of the ironies of this is that too much worry about such potential consequences can make a woman more anxious, and anxiety is on the list of warnings for pregnant women! So before you begin worrying too much, let me try to put this information into perspective.

First, remember again that *most* pregnancies are normal and largely uneventful, and most babies are healthy and normal at birth. Second, there are specific preventive steps that any woman can take to reduce the risks for herself and her unborn child. She can be properly immunized; she can stop smoking and drinking; she can watch her diet and make sure her weight gain is sufficient; and she can get early and regular prenatal care. Many studies show that mothers who receive adequate prenatal care reduce the risks to themselves and their infants. Just one example: Jann Murray and Merton Bernfield (1988), in a study of over 30,000 births, found that the risk of giving birth to a low birth-weight infant was more than three times as great among women who had received inadequate prenatal care as among those receiving adequate care, and this pattern held among both Blacks and Whites (although not, apparently, among Hispanics, as I mentioned in Chapter 1). Unfortunately, inadequate care remains common in the U.S. In 1991, 4.7 percent of White, 10.7 percent of Black, and 11 percent of Hispanic mothers had either no care at all, or first saw a physician in the seventh month or later (Wegman, 1993). In many inner cities in the U.S., and among teenage mothers, these figures are considerably higher (Heagarty, 1991; Wegman, 1993).

Given such statistics, it is perhaps not surprising that the U.S. continues to have a relatively high rate of infant mortality. The good news is that this rate has been declining steadily over the past decades, dropping from 20.0 infant deaths per thousand births in 1970 to 8.9 in 1991 (Wegman, 1993). The bad news is that infant mortality is more than twice as high for Blacks as for Whites (17.6 and 7.3 respectively in 1990). Infant mortality among Native Americans falls in between, at about 11.1 (Rhoades et al., 1992). Even an overall rate of 8.9 places the U.S. twenty-second in the world. Virtually all European countries—where prenatal care is typically free or low cost and universally available—have lower infant mortality rates, as do Japan (with the lowest rate in the world), Hong Kong, and Singapore.

The Black/White difference in infant mortality is so significant a facet of U.S. culture that I need to say a further word about it. This difference has existed at least since record keeping began (in 1915) and has *not* been declining. The difference is considerably smaller in groups that have easy access to free medical care, such as among military personnel (Rawlings & Weir, 1992), but some Black/White difference persists even when researchers compare only infants born to college-educated mothers (Schoendorf et al., 1992). Physicians and physiologists do not yet understand all the reasons for this discrepancy, although it is clear that a significantly higher incidence of low-birth-weight births to Black mothers is a major factor (Kempe et al., 1992; Schoendorf et al., 1992). When we compare only normal-weight babies, infant mortality is about the same in the two groups. But such a statement only pushes the explanation back one step. We still need to know why Blacks in the U.S. have more LBW babies, and the answer to this question is still unclear.

A third point about prenatal problems is that if something does go wrong, chances are good that the negative consequences to the child will be short term rather than permanent. Of course some negative outcomes *are* permanent and have long-term consequences for the child. Chromosomal anomalies are clearly permanent and nearly always associated with lasting mental retardation or school difficulties. Some teratogens also have permanent effects, such as fetal alcohol syndrome, deafness resulting from rubella, or AIDS. And a significant fraction of very low-birth-weight infants experience lasting problems.

But many of the negative outcomes I have talked about in this chapter may be detectable only for the first few years of the child's life, and then only in some families. In fact, the relationship between prenatal or birth problems and long-term outcomes illustrates the very pattern of interaction between nature and nurture that Horowitz suggests in her model, shown in Figure 1.4: a biological problem may be amplified by an unstimulating environment but greatly reduced by a supportive one. For example, there are numerous studies showing that low birth-weight infants, those with poor prenatal nutrition, or those with equivalent difficulties are likely to show persisting problems if they are reared in unstimulating or unsupportive environments but develop much more normally if reared in more intellectually and emotionally nurturing families (Beckwith & Rodning, 1991; Breitmayer & Ramey, 1986; Kopp, 1990). So it is not the prenatal or birth problem alone that is the cause of the child's later problem; rather, a nonoptimal prenatal environment may make the infant more vulnerable to later environmental inadequacy. Such children may require a better family environment to develop normally, but in many cases such normal development *is* possible. So don't despair when you read the long list of cautions and potential problems. The story isn't as gloomy as it first seems.

S U M M A R Y

1. At conception, the 23 chromosomes from the sperm join with 23 from the ovum to make up the set of 46 that will be reproduced in each cell of the new child's body. Each chromosome consists of a long string of deoxyribonucleic acid (DNA), divisible into specific segments, called genes.

2. The child's sex is determined by the twenty-third pair of chromosomes, a pattern of XX for a girl and XY for a boy.

3. Geneticists distinguish between the genotype, which is the pattern of inherited characteristics, and the phenotype, which is the result of the interaction of genotype and environment.

4. During the first days after conception, called the germinal stage of development, the initial cell divides, travels down the fallopian tube, and is implanted in the wall of the uterus.

5. The second stage, the period of the embryo, includes the development of the various structures that support fetal development, such as the placenta, as well as primitive forms of all organ systems.

6. The final 30 weeks of gestation, the fetal period, is devoted primarily to enlargement and refinements in all the organ systems.

7. Normal prenatal development seems heavily determined by maturation—a "road map" contained in the genes. Disruptions in this sequence can occur; the timing of the disruption determines the nature and severity of the effect.

8. Deviations from the normal pattern can be caused at conception by any of a variety of chromosomal anomalies, such as Down syndrome or by the transmission of genes for specific diseases.

9. Prior to conception, it is possible to test parents for the presence of genes for many inherited diseases. After conception, several diagnostic techniques exist that identify chromosomal anomalies or recessive-gene diseases in the fetus.

10. Some diseases contracted by the mother may affect the child, including rubella, AIDS, and CMV. Any of these may (but does not invariably) result in disease or physical abnormalities in the child.

11. Alcohol, nicotine, and cocaine all appear to have significantly harmful effects on the developing fetus; the greater the dose, the larger the potential effect appears to be.

12. The mother's diet is also important. If she is severely malnourished there are increased risks of stillbirth, low birth-weight, and infant death during the first year of life.

13. Older mothers and very young mothers also run increased risks, but in many, if not most cases, these risks are greatly reduced or eliminated if the mother is in good health and receives adequate prenatal care.

14. High levels of anxiety or stress in the mother may also increase the risk of complications of pregnancy or difficulties in the infant, although the research findings here are mixed.

15. Sex differences in prenatal development are few in number. Boys are slower to develop, bigger at birth, and more vulnerable to most forms of prenatal stress.

16. The normal birth process has three parts: dilation, delivery, and placental delivery.

17. Most drugs given to the mother during delivery pass through to the infant's bloodstream and have short-term effects on infant responsiveness and feeding patterns. There may be some longer-term effects, but this is in dispute.

18. In uncomplicated, low-risk pregnancies, delivery at home or in a birthing center is as safe as hospital delivery.

19. The presence of the father during delivery has a variety of positive consequences, including reduced pain experience for the mother, but does not appear to affect the father's attachment to the infant.

20. Nearly one fourth of all deliveries in the United States are now by cesarean section—a statistic that has resulted in considerable debate.

21. Infants born weighing less than 2,500 grams are low birth-weight (LBW); those below 1,500 gm are very low birth-weight; those below 1,000 are extremely low birth-weight. The lower the weight, the greater the risk of significant lasting problems, such as low IQ or learning disabilities.

22. Low birth-weight and infant mortality are considerably more common among African-Americans than among Caucasians or Hispanics.

23. Some prenatal or birth difficulties can produce permanent disabilities or deformities, but many disorders associated with prenatal life or with birth can be overcome if the child is reared in a supportive and stimulating environment.

KEY TERMS

alpha-fetoprotein test
amniocentesis
amnion
axon
cesarean section
chorionic villus sampling
 (CVS)
chromosome
dendrites
deoxyribonucleic acid

dilation
Down syndrome
effacement
fallopian tube
fetal alcohol syndrome
 (FAS)
gametes
gene
genotype
glial cells

low birth-weight (LBW)
neurons
ovum
phenotype
placenta
synapse
ultrasound
uterus

SUGGESTED READINGS

The Boston Women's Health Collective (1992). *The new our bodies, ourselves: A book by and for women* (2nd ed.). New York: Simon & Schuster. This revision of a popular book has an excellent discussion of health during pregnancy and good descriptions and diagrams showing stages of prenatal development and birth. You may not be entirely in sympathy with all of the political views included, but it is nonetheless a very good compact source of information on all facets of pregnancy and delivery.

Nightingale, E. O., & Goodman, M. (1990). *Before birth. Prenatal testing for genetic disease*. Cambridge, MA: Harvard University Press. An extremely informative, clearly written, helpful small book.

Nilsson, L. (1990). *A child is born*. New York: Delacorte Press. A remarkable book, full of the most stunning photographs of all phases of conception, prenatal development, and birth.

Rosenblith, J. F., & Sims-Knight, J. E. (1989). *In the beginning. Development in the first two years of life*. Newbury Park: Sage. A first-rate text covering prenatal development and infancy. It is an excellent next step in your reading if you are interested in this area.

Vorhees, C. V., & Mollnow, E. (1987). Behavioral teratogenesis: long-term influences on behavior from early exposure to environmental agents. In J. D. Osofsky (Ed.), *Handbook of infant development* (2nd ed.) (pp. 913–971). New York: Wiley. A thorough review of the literature on the effects of various commonly discussed teratogens such as alcohol and smoking, this article also covers many other teratogens, such as lead, anticonvulsants, PCBs, hormones, radiation, and aspirin.

Chapter Four

Physical Development in Infancy

I spoke recently with a friend, the new mother of a 6-month-old. When I asked her how things were going she said three very typical things:

"No one told me how much fun it would be; no one told me how much work it would be; and I didn't expect it to be this fascinating. She's changing every day. Now she seems like a real person, sitting up, crawling, beginning to make wonderful noises."

I suspect that someone had indeed told her all those things, but she didn't hear them. Only when you are with a child every day, care for the child and love the child does the reality of the whole amazing process come home to you. I'll do my best to convey that amazement to you, but some of what I am going to say may not be "real" to you unless and until you help to rear a child yourself. Let me begin by describing the child's physical development during the first 18–24 months, starting with a snapshot of the newborn.

The Newborn

Assessing the Newborn

It has become customary in most hospitals to evaluate an infant's status immediately after birth, and then again five minutes later, to detect any problems that may require special care. By far the most frequently used assessment system is something called an **Apgar score,** developed by a physician, Virginia Apgar (1953). In this system, the newborn is rated on the five criteria I've listed in Table 4.1 and given a score of 0, 1, or 2 on each criteria, with a maximum score of 10. A score of 10 is fairly unusual immediately after birth because most infants are still somewhat blue in the fingers and toes at that stage. At the five-minute assessment, however, 85 to 90 percent of infants receive a score of 9 or 10 (National Center for Health Statistics, 1984). Any score of 7 or better indicates

---

TABLE 4.1
Evaluation Method for Apgar Scoring

Aspect of Infant Observed	Score assigned		
	0	1	2
Heart rate	Absent	< 100/min	> 100/min
Respiratory rate	No breathing	Weak cry & shallow breathing	Strong cry & regular breathing
Muscle tone	Flaccid	Some flexion of extremities	Well flexed
Response to stimulation	None	Some motion of feet	Cry
Color	blue	Body pink, extremities blue	Pink all over

Source: After Robinson, 1978, Table 5-2, p. 102.

that the baby is in no danger. A score of 4, 5, or 6 usually means that the baby needs help establishing normal breathing patterns; a score of 3 or below indicates a baby in critical condition, although babies with such low Apgar scores can and often do survive.

Scores in the range of 5–8, like low birth weight and most other types of initial vulnerability, are associated with long-term risk primarily when the infant grows up in nonoptimal circumstances. In stimulating and supportive environments, most children with low Apgar scores appear to develop normally (Breitmayer & Ramey, 1986).

Reflexes

Infants are born with a large collection of **reflexes,** which are physical responses triggered involuntarily by a specific stimulus. Many of these reflexes are still present in adults, so you should be familiar with them, such as the knee jerk the doctor tests for, your automatic eyeblink when a puff of air hits your eye, or the involuntary narrowing of the pupil of your eye when you're in a bright light.

We can roughly group the newborn's reflexes into two categories. First, there are many *adaptive reflexes* that help the baby survive in the world into which he is born. Sucking and swallowing reflexes are prominent in this category, as is the rooting reflex—the automatic turn of the head toward any touch on the cheek, a reflex that helps the baby get the nipple into his mouth during nursing. These reflexes are no longer present in older children or adults, but are clearly highly adaptive for the newborn.

Other adaptive reflexes do persist over the whole life span, including a withdrawal reaction from a painful stimulus, the opening and closing of the pupil of the eye to variations in brightness, and many others. Finally, there are some reflexes that were adaptive in evolutionary history and are still present in newborn humans, even though they are no longer helpful. The grasping reflex is one clear example. If you place your finger across a newborn baby's palm, he will reflexively close his fist tightly around your finger. If you do this with both palms, the baby's grasp is strong enough so that you can lift him up by his hands in this way. We can also see this reflex in monkeys and apes, for whom it is highly useful, since these infants must be able to cling to their mother's body while she moves about, or cling to a tree branch or vine. Most observers assume that this reflex in humans is merely one residual from our evolutionary past.

A second category includes the *primitive reflexes*, so called because they are controlled by the more primitive parts of the brain—the medulla and the midbrain—both of which are close to being fully developed at birth. By about 6 months of age, when the portion of the brain governing such complex activities as perception, body movement, thinking, and language has developed more fully, these primitive reflexes begin to disappear, as if superseded by the more complex brain functions.

For example, if you make a loud noise or startle a baby in some other way, you'll see her throw her arms outward and arch her back, a pattern that is part of the *Moro* or *startle* reflex that you see in Figure 4.1. Stroke the bottom of her foot and she will splay out her toes and then curl them in; this is the *Babinsky* reflex.

What would be different about development and about adult-baby interactions, if babies were born *without* any reflexes, but instead had to learn every behavior?

FIGURE 4.1
These two photos show the Moro reflex very well. In the photo on the left, the baby is fairly relaxed, but when the adult suddenly drops the baby (and catches him again), the baby throws his arms out and arches his back. This reflex is present for about the first six months.

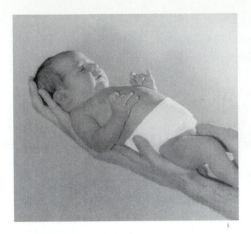
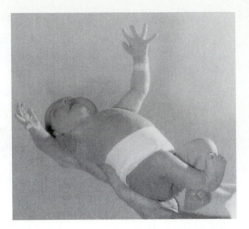

These patterns are of interest primarily because their presence past the age of roughly 6 months may signal the existence of some kind of neurological problem. The Babinsky, in particular, is used as a diagnostic tool by neurologists who may suspect the existence of some dysfunction in a child or adult.

These two categories of reflexes obviously overlap. Many adaptive reflexes—including the sucking and rooting reflexes—begin to fade late in the first year of life, indicating that they are controlled by the more primitive parts of the brain. But I think it is still helpful to distinguish between those reflexes that continue to have daily usefulness for the baby, and those that are more purely reflections of the status of the nervous system, without other adaptive functions.

Perceptual Skills: What the Newborn Sees, Hears, and Feels

Babies also come equipped with a surprisingly mature set of perceptual skills. I'll be describing the development of those skills in the next chapter, but I do want you to have some sense of the starting point. The newborn can:

- Focus both eyes on the same spot, with 8 inches being roughly the best focal distance. Within a few weeks the baby can at least roughly follow a moving object with his eyes. Within the first weeks, possibly at birth, she can discriminate Mom's face from other faces.
- Easily hear sounds within the pitch and loudness range of the human voice; roughly locate objects by their sounds, and discriminate some individual voices, particularly the mother's voice.
- Taste the four basic tastes (sweet, sour, bitter, and salty) and identify familiar body odors. From birth, he can recognize his mother from her smell.

Brief as this summary is, several points nonetheless stand out. First of all, newborns' perceptual skills are a great deal better than most parents believe—better than most psychologists or physicians believed until a few years ago. The better our research techniques have become, the more we have understood just how skillful the new baby is.

Even more striking is how well adapted the baby's perceptual skills are for the interactions he will have with the people in his world. He hears best in the range of the human voice; he can discriminate mother (or other regular care-giver) from others on the basis of smell or sound almost immediately and by sight within a very few weeks; the distance at which he can focus his eyes best, about 8 inches, is roughly the distance between the infant's eyes and the mother's face during nursing.

As you'll see in Chapter 5, there is still a long way to go in the development of sophisticated perceptual abilities. But the newborn begins life able to make key discriminations and to locate objects through various perceptual cues.

Initial Motor Skills: Moving Around

In contrast, the motor skills of the newborn are not very impressive. She can't reach for things she's looking at; she can't hold up her head, roll over, or sit up. These skills emerge only gradually in the early weeks. By one month, the baby can hold her chin up off the floor or mattress. By two months, she is beginning to swipe at objects near her with her hands. But babies start their progress in motor development at a much lower level than they start the development of sophisticated perceptual skills.

A Day in the Life of a Baby

Parents are obviously interested in the various skills and capacities of the newborn infant. They are delighted with his smiles and with each new ability as it emerges. But for most parents, the real questions are more practical: What is it like to live with a newborn? How is the infant's day organized? What sort of natural rhythms occur in the daily cycles? What can you expect from the baby, as you struggle to adapt to and care for this new person in your life?

Researchers who have studied newborns have described five different states of sleep and wakefulness in infants, which they refer to as **states of consciousness;** I've summarized them in Table 4.2. You can see that the baby spends more time sleeping than anything else. Of the time awake, only about two to three hours is either quiet or active awake rather than fussing.

The five main states tend to occur in cycles, just as your own states occur in a daily rhythm. In the newborn, the basic period in the cycle is about 1½ or 2 hours. Most infants move through the states from deep sleep to lighter sleep to fussing and hunger and then to alert wakefulness, after which they become drowsy and drop back into deep sleep. This cycle then repeats itself roughly every two hours: sleep, cry, eat, look; sleep, cry, eat, look. Because the first three parts of this repeating pattern—sleeping, crying, and eating—are so crucial for parents, let me say just a word more about each.

Sleeping

The child's sleep periods are important to parents because they provide breaks in what may otherwise seem like constant care. Newborns sleep about 15 to 16 hours each day, with little day-night rhythm (circadian rhythm); they sleep

Calves, foals, lambs and newborns of virtually all mammals besides humans can stand and walk within a few hours after birth. Can you think of any useful evolutionary function for the greater motor helplessness of the human newborn?

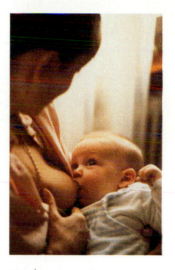

Newborns are pretty near-sighted, but they can focus very well at a distance of about 8 to 10 inches—just about the distance between this baby's eyes and her mother's face while she nurses.

TABLE 4.2
The Basic States of Infant Sleep and Wakefulness

State of Consciousness	Characteristics
Deep sleep	Eyes closed, regular breathing, no movement except occasional startles
Active sleep	Eyes closed, irregular breathing, small twitches, no gross body movement
Quiet awake	Eyes open, no major body movement, regular breathing
Active awake	Eyes open, with movements of the head, limbs, and trunk; irregular breathing
Crying and fussing	Eyes may be partly or entirely closed, vigorous diffuse movement, with crying or fussing sounds

Sources: Based on the work of Prechtl and Beintema, 1964; Hutt, Lenard, & Prechtl, 1969; Parmelee, Wenner, & Schulz, 1964.

about equal amounts at any given time of day. By 6 or 8 weeks of age, the total amount of sleep per day has dropped slightly, and we see the first signs of circadian rhythms—at least among infants in Western countries, where regular sleep/wake cycles are more highly valued. Babies begin to string two or three two-hour cycles together without coming to full wakefulness, at which point we say that the baby can "sleep through the night" (Bamford et al., 1990). By 6 months, babies are still sleeping a bit over 14 hours per day, but the regularity and predictability of the baby's sleep is still more noticeable—at least in Western samples. Not only do most 6-month-olds have clear nighttime sleep patterns, they also begin to nap during the day at more predictable times.

I've given you the average figures, but of course babies vary a lot in their sleep patterns. Of the 6-week-old babies in one recent study, there was one who slept only 8.8 hours per day (now there must be one tired set of parents!) and another who slept nearly 22 hours (Bamford et al., 1990). And some babies, even in Western cultures, do not develop a long nighttime sleep period until late in the first year of life.

All these aspects of the baby's sleep pattern have implications for the emerging parent-infant interaction. Psychologists have also been interested in sleep patterns because marked irregularity of sleep patterns may be a symptom of some disorder or problem. Some babies born to mothers who used cocaine during pregnancy have difficulty establishing a regular pattern of sleeping and waking. Brain-damaged infants often have the same kind of difficulties, so any time an infant fails to develop clear sleep-waking regularity, it *may* be a sign of trouble.

The other interesting thing about sleep in newborns is that they show the external signs that signify dreaming in older children or adults, a fluttering of the eyeballs under the closed lids, called **rapid eye movement** sleep, or REM sleep. REMs are not seen in very young preterm infants, so there is clearly some neurological maturity required for this pattern of activity. Among normal-term newborns, though, REM sleep actually makes up a larger portion of sleep time than is true in adults. In adults, REMs typically occur in brief bursts periodically over the sleep period; in newborns they occur more steadily over the entire sleep period (Berg & Berg, 1987). Just what these differences in pattern may mean about the development of the nervous system or about dreaming in very young infants, is not so clear. But some sort of very busy activity seems to be going on during the baby's sleep time.

Crying

Newborns actually cry less of the time than you might think. One researcher, who was studying normal newborns, found that the figure ranged from 2 to 11 percent of the time (Korner et al., 1981). Crying seems to increase over the first 6 weeks of life and then decreases. Initially, infants cry most in the evening and then shift their crying more toward times just before feedings.

The basic function of the child's cry, obviously, is to signal need. Because babies can't move *to* someone to get care, they have to *bring* someone to them, and crying is the main way they have to attract attention. In fact, infants have a whole repertoire of cry sounds, with different cries for pain, anger, or hunger. The basic cry, which often signals hunger, is usually a rhythmical pattern: cry, silence, breath, cry, silence, breath, with a kind of whistling sound often accompanying the in-breath. An anger cry is typically louder, more intense, and the pain cry normally has a very abrupt onset—unlike the more basic kinds of cries, which usually begin with whimpering or moaning. However, not all infants cry

R E S E A R C H   R E P O R T

Variations in Children's Cries

Parents have always known that some babies had cries that were particularly penetrating or grating; other babies seem to have less-noxious crying sounds. Researchers have confirmed this parental observation in a wide range of studies.

Many groups of babies with known medical abnormalities have different-sounding cries, including those with Down syndrome, encephalitis, meningitis, and those with many types of brain damage. In recent work, Barry Lester has extended this observation to babies who appear physically normal, but are at risk for later problems because of some perinatal problem, such as preterm or small-for-date babies (Lester, 1987; Lester & Dreher, 1989; Zeskind & Lester, 1978). Such babies typically make crying sounds that are acoustically distinguishable from what you hear in a normal, low-risk baby. In particular, the cry of such higher-risk babies has a more grating, piercing quality. Interestingly, the cries of babies with colic also have some of these same qualities (Lester et al., 1992).

On the assumption that the baby's cry may reflect some basic aspect of neurological integrity, Lester also wondered whether one could use the quality of the cry as a *diagnostic* test. Among a group of high-risk babies, for example, could one predict later intellectual functioning from a measure of the gratingness or pitch of the baby's cry? The answer seems to be yes. Lester found that among preterms, those with higher-pitched cries in the first days of life had lower scores on an IQ test at age 5 years (Lester, 1987). Researchers have found the same kind of connection among both normal babies and those exposed to methadone prenatally. In all these groups, the higher the pitch and more grating the cry, the lower the child's later IQ or motor development (Huntington, Hans, & Zeskind, 1990).

Eventually, it may be possible for physicians to use the presence of such a grating or piercing cry as a signal that there may be some underlying physical problem with the infant, or to make better guesses about the long-term outcomes for individual babies at high risk of later problems, such as low-birth-weight babies.

in precisely the same way, so each parent must learn the specific sounds of his or her own baby. Alen Wiesenfeld and his colleagues (Wiesenfeld, Malatesta, & DeLoach, 1981) found that mothers (but not fathers) of 5-month-olds could discriminate between taped episodes of anger and pain cries in their own babies, while neither parent could reliably make the same discrimination with the taped cries of another baby.

In all of this, as with the nature of the cries themselves, there are wide individual differences. Fifteen to twenty percent of infants develop a pattern called *colic*, which involves daily, intense bouts of crying, totalling 3 or more hours a day. The crying is generally worst in late afternoon or early evening—a particularly inopportune time, of course, because parents are tired and need time with one another then, too. Colic typically appears at about 2 weeks of age and then disappears spontaneously at 3 or 4 months of age. Neither psychologists nor physicians know why colic begins, or why it stops without any intervention. It is a difficult pattern to live with, but the good news is that it *does* go away.

Responding to the Baby's Crying.   One of the enduring practical questions for parents about a baby's crying is how they should respond to it. If they pick up the baby right away, every time he cries, will that simply reinforce the baby's crying, so that he will cry more? Or will such an immediate response reassure the child, building the child's expectation that the world is a safe and reliable place?

Ten years ago I was confident that I knew the answer to this question, which was that one should always respond immediately. Early studies showed no sign that such immediate responding increased the child's crying, and there was a lot of evidence that predictable responding was one ingredient in the development of a secure attachment to the parent. More recent studies, though, make the answer less clear-cut. It now looks as if the parents' response may need to depend on the type of crying the child is doing. Intense crying, such as when

> The obvious explanation of the mother's greater ability to discriminate among the different cries of her baby is that she spends more time in caregiving than does the father. What kind of study could you design to test this hypothesis?

FIGURE 4.2
What to do?

the infant is hurt or significantly distressed—very hungry, very wet and uncomfortable, or the like—requires an immediate response. But whimpering and milder crying, such as what a baby may do when she is put down for a nap, is another matter. When a parent consistently responds immediately to such milder cries, babies seem to learn to cry more often (Hubbard & van IJzendoorn, 1987). Thus both reassurance and reinforcement seem to be involved, and it takes real sensitivity on the part of the parent to sort it out.

Eating

Eating is not a "state," but it is certainly something that newborn babies do frequently! Given the normal 2-hour cycle of a newborn baby's day, the infant may eat as many as ten times a day. By 1 month the average number is down to about five-and-a-half feedings, with a very gradual decline from that number over the first year (Barnard & Eyres, 1979). Both breast-fed and bottle-fed babies eat at about the same frequency, but these two forms of feeding do differ in other important ways.

Breast- versus bottle-feeding.   After several decades of extensive research in many countries, physicians and epidemiologists have reached clear agreement that breast-feeding is substantially nutritionally superior to bottle feeding. Breast milk provides important antibodies for the infant against many kinds of diseases, especially gastrointestinal and upper respiratory infections (Cunningham, Jelliffe, & Jelliffe, 1991). Human breast milk also appears to promote the growth of nerves and intestinal tract (Carter, 1988) and may stimulate better immune system function over the long term.

> What specific changes in policies or practices do you think would increase the rate of breast-feeding in the United States (or in your own country)?

Those women who find breast-feeding logistically difficult because of work or other demands may take some comfort from the fact that the research indicates that babies derive some protection from as little as one breast-feeding per day. There is also comfort in the observation that the *social* interactions between mother and child seem to suffer no ill effects from bottle feeding. Bottle-fed babies are held and cuddled in the same ways as are breast-fed babies, and their mothers appear to be just as sensitive and responsive to their babies as are mothers of breast-fed infants (Field, 1977).

I do not want this set of statements to provoke intense guilt in those of you who find that you are physically or otherwise unable to breast-feed. Babies can and do thrive on formula. But it is clear that *if* you have a choice, babies will derive real benefits from breast-feeding.

Physical Changes from Birth to 18 Months

As my friend with the 6-month-old has already observed, one of the remarkable things about babies is just how fast they change. If I need any further reminder of this fact, I need only look in my wallet, where I carry pictures of my grandson's first two years of life. The newborn pictures are (of course!) charming, but by 4 months, Sam was remarkably different. He had begun to sit up with a little

CULTURES & CONTEXTS

Cultural and Social Class Differences in Patterns of Breast-Feeding and their Consequences

If you look at the incidence of breast-feeding in countries around the world over the past 40 or 50 years, you'll find some very curious patterns. In the 1950s and 1960s, breast-feeding declined dramatically in most Western countries, including the United States. By 1971, only 25 percent of United States women breast-fed, even for a few weeks. At the same time, breast-feeding continued to be the normative method of infant-feeding in non-western countries, including virtually all Third World countries (World Health Organization, 1981).

In the decades since, these two trends have reversed. Breast-feeding has risen sharply in most industrialized countries as evidence of its importance came to light; by 1984, 60 percent of United States women breast-fed for at least a few weeks (Ryan et al., 1991). In the same years, however, rates and durations of breast-feeding began to drop in many Third World and developing countries.

It appears that one contributor to the decline of breast-feeding in less-industrialized countries was the marketing of infant formula. Manufacturers of formula often gave free samples or free feeding bottles to new mothers and assured women that formula was as good or better for babies, while frequently failing to provide adequate instruction on how mothers should use the formula. Some women, knowing no better and faced with extreme economic hardship, have diluted their infant's formula with water in order to make it stretch further. Moreover, no one provided a proper explanation of sterilization procedures; for many women, proper sterilization was simply not feasible. Worldwide, this change in normal feeding practices aroused sufficient concern to cause the World Health Organization to issue an "International Code of Marketing of Breast-milk Substitutes" in 1981. Marketing practices have since been modified, although free samples are still given in many countries, and women who receive such free samples are somewhat less likely to breast-feed (Adair, Popkin, & Guilkey, 1993). Overall, despite WHO's efforts, the decline in breast-feeding has continued (Stewart et al., 1991).

Such a decline is cause for real concern, because bottle-fed babies in developing or Third World countries are at far higher risk of serious disease or death. In Bangladesh, for example, the risk of death from diarrhea is three times higher among bottle-fed than among breast-fed babies; in Brazil, the risk of death from various kinds of infections ranges from 2½ to 14 times higher among the bottle-fed babies. In all these studies, the risk associated with bottle-feeding is far higher where the sanitary conditions are poorest (Cunningham et al., 1991). Breast-feeding is thus better for two reasons: it provides the baby with needed antibodies against infection, and it is likely to expose the baby to less infection in the first place.

Patterns in the U.S.

In view of such findings, it is disturbing to find that in the United States the trend line is again downward. Between 1984 and 1989 the percentage of women beginning breast-feeding dropped from 60 percent to 52 percent (Ryan et al., 1991). At both time points, it was the same subgroups that were more likely to breast-feed: older, well-educated, or higher-income mothers. Whites are also more likely than either Blacks or Hispanics to breast-feed. In 1989, the respective rates in the first weeks of the baby's life were 58 percent, 23 percent and 48 percent (Ryan et al., 1991). In all three groups, however, better-educated mothers are more likely to breast-feed, while the less-educated and the poor are least likely to do so (MacGowan et al., 1991). This pattern is of special concern because rates of mortality and illness are already higher among infants born to poor mothers.

A mother's work status also makes some difference in her decision about breast-or bottle-feeding, but it is *not* the deciding factor in many cases. The majority of women who do *not* work also do not breast-feed, while many working women find creative ways to combine employment and breast-feeding (Ryan et al., 1991). If we had societal supports for such a combination, it could be made still easier.

Overall, it is clear that there is still a large public health task remaining, not only in the United States but around the world, to educate women still further about the importance of breast-feeding and to create the cultural and practical supports needed to make breast-feeding easier.

help; he was reaching for things; he smiled a lot more. By the time he was a year old, he had a whole repertoire of striking new abilities. He walked; he understood a few words; he played with objects in a whole new way.

Because motor development is both cephalocaudal and proximodistal, both 7-month-old Helen and 5-month-old Laura are better at reaching and grasping than they are at crawling.

Basic Patterns

The sequence of physical changes we see in these early months follows two broad patterns: Development proceeds from the head downward, called **cephalocaudal,** and from the trunk outward, called **proximodistal.** We see the operation of these two principles in visible behavior, such as the baby's being able to hold up his head before he can sit, and sit before he can crawl. But we also can document the same patterns in the development of the nervous system.

Changes in the Nervous System

Figure 4.3 shows the main structures of the brain. The most completely developed of these structures at birth are the **midbrain** and the **medulla,** which regulate such basic tasks as attention, sleeping, waking, elimination, and movement of the head and neck (but not movement of the trunk or limbs). And as you've just seen, these are all tasks a newborn can perform at least moderately well.

The least-developed part of the brain at birth is the **cortex,** the convoluted gray matter that wraps around the midbrain and is involved in perception, body movement, and all complex thinking and language. Recall from Chapter 3 that all of these structures are composed of two basic types of cells, *neurons* and *glial cells*. Virtually all of both types of cells are already present at birth. The developmental process after birth is primarily the creation of synapses, which involves enormous growth of the dendritic arbor well as of axons and their terminal fibers. Most of that dendritic growth occurs in the cortex, primarily during the first year or two after birth, resulting in a tripling of the overall weight of the brain during those years (Nowakowski, 1987).

Development of Neurons and Synapses.   Dendritic development is not smooth and continuous. Neurophysiologists have found that there is an initial burst of synapse formation, followed by a "pruning" of synapses at about age 2. Redundant connections are eliminated and the "wiring diagram" is cleaned up (Greenough, Black, & Wallace, 1987). Taken together, these two developmental patterns mean that the 1–year-old actually has a *denser* set of dendrites and

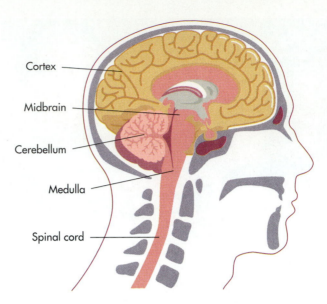

Cortex

Midbrain

Cerebellum

Medulla

Spinal cord

FIGURE 4.3
The medulla and the midbrain are largely developed at birth.
In the first two years after birth it is primarily the cortex that
develops, although increases in the dendritic arbor and in
synapses also occur throughout the nervous system.

Developmental
psychologists have
been very excited about
the discovery of dendritic
pruning in the second year
of life. Why is this such an
intriguing finding?

synapses than an adult does—a piece of information that has surprised many psychologists and raised a whole host of interesting questions. (You can see the rapid increase and get at least a general sense of the pruning from Figure 4.4.)

The pruning process is especially fascinating. Consider this example: early in development each skeletal muscle cell seems to develop synaptic connections with several motor neurons in the spinal cord. But after the pruning process has occurred, each muscle fiber is connected to only one neuron. In an argument reminiscent of the concept of "inborn biases" I mentioned in Chapter 1, some neurophysiologists such as Greenough (Greenough et al., 1987) have suggested that the initial surge of development of dendrites and synapses follows a built-in pattern; the organism is programmed to create certain kinds of neural connections and does so in abundance, creating redundant pathways. According to this argument, the pruning that then takes place at about age 2 is a response to specific experience, so that we selectively retain the most efficient pathways or the ones we use most. Putting it more briefly, "experience does not create tracings on a blank tablet; rather experience erases some of them" (Bertenthal & Campos, 1987). Such pruning appears to continue throughout childhood, with perhaps another peak at adolescence, suggesting that there may be a reorganization of pathways at various times in development.

Greenough and his colleagues do not think that all synaptic development is governed by such built-in programming. He suggests that other synapses are formed entirely as a result of specific experience and go on being created throughout our lives as we learn new skills. But basic motor and sensory processes may initially follow built-in patterns, with pruning then based on experience.

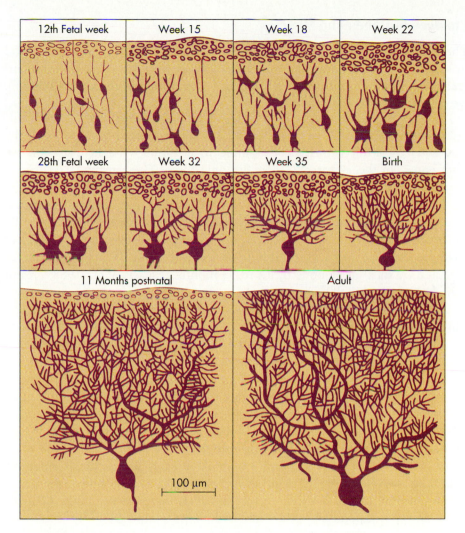

FIGURE 4.4
Nerve cells are almost all present at birth; what changes after birth is an immense growth of the "dendritic arbor" of each neuron, peaking at about 2 years, after which there is a "pruning" of the dendrites and synapses.

Myelinization.   Another crucial process in neuronal development is the development of sheaths around individual axons, which insulate them from one another and improve the conductivity of the nerve. This sheath is made up of a substance called **myelin;** the process of developing the sheath is **myelinization.**

The sequence with which nerves are myelinized follows the familiar cephalocaudal and proximodistal patterns. Thus nerves serving muscle cells in the arms and hands are myelinized earlier than are those serving the lower trunk and the legs. Myelinization is largely complete by age 2, although some continues in the brain well into adolescence.

To understand the importance of myelin, it may help you to know that *multiple sclerosis* is a disease in which the myelin begins to break down. An individual with this disease gradually loses motor control, with the specific symptoms depending on the portion of the nervous system in which the myelin is affected.

Changes in Bones and Muscles

These changes in the nervous system are paralleled by changes in other body structures, including bones and muscles, although here the changes occur fairly gradually from infancy through adolescence, rather than in the remarkable spurt we see in the nervous system.

Bones.   The hand, wrist, ankle and foot all have fewer bones at birth than they will have at full maturity. For example, in an adult's wrist there are nine separate bones. In the 1-year-old, there are only three. The remaining six develop over the period of childhood, with complete growth by adolescence.

In one part of the body, though, the bones fuse rather than differentiating. The skull of a newborn is made up of several bones separated by spaces called **fontanels.** Fontanels allow the head to be compressed without injury during the birth process, and they also give the brain room to grow. In most children, the fontanels are filled in by bone by 12 to 18 months (Kataria et al., 1988) creating a single connected skull bone.

All of the infant's bones are also softer, with a higher water content, than adults' bones. The process of bone hardening, or **ossification,** occurs steadily from birth through puberty, with bones in different parts of the body hardening in a sequence that follows the typical proximodistal and cephalocaudal patterns. So, for example, bones of the hand and wrist harden before those in the feet.

You may well be thinking that bone hardening is pretty boring and unimportant stuff, but it has some fairly direct practical relevance. Soft bones are clearly needed if the fetus is going to have enough flexibility to fit into the cramped space of the uterus. But that very flexibility contributes to a newborn human's relative helplessness. Newborns are remarkably floppy; they cannot even hold their own heads up, let alone sit or walk. As the bones stiffen, the baby is able to manipulate his body more surely, which increases the range of exploration he can enjoy and makes him much more independent.

Muscles.   As is true of neurons, the newborn baby has virtually all the muscle fibers she will ever have (Tanner, 1978). But like the infant's bones, muscle fibers are initially small and watery, becoming longer, thicker, and less watery at a fairly steady rate until adolescence. The sequence is again both proximodistal and cephalocaudal. So the baby gains muscle strength in the neck fairly early, but does not have enough muscle strength in the legs to support walking until some months later.

Size and Shape

All these internal changes obviously affect the baby's size and shape. Babies grow very rapidly in the first months, adding 10 to 12 inches in length and tripling their body weight in the first year. By age 2, after adding another two or three inches, babies are *half as tall as they will be as adults*—a fact I put in italics because it is so surprising to most of us. We are deceived in part by the fact that the baby's body proportions are quite different from those of an adult. Most strikingly, babies have proportionately much larger heads—obviously needed to hold that nearly full-sized brain.

Motor Development

All these physical changes form the substrate on which the child's rapidly improving motor skills are constructed. And of course it is precisely those new physical abilities that are so striking and remarkable to parents (and grandparents!).

Robert Malina (1982) suggests that we can divide the wide range of motor skills into three rough groups: *locomotor* patterns, such as walking, running, jumping, hopping and skipping; *nonlocomotor* patterns such as pushing, pulling, and bending; and *manipulative* skills such as grasping, throwing, catching, kicking, and other actions involving receiving and moving objects. In Table 4.3 I've summarized the developments in each of these three areas over the first 18 months, based primarily on two comparatively recent large studies, one in the United States and one in the Netherlands. The United States study (Capute et al., 1984) involved 381 babies whose pediatricians tested them at regular visits through the first two years; the Dutch study (Den Ouden et al., 1991) included 550 babies who had been tested repeatedly for their first five years. The sequence of milestones the researchers describe in these two studies are highly similar, as were the ages at which babies passed each test.

A baby's achievement of these milestones is striking to watch, but even brief observation of a baby will tell you that there is a lot of other movement going on in addition to creeping or crawling. Young infants also show a lot of

---

TABLE 4.3
Milestones of Motor Development in the first Two Years

Age	Locomotor Skills	Nonlocomotor Skills	Manipulative Skills
1 mo	stepping reflex	lifts head slightly; follows slowly moving objects with eyes	holds object if placed in hand
2–3 mo		Lifts head up to 90 deg when lying on stomach	begins to swipe at objects in sight
4–6 mo	rolls over; sits with some support; moves on hands and knees ("creeps")	holds head erect in sitting position	reaches for and grasps objects
7–9 mo	sits without support; crawls		transfers objects from one hand to the other
10–12 mo	pulls himself to standing; walks grasping furniture ("cruising"); then walks without help	squats and stoops	some signs of hand preference; grasps a spoon across palm but has poor aim of food to mouth
13–18 mo	walks backward and sideways; runs (14–20 mo)	rolls ball to adult	stacks two blocks; puts objects into small containers and dumps them

Sources: Primary sources are Capute et al., 1986, and Den Ouden et al., 1991; Other sources: Connolly & Dalgleish, 1989; The Diagram Group, 1977; Fagard & Jaquet, 1989; Mathew & Cook, 1990; Thomas, 1990.

The rapid pace of motor development is easy to illustrate. Six-month-old Salma is able to crawl; at 11 months, John can walk with some help; only 2 months older, Meredith can walk by herself.

what Esther Thelen (1981) has called *rhythmical stereotypies* (pronounced stare-ee-OTT-uh-peas)—those patterns of kicking, rocking, waving, bouncing, banging, rubbing, scratching, and swaying that the infant repeats over and over and in which he seems to take great delight. These repeated, rhythmical patterns seem to peak at about 6 or 7 months of age, although you can see some such behavior even in the first weeks, particularly in finger movements and leg kicking. While this type of movement does not seem to be totally voluntary or coordinated, it also does not appear to be random. For instance, Thelen has observed that kicking movements peak just before the baby begins to crawl, as if the rhythmic kicking were a part of the preparation for crawling.

Determinants of Growth: Explaining Early Physical Development

When we search for explanations for all these physical changes and emerging motor skills, there are some obvious candidates: maturation, heredity, and various environmental factors, including both diet and practice.

Maturation

Maturational sequences seem necessarily to be part of the explanation, especially for such central patterns as neuronal changes and changes in muscles and bones. In all these areas, while the *rate* of development varies from one child to the next, the *sequence* is virtually the same for all children, even those with marked physical or mental handicaps. Mentally retarded children, for example, typically move through the various motor milestones more slowly than do normal children, but they follow the same sequence. Whenever we find such robust sequences, maturation of some kind seems an obvious explanation.

But Esther Thelen, one of the leading experts on motor development, points out that most of us have an overly simplistic view of the whole idea of maturation (Lockman & Thelen, 1993; Thelen, 1989; Thelen, 1992). There is no "crawling gene" or "walking gene" that somehow "unfolds" in a sequence. Instead, she argues that some new movement or motor skill is a "final common pathway," a result of a complex system of forces operating together, including cognition, perception, and motivation, as well as underlying physical changes.

For example, for the 12-month-old to be able to walk requires not only the growth of leg muscles, but also abdominal muscles, a change in center of gravity downward from the head, and development of visual skills, among many other ingredients (Thelen, 1984). Using a spoon to feed oneself requires development of muscles in the hand and wrist, bone development in the wrist, eye-hand coordination skills that allow one to readjust the aim of the spoon as it moves toward the mouth, and coordination of all of these with properly timed mouth opening (Connolly & Dalgleish, 1989).

Obviously Thelen and her followers are not denying the fundamental significance of the maturation of nerves and muscles. But they are saying that the concept of maturation alone does not *explain* the development of motor skills.

Heredity

Our genetic heritage is individual as well as species-specific. In addition to being programmed for many basic sequences of physical development, each of us also receives instructions for unique growth tendencies. Both size and body shape seem to be heavily influenced by such specific inheritance. Tall parents tend to have tall children; short parents tend to have short children. There are also similarities between parents and children in such things as hip width, arm length (some ancestor certainly passed on a gene for long arms to me!), and long or short trunk. As I mentioned in Chapter 2, rate or tempo of growth, as well as final shape or size, also seems to be an inherited pattern. Parents who were themselves early developers, as measured by such things as bone ossification, tend to have children who are faster developers too (Garn, 1980).

> Can you think of any distinctive physical features, body proportions, or rate of growth patterns that are part of your family genetic heritage?

Environmental Effects: Diet and Practice

On the environmental side, there are two obvious explanatory candidates: diet and practice.

Diet.   I mentioned in the last chapter that serious malnutrition during a pregnancy can have a permanently negative effect on the developing fetus, reducing the number of neurons and retarding the growth of the dendritic arbor. Researchers have had difficulty detecting the effects of malnutrition or chronic subnutrition after birth, because most malnourished babies also grow up in environments that are deficient in other respects as well. What we do know is that poorly nourished children grow more slowly, and then don't end up as large

(Malina, 1982). If their diet later improves, such children may show some catch up in height or growth rate, but they are typically shorter and slower than their peers.

In addition, of course, malnourished or undernourished infants and children have less energy, which in turn can affect the nature of the interactions the child has with both the objects and the people around him. A recent study of school-age children illustrates the point. When Michael Espinosa and his colleagues (Espinosa et al., 1992) observed a group of Kenyan children on the playground, they found that undernourished kids were more solitary and less active than their well-nourished peers. The children in this study were not severely malnourished; they were taking in about 1500 calories per day. This is enough to sustain the child, but not enough to provide the energy needed for play, or perhaps for concentration in school over long periods. I know of no equivalent study of malnourished infants, but my assumption is that researchers would find the same effect. The results of malnutrition may thus be subtle and difficult to detect, but cumulatively substantial for the physical and mental growth of the child.

Practice.   We can also think of environmental influences on physical development in terms of the child's own practice of various physical activities. For example, does a baby who spends a lot of time in a toy called an infant walker, which holds up the baby while he moves around, learn independent walking any sooner than a baby who never has that practice? Does a toddler who has a chance to try to climb stairs learn to climb them sooner, or more skillfully, than a toddler who is rarely exposed to stairs? If you go back and look at Aslin's models of the possible role of early experience from Figure 1.1, you'll see that I am asking whether practice has a *facilitative* effect, or even if it operates as what he calls *attunement*. Alternatively, perhaps practice has no effect at all on the emergence of basic skills.

The answer, as usual, is fairly complicated. Two conclusions are reasonably clear. First, the development of such universal, basic skills as crawling or walking requires some minimum amount of practice just to keep the system working as it should—what Aslin calls a *maintenance* effect of environment. Children who are deprived of such normal practice develop motor skills much more slowly and not in the normal sequence. Wayne Dennis's classic study (1960) of children raised in Iranian orphanages is a good illustration. The babies in one of the institutions Dennis observed were routinely placed on their backs in cribs with very lumpy mattresses. They had little or no experience of lying or moving on their stomachs as a normal baby would, and even had difficulty rolling over because of the hollows in the mattresses. These babies almost never went through the normal sequence of learning to walk—presumably because they didn't have enough opportunity to practice all the on-the-stomach parts of the skill. They did learn to walk eventually, but they were about a year late. It would appear from this and equivalent research (Razel, 1985) that for the development of such universal, basic skills as crawling or walking, babies need some minimum amount of practice just to keep the system working as it should.

We also know that the development of really smooth, coordinated skill in virtually all complex motor tasks requires practice. Maturation may help to determine when a child *can* learn a particular skill, but practice is clearly necessary for

Although the research is not entirely consistent, it looks as though lots of opportunity to practice basic motor skills like stair climbing probably does not speed up a baby's stair-climbing skill a whole lot.

effective performance. As just one example, the strength and coordination required to throw a basketball high enough to reach the basket may develop in predictable ways over the early years, providing the environment is sufficiently rich to provide needed maintenance. But to develop the skill one needs to get the ball through the hoop with regularity, from different angles and distances, requires endless practice.

We are still uncertain about the role of practice in the acquisition of the basic component skills, such as sitting, walking up stairs, climbing, or catching objects. Early studies seemed to show that extra practice in such basic skills didn't speed up their development at all, perhaps because virtually all children have enough opportunity for minimal practice in their ordinary lives. For example, studies of babies using walkers suggest that such infants do not walk any sooner than those who lack such specialized practice (Ridenour, 1982); babies who have practice climbing stairs do not learn skillful stair climbing much, if any, sooner than those with limited stair experience. But there are also recent studies that show the opposite, including one showing that very young babies who are given more practice sitting are able to sit upright longer than those without such practice (Zelazo et al., 1993). The jury is still out on this question.

Health and Death in the First Year of Life

Virtually all babies get sick, most of them repeatedly. Data from the United States indicate that within the first year, babies have an average of seven respiratory illnesses. (That's a lot of nose-wipes!) In the second year of life this actually increases, to about eight illnesses. Interestingly, there is now a whole series of studies showing that the incidence of such disorders is higher among babies in day-care programs than among those reared entirely at home, presumably because there is greater exposure to more germs and viruses in group care settings (Hurwitz et al., 1991). In general, the more different people a baby is exposed to, the more often she is likely to be sick (Wald, Guerra, & Byers, 1991). But this is not the unmitigated negative that it may appear to be. Children reared entirely at home, with low exposure to others, have very high rates of illness at later ages when they first attend school. Attendance at day care simply means that the baby is exposed earlier to the various microorganisms that cause upper respiratory infections.

Infant Mortality. For a small minority of babies, though, the issue is not a few sniffles, but the possibility of death. I mentioned in the last chapter that the infant mortality rate—the number of deaths in the first year of life—now stands at 8.9 deaths per 1,000 live births in the United States. Most of these deaths occur in the first month of life (the *neonatal* period) and are directly linked either to congenital anomalies or low birth weight. Only about 3.5 deaths per 1,000 occur in the remainder of the first year, and nearly half of those are cases of **Sudden Infant Death Syndrome** (SIDS), in which an apparently healthy infant dies suddenly and unexpectedly. In 1991, 5,349 babies in the United States died of SIDS (Wegman, 1993).

SIDS is certainly not unique to the U.S. It occurs worldwide, although for unexplained reasons, the rate varies quite a lot from country to country. SIDS rates are particularly high, for example, in Australia and New Zealand, and particularly low in Japan and Sweden (Hoffman & Hillman, 1992).

Physicians have not yet uncovered the basic cause of these deaths. But we do know a lot more now about the groups that are at higher risk: low-birth-weight babies, males, Blacks, those with young mothers, and those whose mothers smoked during pregnancy or after birth. SIDS is also more common in the winter time and appears to be more common among babies who sleep on their stomachs (Dwyer & Ponsonby, 1992; Hoffman & Hillman, 1992; Ponsonby et al., 1993; Spiers & Guntheroth, 1994). The growing evidence on the role of sleeping position has persuaded pediatricians in some countries to change their standard advice to hospitals and families about the best sleeping position for babies. The American Academy of Pediatrics, for example, has been recommending since 1992 that when healthy infants are put down to sleep, they should be positioned on their sides or backs. Still, sleeping position cannot be the full explanation, because of course *most* babies who sleep on their stomachs do not die of SIDS.

The link between SIDS and maternal (or paternal) smoking is also becoming clearer and clearer: babies whose mothers smoked during their pregnancy or who are exposed to smoke in the months after birth are about four times as likely to die of SIDS as are babies with no smoking exposure (Mitchell et al., 1993; Schoendorf & Kiely, 1992). One more powerful reason not to smoke!

The higher risk of SIDS for Black infants in the United States is part of a persistent pattern. You will remember from the last chapter that infant mortality is more than twice as high among Black infants as among Whites. An equivalent disadvantage exists for Native-American infants (Honigfeld & Kaplan, 1987). These persistent and disturbing differences appear to reflect not only variations in the availability of adequate prenatal care but also a lack of support for poor mothers and their infants after delivery. Poor infants, including both Blacks and Native-Americans, are less likely to receive appropriate immunizations, are more likely to be ill, less likely to receive a doctor's care when they are ill, and four times as likely to die of such entirely preventable diseases as gastroenteritis (Starfield, 1991; Wegman, 1993).

Individual Differences in Early Physical Development

I've already touched on several kinds of differences among babies that affect their physical development in the first few years: diet, feeding experience, specific practice, and adequacy of prenatal and postnatal medical care. Let me sketch several other differences.

Preterm babies.   Preterm or low-birth-weight babies move more slowly through all the developmental sequences I've been describing. You can get some sense of the degree of difference from Table 4.4, which gives several comparisons. The data here are from the Dutch study of normal development I cited in

TABLE 4.4

Comparison of Preterm and Normal-Term Babies in Developmental Milestones in the First Two Years

Developmental Milestone	Age at which 50 percent of babies passed	
	Preterm (< 32 weeks)	Normalterm
Lifts head slightly	10 weeks	6 weeks
Transfers object hand to hand	36 weeks	23 weeks
Rolls over	37 weeks	24 weeks
Crawls	51 weeks	36 weeks
Pulls to standing position	51 weeks	42 weeks

Source: Den Ouden et al., 1991, from Table V, p. 402.

Table 4.3. Den Ouden and her colleagues (1991) tested 555 normal and 555 preterm babies. The latter group included all the otherwise physically normal preterms born at less than 32 weeks gestation in the Netherlands in 1983. You can see that the preterms are about 10–15 weeks behind their full-term peers on most physical skills. This is entirely what we would expect, of course, because the preterm baby is, in fact, maturationally younger than the full-term baby. If you correct for the baby's "gestational age," most (but not all) of the difference disappears. Parents of preterms need to keep this in mind when they compare their baby's progress with that of a full-term baby. By age 2 or 3 years, the physically normal preterm will catch up to his peers, but in the early months he is definitely behind.

Boys and Girls. I'll bet that your first question when you hear that a friend or family member has had a new baby, is: "Is it a boy or a girl?" You might assume that such a preoccupation exists because boy and girl babies are really very different from one another. But in fact they are not. There are remarkably few sex differences in physical development in young infants. As was true at birth, girls continue to be a bit ahead in some aspects of physical maturity, and boys continue to be more vulnerable, with higher infant mortality rates. It is also clear that male infants have more muscle tissue than do girls.

More mixed are the findings on activity level. When researchers observe a difference it is likely to be boys who are found to be more active (Eaton & Enns, 1986), but many investigators report no difference at all (Cossette, Malcuit, & Pomerleau, 1991). There are actually bigger differences between babies from different ethnic groups—which I describe in the *Cultures and Contexts* box on page 118—than there are between boys and girls.

The physical development of infants is probably more clearly governed by built-in sequences and time-tables, and more similar from one baby to another, than any other aspect of development at which we'll be looking. What is striking to the observer is not boy-ness or girl-ness, or black-ness or white-ness, but *baby-ness.*

Why *do* we all ask, immediately, whether a new baby is a boy or a girl? Why does this information seem so vital? Do you think adults in other cultures would be as eager to know a newborn's gender? Why or why not?

CULTURES & CONTEXTS

Differences in Early Physical Development

The sequences of physical changes I've been describing in this chapter do seem to hold true for babies in all cultures. But there are nonetheless interesting differences.

Black babies—whether born in Africa or elsewhere—develop somewhat faster, both prenatally and after birth. In fact, the gestational period for the Black fetus seems actually to be slightly shorter than for the White fetus (Smith, 1978). Black babies also show somewhat faster development of motor skills, such as walking, and are slightly taller than their White counterparts, with longer legs, more muscle, and heavier bones (Tanner, 1978).

In contrast, Asian infants are somewhat slower to achieve many early motor milestones. This could reflect simply differences in rate of maturation. Or it could reflect some ethnic differences in the baby's level of activity or placidity, a possibility suggested by research by Daniel Freedman (1979).

Freedman has observed newborn babies from four different cultures: Caucasian, Chinese, Navaho, and Japanese. Of the four, he found that the Caucasian babies were the most active and irritable and the hardest to console. Both the Chinese and the Navaho infants he observed were relatively placid, while the Japanese infants responded vigorously but were easier to quiet than the Caucasian infants.

Consider one specific illustration. When Freedman tested each baby for the Moro reflex he found that the Caucasian babies showed a pattern in which they reflexively extended both arms, cried vigorously and persistently, and moved their bodies in an agitated way. Navaho babies, on the other hand, showed quite a different pattern. Instead of thrusting their limbs outward they retracted their arms and legs, rarely cried, and showed little or very brief agitation.

Because such differences are visible in newborns they cannot be the result of systematic shaping by the parents. But the parents, too, bring their cultural training to the interaction. Freedman and other researchers have observed that both Japanese and Chinese mothers talk much less to their infants than do Caucasian mothers. These differences in mothers' behavior were present from their first encounters with their infants after delivery, so the pattern is not a response to the baby's quieter behavior. But such similarity of temperamental pattern between mother and child may strengthen the pattern in the child, which would tend to make the cultural differences larger over time.

As one example, Michael Lewis and his colleagues (Lewis, Ramsay, & Kawakami, 1993) have compared 4-month-old Caucasian and Japanese infants' reactions to a routine inoculation. Caucasian-American babies reacted with more visible physical vigor and were more likely to cry. The Japanese infants, in contrast, showed little visible physical reaction, but showed high levels of a chemical called cortisol in their saliva—a chemical that signals the presence of stress. Caucasian babies showed little elevation of cortisol. Thus both groups of babies reacted, but they did so in very different ways.

Of course this study doesn't tell us whether this difference is inborn or the result of specific training in the early months. Most probably, it is some combination of the two influences. The key point is to remember that our own cultural patterns and assumptions may strongly influence what we consider "normal" behavior for an infant.

SUMMARY

1. Doctors and midwives typically assess newborns using the Apgar score, which is a rating on five dimensions.

2. Infants have both adaptive and primitive reflexes. The former group includes such essential reflexes as sucking and rooting; primitive reflexes include the Moro and Babinski, which disappear within a few months.

3. At birth the baby has a far wider array of perceptual skills than psychologists had earlier supposed. In particular, she can see and hear well enough for most social encounters.

4. Babies move through a series of "states of consciousness," from quiet sleep to active sleep to fussing to eating to quiet wakefulness, in a cycle that lasts roughly 1½ to 2 hours.

5. Persistent irregularity of sleep patterns or a particularly high pitched or grating cry may be indications of some neurological problem.

6. Studies repeatedly show breast-feeding to be better for the baby nutritionally, providing needed antibodies and reducing the risk of various infections.

7. Changes in the nervous system are extremely rapid in the first two years. Dendritic and synaptic development reaches its peak between 12 and 24 months, after which there is a "pruning" of synapses. Myelinization of nerve fibers is also largely complete by 2 years.

8. Bones increase in number and density; muscle fibers become larger and less watery.

9. Babies triple their body weight in the first year, and add 12 to 15 inches in length before age 2.

10. Rapid improvement in locomotor and manipulative skills occurs in the first two years, as the baby moves from creeping to crawling to walking to running, and from poor to good ability to grasp objects.

11. These virtually universal sequences of development are clearly influenced strongly by common maturational patterns. But individual heredity also makes a difference, as does diet.

12. Babies require sufficient practice of even basic skills to maintain the physiological system. Whether practice beyond that minimum speeds up basic skill development is still an open question.

13. Most infant deaths in the first weeks are due to congenital anomalies or low birth-weight; past the first weeks, Sudden Infant Death Syndrome is the most common cause of death in the first year.

14. On average, babies have 7 to 8 respiratory illnesses in each of the first two years. This rate is higher among infants in day care.

15. Preterm infants are behind their full-term peers in achieving the milestones of development, but they typically catch up within a few years.

16. There are relatively few differences between boys and girls in early physical development. Ethnic differences do exist, however. Black infants develop somewhat more rapidly, Asian infants somewhat slower.

K E Y   T E R M S

Apgar score	myelin	rapid eye movement
cephalocaudal	myelinization	(REM) sleep
cortex	ossification	states of consciousness
fontanels	proximodistal	sudden infant death
medulla	reflexes	syndrome (SIDS)
midbrain		

SUGGESTED READINGS

The Diagram Group (1977). *Child's Body*. New York: Paddington Press. This nifty book is not new and may be hard to find, but it is worth the effort. Designed as a parents' manual and full of helpful information about physical development, health, and nutrition.

Maurer, D., & Maurer, C. (1988). *The world of the newborn*. New York: Basic Books. An excellent description of the newborn; for the lay reader, but based very clearly and strongly on research.

Rosenblith, J. F., & Sims-Knight, J. E. (1989). *In the beginning. Development in the first two years of life*. Newbury Park, CA: Sage. A fine basic text on infant development.

Slater, A. M., & Bremner, J. G. (Eds.) (1989). *Infant development*. Hillsdale, NJ: Lawrence Erlbaum Associates. Like the Maurer and Maurer book, this one was written by scientists, based on research, but aimed at the lay reader. In this case each chapter was written by a separate expert.

Chapter Five

Perceptual and Cognitive Development in Infancy

I mentioned in the first chapter that I had recently spent a year in Germany. Hoping to learn enough German to be able to speak to my husband's many relatives, I took intensive German classes and struggled to learn new vocabulary and complex grammar. The whole process turned out to be a lot harder than I had expected, but it certainly gave me a chance to observe the ways I go about learning, remembering, and using new information. I had, throughout, an almost physical sense of my brain at work, struggling to create order and sense out of a bombardment of new information. (Periodically my brain would simply go on strike and refuse to take in anything more—a sensation I suspect most of you have had at one time or another!)

In our everyday lives, each of us faces myriad tasks that call for the same kinds of skills I used in my efforts to learn this new language. We study for exams, try to remember what to buy at the grocery store, balance the checkbook, remember phone numbers, or use a map. Not all of us do these things equally well or equally quickly. But all of us perform such activities every day of our lives.

These activities are all part of what we normally describe as *cognitive functioning*, or "intelligence." What I will be exploring here and in the parallel chapters on cognition in each age-period is how we all acquire the ability to do all these things. One-year-olds cannot use maps or balance a checkbook. How do they come to be able to do so? And how do we explain the fact that not all children learn these things at the same rate or become as skilled?

Theoretical Perspectives

Answering questions like these has been complicated by the fact that there are three distinctly different views of cognition, or intelligence, each of which has led to a separate body of research and commentary.

These babies may look like they are playing, but they are also engaged in important cognitive activities—trying to understand the world around them.

Three Views of Intelligence

Historically, the first approach to studying cognitive development, or intelligence, focused on individual differences. It is inescapably true that people differ in their intellectual skill, their ability to remember things, the speed with which they solve problems, the number of words they can define, and their ability to analyze complex situations. When we say someone is "bright" or "very intelligent," it is just such skills we mean, and our label is based on the assumption that we can rank order people in their degree of "brightness." The very same assumption led to the development of intelligence tests, which were designed simply to give us a way of measuring individual differences in intellectual *power*.

Is this what you mean when you say someone is "bright" or "intelligent?" What else do you mean by these terms?

The intellectual power approach, which Robert Sternberg (1979) refers to as the *differential approach* because of its emphasis on individual differences, held sway for many years. But it has one great weakness: it does not deal with the equally inescapable fact that intelligence develops. As children grow, their thinking becomes more and more abstract and complex. If you give a 5-year-old a mental list of things to remember to buy at the grocery store she will have trouble remembering more than a few items. She is also very unlikely to use good strategies to aid her memory, such as rehearsing the list or organizing the items into groups. An 8-year-old would remember more things and probably would rehearse the list under his breath or in his head, as he was walking to the store.

The fact that intelligence develops in this way forms the foundation of the second great tradition in the study of cognitive development, the *cognitive developmental approach* of Jean Piaget and his many followers. Piaget's focus was on the development of cognitive *structures*, rather than on intellectual power, on patterns of development that are *common* to all children, rather than on individual differences.

These two traditions have lived side by side for some years now, rather like not-very-friendly neighbors who smile vaguely at one another when they meet but never get together for coffee. In the past few years, though, the two have developed a mutual friend—a third view, the **information processing** approach, that partially integrates power and structure approaches. Proponents of this third view argue that what we need is an understanding of the *underlying processes* or strategies that make up all cognitive activity. Joseph Fagan (1992) puts it this way:

> Intelligence is not a faculty or trait of the mind. Intelligence is not mental content. *Intelligence is processing.* Knowledge is gained as the result of the assimilation, over time, of information by the intellectual processes (p. 82, emphasis in original).

Researchers in this tradition obviously ask a different kind of question: What are the basic intellectual processes and how should we measure them? One of the strengths of this approach is that once we have identified such basic processes, we can then ask *both* developmental and individual difference questions: do these basic processes change with age, and do people differ in their speed or skill in using them?

These three themes will appear again and again as we look at cognitive development in infancy, in childhood, and in adolescence. But the research in each tradition is not equally distributed across the several age strata. In particular, Piaget's theory has been the most clearly dominant in research on infant intelligence—perhaps because he was really the first theorist to think of the infant's behavior in terms of intelligence. For this reason, much of what I will be talking about in this chapter has been cast in a Piagetian framework, although you will see elements of both cognitive power and information processing approaches entering into the overall theoretical fabric.

Piaget's Views of the Sensorimotor Period

Recall from Chapter 2 that Piaget assumes that from the beginning, the baby is engaged in an *adaptive* process, trying to make sense out of the world around her. She assimilates incoming information to the limited array of schemes she is born with—such as looking, listening, sucking, grasping—and accommodates those schemes based on her experiences. This is the starting point for the entire process of cognitive development, according to Piaget. He called this primitive form of thinking *sensorimotor intelligence*, and the entire stage he called the **sensorimotor period.**

This 2-week-old baby is using two basic sensorimotor schemes at the same time: looking, and grasping.

Basic Features of Sensorimotor Intelligence.   In Piaget's view, the baby is born with only sensory and motor schemes. So that is where she must start. In the beginning, she is entirely tied to the immediate present, responding to whatever stimuli are available. She does not remember events or things from one encounter to the next and does not appear to plan or intend. This gradually changes during these first 18 months as the baby comes to understand that objects continue to exist even when they are out of sight and is able to remember objects, actions, and individuals over periods of time. But Piaget insisted that the sensorimotor infant is as yet unable to *manipulate* these early mental images or memories. Nor does she use *symbols* to stand for objects or events. It is the new ability to manipulate internal symbols, such as words or images, that marks the beginning of the next stage, *preoperational thought*, at roughly 18–24 months of age. John Flavell (1985) summarizes all this very nicely:

> [The infant] exhibits a wholly practical, perceiving-and-doing, action-bound kind of intellectual functioning; she does not exhibit the more contemplative, reflective, symbol-manipulating kind we usually think of in connection with cognition. The infant "knows" in the sense of recognizing or anticipating familiar, recurring objects and happenings, and "thinks" in the sense of behaving toward them with mouth, hand, eye, and other sensory-motor instruments in predictable, organized, and often adaptive ways. . . . It is the kind of noncontemplative intelligence that your dog relies on to make its way in the world (p. 13).

The change from the limited repertoire of schemes available to the newborn to the ability to use symbols at roughly 18 months is gradual. Piaget described six substages, which I've summarized in Table 5.1.

Each stage represents some specific advance over the one that came before. Stage 2 is marked especially by the beginning of those important coordinations between looking and listening, reaching and looking, and reaching and sucking that are such central features of the 2-month-old's means of exploring the world. The term *primary circular reactions* refers to the many simple repetitive actions we see at this stage, each centered around the infant's own body. The baby accidentally sucks his thumb one day, finds it pleasurable, and repeats the action.

TABLE 5.1
Substages of the Sensorimotor Period According to Piaget

Substage	Age	Piaget's label	Characteristics
1	0–1 mo.	Reflexes	Practice of built-in schemes or reflexes, such as sucking and looking. Primitive schemes begin to change through very small steps of accommodation. No imitation; no ability to integrate information from several senses.
2	1–4 mo	Primary circular reactions	Further accommodation of basic schemes, as baby practices them endlessly—grasping, looking, sucking. Beginning coordination of schemes from different senses, so that baby now looks toward a sound and sucks on anything he can reach and bring to his mouth. But the baby does not yet link his body actions to some result outside his body.
3	4–8 mo	Secondary circular reactions	Baby becomes much more aware of events outside his own body and makes them happen again in a kind of trial and error learning. Not clear that there is understanding of the causal links yet, however. Imitation may occur, but only of schemes already in the baby's repertoire. Beginning understanding of the "object concept" also detected in this period.
4	8–12 mo	Coordination of secondary schemes	Clear intentional means-ends behavior. The baby not only goes after what she wants, she may combine two schemes to do so, such as knocking a pillow away to reach a toy. Imitation of novel behaviors occurs, as does transfer of information from one sense to the other (cross-modal transfer).
5	12–18 mo	Tertiary circular reactions	"Experimentation" begins, in which the infant tries out new ways of playing with or manipulating objects. Very active, very purposeful, trial-and-error exploration.
6	18–24 mo	Beginning of representational thought	Development of use of symbols to represent object or events. Child understands that the symbol is separate from the object. Deferred imitation occurs first here, because it requires ability to represent internally the event to be imitated.

Secondary circular reactions, in Stage 3, differ only in that the baby is now repeating some action in order to trigger a reaction outside his own body. The baby coos and Mom smiles, so the baby coos again, apparently in order to get Mom to smile again. These initial connections between body actions and external consequences are pretty automatic, very much like a kind of operant conditioning. Only in Stage 4 do we see the beginnings of real understanding of causal connections, and at this point the baby really moves into exploratory high gear.

In Stage 5 this becomes even more marked with the emergence of what Piaget calls *tertiary circular reactions*. In this pattern the baby is not content merely to repeat the original behavior but tries out variations. The baby in Stage 5 might try out many other sounds or facial expressions to see if they would trigger Mom's smile or try dropping a toy from several heights to see if it made different sounds or landed in different places. There is a purposeful, experimental quality to the baby's behavior. Nonetheless, Piaget thought that even in Stage 5 the baby does not have internal *symbols* to stand for objects. The development of such symbols is the mark of Stage 6.

Table 5.1 also makes clear that Piaget believed the baby's ability to imitate others moved through a series of steps. He thought that the newborn could not or would not imitate at all. By Stage 3, the baby can imitate the actions of others if the action is already in his own repertoire—if he already has that scheme. In Stage 4, the baby can now learn something new from imitation. And in Stage 6, the toddler is capable of deferred imitation in which he sees some action and then imitates it at a later point—a skill that appears to require some ability to represent the action internally and remember it.

Piaget's descriptions of this sequence of development, largely based on remarkably detailed observations of the early months of his own three children's lives, have provoked a very rich array of research, some of which confirms the general outlines of his proposals, some of which does not. Let me illustrate the current findings by focusing on several specific lines of research—on early learning and memory, on early perceptual skills such as the ability to combine data from more than one sense, on imitation, and on the object concept. Not all this research has been done within an explicitly Piagetian framework, but it nonetheless helps us to get a sense of what the baby can do, as well as to evaluate aspects of Piaget's theory.

Learning and Habituation

The broader nature/nurture controversy, rather than Piaget's theory, has stimulated most of the work on learning in infancy. Those who argue that a child's behaviors and characteristics are a product of experience, rather than being genetically patterned, must be able to demonstrate that an infant can indeed learn from such experience.

The question of what and how a baby learns is also important from a practical perspective, if only because it affects the sort of advice parents may receive about suitable stimulation for their child. For example, if a child's perceptual abilities develop largely through maturation rather than learning, experts would be less likely to advise parents to buy mobiles to hang above the baby's crib. But if learning is possible from the earliest days of life, then various kinds of enrichment would be beneficial.

What does the evidence tell us?

Classical Conditioning

The bulk of the research suggests that the newborn can be classically conditioned, although it is difficult. By 3 or 4 weeks of age classical conditioning is quite easy to demonstrate in an infant. In particular, this means that the conditioned emotional responses I talked about in Chapter 2 may begin to develop as early as the first weeks of life. Thus the mere presence of Mom or Dad or other favored person may trigger the sense of "feeling good," a pattern that may contribute to what we see as the child's attachment to the parent. Similarly, a child might develop various classically conditioned negative emotional responses that may be part of what we see as temperament.

Operant Conditioning

Newborns also clearly learn by operant conditioning. Researchers have found that it's possible to increase both the sucking response and head turning with the use of reinforcements such as sweet-tasting liquids or the sound of the mother's voice or heartbeat (DeCasper & Sigafoos, 1983; Moon & Fifer, 1990). At the least, the fact that conditioning of this kind can take place means that whatever neurological "wiring" is needed for learning to occur is present at birth. Results like this also tell us something about the sorts of reinforcements that are effective with very young children; the fact that the mother's voice is an effective reinforcer is surely highly significant for the whole process of mother-infant interaction.

Schematic Learning

The fact that babies can recognize voices and heartbeats in the first days of life is also important because it suggests that another kind of learning is going on as well. This third type of learning, sometimes referred to as *schematic learning*, draws both its name and many of its conceptual roots from Piaget's theory. The basic idea is that from the beginning the baby organizes her experiences into expectancies or into "known" combinations. These expectancies, or *schemas*, are built up over many exposures to particular experiences, but thereafter help the baby to distinguish between the familiar and the unfamiliar. Carolyn Rovee-Collier (1986) has suggested that we might think of classical conditioning in infants as being a variety of schematic learning. When a baby begins to move her head as if to search for the nipple when she hears her Mom's footsteps, this is not just some kind of automatic classical conditioning, but the beginning of the development of expectancies. From the earliest weeks, the baby seems to begin to map links between events in her world—between the sound of her mother's footsteps and the feeling of being picked up, between the touch of the breast and the feeling of a full stomach. Thus early classical conditioning may be the beginnings of the process of cognitive development.

Habituation

A very important related concept is that of **habituation.** Habituation is the automatic reduction in the strength or vigor of a response to a repeated stimulus. An example would probably help. Suppose you live on a fairly noisy street. The sound of cars going by is repeated over and over during each day. But after a while, you not only don't react to the sound, you *do not perceive it as being as loud*. The ability to do this—to dampen down the intensity of a physical response to

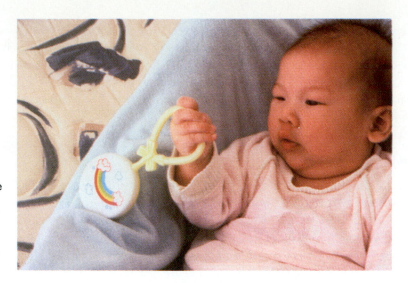

Three-month-old Andrea may be showing a secondary circular reaction here, as she shakes her hand repeatedly to hear the sound of the rattle. But she is probably also habituating to the sound it makes.

some repeated stimulus—is obviously vital in our everyday lives. If we reacted constantly to every sight, sound, and smell that came along, we'd spend all our time responding to these repeated events and not have energy or attention left over for things that are new and deserve attention.

The ability to *dishabituate* is equally important. When there is some change in a habituated stimulus, such as a sudden extra-loud screech of tires on the busy street by your house, you again respond fully. Thus the reemergence of the original response strength is a sign that the perceiver—infant or child or adult—notices some significant change.

The ability to habituate obviously rests on the ability to recognize something as "the same" or "different." Thus if it is present in the newborn, it suggests that the baby has more ability to remember and compare than Piaget thought. In fact, newborns *do* habituate and dishabituate (Lipsitt, 1982). A baby will stop looking at something you keep putting in front of her face; she will stop showing a startle reaction (Moro reflex) to loud sounds after the first few presentations, but will again show a startle response if the sound is changed. Such habituation itself is not a voluntary process; it is entirely automatic. But in order for it to work, the newborn must be equipped with the capacity to "recognize" familiar experiences. That is, she must develop schemas of some kind.

Try to imagine a baby who was unable to habituate. What might be the consequences of such a lack?

The existence of these processes in the newborn has an added benefit for researchers: it has enabled them to figure out just which things an infant responds to as if they were "the same" and which things she responds to as "different." If a baby is habituated to a stimulus, such as a sound or a particular picture, the experimenter can then present slight variations on the original stimulus to see the point at which dishabituation occurs.

Results of research of this type tell us that Piaget underestimated the very young infant. Newborns have a good deal to work with besides just primitive schemes, applied one at a time. From the earliest weeks of life they can learn connections between their own actions and environmental results; they create expectancies about events that go together, and they have some ability—however automatic—to store information about previously occurring events so that habituation and dishabituation are possible.

Memory

Piaget's underestimation of the infant's cognitive skills is also clear from Carolyn Rovee-Collier's fascinating studies of memory in very young infants (1993). She has used an ingenious variation of an operant conditioning procedure to demonstrate that babies as young as 3 months of age can remember specific objects and their actions with those objects, over periods of as long as a week. And if you "remind" them in between times, they can remember their earlier actions over as long as six weeks.

In her standard procedure, Rovee-Collier first hangs an attractive mobile over the baby's crib, and watches to see how the baby responds. In particular, she is interested in how often the baby normally kicks his legs while looking at the mobile. After 3 minutes of this "baseline" observation, she attaches a string from the mobile to the baby's leg, as you can see in Figure 5.1, so that each time the baby kicks his leg, the mobile moves. Babies quickly learn to kick repeatedly in order to make this interesting new thing happen (what Piaget would call a secondary circular reaction). Within 3 to 6 minutes, 3-month-olds double or triple their kick rates, showing that learning clearly occurred. She then tests the baby's memory of this learning by coming back some days later, hanging the same mobile over the crib but *not* attaching the string to his foot. The crucial issue is whether the baby will kick at the mere sight of the mobile. If the baby remembers the previous occasion, he should kick at a higher rate than he did when he first saw the mobile, which is precisely what 3-month-old babies do, even after a delay as long as a week.

In some experiments, Rovee-Collier also "reminds" the baby of the original learning by coming back some time after the first training, hanging the mobile over the crib, and tugging on the string herself at the same rate that the baby had learned to kick. So the baby sees the mobile moving in a rhythmic pattern, but has no chance to move the mobile himself. Then the experimenter comes back a third time and merely hangs the mobile over the crib, watching the rate of the baby's kicks. With the reminder in between, babies as young as 3 months remember the original learned connection between kicking and the mobile over several weeks.

Why is this so interesting? Primarily because it contradicts Piaget's view of the sensorimotor infant, whom he saw functioning pretty much in the here-and-now. It shows us, once again, that the young infant is cognitively a whole lot more sophisticated than we had supposed. At the same time, Rovee-Collier's work also offers some kind of support for Piaget's views, since she finds that there are systematic gains in the baby's ability to remember over the months of infancy. Two-month-olds can remember their kicking action for only one day; 3-month-olds can remember over a week, and by 6 months the baby can remember over two weeks. Similarly, reminders work better and better as the

FIGURE 5.1
This 3-month-old baby in one of Rovee-Collier's memory experiment will quickly learn to kick her foot in order to make the mobile move. And she will remember this connection between kicking and the mobile several days later.

Rovee-Collier's findings have surprised a lot of developmental psychologists. Do you find them surprising? Why or why not?

baby gets older. But all these early infant memories are *strongly* tied to the specific context in which the original experience occurred. Even 6-month-olds do not recognize or remember the mobile if you change the context even slightly, such as hanging a different cloth around the playpen in which the child was originally tested. Thus babies do remember—far more than Piaget believed—but their memories are highly specific. With age, their memories become less and less tied to specific cues or contexts.

Perceptual Development in the First Two Years

Unexpectedly good infant skill has also been vividly demonstrated in research on early perception. You already know from Chapter 4 that at birth, or in the early weeks of life, the baby can focus his eyes, follow a moving object at least roughly, taste the major tastes, and hear most pitches. These are obviously important skills. They enable the baby to enter into the key interactions with the caregivers and to react to objects around him. Far more interesting, though, is the recent evidence that very young infants can make remarkably fine discriminations among sounds, sights, and feelings, and that they pay attention to and respond to *patterns*, not just to individual events. We can only sample this fascinating new body of research, but a few examples will give you the flavor—and may amaze you as much as it amazes most researchers.

Discriminating Mom From Other People

For years I have been telling my friends and relatives that there was clear research showing that babies can't recognize their mothers' faces until at least a month or two of age, but that they can recognize the mother by sound or smell immediately. None of my friends or relatives believed me; they all said, "I don't care what the research says; I know my baby could recognize my face right away." Well, it looks like they were right and the older research (and I) was wrong.

We have known for some time that newborns can distinguish between one person and another, particularly between Mom and other people, by using their hearing. DeCasper and Fifer (1980) have found that newborns can tell their mother's voice from another female voice (but not their father's voice from another male voice) and prefer the mother's, possibly because the baby has become familiar with the mother's voice while still in utero. By 6 months, babies can even match voices with faces. If you put an infant of this age in a situation where she can see both her father and mother and can hear a tape recorded voice of one of them, she will look toward the parent whose voice she hears (Spelke & Owsley, 1979).

The ability to discriminate by smell also seems to be part of the baby's very early repertoire. Babies as young as a week old can tell the difference between their mother's smell and the smell of a stranger, although this seems to be true only for babies who are being breast-fed and spend quite a lot of time with their noses against the mother's bare skin (Cernoch & Porter, 1985).

> Does this mean that researchers ought to believe mothers and fathers more often, when they describe their infants and what the babies can do? How should scientists weigh anecdotal evidence against research evidence?

What has been most surprising is the discovery that newborns can also recognize their mothers by sight. There are several new studies that show this, but the clearest and cleanest is Gail Walton's (Walton, Bower, & Bower, 1992). She videotaped the faces of 12 mothers of newborns, and then matched each of these faces with the face of another woman whose hair color, eye color, complexion and hair style were the same as the Mom's. Each baby was then given a chance to look at each of the videos. These babies, who were only a day or two old at the time of the testing, looked longer at the video of their Mom, which shows not only that they could tell the difference between the two faces, but that they preferred the mother's face. Walton also has some preliminary information that babies do *not* discriminate, or do not prefer, their fathers' faces as early as this.

This is a fascinating result. A baby might learn the sound of the mother's voice in utero, but obviously has to learn the details of the mother's features after birth. Walton's study tells us that babies achieve such learning within hours of birth. But how is this possible? Is there some kind of imprinting going on here to the first face the baby sees after it is born? If so, then the process should be affected by birth practices or by the amount of contact the baby has had with various individuals. As is often the case, this one study seems to settle one question but raises many more.

Beyond the question of preference, there is also the issue of just what it is that babies are looking at when they scan a face. Before about 2 months of age, babies seem to look mostly at the edges of the faces (the hairline and the chin); after 2 months they seem to look more at the internal features, particularly the eyes.

At age 2 weeks, Rosa can already discriminate her Mom's face from the face of another woman, and can also recognize her Mom's voice and smell.

What Babies Look At

This change illustrates a more general pattern. From the first days of life babies scan the world around themselves—not very smoothly or skillfully, to be sure, but nonetheless regularly, even in the dark (Haith, 1980). They will keep moving their eyes until they come to a sharp light/dark contrast, which typically signals the edge of some object. Having found such an edge, the baby stops searching and moves his eyes back and forth across and around the edge. These strategies (which Haith [1980] calls "rules babies look by") seem to change at about 2 months, perhaps because the cortex has then developed more fully, or perhaps because of experience, or both. Whatever the cause, at about this time the baby's attention seems to shift from *where* an object is to *what* an object is. Put another way, the baby seems to move from a strategy primarily to *find things* to a strategy primarily to *identify* things. Babies this age begin to scan rapidly across an entire figure, rather than getting stuck on edges.

Discriminating Emotional Expressions

Not long after, babies begin to respond differently to various emotional expressions as well as to facial features. For example, Haviland and Lelwica (1987) found that when mothers expressed happiness, 10-week-old babies looked happy and interested and gazed at the mother; when the mother expressed sadness,

Langlois' Studies of Babies' Preferences for Attractive Faces

Of all the current research on infant perception that seems to point toward the conclusion that there are many more built-in abilities and preferences than we had supposed, the most surprising and intriguing to me have been Judith Langlois' studies of infant preferences for attractive faces. Langlois has found that babies as young as 2 months will look longer at a face that adults judge to be attractive than at one adults judge to be less attractive.

In the first study in this series, Langlois and her colleagues (Langlois et al., 1987) tested 2–3-month-olds and 6–8-month-olds. Each baby, while seated on Mom's lap, was shown pairs of color slides of 16 adult Caucasian women, half rated by adult judges as attractive, half rated as unattractive. On each trial, the baby saw two slides simultaneously shown on a screen in front of him/her, with each face approximately life-size, while the experimenter peeked through a hole in the screen to count the number of seconds the baby looked at each picture. Each baby saw some attractive/attractive pairs, some unattractive/unattractive pairs, and some mixed pairs.

The crucial trials are obviously those in which there was one attractive and one unattractive face. The results, which are on the left side of the table below, show that even the 2–3-month-olds preferred to look at the attractive faces.

One of the nice features of this study is that the researchers used a variety of attractive and unattractive faces, which makes the conclusion clearer. But because they used only Caucasian females, that leaves open the generality of the result. In a still-newer study (Langlois et al., 1991), Langlois used the same procedure but showed some 6-month-old infants

pictures of a) both unattractive and attractive men and women, or b) attractive and unattractive Black women's faces, or c) baby faces varying in attractiveness, all with neutral expressions. You can see the results on the right half of the table below.

Once again the results are consistent: in every case babies look significantly longer at the attractive than the unattractive faces.

In another exploration of this same issue, Langlois, Roggman, and Rieser-Danner (1990) observed 1-year-old babies interacting with an adult wearing either an attractive or an unattractive mask. They found that the toddlers showed more positive affective tone, less withdrawal, and more play involvement with the stranger in the attractive mask. These 1-year-olds also played more with an attractive than an unattractive doll.

It is hard to imagine what sort of learning experiences could account for such a preference in a 2-month-old. Instead, these findings raise the possibility that there is some in-born template for the "correct" or "most desired" shape and configuration for members of our species, and that we simply prefer those who match this template better. If that's true, what kind of consequences might it have for child and adult development, especially the development of the less-attractive baby, child, or adult?

Results from Two Langlois Studies

	Average Looking Time				
	2–3 mo. olds	6–8 mo. olds	Male & female	Black women	Baby faces
Attractive faces	9.22*	7.24*	7.82*	7.05*	7.16*
Unattractive faces	8.01	6.59	7.57	6.52	6.62

* contrast between attractive and unattractive faces is statistically significant

Sources: Langlois et al., 1987, from Table 1, p. 365; Langlois et al., 1991, Table 1, p. 81.

babies showed increased mouth movements or looked away; when the mother expressed anger, some babies cried vigorously, while others showed a kind of still or "frozen" look. These responses did not seem to be merely imitation, but rather responses to the parent's specific emotions.

By 5 or 6 months, babies can discriminate among strangers' faces displaying different emotions. At the same age they respond differently to voices speaking with varying emotional tones. They can tell the difference between happy and sad voices (Walker–Andrews & Lennon, 1991), and between happy, surprised, and fearful faces (Nelson, 1987). By roughly 10 months, infants use such emotional cues to help them figure out what to do in novel situations, such as when a stranger comes to visit, or in the doctor's office, or even when someone puts a new toy in front of them. Babies this age will first look at Mom's or Dad's face to check for the adult's emotional expression. If Mom looks pleased or happy the baby is likely to explore the new toy with more ease or to accept the stranger with less fuss. If Mom looks concerned or frightened, the baby responds to those cues and reacts to the novel situation with equivalent fear or concern. Researchers have described this as a process of **social referencing** (Hirshberg & Svejda, 1990; Walden, 1991).

How might a parent use knowledge of the process of social referencing?

Responding to Patterns

To me, the most surprising discoveries to come out of the surge of new research on infant perception is that babies as young as 3 or 4 months old pay attention to *relationships* among objects or among features of objects. For example, suppose you show babies a series of drawings, one at a time, each of which shows a small object above a larger object of the same shape—something like the ones in the top row of Figure 5.2. After seeing a series of such pictures, babies will habituate. That is, they will look for shorter and shorter periods of time until they are barely glancing at a new version of the figure before looking away. "Ho hum,

Habituation stimuli

Test stimulus

FIGURE 5.2
Caron and Caron used pictures like this in a study designed to check whether babies were paying attention to the patterns or the relationships among stimuli. Babies were first habituated to a series of pictures, each of which displayed the same pattern, like those in the upper row. Then they were tested either on more of the same or on one with a reverse pattern, like the one on the bottom. Three- and 4-month-old babies show renewed interest in the test stimulus, which indicates that they notice the pattern and see that it has now changed.

another one of those." Once habituation is established, you can then throw in a test picture, like the one shown at the bottom of Figure 5.2, that illustrates the opposite pattern, in this case big-over-small. What you are likely to find is that babies of 3 and 4 months will show renewed interest in this different pattern, which tells us that the baby's original habituation had not been to the *specific* stimuli but to a *pattern* (Caron & Caron, 1981).

Using auditory stimuli, you can find the same awareness of pattern in even younger babies. A study by DeCasper (DeCasper & Spence, 1986) is a particularly striking example. He had pregnant women read a children's story like Dr. Seuss's *The Cat in the Hat* out loud each day for the final six weeks of their pregnancy. After the infants were born, he played recordings of the mother reading this same story or another previously-unheard story to see which the infant preferred. The newborns clearly preferred the sound of the story they had heard in utero. A still newer study (Moon, Cooper, & Fifer, 1993) using a similar method tells us that newborns recognize and prefer to listen to their native language. Babies with Spanish-speaking mothers would suck harder in order to turn on a tape recording of a female voice (not the mother) reading Spanish than one reading English, while newborns with English-speaking mothers showed the reverse. I find both of these studies amazing.

Still further evidence that infants pay attention to patterns comes from the observation that babies as young as 6 months listen to melodies and recognize the patterns. Sandra Trehub and her colleagues (Trehub, Bull, & Thorpe, 1984; Trehub, Thorpe, & Morrongiello, 1985) trained 6-month-old babies to turn their heads toward a loudspeaker for a particular six-tone melody; the researchers then tested to see if the babies would still turn their heads when they heard melodies that varied in a number of ways. The babies kept turning their heads to new melodies if they had the same contour (notes going up and down in the same sequence) and were in approximately the same range. They did not turn their heads if the contour (melody) changed or if the notes were much higher or much lower.

Collectively, all this evidence tells us not only that key features of the auditory system must be well developed some weeks before birth, but more significantly, they make clear that within the first days and weeks of life, babies pay attention to and respond to pattern, not just to specific sounds.

> At older ages, children vary quite a lot in how easily they are able to "carry a tune." You might hypothesize that babies who were especially good at discriminating melodies would also be better at keeping to a tune at later ages. How might you test this hypothesis with research?

Cross-Modal Transfer: Combining Information From Several Senses

So far I have mostly talked about seeing, hearing and smelling as if we experience the world through only once sense at a time. But if you think about the way you receive and use perceptual information, you'll realize quickly that you rarely receive information in such a limited way. Ordinarily you have *both* sound and sight, or touch and sight, or still more complex combinations of smell, sight, touch, and sound. Psychologists have been interested in knowing how early an infant can combine such information. For example, how early does an infant figure out which mouth movements go with which sounds? How early can a baby recognize by feel a toy he has only seen before, a process involving **cross-modal transfer.**

If you look again at Table 5.1, you'll see that Piaget believed that the most primitive integration of sensory information, such as looking in the direction of some sound or watching your hand as you touch or grasp something, did not happen until at least stage 2, and that cross-modal transfer did not develop until stage 4, at about 8 months of age or later. Other theorists, including James and Eleanor Gibson, have argued that some intermodal coordination of perceptual information is built in from birth. The baby then builds on that inborn set of skills with specific experience with objects. Research favors the Gibsonian view: empirical findings show that cross-modal transfer is possible as early as 1 month and becomes common by 6 months (Rose & Ruff, 1987).

For example, if you attach a nubby sphere to a pacifier and let a baby suck on it, you can test for cross-modal transfer by showing the baby pictures of the nubby sphere and a smooth sphere. If the baby looks longer at the picture of the nubby sphere it would indicate cross-modal transfer. When Meltzoff and Borton (1979) did this, they found that 1-month-old babies preferred to look at the picture of the object they had sucked on earlier. Other investigators have not always found such transfer in infants as young as 1 month, so the phenomenon is not robust at this age.

Intersensory integration and transfer are more consistently found in older infants, not only between touch and sight, but between other modalities like sound and sight. For instance, in several delightfully clever experiments, Elizabeth Spelke showed that 4-month-old infants can connect sound rhythms with movement (1979). She showed babies two films simultaneously, one showing a toy kangaroo bouncing up and down, the other a donkey bouncing up and down, with one of the animals bouncing at a faster rate. Out of a speaker located between the two films the infant heard a tape recording of a rhythmic bouncing sound that matched one of the two rates. In this situation, babies spent more time watching the film that had the rhythm matching the sound they were hearing.

In the same vein, researchers have shown that 4- to 5-month-old babies will look longer at a face of a person mouthing a vowel they are hearing over a loudspeaker than at the face of a person mouthing another vowel (Kuhl & Meltzoff, 1984; Walton & Bower, 1993). Even more remarkable is a study in which 7-month-olds saw pairs of faces displaying happy and angry expressions, while listening to words spoken either in a happy or angry voice. The babies looked longer at the face that matched the *emotion* in the speaking voice—a finding that suggests remarkable sophistication of intermodal transfer in these young infants (Soken & Pick, 1992).

All of this burgeoning (and I think fascinating) research on combining of information from several senses has raised some interesting theoretical issues. For one thing it is now perfectly clear that the baby does not need language to transfer information from one mode to another. And the fact that at least some transfer is possible within the first few weeks of life, before the infant has had much direct experience with either mode, certainly points rather strongly to the possibility that *some* connections may be built in.

All in all, Piaget seems to have been wrong not only about the specific ages at which things develop, but perhaps even in whether they need to "develop" at all. It begins to look as if there is a great deal of basic understanding about the

Even if 3-month-old Nellie does not look at this toy while she is chewing on it, she is nonetheless learning something about how it *ought* to look, just based on how it feels in her mouth and in her hands—an example of cross-modal transfer.

events in the world that is already "built in" at birth—a conclusion buttressed by recent studies of the object concept.

Development of the Object Concept

One of Piaget's most striking observations of infants was that they seemed not to have a grasp of certain basic properties of objects that we all take completely for granted. You and I know that objects exist outside of our own actions on them. My computer exists independent of my looking at it and I know that it continues to sit here in my office even if I am somewhere else—an understanding that Piaget called **object permanence.** Piaget thought that babies did not initially know any of these things about objects and acquired this understanding only gradually during the sensorimotor period (Flavell, 1985; Piaget, 1952; 1954).

In Stages 1 and 2, the baby may follow a person or object with his eyes until it is out of view, but then appears to lose interest. Out of sight, literally out of mind. Piaget believed that a young infant did not understand in any way that other people or objects have independent existence and that they continue to exist even when he cannot see them or act on them.

In Stage 3, he begins to anticipate the movement of objects. If he drops a toy over the edge of his highchair, he may look over the edge to the place where it is likely to have dropped. If you cover part of a toy with a cloth while the baby is reaching for it, he may continue to reach for it. But if you fully cover the toy he will stop reaching and show no further interest—a pattern you can see in the photos in Figure 5.3.

In Stage 4, starting at roughly 8 months of age, the baby will continue reaching for the object or will pull away a cover he has seen you put over some desired object. But babies this age show a curious limitation in this new behavior. Suppose you hide a toy several times in one place and the baby successfully uncovers it each time. Then—in full view of the baby—you now hide the toy in a second place or cover it with a different cloth. Babies in Stage 4 will now search for the toy in the *first* location. Piaget thought that this showed that the baby doesn't yet have a full internal representation of the object, or an understanding that the object can be moved around. Instead, he has developed a sensorimotor scheme that links the toy with reaching in the first location. In learning theory terms, he has developed a simple sensorimotor habit, rather than a full understanding of the permanence of objects.

In Stage 5, the baby searches wherever he saw the toy most recently. Thus the baby is separating the objects from his own actions to retrieve it, a major new step on the road to object permanence.

This sequence of development has been so compelling, so interesting, and so surprising to many researchers (and parents) that researchers have conducted reams of research on the subject. Until recently, most researchers had concluded that Piaget's description of the sequence of development of the object concept was correct. Certainly, if you follow Piaget's procedures, you will see essentially the same results among children in all cultures.

FIGURE 5.3
A baby in substage 3 of the development of object constancy. She stops reaching as soon as the screen is put in front of the toy and shows no sign that she knows that the toy is still there.

CULTURES & CONTEXTS

Object Permanence in Zambian Infants

Piaget believed that the emergence of the child's understanding of object permanence followed a universal sequence. One way to test this assumption, of course, is to observe or test children in nonwestern societies, particularly infants or children whose early experiences are different from what we see in the U.S. or Europe. Susan Goldberg's longitudinal study of 38 Zambian infants (1972) gives us one such cross-cultural look.

Goldberg's two years of observations in Zambia made clear that the typical experience of a Zambian baby was quite different in a number of respects from that of most Western infants. From shortly after birth, Zambian mothers carry their babies about in a sling on their back. They spend very little time on the floor or in any position in which they have much chance of independent movement until they are able to sit up at about 6 months. At that point they are usually placed on a mat in the yard of the house. From this vantage the baby can watch all the activity around the house and in the neighborhood, but he has few objects with which to play. Goldberg reports that the Zambian mothers did not see it as their task to provide play objects for their infants, nor to structure the child's play in any way. And in fact Goldberg says she rarely saw the babies playing with objects, even those that might have been available in the yards.

Yet despite this very limited experience manipulating objects, tests of object permanence showed that the Zambian babies were *ahead* of the American averages on a measure of the object concept at 6 months of age. At 9 and 12 months of age, this pattern was reversed, and the Zambian babies were slightly behind the U.S. norms, but Goldberg believes this difference is due not to any cognitive failure but to the fact that at these ages the Zambian babies were quite unresponsive and passive toward objects, and thus very difficult to test. One possible explanation of this is that in Zambian culture, at least as Goldberg observed it, obedience is a highly valued quality in a child. The babies are trained from very early on to be particularly obedient to prohibitions of various kinds. When the baby plays with some forbidden object, the parent takes the object away. Perhaps, then, the infants learn that when an object is removed, it means "don't play with that" and he makes no further move to reach for the toy during the object permanence test. This does not necessarily mean that the baby has not understood these later stages of object permanence; it could also mean that our traditional ways of measuring this understanding would need to be modified for these children.

Goldberg's observations thus illustrate both the robustness of some basic developmental patterns *and* the impact of culture on the ways children display those patterns. Babies in Zambia appear to develop the early steps of the understanding of object permanence even though they have little chance to manipulate objects. But their training and experience also affect their response to objects.

Newer research, though, points to the possibility that very young babies have far more understanding of the properties of objects, including their permanence, than Piaget supposed. For example, Renée Baillargeon (1987; Baillargeon & DeVos, 1991; Baillargeon, Spelke, & Wasserman, 1985), in a series of clever studies, has shown that babies as young as 3½ or 4 months show clear signs of object permanence if you use a *visual* response rather than a reaching response to test it. Similarly, in a whole series of experiments, Elizabeth Spelke (1991) has shown that young infants respond to objects in a far less transitory and ephemeral way than Piaget thought. In particular, 2- and 3-month-olds are remarkably aware of what kinds of movements objects are capable of—even when they are out of sight. They expect objects to continue to move on their initial trajectory and show surprise if the object appears somewhere else. They also seem to have some awareness that solid objects cannot pass through other solid objects.

In one experiment, Spelke (1991) used the procedure shown schematically in the upper part of Figure 5.4. Researchers repeatedly showed 2-month-old babies a series of events like that in the "familiarization" section of the figure: they rolled a ball starting from the left-hand side to the right where it disappeared behind a screen. When the researchers took the screen away, the baby could see that the ball was stopped against the wall on the right. After the baby got bored looking at this sequence (habituated), they tested the baby with two variations, one "consistent" and one "inconsistent." In the consistent variation, the researchers placed a second wall behind the screen and the sequence ran as before, except that when they removed the screen, the babies could see the ball resting up against the nearer wall. In the inconsistent variation, the researchers surreptitiously placed the ball on the *far* side of the new wall. When they removed the screen the ball was visible in this new and presumably impossible place. Babies in this experiment were quite uninterested in the consistent condition, but showed sharply renewed interest in the inconsistent condition, as you can see in the lower part of Figure 5.4, which shows the actual results of this experiment.

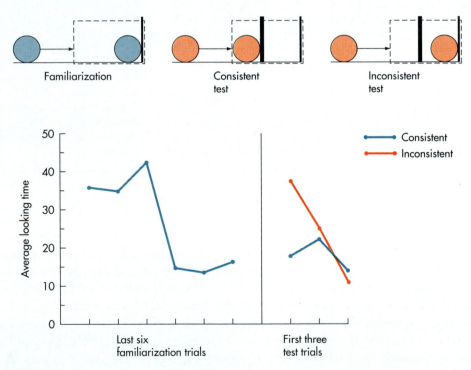

FIGURE 5.4

The top part of the figure shows a schematic version of the three conditions Spelke used. The bottom half shows the actual results. You can see that the babies stopped looking at the ball and screen after a number of familiarization trials, but showed renewed interest in the inconsistent version—a sign that the babies saw this as somehow different or surprising. The very fact that the babies found the inconsistent trial surprising is itself evidence that infants as young as 2 months have far more knowledge of objects and their behavior than most of us had thought. (Source: Spelke, 1991, Figure 5.3 and 5.4.)

Findings like this have reopened the debate about Piaget's description of the development of object constancy. More generally, they have sparked a new discussion of that old friend, the nature-nurture issue (Diamond, 1991; Fischer & Bidell, 1991; Karmiloff-Smith, 1991). Just how much is built in at birth? Piaget, of course, never said that *nothing* was built in. He assumed that the baby came equipped with a repertoire of sensorimotor schemes. But his most fundamental theoretical proposal was that the child *constructed* his understanding of the world, based on experience. On the other side of this new argument are those who see the baby as being endowed not only with specific knowledge about the world, but with built-in constraints in the ways he processes information.

Spelke's own conclusion is that the development of the understanding of objects is more a process of elaboration than discovery. Newborn or very young babies may have considerable awareness of objects as separate entities, following certain rules. Certainly all the research on the perception of patterns suggests that babies pay far more attention to relationships between events than Piaget's model had led us to suppose. Indeed the research on babies' preferences for attractive faces, which I talked about in the *Research Report* box on page 132, suggests that there may be built-in *preferences* for particular patterns. Still, even Spelke would not argue that the baby comes equipped with full-fledged knowledge of objects or a well-developed ability to experiment with the world. Just how much Piaget's model will need to be altered because of work of this type is unclear, but it has raised a whole host of new questions.

> Spelke contends that her research shows that babies have a great deal of knowledge about objects built-in from the beginning. How might a confirmed Piagetian reply?

Imitation

As a final example of research on infant cognition that has flowed from Piaget's theory, let me say just a word about studies of imitation. Piaget thought that infants could imitate actions they could see themselves make, such as hand gestures, as early as the first few months of life. But it wasn't until stage 4 (8–12 months) that Piaget thought the baby could imitate someone else's facial expressions. To do this seems to require some kind of cross-modal transfer: you must transfer information from the visual cues you get from seeing the other's face to the kinesthetic cues you get from your own facial movement. Otherwise, how could you match the expression? Finally, Piaget thought that deferred imitation, in which the baby sees something at one time but imitates it at a later time, did not occur until stage 6, when internal representation has already begun.

The issue of how soon a baby can imitate is important not just as a test of Piaget's theory. It may also tell us how soon a baby can learn from modeling—a major form of learning proposed by social-cognitive theorists like Bandura. In broad terms Piaget's proposed sequence has been supported. Imitation of someone else's hand movements or their actions with objects seems to improve steadily during the months of infancy, starting at 1 or 2 months of age; imitation of two-part actions develops much later, perhaps at 15–18 months (Poulson, Nunes, & Warren, 1989). Yet there are also two important exceptions to this general confirmation of Piaget's theory: infants imitate some facial gestures in the first weeks of life, and deferred imitation seems to occur earlier than Piaget proposed.

Several researchers have found that newborn babies will imitate certain facial gestures, particularly tongue protrusion (Anisfeld, 1991; Field et al., 1982; Meltzoff & Moore, 1983). This only seems to work if the model sits there with his tongue out looking at the baby for a fairly long period of time, perhaps as long as a minute. But the fact that babies this young imitate at all is striking—although it is entirely consistent with the observation that quite young babies are capable of tactual/visual cross-modal transfer.

Studies of deferred imitation are not so strikingly discordant with Piaget's description, but there is at least one study (Meltzoff, 1988) showing that babies as young as 9 months can defer their imitation over as long as 24 hours. By 14 months, toddlers recall others' actions over periods of 2 days. In one recent study, Elizabeth Hanna and Andrew Meltzoff (1993) trained a 14-month-old to play with 5 particular toys in distinctive ways, such as collapsing a collapsible cup or picking up a string of beads and placing it a cup. Other babies watched these play behaviors in a laboratory setting. Two days later, an adult unfamiliar to the baby went to the child's home, bringing along the set of toys and giving them to the child one at a time, to see if the child would imitate the actions he had seen the other child perform 2 days earlier. The majority of the 14-month-olds imitated at least 2 of these behaviors, while a control group who received the toys but had not seen the model typically did not use the toys in these particular ways.

These findings are significant for several reasons. First, they make it clear that children of this age can and do learn specific behaviors through modeling, even when they have no chance to imitate the behavior immediately. Second,

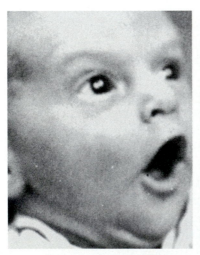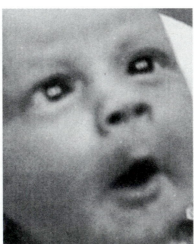

FIGURE 5.5
This Mom was asked to model an exaggerated "surprise" expression to her newborn—an expression the baby imitated, providing further evidence that at least some complex kinds of imitation may be possible far earlier than Piaget thought. (Source: T. M. Field, Social perception and responsivity in early infancy. In T. M. Field, A. Huston, H. C. Quay, L. Troll & G. E. Finley (Eds.), *Review of human development*. Copyright 1982 by John Wiley & Sons, New York, p. 26.)

deferred imitation clearly requires that the baby remember what he saw and connect that memory to the object, all of which seems to require internal representation—which Piaget did not think was present this early. The fact that they are present in children as young as 14 months and that the children were even able to imitate the action when the imitation occurred in a different setting (at home) from the setting in which the observation occurred (the laboratory) suggests that Piaget was simply wrong about when babies are first able to use some kind of internal representation to remember actions and events.

Overall, the research I have described so far points to the inescapable conclusion that babies are more skillful than Piaget thought, and that there may be more abilities built in from the beginning than he suggested. But that still leaves open the deeper question of whether the baby is *constructing* his understanding of the world through his experience, or whether both his understanding and his experience is *constrained* by powerful built-in biases. You will not be surprised to know that many of these same issues arise yet again when we look at the early stages of the development of language in these same months.

The Precursors of Language

Most of us think of "language" as beginning when the baby uses her first words, which happens (to the delight of most parents) at about 12 months of age. But there are all sorts of important developments that precede the first words.

Perception of Speech Sounds

Let's start with the basic perceptual skills. A baby cannot learn language until he can hear the individual sounds as distinct. Just how early can he do that? If you hadn't just read the rest of this chapter you might be surprised by the answer. But by now, you know how this song goes. The answer is "remarkably early."

As early as 1 month, babies can discriminate between speech sounds like *pa* and *ba* (Trehub & Rabinovitch, 1972). By perhaps 6 months of age, they can discriminate between two-syllable "words" like *bada* and *baga* and can even respond to a syllable that is hidden inside a string of other syllables, (like ti*ba*ti or ko*ba*ko) (Fernald & Kuhl, 1987; Goodsitt et al., 1984; Morse & Cowan, 1982). It doesn't even seem to matter what voice quality the speaker uses. By 2 or 3 months of age, babies respond to individual sounds as the same, whether spoken by a male or a female or a child (Marean, Werner, & Kuhl, 1992).

Even more striking is the finding that babies are actually better at discriminating some kinds of speech sounds than adults are. Each language uses only a subset of all possible speech sounds. Japanese, for example, does not use the *l* sound that appears in English; Spanish makes a different distinction between the *d* and *t* sound than we do in English. It turns out that up to about 12 months of age, babies can accurately discriminate all sound contrasts that appear in *any* language, including sounds they do not hear in the language spoken to them. By 1 year of life, this ability has faded although it does not disappear altogether. Adults

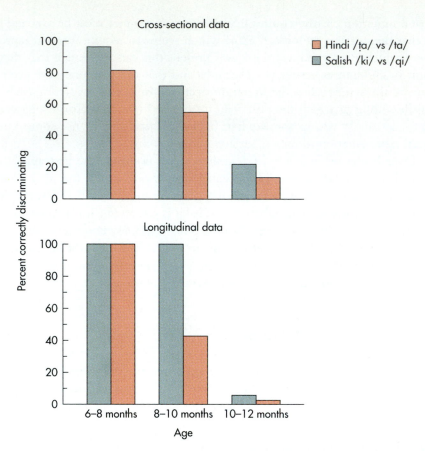

FIGURE 5.6

In these studies, babies growing up in English-speaking environments were tested for their ability to make two discriminations: between two speech sounds that are used differently in Hindi but that are treated the same in English and between a pair of sounds used differently in Salish but treated as the same in English. The upper part of the figure shows a cross-sectional comparison, with 12 babies tested at each age. The lower part of the figure shows what happened to the discrimination ability of six babies studied longitudinally. You can see that virtually all the babies could make these discriminations at 8 months, but that this ability rapidly disappeared. (Source: Werker & Tees, 1984, p. 61, Figure 4.)

can learn to "hear" such sound variations if they work very hard at it, such as when trying to learn to speak a foreign language without an accent. But the infant appears to hear all these distinctions naturally.

The unusually complete study by Janet Werker and Richard Tees (1984) illustrates the point. Combining cross-sectional and longitudinal designs, they first studied separate groups of 6–8-month-old, 8–10-month-old, and 10–12-month-old babies being raised in English-speaking homes. Researchers tested each baby on three sound pairs, one heard in English (*ba* versus *da*), one from a North-American Indian language, Salish (*ki* versus *qi*), and one from Hindi, a language from the Indian subcontinent (*ṭa* versus *ta*). You can see in Figure 5.6 that the 6–8-month-old English-environment babies could easily hear and respond to both the Hindi and Salish contrasts, but very few of the 10–12-month-olds could do so. When Werker and Tees later retested some of the 6-month-olds at 9 and 12 months, they found that these babies *lost* the ability to make these discriminations. In separate tests, Werker and Tees also tested Hindi- and Salish-environment infants, and found that 12-month-old Hindi infants could easily discriminate the Hindi contrast, and Salish toddlers could still hear the Salish contrast.

It seems to me that these findings are consistent with what we now know about the pattern of rapid, apparently pre-programmed, growth of synapses in the early months of life, followed by synaptic pruning. Many connections are initially created, permitting discriminations along all possible sound continua. But only those pathways that are actually used in the language the child hears are retained. Whether this turns out to be the right explanation or not, it is certainly clear that the baby is paying attention to very detailed aspects of speech sounds, from the earliest days of life.

Early Sounds and Gestures

This early perceptual skill is not matched right away by much skill in producing sounds. From birth to about 1 month of age, the most common sound an infant makes is a cry, although there are other fussing, gurgling, and satisfied sounds. This sound repertoire expands at about 1 or 2 months, when we begin to hear some laughing and **cooing** vowel sounds, like *uuuuuu*. Sounds like this are usually signals of pleasure in babies and may show quite a lot of variation in tone, running up and down in volume or pitch.

Consonant sounds appear only at about 6 or 7 months, frequently combined with vowel sounds to make a kind of syllable. Babies this age seem to begin to play with these sounds, often repeating the same sound over and over (such as *bababababababa* or *dahdahdah*). This new sound pattern is called **babbling,** and it makes up about half of babies' noncrying sounds from about 6 to 12 months of age (Mitchell & Kent, 1990).

Any parent can tell you that babbling is a delight to listen to. It also seems to be an important part of the preparation for spoken language. For one thing, we now know that infants' babbling gradually acquires some of what linguists call the *intonational pattern* of the language they are hearing—a process Elizabeth Bates refers to as "learning the tune before the words" (Bates, O'Connell, & Shore, 1987). At the very least, infants do seem to develop at least two such "tunes" in their babbling. When they babble with a rising intonation at the end of a string of sounds it seems to signal a desire for a response; a falling intonation requires no response.

A second important thing about babbling is that when babies first start babbling, they typically babble all kinds of sounds, including some that are not part of the language they are hearing. But at about 9 or 10 months, their sound repertoire gradually begins to drift toward the set of sounds they are listening to, with the nonheard sounds dropping out (Oller, 1981)—a pattern that clearly parallels the findings from the Werker and Tees study I just talked about (Figure 5.6).

Why do you suppose babies babble? Do you think it is just the vocal equivalent of rhythmic foot kicking, or can you think of some other purpose it might serve?

Findings like these do not tell us that babbling is *necessary* for language development, but they certainly make it look as if babbling is part of a connected developmental process that begins at birth.

Gestures in the First Year.   Another part of that connected developmental process may be a kind of gestural language that develops at around 9 or 10 months. At this age we first see babies "demanding" or "asking" for things using gestures or combinations of gestures and sound. A 10-month-old baby who apparently wants you to hand her a favorite toy may stretch and reach for it, opening and closing her hand, accompanied by whining sounds or other heart-rending noises. There is no mistaking the meaning. At about the same age, babies will enter into those gestural games much loved by parents, like "patty-cake", or "soooo-big", or "wave bye-bye." (Bates, Camaioni, & Volterra, 1975; Bates et al., 1987).

Interestingly, the infant's ability to *understand* the meaning of individual words (which linguists call **receptive language**) also seems to begin at about 9 or 10 months. In one study, Elizabeth Bates and her colleagues asked mothers about their 10-month-old babies' understanding of various words (Bates, Bretherton, & Snyder, 1988). On average, the mothers listed 17.9 words understood. By 13 months, that number was up to nearly 50 words. Because infants of 9 to 13 months typically do not speak any individual words, findings like these make it clear that receptive language comes before **expressive language**. Children understand before they can speak.

Adding up these bits of information, we can see that a whole series of changes seems to come together at 9 or 10 months: the beginning of meaningful gestures, the drift of babbling toward the heard language sounds, imitative gestural games, and the first comprehension of individual words. It is as if the child now understands something about the process of communication and is intending to communicate to the adult.

At 9 months, Alexandra probably hasn't yet spoken her first word, but chances are she already understands quite a few. Receptive language is usually ahead of expressive language.

The First Words

Somewhere in the midst of all the babbling, the first words appear, typically at about 12 or 13 months (Capute et al., 1986). The baby's first word is an event that parents eagerly await, but it's fairly easy to miss. A *word*, as linguists usually define it, is any sound or set of sounds that is used consistently to refer to some thing, action, or quality. But it can be *any* sound. It doesn't have to be a sound that matches words the adults are using. Brenda, a little girl whom Ronald Scollon studied, (1976) used the sound *nene* as one of her first words. It seemed to mean primarily liquid food, because she used it for milk, juice, and bottle. But she also used it to refer to mother and sleep. (You can see some of Brenda's other early words in the Table 5.2).

Often, a child uses her earliest words only in one or two specific situations and in the presence of many cues. The child may say "doggie" or "bow-wow" only to such promptings as "How does the doggie go?" or "What's that?" Some

TABLE 5.2
Brenda's Vocabulary at 14 Months

Sound	Apparent meaning
aw u	I want, I don't want
nae	no
daedi	daddy, baby, picture in magazine
daeyu	down, doll
nene	liquid food
e	yes
maem	solid food
ada	another, other

Source: R. Scollon, *Conversations with a one year old.* Honolulu: The University Press of Hawaii, 1976, p. 47.

linguists describe this period as one in which the child "learns what words do" (Nelson, 1985). The child learns a few words that communicate in particular interactional situations, but has not yet understood that words are *symbolic*—that they refer to objects or events. In this early period children typically learn words very slowly, after many repetitions. It is quite common for children to take 6 months to acquire a vocabulary of 30 words.

R E S E A R C H   R E P O R T

Early Gestural "Language" in the Children of Deaf Parents

Deaf children of deaf parents are a particularly interesting group to study if we want to understand language development. These children do not hear oral language, but their parents expose them to *language*—sign language. Do these children show the same early steps in language development as do hearing children, only using gestural language?

The answer seems to be yes. Deaf children show a kind of "sign babbling" between about 7 and 11 months of age, much as hearing children babble sounds in these same months. Then at 8 or 9 months of age, deaf children begin using simple gestures, such as pointing, which is just about the same time that we see such gestures in hearing babies of hearing parents. At about 12 months of age, deaf babies seem to display their first *referential* signs—that is signs in which a gesture appears to stand for some object or event, such as signalling that they want a drink by making a motion like bringing a cup to the mouth (Petitto, 1988; 1992).

Folven and Bonvillian (1991) have studied an equally interesting group—hearing children of deaf parents. These babies are exposed to sign language from their parents and to spoken language from their contacts with others in their world, including TV, teachers, other relatives, playmates. In this small sample of nine babies, the first sign appeared at an average age of 8 months, the first referential sign at 12.6 months and the first spoken word at 12.2 months. What is striking here is that the first referential signs and the first spoken words appear at such similar times, and the spoken words appear at such a completely normal time, despite the fact that these children of deaf parents hear comparatively little spoken language.

This marked similarity in the sequence and timing of early language steps in the deaf and the hearing child provides strong support for the argument that the baby is somehow primed to learn "language" in some form, be it spoken or gestural.

The Naming Explosion

Somewhere between 18 and 24 months this pattern shifts, and most children add new words rapidly, as if they had figured out that "things have names." Many toddlers in this phase add 10, 20, or 30 words in a period of weeks. At this point children seem to learn new words with very few repetitions, and they generalize these new words to many more situations.

You can see both aspects of this pattern—the early slow growth and then the vocabulary spurt—in Figure 5.7, which shows the vocabulary growth curves of six of the subjects whom Goldfield and Reznick studied longitudinally (1990).

I should point out that not all children show precisely this pattern. In Goldfield and Reznick's study, for example, 13 out of 24 children showed a vocabulary spurt, while the remaining 11 followed varying growth patterns. A few showed no spurt at all, only gradual acquisition of vocabulary. So we need to be careful here about assuming that the same processes are involved for every child. Still, the most common pattern is like the ones in Figure 5.7.

During the naming explosion, children mostly learn words that are names for things or people, like ball, car, milk, doggie, he, or that. Verblike words tend to develop later, perhaps because they label *relationships* between objects rather than just a single object (Gleitman & Gleitman, 1992). For example, over half the first 50 words of the eight children Katherine Nelson studied were nounlike words while only 13 percent were action words (Nelson, 1973). Researchers have found the same pattern in studies of children learning other languages as well, as you can see in the *Cultures and Contexts* box on page 147.

However, just as all children do not show a vocabulary spurt, all children do not follow a noun-before-verb pattern either. Katherine Nelson (1973) first noticed that some toddlers use what she called an **expressive style.** For them, most early words are linked not to objects but to social relationships. They often learn pronouns (you, me) early and use many more of what Nelson calls "personal-social" words, such as *no, yes, want,* or *please.* Their early vocabulary may also include some multiword strings, like *love you* or *do it* or *go away.* This is in sharp

FIGURE 5.7

Each of the lines in this figure represents the vocabulary growth of one of the children studied by Goldfield and Reznick in their longitudinal study. (Source: Goldfield & Reznick, 1990, Figure 3, p. 177.)

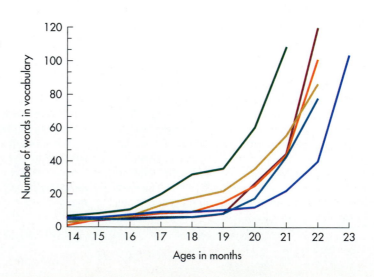

CULTURES & CONTEXTS

Early Words by Children in Many Cultures

Children in every culture studied by linguists have shown the same tendency to learn words for people or things before they learn words for actions or other parts of speech. Here are some (translated) samples from the very early vocabularies of one child from each of four cultures, all studied by Dedre Gentner (1982).

Isn't it impressive how very similar these early vocabularies are? Of course there

	German boy	English girl	Turkish girl	Chinese girl
Some of the words for people or things	Mommy	Mommy	Mama	Momma
	Papa	Daddy	Daddy	Papa
	Gaga	babar	Aba	grandmother
	baby	baby	baby	horse
	dog	dog	food	chicken
	bird	dolly	apple	uncooked rice
	cat	kitty	banana	cooked rice
	milk	juice	bread	noodles
	ball	book	ball	flower
	nose	eye	pencil	wall clock
	moon	moon	towel	lamp
Total Percentage of Naming words	67%	69%	57%	59%
Some of the non-naming words	cry	run	cry	go
	come	all gone	come	come
	eat	more	put on	pick up
	sleep	bye-bye	went pooh	not want
	want	want	want	afraid
	no	no	hello	thank you

are some variations, but all these children had names for Mommy and Daddy, for some other relative, for other live creatures, and for food. All but the Chinese child had words for toys or clothes. All four had also learned more naming words than any other type, with very similar proportions. They don't know the *same* words, but the pattern is remarkably similar.

---

contrast to the children who use what Nelson calls a **referential style,** whose early vocabulary is made up predominantly of nounlike words. Observations like this remind us that we need to search not just for common developmental pathways, but also to note and try to understand individual variations.

Individual Differences in Sensorimotor Development

Discussions of individual differences in cognitive skill are nearly always cast in "cognitive power" terms. We ask whether there are differences in *rate* of development, and whether such differences in rate are consistent over time. Questions of this kind about infant development have an important practical implication: If we could accurately measure differences in infants' rate (or pattern) of development in the early months of life, then it might be possible to identify infants who are later going to have problems learning to read or to perform in school in other ways. Early identification might also make it possible to intervene very early, perhaps thereby averting or, at least, ameliorating the problem.

One of the motivations behind the development of the various infant IQ tests was just such a hope that test scores could help identify infants with current or prospective problems. Typically, these tests are constructed rather like IQ tests for older children: They include a series of items identified as suitable for children of particular ages, or a series of items of increasing difficulty. The child's performance is then compared to the average performance of other children the same age to yield an IQ-like score. In the case of infant tests, the items measure primarily sensory and motor skills, such as:

- Reaching for a dangling ring (a 3-month-old item)
- Uncovering a toy hidden by a cloth (8 months)
- Putting cubes in a cup on request (9 months)
- Building a tower of three cubes (17 months)

In the most widely used modern version of such a test, the **Bayley Scales of Infant Development** (Bayley, 1969, revised 1993), the score is subdivided into two parts, one reflecting mental development and the other motor development.

Many (but not all) of those who devised such infancy tests assumed that they were measuring the same basic intellectual processes as the tests for older children measure. But the empirical results do not support that assumption. Scores on infant tests do not predict later IQ test scores at all well. The typical correlation between a 12-month Bayley mental test score and a 4-year-old IQ score is only about .20 to .30 (Bee et al., 1982)—significant, but not robust. Bayley's test and others like it, such as the Denver Developmental Screening Test, are effective in identifying children with serious developmental delays (Frankenberg et al., 1975; Lewis & Sullivan, 1985). But as a more general predictive tool to forecast later IQ or school performance, such tests have not been nearly as useful as many had hoped. On the whole, it looks as if what is being measured on typical infant tests is not the same as what common childhood or adult intelligence tests tap (Colombo, 1993).

However, new work emerging from an information processing framework has reopened the debate about "infant intelligence" and how to measure it. Beginning about 20 years ago, a number of researchers argued that what we need to measure is not the baby's ability to perform on such tasks as putting cubes in cup, but rather the infant's ability to process information in some very fundamental way (Fagan & McGrath, 1981; Lewis & Brooks-Gunn, 1981; Miranda & Fantz, 1974). The strategy they suggested was to measure the rate of habituation in 3- and 4-month-old infants. In the typical procedure, researchers count how many repeated exposures it takes before a baby stops responding with interest to a stimulus. The speed with which such habituation takes place may tell us something about the efficiency of the perceptual/conceptual system and its neurological underpinnings. And if such efficiency lies behind some of the characteristic we normally call "intelligence," then it is possible that individual differences in rate of habituation in the early months of life might predict later intelligence test scores.

That is exactly what researchers have now found. The rate of habituation shown by 4- to 6-month-old babies is correlated positively with IQ and language development in preschool and elementary school. That is, slower habituation is associated with lower IQ and poorer language and faster habituation is associated with better IQ (McCall & Carriger, 1993; Rose, 1993) The average correlation is in the range of .45 to .50. This is certainly not perfect, but is notably higher than the correlations we see between standard infant IQ scores and later IQ or school performance. Given the difficulties involved in measuring habituation rate in babies, the correlations are actually quite remarkably high.

Alina, at 17 months, would no doubt be able to pass the 17-month-old item on the Bayley Scales of Infant Development that calls for building a tower of three cubes.

Certainly these correlations do not prove that intelligence, as we measure it on an IQ test, is only a reflection of some kind of "speed of basic processing." But results like these underline the potential importance of looking at the underlying components of information processing if we want to understand individual differences in skills in early infancy. They also suggest the direction we might go to devise more predictive tests of infant intelligence. In fact, Fagan has developed just such a test, based heavily on measures of habituation rate in early infancy (Fagan & Shepherd, 1986).

Cognitive Development in Infancy: An Overall Look

In a number of important respects, Piaget seems to have underestimated the ability of infants to store, remember, and organize sensory and motor information. Very young babies pay much more attention to patterns, sequence, and prototypical features than Piaget thought; moreover, they can apparently remember them over at least short intervals. Many current theorists have taken this evidence to mean that the baby comes equipped with a wide range of built-in knowledge or inborn constraints on his ways of understanding the world around him.

On the other side of the argument, however, is the obvious fact that newborns, despite their remarkable perceptual and cognitive abilities, are *not* as skilled as 6-month-olds or 12-month-olds. Newborns do not use gestures to communicate, they do not talk, they do not show deferred imitation. Six-month-olds do not combine several strategies to achieve some goal and do not seem to experiment with objects in the same way as we see later. Even at 12 months toddlers do not seem to use symbols to stand for things in any general way. They use a few words, but don't yet show pretend play, for example. So despite all the new and fascinating evidence that casts some doubt on some of Piaget's basic theorizing, it still appears to be correct to describe the infant as *sensorimotor* rather than *symbolic* in her thinking. Over the first 18–24 months the baby seems to be building toward such symbol use, a shift that John Flavell correctly sees as remarkable:

> . . . a cognitive system that uses symbols just seems . . . to be radically, drastically, qualitatively different from one that is not. So great is the difference that the transformation of one system into the other during the first 2 years of life still seems nothing short of miraculous to me, no matter how much we learn about it (1985, p. 82).

SUMMARY

1. When we study the development of intelligence or cognition, we need to distinguish between three traditions: one focusing on intellectual power, one on intellectual structure, and the third on information processing skills.

2. Studies of infant cognition have been most strongly influenced by Piaget's structural view of intelligence.

3. Piaget described the sensorimotor infant as beginning with a small repertoire of basic schemes, from which she moves toward symbolic representation in a series of six sub-stages.

4. Stage 1 is essentially automatic pilot; stage 2 includes coordination of different modalities; in stage 3 the baby focuses more on the outside world; in stage 4 the baby understands causal connections and grasps the object concept in a preliminary way; in stage 5, the baby begins to experiment more fully, and in stage 6, we see first signs of symbol usage.

5. Babies are able to learn by both classical and operant conditioning within the first few weeks of life, earlier than Piaget thought.

6. Newborns are also able to habituate to repeated stimuli, indicating that they have the ability to "recognize" that they have experienced something before.

7. Three- and 4-month-old infants show signs of remembering specific experiences over periods of as long as a few days or a week, a sign that they must have some form of internal representation well before Piaget supposed.

8. In the first weeks of life, infants appear to be intent on locating objects; after about 2 months, they seem intent on identifying objects, so their method of scanning changes.

9. Newborns can also discriminate Mom from other people in the first days or weeks of life, by sight, sound, and smell. By 3 months they respond differently to varying emotional expressions.

10. From the earliest weeks, babies respond to the patterns of stimuli, or to relationships among stimuli, such as "big over small," or the sound of a particular story or melody. They also prefer to look at attractive rather than at less attractive faces.

11. Babies also show cross-modal transfer as early as 1 month, far earlier than Piaget supposed.

12. Piaget described a sequence of development in the child's understanding of the concept of object permanence—that objects continue to exist when they are out of sight or not being acted on by the child. In Piaget's experiments, babies began to show real comprehension of this only at about 8 months.

13. Newer research suggests that babies may have far more elaborate understanding of the properties of objects—including their permanence—at much earlier ages than Piaget supposed, although researchers are still debating this.

14. Babies are able to imitate some facial expressions in the first days of life. But they do not show deferred imitation until much later.

15. First words, at about 12 months of age, are preceded by a number of important steps.

16. Babies can discriminate among speech sounds in the first weeks. They can, in fact, make discriminations that adults cannot make.

17. Babies' earliest sounds are cries, followed at about 2 months by cooing, then babbling at about 6 months. At 9 months babies typically use meaningful gestures and can understand a small vocabulary of spoken words.

18. After the first word, babies add words slowly for a few months and then rapidly. Most have a vocabulary of about 50 words by 18 months, at which point a "vocabulary explosion" occurs for the majority of infants.

19. The earliest words are more often names for people or objects than they are words to describe actions.

20. The construction of IQ-like tests to measure individual differences in senso-rimotor development has not been as successful as researchers hoped; such tests are not strongly related to later measures of IQ.

21. Much more predictive are measures of more basic information processing skills in infancy, such as rate of habituation at 4 months, which is correlated with later IQ.

22. On the whole, Piaget seems to have underestimated the infant; it may also be that there is far more built in at birth than Piaget supposed. But all would agree that there is progressive development, built upon the base with which the baby begins. The early development culminates in the emergence of the ability to use symbols in play and in thought, at about 18–24 months of age.

KEY TERMS

babbling	expressive language	receptive language
Bayley Scales of Infant Development	expressive style	referential style
cooing	habituation	sensorimotor period
cross-modal transfer	information processing	social referencing
	object permanence	

SUGGESTED READINGS

Aslin, R. N. (1987b). Visual and auditory development in infancy. In J. D. Osofsky (Ed.), *Handbook of infant development*, 2nd ed. New York: Wiley-Interscience. Aslin has written a number of relatively recent summaries and reviews of the research on early perceptual development, of which this is perhaps the one nonexperts can most easily understand. Even so, this is quite technical and considerably more detailed than I have been in this chapter.

Bower, T. G. R. (1989) *The rational infant.* New York: Freeman. This is the most recent description and theory about infant perception from one of the major researchers and theorists in this area.

Field, T. (1990). *Infancy.* Cambridge, MA: Harvard University Press. One of an excellent series of books on topics in child development, written by experts but intended for lay readers. Field covers many of the topics I have discussed in this chapter as well as in Chapter 6.

Flavell, J. H. (1985). *Cognitive development.* (2nd ed.) Englewood Cliffs, NJ: Prentice-Hall. This is a first-rate basic text in the field, written by one of the major current figures in cognitive developmental theory. The introductory chapter and the chapter on infancy may be especially helpful if you find Piaget's theory somewhat hard to grasp.

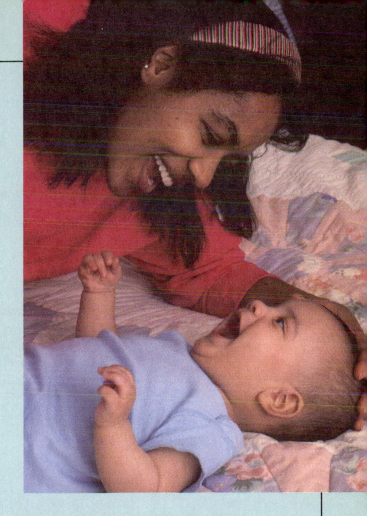

Chapter Six

Social and Personality Development in Infancy

t a social gathering several years ago I watched two young friends, Mark and Marcie, with their 4-month-old son Alexander. With very little effort, Alexander managed to attract everyone's attention. He looked around him, occasionally gave brief smiles, kicked his feet, shook a rattle, and cried once in a while. Those simple behaviors were enough to have all the adults in the room hovering over him, trying their best to entice a smile. I was not immune to his charms. I trotted out all my playing-with-baby tricks, raising my eyebrows, smiling broadly, calling his name, tickling him a bit on the cheek or on his feet, making clucking noises. My reward was one very small smile and a brief gaze.

Alex's parents, after 4 months of practice, were much more successful in this game. Either Mom or Dad could coax a smile from him within just a few seconds; either of them could easily soothe him if he cried.

My most immediate reaction to this scene was simple pleasure at seeing loving and attentive parents with their infant. But the psychologist in me was watching too. I could see all of Alex's social skills, his ability to entice. And I could see how much Alex and his parents had already learned about one another, how smoothly they performed a kind of "dance" of interaction. The baby brings his inborn and emerging physical and cognitive skills to this interaction; the parents bring their own skills and qualities as well as their instinctive responses to babies. To understand infants, we need to look at the development of these earliest relationships.

Attachment Theory

The strongest theoretical influence in modern-day studies of infant-parent relationships is attachment theory, particularly the work of John Bowlby (1969; 1973; 1980; 1988a; 1988b), whose approach I mentioned briefly in Chapter 2. His ideas were rooted in psychoanalytic thought, particularly in the emphasis on the significance of the earliest relationship between mother and child. But he added important evolutionary and ethological concepts. In his view, "the propensity to make strong emotional bonds to particular individuals [is] a basic component of human nature, already present in germinal form in the neonate" (1988a, p. 3). Such relationships have *survival* value because they bring nurturance to the infant. They are built and maintained by an interlocking repertoire of instinctive behaviors that create and sustain proximity between parent and child or between other bonded pairs.

In Bowlby's writings, and in the equally influential writings of Mary Ainsworth (1972; 1982; 1989; Ainsworth et al., 1978), the key concepts are that of an affectional bond, an attachment, and attachment behaviors.

Ainsworth defines an **affectional bond** as "a relatively long-enduring tie in which the partner is important as a unique individual and is interchangeable with none another. In an affectional bond, there is a desire to maintain closeness to the partner" (1989, p. 711). An **attachment** is a subvariety of emotional bond in which a person's sense of security is bound up in the relationship. When you are attached, you feel (or hope to feel) a special sense of security and com-

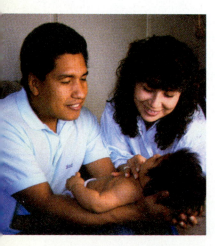

This Mom and Dad can probably easily coax a smile from their baby; even at this early stage they have learned each other's cues.

fort in the presence of the other, and you can use the other as a "safe base" from which to explore the rest of the world.

In these terms, the child's relationship with the parent is an attachment, but the parents' relationship with the child is not, since the parent presumably does not feel a greater sense of security in the presence of the infant or use the infant as a safe base. A relationship with one's adult partner or with a very close friend, however, is likely to be an attachment in the sense Ainsworth and Bowlby mean the term.

Since affectional bonds and attachments are internal states, we cannot see them directly. Instead we deduce their existence by observing **attachment behaviors,** which are all those behaviors that allow a child or adult to achieve and retain proximity to someone else to whom he is attached. This could include smiling, making eye contact, calling out to the other person across a room, touching, clinging, or crying.

It is important to make clear that there is no one-to-one correspondence between the number of different attachment behaviors a child (or adult) shows on any one occasion and the strength of the underlying attachment. Attachment behaviors are elicited primarily when the individual has need of care, support, or comfort. An infant is in such a needy state a good deal of the time; but an older child will be likely to show attachment behaviors only when he is frightened, tired, or otherwise under stress. It is the *pattern* of these behaviors, not the frequency, that tells us something about the strength or quality of the attachment or the affectional bond.

To understand the early relationship between the parent and the child, we need to look at both sides of the equation—at the development of the parents' bond to the child and the child's attachment to the parent.

> Think about your own relationships. In Bowlby's and Ainsworth's terms, which are attachments and which are affectional bonds?

> Pick one of your attachment relationships and make a list of all the attachment behaviors you show toward that person. Are any of these the same as the kind of attachment behaviors we see in an infant?

Adapting to the Newborn

Let me begin by looking at the social and emotional context in which infants and parents must form these early bonds. The baby is born; Mom, Dad, and infant return home and must now adapt to one another and to the massive changes in their lives occasioned by this new member of the family. For most adults, the role of parent brings profound satisfaction, a greater sense of purpose and self-worth, and a feeling of being a grownup. It may also bring a sense of shared joy between husband and wife (Umberson & Gove, 1989). In one large study in the U.S., 80 percent of the parents sampled said their lives had been changed for the better by the arrival of children (Hoffman & Manis, 1978). But it is also true that the birth of the first child signals a whole series of changes in parents' lives, and not all these changes are without strain.

In particular, marital satisfaction typically goes down in the first months and years after the first child is born (Rollins & Feldman, 1970). Individuals and couples report a sense of strain made up partly of fatigue, partly of a feeling that there is too much to cope with, anxiety about not knowing how best to care for the child, and a strong sense of loss of time and intimacy in the marriage relationship itself (Feldman, 1987). In longitudinal studies in which couples have been observed or interviewed during pregnancy and then again in the months after the first child's birth, spouses typically report fewer expressions of love, fewer positive actions intended to maintain or support the relationship, and more expressions of ambivalence after the child's birth than before (Belsky, Lang, & Rovine, 1985). Such strains and reduced satisfaction are less noticeable when the child was planned rather than unplanned and among those couples whose marriage was strong and stable before the birth of the child. But virtually all couples experience some strain.

The Formation of the Parent's Bond to the Infant

The Initial Bond

In the midst of this complex adaptive process, the parents need to develop a bond to the new baby in their midst. How does that occur? If you read the popular press at all, I am sure you have come across articles proclaiming that mothers (or fathers) must have immediate contact with their newborn infant if they are to become properly bonded with the baby. This belief has been based primarily on the work of two pediatricians, Marshall Klaus and John Kennell (1976), who proposed the hypothesis that the first few hours after an infant's birth is a "critical period" for the mother's development of a bond to her infant. Mothers who are denied early contact, Klaus and Kennell thought, are likely to form weaker bonds and thus be at higher risk for a range of parenting disorders.

Their proposal was one of many factors leading to significant changes in birth practices, including the now-normal presence of fathers at delivery. I would certainly not want to turn back the clock on such changes. But it now looks as if Klaus and Kennel's hypothesis is probably incorrect. Immediate contact does not appear to be either necessary or sufficient for the formation of stable long-term affectional bond between parent and child (Myers, 1987).

A few studies show some short-term beneficial effects of very early contact. In the first few days after delivery, mothers with such contact may show more tender fondling or more gazing at the baby than is true of mothers who first held their babies some hours after birth (Campbell & Taylor, 1980; de Chateau, 1980). But there is little indication of a lasting effect. Two or three months after delivery, mothers who have had immediate contact with their newborns do not smile at them more, or hold them differently than do mothers who had delayed contact.

Only in a certain subgroup of mothers, such as first-time mothers, mothers living in poverty, or very young mothers—all groups who are at somewhat higher risk for problems with parenting—are there a few signs that early contact may make a difference.

For example, Susan O'Connor and her colleagues (O'Connor et al., 1980) randomly assigned some poverty-level mothers to a "rooming in" arrangement in which the mother cared for her infant in her own hospital room and thus had extended contact. Other mothers saw their infants only at feeding times. *Neither* group had immediate contact with the infant after birth, so the difference here is

An added difficulty for many women after the birth of a child is a period of depressed mood, often called the "maternity blues" or "postpartum blues." Estimates vary, but Western studies suggest that something between half and three quarters of all women go through a brief period in which they find themselves crying often and feeling unexpectedly low in mood (Hopkins, Marcus, & Campbell, 1984). Most women pass through this depression in a few days and then return to a more positive and more stable mood state. But approximately 10 percent of women appear to experience a longer-lasting and more severe postpartum mood disturbance, commonly called a **postpartum depression** (Campbell et al., 1992).

The Real World
Postpartum Depression

Clinicians use the term *depression*, or the phrase *clinical depression*, to describe more than just the blues, although sadness or persisting low mood is one of the critical ingredients. To be diagnosed as suffering from a clinical depression, including postpartum depression, you must also show some other symptoms, such as poor appetite, sleep disturbances (inability to sleep or excessive sleep), loss of pleasure in everyday activities, feelings of worthlessness, complaints of diminished ability to think or concentrate, or recurrent thoughts of death or suicide. An individual must show at least half of these symptoms to be diagnosed as clinically depressed.

You can see from this description that such a depressive episode is not a trivial experience. So the fact that as many as one woman out of every ten experiences such feelings after the birth of a child is striking. Fortunately, postpartum depression is normally shorter than other forms of clinical depression. A duration of six to eight weeks seems to be typical, after which the woman gradually recovers her normal mood (Hopkins et al., 1984),

although for perhaps one or two percent of women the depression persists for a year or longer.

Such depressions seem to be more common in women who did not plan their pregnancy, who were high in anxiety during the pregnancy, or whose partner is not supportive of them or is displeased with the arrival of the child (Campbell et al., 1992; O'Hara et al., 1992). They are also more likely to occur in any woman who has experienced high levels of life changes during the pregnancy and immediately after the birth—changes such as moving, death of someone close, or loss of a job. Interestingly, though, postpartum depression does not seem to be more common after a first child than after later children, although a woman who experienced such a depression after her first child is more likely to have a repeat episode after later births (Hopkins et al., 1984).

Understandably, mothers who are in the midst of a significant postpartum depression interact differently with their infants than do mothers whose mood is more normal. For example, Alison Fleming and her colleagues (1988) found that depressed mothers stroked and touched their infants with affection less frequently in the first three months after delivery than did nondepressed mothers. However, these differences did *not* persist after the mother's depression lifted; at 16 months, Fleming could find no differences in mother-child interaction between the mothers who had been depressed and those who had not.

I think it is quite common in our society to pass off a woman's postpartum depression as if it were a minor event, "just the blues." And of course for many women, it is. But for a minority the arrival of a child ushers in a much more significant depressive episode, requiring at the very least a sympathetic and supportive environment, if not clinical intervention.

---

in the amount of contact in the first few days, not the timing of the first contact. Researchers then tracked these two groups through the first 18 months of the children's lives. O'Connor was especially looking for any signs of "inadequacy of parenting," such as abuse of the child or the baby's failure to thrive. You can see the results in Table 6.1.

Obviously, very few mothers in either the rooming-in or normal-hospital groups showed inadequate parenting, but the rate was higher for the group that had had less contact with the infant in the early days. These findings raise the possibility that extended early contact may help *prevent* later parenting problems, but only among those mothers who are at high risk for such problems in the

If you were a hospital administrator and had to decide whether to have "rooming in" as a standard procedure for all mothers and babies, would you be persuaded by O'Connor's results? What other factors would you consider?

TABLE 6.1
Effect of Extended Early Contact on Adequacy of Parenting

	Rooming-in group (143 cases)	Regular-hospital care group (158 cases)
Number of children referred to Children's Protective Services for suspicion of abuse	1	5
Number of children hospitalized for illness or "failure to thrive"	1	8

Source: O'Connor et al., 1980, pp. 356–357.

These two Moms show almost identical expressions—the classic "mock surprise" expression—characteristic of adults when interacting with a baby: raised eyebrows, open mouth, semismile.

first place. For the majority of mothers, early contact does not seem to be an essential ingredient in the formation of a strong affectional bond between mother and infant.

Meshing of Attachment Behaviors

What *is* essential is the opportunity for the parent and infant to develop a mutual, interlocking pattern of attachment behaviors—just what young Alex and his parents had already achieved. The baby signals his needs by crying or smiling; he responds to being held by soothing or snuggling; he looks at the parents when they look at him. The parents, in their turn, enter into this two-person "dance" with their own repertoire of caregiving behaviors. They pick the baby up when he cries, wait for and respond to his signals of hunger or other need, smile at the baby when he smiles, gaze into his eyes when he looks at them. Some researchers and theorists have described this as the development of *synchrony* (Isabella, Belsky, & von Eye, 1989).

One of the most intriguing things about this process is that we all seem to know how to do this particular dance and we do it in very similar ways. In the presence of a young infant most adults will automatically display a distinctive pattern of interactive behaviors, including smiling, raised eyebrows, and very wide open eyes. And we all seem to use our voices in special ways with babies as well. Parents all over the world use a characteristic high pitched and lilting pattern of speaking to babies; they also use similar intonation patterns. In a study of mother-infant interactions among Chinese, German, and United States mothers, Hanus and Mechthild Papousek (1991) found that all three groups tended to use a rising voice inflection when they wanted the baby to "take a turn" in the interaction and a falling intonation when they wanted to soothe the baby.

But while we can perform all these attachment *behaviors* with many infants, we do not form a bond with every baby we coo at in the grocery store. For the adult, the critical ingredient for the formation of a bond seems to be the opportunity to develop real mutuality—to practice the dance until the partners follow one another's lead smoothly and pleasurably. This takes time and many rehearsals, and some parents (and infants) become more skillful at it than others. In general, the smoother and more predictable the process becomes, the more satisfying it seems to be to the parents and the stronger their bond to the infant becomes.

This second step appears to be *far* more important than the initial contact at birth in establishing a strong parental bond to the child. But this second process, too, can fail. I've explored some of the possible reasons for such a failure in *The Real World* box on page 160.

Father-Child Bonds

Most of the research I have talked about so far has involved studies of mothers. Still, many of the same principles seem to hold for fathers as well. The father's bond, like the mother's, seems more dependent on the development of mutuality than on contact immediately after birth. Aiding the development of such mutuality is the fact that fathers seem to have the same repertoire of attachment behaviors as do mothers. In the early weeks of the baby's life, Dads touch, talk to, and cuddle their babies in the same ways that mothers do (Parke & Tinsley, 1981).

Past these first weeks of life, however, we see signs of a kind of specialization of parents' behaviors with their infants and toddlers—at least among parents in the industrialized societies in which researchers have conducted these observations. Dads spend more time playing with the baby, with more physical rough-housing. Moms spend more time in routine caregiving and also talk and smile more at the baby (Walker et al., 1992). This does not mean that fathers have a weaker affectional bond with the infant; it does mean that the attachment behaviors they show toward the infant are typically somewhat different from those mothers show.

Brandon's Dad, like most fathers, is far more likely to toss the baby in the air or play with him in this vigorous physical way than is his Mom.

In any given year, roughly one million children in the United States suffer from neglect, or from physical or sexual abuse (National Research Council, 1993). Most such abuse is inflicted on older children; the average age of children in cases reported to Child Protective Services is seven. But in many cases the origins of later abuse or neglect may lie in a failure of the parent to form a strong affectional bond to the baby in the first months of life. Such a failure can occur if either the baby or the parents lack the skills to enter into the "dance" of interaction fully. Of the two, the more serious problems seem to arise if it is the parent who lacks skills, but problems can also arise when the baby is handicapped in some way or otherwise lacks the full repertoire of attachment behaviors, such as might be the case for a preterm baby (van IJzendoorn et al., 1992).

The Real World
Child Abuse and Other Consequences of Failure of Bonding

For example, blind babies smile less and do not show mutual gaze, and preterm infants are typically very unresponsive in the early weeks and months (Fraiberg, 1974; 1975). *Most* parents of handicapped or premature infants form a strong bond to the child despite the baby's problems, but the rate of abuse is higher among preterm than term infants and higher among families whose babies who are sick a lot in the first few months (Belsky, 1993; Sherrod et al., 1984).

On the other side of the interaction, a parent might lack "attachment skill" because she or he did not form a secure attachment with her or his own parents, perhaps because of abuse (Crittenden et al., 1991). Many parents who abuse their children were themselves abused as children—although it is important to emphasize that many adults who experienced abuse in childhood manage to break the cycle of violence and refrain from abusing their own children (Zigler & Hall, 1989). Still, there appears to be a significant "intergenerational transmission" of such violence (Belsky, 1993). Those who are unable to break this cycle are typically those who lack other social skills, who have no adequate social supports or are living under high levels of stress.

Another serious problem on the parents' side of the equation is depression, which disrupts not only the parent's nurturing behavior, but affects the child's response as well. Babies interacting with depressed mothers, or even with mothers who have been told to look depressed or "blank-faced," smile less, show more sad and angry facial expressions, and are more disorganized and distressed (Field et al., 1990; Pickens & Field, 1993). Depressed mothers, for their part, are slower to respond to their infant's signals and are more negative—even hostile—to their infants (Rutter, 1990). Overall, these relationships appear to lack synchrony. That is, the mother and infant are not "dancing" well together. These deficiencies in the mother's behavior with the infant even persist after the mother is no longer depressed, and they generalize beyond the mother-infant dyad; babies with depressed mothers show similar distressed or nonsynchronous behaviors when they interact with a nondepressed adult (Field et al., 1988). Such children are also at higher risk for later behavior problems, including either heightened aggression or withdrawal (Cummings & Davies, 1994).

Not all depressed mothers show this pattern of behavior. If they have a good marriage, good support from friends and other family, and if the baby has good interactive skills, depressed moms seem to be able to develop positive patterns of interaction with their babies. (Teti, Gelfand, & Pompa, 1990).

One common theme in all these findings is that a parent, regardless of depression or history or abuse, is more likely to abuse a child when her current life conditions are highly stressful. So abuse is more likely in families in which there is alcoholism in one parent (Famularo et al., 1986), in large families, in single-parent households, and among families living in poverty or in extremely crowded conditions (Garbarino & Sherman, 1980; Pianta, Egeland, & Erickson, 1989; Sack, Mason, & Higgins, 1985). Parents can even surmount these adverse conditions, though, if they have adequate emotional support, either from one other or from others outside the family. At highest risk are those families living in adverse economic and physical conditions who also lack adequate emotional or social support from peers, extended family, or community (Belsky, 1993).

We do not yet know whether such sex differences in parenting behaviors are reflections of culturally based role definitions, or whether they might be instinctive, built-in differences. One crucial test would be to study families in which the father is the primary caregiver to see if the parental behavioral roles are reversed. So far we have only pale imitations of this crucial test—studies in which the father had been a major caregiver for a few months of the child's early life. The three such studies I know of, done in Sweden, the United States, and Australia, have yielded totally contradictory results (Field, 1978; Lamb et al., 1982; Russell, 1982), which leaves the question still open.

The Development of the Infant's Attachment to the Parents

Like the parent's bond to the baby, the baby's attachment emerges gradually. Bowlby (1969) suggested three phases in the development of the infant's attachment, which I've sketched schematically in Figure 6.1.

Phase 1: Nonfocused Orienting and Signaling. Like Piaget, Bowlby thought the baby begins life with a set of innate behavior patterns that orient him toward others and signal his needs. Mary Ainsworth describes these as "proximity promoting" behaviors—they bring people closer. In the newborn's repertoire, these include crying, making eye contact, clinging, cuddling, and responding to caregiving efforts by being soothed. But at first, as Ainsworth says, "these attachment behaviors are simply emitted, rather than being directed toward any specific person" (1989, p. 710).

At this stage there is little evidence of an attachment. Nonetheless, the roots of attachment are to be found in this phase. The baby is building up expectancies, schemas, the ability to discriminate Mom and Dad from others. The smooth, predictable interactions that strengthen the parent's bond also form the base for the baby's emerging attachment.

Phase 2: Focus on One or More Figure(s). By 3 months of age, the baby begins to aim her attachment behaviors somewhat more narrowly. She may smile more to the people who regularly take care of her and may not smile readily to a stranger. Yet despite the change, Bowlby and Ainsworth have argued that the

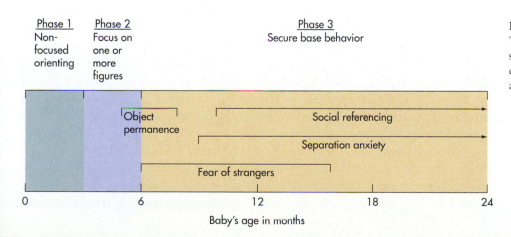

FIGURE 6.1
This schematic may help you see how the various threads of development of attachment are woven together.

infant does not yet have a full-blown attachment. There are still a number of people who are favored with the child's "proximity promoting" behaviors and no one person has yet become the "safe base." Children in this phase show no special anxiety at being separated from their parents and no fear of strangers.

Phase 3: Secure Base Behavior.   Bowlby thought that the baby forms a genuine attachment only at about 6 months of age. At the same time, the dominant mode of the baby's attachment behavior changes. Because the 6- to 7-month-old begins to be able to move about the world more freely by creeping and crawling, she can move *toward* the caregiver as well as enticing the caregiver to come to her. Her attachment behaviors therefore shift from mostly "come here" signals (proximity promoting) to what Ainsworth calls "proximity seeking," which we might think of as "go there" behaviors. We also see a child of this age using the "most important person" as a safe base from which to explore the world around her—one of the key signs that an attachment exists.

I should note that not all infants have a *single* attachment figure, even at this early point. Some may show strong attachment to both parents, or to a parent and another caregiver, such as a baby-sitter or a grandparent. But even these babies, when under stress, usually show a preference for one of their favored persons over the others.

Once the child has developed a clear attachment, at about 6 to 8 months, several related behaviors also appear. One of these is social referencing, which I talked about in the last chapter. The 10-month-old begins to check out Mom's or Dad's expression before deciding whether to venture forth into some novel situation. At about the same age, babies also typically show both fear of strangers and separation protest.

Fear of Strangers and Separation Protest.   Both these forms of distress are rare before 5 of 6 months, rise in frequency until about 12 to 16 months, and then decline. The research findings are not altogether consistent, but it looks as though fear of strangers normally appears first, while separation anxiety starts a bit later but continues to be visible for a longer period, a pattern I've marked in Figure 6.1.

Such an increase in fear and anxiety has been observed in children from a number of different cultures, and in both home-reared and day-care-reared children in the United States, all of which makes it look as if there are some basic cognitive or other age-related developmental timetables underlying this pattern (Kagan, Kearsley, & Zelazo, 1978). But while the general timing of these two phenomena may be common to virtually all children, the intensity of the fearful reaction is not. Children differ widely in how much fear they show toward strangers or toward novel situations. Some of this difference may reflect basic temperamental variations (Berberian & Snyder, 1982). Heightened fearfulness may also be a response to recent upheaval or stress in the child's life, such as a recent move or a parent changing jobs. It is also clear that the stranger's behavior makes a considerable difference. When a substitute caregiver is responsive and warm but does not approach too closely, babies show less fear than when the

CULTURES & CONTEXTS

Attachment in a Very Different Cultural System

Is the sequence of phases Bowlby and Ainsworth describe universal? Do all babies go through this same sequence, no matter what kind of family or culture they live in? Maybe yes, maybe no. Ainsworth herself observed the same basic three phases in forming a clear attachment among children in Uganda, although children in this culture showed a more intense fear of strangers than is usually found in American samples. But among the Ganda, as in American and other Western families, the mother is the primary caregiver. What would we find in a culture in which the child's early care is much more communal?

Edward Tronick and his colleagues (Tronick, Morelli, & Ivey, 1992) have studied just such a culture, a pygmy group called the Efe, who forage in the forests of Zaire. They live in camps in small groups of perhaps 20 individuals, each camp consisting of several extended families, often brothers and their wives.

Infants in these communities are cared for communally in the early months and years of life. They are carried and held by all the adult women, and interact regularly with many different adults. If they have needs, they are tended by whichever adult or older child is nearby; they may even be nursed by women other than the mother, although they normally sleep with the mother.

Tronick and his colleagues report two things of particular interest about early attachment in this group. First, Efe infants seem to use virtually any adult or older child in their world as a safe base, which suggests that there is no single central attachment. But at the same time, beginning at about 6 months, the Efe infants nonetheless seem to insist on being with their mother more and to prefer her over other women, although other women continue to help care for the child.

Thus even in an extremely communal rearing arrangement, there is still some sign of a central attachment, albeit perhaps less dominant. At the same time, it is clear, as Inge Bretherton says, that "attachment behavior is never purely instinctive, but is heavily overlain with cultural prescriptions" (1992b, p. 150).

babysitter pays little attention to the child or touches the child too soon (Gunnar et al., 1992; Mangelsdorf, 1992). Whatever the origin of such variations in fearfulness, the pattern does eventually disappear in virtually all toddlers, typically by the middle of the second year. And while it is going on, parents can take advantage of the existence of social referencing to try to reduce the child's fear: your child is more likely to accept a stranger if he sees you talking and smiling to the stranger first.

Attachments to Mothers and Fathers

I pointed out earlier that both fathers and mothers appear to form strong bonds to their infants, although their behavior with infants varies somewhat. But what about the child's half of this relationship? Are infants and children equally attached to their fathers and mothers?

In general, yes. From the age of 7–8 months, when strong attachments first appear, infants prefer *either* the father or the mother to a stranger. And when both the father and the mother are available, an infant will smile at or approach either or both, *except* when he is frightened or under stress. When that happens, especially between 8 and 24 months, the child typically turns to the mother rather than the father (Lamb, 1981).

As you might expect, the strength of the child's attachment to the father at this early age seems to be related to the amount of time the Dad has spent with

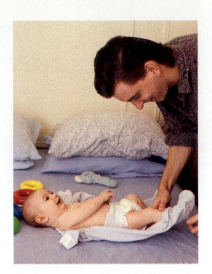

If Gail Ross is right, then young Edwin will be likely to form a strong attachment to his Dad because his Dad changes his diapers.

the child. Gail Ross (Ross et al., 1975) found she could predict a baby's attachment to the father by knowing how many diapers the dad changed in a typical week. The more diapers the father changed, the stronger the attachment! But greatly increased time with the father does not seem to be the only element, since Michael Lamb and his Swedish colleagues have found that infants whose father was the major caregiver for at least a month in the first year of the child's life were nonetheless more strongly attached to their mothers than their fathers (Lamb et al., 1983). For the father to be consistently *preferred* over the mother would probably require essentially full-time paternal care. As this option becomes more common in our society, it will be possible to study such father-child pairs to see if a preference for the father develops.

Internal Working Models of Attachment

Go to a day-care center some time and watch the way the babies or toddlers greet their parents at the end of the day. Some are calmly pleased to see Mom or Dad, running for a hug, showing a new toy, or smiling when Mom or Dad picks them up, showing no distress. Others may cry or cling strongly to the parent. All these babies have moved through the typical sequence from preattachment to attachment, but the *quality* of their attachments differ. In Bowlby's terminology, infants have different **internal working models** of their relationship with parents and key others. This internal working model of attachment relationships includes such elements as the child's confidence (or lack of it) that the attachment figure will be available or reliable, the child's expectation of rebuff or affection, and the child's sense of assurance that the other is really a safe base for exploration.

   The internal model begins to be formed late in the child's first year of life and continues to become more complex and firmer through the first 4 or 5 years. By age 5, most children have clear internal models of the mother (or other caregiver), a self model, and a model of relationships. Once children have formed these models, they shape and explain experiences and affect memory and attention. We notice and remember experiences that fit our models and miss or forget experiences that don't match. In Piaget's terms, we more readily assimilate data that fit the model. More importantly, the model affects the child's behavior: The child essentially attempts to recreate, in each new relationship, the pattern with which he is familiar. Alan Sroufe gives a nice example that may make this point clearer:

> What is rejection to one child is benign to another. What is warmth to a second child is confusing or ambiguous to another. For example, a child approaches another and asks to play. Turned down, the child goes off and sulks in a corner. A second child receiving the same negative reaction skips on to another partner and successfully engages him in play. Their experiences of rejection are vastly different. Each receives confirmation of quite different inner working models (1988, p. 23).

Secure and Insecure Attachments

All the theorists in this tradition share the assumption that the first attachment relationship is the most influential ingredient in the creation of the child's working model. In describing variations in that first attachment relationship researchers almost universally use Mary Ainsworth's category system (Ainsworth et al., 1978; Ainsworth & Wittig, 1969). She distinguishes between **secure attachment** and two types of **insecure attachment,** which she has assessed using a procedure she called the **Strange Situation.**

The Strange Situation consists of a series of episodes in a laboratory setting, typically used when the child is between 12 and 18 months of age. The child is first with the mother, then with the mother and a stranger, alone with the stranger, completely alone for a few minutes, reunited with the mother, left alone again, and then reunited first with the stranger, and then the mother. Ainsworth classifies children's reactions to this situation into three types: *securely attached*, *insecure/avoidant*, and *insecure/ambivalent* (also sometimes called resistant). Mary Main (Main & Solomon, 1990) has suggested a fourth group, which she calls insecure/disorganized/disoriented. I have listed some of the characteristics of the different types in Table 6.2.

TABLE 6.2

Categorization of Secure and Insecure Attachment in Ainsworth's Strange Situation

Securely attached.	Child shows low to moderate levels of proximity seeking to mother; does not avoid or resist contact if mother initiates it. When reunited with mother after absence, child greets her positively, or is easily soothed if upset. Clearly prefers mother to stranger.
Insecurely attached: detached/avoidant.	Child avoids contact with mother, especially at reunion after an absence. Does not resist mother's efforts to make contact, but does not seek much contact. Treats stranger and mother about the same throughout.
Insecurely attached: resistant/ambivalent.	Greatly upset when separated from mother, but mother cannot successfully comfort child when she returns. Child both seeks and avoids contact, at different times. May show anger toward mother at reunion, and resists both comfort from and contact with stranger.
Insecurely attached: disorganized/disoriented.	Dazed behavior, confusion, or apprehension. Child may show contradictory behavior patterns simultaneously, such as moving toward mother while keeping gaze averted.

Sources: Ainsworth et al., 1978; Main & Solomon, 1990.

CULTURES & CONTEXTS

Secure and Insecure Attachments in Different Cultures

Studies in a variety of countries have pointed to the possibility that secure attachments may be more likely in certain cultures than others. The most thorough analyses have come from a Dutch psychologist, Marinus van IJzendoorn, who has examined the results of 32 separate studies in eight different countries. You can see the percentage of babies that researchers classified in each category for each country in the table below (van IJzendoorn & Kroonenberg, 1988).

We need to be cautious about over interpreting the information in this table, because in most cases there are

One possibility is that the Strange Situation is simply not an appropriate measure of attachment security in all cultures. For example, because Japanese babies are rarely separated from their mothers in the first year of life, being left totally alone in the midst of the Strange Situation may be far more stressful for them, which might result in more intense, inconsolable crying and hence a classification of ambivalent attachment. The counter argument is that comparisons of toddlers' actual behavior in the Strange Situation suggest few cultural differences in such things as proximity seeking or avoidance of Mom, all of which gives us more confidence that the Strange Situation is tapping similar processes among children in many cultures (Sagi, van IJzendoorn, & Koren-Karie, 1991).

Cross-cultural comparisons of secure and insecure attachments

Country	Number of Studies	Percentage of Each Attachment Type		
		Secure	Avoidant	Ambivalent
West Germany	3	56.6	35.3	8.1
Great Britain	1	75.0	22.2	2.8
Netherlands	4	67.3	26.3	6.4
Sweden	1	74.5	21.6	3.9
Israel	2	64.4	6.8	28.8
Japan	2	67.7	5.2	27.1
China	1	50.0	25.0	25.0
United States	18	64.8	21.1	14.1
Overall Average		65.0	21.3	13.7

Source: Based on Table 1 of van IJzendoorn & Kroonenberg, 1988, p. 150–151.

It is also possible that the *meaning* of a "secure" or "avoidant" pattern is different in different cultures, even if the percentages of each category are similar. German researchers, for example, have suggested that an insecure avoidant classification in their culture may reflect not indifference by mothers, but explicit training toward greater independence in the baby (Grossmann et al., 1985).

On the other hand, research in Israel (Sagi, 1990) shows that the Strange Situation attachment classification predicts the baby's later social skills in much the same way as is found in United States samples, which suggests that the classification system is valid in both cultures.

only one or two studies from a given country, normally with quite small samples. The single study from China, for example, included only 36 babies. Still, the findings are thought provoking.

The most striking thing about these data is actually its consistency. In each of the eight countries, a secure attachment is the most common pattern, found in more than half of all babies researchers studied; in six of the eight, an avoidant pattern is the more common of the two forms of insecure attachment. Only in Israel and Japan is this pattern significantly reversed. How can we explain such differences?

At the moment the most plausible hypothesis is that the same factors in mother-infant interaction contribute to secure and insecure attachments in all cultures, and that these patterns reflect similar internal models. But it will take more research like the Israeli work, in which the long-term outcomes of the various categories are studied, before we can be sure if this is correct

Roughly two-thirds of children are rated as securely attached. The probability that a child will be insecurely attached is much higher among children reared in poverty-level families, in families with a history of abuse, or in families in which the mother is diagnosed as seriously depressed (Cicchetti & Barnett, 1991; Spieker & Booth, 1988). A disorganized/disoriented pattern seems especially likely in families in which the parents had some unresolved trauma in their own childhoods, such as either abuse or their own parents' death (Main & Hesse, 1990).

The category system Ainsworth devised and the theory that lies behind it have prompted an enormous amount of research and new theory, much of it fascinating, and much of it with practical ramifications. So let me take some time to explore a few of the issues and implications.

Stability of Attachment Classification.   One of the key questions is whether security of attachment is stable over time. Does a child who is securely attached to his mother at 12 months still show the same secure attachment at 24 or 36 months? Is it still present at school age? This is a particularly important question for those researchers and therapists who are concerned about the possible permanent effects of early abuse, neglect, or other sources of insecure attachment. Can children recover from such early treatment? Does an initial secure attachment permanently buffer a child from the effects of difficult life circumstances at a later point?

The answer—as usual—is yes and no. When the child's family environment or life circumstances are reasonably consistent, the security or insecurity of attachment does remain stable. For example, in a stable, middle-class sample, Mary Main and her colleagues (Main & Cassidy, 1988; Main, Kaplan, & Cassidy, 1985) found strong correlations between ratings of security of attachment at 18 months and at 6 years. But when the child's circumstances change in some major way—such as when she starts going to day care or nursery school, or grandma comes to live with the family, or the parents divorce or move—the security of the child's attachment may change as well, either from secure to insecure or the reverse. In poverty-level families, in which instability of circumstances is more common, changes in attachment security are also common.

The very fact that a child's security can change from one time to the next does not refute the notion of attachment as an "internal working model." Bowlby suggested that for the first two or three years, the particular pattern of attachment a child shows is in some sense a property of each specific *relationship*. For example, recent studies of toddlers' attachments to mothers and fathers show that about 30 percent of the time the child is securely attached to one parent and insecurely attached to the other, with both possible combinations equally represented (Fox, Kimmerly, & Schafer, 1991). It is the quality of each relationship that determines the child's security in that pair. If that relationship changes markedly, the security of the baby's attachment to that individual may change too. But by age 4 or 5, Bowlby argued that the internal working model becomes more general, more a property of the *child*, more generalized across relationships, and thus more resistant to change. At that point, the child tends to impose it upon new relationships, including relationships with teachers or peers.

Thus a child may "recover" from an initially insecure attachment or lose a secure one. But consistency over time is more typical, both because children's relationships tend to be reasonably stable for the first few years, and because once the internal model is clearly formed, it tends to perpetuate itself.

Origins of Secure and Insecure Attachments.   Where do these differences come from? For the development of a secure attachment, the common denominators seem to be both parental acceptance of the infant and *contingent responsiveness* from the parents to the infant (Isabella et al., 1989; Pederson et al., 1990).

Contingent responsiveness does not just mean that the parents love the baby or take care of the baby well, but rather that in their caregiving and other behavior toward the child they are sensitive to the child's own cues and respond appropriately. They smile when the baby smiles, talk to the baby when he vocalizes, pick him up when he cries, etc. Parents of securely attached babies are also likely to be more emotionally expressive toward their babies—smiling more, using their voices in more expressive ways, touching the infant more (Egeland & Farber, 1984; Izard et al., 1991).

In contrast, mothers of babies researchers rated as insecure/avoidant are likely to be "psychologically unavailable" to their infants (to use Alan Sroufe's phrase). Mothers may show such a withdrawn or neglecting pattern for a variety of reasons, but a common ingredient is depression in the mother—a phenomenon I have already mentioned.

Infants rated as insecure/ambivalent are likely to have mothers who are inconsistent in their responses to the infant, rejecting the infant's bids for contact some of the time, responding positively at other times. Classifications in the fourth group, the insecure/disorganized/disoriented, are common among children who are maltreated (Carlson et al., 1989; Lyons-Ruth et al., 1991).

The Role of the Parents' Own Internal Attachment Model.   Researchers who study attachment have begun to ask a new set of questions about the origins of the child's attachment pattern: Does the *parent's* internal model of attachment—which is presumably a product of his or her own early history—affect the security of the child's attachment?

Mary Main and her colleagues (Main et al., 1985) have devised an interview measure of the security of adult attachment in which researchers asked adults about their childhood experiences and their current relationship with their parents. In one question, the adults are asked to choose five adjectives to describe their relationship with each parent, and to say why they chose each adjective. They are also asked whether they ever felt rejected in childhood, and how they feel about their parents currently. On the basis of the interview, researchers classified the adult's internal working model of attachment as being in one of three categories:

- *Secure/autonomous/balanced*: The adult values attachment relations, views those relationships as having been influential in her current personality. The subject speaks freely and coherently about her early experiences and has thought about what had motivated her parents' behavior.
- *Dismissing or Detached*: These adults minimize the importance or the effects of their early experience. They may idealize their parents, but have poor recall of their childhood, often denying negative experiences and emotions or calling them normal or typical. Their emphasis is on their own personal strengths.
- *Preoccupied or Enmeshed*: The adult often talks about inconsistent or role-reversed parenting. She may be confused about her experiences or about what had been expected of her. As adults, those in this group are still caught up in their family and in their relationships, either still struggling with anger or with the desire to please.

R E S E A R C H   R E P O R T

Promoting Secure Attachments With Infant Carriers

In many parts of the world, particularly in the Third World, mothers carry their babies with them most of the time, using some kind of sling or wrap that keeps the child against the mother's body. In the United States, in recent years, variations on such a system have become a fairly common sight as well. We see Moms or Dads with a young infant snuggled against them, held by some kind of soft baby carrier. This not only allows Moms or Dads to have hands free to work or move while keeping the baby nearby, it also seems to foster a more secure attachment. Mary Ainsworth observed such a link in her studies in Uganda (Ainsworth, 1967). Now we have experimental data from the United States demonstrating the same effect.

Elizabeth Anisfeld and her colleagues (Anisfeld et al., 1990) gave each of a group of low-income mothers a gift right after the birth of their baby. Half received a soft baby carrier, the other half received a plastic infant seat. Both groups were encouraged to use the item daily, and most did use the item at least some of the time. When researchers tested the infants in the Strange Situation at 13 months, Anisfeld found that 87 percent of those babies whose moms had carried them in the soft carrier were securely attached, compared to only 38 percent of the children of the moms in the group that received the infant seat. Because the mothers had been assigned randomly to these two conditions, we can be more confident of the causal link between the expanded physical contact fostered by the baby carrier and the child's secure attachment.

The application to everyday life seems straightforward: more physical contact between baby and parents is beneficial, and a baby carrier is a particularly good way to achieve such contact. It is also a pleasure!

When researchers link these adult models to the security of attachment the *children* of those adults display, the expected pattern emerges: Adults with secure models of attachment to their own parents are much more likely to have infants or toddlers with secure attachments. Those with dismissing models are more likely to have infants with avoidant attachments, while adults with preoccupied attachments are more likely to have infants with ambivalent attachment (Crittenden, Partridge, & Claussen, 1991; Crowell & Feldman, 1991; Main et al., 1985). Such a pattern has also been found in at least one prospective study in which the mother's attachment model was assessed *before* she gave birth to her first child (Fonagy, Steele, & Steele, 1991).

A good illustration of how the mother's internal model can affect her behavior comes from a study by Judith Crowell and Shirley Feldman (1991). They observed Moms with their preschoolers in a free-play setting. In the middle of the play period, the mother left the child alone for several minutes and then returned. Mothers who were themselves rated as secure in their attachment model were more likely to prepare the child ahead of time for the impending separation, had less difficulty themselves with the separation, and were most physically responsive to the child during reunion. Their children were least likely to avoid them during the reunion as well. Preoccupied moms were themselves more anxious about separating from the child and prepared the child less. Dismissing mothers also prepared the child very little, but left without difficulty, and remained physically distant from their children after returning to the playroom. Crowell and Feldman also noted that mothers with dismissing or preoccupied internal models interpreted the child's behavior very differently than did the secure moms.

> One mother observed her crying child through the observation window and said, "See, she isn't upset about being left." At reunion, she said to the child, "Why are you crying? I didn't leave." (1991, p. 604).

Thus not only does the mother's own internal model affect her actual behavior, it affects the meaning she ascribes to the child's behavior, both of which will affect the child's developing model of attachment.

Long-Term Consequences of Secure and Insecure Attachment. One of the reasons I have spent so much time talking about secure and insecure attachment is that this classification system has proven to be extremely helpful in predicting a remarkably wide range of other behaviors in children, both as toddlers and in later childhood. Dozens of studies show that children rated as securely attached to their mothers in infancy are later more sociable, more positive in their behavior toward others, including friends and siblings, less clinging and dependent on teachers, less aggressive and disruptive, more empathetic, and more emotionally mature in their approach to school and other nonhome settings (e.g., Frankel & Bates, 1990; Lyons-Ruth, Alpern, & Repacholi, 1993; Youngblade & Belsky, 1992).

Most of this research has been on preschool or early elementary school children, so we cannot say with certainty that these early effects persist longer than age 6 or 7. But in the one study I know of in which children with known early attachment histories have been followed as far as preadolescence, the pattern of findings is the same.

Alan Sroufe and his colleagues, in a study I described briefly in Chapter 1, have now followed 47 of the several hundred children in their larger sample up to age 10 and 11 (Sroufe, 1989; Sroufe, Carlson, & Schulman, 1993; Urban et al., 1991). At that age, the children were observed during a specially designed summer camp. The counselors rated each child on a range of characteristics, and observers noted how often children spent time together or with the counselors. Naturally, neither the counselors nor the observers knew what the children's initial attachment classification had been. The findings are clear: those with histories of secure attachment were rated as more self-confident and as having more social competence. They complied more readily with counselor requests, expressed more positive emotions, and had a greater sense of their ability to accomplish things—something Bandura calls *self-efficacy* and Sroufe calls *agency*. They created more friendships, especially with other securely attached youngsters, and engaged in more complex activities when playing in groups. The majority of those with histories of insecure attachment showed some kind of deviant behavior pattern at age 11, such as isolation from peers, bizarre behavior, passivity, hyperactivity, or aggressiveness. Only a few of the originally securely attached children showed any of these patterns.

I should emphasize again that these 47 children are the only ones yet studied over this length of time, and it is risky to build too tall a theoretical edifice on such a small empirical foundation. But Sroufe's data fit very well with the results from studies of younger children as well as with newer studies that show links between adolescents' *current* attachment status (measured with an interview) and emotional health or effective functioning. Collectively the findings point to potentially long-term consequences of attachment patterns or internal working models of relationship that children construct in the first year of life. But fluidity and change also occur, and we need to know much more about the factors that tend to maintain, or alter, the earliest models.

Temperament and Attachment. One last point: It may have occurred to some of you that there is a certain similarity in the description of a "difficult" temperament and of an ambivalent attachment. In fact Chess and Thomas have themselves noted this similarity (1982), and argued that the Strange Situation is really only tapping temperamental differences.

I am not persuaded by this argument for several reasons. For one thing, if security of attachment were only temperament, how could we explain the repeated observation that a child can be simultaneously securely attached to one person and insecurely attached to another?

Nonetheless, there must clearly be some link between temperament and attachment. Babies with different temperaments not only react differently to the world around them, they also trigger different reactions from the people taking care of them. But the process is complex. Buss and Plomin (1984) have proposed that children in the middle range on temperament dimensions typically adapt *to* their environment, while those children whose temperament is extreme—like extremely difficult children—force their environment to adapt to them. So, for example, parents punish temperamentally difficult children more (Rutter, 1978) than more adaptable children. But even this statement is too simple. A parent's own child-rearing skills, the stress she experiences, and the amount of social or emotional support she has, all affect her ability to deal with an irritable or difficult child.

For example, Susan Crockenberg (1981; 1986) has found that babies with difficult temperaments are more likely to be insecurely attached *only* if their mothers see themselves as having inadequate social support. Equivalently difficult babies whose mothers have adequate support are no more likely than are easy babies to be insecurely attached.

Crockenberg's study illustrates that the security or insecurity of the child's attachment is a complex outcome of the interaction of a great many elements in the system—the child's innate qualities (such as temperament), the skills and patterns the parents bring to the equation, and the setting in which the whole family is embedded.

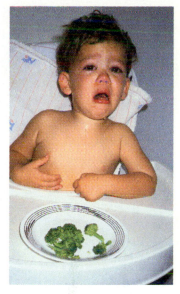

If Chess and Thomas are right, then we might assume that this toddler with a "difficult" temperament is also insecurely attached to his parents. But the relationship between temperament and attachment is a good deal more complicated than that.

The statement that difficult babies are more often punished is open to several possible interpretations. What are they?

The Development of the Sense of Self

During the same months that the baby is developing an attachment to Mom or Dad and creating an initial, primitive internal working model of attachment, she is also developing a parallel internal model of *self*. Just as she is figuring out that

Mom or Dad continue to exist when they are out of sight, she is figuring out that *she* exists separately, and that she has qualities and properties.

Our thinking about the child's emerging sense of self has been strongly influenced by both Freud and Piaget, each of whom assumed that the baby begins life with *no* sense of separateness. Freud emphasized what he called the *symbiotic* relationship between the mother and young infant in which the two are joined together as if they are one. He believed that the infant does not understand himself to be separate from the mother. Piaget emphasized that the infant's understanding of the basic concept of object permanence was a necessary precursor for the child's attaining *self*-permanence—a sense of himself as a stable, continuing entity. Both of these aspects of early self-development reappear in current descriptions of the emergence of the sense of self. Michael Lewis, for example (1990; 1991; Lewis & Brooks-Gunn, 1979), divides the process into two main steps or tasks.

The First Step: The Subjective Self

Lewis argues that the child's first task is to figure out that he is separate from others and that this separate self endures over time and space. He calls this aspect of the self-concept the **subjective self,** or sometimes the *existential self* because the key awareness seems to be that "I exist." Agreeing with Freud, Lewis places the beginnings of this understanding in the first 2 or 3 months of life. At that time, the baby grasps the basic distinction between self and everything else. In Lewis' view, the roots of this understanding lie in the myriad everyday interactions the baby has with the objects and people in his world. Over the early months, the baby learns that he has effects on things. When he touches the mobile, it moves; when he cries, someone responds; when he smiles, his mother smiles back. By this process the baby separates out self from everything else and a sense of *I* begins to emerge. But it is not until the baby also grasps the concept of object permanence, at about 9 to 12 months, that we can say a subjective self has really emerged.

The Second Step: The Objective Self

This is not the end of the story. It is not enough merely to understand yourself as an agent in the world or a person who has experiences. For a full sense of self, the toddler must also understand herself to be an *object* in the world. Just as a ball has properties—roundness, the ability to roll, a certain feel in the hand—so the "self" also has qualities or properties, such as gender, size, a name, or qualities like shyness or boldness, coordination or clumsiness. It is this *self-awareness* that is the hallmark of the second phase of identity development. Lewis refers to this as the **objective self,** or sometimes the *categorical self*, because once the child achieves self-awareness the process of defining the self involves placing oneself in a whole series of categories.

Studying Self-Awareness.   It has not been easy to determine just when a child has developed such self-awareness. The most commonly used procedure involves a mirror. First the baby is placed in front of a mirror, just to see how she behaves. Most infants of about 9–12 months will look at their own images, make faces, or try to interact with the baby-in-the-mirror in some way. After allowing this free exploration for a time, the experimenter, while pretending to wipe the baby's face with a cloth, puts a spot of rouge on the baby's nose and then again lets the baby look in the mirror. The crucial test of self-recognition, and thus of awareness of the self, is whether the baby reaches for the spot on her *own* nose, rather than the nose on the face in the mirror.

The results from one of Lewis' studies using this procedure are in Figure 6.2. As you can see, none of the 9–12 month old children in this study touched their noses, but by 21 months, three quarters of the children showed that level of self-recognition. The figure also shows the rate at which children refer to themselves by name when they are shown a picture of themselves, which is another commonly used measure of self-awareness. You can see that this development occurs at almost exactly the same time as self-recognition in a mirror. Both are present by about the middle of the second year of life, a finding confirmed by other investigators (Bullock & Lütkenhaus, 1990).

We can see signs of this new self-awareness in a whole range of other behavior. It is only at this point in toddlerhood, for example, that we see such self-conscious emotions as embarrassment, pride, or shame, all of which involve some aspect of self-evaluation (Lewis, Allesandri, & Sullivan, 1992). It is also at this point that toddlers begin to insist on doing things for themselves and show a newly proprietary attitude toward toys ("Mine!") or other treasured objects. Looked at this way, much of the legendary "terrible twos" can be understood as an outgrowth of self-awareness.

The Emergence of Emotional Expression. The developmental shifts in the child's understanding of self are matched by parallel progressions in the baby's expression of emotions. You already know from Chapter 5 that babies are able to read others' emotions to at least some extent. They respond differently to their mothers' happy or sad expressions and by 10 months show social referencing. During the months of infancy, infants also develop a repertoire of their own emotional expressions.

At 4 months, Lucy's pleasure at looking at herself in a mirror comes from the fact that this is an interesting moving object to inspect, not from any understanding that this is *herself* in the mirror.

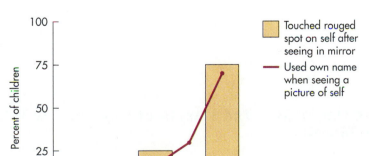

Touched rouged spot on self after seeing in mirror

Used own name when seeing a picture of self

FIGURE 6.2
Mirror recognition and self-naming develop at almost exactly the same time. (Source: Lewis & Brooks, 1978, pp. 214–215.)

At birth, infants already have a range of facial expressions that match happy or unhappy circumstances. By 3 or 4 months of age, adult observers are able to distinguish several other emotional expressions in the baby's repertoire: interest, anger, surprise, and sadness. A clear facial expression representing fear is distinguishable a few months later (Harris, 1989; Izard et al., 1980). But it is only early in the second year of life, at about the same time that a child shows self-recognition in the mirror, that we see the emergence of those self-conscious emotions like embarrassment or empathy.

Early Self-Definitions.   Having achieved an understanding of herself as *object* with qualities or properties, the toddler now begins to *define* herself, to label herself in various ways. One of the earliest dimensions of such self-definition is gender. Two-year-olds can label themselves accurately as boys or girls, and their behavior begins to diverge in clear ways at about this age. For example, if you observe children while they play in a room stocked with a wide range of attractive toys, 2- and 3-year old girls are more likely to play with dolls or at various housekeeping games, including sewing, stringing beads, or cooking. Boys the same age will more often choose to play with guns, toy trucks, fire engines, and with carpentry tools (O'Brien, 1992). At the same ages we also see the beginnings of a preference for playmates of the same gender (Maccoby, 1988; 1990; Maccoby & Jacklin, 1987)—a pattern that gets progressively stronger through the preschool and early elementary school years.

Toddlers also categorize themselves on other simple dichotomous dimensions, such as big versus little, smart versus dumb, good or bad. At this early stage, they see themselves as one or the other, not both at different times.

In Bowlby's language, what seems to be happening here is that the child is creating an internal model of self, just as he creates an internal model of relationships. He first learns that he exists separately, that he has effects on the world. Then he begins to understand that he is also an object in the world, with properties, including size and gender. The internal model of self, or the self-scheme as it is often labeled, does not develop fully at this early age. But the toddler is already building up an image of himself, his qualities, his abilities. Like the internal model of attachment, this self-model or *self-scheme* affects the choices the toddler makes—such as choosing to play with other children of the same gender—as well as influencing the way the toddler will interpret experiences. In this way the internal model is not only strengthened but tends to carry forward.

Beyond the Family: The Effects of Day Care on Infants and Toddlers

In all of what I have said so far about infant development, I have talked as if every infant is reared largely or entirely within an individual family, cared for by one or both parents. But of course in many countries, and certainly in the United States, that is no longer the case.

In virtually every industrialized country in the world, women have gone into the work force in great numbers in the past two decades. In the United States the change has been particularly rapid and massive: In 1972, only 24 percent of women with children under age 1 were in the labor force; by 1991 the *majority* of such women were working outside the home at least part-time, a rate that appears to be higher than for any other country in the world (Cherlin, 1992). It is now typical for infants as well as school-age children to spend a significant amount of time in the care of someone other than a parent. Similar, although less massive, changes have occurred in other countries, but in the discussion to follow I'm going to be talking almost exclusively about day care as it exists in the United States.

What effect does such nonparental care have on infants and young children? As you can easily imagine, this is *not* a simple question to answer, for a whole host of reasons:

- There is an enormous variety of different care arrangements all lumped under the general title of "day care."
- Children enter these care arrangements at different ages and remain in them for varying lengths of time. Some children have the same alternate caregiver over many years; others shift often from one care setting to another.
- Day care varies hugely in quality.
- Families who place their children in day care are undoubtedly different in a whole host of ways from those who care for their children primarily at home. How can we be sure that effects attributed to day care are not the result of family differences instead?

Most of the research we have to draw on does not really take these complexities into account. Typically, researchers have compared children "in day care" with those "reared at home," and assumed that any differences between the two groups were attributable to the day-care experience. Recent studies are often better, but we are still a long way from having clear or good answers to even the most basic questions about the impact of day care on children's development. Nonetheless, because the question is so critical, you need to be aware of what we know, as well as what we do not yet know.

The majority of children in the U.S. have at least some experience with nonparental care, although group care like this day care center is not the most common form.

Who Is Taking Care of the Children?

Let me begin at the descriptive level. Just who is taking care of all those children while their parents work? In some countries, such as France or Belgium, the government organizes and subsidizes child care and it is free to all parents. At the other end of the continuum lies the United States, where we have no national standards for care and only minimum government subsidies, primarily in the form of income tax credits for the poor, and support for the Head Start program for 3- and 4-year-olds. In our culture, each family must make its own arrangements as best it can.

Figure 6.3 shows the solutions parents have found. The figure includes data for all children under age 5 in the United States in 1991 whose mothers were employed at least part time outside the home. The most common pattern is

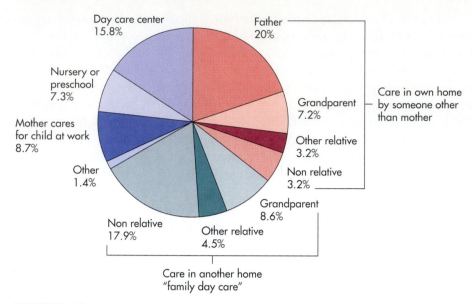

FIGURE 6.3

Child care arrangements for children 5 and under in the United States in 1991. The most common arrangement is what is usually called *family day care*, that is, care in someone else's home. (Source: U.S. Bureau of the Census, 1993, Table 610.)

obviously for a child to be cared for in another person's home, most often by another mother who takes in a few children for care—a pattern usually called **family day care.** Care in the child's own home by someone other than a parent is next most common, with day-care *centers* actually relatively unusual. This pattern varies somewhat with age. Among 3- and 4-year-olds, center care is the most frequent choice; for infants under one year of age, care by a relative and family day care are much more common (Hayes, Palmer, & Zaslow, 1990).

High-quality care is possible in any of these settings, although they do differ from one another in systematic ways. For example, center care typically provides the most cognitive enrichment, while family day-care homes typically provide the least; both center care and family day care give the child an opportunity to play with same-age peers, while at-home care does not (Clarke-Stewart, 1987). Such variations make it very difficult to talk about global effects of day care, because the systems are quite different. Furthermore, the bulk of the research evidence is based on studies of children in center care, and we cannot be sure that these findings will generalize to children in family day care or with at-home care by someone other than a parent.

Effects of Day Care on Cognitive Development

Early research suggested that day care of any variety had little effect of any kind on the cognitive development of children from advantaged families, while children from disadvantaged families often show some cognitive gains (Scarr & Eisenberg, 1993). When the child care is highly cognitively enriched, the latter effect is especially clear (1992; 1993; Ramey, Lee, & Burchinal, 1989).

Several recent studies, however, suggest that this apparently clear conclusion requires some qualification. On the positive side, a study in Sweden, where day care is typically of very high quality, suggests that even middle-class children may benefit intellectually from day care, especially when they begin such care in infancy. Andersson (1992) found that among a large group of 13-year-olds, those who had spent the most time in day-care centers had better school performance throughout elementary school compared to those totally home-reared, or those with only minimal day-care experience.

On the other side, there is a very good, large, new study in the United States (Baydar & Brooks-Gunn, 1991) that suggests exactly the opposite: that white middle-class children who enter child care in the first year of life, compared to those reared at home, do *less* well on cognitive tests at age 3 or 4. Baydar and Brooks-Gunn studied 1,181 3- and 4-year-olds, all children of a nationally representative sample of young adults who have participated in a large longitudinal study—the National Longitudinal Study of Youth. In this large sample, the researchers were able to compare children who had entered day care at various ages with those who had been cared for largely or entirely by parents. They found that among the White children—but *not* among the Black children—those who began some kind of alternative care in the first year of life had the lowest vocabulary scores later in preschool, whether they were from advantaged or poverty level families. The most negative effects were found for White children who began day care between 3 months and 9 months of age, and no negative effects were found for those who entered day care after age 1.

It is not clear how we can reconcile these discrepant findings. Perhaps the quality of care is crucial, especially when the child is under age 1. We do know that most alternative care is not highly cognitively enriched, and this may be especially important early on. Consistency of care—present in Sweden, but perhaps not available to many in the United States—may also be critical. Or perhaps White mothers who return to work soon after their child's birth are different in systematic ways from those who do not—ways that would contribute to the differences in later IQ measures. At this point, we cannot settle the question.

> Of all these possible explanations of the discrepant findings, which one(s) do you think are most likely to be correct? How could you check your hypothesis with research?

Effects of Day Care on Personality

Findings on the impact of day care on children's personality are even more varied. A number of investigators have found that children in day care are more sociable, more popular, and have better peer-play skills than do those reared primarily at home. Andersson found this in his longitudinal study in Sweden (1989; 1992), as have researchers in the United States (Scarr & Eisenberg, 1993). In general, this positive effect seems to be larger for children who enter day care in infancy as opposed to later—precisely the opposite of the Baydar findings for cognitive effects. However, the positive effect of day care on sociability and peer skills seems to hold only for *good-quality* care (Field, 1991; Howes, 1990).

On the negative side of the ledger is the fairly common finding that children who have been in day care, compared to those reared by parents at home, are more aggressive with peers and less compliant with teachers and parents at later ages (Belsky & Eggebeen, 1991; Haskins, 1985). Not everyone reports such an effect, and the level of aggressiveness described by most authors is not extreme. But the very fact that *some* day-care experiences are linked to increased aggressiveness and noncompliance has raised a cautionary note.

Again, how should we interpret such varied findings? By some measures day-care children seem to be *more* socially competent; by other measures, they seem less so. One possibility is that teachers in many day-care centers, in an effort to encourage children to be independent, have also inadvertently reinforced aggressiveness and excessive assertiveness. Maybe. In one day-care center whose children had shown heightened aggressiveness, the center staff deliberately altered its program to emphasize positive social skills. After this change, the heightened aggressiveness disappeared (Finkelstein, 1982).

Alternatively, some have interpreted the aggressiveness as a sign that children in day care learn to think for themselves more, are more independent, and assertive (Clarke-Stewart, 1990; 1992). Others argue that the key may be the quality of the day care, not day care itself, as suggested by the very positive outcomes Field observed for children who had been in stable, good-quality care. Still others, such as Jay Belsky—a psychologist who has generally taken the most pessimistic view of all the findings on day care—conclude that we should take these hints of behavioral maladjustment among children in day care very seriously (Belsky, 1990; 1992) and that they reflect more basic difficulties in the child, such as problems with attachment.

Effects of Day Care on Children's Attachments to Parents

The hottest debate concerns just this question of attachment. Specifically, can an infant or toddler develop a secure attachment to her mother or father if she is repeatedly separated from them? We know that the majority of infants develop secure attachments to their fathers, even though the father typically goes away every day to work, so it is clear that such regular separations do not *preclude* secure attachment. Still, perhaps separation from both parents on a daily basis might adversely affect the security of the child's attachment.

We can narrow the window of uncertainty a good deal if we consider the child's age at the time she or he first enters day care. All parties to the current dispute agree that children who enter day care after the first year of life show *no* consistent loss of security of attachment to their parents. Where there is disagreement is about those infants who enter day care before 12 months of age.

Only when babies enter day care before age 1, as some of these youngsters seem to have done, is there a slightly increased likelihood of an insecure attachment. There is still a major dispute about how to interpret this finding.

Until about a decade ago, most psychologists reading the relevant research had concluded that there was no negative effect of infant day care. But then Belsky, in a series of papers and in testimony before a Congressional committee, sounded an alarm (Belsky, 1985; 1987; 1990; 1992; Belsky & Rovine, 1988). Combining data from several studies, he concluded that there was a heightened risk of an insecure attachment among infants who enter day care before their first birthday. Controversy erupted. Since that time, a number of other researchers have analyzed the combined results from larger numbers of studies and confirmed Belsky's original conclusion.

Summing across the findings from 13 different studies involving 897 infants, Michael Lamb (Lamb, Sternberg, & Prodromidis, 1992) finds that 35 percent of infants who had experienced at least 5 hours per week of nonmaternal care were insecurely attached, compared to 29 percent of the infants with exclusively non-maternal care—a finding I mentioned briefly in Chapter 2. He also found that the risk of an insecure attachment did *not* rise as the number of hours of the mother's employment increased. That is, babies whose mothers worked 40 hours a week, or 20 hours a week were not more likely to be insecurely attached than those whose mothers worked 5 hours a week.

This is clearly not a huge difference, although it is statistically significant. The present controversy swirls around how to interpret or explain this difference.

Belsky has his supporters. Alan Sroufe, one of the major figures in studies of early attachment, points out that we know that security of attachment is fostered both by the child's sense of the responsiveness of care, and by the opportunity for parent and child to fine-tune their interactive dance. Both of these may be disrupted by placing the child in day care, although clearly in the majority of cases, parents find ways to counteract such disruptions, because the majority of children in day care are nonetheless securely attached (Sroufe, 1990).

On the other side of the argument are ranged a group of researchers who either don't believe that there is a serious problem or who argue that there are so many confounding variables that it is impossible to draw any clear conclusion. For one thing, there is a serious problem of self-selection involved in any comparison of day-care and parent-reared infants. Mothers who work are different in other ways from mothers who do not. More are single mothers, more prefer to

The Need for a Family Policy in the United States

In a recent paper, Louise Silverstein (1991) makes a number of compelling points:

> In 1990, fewer than 7% of American families reflected the two-parent model of husband as breadwinner and mother as homemaker (Braverman, 1989). Thus, the question of *whether* mothers should work is essentially irrelevant to modern family life. Mothers *do* work, and "child care is now as essential to family life as the automobile and the refrigerator" (Scarr, 1990, p. 26). (p. 1028) . . .

> However, the United States remains the only one of 75 industrialized nations that does not have a government-sponsored family policy that provides some form of paid maternity benefits, parental leave, and subsidized child care (p. 1025).

Silverstein's central argument is that psychologists have contributed to this lack of official support for the modern family by continuing to focus so much research attention on the question of the potential ill effects of mothers' employment or of day care. Instead, she argues, we must devote our research attention to the "negative consequences of the lack of affordable, government-subsidized, high-quality programs" (p. 1030).

A panel convened by the National Academy of Sciences to study child care in the United States, echoes these concerns. Its basic conclusions include:

> 1. Existing child care services in the United States are inadequate to meet current and likely future needs of children, parents, and society as a whole. . . . The general accessibility of high-quality, affordable child care has immediate and long-term implications for the health and well-being of children, parents, and society as a whole. . .

> 2. Of greatest concern is the large number of children who are presently cared for in settings that do not protect their health and safety and do not provide appropriate developmental stimulation" (Hayes et al., 1990, p. xii).

Assuming that these statements are accurate, what do you think we ought to do about it? What new policies or programs would we need?

What other differences might you expect between working and nonworking mothers of infants? How might those differences affect the likelihood that a child would be securely or insecurely attached?

work or find child care onerous. So how can we be sure that any heightened probability of insecure attachment is due to the day-care experience and not to other experiences?

There may also a problem with using the Strange Situation as a measure of attachment security for children in day care. To assess security, the child must be at least mildly stressed—otherwise we simply don't see enough attachment behaviors to make a judgment. A child in day care, who is used to repeated separations from Mom, may simply not experience the episodes of the Strange Situation as stressful and thus may show behavior that looks like avoidance but is really an indication of relative comfort in the situation (Clarke-Stewart, 1990).

For these and other reasons, Alison Clarke-Stewart (1990) concludes that "at the present time. . . it is not appropriate to interpret the difference, as Belsky appears to, as suggesting that these children are emotionally insecure" (p. 69). Others have concluded that there may indeed be a link between some aspect of day care and security of attachment, but that we simply don't yet know what the link might be (Lamb et al., 1992).

One can also argue that Belsky is asking the wrong question. For the vast majority of families, the question is not "Should I put my child in day care?" but rather: "Given that I have to work to help support my family, how do I find good quality, affordable care for my child?"

We do know that the quality of the child's care makes a difference. Indeed, most of the positive outcomes of day care I have been describing occur *only* in high-quality programs, while inconsistent care or poor quality custodial care can be actively detrimental to the child. In Table 6.3 I've listed the characteristics of good quality programs, a list that might serve as a starting point in your evaluation of alternatives if and when you face this choice with your own children.

TABLE 6.3
Ideal Characteristics of a Day-Care Setting

- **A low teacher/child ratio:** For children younger than 2, the ratio should be no higher than 1:4; for 2- to 3-year-olds, ratios between 1:4 and 1:10 appear to be fine.
- **A small group size.** The smaller the number of children cared for together—whether in one room in a day-care center or in a home—the better for the child. For infants, a maximum of 6 to 8 per group appears best; for 1- to 2-year olds, between 6 and 12 per group; for older children, groups as large as 15 or 20 appear to be o.k.
- **A stable relationship with a single caregiver.**
- **A clean, colorful space, adapted to child play.** Lots of expensive toys are not critical, but there must be a variety of activities that children will find engaging, organized in a way that encourages play.
- **A daily plan with at least some structure, some specific teaching, some supervised activities.** Too much regimentation is not ideal, but children are better off with *some* structure.
- **A caregiver with some knowledge of child development.**
- **A caregiver who is positive, involved, and responsive to the child, not merely a custodian.**

Sources: Clarke-Stewart, 1992; Howes, Phillips & Whitebook, 1992; Scarr & Eisenberg, 1993.

SUMMARY

1. Most parents are delighted with their new baby, but marital satisfaction does typically decline somewhat after the birth of the first child.

2. The majority of women experience a period of "the blues" after giving birth; a minority suffer a more serious postpartum depression.

3. In attachment theory, an important distinction is made between an affectional bond (an enduring tie to a uniquely viewed partner) and an attachment, which additionally involves the element of security and a safe base. An attachment is deduced from the existence of attachment behaviors.

4. The parents' bond to the infant may develop in two phases, but the second of these appears to be far more significant than the first: (1) An initial strong bond may form in the first hours of the child's life (2) the bond is strengthened by the repetition of mutually reinforcing and interlocking attachment behaviors.

5. A failure of parents to form a bond to the infant can occur either because the infant lacks the needed enticing skills or the parent lacks skills. In either case the consequence may be neglect or abuse.

6. Fathers as well as mothers form strong bonds to their infants, but fathers show more playful behaviors with their children than do mothers.

7. Bowlby proposed that the child's attachment to the caregiver develops through a series of steps, beginning with rather indiscriminate aiming of attachment behaviors toward anyone within reach, then through a focus on one or more figures, and finally "secure base behavior," beginning at about 6 months of age, which signals the presence of a clear attachment.

8. In the second half of the first year, babies also typically show fear of strangers and protest at separation from their favored person.

9. Children typically develop strong attachments to both father and mother.

10. Children differ in the security of their first attachments and thus in the internal working model they develop. The secure infant uses the parent as a safe base for exploration and can be readily consoled by the parent.

11. Studies in many countries suggest that a secure attachment is the most common pattern everywhere, but cultures differ in the frequency of different types of insecure attachment.

12. The security of the initial attachment is reasonably stable; contingent responsiveness and parental acceptance fosters a secure attachment.

13. Securely attached children appear to be more socially skillful, more curious and persistent in approaching new tasks, and more mature.

14. There is no one-to-one correspondence between temperament and security or insecurity of attachment.

15. During the second half of the first year, the infant is also developing the first step of a sense of self, the subjective self. The infant understands himself to exist separately and to be able to cause things to happen.

16. In the second year of life the baby develops a sense of self as a lasting object with properties, such as gender and size.

17. The majority of children in the United States now spend some part of their infancy or preschool years in some form of nonparental care. The most common form of such care is family day care.

18. The impact of day care on cognitive development is somewhat unclear, although good-quality day care appears to provide some cognitive benefit to children from poor families. There is similar dispute about the impact on personality. Some studies show children in day care to be more aggressive; others show them to be more socially skillful.

19. Numerous studies show a small difference in security of attachment between children in day care and those reared at home. Interpreting this difference has proven difficult and contentious.

20. The quality of care appears to be a highly significant element. Good quality care involves small groups of children, clean spaces designed for children's play, and responsive caregivers trained in child development.

K E Y   T E R M S

affectional bond
attachment
attachment behaviors
family day-care

insecure attachment
internal working model
objective self
postpartum depression

secure attachment
Strange Situation
subjective self

S U G G E S T E D   R E A D I N G S

Booth, A. (Ed.) (1992). *Child care in the 1990s. Trends and consequences.* Hillsdale, NJ: Erlbaum. If you want to get the day-care debate from the horses' mouths, this is an excellent source. It includes Alison Clarke-Stewart's summary of the effects of day care on children, along with a reply by Belsky and others. If nothing else, this book will persuade you that academic arguments are not always dry and dull; there is plenty of heat here!

Bowlby, J. (1988b). *A secure base.* New York: Basic Books. This splendid small book, Bowlby's last before his recent death, includes a number of his most important papers as well as new chapters that bring his theory up-to-date. See particularly Chapters 7 and 9.

Bretherton, I. (1992a). The origins of attachment theory: John Bowlby and Mary Ainsworth. *Developmental Psychology, 28,* 759–775. A clear, current, and thoughtful review of both Bowlby's and Ainsworth's ideas, including new data from anthropology and other cross-cultural analyses.

Grusec, J. E., & Lytton, H. (1988). *Social development. history, theory, and research.* New York: Springer-Verlag. This is a good basic text on social development. A very good source for further detail on almost any of the topics I've covered in this chapter.

National Research Council (1993). *Understanding child abuse and neglect.* Panel on Research on Child Abuse and Neglect, Commission on Behavioral and Social Sciences and Education. Washington, DC: National Academy Press. This is not light reading but it is an excellent source of current information. It includes chapters on the scope of the problem, etiology, consequences, and treatments.

Schaffer, H. R. (1990). *Making decisions about children. Psychological questions and answers.* Oxford: Basil Blackwell. An unusual and potentially very helpful book. Schaffer has taken up a series of practical questions about children's early development, many of which touch on issues I talked about in this chapter, such as whether early contact is essential for the parent's bond or whether the mother's employment has any detrimental effect on the child. For each question, he summarizes a few key studies and then provides his own conclusion.

Interlude One

Summing Up Infant Development

Because this is the first of these age summaries, let me say a word about their purpose. Because I have organized this book chronologically, with a set of chapters describing each age period, you might think that you will automatically gain a sense of the basic characteristics of each era. But because psychological research tends to focus on only one system at a time, such as attachment, perceptual skills, or language, my descriptions tend to follow the same pattern. In these interludes, I want to try to put the baby (or child or adult) back together, to look at all the threads at once.

BASIC CHARACTERISTICS OF INFANCY

The table overleaf summarizes the various developmental patterns I've described in the past three chapters. The rows in the figure correspond to the various threads of development; what we need to do now is read up and down the figure in addition to looking across the rows.

The overriding impression one gets of the newborn—despite her remarkable skills and capacities—is that she is very much on automatic pilot. There seem to be built-in rules or schemas that govern the way the infant looks, listens, explores the world, and relates to others.

One of the really remarkable things about these rules is how well designed they are to lead both the child and the caregivers into the "dance" of interaction and attachment. Think of an infant being breast-fed. The baby has the necessary rooting, sucking, and swallowing reflexes to take in the milk; in this position, the mother's face is at just about the optimum distance from the baby's eyes for the infant's best focusing. The mother's facial features, particularly her eyes and mouth, are just the sort of visual stimuli that the baby is most likely to look at; the baby is particu-

larly sensitive to the range of sounds of the human voice, particularly the upper register, so the higher-pitched, lilting voice most mothers use is easily heard by the infant.

Sometime around 6 to 8 weeks there seems to be a change, with these automatic, reflexive responses giving way to behavior that looks more volitional. The child now looks at objects differently, apparently trying to identify what an object is rather than merely where it is; at this age she also begins to reliably discriminate one face from another, smiles more, sleeps through the night, and generally becomes a more responsive creature.

These changes in the baby alter the parent-infant interaction patterns as well. As the child stays awake for longer periods, smiles and makes eye contact more, exchanges between parent and child become more playful and smoother-paced.

Somewhere in the middle of the first year, between roughly 6 and 8 months, there seems to be another shift, marked by the emergence of a remarkably wide range of new skills or behaviors: (1) The baby forms a strong central attachment, followed a few months later by separation anxiety and fear of strangers. (2) The infant begins to move around independently (albeit very slowly and haltingly at first). (3) The baby babbles, then begins to use meaningful gestures, to engage in imitative gestural games, and to comprehend individual words. (4) The baby understands, in at least a preliminary way, that objects and people can continue to exist even when they are out of sight. At the very least, these changes profoundly alter the parent–child interactive system, requiring the establishment of a new equilibrium.

The baby continues to build gradually on this set of new skills—learning a few spoken words, learning to walk, consolidating the basic attachment—until 18 or 20

months of age, at which point the child's language and cognitive development appear to take another major leap forward—a set of changes I'll be talking about in chapters yet to come.

CENTRAL PROCESSES

So what is causing all these changes? Any short list of such causes is inevitably going to be a gross oversimplification. Still, undaunted, let me suggest four key processes that seem to me to be shaping the patterns shown in the summary table.

Physical Maturation. First and most obviously, the biological clock is ticking very loudly indeed during these early few months. Only at adolescence, and again in old age, do we see such an obvious maturational pattern at work. In infancy, it is the prepatterned growth of neural dendrites and synapses that appears to be the key. The shift in behavior we see at 2 months, for example, seems to be governed by just such built-in changes, as synapses in the cortex develop sufficiently to control behavior more fully.

Important as this built-in program is, it nonetheless *depends on* the presence of a minimum "expectable" environment (Greenough, Black, & Wallace, 1987). The brain may be wired to create certain synapses, but the process has to be triggered by exposure to particular kinds of experience. Because such a minimum environment exists for virtually all infants, the perceptual, motor, and cognitive developments we see are virtually identical from one baby to the next. But that does not mean that the environment is unimportant.

The Child's Explorations. A second key process is the child's own exploration of the world around her. She is born *ready* to explore, to learn from her experience, but she still has to learn the specific connections between seeing and hearing, to tell the differences between Mom's face and someone else's, to pay attention to the sounds emphasized in the language she is hearing, to discover that her actions have consequences, and on and on.

Clearly, physiological maturation and the child's own exploration are intimately linked in a kind of perpetual feedback loop. The rapid changes in the nervous system, bones, and muscles, permit more and more exploration, which in turn affects the child's perceptual and cognitive skills,

which in turn affects the architecture of the brain.

For example, there is now a good deal of evidence that the ability to crawl—a skill that rests on a whole host of maturationally-based physical changes—profoundly affects the baby's understanding of the world. Before the baby can move independently, he seems to locate objects only in relation to his own body; after he can crawl, he begins to locate objects with reference to fixed landmarks (Campos & Bertenthal, 1989). This shift, in turn, probably con-

tributes to the infant's growing understanding of himself as an object in space.

Attachment. A third key process seems obviously to be the relationship between the infant and the caregiver(s). I am convinced that Bowlby is right about the built-in *readiness* of all infants to create an attachment. But in this domain, the quality of the specific experience the child encounters seems to have a more formative effect than is true for other aspects of development. A wide range of environments are

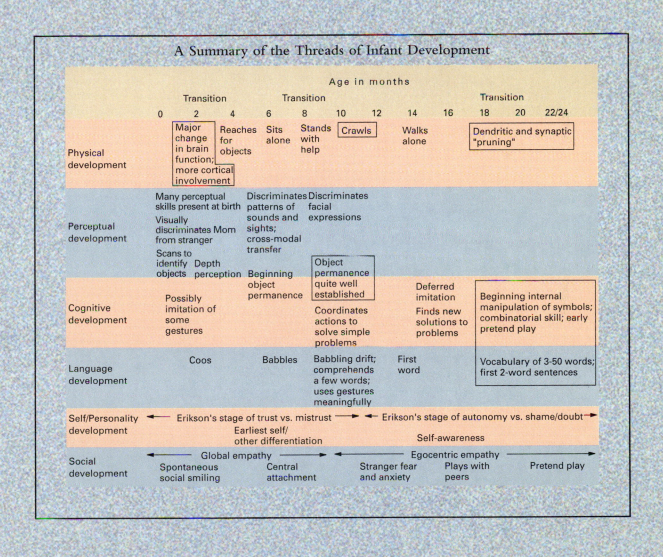

A Summary of the Threads of Infant Development

"good enough" to support physical, perceptual, and cognitive growth in these early months. But for the establishment of a secure central attachment, the acceptable range seems to be narrower.

Still, attachment does not develop along an independent track. Its emergence is linked both to maturational change and to the child's own exploration. For example, the child's understanding of object permanence may be a necessary precondition for the development of a basic attachment. As John Flavell puts it, "how ever could a child persistently yearn and search for a specific other person if the child were still cognitively incapable of mentally representing that person in the person's absence?" (1985, p. 135).

We might also turn this hypothesis on its head and argue that the process of establishing a clear attachment may cause, or at least affect, the child's cognitive development. For example, securely attached youngsters appear to persist longer in their play and develop the object concept more rapidly (Bates et al., 1982). Such a connection might exist because the securely attached child is simply more comfortable exploring the world around him from the safe base of his secure person. He thus has a richer and more varied set of experiences, which may stimulate more rapid cognitive (and neurological) development.

Internal Working Models. We could also think of attachment as being a subcategory of a broader process, namely the creation of internal working models. Seymour Epstein (1991) proposes that what the baby is doing is nothing less than beginning to create a "theory of reality." In Epstein's view, such a theory includes at least four elements:

- A belief about the degree to which the world is a place of pleasure or pain;
- A belief about the extent to which the world is meaningful—predictable, controllable and just versus capricious, chaotic, or uncontrollable;
- A belief about whether people are desirable or threatening to relate to;
- A belief about the worthiness or unworthiness of the self.

The roots of this theory of reality, so Epstein and others argue (Bretherton,

1991), lie in the experiences of infancy, particularly the experiences with caregivers and other humans. Indeed, Epstein suggests that the beliefs created in infancy are likely to be the most basic, and therefore the most durable and resistant to change at later ages. Not all psychologists would agree with Epstein about the broadness of the infant's "theory" of reality. But virtually all would now agree that the baby begins to create at least two significant internal models, one of the self and one of relationships with others (attachment). Of the two, the attachment model seems to be the most fully developed at 18 or 24 months; the model of the self undergoes many elaborations in the years that follow. It is only at about age 6 or 7 that the child seems to have a sense of his *global* worth—a characteristic we usually call self-esteem (Harter, 1987; 1990).

INFLUENCES ON THE BASIC PROCESSES

Perhaps the most important thing for you to remember about infant development is how robust and well buffered it is (Masten, Best, & Garmezy, 1990). Nonetheless, several kinds of circumstances can deflect infants from this common trajectory.

Organic Damage. The most obvious potential influence is some kind of damage to the physical organism, either from genetic anomalies, inherited disease, or teratogenic effects in utero. But even here, there is an interaction between nature and nurture. Recall from Chapter 3 that the long-term consequences of such damage may be more or less severe, depending on the richness and supportiveness of the environment the baby grows up in.

Family Environment. There are (at least) two ways to analyze the effect of the family environment. On the one hand, we can try to define an "ideal" environment—one that maximally supports, enriches, and furthers optimal development in the infant. Research in this tradition confirms that the ideal environment is one with a variety of objects for the baby to explore, at least some free opportunity to explore, and loving, responsive, and sensitive adults who talk to the infant often and respond to the infant's cues (Bradley et al., 1989).

Alternatively, we can look at the effects of very poor environments. Many theorists such as Horowitz, whose model I showed in Figure 1.4, argue that most environments are sufficient to support normal development. Only environments which deviate widely from the norm will cause serious and lasting problems, especially if the infant brings some vulnerability to the process as well. Severe neglect or abuse would fall into this category, as might deep or lasting depression in a parent or persisting upheaval or stress in family life. Paradoxically, both these ways of looking at the family seem accurate to me. For most aspects of development in infancy, most environments are "good enough" for normal growth. But that does not mean that all babies whose family environment is above the cutoff point will develop optimally. Variations in enrichment, in responsiveness, in loving support affect not only the pattern of attachment, but probably also the child's motivation, the content of his self-concept, his willingness to explore, as well as his specific knowledge. We see the consequences of such differences further down the developmental road, when the child is facing the challenging tasks of school and the demands of relating to other children.

Influences on the Family. I've made the point before, but let me make it again: the baby is embedded in the family, but the family is part of a larger economic, cultural, and social system, all of which can have both direct and indirect effects on the infant. Let me give you just two examples.

The most obvious point is that the parents' overall economic circumstances may have a very wide ranging impact on the baby's life experience. Poor families are less able to provide a safe and secure environment. Their infants are more likely to be exposed to environmental toxins such as lead, less likely to have regular health care, including immunizations, and more likely to have nutritionally inadequate diets. If they place their infant in day care, they may be unable to afford good quality care, and they are more likely to have to shift their baby from one care arrangement to another. Collectively, these are large differences. We do not see the effects immediately; babies reared in poverty-level families do not look much different from babies reared in more affluent circumstances. But the differences begin to be obvious at age 2 or 3 or 4.

Another example, one that cuts across all social classes, is the effect of the parents' own social support on the infant's development. Mothers or fathers who feel that they have adequate support are more likely to have securely attached infants, are better able to handle the extra strain of a low-birth-weight infant or an infant with a difficult temperament (Crockenberg, 1981).

This effect can even be demonstrated experimentally. Jacobson and Frye (1991) randomly assigned 46 poverty-level mothers either to a control group or to participate in an experimental support group that met both prenatally and for the first year after delivery. When Jacobson and Frye evaluated the infants' attachment at 14 months, they found that the babies whose Moms had been in the support group were more securely attached than those whose Moms had had no such special help.

One Last Word. One of the strongest impressions one gets from so much of the current research on babies is that they are far more capable than we had thought. They appear to be born with many more skills, many more templates for handling their experiences. But they are not 6-year-olds, and we need to be careful not to get too carried away with our statements about how much the baby can do. As you will see in the next two chapters, the preschooler makes huge strides in every area.

Chapter Seven

Physical and Cognitive Development from 2 to 6

atch an 18-month-old playing near his Mom or Dad, and you'll notice that he doesn't go too far away. He may also glance at the parent regularly, as if checking to make sure his safe base is still there. Watch the same child a few years later and he is probably playing in a separate room, maybe with a chum. He may call out to Mom or Dad once in a while, asking them to come and see something he has created. He walks with confidence, runs, climbs, chatters, plays with toys in a new way. Changes like this may be less dramatic and obvious than the physical and cognitive changes in infancy, but they are nonetheless profound. In the years from 2 to 6 the child moves from still-dependent toddler, able to communicate only in very primitive ways, to a remarkably competent, communicative, social creature, who is ready to begin school.

Physical Changes Between 2 and 6

In Chapter 4, I chronicled the many rapid changes in the infant's body. When we look at physical changes between 2 and 6 years, the story is much briefer. In the nervous system, new synapses are still formed as the child explores the world more fully and some myelinization still continues. But the rate of change is vastly slower than what occurs in the early months of life.

Similarly, changes in height and weight are far slower in these preschool years than in infancy. Between about age 2 and adolescence, children add about 2 to 3 inches in height and about 6 pounds in weight per year. Children growing up in poverty environments typically gain less in height (Reading, Raybould, & Jarvis, 1993), but for every socioeconomic group—barring frank starvation—there is steady physical growth in these years.

Motor Development

These more gradual changes nonetheless combine to enable the child to make steady progress in motor development. The changes are not so dramatic as the beginning of walking. But they are significant because they enable the toddler and preschooler to acquire skills that markedly increase his independence and exploratory ability.

Table 7.1, which parallels Table 4.3, shows the major locomotor, nonlocomotor, and manipulative skills that emerge in these preschool years. You can see that by age 5 or 6, the child is able to move confidently in all directions, to ride a trike, and to use her hands for quite small motions and actions, including picking up, holding, and using small objects such as pencils or scissors. Children of 5 and 6 also have the hand-eye coordination to kick and bat at balls—abilities that may be important for those parents who are eager to have their children acquire specific sports skills.

Health in the Preschool Years

Those of us who live in countries with relatively low infant and childhood mortality rates are used to thinking of childhood as a basically healthy time. But in fact, 42 percent of the children in the world are born in countries in which one

TABLE 7.1
Milestones of Motor Development from 2 to 6

Age	Locomotor Skills	Nonlocomotor Skills	Manipulative Skills
18–24 mo	Runs (20 mo); walks well (24 mo); climbs stairs with both feet on each	Pushes and pulls boxes or wheeled toys; unscrews lid on a jar; typically has enough sphincter muscle control to be toilet trained at about 20–24 months	Shows clear hand preference; stacks 4 to 6 blocks; turns pages one at a time; picks things up without overbalancing
2–3 yrs	Runs easily; climbs up and down from furniture unaided	Hauls and shoves big toys around obstacles	Picks up small objects, e.g. Cheerios; throws small ball forward while standing
3–4 yrs	Walks upstairs one foot per step; skips on both feet; walks on tiptoe	Pedals and steers a trike; walks in any direction pulling a big toy	Catches large ball between outstretched arms; cuts paper with scissors; holds pencil between thumb and first two fingers
4–5 yrs	Walks up *and* downstairs one foot per step; stands, runs and walks well on tiptoe		Strikes ball with bat; kicks and catches ball; threads beads but not needle; grasps pencil maturely
5–6 yrs	Skips on alternate feet; walks a thin line; slides, swings		Plays ball games quite well; threads needle and sews stitches

Sources: Connolly & Dalgliesh, 1989; The Diagram Group, 1977; Fagard & Jaquet, 1989; Mathew & Cook, 1990; Thomas, 1990.

in five children dies before age 5 (Wegman, 1992), often from readily curable diseases, such as diarrhea. In contrast, in the United States in 1990, only slightly more than one child out of a hundred dies before age 5, and of these, the great majority die in infancy. Less than two children out of a thousand die between the ages of 1 and 5. Still, even in such advantaged circumstances, children do get sick; some die.

Brief sicknesses, such as colds or viruses (called *acute* illnesses by physicians) are common among young children. Preschool children have fewer of these acute illnesses than infants do, but still perhaps six each year (Parmelee, 1986). In contrast, only roughly ten percent of children have any kind of *chronic* illness (an illness lasting 6 months or longer) during childhood (Starfield & Pless, 1980). The most common types are allergies, asthma, visual and hearing impairments, and diabetes (Starfield, 1991).

Another danger for children is accidents. In any given year, about a quarter of all children under 5 in the United States have at least one accident that requires some kind of medical attention (U.S. Bureau of the Census, 1993). Accidents are also the major cause of death between the ages of 1 and 5 (Starfield, 1991). At every age, such accidents are more common among boys

Most kids this age are sick in bed like this about six times a year.

Children who are sick a lot early in life have a higher risk of having health problems in adolescence and adulthood. How many different explanations can you think of for such a link?

than among girls. Among preschoolers, home-based accidents are most common—falls, cuts, accidental poisonings, and the like. Automobile accidents are the second leading source of injuries among children this age, although the rate of serious injury and death from auto accidents has been dropping dramatically in recent years because of new laws mandating the use of restraint devices for infants and toddlers travelling in cars (Christophersen, 1989).

Talking in Sentences: The Next Steps in Language Development

When we left the infant in Chapter 5, he was just beginning to use a few individual words. This is no small accomplishment, but the next step—the construction of sentences—is even more remarkable. The toddler moves with amazing rapidity from single words to complex sentences. By age 3, most children have acquired all the basic tools needed to make conversation (Bloom, 1991).

First Sentences: 18 to 27 Months

The first sentences have several distinguishing features. They are *short*—generally two or three words—and they are *simple*. Nouns, verbs and adjectives are usually included, but virtually all the purely grammatical markers (which linguists call **inflections**) are missing. At the beginning, for example, children learning English do not normally use the *s* for plurals or put the *ed* ending on verbs to make the past tense, nor do they use the *'s* of the possessive or auxiliary verbs like *am* or *do*.

It is also clear that even at this earliest stage children create sentences following rules. Not adult rules, to be sure, but rules nonetheless. They focus on certain types of words and put them together in particular orders. They also manage to convey a variety of different meanings with their simple sentences.

For example, young children frequently use a sentence made up of two nouns, such as *Mommy sock* or *sweater chair* (Bloom, 1973). We might conclude from this that a "two noun" form is a basic grammatical characteristic of early child language. But that misses the complexity. For instance, the child in Bloom's study who said *Mommy sock* said it on two different occasions. The first time was when she picked up her mother's sock and the second was when the mother put the child's own sock on the child's foot. In the first case, *Mommy sock* seems to mean Mommy's sock (a possessive relationship). But in the second instance the child seems to convey "Mommy is putting a sock on me," which is an *agent* (Mommy)-*object* (sock) relationship.

Grammar Explosion: 27 to 36 months

Just as there is a vocabulary explosion following an early, slow beginning, so there is also a grammar explosion following these first simple sentences. Beginning some time between 24 and 36 months of age, most children rather

TABLE 7.2
Examples of Daniel's Simple and More Complex Sentences

Simple Sentences (Age 21 months)	More Complex Sentences (age 23 months)	
a bottle	a little boat	cat there
here bottle	doggies here	boat here
horse doggie	give you the book	it's a boy
broke it	it's a robot	it's cat
it a bottle	little box there	no book
kitty cat	oh cars	oh doggie
Oh a doggie	sit down	this a bucket
poor Daddy	that flowers	there's a boat there
thank you	those little boat	what those?
that hat?	what's that?	what this?
that monkey	where going?	where the boat?
want a bottle		
want bottle		
want that?		

Source: Reprinted by permission of the publisher from "Early patterns of grammatical development" by D. Ingram, in R. E. Stark (Ed.), *Language behavior in infancy and early childhood,* Tables 6 and 7, pp. 344–345. Copyright 1981 by Elsevier Science Publishing Co., Inc.

quickly add many of the inflections and function words. Within a few months, children use plurals, past tenses, auxiliary verbs such as "is" or "does," prepositions, and the like. They also begin to create negative sentences, and to ask questions with the auxiliary verb in the correct order. You can get a feeling for the sound of the change from Table 7.2, which lists some of the sentences of a little boy named Daniel, recorded by David Ingram (1981). The left-hand column lists some of Daniel's sentences at about 21 months of age, when he was still using the simplest forms; the right-hand columns list some of his sentences only 2½ months later (age 23–24 months), when he had shifted into higher gear.

Adding Inflections. Daniel did not add all the inflections at once. In this sample of his speech shown in the Table, he uses only a few, mostly the *s* for plural. It turns out that within each language community, children seem to add inflections and more complex word orders in fairly predictable sequences. Among children learning English, Roger Brown (1973) found that the earliest inflection is most often the *ing* added onto a verb, such as in *I playing* or *doggie running*. Then come (in order) prepositions like *on* and *in*, the plural *s* on nouns, irregular past tenses (such as *broke* or *ran*), possessives, articles (*a* and *the* in English), the *s* that we add to third person verbs such as *he wants*, regular past tenses like *played* and *wanted*, and the various forms of the auxiliary verb, as in *I am not going*.

Questions and Negatives. There are also predictable sequences in the child's developing use of questions and negatives. In each case, the child seems to go through periods when he creates types of sentences that he has not heard adults use, but that are consistent with the particular set of rules he is using. For example, in the development of questions there is a point at which the child gets a *wh* word (who, what, when, where, why) at the front end of a sentence, but doesn't yet have the auxiliary verb put in the right place, such as: *Why it is resting now?* Similarly, in the development of negatives, there is a stage in which the *not* or *n't* or *no* is put in, but the auxiliary verb is omitted, as in *I not crying*, or *there no squirrels*.

Overregularization.   Another intriguing phenomenon of this second phase of sentence construction that underlines the rule-making and rule-following quality of even the earliest sentences is **overregularization** or overgeneralization. In English, this is especially clear in children's creation of past tenses like *wented* or *goed* or *ated*. Stan Kuczaj (1977; 1978) pointed out that young children initially learn a small number of irregular past tenses and use them correctly for a short time. But then rather suddenly the child seems to discover the rule of adding *ed* and overgeneralizes this rule to all verbs. Then they relearn the exceptions one at a time. Even among preschoolers this type of "error" is not hugely common (only about 2 to 3 percent of all past tenses in English, according to one recent study (Marcus et al., 1992)). But these overregularizations stand out because they are so distinctive, and because they illustrate yet again that children create forms that they have not heard but that are logical within their current grammar.

Complex Sentences: 36 to 48 Months

After children have figured out the inflections and basic sentence forms like negation and questions, they soon begin to create remarkably complex sentences, with embedded clauses, tag questions, and sentences combined with conjunctions like *and* and *but*. Here are some examples from de Villiers and de Villiers (1992).

> "I didn't catch it but Teddy did!"
> "I'm gonna sit on the one you're sitting on."
> "Where did you say you put my doll?"
> "Those are punk rockers, aren't they?"

When you remember that only about 18 months earlier, the child had been saying little more complex than *see doggie* you can appreciate how far he has come in a short time.

The Development of Word Meaning

To understand language development, it is not enough to know how children learn to string words together to form sentences. We also have to understand how the words in those sentences come to have meaning. Linguists are still searching for good ways to describe (or explain) children's emerging word meaning. So far, several sets of questions have dominated the research.

What Comes First, the Meaning or the Word?   The most fundamental question is whether the child learns a word to describe a category or class he has

What I've said in the main text about early language describes what happens when a child learns a *single* language. But what about children who are exposed to two or more languages from the beginning? There are at least two important practical questions surrounding this issue of bilingualism:

- Should parents who speak different native languages try to expose their children to both, or will that only confuse the child and make any kind of language learning harder? What's the best way to do this?

- If a child arrives at school age without speaking the dominant language of schooling, what is the best way for the child to acquire that second language?

LEARNING TWO LANGUAGES AT THE SAME TIME

Parents should have no fears about exposing their child to two or more languages from the very beginning. Such simultaneous exposure does seem to result in slightly slower early steps in word learning and sentence construction, and the child will initially "mix" words or grammar from the two languages in individual sentences (Genesee, 1993). But bilingual children catch up rapidly to their monolingual peers.

The experts agree that the best way to help a child to learn two languages fluently is to speak both languages to the child from the beginning, *especially* if the two languages come at the child from different sources. For example, if Mom's native language is English and Dad's is Italian, Mom should speak only English to the infant/toddler and Dad should speak only Italian. (The parents will of course speak to each other in whatever language they have in common.) If both parents speak both languages to the child, or mix them up in their own speech, this is a much more difficult situation for the child and more "mixing" will occur (McLaughlin, 1984). It will also work if one language is always spoken at home and the other in a day-care center, or with playmates, or in some other outside situation.

BILINGUAL EDUCATION

For many children, the need to be bilingual does not begin in the home, but only at school age. In the United States

The Real World
Bilingual Children

today, there are 2.5 million school-age children for whom English is not the primary language of the home (Hakuta & Garcia, 1989). Many of those children arrive at school with little or no facility in English. Educators have had to grapple with the task of teaching children a second language at the same time that they are trying to teach them subject matter such as reading and mathematics. The problem for the schools has been to figure out the best way to do this. Should the child be immediately immersed in the new language? Should the child learn basic academic skills in his native language and only later learn English as a second language? Or is there some combination of the two that will work?

The research findings are messy. Still, one thread does run through it all: neither full immersion nor English-as-a-second-language programs are as effective as truly bilingual programs in which the child is given at least some of her basic instruction in subject matter in her native language in the first year or two of school, but is also exposed to the second language in the same classroom (Padilla et al., 1991; Willig, 1985). After several years of such combined instruction, the child then makes a rapid transition to full use of the second language for all instruction. Interestingly, in her analysis of this research, Ann Willig has found that the ideal arrangement is very much like what works best at home with toddlers: if some subjects are always taught in one language and other subjects in the other language children learn both most easily. But if each sentence is translated, children do not learn the new language as quickly or as well.

Note, though, that even such ideal bilingual education programs will not be effective for children who come to school without good spoken language in their native tongue. Learning to read, in any language, requires that the child have a fairly extensive awareness of the structure of language —a point I'll be exploring more fully in Chapter 9. Any child who lacks such awareness— because she has been exposed to relatively little language, was not read to or talked to in infancy and preschool years—will have difficulty learning to read, whether the instruction is given in the native language or in English.

already created through his manipulations of the world around him or whether the existence of a word forces the child to create new cognitive categories. This may seem like a highly abstract argument, but it touches on the fundamental issue of the relationship between language and thought. Does the child learn to

Does this 18-month-old know the word *doll* because she first had a concept of doll and later learned the word, or did she learn the word first and then create a category or concept to go with the word?

To many students, discussions of the relationship between language and thought seem abstruse and uninteresting. See if you can put into your own words why this issue might be important or interesting. Can you think of a reason, in real life, why it would matter whether language or thought dominates?

represent objects to himself *because* he now has language, or does language simply come along at about this point and make the representations easier?

Not surprisingly, the answer seems to be both (Clark, 1983; Cromer, 1991; Greenberg & Kuczaj, 1982). On the cognitive side of the argument are several pieces of evidence I described in Chapter 5, such as the fact that young babies are able to remember and imitate objects and actions over periods of time—long before they have language to assist them.

The naming explosion may also rest on new cognitive understandings, in particular the new ability to categorize things. In several studies, Alison Gopnik and Andrew Meltzoff (1987; 1992) have found that the naming explosion typically occurs just after, or at the same time as, children first show spontaneous categorization of mixed sets of objects. Having discovered "categories," the child may now rapidly learn the names for already existing categories. But at the same time, once the child now understands in some primitive way that names refer to categories, then learning a new name suggests the existence of a new category (Waxman & Hall, 1993), and thus the name affects the child's thinking.

Extending the Class.   What kind of concepts does the child start with? Suppose your 2-year-old, on catching sight of the family tabby, says, "*See kitty.*" No doubt you will be pleased that the child has the right word applied to the animal. But what does the word "kitty" mean to the child? Does he think it is a name only for that particular fuzzy beast? Or does he think it applies to all furry creatures, all things with four legs, things with pointed ears, or what?

One way to figure out the kind of class or category the child has created is to see what other creatures or things he also calls *kitty*. That is, we can ask how the class is *extended* in the child's language. If the child has a kitty category based on furriness then many dogs and perhaps sheep would also be called kitty. If having a tail is a crucial feature, then she might exclude sheep, as well as some breeds of cat. Or perhaps the child uses the word kitty only for the family cat. This would imply a very narrow category indeed. The general question for researchers has been whether children tend to use words narrowly or broadly, overextending or underextending them.

Our current information tells us that underextension is most common at the earliest stages, particularly before the naming explosion (Harris, 1992)—although even at this early point, overextension also can occur. Once the naming explosion starts, however, overextension seems to be more common. At that stage, we're more likely to hear the word cat applied to dogs or guinea pigs than we are to hear the child use it for just one animal or for a very small set of animals or objects (Clark, 1983). All children seem to show overextensions, but the particular classes the child creates are unique to each child. One child observed by Eve Clark used the word *moon* for cake, round marks on windows, writing on windows and in books, round shapes in books, tooling in leather book covers, round postmarks, and the letter *O*. Another used the word *ball* to refer to toy balls, radishes, and stone spheres at park entrances, while another child used the word *ball* to refer to apples, grapes, eggs, squash, and a bell clapper (Clark, 1975).

These overextensions *may* tell us something about the way children think, such as, that they have broad classes. But linguists like Clark remind us that part of the child's problem is that he simply doesn't know very many words—a state of affairs with which I have a lot of sympathy, having spent many months in Germany trying to speak intelligently with a vocabulary of about 1,000 words! A child who wants to call attention to a horse may not know the word horse, so may say "dog" instead. Overextensions may thus arise from the child's desire to communicate and may not tell us that the child fails to make the discriminations involved (Clark, 1977; 1987).

Parents may also contribute to a child's overextensions. Carolyn and Cynthia Mervis (1982) found that mothers use the labels that they think the child will understand, rather than using the more precise labels. So they may call leopards and lions "kitty cats" or a toy fire engine a "car." Such a pattern may aid communication between mother and child, but it also may contribute to what we hear as overextensions in the child's early language.

Constraints on Word Learning.   One of the most fundamental questions about word meanings, the subject of hot debate among linguists in recent years, is just how a child figures out which part of some scene a word may refer to. The classic example: A child sees a brown dog running across the grass with a bone in its mouth. An adult points and says *doggie*. From such an encounter the toddler is somehow supposed to figure out that *doggie* refers to the animal, and not to running, bone, dog-plus-bone, brownness, ears, grass, or any other combination of elements in the whole scene.

Many linguists have proposed that a child could only conceivably cope with this monumentally complex task if he operated with some built-in biases or *constraints* (Markman, 1989; Markman, 1992; Waxman & Kosowski, 1990; Woodward & Markman, 1991). For example, the child may have a built-in initial

If Dad says "goose" while he and his toddler are looking at this scene, how does the boy know that "goose" means the animal and not "white," or "dirt," or "honk honk," or some other feature? In fact, in this case as in most instances, the child first *points* and then the father labels, which greatly simplifies the problem.

assumption that words refer to objects *or* events but not both, or an assumption that words refer to whole objects and not to their parts or attributes. Toddlers of 19 to 20 months, for example, already know that if you point at something and give a word, it is the label for that object, not a name for some other feature of the scene (Baldwin, 1993).

Another possible built-in assumption or constraint is the *principle of contrast*, namely that every word has a different meaning, so if a different word is used, it must refer to some different object or a different aspect of an object (Clark, 1990). For example, in a widely quoted study, Carey and Bartlett (1978) interrupted a play session with 2- and 3-year-old children by pointing to two trays and saying, "bring me the chromium tray, not the red one, the chromium one." These children already knew the word *red* but did not know the word *chromium*. Nonetheless, most of the children were able to follow the instruction by bringing the nonred tray. Furthermore, a week later about half of the children remembered that the word chromium referred to some color, and that the color was "not red." Thus they learned the meaning by contrast.

The majority of linguists today appear to accept the idea of built-in constraints (Maratsos, 1992). Doubters, such as Katherine Nelson (1988), point out that most of the research on language constraints has been done with children who were well past the one-word stage of language. It is possible that such biases, if they exist, are not built in but emerge as the child is learning language. Furthermore, Nelson suggests that the child rarely encounters a situation in which the adult points vaguely and gives some word. By far the most common scenario is that the parent follows the child's lead, labeling things the child is already playing with or pointing at (Harris, 1992). In fact, children's whose parents do more of such responsive, specific labeling seem to learn language somewhat faster (Dunham, Dunham, & Curwin, 1993; Harris, 1992). To the extent that this is true, then the constraints on the process may be the child's own conceptual system and the ability of the adult to interpret the child's meaning, rather than some built-in tendencies within the child.

On the basis of this very brief presentation, do you find yourself persuaded by Clark's constraint argument or Nelson's counterargument? What more would you want to know?

Using Language: Communication and Self-Direction

In the past decade or so, linguists have also turned their attention to a third aspect of children's language, namely the way children learn to *use* speech, either to communicate with others (an aspect of language linguists call **pragmatics**) or to regulate their own behavior.

Language Pragmatics.   Children seem to learn the pragmatics of language at a remarkably early age. For example, children as young as 18 months show adult-like gaze patterns when they are talking with a parent: they look at the person who is talking, look away at the beginning of their own speaking turn, and then look at the listener again when they are signaling that they are about to stop talking (Rutter & Durkin, 1987).

Furthermore a child as young as 2 years adapts the form of his language to the situation he is in or the person he is talking to. He might say "gimme" to another toddler as he grabs the other child's glass, but might say "more milk" to an adult (Becker, 1982). Among older children, language is even more clearly

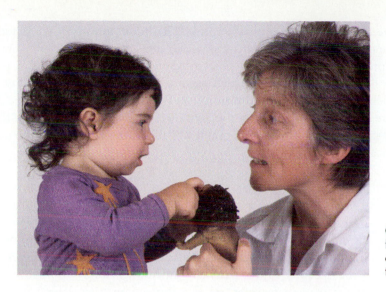

Clare, at 20 months, already follows some of the social rules of conversation, such as taking turns and gaze patterns.

adapted to the listener: 4-year-olds use simpler language when they talk to 2-year-olds than when they talk to adults (Tomasello & Mannle, 1985). Thus from very early, probably from the beginning, the child's language is meant to *communicate*, and the child adapts the form of his language in order to achieve better communication.

Language and Self-Control.   Children also use language to help control or monitor their own behavior. Such "private speech," which may consist of more fragmentary sentences, muttering, or instructions to the self, is detectable from the earliest use of words and sentences. For example, when 2- or 3-year-olds play by themselves, they give themselves instructions, stop themselves with words, or describe what they are doing: "No, not there." "I put that there," or "put it" (Furrow, 1984). Such self-regulatory language has largely gone "underground" by age 9 or 10, but we can still hear it in older children—even in adults—when they are working on hard problems (Bivens & Berk, 1990).

Even this brief foray into the research on the child's use of language points out that a full understanding of language development is going to require understanding of both cognitive development and of the child's social skills and understanding. It reminds us once again that the child is not divided up into tidy packages labeled "physical development," "social development," or "language development," but is a coherent, integrated system.

> Does this sound familiar? I talk to myself when I'm trying to figure out how to get some reluctant machine to work. Under what conditions do you use language this way?

Explaining Language Development

Explaining how a child learns language has proven to be one of the most compelling, and one of the most difficult, challenges within developmental psychology. This may surprise you. I suspect that most of you just take for granted that a child learns to talk by listening to the language she hears. What is magical or complicated about that? Well the more you think about it, the more amazing and mysterious it becomes. For one thing, as Steven Pinker (1987) points out, there is a veritable chasm between what the child hears as language input and the language the child must eventually speak. The input consists of some set of sentences spoken to the child, with intonation, stress, and timing. They are spoken in the presence of objects and events, and the words are given in a particular order. All that may be helpful, even essential. But what the child must acquire from such input is nothing less than a set of rules for *creating* sentences. And the rules are not directly given in the sentences she hears. How does the child accomplish this feat? Theories abound. Let me start on the nurture end of the theoretical continuum.

Imitation and Reinforcement.   The earliest theories of language acquisition were based either on learning theory or on the common sense idea that language was learned by imitation. Imitation obviously has to play some part, because the child learns the language she hears. Babbling drifts toward the sounds in the heard language; children imitate sentences they hear; they learn to speak with the accent of their parents. And those babies who show the most imitation of actions and gestures are also those who learn later language most quickly (Bates et al., 1982). So the tendency to imitate may be an important ingredient. Still, imitation alone can't explain the fact that children consistently create types of sentences and forms of words that they have never heard—words like *goed* or *beated*.

Reinforcement theories such as Skinner's (1957) fare no better. Skinner argued that parents shape language through systematic reinforcements, gradually rewarding better and better approximations of adult speech. But in fact there is little evidence that parents do anything like this. Instead, parents are remarkably forgiving of all sorts of peculiar constructions and meaning (Brown & Hanlon, 1970; Hirsh-Pasek, Trieman, & Schneiderman, 1984). In addition, children learn many forms of language, such as plurals, with relatively few errors, so some process other than shaping has to be involved.

Newer Environmental Theories: Talking to the Child.   Still, it seems obvious that what is said to the child has to play *some* role in the process. At the simplest level, we know that children whose parents talk to them often, read to them regularly, and respond to the child's own verbalizations have children who begin to talk a little sooner. So at least the *rate* of development is affected by the amount of input.

The quality of the parents' language may also be important. In particular, we know that adults talk to children in a special kind of very simple language, often called **motherese**—a pattern I mentioned briefly in Chapter 1. This simple language is spoken in a higher-pitched voice, and at a slower pace, than is talk between adults. The sentences are short, with simple, concrete vocabulary, and they are grammatically simple. When speaking to children, parents also repeat a lot, with minor variations ("Where is the ball? Can you see the ball? Where is the ball? There is the ball!"). They may also repeat the child's sentence but in a slightly longer, more grammatically correct form—a pattern referred to as an *expansion* or a *recasting*.

Parents don't talk this way to children in order to teach them language. They do so with the hope that they will communicate better that way. But it may

R E S E A R C H   R E P O R T

The Importance of Reading to the Child

One intriguing piece of evidence showing the importance of the child's environment in early language learning is a study that G. J. Whitehurst and his colleagues conducted (Whitehurst et al., 1988). They trained some parents to read picture books to their toddlers and to interact with them in a special way during the reading, a pattern they called *dialogic* reading. Specifically, the researchers trained parents to use questions that children could not answer just by pointing. So a mother reading Winnie the Pooh might say, "There's Eeyore. What's happening to him?" Or the parent might ask, pointing to some object shown in a book, "What's the name of that?" or inquire about some character in a story, such as, "Do you think the kitty will get into trouble?" The researchers encouraged parents in a control group to read to the child, but gave them no special instructions. After a month, the children in the experimental group had shown a larger gain in vocabulary than had the children in the comparison group.

Whitehurst has now replicated this study in Mexico (Valdez-Menchaca & Whitehurst, 1992). One teacher in a day-care center received training in dialogic reading. She then spent 10 minutes each day reading with each of 10 2-year-olds, all from working-class families. This continued for a period of 6 to 7 weeks. A comparison group of children in the same day-care center spent an equivalent amount of time with the same teacher each day, but these children received arts and crafts instruction rather than reading. At the end of the intervention, the children who had been read to had higher vocabulary scores on a variety of standardized tests and used more complex grammar in a special test conversation with another adult than did the children in the group receiving arts and crafts instruction.

The fact that Whitehurst finds the same types of effects in two different cultures, with two different languages, strengthens the argument that richer interactive language between parent and child is one ingredient in fostering the child's language growth.

---

well be very useful, even necessary, for the child's language acquisition. We know, for example, that some kind of higher-pitched, simplified, repetitious language to babies and children occurs in virtually all cultures and language communities.

We also know that babies as young as a few days old can discriminate between motherese and adult-directed speech and *that they prefer to listen to motherese*, whether it is spoken by a female or a male voice (Cooper & Aslin, 1990; Pegg, Werker, & McLoed, 1992). In particular, it seems to be the higher pitch of motherese that babies prefer. Once the child's attention is drawn by this special tone, the very simplicity and repetitiveness of the adult's speech may help the child to pick out repeating grammatical forms.

Children's attention also seems to be drawn to recast sentences. In one recent study, for example, Farrar (1992) found that 2-year-old children were two to three times as likely to imitate a correct grammatical form after they had heard their mother recast their own sentences than they were when that same correct grammatical form appeared naturally in the mother's conversation. Experimental studies confirm this effect of recastings. Children who are deliberately exposed to higher rates of specific types of recast sentences seem to learn those grammatical forms more quickly (Nelson, 1977).

Sounds good, doesn't it? But there are some holes in this theory. For one thing, while children who hear more expansions learn grammar sooner, children who rarely hear such forms nonetheless acquire a complex grammar, albeit more slowly. And while motherese does seem to occur in the vast majority of cultures and contexts, it does not occur in *all*. For example, Pye (1986) could find no sign of motherese in one Mayan culture, and studies in the United States show it is greatly reduced among depressed mothers (Bettes, 1988). Children of these mothers nonetheless learn language. Thus while motherese may be helpful, it cannot be *necessary* for language.

Innateness theories.   On the other side of the theoretical spectrum we have the innateness theorists who argue that much of what the child needs for learning language is built into the organism. Early innateness theorists like Noam Chomsky (1965; 1975; 1986; 1988) were especially struck by two phenomena: the extreme complexity of the task the child must accomplish, and the apparent similarities, across languages and across children, in the steps and stages of children's early language. Newer cross-language comparisons now make it clear that there is more variability than first appeared—a set of findings I've described in the *Cultures and Contexts* box on page 203. Nonetheless, innateness theories are alive and well and highly influential.

One influential current innateness theorist is Dan Slobin (1985a; 1985b). Slobin assumes a basic language-making capacity in any child, made up of a set of fundamental *operating principles*. Just as the newborn infant seems to come programmed "with rules to look by," so Slobin is arguing that infants and children are programmed "with rules to listen by."

You've already encountered a good deal of evidence in Chapter 5 that is consistent with this proposal. We know that from earliest infancy, babies focus on individual sounds and on syllables in the stream of sounds they hear, that they pay attention to sound rhythm, and that they prefer speech of a particular pattern, namely motherese. Slobin also proposes that babies are preprogrammed to pay attention to the beginnings and endings of strings of sounds and to stressed sounds. Together, these operating principles would help to explain some of the features of children's early grammars.

The fact that this model is consistent with the growing information about apparently built-in perceptual skills and processing biases is certainly a strong argument in its favor. But it is still early days in the exploration of this approach, and there are other compelling alternatives. In particular, there are theorists who argue persuasively that what is important are not the built-in biases, but the child's *construction* of language as part of the broader process of cognitive development. In this view, the child is a "little linguist," applying her emerging cognitive understanding to the problem of language, searching for regularities and patterns.

Constructivist Theories of Language.   Melissa Bowerman (1985) is the clearest proponent of this view. She puts the proposition this way: "When language starts to come in, it does not introduce new meanings to the child. Rather, it is used to express only those meanings the child has already formulated independently of language" (1985, p. 372).

If this is true, then we should observe clear links between achievements in language development and the child's broader cognitive development. And, in

CULTURES & CONTEXTS

Universals and Variations in Early Language

In the early years of research on children's language development, linguists and psychologists were strongly impressed by the apparent similarities across languages in children's early language. You've already seen some of the evidence that supports this impression in an earlier *Cultures and Contexts* box in Chapter 5, illustrating large similarities in early vocabularies. Studies in a wide variety of language communities, including Turkish, Serbo-Croatian, Hungarian, Hebrew, Japanese, Kaluli (a New Guinean language), German, and Italian, have revealed other important similarities in early language:

- The prelinguistic phase seems to be identical in all language communities. All babies coo, then babble; all babies understand language before they can speak it; babies in all cultures begin to use their first words at about 12 months.

- In all language communities that linguists have studied so far, a one-word phase precedes the two-word phase, with the latter beginning at about 18 months.

- In all languages researchers have studied so far, children add prepositions describing locations in essentially the same order. Children learn the words for *in*, *on*, *under* and *beside* first. Then the child learns the words *front* and *back* (Slobin, 1985a).

- Children seem to pay more attention to the ends of words than the beginnings, so they learn suffixes before they learn prefixes.

At the same time, cross-linguistic comparisons show that children's beginning sentences are not nearly so similar as the early innateness theorists had supposed. For example:

- The specific word order that a child uses in early sentences is not the same for all children in all languages. In some languages a noun/verb sequence is fairly common, in others a verb/noun sequence may be heard.

- Children learn particular inflections in highly varying orders from one language to another. Japanese children, for example, begin very early to use a special kind of marker, called a *pragmatic* marker, which tells something about the feeling or the context. For instance, in Japanese, the word *yo* is used at the end of a sentence when the speaker is experiencing some resistance from the listener; the word *ne* is used when the speaker expects approval or agreement. Japanese children begin to use these markers very early, much earlier than other inflections appear in most languages.

- Most strikingly, there are languages where there seems to be no simple two-word sentence stage in which the sentences are without inflections. Children learning Turkish, for example, use essentially the full set of noun and verb inflections by age 2 and never go through a stage of using uninflected words. Their language is simple but it is rarely ungrammatical from the adult's point of view (Aksu-Koc & Slobin, 1985).

Obviously any theory of language acquisition must account for both the common ground and the wide variations from one language to the next.

---

fact, we do. For example, symbolic play such as drinking from an empty cup and imitation of sounds and gestures, both appear at about the same time as the child's first words, suggesting some broad "symbolic" understanding that is reflected in a number of behaviors. In children whose language is significantly delayed, both symbolic play and imitation are normally delayed, too (Bates, O'Connell, & Shore, 1987; Snyder, 1978; Ungerer & Sigman, 1984).

A second example occurs later: at about the point when two-word sentences appear, we can also see children begin to combine several gestures into a sequence in their pretend play, such as pouring imaginary liquid, drinking, then wiping the mouth. Those children who are the first to show such sequencing in their play are also the first to show two-or three-word sentences in their speech (Bates et al., 1987; Brownell, 1988; Shore, 1986).

Obviously, we do not have to choose between Slobin's and Bowerman's approaches. Both may be true. The child may begin with built-in operating principles that aim the child's attention at crucial features of the language input. The child then processes that information according to her initial (perhaps built-in) strategies or schemes. But then she modifies those strategies or rules as she receives new information. The result is a series of rules for understanding and creating language. The strong similarities we see among children in their early language constructions come about both because all children share the same initial processing rules, and because most children are exposed to very similar input from the people around them. But because the input is not identical, because languages differ, language development follows less and less common pathways as the child progresses.

As these brief descriptions of theory make clear, linguists and psychologists who have studied language have clearly made progress. We know a lot more now about how *not* to explain language. But we have not yet cracked the code. The fact that children learn complex and varied use of their native tongue within a few years remains both miraculous and largely mysterious.

The broader changes in the child's cognitive skills over the same years seem less mysterious, but we continue to learn more about the remarkable cognitive accomplishments of the preschool child, as well as the limitations on her thinking.

Changes in Thinking Between 2 and 6

Let me begin, as I did in Chapter 5, with a look at Piaget's view of the cognitive changes during these years, because his thinking has formed the framework of so much of our research on this age period.

Piaget's View of the Preoperational Period

According to Piaget, at about age 2 the child begins to use *symbols*—images or words or actions that *stand for* something else. What is more, she can now manipulate those symbols mentally. Both these changes mark the beginning of what Piaget calls the **preoperational period.**

We can see this shift clearly in children's pretend play, which I have talked about in the *Research Report* on page 207. Among preschoolers, a broom may become a horsie, or a block may become a train. We can also see such symbol use in the emergence of language at about the same time. And we see the child's improving ability to manipulate these symbols internally in such things as her improving memory or in her ability to search more systematically for lost or hidden objects.

Beyond the accomplishment of symbol use, Piaget focused mostly on all the things the preschool age child still *cannot* do, which gives an oddly negative tone to his description of this period. Even the term he used to describe this stage conveys some of this tone: it is *pre*operational.

For example, Piaget described the preoperational child as one who looks at things entirely from her own perspective, her own frame of reference, a characteristic Piaget called **egocentrism** (Piaget, 1954). The child is not being selfish; rather she simply thinks (assumes) that everyone sees the world as she does.

Figure 7.1 is a photo of a classic experiment illustrating this kind of egocentrism. The child is shown a three-dimensional scene with mountains of different sizes and colors. From a set of drawings, he picks out the one that shows the scene the way he sees it. Most preschoolers can do this without much difficulty. Then the examiner asks the child to pick out the drawing that shows how someone *else* sees the scene, such as the little clay man or the examiner. At this point preschool children have difficulty. Most often they again pick the drawing that shows their *own* view of the mountains (Flavell et al., 1981; Gzesh & Surber, 1985).

Piaget also pointed out that the preschool age child was captured by the appearance of objects—a theme that still dominates the research on children of this age. In Piaget's work, this theme is evident in some of the most famous of his studies, those on **conservation,** which I described in Chapter 2.

His measurement technique involved first showing the child two equal sets or objects, getting the child to agree they were equal in some key respect such as weight or quantity or length or number, and then shifting or deforming one of the objects and asking the child if they were still the same in some way. Children rarely show any type of conservation before age 5, which Piaget took to be a sign that they were still captured by the *appearance* of change and did not focus on the underlying, unchanging aspect.

A third limitation Piaget saw in the preoperational child's thinking was in her ability to classify—to put things together that go together. His observations led him to believe that only at about age 4 does a child begin to group objects consistently into categories or classes, at first using only one dimension (e.g., shape, such as round things versus square things) and later two or more dimensions at once.

FIGURE 7.1
One of the types of experimental arrangements used to study egocentrism in children.

Can you think of any examples of egocentrism in your own behavior? What about buying someone else the gift you were hoping to receive yourself? Other examples?

The 3-year-old on the right is able to adapt her speech and her play to the needs of her blind friend, which is one sign that preschoolers are less egocentric than Piaget thought.

Newer Research on the Preoperational Child

In Chapter 5 I pointed out again and again that Piaget had underestimated babies' abilities to discriminate, compare, and imitate. The same point emerges very strongly from recent research on the thinking of children from ages 2 to 6. A rich and intriguing body of evidence suggests that preschoolers are a great deal less egocentric than Piaget thought. At the same time, it is clear from this newer work that children this age do indeed struggle with the problem of distinguishing between appearance and reality. Let me walk you through some of the evidence.

Perspective Taking and Egocentrism.   Research on the child's ability to take others' perspectives shows that children as young as 2 and 3 have at least *some* ability to understand that other people see things or experience things differently than they do. For example, I already pointed out that children this age will adapt their speech or their play to the demands of their companion. They also play differently with older or younger playmates and talk differently to a younger or a handicapped child (Brownell, 1990; Guralnick & Paul-Brown, 1984).

But such understanding is clearly not perfect at this young age. John Flavell has proposed that there are two levels of such perspective taking ability. At Level 1, the child knows *that* some other person experiences something differently. At Level 2, the child develops a whole series of complex rules for figuring out precisely *what* the other person sees or experiences (Flavell, 1985; Flavell, Green, & Flavell, 1990). Two- and 3-year-olds have Level 1 knowledge but not Level 2. We begin to see some Level 2 knowledge in 4- and 5-year-olds.

Appearance and Reality.   This shift seems to be part of a much broader change in the child's understanding of appearance and reality. Flavell has studied this in a variety of ways such as showing objects under colored lights to change the apparent color or putting masks on animals to make them look like another animal. He finds that 2- and 3-year-olds consistently judge things by their appearance; by 5, the child begins to be able to separate the appearance from the underlying reality and knows that some object isn't "really" red, even though it looks red under a red-colored light, or that a cat with a dog mask is still "really" a cat (Flavell, Green, & Flavell, 1989; Flavell et al., 1987).

In the most famous Flavell procedure, the experimenter shows the child a sponge that has been painted to look like a rock. Three-year-olds, faced with this odd object, will either say that the object looks like a sponge and is a sponge, or it looks like a rock and is a rock. But 4- and 5-year-olds can distinguish the two; they realize it looks like a rock but *is* a sponge (Flavell, 1986). Thus the older child now understands that the same object can be represented differently, depending on one's point of view.

Using the same type of materials, investigators have also asked if a child can grasp the principle of a *false belief*. After the child has felt the sponge/rock and has answered questions about what it looks like and what it "really" is, you can ask something like this: "John [a playmate of the subject's] hasn't touched this, he hasn't squeezed it. If John just sees it over here like this, what will he think it is? Will he think it's a rock or will he think that it's a sponge?" (Gopnik &

Young Children's Play

If you watch young children during their unstructured time you'll see them building towers out of blocks, talking to or feeding their dolls, making "tea" with the tea set, racing toy trucks across the floor, dressing up in grown-up clothes. They are, in a word, *playing*. This is not trivial or empty activity; it is the stuff on which much of the child's cognitive development seems to be built.

The form of this play changes in very obvious ways during the years from 1 to 6, following a sequence that matches Piaget's stages rather well (Rubin, Fein, & Vandenberg, 1983).

Sensorimotor play. The child of 12 months or so spends most of her play time exploring and manipulating objects using all the sensorimotor schemes in her repertoire. She puts things in her mouth, shakes them, moves them along the floor.

Constructive Play. Such exploratory play with objects does continue past 12 months, especially with some totally new object, but by age 2 or so children begin to use objects to build or construct things—creating a block tower, putting together a puzzle, making something out of clay or with tinkertoys. Such "constructive" play makes up nearly half of the play of children aged 3 to 6 (Rubin et al., 1983).

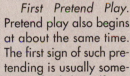

Constructive Play

First Pretend Play. Pretend play also begins at about the same time. The first sign of such pretending is usually something like a child using a toy spoon to "feed" himself or a toy comb to comb his hair. In this early phase children still use toys for their actual or typical purposes (spoon for feeding) and their actions are still oriented to the *self*, but there is pretend involved. Between 15 and 21 months, there is a shift: the recipient of the pretend action now becomes another person or a toy, most often a doll. The child is still using objects for their usual purposes (such as drinking from a cup), but now she is using the toy cup with a doll instead of herself. Dolls are especially good toys

for this kind of pretend, because it is not a very large leap from doing things to yourself to doing things with a doll. So children feed dolls imaginary food, comb their hair, soothe them.

First Pretend Play

Substitute Pretend Play. Between 2 and 3 years of age children begin to use objects to stand for something altogether different. They may comb the doll's hair with a baby bottle while saying that it is a comb, or use a broom to be a horsie, or make "trucks" out of blocks. By age 4 or 5, children spend as much as 20 percent of their play time in this new, complicated kind of pretending (Field, De Stefano, & Koewler, 1982).

Sociodramatic Play. Somewhere in the preschool years children also begin to play parts or take roles. This is really still a form of pretending, except that now several children create a mutual pretense. They play "daddy and mommy," "cowboys and indians," "doctor and patient" and the like. At first children simply take up these roles; later they name the roles to one another and may give each other explicit instructions about the right way to pretend a particular role. You can begin to see this form of play in a some 2-year-olds; by age 4 virtually all children engage in some play of this type (Howes & Matheson, 1992). Interestingly, at about the same ages a great many children seem to create imaginary companions (Taylor, Cartwright, & Carlson, 1993). For many years psychologists believed that the existence of such an imaginary companion was a sign of disturbance in a child; now it is clear that such a creation is a normal part of the development of pretense in many children.

Children clearly get great delight out of all of these often elaborate fantasies. Equally important, by playing roles, pretending to be someone else, they also become more and more aware of how things may look or feel to someone else, and their egocentric approach to the world declines.

Astington, 1988, p. 35). By and large, 3-year-olds think that John will believe it is a sponge, while 4- and 5-year-olds realize that because John hasn't felt the sponge, he will have a false belief that it is a rock. Thus the child of 4 or 5 understands that someone else can believe something that isn't true *and will act on that belief.*

Theories of Mind. Evidence like this has led a number of theorists (Astington & Gopnik, 1991; Harris, 1989; Perner, 1991) to propose that the 4- or 5-year-old has developed a new and quite sophisticated **theory of mind.** The child this age has begun to understand that you cannot predict what other people will do solely from observing the situation itself; the other person's desires and beliefs also enter into the equation. So the child develops various theories about other people's ideas, beliefs, and desires, and about how they will affect someone else's behavior.

Such a theory of mind does not spring forth full blown at age 4. Three-year-old children already understand some aspects of the links between people's thinking or feeling and their behavior. They know that a person who wants something will try to get it. They also know that a person will feel sad if she fails and happy if she succeeds (Wellman, 1988), and that she may still want something even if she can't have it (Lillard & Flavell, 1992). But they do not yet understand the basic principle that each person's actions are based on his own *representation* of reality, and a person's representation may differ from what is "really" there. People act based on what they believe or feel, even if what they believe is incorrect or what they feel is unexpected or apparently inconsistent in a given situation. Thus a person who feels sad even though she has succeeded at something will act on that sadness, not on the visible success. It is this new aspect of the theory of mind that is clearly absent in the 3-year-old, but that we can see emerging at about 4 or 5.

Such an increased awareness of the ways in which thinking operates is also apparent in other areas. For example, between 3 and 5, children figure out that in order to tell if a rock painted like a sponge is really a sponge or a rock, a person would need to touch or hold it. Just looking at it doesn't give you enough information (Flavell, 1993; O'Neill, Astington, & Flavell, 1992). These developments are important because they seem to be the first signs of what psychologists now call **metamemory** and **metacognition**—knowing about the process of memory and the process of thinking—which I'll talk more about in Chapter 9.

All of this new work on the child's theory of mind has not only opened up a fascinating new area of research, it has clearly demonstrated that the preschool child is vastly less egocentric than Piaget supposed. By age 4, and in more limited ways at earlier ages, the child has a remarkably sophisticated ability to understand other points of view and can predict other people's behavior based on deductions about their beliefs or feelings. I don't know about you, but I find this an amazing—and surprising—achievement.

Conservation and Classification. Piaget's underestimation of the cognitive abilities of the preschool child is also evident in research on classification. Three-

> Consider your own theory of mind. What assumptions do you make about the way other people's behavior is affected by their beliefs or feelings or ideas? You operate on the basis of such a theory all the time, but can you articulate it?

CULTURES & CONTEXTS

Understanding of Appearance and Reality in Other Cultures

A number of studies from widely differing parts of the globe and in widely different cultures suggest that the shift at about age 4 in children's understanding of appearance and reality and of false belief may well be a universal developmental pattern.

Jeremy Avis and Paul Harris (1991) adapted the traditional false belief testing procedure for use with a pygmy tribe, the Baka, who live in Cameroon. The Baka are a hunter-gatherer people who live together in camps. Each child was tested in his or her own hut, using materials with which they were completely familiar. They watched one adult, named Mopfana (a member of the tribe), put some mango kernels into a bowl. Mopfana then left the hut, and a second adult (also a tribe member) told the child they were going to play a game with Mopfana: they were going to hide the kernels in a cooking pot. Then this second adult asked the child what Mopfana was going to do when he came back. Would he look for the kernels in the bowl or in the pot? Would Mopfana's heart feel good or bad before he lifted the lid of the bowl and after he lifted the lid? Younger children—2-, 3-, and early 4-year-olds—were much more likely to say that Mopfana would look for the seeds in the pot or to say that he would be sad before he looked in the bowl, while older 4- and 5-year-olds were nearly always right on all three questions.

Similarly, when Flavell used his sponge/rock task with children in mainland China, he found that Chinese 3-year-olds were just as confused about this task as are American or British 3-year-olds, whereas 5-year-old Chinese children had no difficulty with the problem (Flavell et al., 1983).

Using a somewhat different kind of problem, but one that still touches on the difference between appearance and reality, Paul Harris and his colleagues (Harris, 1989) have asked children in several cultures how characters in a story *really* feel, and what emotion *appears* on their faces. For example:

> Diana is playing a game with her friend. At the end of the game Diana wins and her friend loses. Diana tries to hide how she feels because otherwise her friend won't play any more (Harris, 1989, p. 134).

Four-year-old children in Britain and the United States, faced with such stories, have no trouble saying how the character will really feel, but more trouble saying how the character would look, while by 5 or 6, the child grasps the possible difference. Harris has found that the same shift occurs in Japan at about the same age (Gardner et al., 1988), despite the fact that the Japanese culture puts far more emphasis on the disguising of emotions.

In these very different cultures, then, something similar seems to be occurring between age 3 and age 5. In these years, all children seem to understand something general about the difference between appearance and reality.

---

and 4-year-olds are able to classify objects into groups quite readily if you simplify the task or if you make it clear that you want them to use some kind of superordinate category for classifying. In one study, Sandra Waxman and Rochel Gelman (1986) told 3- and 4-year-olds that a puppet really liked pictures of food (or animals, or furniture). The experimenters then gave the children 12 pictures and asked them to put the ones the puppet would like in one bin and the ones the puppet would not like in another bin. When they were given the category label in this way, these young children could quite easily classify the pictures into food and nonfood categories, or furniture and nonfurniture categories.

Even at 18 months babies may be capable of some classification. Alison Gopnik and Andrew Meltzoff (1992) gave toddlers this age sets of objects to play with, such as four different finger rings and four different rocks. The objects were laid out in front of the child in a random array, and the child was encouraged to handle the objects, but given no other specific instructions. Fully half of these young children physically separated the two types of objects into distinct piles or groups.

In contrast, studies of conservation have generally confirmed Piaget's basic observations. Although younger children can demonstrate some understanding of conservation if the task is made very simple (Gelman, 1972; Wellman, 1982), most children cannot consistently solve conservation problems until age 5 or 6 or later.

The relatively late development of the child's understanding of conservation makes sense if we think of conservation tasks as a particularly sophisticated form of questions about appearance and reality; the amount of juice appears to change, even though in reality it does not. In addition, to grasp the basic principle of conservation the child also has to understand rules about what kinds of manipulations will change quantities (that adding makes something more, for example). But the understanding of the distinction between appearance and reality seems to be a precursor or requirement for conservation tasks.

Overview of the Preschool Child's Thinking

How can we add up the bits and pieces of information about the preschool child's thinking? At the least, we can say that preschool children are capable of forms of logic that Piaget thought impossible at this stage. In particular, by age 4, and certainly by age 5, they not only can take others' perspectives, they understand at least in a preliminary way that other people's behavior rests on inner beliefs and feelings.

One possibility is that Piaget simply got the age wrong, and that the transition he saw at 6 or 7 really happens at around age 4 or 5. Certainly the various understandings that children seem to come to at about that age—about false belief, about appearance and reality, and the ability to take another person's physical perspective—are remarkably stagelike.

Another possibility is that while preschoolers can do some sophisticated-looking things, their understanding remains specific rather than general. It is still tied heavily to specific situations or displayed only with a good deal of support. Studies of both conservation and children's logic show that researchers can *elicit* sophisticated performances in 2-, 3-, and 4-year-old children, but preschoolers do not typically show such understandings spontaneously. In order for the preschool child to demonstrate these relatively advanced forms of thinking, you have to make the task quite simple, eliminate distractions, or give special clues. The fact that children this age can solve these problems at all is striking, but it is still true that preschool children think differently from older children. The very fact that they can perform certain tasks *only* when the tasks are made very simple or undistracting is evidence for such a difference.

More broadly, preschoolers do not seem to experience the world or think about it using such a general set of rules or principles as we see in older children. Thus, they do not easily generalize something they have learned in one context to a similar but not identical situation. It is precisely such a switch to general rules that Piaget thought characterized the thinking of the school age child.

Individual Differences in Language and Cognitive Functioning

The sequences and patterns of language and cognition I've been describing give you a general picture, but it is nonetheless a somewhat misleading picture. There are also important variations from one child to the next, particularly in the rate of development the child shows and in the child's relative ability to perform intellectual tasks. We see such differences not only in the speed of the child's language development, but in measures of cognitive power such as IQ tests.

Differences in Rate and Style of Language Development

Some children begin using individual words at 8 months, others not until 18 months; some do not use two-word sentences until 3 or even later. You can see the range of normal variation very clearly in the behavior of the three children Roger Brown has studied intensively—Eve, Adam and Sarah. Figure 7.2 shows the average sentence length, which linguists refer to as the *mean length of utterance*, or MLU, of each of the children at each age. I have drawn a line at the MLU level that normally signifies a switch from the simplest to more complex

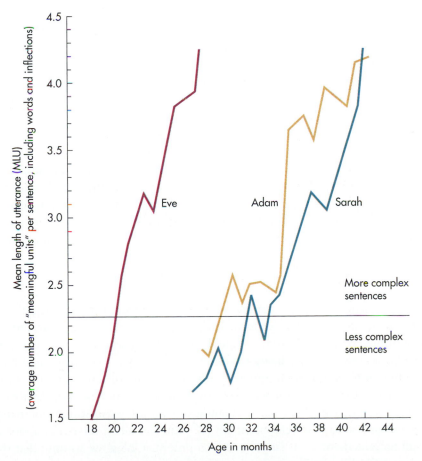

FIGURE 7.2

Children go through the various steps and stages of language development at markedly different rates, as you can see clearly here. Eve began to use grammatical inflections in her language (noted by the horizontal line across the graph) at about 21 months, while Adam and Sarah were much slower. (Source: Brown, 1973, Figure 1, p. 55.)

sentences. You can see that Eve made this transition at about 21 months, while Adam and Sarah passed over this point about a year later.

I should point out that most children who talk late catch up later, and earliness or lateness of complex speech is *not* predictive of later IQ or later reading ability. The exception to this statement is a small group of late talkers who also have poor *receptive* language. This group appears to remain behind in language development, and perhaps in cognitive development more generally (Bates, 1993).

Such variations seem to have at least some genetic basis (Mather & Black, 1984; Plomin & DeFries, 1985a; 1985b), but they are also at least partly a response to differences in the richness of the language environment. Among adoptive families, for example, those who read to their children more and talk to them more have children who develop language more quickly.

Perhaps more importantly, there are also differences among children in their *style* of early language. You'll recall from Chapter 5 that Katherine Nelson first noticed such differences in her studies of early vocabulary. She identified two styles, which she called "referential" and "expressive." Later researchers have found further signs of such a difference in both grammar and articulation.

Elizabeth Bates and her colleagues (Bates, Bretherton, & Snyder, 1988; Thal & Bates, 1990) argue that the difference may run fairly deep. Referential-style children are, in some sense, more cognitively oriented children. They are drawn to objects, spend more of their time in solitary play with objects, and interact with other people more often around objects, too. They are much more likely to show a clear spurt in vocabulary development in the early stages, adding a whole lot of object names in a very short space of time, as if they—more than expressive children—had understood the basic principle that things have names. Such children are also advanced in their ability to understand complex adult language and have good articulation.

> There are some indications that girls are more likely to follow a referential pattern, while boys may be more often expressive. Can you think of any possible explanations of such a difference?

The expressive-style toddler, on the other hand, is oriented more toward people, toward social interactions. His early words and sentences include a lot of "strings" of words that are involved in common interactions with adults, like "What do you want?" Since many such strings include grammatical inflections, expressive children's early language often sounds more advanced than that of a referential child. But their vocabularies develop more slowly, with no obvious spurt. They are also generally harder to understand because their pronunciation is not as clear.

Just how these differences come about is still being hotly debated. It could be that such children are simply matching the quality of the language they are hearing. For example, there are a few hints that first-born children may be more likely to follow the referential pattern. Perhaps they receive much more intensive language input, with much more emphasis on learning names. Later-borns, who seem to be somewhat more likely to follow an expressive style, may encounter a rather different linguistic environment, with more emphasis on communication.

Whatever the source, the existence of such large differences in the form or style of early language raises serious questions about the assumption that the early stages of language development are the same for all children and about virtually all nativist theories of language development. Unless we assume that there are rather radical variations in the input with which the child is working, it is difficult to account for such style differences from a base of common operating principles or other built-in processes. All in all, the literature on style differences in language learning, which seemed like an interesting sidelight when Nelson first described the phenomenon, has turned out to lead to a fascinating set of new questions.

Differences in Intelligence Among Preschoolers

In Chapter 5, I mentioned that so-called infant IQ tests were not strongly related to later measures of IQ. But I did not give you a full description of such later measures, nor define IQ. It is now time to do both.

Remember from Chapter 5 that the study of intelligence is part of the "cognitive power" tradition. Those who approached the study of thinking in this way were struck by the obvious variations among individuals in their ability to think, analyze, solve problems, or learn new material. These researchers sought ways to measure and to understand those differences.

If you had to guess, which of the two styles of early language learning would you bet young Shifra shows?

The First IQ Tests.   The first modern intelligence test was published in 1905 by two Frenchmen, Alfred Binet and Theodore Simon. From the beginning, the test had a practical purpose, which was to identify children who might have difficulty in school. For this reason, the tests Binet and Simon devised were very much like some school tasks, including measures of vocabulary, comprehension of facts and relationships, and mathematical and verbal reasoning. For example, can the child describe the difference between wood and glass? Can the young child touch his nose, his ear, his head? Can he tell which of two weights is heavier?

Lewis Terman and his associates at Stanford University (Terman, 1916; Terman & Merrill, 1937) modified and extended many of Binet's original tests when they translated and revised the test for use in the United States. The several Terman revisions, called the **Stanford–Binet,** consist of a series of six individual tests for children of each age. A child taking the test is given the age tests beginning below his actual age, then those for his age, then those for each successively older age until the child reaches a level at which he fails all six tests.

Terman initially described a child's performance in terms of a score called an **Intelligence Quotient,** later shortened to IQ. This score was computed by comparing the child's chronological age (in years and months) with his *mental age,* defined as the level of questions he could answer correctly. For example, a child who could solve the problems for a 6-year-old but not those for a 7-year-old would have a mental age of 6. The formula used to calculate the IQ was

$$\frac{\text{Mental Age}}{\text{Chronological age}} \times 100 = IQ$$

This formula results in an IQ above 100 for children whose mental age is higher than their chronological age and an IQ below 100 for children whose mental age is below their chronological age.

This old system for calculating the IQ is not used any longer, even in the modern revisions of the Stanford–Binet. IQ score calculations are now based on a direct comparison of a child's performance with the average performance of a large group of other children his own age. But an IQ of 100 is still average, and higher and lower scores still mean above and below average performance. Two-thirds of all children achieve scores between 85 and 115; roughly 95 percent of scores fall between 70 and 130. Children who score below 70 are normally referred to as *retarded*, while those who score above 130 are often called *gifted*.

Modern IQ Tests.   The tests psychologists use most often today are the Revised Stanford–Binet and the Wechsler Intelligence Scales for Children, or **WISC** (Wechsler, 1974), of which the most recent version is the WISC-III. It includes five types of "verbal" tests: general information (e.g., How many eyes have you?), general comprehension (e.g., What is the thing to do when you scrape your knee?), arithmetic, similarities (e.g., In what way are an orange and a pear alike?), and vocabulary. The other half of the WISC consists of five "performance" tests, which rely much less on verbal skills and include such things as arranging pictures in a correct order to make a story or copying designs using colored blocks, as in the photo.

Stability and Predictive Value of IQ Tests.   Because these tests were originally designed to predict a child's ability to perform in school, it is obviously crucial to know whether they do this job well. The research findings on this point are quite consistent: The correlation between a child's test score and her current or later grades in school is about .50 to .60 (Brody, 1992; Carver, 1990). This is a strong but by no means perfect correlation. It tells us that on the whole, children with top IQ scores will also be among the high achievers in school, and those who score low will be among the low achievers. Still, some children with high IQ scores don't shine in school while some lower IQ children do.

I am *not* saying here that IQ *causes* good or poor performance in school—although that is one possibility and one that has been widely believed. All we are sure of is that the two events—high or low IQ scores and high or low school performance—tend to go together so that we can use one to predict the other. IQ scores are also quite stable. If two tests are given a few months or a few years apart, the scores are likely to be very similar. The correlations between adjacent-year IQ scores in middle childhood, for example, are typically in the range of .80 (Honzik, 1986). Yet this high level of predictability masks an interesting fact: many children show quite wide fluctuations in their scores. Robert McCall, analyzing several longitudinal studies in which children have been given IQ tests repeatedly over many years, concludes that about half of children show little or no significant fluctuation in their scores. The remaining half, however, show changes from one test to another and over time (McCall, 1993). Some show steadily rising scores, some declining, some show a peak in middle childhood and then a decline in adolescence. In individual cases, the shifts may cover a range as large as 40 points.

Such wide fluctuations are more common in young children. The general rule of thumb is that the older the child the more stable the IQ score becomes, although even in older children, scores may still show fluctuations in response to major stresses such as parental divorce, changing schools, or the birth of a sibling.

This second grader is working on one of the subtests of the WISC, in which he must use a set of blocks to try to copy the design shown in the book.

Limitations of IQ tests.   Before I move on to the question of the possible origins of differences in IQ, it is important to emphasize a few key limitations of such tests or the scores derived from them.

IQ tests do not measure underlying competence. An IQ score cannot tell you (or a teacher, or anyone else) that your child has some specific, fixed, underlying capacity. It reflects only performance on some given day.

The scores are not etched on a child's forehead at birth, never to change. Individual children can and do shift, particularly in response to any stress in their lives.

Perhaps most important, traditional IQ tests simply do not measure a whole host of skills that are likely to be highly significant for getting along in the world. IQ tests were originally designed to measure only the specific range of skills that are needed for success in school. This they do reasonably well. What they do not tell us is how good a particular person may be at other cognitive tasks requiring skills such as creativity, insight, street-smarts, reading social cues, or understanding spatial relationships (Gardner, 1983; Sternberg & Wagner, 1993).

Given what I have said so far about IQ tests, do you think it would be worthwhile to test every preschool child? How would you use such scores? What would be the drawbacks of such universal testing?

Explaining Differences in IQ

You will not be surprised to discover that the arguments about the origins of differences in IQ nearly always boil down to a dispute about nature versus nurture. When Binet and Simon wrote the first IQ test, they did not assume that intelligence as measured on an IQ was fixed or inborn. But many of the American psychologists who revised and promoted the use of the tests *did* believe that intellectual capacity is inherited and largely fixed at birth. Those who took this view, and those who believed that the environment was crucial in shaping a child's intellectual performance, have been arguing for at least 60 years.

Evidence for the Importance of Heredity.   Both twin studies and studies of adopted children show strong hereditary influences on IQ, as you already know from Chapter 2. Identical twins are more like one another in IQ than are fraternal twins, and the IQs of adopted children are better predicted from the IQs of their natural parents than their adoptive parents. These are precisely the findings we would expect if there were a strong genetic element at work.

Evidence for the Importance of Environment.   Adoption studies also provide some strong support for an environmental influence on IQ scores, because the actual *level* of IQ scores of adopted children is clearly affected by the environment in which they have grown up. Early studies of adopted children involved mostly children born to poverty-level parents who were adopted into middle-class families. Such children typically have IQs that are 10–15 points higher than that of their birth mother (Scarr, 1983) suggesting that the effect of the middle-class adoptive family was to raise the child's IQ. But this doesn't tell us whether a *less*–stimulating adoptive family would *lower* the IQ of a child born to average- or above-average-IQ parents. That piece of information is now available from a French study by Christiane Capron and Michel Duyme (1989), who studied a group of 38 French children all adopted in infancy. What makes the study

TABLE 7.3
IQ Scores at Adolescence for Capron and Duyme's Adopted Children

Social Class of Biological Parents	Social Class of Adoptive Parents	
	High	Low
High	119.60	107.50
Low	103.60	92.40

Source: Capron & Duyme (1989), Table 2, p. 553.

unusual is that these children represent all possible combinations of high- and low-social class and education in the birth parents and the adoptive parents. Table 7.3 shows the children's IQ scores in adolescence. If you look across both rows, you can see that there is a difference of 11 or 12 points between the IQs of children reared in upper-class homes and those reared in lower-class families, no matter what the social class level or education of the birth parents. At the same time, the data also show a genetic effect, because the children *born to* upper-class parents have higher IQs than do those from lower-class families, no matter what kind of rearing environment they encountered.

Combining the Information.   Virtually all psychologists would now agree that heredity is a highly important influence on IQ scores. Studies around the world consistently yield estimates that roughly half of the variation in IQ within the population is due to heredity (Plomin, 1989; Plomin & Rende, 1991). The remaining half is clearly due to environment or to interactions between environment and heredity.

One useful way to conceptualize this interaction is with the concept of *reaction range*. The basic idea is that genes establish some range of possible reactions, upper and lower boundaries of functioning. Where a child will fall within those boundaries will be determined by environment. Richard Weinberg (1989) estimates that the reaction range for IQ is about 20 to 25 points. That is, given some specific genetic heritage, each child's actual IQ test performance may vary as much as 20 or 25 points, depending on the richness or poverty of the environment in which he grows up. When we change the child's environment for the better, the child moves closer to the upper end of his reaction range. When we change the environment for the worse, the child's effective intellectual performance falls toward the lower end of his reaction range. Thus even though intelligence as measured on an IQ test is highly heritable, the absolute score within the reaction range is determined by environment. But just what is it about family environments that seems to make a difference?

Specific Family Characteristics and IQ.   When we watch the ways individual families interact with their infants or young children and then follow the children over time to see which ones later have high or low IQs, we can begin to get some sense of the kinds of specific family interactions that foster higher scores. At least five dimensions of family interaction or stimulation seem to make a difference. Families with higher IQ children:

1. provide an *interesting and complex physical environment* for the child, including play materials that are appropriate for the child's age and developmental level (Bradley et al., 1989).

2. are *emotionally responsive* to and *involved* with their child. They respond warmly and contingently to the child's behavior, smiling when the child smiles, answering the child's questions, and in myriad ways respond to the child's cues (Barnard et al., 1989; Bradley & Caldwell, 1984; Lewis, 1993).

3. *talk to their child*, using language that is descriptively rich and accurate (Sigman et al., 1988).

4. *avoid excessive restrictiveness*, punitiveness, or control, instead giving the child room to explore, even opportunities to make mistakes (Bradley et al., 1989; Olson, Bates, & Kaskie, 1992).

5. *expect* their child to do well and to develop rapidly. They emphasize and press for school achievement (Entwisle & Alexander, 1990).

You'll remember from Chapter 2 that there is a problem in research of this type. Because parents provide *both* the genes and the environment, we can't be sure that these environmental characteristics are really causally important. Perhaps this is the kind of environment that brighter parents provide, but the genes and not the environment cause the higher IQs in their children. The way around this problem is to look at the link between environmental features and IQ in adopted children. Fortunately we have a few studies of this type, and they point to the same critical environmental features. That is, among adoptive families, those that behave in the ways listed above have adopted children who score higher on IQ tests (Plomin, Loehlin, & DeFries, 1985).

School Experience and Special Interventions.   Home environments and family interactions are not the only source of environmental influence. Many children also spend a very large amount of time in group care settings, including day care, special programs like Head Start, or regular preschools. How much effect do these environments have on the child's intellectual growth? I talked about some of the day care effects in the last chapter, but I need to expand a bit.

On a theoretical level, this question is of interest because it may tell us something about early experience in general and about the resilience of children. Are the effects of an initially impoverished environment permanent, or can they be offset by an enriched experience, such as a special preschool? At a practical level, programs like Head Start are based squarely on the assumption that it *is* possible to modify the trajectory of a child's intellectual development, especially if you intervene early.

Attempts to test this assumption have led to a messy body of research. In particular, children are rarely assigned randomly to Head Start or non–Head Start groups (Lee et al., 1990), making interpretation difficult. Still, there is some agreement on the effects. Children enrolled in Head Start or other enriched preschool programs, compared to similar children without such preschool, normally show a gain of about 10 IQ points during the year of the

Children in Head Start Programs or other enriched preschools don't have higher IQs later, but they are less likely to repeat a grade or to be assigned to special education classes.

Head Start experience. This IQ gain typically fades and then disappears within the first few years of school (McKey et al., 1985), but there is nonetheless a clear residual effect. Children with Head Start or other enriched preschool experience are less likely to be placed in special education classes, somewhat less likely to repeat a grade, and somewhat more likely to graduate from high school (Darlington, 1991; Haskins, 1989). So although the children with preschool experience do not typically *test* much higher (and do *not* differ in IQ), they *function* better in school.

Even larger and more lasting effects are found when the child begins the special program in infancy rather than at age 3 or 4 or 5. Craig Ramey and his colleagues at North Carolina have conducted the best-designed and most meticulously reported of the infancy intervention studies (1993; Ramey & Campbell, 1987; Ramey & Haskins, 1981a; 1981b; Ramey, Lee, & Burchinal, 1989). These researchers randomly assigned infants from poverty-level families, whose mothers had low IQs, to either a special day-care program, 8 hours a day, 5 days a week, or to a control group, which received nutritional supplements and medical care but no special enriched day care. The special care program, which began when the infants were 6 to 12 weeks of age and lasted until they began kindergarten, involved very much the kinds of "optimum" stimulation I just described.

In Figure 7.3, you can see the average IQ scores of the children at various ages. It shows that IQs of children in the special program were higher at every age, although the scores declined for both groups in the elementary school years.

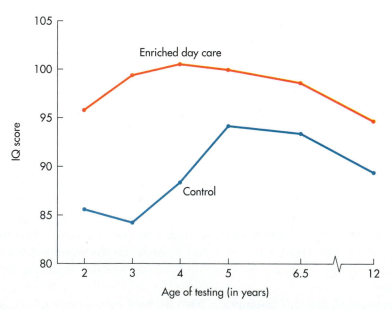

FIGURE 7.3

In the Ramey study, children were randomly assigned to an experimental group with special day care or to a control group. At kindergarten, both groups entered public school. The difference in IQ between the experimental and control groups remained statistically significant even at age 12, seven years after the intervention ended. (Source: Ramey & Campbell, 1987, Figure 3, p. 135, with additional data from Ramey, 1993, Figure 2, p. 29.)

What is perhaps more important is the observation that fully 44 percent of the control group children had IQ scores that the researchers classified as borderline or retarded (scores below 85), compared to only 12.8 percent of the children who had been in the special program. In addition, the enriched day-care group had significantly higher scores on both reading and mathematics tests at age 12 and were only half as likely to have repeated a grade (Ramey, 1992; Ramey, 1993).

These results do *not* mean that all mental retardation could be "cured" by providing children with heavy doses of special education in infancy. What they do show is that the intellectual power of those children who begin life with few advantages can be significantly increased if richer stimulation is provided. At a more general level, they tell us that environment as well as heredity can effect the level of intellectual functioning a child achieves.

Racial Differences in IQ

So far I have side-stepped an extremely difficult set of questions, namely racial differences in IQ or cognitive power. Because these questions can easily be blown out of proportion, I do not want to place too much emphasis on this topic. But you need to see what we know, what we don't know, and how psychologists have tried to explain the differences.

A number of racial differences in intellectual performance have been found, including consistently higher performance on achievement tests—particularly math tests—by Asian and Asian-American children (Stevenson et al., 1990; Sue & Okazaki, 1990). But the basic finding that has given researchers and theorists the most difficulty is that in the United States, Black children score lower than White children on measures of IQ. This difference, which is on the order of 12 IQ points, is *not* found on infant tests of intelligence or on measures of infant habituation rate (Fagan & Singer, 1983), but a difference becomes apparent by the time children are 2 or 3 years old (Brody, 1992).

Some scientists have argued that these findings reflect basic genetic differences between the races (Jensen, 1980). Other scientists, even granting that IQ is highly heritable, point out that the 12 point difference falls well within the presumed reaction range of IQ. They emphasize that there are sufficiently large differences in the environments in which Black and White children are typically reared to account for the average difference in score (Brody, 1992).

Some of the most convincing research supporting the latter view comes from Sandra Scarr and her colleagues (Scarr & Kidd, 1983; Weinberg, Scarr, & Waldman, 1992). For example, she has found that Black children adopted at an early age into White middle-class families, and thus reared in the majority environment, scored only slightly less well on IQ tests than did White children adopted into the same families. In another study of adopted Black children, Moore (1986) found that those who had been reared in White families not only had higher IQ scores than those adopted into Black families (117 versus 103), they also approached the IQ testing situation quite differently. They stayed more focused on the task and were more likely to try some task even if they didn't think they could do it. Black children adopted into middle-class Black families did not show this pattern of persistence and effort. They asked for help more

Some psychologists have argued that the reason Blacks achieve lower IQ scores than Whites is that the tests are systematically biased against Blacks or other minority group members. What kind of research results would demonstrate such a bias? What kind would argue against it?

often and gave up more easily when faced with a difficult task. When Moore then observed each adoptive mother teaching her child several tasks, he could see parallel differences. The White mothers were more encouraging and less likely to give the child the answer than were the Black mothers.

Findings like these persuade me that the IQ difference we see is primarily a reflection of the fact that the tests, and the school, are designed by the majority culture to promote a particular form of intellectual activity and that many Black or other minority families rear their children in ways that do not maximize (or emphasize) this particular set of skills. In a similar vein, Harold Stevenson has argued that the differences between Asian and Caucasian children in performance on mathematics tests results not from genetic differences in capacity, but from differences in cultural emphasis on the importance of academic achievement, number of hours spent on homework, and differences in the quality of the math instruction in the schools (Stevenson & Lee, 1990; Stigler, Lee, & Stevenson, 1987)—points I'll come back to in Chapter 9.

The fact that we may be able to account for such racial differences in IQ or achievement test performance by appealing to the concept of reaction range and to cultural or subcultural variations does not make the differences disappear, nor does it make them trivial. But perhaps it puts such findings into a less explosive framework.

The Measurement of Intelligence: A Last Look

One of the questions that students often ask at about this point is whether, given all the factors that can affect a test score, it worth bothering with IQ tests at all. I think that these tests do assess some important aspects of children's intellectual performance and that they can be helpful in identifying children who may have difficulties in school. But it is worth emphasizing again that they do *not* measure a lot of other things we may be interested in. An IQ test is a specialized tool, and like many such tools, it has a fairly narrow range of appropriate use. I wouldn't want to throw out this tool, but we have to keep its limitations very firmly in mind when we use it.

S U M M A R Y

1. Physical development is slower from 2 to 6 years than in infancy, but is still steady. Motor skills continue to improve gradually.

2. Preschool children average 4 to 6 acute illnesses each year. Chronic illnesses are less common.

3. Language development moves at rapid pace between ages 2 and 3. Children begin forming two-word sentences and then move swiftly to more complex sentences, adding various grammatical inflections. Even their simplest sentences convey a variety of meanings.

4. From the earliest sentences, children's language is creative, including forms and combinations the child has not heard but that follow apparent rules.

5. Studies of word meaning suggest that children learn many words only when they already understand the underlying concept. Children's early word categories are more often overextended than underextended.

6. Most linguists now agree that children have some built-in constraints on their word learning, such as the principle of contrast.

7. Simple imitation or reinforcement theories of language development are not adequate to explain the phenomenon. More complex environmental theories, emphasizing the role of environmental richness or motherese, are more helpful, but also not sufficient.

8. Innateness theories, positing built-in operating principles or "rules to listen by," are more persuasive, but they omit the role of the child as analyzer and synthesizer of linguistic information.

9. Piaget marked the beginning of the preoperational period at the point when the child, at about 18–24 months, begins to use mental symbols. Despite this advance, he saw the preschool child as lacking many sophisticated cognitive characteristics. In Piaget's view, such children are still egocentric, lack understanding of conservation, and have only primitive classification abilities.

10. Recent research on the cognitive functioning of preschoolers makes it clear that Piaget underestimated these children. They are much less egocentric than he thought, and in fact they have remarkably sophisticated theories of mind by age 4 or 5. At about that age children also understand the difference between appearance and reality.

11. Preschoolers also show more sophisticated classification ability than Piaget described, but he was generally correct about the timing of understanding of conservation.

12. Language development proceeds at varying speeds in different children, with faster development associated with linguistically richer environments.

13. Differences in style of language learning—expressive and referential—may turn out to be quite pervasive and important.

14. Children also differ in cognitive power, as measured by standard intelligence tests. Scores on such tests are predictive of school performance and are quite consistent over time.

15. Differences in IQ have been attributed to both heredity and environment. Twin and adoption studies make it clear that at least half of the variation in IQ scores is due to genetic differences, the remainder to environment and the interaction of heredity and environment.

16. Qualities of the environment that appear to make a difference include the complexity of stimulation, the responsiveness and involvement of parents, the relative lack of parental restrictiveness, and high expectations for the child's performance.

17. Children's IQs can be raised by providing specially stimulating environments, such as enriched day care or preschools.

18. Several kinds of racial differences in IQ or test performance have been found consistently. We can attribute such differences most appropriately to environmental variation, rather than genetics.

K E Y   T E R M S

conservation

egocentrism

inflections

Intelligence Quotient
  (IQ)

metacognition

metamemory

motherese

overregularization

pragmatics

preoperational period

Stanford–Binet

theory of mind

WISC

S U G G E S T E D   R E A D I N G S

Brody, N. (1992). *Intelligence* (2nd ed.) San Diego, CA: Academic Press. Dense and detailed, but the best current source I know of for further information about all aspects of this subject.

de Villiers, P. A., & de Villiers, J. G. (1992). Language Development. In M. H. Bornstein & M. E. Lamb (Eds.), *Developmental psychology. An advanced textbook* (3rd ed.) (pp. 337–418). Hillsdale, NJ: Erlbaum. A remarkably thorough and clear review of this subject, much easier to read than many current discussions or descriptions of language development, touching on many of the issues I have raised here. I strongly recommend it as a next source.

Flavell, J. H. (1992). Cognitive development: Past, present, and future. *Developmental Psychology*, *28*, 998–1005. This brief paper by one of the leading thinkers and researchers in the field of cognitive development gives you a quick tour of what Flavell thinks we now know, don't know, and are still arguing about. Flavell's 1985 book, *Cognitive Development*, which I listed as a suggested reading in Chapter 5, is also a wonderful source.

Hakuta, K. (1986). *Mirror of language: The debate on bilingualism*. New York: Basic Books. An elegant and comprehensible discussion of many of the issues about bilingualism and bilingual education I have discussed in *The Real World* box on page 195.

Pinker, S. (1994). *The language instinct. How the mind creates language*. New York: William Morrow. This splendid book, written by one of the most articulate and easy-to-understand linguists, lays out the argument for a built-in language instinct.

Chapter Eight

Social and Personality Development from 2 to 6

I f you asked a random sample of adults to tell you the most important characteristics of children between the ages of 2 and 6, my hunch is that the first thing on the list would not be the child's growing physical skill or her newly developing theory of mind. New language abilities might make the list, but I'd lay odds that most people would first mention the "terrible twos"—the nay-saying, newly oppositional toddler who wants to do things for herself. This public characterization of the toddler is exaggerated, but it is still true that some of the most obvious changes during the preschool years are in the realm of social behavior.

Theoretical Perspectives

It was just such changes in the child's relationships with others, and in personality, that Freud and Erikson attempted to describe in their theories. I talked about both these theories in Chapter 2, but let me review briefly.

Freud and Erikson

If you go back and look at Table 2.3 (page 46), you'll see that Freud described two stages during these preschool years, each highlighting a different aspect of sexual sensitivity. The first of these, the *anal stage*, he thought was dominant between roughly ages 1 and 3. It is characterized by increased sensitivity in the anal region, and is significant particularly because it typically coincides with the parents' desire to toilet train the child.

The *phallic stage* occurs between ages 3 and 5, when the genitals increase in sensitivity. It is during this stage that Freud thought the Oedipus conflict occurred, resulting in identification with the same-sex parent—a process I described in some detail in Chapter 2.

Erikson places the emphasis somewhat differently. Both of the stages he lists within this period are triggered by new physical, cognitive, or social skills of the child, rather than changes in sexual sensitivity as Freud suggests. The stage he calls *autonomy versus shame and doubt*, for example, is centered around the toddler's new mobility and the desire for autonomy that comes with that mobility. The stage of *initiative versus guilt* is ushered in by new cognitive skills, particularly the preschooler's ability to plan, which accentuates his wish to take the initiative.

Both theorists seem to be saying that the key to this period is the balance between the child's emerging skills and desire for autonomy, and the parent's need to protect the child and control the child's behavior. Thus the parent's task changes rather dramatically after the baby leaves infancy. In the early months of life, the key task for the parents is to provide enough warmth, predictability, and responsiveness to foster a secure attachment and support the basic physiological programming. But once the child becomes physically, linguistically, and cognitively more independent, the need to control becomes a central aspect of the parents' task. Too much control and the child will not have sufficient opportunity to explore; too little control and the child will become unmanageable and fail to learn the social skills he will need to get along with peers as well as adults.

I want to do it myself! The issues of independence and control are central to children in the preschool period.

Other Theoretical Perspectives

Neither Freud nor Erikson talked much about the role of the child's peers in development, but in recent years a number of theorists have emphasized the vital significance of such encounters. Willard Hartup suggests that each child needs experience in two different kinds of relationships: *vertical* and *horizontal* relationships (1989). A vertical relationship involves an attachment to someone who has greater social power or knowledge, such as a parent, a teacher, or even an older sibling. Such relationships are complementary rather than reciprocal. The bond may be extremely powerful in both directions, but the actual behaviors the two partners show toward one another are not the same. Horizontal relationships, in contrast, are reciprocal and egalitarian. The individuals involved, such as same-age peers, have equal social power and their behavior toward one another comes from the same repertoire.

Hartup's point is that these two kinds of relationships serve different functions for the child, and both are needed for the child to develop effective social skills. Vertical relationships are necessary to provide the child with protection and security. In these relationships the child creates his basic internal working models and learns fundamental social skills. But it is in horizontal relationships—in friendships and in peer groups as well as in relationships with siblings—that the child tries out those basic skills. And it is in horizontal relationships that the child acquires those social skills that can only be learned in a relationship between equals: cooperation, competition, and intimacy.

These two kinds of relationships obviously affect one another, but the theory and data tend to be separate, so let me begin by talking about the vertical relationships, in particular the core relationship between child and parent.

Relationships with Parents in the Preschool Years

Attachment

You'll remember from Chapter 6 that by 12 months of age, the baby normally has established a clear attachment to at least one caregiver. The baby displays this attachment with a wide variety of attachment behaviors, including smiling, crying, clinging, social referencing, and "safe base behavior." By age 2 or 3, the attachment appears no less strong, but many of these attachment behaviors have become less continuously visible. Children this age are cognitively advanced enough to understand Mom if she explains why she is going away and that she will be back, so their anxiety at separation wanes. They can even use a photograph of their mother as a "safe base" for exploration in a strange situation (Passman & Longeway, 1982), which reflects the major cognitive advance of symbolic representation. Of course attachment behaviors have not completely disappeared. Three- and 4-year-olds still want to sit on Mom's or Dad's lap; they are still likely to seek some closeness or proximity when Mom returns from an absence. But in nonfearful or nonstressful situations, the child is able to wander further and further from her safe base without apparent distress.

Off she goes, into greater independence. Children this age, especially those with secure attachments, are far more confident about being at a distance from their safe base.

An even broader change occurs at about age 4, when the child's attachment seems to change in quality. Bowlby describes this new stage or level as a *goal-corrected partnership*. Just as the first attachment probably requires that the baby understand his mother will continue to exist when she isn't there, so now the preschooler grasps that the *relationship* continues to exist even when the partners are apart. Children this age are much less distressed at separation; but they get upset if they don't know what's happening or haven't shared in the planning (Marvin & Greenberg, 1982).

At about the same age, the child's internal model of attachment appears to generalize, a process I mentioned in Chapter 6. Bowlby argued that the child's model becomes less a property of each individual relationship and more a property of relationships in some more general sense. Four- and 5-year-olds are thus more likely to apply their internal model to new relationships, including relationships with peers.

What effect do you think the child's increasingly complex theory of mind has on the child's relationship with her parents?

Conflict and the Oedipal Period

Interestingly, at about the same age, children also show an increase in aggression toward the same-sex parent and a peak in affection toward the opposite-sex parent, just as Freud suggested (Watson & Getz, 1990a; 1990b). One 4-year-old in Watson and Getz's studies of this phenomenon, after his mother told him that she loved him, said "And I love you too, and that's why I can't ever marry someone else"—a statement that would surely gladden the heart of any true Freudian! (Watson & Getz, 1990a, p. 29).

Figure 8.1 shows you the results for aggression from Watson and Getz' studies. For each instance of their child's aggression, parents reported which parent had been the recipient of the aggression. Scores above the line signify that the child showed more aggression toward the *same-sex* parent—a pattern that clearly peaked at age 4 for both boys and girls. Whether one needs to rely on the concept of an Oedipal conflict to account for these results is not clear. But these findings do point to complex changes in children's relationships with their mothers and fathers during these years.

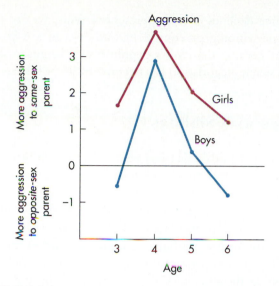

FIGURE 8.1

The data in this figure are based on the detailed reports of parents on the aggressive behavior of their child toward them. Scores above 0 mean that the child was more aggressive toward the same-sex parent than toward the opposite-sex parent, while scores below 0 mean the reverse. (Source: Watson & Getz, 1990b, from Table 3, p. 499.)

Compliance and Defiance

Despite the rise of aggression shown in Figure 8.1, it is a mistake to characterize the parent-preschooler relationship in general terms as increasingly negative or confrontational. Certainly it is true that the 2-year-old's greater autonomy brings him into more and more situations in which the parent wants one thing and the child another. But contrary to the popular image of the "terrible twos," 2-year-olds actually comply with parents' requests more often than not. They are more likely to comply with safety requests ("Don't touch that, it's hot!") or with prohibitions about care of objects ("Don't tear up the book"), than they are with requests to delay ("I can't talk to you now, I'm on the phone") or self-care, such as washing of hands or going to bed when requested. But on the whole, children this age comply fairly readily (Gralinski & Kopp, 1993). When they resist, it is most likely to be passively, by simply not doing what is asked. Only a small percentage of the time does the child say "NO" or actively defy the parent (Kuczynski et al., 1987). Overt refusals become *more* common by age 3 or 4, as does active negotiation with the parent.

Many psychologists think there is an important distinction between simple refusals ("I don't want to," or "No") and defiance, in which the child's refusal is accompanied by anger, temper tantrums, or whining (Crockenberg & Litman, 1990). The former seems to be an important and healthy aspect of self-assertion and has been linked both to secure attachments and to greater maturity (Matas, Arend, & Sroufe, 1978). Defiance, on the other hand, has been linked to insecure attachment, or to a history of abuse.

Direct defiance declines over the preschool years; we are less likely to see temper tantrums or whining or equivalent outbursts in a 6-year-old than in a 2-year-old, in part because the child's cognitive and language skills have developed to the point where negotiation has become more possible.

Relationships with Siblings

The family contains not just the vertical relationships with parents, but also—for many preschoolers—a highly formative type of "horizontal" relationship with brothers and sisters. In these early years, in fact, interactions with siblings may be a more important part of a child's social world than at any other age. Recent studies of sibling relationships have focused on several issues, including the following: (1) what is the nature of sibling relationships during the preschool years? and (2) why are siblings often so very different from one another?

Folklore, such as the story of Cain and Abel, might lead us to believe that rivalry or jealousy is the key ingredient of sibling relationships. But observations of preschoolers with their siblings point toward other ingredients. Toddlers and preschoolers help their brothers and sisters, imitate them, and share their toys. Judy Dunn (1982), in a detailed longitudinal study of a group of 40 families in England, observed that the older child often imitated a baby brother or sister. But by the time the younger child was a year old, he or she began imitating the older sib, and from then on most of the imitation flows in that direction, with the younger child copying the older one.

At the same time, brothers and sisters also hit one another, snatch toys, threaten, and insult each other. The older child in a pair of preschoolers is likely to be the leader, and is therefore more likely to show both aggressive and helpful behaviors (Abramovitch, Pepler, & Corter, 1982). For both members of the pair, however, the dominant feature seems to be ambivalence. Both supportive and negative behaviors are evident in about equal proportions. In Abramovitch's research, such ambivalence occurred whether the pair were close in age or further apart and whether the older child was a boy or a girl. Naturally there are variations on this theme; some pairs show mostly antagonistic or rivalrous behaviors, while some show mostly helpful and supportive behaviors.

One apparent cause of such variations in sibling relationships seems to be the extent to which parents treat their children differently. Some of the best evidence comes from several studies by Judy Dunn (Dunn & McGuire, 1994) in both England and the United States. She has found that parents may express warmth and pride toward one child and scorn toward another, may be lenient toward one and strict with another. Here's an example from one of Dunn's observations, of 30-month-old Andy and his 14-month-old sister Susie.

> Andy was a rather timid and sensitive child, cautious, unconfident, and compliant. . . Susie was a striking contrast—assertive, determined, and a handful for her mother, who was nevertheless delighted by her boisterous daughter. In [one] observation of Andy and his sister, Susie persistently attempted to grab a forbidden object on a high kitchen counter, despite her mother's repeated prohibitions. Finally, she succeeded, and Andy overheard his mother make a warm, affectionate comment on Susie's

action: "Susie, you *are* a determined little devil!" Andy, sadly, commented to his mother, "*I'm* not a determined little devil!" His mother replied, laughing, "No! What are you? A poor old boy!" (Dunn, 1992, p. 6).

Not only are such episodes common in family interactions, children are highly sensitive to such variations in treatment. Notice how Andy had monitored his mother's interaction with Susie and then compared himself to his sister. Children this age are already aware of the emotional quality of exchanges between themselves and their parents, as well as the exchanges between their siblings and parents. Dunn finds that those who receive less affection and warmth from their mothers are likely to be more depressed, worried, or anxious than are their siblings. And the more differently the parents treat siblings, the more rivalry and hostility there is likely to be between the brothers and sisters (Brody et al., 1992).

Of course parents treat children differently for many reasons, including the child's age. Susie's and Andy's mother may be accepting of Susie's naughty behavior simply because she is so young. They also respond to temperamental differences in the children. But whatever the cause, it now seems clear that such differences in treatment are an important ingredient in the child's emerging internal model of self and contribute greatly to variations in behavior between children growing up in the same families.

Relationships with Peers

Relationships within the family, with both parents and siblings, are certainly central to the young child's emerging personality and social skills, particularly in these early years when children still spend a good portion of their time at home. But over the years from 2 to 6, relationships with nonsibling peers become increasingly important.

Children first begin to show some positive interest in other infants as early as 6 months of age. If you place two babies that age on the floor facing each other, they will look at each other, touch, pull each other's hair, imitate each

These 2-year-olds are playing next to each other, but they are not playing *with* each other—a pattern sometimes called *parallel play*.

other's actions, and smile at one another. By 10 months these behaviors are even more evident. Children this age apparently still prefer to play with objects, but will play with each other if no toys are available. By 14 to 18 months, we begin to see two or more children playing together with toys—sometimes cooperating together, sometimes simply playing side by side with different toys, a pattern often called *parallel play*. Toddlers this age express interest in one another, gazing at or making noises at each other. But it isn't until around 18 months that we begin to see much coordinated play, such as when one toddler chases another or one imitates the other's action with some toy.

By 3 or 4, children appear to prefer to play with peers rather than alone and their play with one another is much more cooperative and coordinated. They build things together, play in the sandbox together, or with dolls, trucks, or dress-up clothes. In all these interactions, we can also see both positive and negative behaviors, both aggression and altruism. (Hartup, 1992).

Aggression

The most common definition of **aggression** is behavior with the apparent intent to injure another person or object (Feshbach, 1970). Every child shows at least some behavior of this type, most often after some kind of frustration. But the form and frequency of aggression changes over the preschool years, as you can see in the summary in Table 8.1.

When 2- or 3-year-old children are upset or frustrated, they are most likely to throw things or hit each other. As their verbal skills improve, however, there is a shift away from such overt physical aggression toward greater use of verbal aggression, such as taunting or name calling, much as their defiance of their parents shifts from physical to verbal strategies.

TABLE 8.1
Changes in the Form and Frequency of Aggression between Age 2 and 6

	2- to 4-year-olds	4- to 8-year-olds
Physical aggression	At its peak from 2 to 4.	Declines over the period from 4 to 8.
Verbal aggression	Relatively rare at 2; increases as the child's verbal skill improves.	Dominant form of aggression from 4 to 8.
Goal of aggression	Primarily "instrumental aggression," aimed at obtaining or damaging an object rather than directly hurting someone else.	More "hostile aggression," aimed at hurting another person or another's feelings.
Occasion for aggression	Most often after conflicts with parents.	Most often after conflicts with peers.

Sources: Goodenough, 1931; Hartup, 1974; Cummings et al., 1986.

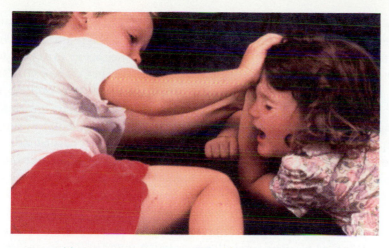

Six-year-old Christopher and his 4-year-old sister Helen may be less likely to get into this kind of physical fight than they were a few years ago, but clearly this kind of physical aggression does not disappear in the preschool years.

A related, but distinct, aspect of "negative" encounters between children is competition or **dominance.** Whenever there are too few toys for the number of children, not enough time with the teacher to go around, or some other scarcity of desired objects, there will be competition. Sometimes competition results in outright aggression. More often, competition results in the development of a clear **dominance hierarchy,** more popularly known as a "pecking order." Some children seem to be more successful than others at asserting their rights to desired objects, time, or space.

Clear dominance hierarchies are already visible at preschool age (Strayer, 1980). That is, among a group of children who play together often, some regularly win out over nearly all other children. Others, lower in the dominance hierarchy, lose to everyone. Interestingly, among 3- and 4-year-olds, a child's place in the group dominance system is *not* related to popularity or to positive interactions to or from the child. But among 5- and 6-year-olds, the dominance and popularity/friendship systems may be linked. In this age group, the dominant children are also the most popular—*so long as they are not bullies* (Pettit et al., 1990; Strayer, 1980). Among 5-year-olds, as among school-age children, bullies are consistently rejected by their peers. The overall picture that emerges is that past the age of 4 or 5, *socially competent* children are those who are at the middle to higher end of the dominance hierarchy, who are positive, helpful and supportive of others, and who refrain from overt acts of physical aggression.

Think about the groups to which you belong. Do they have clear dominance hierarchies? Now imagine a group of adults coming together for the first time. Within a few weeks there is likely to be a pecking order. What determined that order? How does a dominant person establish such dominance?

Prosocial Behavior

Another important facet of peer relationships in these preschool years is a set of behaviors psychologists call **prosocial behavior:** "Voluntary behavior intended to benefit another, such as helping, sharing, and comforting behaviors" (Eisenberg, 1992, p. 3). In everyday language, this is roughly what we mean by **altruism.**

We first see such prosocial behaviors in children of about 2 or 3—at about the same time that they begin to show real interest in play with other children. They will offer to help another child who is hurt, offer a toy, or try to comfort another person (Marcus, 1986; Zahn-Waxler & Radke-Yarrow, 1982). As I pointed out in Chapter 7, children this young have only a beginning understanding of the fact that others feel differently from themselves, but they obviously understand enough about the emotions of others to respond in supportive and sympathetic ways when they see other children or adults hurt or sad.

We don't yet have a good enough base of data to be sure about the developmental patterns past these early years. Some kinds of prosocial behaviors seem to increase with age. For example, if you give children an opportunity to donate some treat to another child whom you describe as needy, older children donate more than younger children do. Helpfulness, too, seems to increase with age up through adolescence. But not all prosocial behaviors show this pattern. Comforting another child, for example, seems to be more common among preschool and early elementary school children than at older ages (Eisenberg, 1988; 1990).

We also know that children vary a lot in the amount of such altruistic behavior—variations that seem to be related to interaction patterns within the family. I've translated some of the relevant research into concrete advice in *The Real World* box on page 233.

Friendships

Beginning at about age 18 months, toddlers also begin to show the first signs of playmate preferences (Brownell & Brown, 1992), even some signs of individual friendships. For example, Carollee Howes (1983; 1987) noted that many children this young showed consistent preferences for one or more playmates over a full year period in a day-care center. Using a somewhat stricter definition of friendship—that the pair spend at least 30 percent of their time together—Robert Hinde and his co-workers (1985) found that only about 20 percent of a group of 3½-year-olds showed signs of a stable friendship; but by age 4, half of these same children regularly played this often with one child.

To be sure, these early peer interactions are still quite primitive. Most of the time, toddlers ignore one another's bids for interaction, and when they play together it is mostly around common toys. And early friendships are more based on sheer proximity and shared play interests than is true of friendships among older children. Still, it is noteworthy that preschool friend pairs nonetheless show more mutual liking, more reciprocity, more extended interactions, more positive and less negative behavior, and more supportiveness in a novel situation than is true between nonfriend pairs at this same age, all signs that these relationships are more than merely passing fancies.

One of the really intriguing facts about such early friendships is that they are more likely between same-sex pairs, even among children as young as age 2 or 3. John Gottman (1986) reports that perhaps 65 percent of friendships in preschool children in the United States are with a same-sex peer. Social interactions with children other than the chosen friend(s) are also more likely to be

How many explanations can you think of for the fact that children begin to prefer to play with same-sex peers as early as age 3 or 4?

The Real World
Rearing Helpful and Altruistic Children

If you wish to encourage your own children to be more generous or altruistic, here are some specific things you can do, based on the work of Eisenberg and others (1992):

1. Create a Loving and Warm Family Climate. This is especially effective if such warmth is combined with clear explanations.

2. Explain Why and Give Rules. Clear rules about what *to* do as well as what *not* to do are important. Explaining the consequences of the child's action in terms of its effects on others is also good, such as: "If you hit Susan it will hurt her". Equally important is stating *positive* rules or guidelines, e.g., "It's always good to be helpful to other people," or "We should share what we have with people who don't have so much."

3. Provide Prosocial Attributions. Attribute your child's helpful or altruistic action to the child's own internal character: "You're such a helpful child!" or "You certainly do a lot of nice things for other people." This strategy begins to be effective with children at about age 7 or 8, at about the same time that they are beginning to develop global notions of self-esteem. In this way you may be able to affect the child's self-scheme.

4. Have Children Do Helpful Things. Children can help cook, take care of pets, make toys to give away, teach younger siblings or tutor in school, and so forth. This can backfire if the coercion required to get the child to do the helpful thing is too strong: the child may now attribute his "good" behavior to the coercion ("mother made me do it"), rather than to some inner trait of his own ("I am a helpful/kind person") and no future altruism is fostered.

5. Model Thoughtful and Generous Behavior. Stating the rules clearly will do little good if your own behavior does not match what you say!

with children of the same sex, beginning as early as age 2½ or 3 (Maccoby, 1988; 1990; Maccoby & Jacklin, 1987). By school age, peer relationships are almost exclusively same-sex.

You can see the early development of this preference in Figure 8.2, which shows the results of a study of preschool play groups by La Freniere, Strayer and Gauthier (1984). By age 3, about 60 percent of play groups were same-sex groupings and the rate rose from there.

Sex Differences in Social Interactions.   Not only are preschoolers' friendships and peer interactions increasingly sex-segregated, it is also becoming clear that boy-boy interactions and girl-girl interactions differ in quality, even in these early years. Eleanor Maccoby, one of the leading theorists in this area (1990), describes the girls' pattern as an *enabling style*. Enabling includes such behaviors as supporting the partner, expressing agreement, making suggestions. All these behaviors tend to foster a greater equality and intimacy in the relationship and keep the interaction going. In contrast, boys are more likely to show what Maccoby calls a *constricting* or *restrictive* style. "A restrictive style is one that tends to derail the interaction—to inhibit the partner or cause the partner to withdraw, thus shortening the interaction or bringing it to an end" (1990, p. 517). Contradicting, interrupting, boasting or other forms of self-display are all aspects of this style. You can get some sense of the difference from two examples drawn from Campbell Leaper's observations of pairs of previously unacquainted 7-year-olds, given in

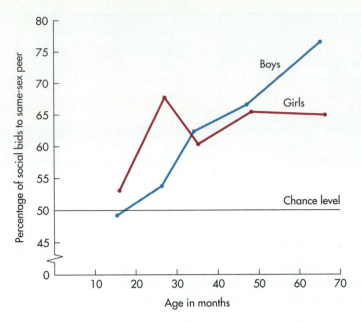

FIGURE 8.2

Same-sex playmate preference among preschoolers. (Source:
La Freniere, Strayer, & Gauthier, 1984. Figure 1, p. 1961. Copyright
by The Society for Research in Child Development, Inc.)

Table 8.2 (Leaper, 1991). Leaper's labels for these two exchanges are *cooperative* and
domineering, but they seem clearly to match Maccoby's distinction between constricting and restrictive styles.

   These two patterns begin to be visible in the preschool years. For example,
Maccoby (1990) points out that beginning as early as age 3 or 4, boys and girls
use quite different strategies in their attempts to influence each other's behavior.
Girls generally ask questions or make requests; boys are much more likely to

TABLE 8.2
Examples of Enabling and Constricting Styles of Interaction

	Girl's Interaction		Boys' Interaction
Jennifer	Let's go play on the slide [sliding noises]	Andy	Mm, I don't like this
		Patrick	[4 sec. silence; coughs, laughs]
Sally	Okay [sliding noises]	Andy	Do this
	I'll do a choo-choo train with you	Patrick	[4 sec. silence]
Jennifer	Okay	Andy	Do this.
Sally	You can go first	Patrick	I wish I could go
Jennifer	Ch (gasp)	Andy	Do this. Kick your chair [kicking sounds]. Kick your chair!
Sally	Ch (gasp)		
		Patrick	I can't
		Andy	Mm huh (sigh)
		Patrick	[7 sec. silence]

Source: Leaper, 1991, from Tables 2 and 3, page 800.

make demands or phrase things using imperatives ("Give me that!"). The really intriguing finding is that even at this early age, boys simply don't comply very much to the girls' style of influence attempt. So playing with boys yields little positive reinforcement for girls, and they begin to avoid such interactions and band together.

Similar differences in relationship style are evident in older children and adults. Girls and women have more intimate relationships with their friends. And in pairs or groups, girls and women seem to focus their attention on actions that will keep the interaction going. Adult men are more likely to be task oriented, women to be relationship oriented. I'll have more to say about these differences in later chapters. For now I only wanted to point out that these subtle and profound differences seem to begin in very early childhood.

How might such differences arise so early? We are a long way from being able to answer that question, but part of the answer must surely lie in the process by which a child figures out whether he is a boy or she is a girl. Such an understanding is, in turn, part of the more general emergence of the preschool child's sense of self.

Do your observations of adult relationships match the distinction Maccoby is making here? What do you think happens when one man and one woman interact in some nonromantic encounter? Is the resulting style some combination of enabling and constricting or does one style dominate?

The Emergence of the Sense of Self

The Objective Self.   When we left the 18- to 24-month-old in Chapter 6, he was beginning to develop what Lewis calls the *objective self*. The toddler already understands himself to be an object in the world, with various properties. Between 2 and 6 the child certainly continues to define herself in this way. By the end of this period, a child can give you quite a full description of herself on a whole range of dimensions. Still, these early self-concepts remain highly concrete. For example, Susan Harter (1987; 1990; Harter & Pike, 1984) has found that children between 4 and 7 have clear notions of their own competence on a range of physical, intellectual, and social tasks, such as solving puzzles, being able to count, knowing a lot in school, climbing or skipping or jumping rope, or having lots of friends. But these separate aspects of the *self-scheme* or internal working model of the self have not yet coalesced into a global assessment of self-worth. Children this age do not say things like "I am a terrible person," or "I really like myself." Their perceptions of themselves are more tied to specific settings, specific tasks. The self-perceptions of a preschool-age child are also tied to visible characteristics, such as what he looks like, what or who he plays with, where he lives, what he is good or bad at doing, rather than to more enduring, inner qualities, such as personality traits or basic abilities. This pattern obviously parallels what we see in cognitive development at the same ages since it is in these same years that children's attention tends to be captured by the external appearance of objects rather than by their enduring properties.

The Social Self.   Another facet of the child's emerging sense of self is an increasing awareness of himself as a player in the social game. By age 2, the toddler has already learned a variety of social "scripts"—routines of play or interaction with others in her world. Case (1991) points out that the toddler now

Through their pretend play, Lucy and Rachel, at age 3, are not only learning about how to interact with a peer, they are also rehearsing various social scripts.

begins to develop some implicit understanding of her own roles in these scripts. So she begins to think of herself as a "helper" in some situations or as "the boss" when she is telling some other child what to do. You can see this clearly in children's sociodramatic play, as they begin to take explicit roles: "I'll be the daddy and you be the mommy" or "I'm the boss." As part of the same process, the preschool child also gradually understands her place in the a network of family roles. She has sisters, brothers, father, mother, etc.

The Gender Concept

One of the most fascinating aspects of the preschool child's emerging sense of self is the development of the child's sense of gender. How do children come to understand that they are a boy or a girl, and when and how do they learn to identify behaviors and attitudes that are considered normal and appropriate for their gender in their particular culture? The child has several related tasks. On the cognitive side, she must learn the nature of the gender category itself—that boyness or girlness is permanent, unchanged by such things as modifications in clothing or hair length. This understanding is usually called the **gender concept.** On the social side, she has to learn what behaviors go with being a boy or a girl. That is, she must learn the **sex role** appropriate for her gender.

The Development of the Gender Concept. How soon does a child figure out that she is a girl or he is a boy? It depends on what we mean by "figure out." There seem to be three steps. First, there is **gender identity,** which is simply a child's ability to label his own sex correctly and to identify other people as men or women, boys or girls. By 9 to 12 months, babies already treat male and female faces as if they were different categories (Fagot & Leinbach, 1993). Within the next year, they begin to learn the verbal labels that go with these different categories. By age 2, if you show them a set of pictures of a same-sex child and several opposite-sex children and say "which one is you?," most children can correctly pick out the same-sex picture (Thompson, 1975). By 2½ or 3, most children can correctly label and identify the sex of others as well (point out "Which one is a girl?" or "Which one is a boy?" in a set of pictures). Hair length and clothing seem to be especially important cues in these early discriminations.

Accurate labeling, though, does not signify complete understanding. As is true with all the concepts I talked about in Chapter 7, which show increasing subtlety and complexity over the preschool and early school years, the gender concept undergoes further refinements. The second step is **gender stability,** the understanding that you stay the same gender throughout life. Researchers have measured this by asking children such questions as "When you were a little baby, were you a little girl or a little boy?" or "When you grow up will you be a mommy or a daddy?" Most children understand the stability aspect of gender by about age 4 (Slaby & Frey, 1975).

Finally, there is the development of true **gender constancy,** which is the recognition that someone stays the same gender even though he may appear to change by wearing different clothes or having a different hair length. For example, girls don't change into boys by cutting their hair very short or by wearing boys' clothes. It may seem odd that a child who understands that he will stay the same gender throughout life (gender stability) can nonetheless be confused about the effect of changes in dress or appearance on gender. But numerous studies show this sequence, including studies of children growing up in other cultures, such as Kenya, Nepal, Belize, and Samoa (Munroe, Shimmin, & Munroe, 1984).

The underlying logic of this sequence may be a bit clearer if I draw a parallel between gender constancy and the concept of conservation I described in Chapter 7. Conservation of mass or number or weight involves recognition that an object remains the same in some fundamental way even though it changes externally in some fashion. Gender constancy is thus a kind of "conservation of gender," and is not typically understood until about 5 or 6, when the other conservations are first grasped.

The Development of Sex-Role Concepts and Stereotypes. Obviously, figuring out your gender and understanding that it stays constant is only part of the story. Learning what goes with, or ought to go with, being a boy or a girl is also a vital part of the child's task.

Researchers have studied this in two ways—by asking children what boys and girls (or men and women) like to do and what they are like (which is an inquiry about sex-role *stereotypes*), and by asking children if it is *o.k.* for boys to play with dolls or girls to climb trees or to do equivalent cross-sex things (an inquiry about *sex roles*).

In our society, adults have clear sex-role stereotypes. We think of men as being competent, skillful, assertive, aggressive, and able to get things done. Adults see women as warm and expressive, tactful, quiet, gentle, aware of others' feelings, and lacking in competence, independence, and logic (Broverman et al., 1972; Ruble, 1983). Cross-cultural studies, such as Williams and Best's comparison of 26 cultures, show that highly similar stereotypes exist everywhere (Williams & Best, 1990).

Studies of children show that such stereotyping occurs early. The 3-year-old daughter of a friend of mine announced one day that Mommies use the stove and Daddies use the grill. Even 2-year-olds already associate certain tasks and possessions with men and women, such as vacuum cleaner or food with women and cars and tools with men. By age 3 or 4, children can assign a wide range of occupations, toys, and activities to the stereotypic gender. By age 5, children begin to associate certain personality traits with males or females, and such knowledge is well developed by age 8 or 9 (Martin, 1993; Serbin, Powlishta, & Gulko, 1993)— a pattern Williams and Best found in all the cultures they studied. The most clearly stereotyped traits are weakness, gentleness, appreciativeness, and softheartedness for women, and aggression, strength, cruelty, and coarseness with males.

Studies of children's ideas about what men and women (or boys and girls) *ought* to be like add an interesting additional element. For example, William Damon (1977) told a story to children aged 4 through 9 about a little boy named George who likes to play with dolls. He then asked each child a series of questions about George and the dolls. Four-year-olds in this study thought it was o.k. for George to play with dolls. There was no rule against it, and he should do it if he wanted to. Six-year-olds, in contrast, thought it was *wrong* for George to play with dolls. By about age 9, children had differentiated between what boys and girls usually do, and what is "wrong." One boy said, for example, that breaking windows was wrong and bad, but that playing with dolls was not bad in the same way: "breaking windows you're not supposed to do. And if you play with dolls, well you can, but boys usually don't."

What seems to be happening is that the 5- and 6-year-old, having figured out that she is permanently a girl or he is a boy, is searching for a *rule* about how boys and girls behave (Martin & Halverson, 1981). The child picks up information from watching adults, from watching TV, from listening to the labels that are attached to different activities (e.g., "boys don't cry"). Initially they treat these as

> In Western cultures, it is far more common for young girls to be "tomboys" than it is for boys to show "girlish" behavior. Does this mean girls have a less clear gender concept? What do you think might be causing such a difference?

Does this little boy, like the mythical George in Damon's studies, have a right to play with dolls? Four-year-olds and 9-year-olds are likely to think that he does, but many 6-year-olds think it is simply wrong for boys to do girl things or for girls to do boy things.

absolute, moral rules. Later they understand that these are social conventions, at which point sex-role concepts become more flexible, even while the child's understanding of the societal stereotype becomes more and more sharply defined.

The Development of Sex-Role Behavior.   The final element in the equation is the actual behavior children show with their own sex and with the opposite sex. The unexpected finding here is that children's *behavior* is sex typed earlier than are their ideas about sex roles.

By 18 to 24 months, children begin to show some preference for sex-stereotyped toys, such as dolls for girls or trucks or building blocks for boys, which is some months *before* they can consistently identify their own gender (O'Brien, 1992). By age 3, children begin to show a preference for same-sex playmates and are much more sociable with playmates of the same sex—at a time when they do not yet have a concept of gender stability (Maccoby, 1988; 1990; Maccoby & Jacklin, 1987).

The other intriguing pattern is that children in early elementary school seem to begin to pay more attention to the behavior of same-sex than opposite-sex adults or playmates, and to play more with new toys that are labeled as being appropriate for their own sex (Bradbard et al., 1986; Ruble, Balaban, & Cooper, 1981). Overall, then, we see many signs that children are both aware of and affected by gender from very early, perhaps by age 1, certainly by age 2. But gender becomes a still more potent force in guiding behavior and attitudes at around age 5 or 6.

Explaining Sex-Role Development.   Theorists from most of the major traditions have tried their hand at explaining this pattern of development. Freud relied on the concept of identification to explain the child's adoption of appropriate sex-role behavior, but his theory founders on the fact that children begin to show clearly sex-typed behavior long before age 4 or 5, when Freud thought identification occurred.

Social-learning theorists, such as Bandura (1977) and Mischel (1966; 1970) naturally emphasized the role of both direct reinforcement and of modeling in shaping children's sex-role behavior and attitudes. This notion has been far better supported by research. Parents do seem to reinforce sex-typed activities in children as young as 18 months old, not only by buying different kinds of toys for boys and girls, but by responding more positively when their sons play with blocks or trucks or when their daughters play with dolls (Fagot & Hagan, 1991; Lytton & Romney, 1991). Such differential reinforcement is particularly clear with boys and particularly from fathers (Siegal, 1987). There is also new evidence suggesting that toddlers whose parents are more consistent in rewarding sex-typed toy choice or play behavior, and whose mothers favor traditional family sex roles, learn accurate gender labels earlier than do toddlers whose parents are less focused on the gender-appropriateness of the child's play (Fagot & Leinbach, 1989; Fagot, Leinbach, & O'Boyle, 1992)—findings clearly consistent with the predictions of social-learning theory.

Cross-cultural evidence also supports a social-learning view. Anthropologist Beatrice Whiting (Whiting & Edwards, 1988), after examining patterns of

By age 2 or 3 we already see clear sex differences in children's toy choices. Left to their own devices, boys like this will select blocks or trucks to play with. Girls the same age are more likely to choose dolls or tea sets or dress-up clothes.

gender socialization in 11 different cultures, concludes that "we are the company we keep." In most cultures, girls and boys keep different company, beginning quite early, with girls spending more time with women as well as in child-care responsibilities. To the extent that this is true, it would provide each sex with more same-sex than opposite-sex models, and more opportunity for reinforcement of sex-appropriate behavior such as nurturance directed at younger siblings.

Still, helpful as it is, a social-learning explanation is probably not sufficient. In particular, there is less differential reinforcement of boy- versus girl-behavior than you'd expect and probably not enough to account for the very early and robust discrimination children seem to make on the basis of gender. Even children whose parents seem to treat their young sons and daughters in highly similar ways nonetheless learn gender labels and show same-sex playmate choices.

A third alternative, based strongly on Piagetian theory, is Lawrence Kohlberg's suggestion that the crucial aspect of the process is the child's understanding of the gender concept (1966; Kohlberg & Ullian, 1974). Once the child realizes that he is a boy or she is a girl forever, then it becomes highly important for the child to learn how to behave in a way that fits the category he or she belongs to. Specifically, Kohlberg predicts that we should see systematic same-sex imitation only *after* the child has shown full gender constancy. And in fact, children do seem to become much more sensitive to same-sex models after they have understood gender constancy (Frey & Ruble, 1992; Ruble et al., 1981). But Kohlberg's theory cannot easily handle the obvious fact that children show clear differential sex-role behavior, such as toy preferences, long before they have achieved full understanding of the gender concept.

The most fruitful current explanation is usually called **gender schema** theory (Martin, 1991; Martin & Halverson, 1981; 1983; Ruble, 1987). Just as the self-concept can be thought of as a "scheme" or "self-theory," so the child's understanding of gender can be seen in the same way. The gender schema begins to develop as soon as the child notices the differences between male and female, knows his own gender, and can label the two groups with some consistency—all of which happens by age 2 or 3. Perhaps because gender is clearly an either/or category, children seem to understand very early that this is a key distinction, so the category serves as a kind of magnet for new information (Maccoby, 1988). In Piaget's terms, once the child has established even a primitive gender-scheme, a great many experiences are assimilated to it. Thus as soon as this scheme begins to be formed, children may begin to show preference for same-sex playmates or for gender-stereotyped activities (Martin & Little, 1990).

Preschoolers first learn some broad distinctions about what kinds of activities or behavior go with each gender, both by observing other children and through the reinforcements they receive from parents. Then between age 4 and 6 the child learns a more subtle and complex set of associations for his or her *own* gender—what children of his own gender like and don't like, how they play, how they talk, what kinds of people they associate with. Only at about age 8 to 10 does the child develop an equivalently complex view of the opposite gender (Martin, Wood, & Little, 1990).

The key difference between this theory and Kohlberg's is that for a gender schema to be formed it is not necessary that the child understand that gender is permanent. When gender constancy is understood at about 5 or 6, she develops a more elaborated rule or schema of "what people who are like me do" and treats this "rule" the same way she treats other rules—as absolutes. Later, the child's application of the "gender rule" becomes more flexible. She knows, for example, that most boys don't play with dolls, but that they *can* do so if they like.

The Development of Self-Control

Along with a self-concept, the preschooler must also develop another aspect of the self—self-control. Toddlers live in the here-and-now. When they want something, they want it immediately. When they are tired, they cry; when they are hungry, they insist on food. They are bad at waiting or at working toward distant goals and find it hard to resist temptation. There is a joyous side to this same quality: because they live in the moment, they see things with new eyes—the bug on a leaf, the color of a particular flower, the delight in a favored food. But to function as acceptable social beings, they must learn self-control. Ultimately, the child must learn how to *inhibit* some unacceptable behavior and how to *direct* his own behavior toward some goal.

The process of acquiring such self-control is fundamentally one in which control shifts slowly from the parents to the child. With toddlers, parents provide most of the control, through the use of prohibitions and requests of various kinds. Over the years from 2 to 6, as the child gradually internalizes the various standards and expectations, the child takes on more of the control task for himself.

Such internalization, and the accompanying improvement in self-control, is obviously built on many earlier developments, including the growth of language. You'll recall from the last chapter that toddlers and preschool age children quite specifically use language to aid in their self-regulation and control, and language also makes it a great deal easier for parents to communicate clearly with their child. Internalization is also fostered by particular kinds of family interactions: parental warmth, sensitivity, responsiveness, and child-centered methods of control—qualities I'll have more to say about in a moment. For now, I merely want to point out that this list of family qualities should sound at least vaguely familiar: many of these same qualities also seem to foster secure attachments during the first year of life.

> If you had as one of your goals of child rearing to rear totally "nonsexist" children, how might you try to go about it, given what you have read about the emergence of the child's gender concept?

Understanding of Emotion

Still another ability that expands greatly in the preschool years and that has major repercussions for social relationships, is the ability to understand emotions. Think back, for example, to the description of young Andy and his sister Susie I quoted a few pages ago. Andy's reaction to the conversation between his mother and his baby sister was strongly affected by his reading of the emotions expressed in the interaction, including his mother's pleasure at Susie's behavior.

An ability to grasp others' emotions is also no doubt an important ingredient in the preschool child's emerging ability to form individual friendships

(Dunn & Brown, 1994; Hubbard & Coie, 1994). But the reverse is also true: social interactions are the arena in which the child learns about the meaning of emotional expressions.

The emergence of the child's understanding of emotions begins in infancy and rests on many of the cognitive changes I talked about in Chapter 7. You already know that by 10 to 12 months, babies can tell the difference between positive or negative facial expressions on others' faces, because at that age they already show *social referencing*. And by age 3, the child has begun to develop a theory of mind that includes the understanding that another person will feel sad if she fails or happy if she succeeds. A year or so later, at about age 4, the child begins to understand that others' behavior is governed by their beliefs and desires. Further, the preschool child begins to figure out that particular emotions occur in situations involving specific relationships between desire and reality. Sadness, for example, normally occurs when someone fails to acquire some desired object or loses something desired (Harris, 1989).

All of this may make it sound as if 4- and 5-year-olds have already understood everything they need to know about others' emotions. In fact, there is a good deal of more sophisticated knowledge still to come, such as understanding more complex or subtle emotions, and in grasping the fact that a person can have more than one emotion at the same time, even competing emotions.

For example, 4-year-olds can easily recognize facial expressions and situations that convey the emotions happy, sad, mad, loving, and scared. But feelings like pride or shame are understood only in middle childhood (Harter & Whitesell, 1989). Similarly, by age 6, children understand that a person can switch rather rapidly from sadness to happiness if circumstances change, but it is only at about age 10 that children begin to understand that a person can feel opposite feelings (ambivalence) at the same moment (Harter & Whitesell, 1989).

Cross-Cultural Comparisons.   One might reasonably ask—as with virtually all the developmental sequences I have given you in this book—whether children in every culture learn about emotions in this same way. In this case, we have a bit of evidence.

The Utka, an Inuit band in northern Canada, have two words for fear, distinguishing between fear of physical disaster and fear of being treated badly. In some African languages, there are no separate words for fear and sorrow. Samoans use the same word for love, sympathy, and liking, and Tahitians have no word at all that conveys the notion of guilt. These examples, drawn by James Russell (1989) from the anthropological literature, remind us that we need to be very careful when we talk about the "normal" process of a child learning about emotional expression and emotional meaning. From an English-speaking, Western perspective, emotions like fear or anger seem like "basic" emotions that all infants would understand early and easily. But what would be the developmental sequence for a child growing up in a culture in which fear and sorrow are not distinguished?

At the same time, the work of Paul Ekman (1972; 1973; 1989) has given us evidence of a strong cross-cultural similarity in people's facial expressions when conveying certain of these same "basic" emotions, such as fear, happiness, sad-

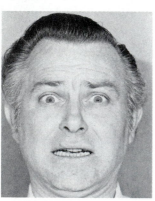

FIGURE 8.3
What emotion is being expressed in each of these photos? If you said happiness and fear, you agree with virtually all observers, in many countries, who have looked at these pictures. (Source: Copyright Paul Ekman.).

ness, anger, and disgust. (Figure 8.3 shows two such common expressions). In all cultures studied so far, adults understand these facial expressions as having the same core meaning. Cultural variations are laid on top of these basic expressive patterns, and cultures have different rules about which emotions may be expressed and which must be masked. But there appears to be some common ground as well. One could argue that infants and toddlers are already quite good at discriminating and understanding these shared patterns. Even 2-year-olds can recognize and categorize happy and sad expressions. The child must then slowly learn all the cultural overlays—the links between emotion and situation that hold for each culture, the specific meanings of emotional language, the scripts that govern the appropriate expression of emotion in a given culture. No small task. What is remarkable is just how much of this information the preschooler already comprehends and reflects in his own behavior.

Individual Differences in Social Behavior and Personality

So far I've been talking primarily about shared developmental patterns. But I am sure it is obvious to you that in the preschool years, children's relationships, social behavior, and personalities become even more divergent than was true among infants. Some toddlers and preschoolers are highly aggressive, defiant, and difficult to manage (Campbell & Ewing, 1990; Patterson, Capaldi, & Bank, 1991). Some are shy and retiring, while others are sociable and outgoing. These differences clearly have a variety of sources. Inborn temperament seems to play some role in creating such differences, although by this age the child's temperamental tendencies have also been shaped by the parents' behavior. The security or insecurity of the child's first attachment is also part of the equation, as you have already seen in Chapter 6. Yet another causal element seems to be the parents' style of child rearing—the way they deal with the need to discipline and control the child, the extent to which they show affection and warmth, the contingency of their responses.

Temperament Differences

As I mentioned in Chapter 2, variations in the child's temperament, such as "easiness" or "difficultness," become reasonably stable in the preschool years. At this same age, we also begin to see a link between difficultness of temperament and both concurrent and future behavior problems: Three- or 4-year-olds with difficult temperaments are more likely to show heightened aggressiveness, delinquency, or other forms of behavior problems in school, both as teenagers and adults (Bates, 1989; Bates, Maslin, & Frankel, 1985; Chess & Thomas, 1984). It is important to understand, though, that this is a *probability* statement. The majority of preschoolers who are classed as having difficult temperaments do *not* develop later behavior problems, although the likelihood of such an outcome is greater. Probably the easiest way to think of it is that a difficult temperament

If young Frank's tantrum is part of a regular pattern of difficult behavior, then the chances are higher that he will have behavior problems later in elementary school or adolescence. But such an outcome is not inevitable.

creates a *vulnerability* in the child. If this vulnerable child has supportive and loving parents who are able to deal effectively with the child's difficultness, the trajectory is altered and the child does not develop broader social problems. But if the parents do not like the child, or lack suitable child rearing skills, or if the family is facing other stresses, the vulnerable, difficult child is highly likely to emerge from the preschool years with serious problems relating to others (Bates, 1989; Fish, Stifter, & Belsky, 1991).

The Impact of the Family: Styles of Parenting

The research on temperament gives us but one of many illustrations of the importance of understanding the family's role in the child's emerging personality or social behavior. Psychologists have struggled over the years to identify the best ways of describing the many dimensions along which families may vary. At the moment, the most fruitful conceptualization is one offered by Diana Baumrind (1972), who focuses on four aspects of family functioning: nurturance or warmth, firmness and clarity of control, level of maturity demands, and degree of communication between parent and child.

Each of these four dimensions has been independently shown to be related to various child behaviors. Children with nurturant and warm parents, as opposed to those with more rejecting parents, are more securely attached in the first two years of life, have higher self-esteem, are more empathetic, more altruistic, more responsive to others' hurts or distress, have higher measured IQs in preschool and elementary school, and are less likely to show delinquent behavior in adolescence or criminal behavior in adulthood (Maccoby, 1980; Schaefer, 1989; Simons, Robertson, & Downs, 1989). High levels of affection can even buffer the child against the negative effects of otherwise disadvantageous environ-

The Long-Term Consequences of Hostility and Abuse

The other end of the warmth continuum is, of course, hostility, a pattern of parental behavior associated with a whole range of lousy outcomes for children, especially when that hostility takes physical form, as abuse. I talked a bit about abuse and some of its causes in a box in Chapter 6. Let me touch here on some of the consequences.

Physically abused children are far more likely than are nonabused children to become aggressive or delinquent later in childhood or violent as an adult—including such behaviors as date rape or spousal abuse. They are more likely to be substance abusers in adolescence and adulthood, to attempt suicide, to have emotional problems such as anxiety or depression or more serious forms of emotional illness, and to have lower IQs, and poorer school performance (Malinosky-Rummell & Hansen, 1993).

Sexually abused children also show a wide variety of disturbances, including fears, posttraumatic stress disorder, behavior problems, and poor self-esteem (Kendall-Tackett, Williams, & Finkelhor, 1993). Children who suffer either type of abuse do not typically show *all* these symptoms, but they are far more likely than are their nonabused peers to show some form of significant disturbance. The more lasting and severe the abuse, the greater the likelihood of problems of these types.

The picture is not totally bleak. Some abused children show no measurable symptoms, and when the abuse is stopped, many children show a decline in symptoms of distress, especially when the mother was supportive and protective toward the child. But let us not lose sight of the fact that long-term problems are common among children who experience this degree of hostility or hurt, nor of the fact that our society has not yet found good ways of reducing the incidence of such abuse.

---

ments. McCord, for example (1982) has found that among boys growing up in single-parent families in poor, tough neighborhoods, those whose mothers were rejecting were three times as likely to become delinquent or criminal as were those with affectionate and warm mothers.

I suspect that the role of warmth in fostering a secure attachment of the child to the parent is one of the key elements in this picture. You already know from Chapter 6 that securely attached children are more skillful with their peers, more exploratory, more sure of themselves. Warmth also makes children generally more responsive to guidance, so the parents' affection and warmth increase the potency of the things that parents say to their children and the efficiency of their discipline (MacDonald, 1992).

The degree and clarity of the parents' control over the child is also a highly significant aspect of family style. Parents with clear rules, consistently applied, have children who are much less likely to be defiant or noncompliant—a pattern you'll remember from Gerald Patterson's research, which I talked about in Chapter 1 (Figure 1.2). But such clarity does not produce little robots. Children from families with consistent rules are also more competent and sure of themselves (Baumrind, 1973), and less aggressive (Patterson, 1980).

Equally important is the *form* of control the parent uses. The most optimal outcomes for the child occur when the parent is not overly restrictive, explains things to the child, and avoids the use of physical punishments.

We also find more optimal outcomes for children whose parents have high expectations, or high "maturity demands" in Baumrind's language. Such children have higher self-esteem, show more generosity and altruism toward others, and lower levels of aggression.

Finally, open and regular communication between parent and child has been linked to more positive outcomes. Listening to the child is as important as talking. Ideally, the parent needs to convey to the child that what the child has to say is *worth* listening to, that his ideas are important and should be considered in family decisions. Children from such families have been found to be more emotionally and socially mature (Baumrind, 1971; 1973; Bell & Bell, 1982).

To Spank or Not to Spank

The short, emphatic answer to the question, "Should I spank my child?" is NO. I am well aware that this is easier to say than to do, (and I admit to having applied a hand to my own children's rear ends on one or two occasions, even knowing that it would do little good and some potential damage). But the information we have about the effects of physical punishment, including spanking, seems to me to be so clear that a firm answer to the question is possible.

Note please: I am not talking here about physical abuse, although certainly some parents do abuse their children by spanking excessively with a switch or a brush or other objects. I'm talking about the ordinary kind of spanking—two or three hard swats on the rear—that most people think of as normal and helpful. Even physicians generally approve physical punishment of this kind. In one recent survey of family physicians and pediatricians, roughly two-thirds said they approved of spanking (McCormick, 1992). But in my view they are wrong.

In the short term, spanking a child usually *does* get the child to stop the particular behavior you didn't like, and it seems to have a *temporary* effect of reducing the chance that the child will repeat the bad behavior. Since that's what you wanted, it may seem like a good strategy. But even in the short term there are some negative side effects. The child may have stopped misbehaving, but after a spanking he is likely to be crying, which may be almost as distressing as the original misbehavior. And crying is a behavior that spanking does not decrease: it is virtually impossible to get children to stop crying by spanking them! So you have exchanged one unpleasantness for another, and the second unpleasantness (crying) can't be dealt with by using the same form of punishment.

Another short-term side effect is that *you* are being reinforced for spanking whenever the child stops misbehaving after you spank her. Thus you are being "trained" to use spanking the next time, and a cycle is being built up.

In the longer term, the effects are uniformly negative. First, when you spank, the child observes you using physical force or violence as a method of solving problems or getting people to do what you want. You thus serve as a model for a behavior you do *not* want your child to use with others.

Second, by repeatedly pairing your presence with the unpleasant or painful event of spanking, you are undermining your own positive value for your child. Over time, this means that you are less able to use *any* kind of reinforcement effectively. Eventually even your praise or affection will be less powerful in influencing your child's behavior. That is a very high price to pay.

Third, there is frequently a strong underlying emotional message that goes with spanking—anger, rejection, irritation, dislike of the child. Even very young children read this emotional message quite clearly (Rohner, Kean, & Cournoyer, 1991). Spanking thus helps to create a family climate of rejection instead of warmth, with all the attendant negative consequences.

Finally, there is research evidence that children who are spanked—just like children who are abused—more often show higher levels of aggression and less popularity with their peers, lower self-esteem, and more emotional instability (Rohner et al., 1991). These are not outcomes parents intend for their children.

I am *not* saying that you should never punish a child. I *am* saying that *physical punishment*, such as spanking, is not a good way to go about it. If you have been brought up in a family in which spanking was the standard method, you may simply not know other ways. If you find yourself in this position, a parenting class—often offered by community colleges or other community organizations—might be of help.

While each of these characteristics of families may be significant individually, in fact they do not occur in isolation. They occur in combinations and patterns. Baumrind has identified three such patterns or styles:

- The **permissive style** is high in nurturance, but low in maturity demands, control, and communication;
- The **authoritarian style** is high in control and maturity demands, but low in nurturance and communication;
- The **authoritative style** is high in all four.

Eleanor Maccoby and John Martin (1983) have proposed a variation of Baumrind's category system, shown in Figure 8.4, which I find even more helpful. They categorize families on two dimensions, the degree of demand or control and the amount of acceptance/rejection. The intersection of these two dimensions creates four types, three of which correspond quite closely to Baumrind's authoritarian, authoritative, and permissive types. Maccoby and Martin's conceptualization adds the fourth type, the **neglecting** or uninvolved style, which current research tells us may be the most detrimental of the four. Let me talk briefly about each style.

The Authoritarian Type. Children growing up in authoritarian families—with high levels of demand and control but relatively low levels of warmth or responsiveness—typically are less skilled with peers than are children from other types of families and have lower self-esteem. Some of these children appear subdued; others may show high aggressiveness or other indications of being out of control. Which of these two outcomes occurs may depend in part on how skillfully the parents use the various disciplinary techniques. Patterson finds that the "out of control" child is most likely to come from a family in which the parents are authoritarian by inclination, but lack the skills to enforce the limits or rules they set. Studies of older children and adolescents show the same patterns. In

	LEVEL OF ACCEPTANCE	
	Accepting, responsive	Rejecting, unresponsive
LEVEL OF DEMAND AND CONTROL — Demanding, controlling	Authoritative, reciprocal	Authoritarian, power-assertive
Undemanding, low in control attempts	Indulgent, permissive	Neglecting, uninvolved

FIGURE 8.4

Maccoby and Martin expanded on Baumrind's categories in this two-dimensional typology. (Source: Adapted from E. E. Maccoby & J. A. Martin, 1983. Socialization in the context of the family. Parent-child interaction. In E. M. Hethrington (Ed.), *Handbook of child psychology*, Figure 2, p. 39. New York: Wiley.)

a study of nearly 8,000 high school students, Sanford Dornbusch and his co-workers (Dornbusch et al., 1987; Lamborn et al., 1991) have found that teenagers from authoritarian families have poorer grades in school and more negative self-concepts than do teenagers from authoritative families.

It is somewhat surprising that children reared in permissive families are *less* independent and take *less* responsibility. You might think that such children have been specifically encouraged and reinforced for independence and decision making. Can you think of any reason why this pattern of results might occur?

The Permissive Type.   Children growing up with indulgent or permissive parents, too, show some negative outcomes. Dornbusch finds that they do slightly worse in school during adolescence, are likely to be more aggressive— particularly if the parents are specifically permissive toward aggressiveness—and to be somewhat immature in their behavior with peers and in school. They are less likely to take responsibility and are less independent.

The Authoritative Type.   The most consistently positive outcomes have been associated with the authoritative pattern, in which the parents are high in both control and warmth, setting clear limits but also responding to the child's individual needs. Children reared in such families typically show higher self-esteem, are more independent but at the same time are more likely to comply with parental requests, and may show more altruistic behavior as well. They are self-confident and achievement oriented in school and get better grades (Boyes & Allen, 1993; Crockenberg & Litman, 1990; Dornbusch et al., 1987; Lamborn et al., 1991; Steinberg, Elmen, & Mounts, 1989).

The Neglecting Type.   In contrast, the most consistently negative outcomes are associated with the fourth pattern, the neglecting or uninvolved type. You may remember from the discussion of secure and insecure attachments in Chapter 6 that one of the family characteristics often found in children rated as insecure/avoidant is the "psychological unavailability" of the mother. The mother may be depressed or may be overwhelmed by other problems in her life and simply not have made any deep emotional connection with the child. Whatever the reason, such children continue to show disturbances in their relationships with peers and with adults for many years. At adolescence, for example, youngsters from neglecting families are more impulsive and antisocial, less competent with their peers, and much less achievement oriented in school (Block, 1971; Lamborn et al., 1991; Pulkkinen, 1982).

Several conclusions from this research are important. First, it seems clear that children are affected by the family "climate" or style. It seems highly likely that these effects persist well into adulthood, although we do not have the sort of longitudinal data we would need to be sure. Second, many of us are accustomed to thinking about family styles as if permissive and authoritarian patterns were the only options. But research on the authoritarian pattern shows clearly that one can be *both* affectionate and firm, and that children respond to this combination in very positive ways.

Family Structure: Divorce and Other Variations

Beyond parenting style, another obvious aspect of the family system is the particular configuration of people who live together in a given family unit—an aspect usually called *family structure*. I suspect that many of us still harbor the illusion that the most common family structure is a father, a mother, and several children. And no doubt many of us still think that the majority of children spend all of their childhood and adolescence with the same Mom and Dad. But in the United States today, both those assumptions are wrong.

Sandra Hofferth (1985) has generated some particularly startling estimates, based on a longitudinal study of over 5,000 American families who have been followed since 1968. She projects that only 30 percent of White children in the United States born in 1980 will still be living with their two natural parents at age 17. For Black children, the figure is only 6 percent. Other estimates are somewhat more optimistic (Bumpass, 1984; Norton & Glick, 1986), but there is agreement that a minimum of 60 percent of children born in the United States today will spend at least *some* part of their childhood in a single-parent household. Perhaps 35 percent will spend at least a part of their childhood with a step-parent.

An equally striking look at the enormous variety of family structures comes from a study of a large sample of children from a poor, Black Chicago neighborhood whose family patterns were first observed when they were in first grade in 1967 (Kellam, Ensminger, & Turner, 1977), and then again in 1976, when they were adolescents (Hunter & Ensminger, 1992). Figure 8.5 shows the results for both time points so that you can see the changes that occurred and the enormous

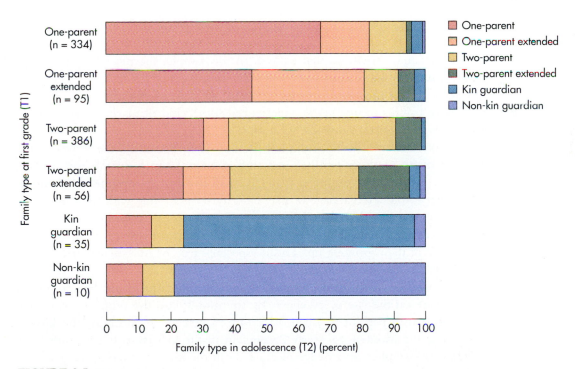

FIGURE 8.5

This figure is complicated, but it is worth your study. Each row represents a group of Black children who had been in a particular form of family in first grade. The divisions on each row then indicate what kind of family structures those children lived in at adolescence. You can also get some sense of the proportions of each type of structure by looking at the numbers of families of each type at first grade (given as n = xxx along the left). (Source: Hunter & Ensminger, 1992, Figure 1, p. 443.)

CULTURES & CONTEXTS

The Benefits of Extended Families

Because single-parent families have become so common in the United States, researchers here tend to develop a kind of tunnel vision when it comes to studies of "family structure." For us, the question nearly always translates to a comparison of single-parent families with two-parent families. But in many parts of the world, the normative form of family life is not the nuclear or two-parent family, but rather an *extended* family, in which several generations live together in the same household. One recent study from the Sudan provides a kind of antidote to our typical cultural myopia.

Al Hassan Al Awad and Edmund Sonuga-Barke (1992) compared the incidence of childhood problems for children who lived in Western-style nuclear families (mother and father only) versus those who lived in traditional extended families, in which three generations lived in the same household. All these families lived in towns near Khartoum (the capital of Sudan), and the two groups were matched for social status and approximate income. The mothers were interviewed about their child's behavior and problems.

The findings are very clear: children reared in extended households were described as better off than were those living in nuclear households. They had fewer conduct problems, fewer sleep problems, better self-care, and were less likely to be overly dependent. The best single predictor of these good outcomes was the involvement of the child's grandmother in the child's care, and this was true within the group of nuclear families as well as in the comparison of nuclear and extended families.

How many different explanations for this result can you think of? Should we generalize this finding to Western cultures and conclude that extended families would typically be better for children? How could you check out such a hypothesis?

variety of family structures that existed. In this sample, the most frequent stable family structure was a single-parent family. Two-parent families were somewhat less likely to have persisted over the 10 years; 42 percent of those who still lived with both parents in first grade experienced some kind of marital dissolution in the following 10 years—divorce, separation, or death.

Even this remarkably complex picture doesn't convey the whole story, because many of these families had shifted several times during the decade. Divorced mothers, for example, may have had live-in relationships with one or more men before a remarriage or may have lived for a while with their own parents. All in all, it is clear that the *majority* of children in the United States today experience at least two different family structures, often many more than that in the course of their growing up. This is especially true of African-Americans, but is increasingly true of other ethnic groups in our culture as well.

In other industrialized countries, single-parent families are less common, but they are on the rise everywhere. By the mid-1980s, the proportions ranged from less than 5 percent in Japan, to about 15 percent in Australia, the United Kingdom, and Sweden, to nearly 25 percent in the U.S (Burns, 1992). Because cultures are complex, knowledge gleaned about the impact of family structure on children's development in one country may not hold elsewhere. But the issue is growing in importance in many parts of the world

What do we know about the impact on children of being reared in such varied or varying family structures? Not as much as we'd like, but let me explore several issues.

The Impact of Divorce Itself.   Any change in the family structure is accompanied by dislocation and stress. In the case of divorce or separation, when an adult is subtracted from the family, the dislocation seems to be especially severe. In the several years immediately after a divorce, children become more defiant, more negative, more aggressive, depressed, or angry. If they are of school age, their school performance typically drops for at least a while (Furstenberg & Cherlin, 1991; Hetherington, 1989; Hetherington & Clingempeel, 1992). There is some disagreement about how long this negative effect may last for the child. Some investigators report lingering effects 5 and 10 years later (1989; Wallerstein, 1984). Others do not find such lasting effects (Hetherington, 1989), but all agree that in the short term, children are disturbed.

These negative effects are considerably larger for boys than for girls. Age differences in the severity of the reaction, however, are typically not found. Specifically, contrary to predictions from Freudian theory, preschoolers are *not* more severely affected than those of other ages.

The parents' behavior is also disrupted. The adults may show wide mood swings, experience problems at work, or poor health. Their parenting style also changes, becoming much less authoritative, almost neglectful (Hetherington, 1989). In particular, they do much less well at monitoring their children's

> Why would Freud's theory lead to a prediction that the impact of divorce would be greater for preschool-age children?

The Real World
Softening the Effects of Divorce

Given the rate of divorce in our culture, a significant percentage of you reading these words will go through a divorce when you have children still living at home. There is no way to eliminate all the disruptive effects of such an event on your children, but here are some specific things you can do that are likely to soften or shorten the effects:

1. Try to keep the number of separate changes the child has to cope with to a minimum. If at all possible, keep the children in the same school, in the same home, and the same day-care setting, etc.

2. Maintain your own network of support and use that network liberally. Stay in touch with friends, seek out others in the same situation, join a support group. In whatever way you can, nurture yourself and your own needs (Hetherington & Camera, 1984).

3. Help your child(ren) stay in touch with the noncustodial parent. If you are the noncustodial parent, maintain as much contact as possible with your child(ren), calling regularly, seeing them regularly, attending school functions, etc. I should tell you that the evidence on this point is actually quite mixed; some studies show no positive benefit to the child of continued regular contact with the non-

custodial parent (Emery, 1988). The difficulty in interpreting these results is that contact with the noncustodial parent is often confounded with the quality of the relationship between the now-divorced parents, which leads to the next point:

4. If you and your ex-spouse continue to have conflict, try very hard not to fight in front of the children. Conflict between the spouses itself seems not to be inevitably detrimental; it is the conflict that the child actually sees and hears that adds to the child's level of stress and disruption (Emery, 1988). If such conflict is low, then increased contact with the noncustodial parent seems most likely to be beneficial to the child.

5. Whatever else you do, do not use the child as a go-between or talk disparagingly about your ex-spouse to your child. Children who feel caught in the middle between the two parents are more likely to show various kinds of negative symptoms, such as depression or behavior problems (Buchanan, Maccoby, & Dornbusch, 1991).

In the midst of your own emotional upheaval from a divorce, these are not easy prescriptions to follow. But if you are able to do so, your children will suffer less.

Stepfamily structures like this one are extremely complex, full of strains and difficulties not found in original families.

behavior and setting clear rules or limits, a pattern that typically persists for several years, even if the mother remarries (Hetherington & Clingempeel, 1992).

In all of this, it is not clear yet just what the causal agent is, because there are so many changes that happen at the same time a couple divorces: the loss of one member of the family system, a rise in conflict between the parents, economic hardship (especially for the single mother, in most cases), and other stressful life changes. The disruption in the children's behavior and in the adults' behavior seems to result from some combination of these factors, although of them all, open conflict between the parents may well be the most critical (Amato, 1993).

Interestingly, it appears that many of these negative effects for both the adult and the children are mitigated when the mother has another adult in the home—her own mother, a friend, a live-in boyfriend (Dornbusch et al., 1985; Kellam et al., 1977), which suggests that a two-adult system in a family may simply be more stable or easier to manage.

Step-parent Families.   However—and this is an important however—there are various indications that this buffering effect of a second adult in the home may *not* extend to step-parent family structures (mother/stepfather or father/stepmother). For example, Dornbusch, in his large study of adolescents, finds that step-parent families show higher levels of authoritarian and lower levels of authoritative child-rearing styles (Dornbusch et al., 1987), and the children have lower school grades and higher rates of delinquency than do children in two-natural-parent families. Mavis Hetherington, one of the key researchers in this field, has found something similar in a major study comparing intact, single-mother, and mother-stepfather families, all with adolescent children (Hetherington & Clingempeel, 1992). The stepfathers in this study were consistently less likely to be authoritative than were nondivorced fathers. Indeed, stepfathers were typically disengaged from the child-rearing role, with little involvement or rapport with their stepchildren. These patterns persisted even several years after the remarriage, suggesting that the process of adaptation in these families is extremely difficult. For remarried families with younger children, the process appears to be somewhat easier, although just why that should be so is not yet clear (Hetherington, 1989).

In the end, the research on divorced and step-parent families may point us to the conclusion that the family *process* is more important than the family structure. For example, authoritative child rearing is linked to low levels of disturbed behaviors and higher levels of psychological adjustment in the child whether the child is growing up with a single mother, with a mother and stepfather, with two natural parents, or in any other family structure. Similarly, any time the relationship between the two adults in the family system weakens in some fashion, such as when the husband and wife are experiencing stress or heightened conflict, behavior standards for children decline, and this is true whether the couple divorces or not (Goldberg, 1990).

It is still early days in our understanding of the impact of various types of family structure. But even these preliminary findings illustrate once again just how complex the family system really is. It is not enough merely to contrast "intact" and "divorced" families, or "single-parent" and "two-parent" families. We need to understand what goes on *inside* the families, and how that process is affected by structure.

S U M M A R Y

1. Freud and Erikson each described two stages of personality development during the preschool years—the anal and phallic in Freud's theory, autonomy and initiative in Erikson's theory.

2. Both vertical relationships, such as with parents and teachers, and horizontal relationships with peers are highly important in these years. Only in play with peers can the child learn about reciprocal relationships, both cooperative and competitive.

3. The child's attachment to the parent(s) remains strong, but attachment behaviors become less visible as the child gets older, except in stressful situations.

4. At about age 4, the child's attachment appears to change in quality, and there is also a peak of aggression toward the same-sex parent and of affection toward the opposite-sex parent.

5. Although preschoolers show more refusals and defiance of parental influence attempts than do infants, compliance is actually the most common pattern. Outright defiance declines from 2 to 6.

6. Both these changes are clearly linked to the child's language and cognitive gains.

7. Sibling relationships in these years are complex and full of ambivalence. The younger sib typically imitates the elder sib more; both express both antagonistic and positive behaviors and feelings toward one another.

8. Parents often treat siblings quite differently. The more this is so, the more rivalry or hostility is likely to exist between siblings.

9. Play with peers is visible before age 2 and becomes increasingly central through the preschool years. Aggression with peers is also evident, more physical in the 2- and 3-year-old, more verbal in the 5- and 6-year-old.

10. Children as young as 2 also show altruistic behavior toward others, and this behavior seems to grow as the child's ability to take another's perspective increases.

11. Short-term friendships are also evident in children in this age range. The majority of such pairs are same-sex.

12. The preschooler continues to define himself along a series of objective dimensions, but does not yet have a global sense of self-esteem.

13. Between 2 and 6, most children move through a series of steps in their understanding of gender constancy, first labeling their own and others' gender, then understanding the stability of gender, and finally the constancy of gender at about age 5 or 6.

14. In these same years, children begin to learn what is "appropriate" behavior for their gender. By age 5 or 6, most children have clear gender stereotypes and have developed fairly rigid rules about what boys or girls are supposed to do or be.

15. The earliest to develop is sex-role behavior. Sex-typed toy choices are evident from age 2; same-sex playmate preference is clear by 3.

16. Neither Freud's nor Kohlberg's explanations of gender development has fared well. Social learning explanations are more persuasive, because parents do appear to do some differential reinforcement of sex-appropriate behavior. The most useful current theory is gender schema theory, which combines some elements of Piagetian and social-learning models.

17. As early as age 3 or 4, boys and girls show different patterns or styles of interaction with peers, with girls showing an "enabling" style and boys a "constricting" style.

18. Preschoolers must also learn the rudiments of self-control, a process involving the transfer of control from parents to the child. Language and cognitive skills are an important ingredient.

19. The child's understanding of others' emotions grows rapidly in these years and is a critical ingredient in social relationships. By age 4 or 5, children understand some of the links between specific situations and others' likely emotions.

20. Cross-cultural research suggests some core or basic emotions common to all cultures; children must then learn the cultural specifics.

21. Children also differ widely in social behavior and personality. Temperament plays some role. Children with more difficult temperaments are more likely to show later behavior problems or delinquency.

22. Parental styles are also significant. Authoritative parenting, combining high warmth, clear rules and communication, and high maturity demands, is associated with the most positive outcomes. Neglecting parenting is associated with the least positive. Two other patterns, each with specific effects, are the authoritarian and the permissive.

23. Family structure also affects children. Following a divorce, children typically show disrupted behavior for several years. Parental styles become less authoritative.

24. Probably family process is more significant than family structure in affecting the child's development.

KEY TERMS

aggression	dominance hierarchy	gender stability
altruism	gender concept	neglecting style
authoritarian style	gender constancy	permissive style
authoritative style	gender identity	prosocial behavior
dominance	gender schema	sex role

SUGGESTED READINGS

Boer, F., & Dunn, J. (Eds.) (1992). *Children's sibling relationships. Developmental and clinical issues*. Hillsdale, NJ: Erlbaum. A first-rate collection of papers on a subject that is of growing interest to many psychologists. Each paper is relatively brief and reviews the available literature on one aspect of sibling relationships.

Cherlin, A. J. (1992). *Marriage, divorce, remarriage*. Cambridge, MA: Harvard University Press. An excellent, current review of all aspects of family formation, dissolution, and structural variations. It includes a long discussion of the impact of both race and poverty on the various trends.

Eisenberg, N. (1992). *The caring child*. Cambridge, MA: Harvard University Press. This is one of a series of excellent books aimed at the thoughtful lay reader rather than fellow professors.

Grusec, J. E., & Lytton, H. (1988). *Social development. History, theory, and research*. New York: Springer-Verlag. I recommended this in Chapter 6 and recommend it again here as an excellent, current text.

Lickona, T. (1983). *Raising good children*. Toronto: Bantam Books. One of the very best "how to" books for parents I have ever seen, with excellent, concrete advice as well as theory. His emphasis is on many of the issues I raised in *The Real World* discussion of rearing altruistic children.

Lieberman, A. F. (1993). *The emotional life of the toddler*. New York: The Free Press. Written for parents, this is an excellent discussion of many of the challenges and joys of this period of development.

Summing Up Preschool Development

BASIC CHARACTERISTICS OF THE PRESCHOOL PERIOD

The sense one gets of this period, summarized in the Table, is that the child is making a slow but immensely important shift from dependent baby to independent child. The toddler and preschooler can now move around easily, can communicate more and more clearly, has a sense of himself as a separate person with specific qualities, and has the beginning cognitive and social skills that allow him to interact more fully and successfully with playmates. At the same time, to use Piaget's term, the

child's thinking is *decentering*. She is shifting from using herself as the only frame of reference, and has become less tied to the outside appearances of things.

In the beginning, these new-found skills and new independence are not accompanied by impulse control. Two-year-olds are pretty good at doing; they are lousy at *not* doing. A large part of the conflict parents experience with children at this age comes about because the parent *must* limit the child, not only for the child's own survival, but to help teach the child impulse control (Excalona, 1981).

The preschool years also stand out as the period in which the seeds are sown for the child's—and perhaps the adult's—social skills and personality. The attachment process in infancy continues to be formative because it helps to shape the internal working model of social relationships the child creates. But in the years from 2 to 6, the child revises, consolidates, and establishes this early model more firmly. The resultant interactive patterns tend to persist into elementary school and beyond. The 3-, 4-, or 5-year-old who develops the ability to share, to read others' cues well, to

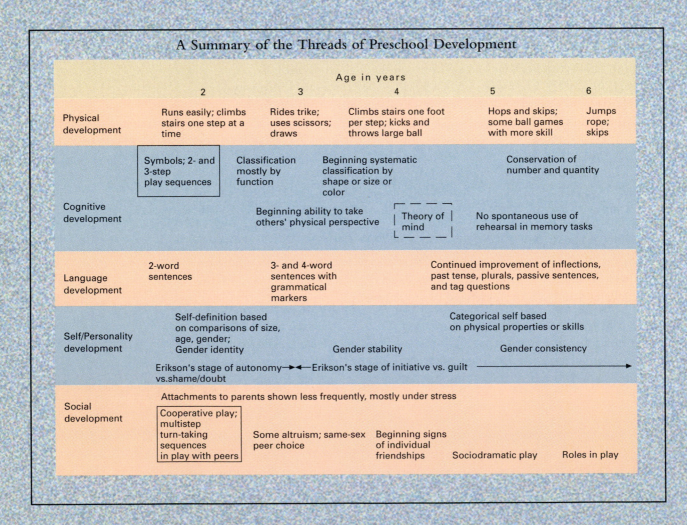

A Summary of the Threads of Preschool Development

	Age in years				
	2	3	4	5	6
Physical development	Runs easily; climbs stairs one step at a time	Rides trike; uses scissors; draws	Climbs stairs one foot per step; kicks and throws large ball	Hops and skips; some ball games with more skill	Jumps rope; skips
Cognitive development	Symbols; 2- and 3-step play sequences	Classification mostly by function	Beginning systematic classification by shape or size or color	Conservation of number and quantity	
		Beginning ability to take others' physical perspective	Theory of mind	No spontaneous use of rehearsal in memory tasks	
Language development	2-word sentences	3- and 4-word sentences with grammatical markers	Continued improvement of inflections, past tense, plurals, passive sentences, and tag questions		
Self/Personality development	Self-definition based on comparisons of size, age, gender; Gender identity		Gender stability	Categorical self based on physical properties or skills	
				Gender consistency	
	Erikson's stage of autonomy vs.shame/doubt → ← Erikson's stage of initiative vs. guilt →				
Social development	Attachments to parents shown less frequently, mostly under stress				
	Cooperative play; multistep turn-taking sequences in play with peers	Some altruism; same-sex peer choice	Beginning signs of individual friendships	Sociodramatic play	Roles in play

respond positively to others, and to control aggression and impulsiveness, is likely to be a socially successful, popular 8-year-old. In contrast, the noncompliant, hostile preschooler is far more likely to become an unpopular, aggressive school child (Campbell et al., 1991; Patterson, Capaldi, & Bank, 1991).

CENTRAL PROCESSES

There are clearly many forces at play in creating these changes, beginning with two immense cognitive advances in this period: the 18- or 24-month-old child's new ability to use symbols and the rapid development, between ages 3 and 5, of a more sophisticated theory of mind.

Symbol Use. The development of symbol use is reflected in many different aspects of the child's life. We see it in the rapid surge of language development, in the child's approach to cognitive tasks, and in play, where the child now pretends, having an object *stand for* something else. The ability to use language more skillfully, in turn, affects social behavior in highly significant ways, such as the increasing use of verbal rather than physical aggression, and the use of negotiation with parents in place of tantrums or defiant behavior.

Theory of Mind. The emergence of the child's more sophisticated theory of mind has equally broad effects, especially in the social arena, where the child's new found abilities to read and understand others' behaviors form the foundation for new levels of interactions with peers and parents. It is probably not accidental that individual friendships between children are first visible at about the time that they also show the sharp drop in egocentrism that occurs with the emergence of the theory of mind.

We also see the seminal role of cognitive changes in the growing importance of several basic schemes. Not only does the 2- or 3-year-old have a more and more generalized internal model of attachment, she also develops a self-scheme and a gender-scheme, each of which forms part of the foundation of both social behavior and personality.

Play with Peers. Important as these cognitive changes are, they are clearly not the only causal forces. Equally central is the child's play with peers, which is itself made possible by the new physical and cognitive skills we see in the 2-year-old. When children play together they expand each other's experience with objects and suggest new ways of pretending to one another, thus fostering still further cognitive growth. Conflict and disagreement are also key parts of children's play, affecting not only the child's emerging social skills, but stimulating the growth of theory of mind (Bearison, Magzamen, & Filardo, 1986). When two children disagree about how to explain something or insist on their own different views, it enhances each child's awareness that there *are* other perspectives, other ways of thinking or playing.

Of course play with other children is also a part of the child's developing gender schema. Noticing whether other people are boys or girls and what toys boys and girls play with is itself the first step in the long chain of sex role learning.

Family Interactions. It is also in social interactions, especially those with parents, that the child's initial social behaviors are modified or reinforced. The parents' style of discipline becomes critical here. Gerald Patterson's work shows clearly that parents who lack the skills to control the toddler's impulsivity and demands for independence are likely to end up strengthening noncompliant and disruptive behavior, even if the parent's intention is the reverse (Patterson & Bank, 1989; Patterson et al., 1991).

INFLUENCES ON THE BASIC PROCESSES

The family's ability to support the child's development in these years is affected not only by the skills and knowledge the parents bring to the process, but also by the amount of stress they are experiencing from outside forces and the quality of support they have in their personal lives (Crockenberg & Litman, 1990; Morisset et al., 1990). In particular, mothers who are experiencing high levels of stress are more likely to be punitive and negative toward their children, with resulting increases in the child's defiant and noncompliant behavior (Webster-Stratton, 1988). And maternal negativity, in turn, is implicated in the persistence of noncompliant behavior into elementary school. This link is clear in Susan Campbell's longitudinal study of a group of such noncompliant children (Campbell & Ewing, 1990; Campbell et al., 1986; Campbell et al., 1991). She finds that among a group of 3-year-olds who were labeled as "hard-to-manage," those who improved by age 6 had mothers who had been less negative.

The mother's stress is obviously not the only factor in her level of negativity toward the child. Depressed mothers are also more likely to show such behavior (Conrad & Hammen, 1989), as are mothers from working-class or poverty-level families, who may well have experienced such negativity and harsh discipline in their own childhoods. But stress and lack of personal social support are part of the equation. Thus the preschooler, like children of every age, is affected by broader social forces outside the family as well as by the family interaction itself.

Chapter Nine

Physical and Cognitive Development from 6 to 12

T he years of middle childhood, marked on one side by the beginning of schooling and on the other by the onset of puberty, are often passed over rather briefly as if they were somehow insignificant. Far less research has been done on children this age than on either preschoolers or adolescents. Even theorists often give less emphasis to this period. Freud, for example, referred to this as the "latency" period, as if development had gone underground. Yet it is clear that there are major cognitive advances in these years, and that patterns and habits established during this time will affect not only adolescent experience, but also adulthood.

The beginning of formal schooling is itself a remarkable change. To be sure, the ever-growing proportion of children who have spent time in day care or preschool arrive at school with a good deal of school-like experience. This may make the transition to school less dramatic, but even for these children, school represents a major change in the level of expectation for performance that the child must try to meet. School signifies the beginning of the time when the child is expected to learn all those specific competencies and roles that are part of his culture, including the three Rs. Erikson focused on precisely this aspect of the period from 6 to 12, calling this stage *industry versus inferiority*.

What hypotheses can you generate to explain why developmental psychologists have studied middle childhood less than any other age period of childhood?

Physical Changes in Middle Childhood

Perhaps one reason that middle childhood has been such a neglected area of study is that there is no remarkable physical change in children in this period. Change is steady, but not striking. The growth patterns established in the late preschool years continue, with 2 to 3 inches and about 6 lbs added each year. Most of the significant motor skills have been developed in at least basic form by age 6 or 7, so what we see between 6 and 12 is increasing speed and strength, better and better coordination, and greater skill at specific physical tasks. As just

Children all over the world start school at about the same age. Here you can see a Czech classroom and one in an aboriginal school in Australia.

In the U.S., and increasingly in other industrialized countries, children no longer play much in the street or in backyards; they play on organized teams and groups: soccer teams, Little League baseball, Pee Wee League football, swimming clubs and the like. Many children begin such programs when they are 6 or 7, often with great enthusiasm. But participation peaks by age 10 or 11, and then declines rapidly. Why?

Kids drop out of such programs because the emphasis on competition and winning is so great (Harvard Education Letter, 1992). Amateur coaches often have no good idea what kinds of motor skills are normal for a 6- or 7-year-old, so when they see a child who does not yet throw a ball skillfully or who kicks a ball awkwardly, they label this child as clumsy or uncoordinated. From then on, these perfectly normal kids get little playing time or encouragement. Only the stars—children with unusually good or early motor skill development—get maximum attention and exercise.

In fact 6 or 7 is really too early for most children to be playing on full-sized playing fields or in competitive games (Kolata, 1992). It would be far better to wait until age 9 or 10—if then— for competitive games and to have kids spend the earlier years learning and perfecting basic skills in activities that are fun regardless of a child's skill level; these activities should involve as much movement as possible. One expert, Vern Seefeldt, the director of the Institute for the Study of Youth Sports at Michigan State University, says:

The Real World
Sports for Children

Children need to be in situations where their participation and ability to learn skills are maximized. In an adult game, you try to throw the ball so the batter can't hit it or kick the ball where it can't be retrieved. With kids, you need to do just the opposite (Kolata, 1992, p.40).

If children begin with organized sports activities as young as 6 or 7, the early experiences should be carefully selected. Soccer or swimming are particularly good, not only because everyone is likely to get at least some aerobic exercise, but also because the basic skills are within the abilities of children of this age. Baseball, in contrast, is *not* a good sport for the average 6- or 7-year-old, because it requires real eye-hand coordination to hit or catch the ball, and most 7-year-olds are not yet proficient at such coordination. By age 10 or so, many children will be ready to play sports such as basketball, but many organized sports, such as tennis, are still difficult for the average child of this age. (Jennifer Capriati, who began her professional tennis career at age 14 is, after all, an *exception*, and not the rule.) Only in adolescence do most young people have the strength and coordination for sports like football.

If you want to encourage your children to be involved in sports, choose carefully. Let the child try several sports to see which one or ones he or she may enjoy, and be sure to select programs in which *all* children are given skill training and encouragement and in which competition is initially deemphasized. And don't push too fast or too hard. If you do, your child is likely to drop out of any type of organized sport by age 10 or 11, saying—as many do—that they feel inadequate or that it isn't fun anymore.

---

one example: 5-year-olds can jump about 34 inches in a standing broad jump. By age 11, the average child can jump almost twice as far (about 64 inches) (Cratty, 1979).

Girls in this age range are still ahead of boys in their overall rate of maturation, but they also have slightly more body fat and slightly less muscle tissue than do boys. Boys are therefore, on average, slightly faster and stronger, but the differences are small, and there is a great deal of overlap in the distributions. For example, a 9-year-old boy can run 16.5 feet per second; a 10-year-old girl can run 17 feet per second (Cratty, 1979).

What does begin during this period is the set of changes that eventually lead to puberty. Pubertal hormone changes may begin as early as age 8 in girls, and at 9 or 10 for boys. But although the process begins in the school years, it is not until adolescence that we see it in full flower, so I will save the discussion of these pubertal changes until Chapter 11, where I will describe the whole process in one connected discussion.

Health

The rate of illnesses in these years is slightly lower than what we see in preschool children. In the United States, most elementary school youngsters have 4 to 6 short-term illnesses each year, mostly colds and flu. As at every age, children who are experiencing high levels of stress or family upheaval are more likely to become ill. For example, a large nationwide study in the United States shows that children living in mother-only families have more asthma, more headaches, and a generally higher vulnerability to illnesses of many types than do those living with both biological parents (Dawson, 1991). Figure 9.1 shows one comparison from this study, using a "health vulnerability score." This score is the sum of nine questions answered by parents about their child's health. You can see in the figure that the average score is only about 1.0 out of a possible 9, which implies that most children are quite healthy. But it is clear that children living in more stressful family structures have higher health vulnerability—and this is true even when such other differences between the families as race, income, and mother's level of education are factored out. It is also evident in the figure that the stepfamily structure is also associated with somewhat increased health risks, a finding that is consistent with the point I made in the last chapter about stepfamilies.

The risk of injuries from accidents also rises in this age range—broken arms or legs from falls, cuts and abrasions from active play, injuries from fires, or auto accidents. The annual rate of such injuries is about .4 for preschool children. Among elementary school boys, the rate is about .8, and among girls about .6 (Schor, 1987)—illustrating the general point that boys are consistently at higher risk for almost all kinds of physical injuries.

Other Health Hazards: Obesity.   Acute or chronic diseases are not the only health hazards for children. Beyond accidents, one of the most significant risks is obesity. Estimates of the frequency of obesity among children vary quite a lot, depending in part on how it is defined. One typical definition is a body weight 20 percent or more above the normal weight for height, and by this definition,

FIGURE 9.1
Dawson finds that children from single-parent and step-parent families are more likely to be sick, even when poverty and race are held constant. (Source: Dawson, 1991, from Table 3, p. 577.)

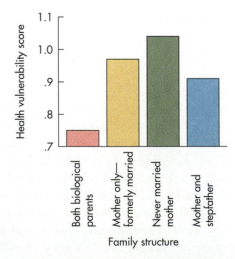

perhaps 15 percent of U.S. youngsters are obese, with the incidence rising steadily in the past 30 years (Gortmaker et al., 1987). Between 1963 and 1980, obesity increased by more than 50 percent among school-age children.

High rates of obesity are common in other Western countries as well. For example, researchers in Italy reported that among 10-year-olds, 23.4 percent of the males and 12.7 percent of the girls were classed as obese (Maffeis et al., 1993).

Obesity is *not* ordinarily more common among poor children, although there are individual ethnic groups in which the incidence is unusually high, including many Native-American groups and—perhaps—inner city Blacks (Bandini & Dietz, 1992; Gilbert et al., 1992; Okamoto, Davidson, & Conner, 1993; Sherry et al., 1992).

Obesity is a significant long-term health problem. Among adults, the obese have shorter life expectancies and higher risk of heart disease and high blood pressure. We also know that there is a correlation between fatness in childhood and obesity in adulthood. Only about a third to a fifth of obese preschoolers are still obese as adults, but by school age the relationship has become much stronger: about half of those who are obese in these years are still obese as adults (Serdula et al., 1993). Put another way, an obese child has three to five times the risk of being an obese adult. This does not mean, by the way, that all fat adults were fat children. More than half of obese adults were *not* fat as children. But being obese in childhood significantly increases the risk.

Obesity in childhood or adulthood appears to result from an interaction between a genetic predisposition and environmental factors that promote overeating or low levels of activity. The genetic component is clear from both twin and adoption studies. Adult identical twins, for example, have extremely similar adult weights even if they are reared apart, while fraternal twins differ much more (Stunkard et al., 1990). Similarly, adopted children reared by obese parents are less likely to be obese than are the natural children of obese parents (Stunkard et al., 1986).

This overweight boy not only has different kinds of encounters with his peers, he is also more likely to be fat as an adult, with accompanying increased health risks.

Whether a child with a genetic propensity to fatness will actually become obese, however, depends on "energy balance"—the balance between the calories taken in and the number expended by exercise. On the "intake" side of this balance, the data are just plain confusing. Most studies of eating patterns show little or no difference in food intake between obese and nonobese children (Bandini & Dietz, 1992; Klesges, Shelton, & Klesges, 1993)—although there are some newer studies that suggest that obese children may take in higher proportions of dietary fat (Gazzaniga, 1993). On the "outgo" side, the evidence is somewhat clearer. There are various indications that obese children choose more sedentary activities, or exercise somewhat less. In particular, recent studies show a link between amount of TV watching and obesity.

One group of researchers, studying a national sample of over 6,000 children, estimates that the prevalence of obesity increases roughly 2 percent for each additional hour of television a child or teenager watches per day, even when prior weight, family influences, and other background variables are taken into account (Dietz & Gortmaker, 1985). These investigators are not arguing that watching TV makes you fat; they are suggesting that the more TV a child watches, the less exercise he or she is getting and the greater the likelihood that the youngster will eat high-fat junk food.

Obesity obviously affects a child's social experiences during the school years, which may have effects detectable into adulthood. At the same time, I should point out that *fear* of fatness may also become a significant problem for some children, especially girls from White, middle-class families. Serious eating disorders such as bulimia and anorexia—which I'll talk about in Chapter 11— don't become common until adolescence, but many school-age children are already well aware of current cultural norms of thinness, particularly for women. Some normal-weight girls of 8 or 9 are already preoccupied with their weight, even dieting (Mellin, Irwin, & Scully, 1992). When they hit puberty, with its large increase in body fat, a significant fraction of these girls develop eating disorders as a way of trying to control their weight and fat level. The balancing act required for the parents of an overweight child, then, is to try to help the child develop better eating and exercise habits without so emphasizing the importance of thinness that the child develops pathological patterns of dieting. In either case, it is clear that both health habits and body images established in these early years will tend to persist into adolescent adulthood, with potentially pervasive health consequences.

Language Development in Middle Childhood

By age 5 or 6, virtually all children have mastered the basic grammar and pronunciation of their native tongue. They can create remarkably complex sentences and have a vocabulary of perhaps 15,000 words. But anyone who has talked recently with a 6-year-old is well aware of the fact that there is still a fair distance to go for the child to acquire adultlike facility with language. During middle childhood, children learn a great many conversational skills, such as how to maintain the topic of conversation, how to create unambiguous sentences, and how to speak politely or persuasively (Anglin, 1993).

They also continue to add new vocabulary at a fairly astonishing rate of 5,000 to 10,000 words per year. This estimate comes from a recent, careful study by Jeremy Anglin (1993), who tested the vocabulary knowledge of first, third, and fifth grade children on a sample of words drawn at random from a large dictionary. Anglin's analysis is especially interesting because he broke down the total vocabulary into several different types of words. *Root words* are those basic, uninflected words, such as *closet*, *flop*, *hermit*, and *pep*. *Inflected words* are those to which at least one inflection has been added, such as an *ed* for a past tense, an *s* for plural, or *ing*. The third category, *derived words*, often have a root word as a base, to which some other piece has been added, such as happ*ily* or happ*iness*. You can see in Figure 9.2 that between first and fifth grade children increased in their knowledge of all three types of words, but the biggest increase, occurring between third and fifth grade, was in derived words.

Anglin argues that what is happening is that at about third grade, the child shifts to a new level of understanding of the structure of language, figuring out relationships between whole categories of words, such as between adjectives and

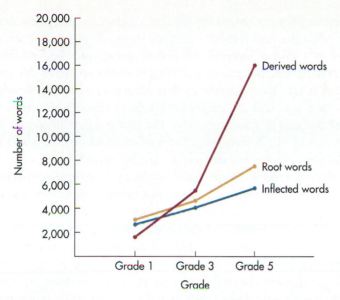

FIGURE 9.2

Anglin's study shows a very large overall increase in children's vocabularies during the school years, but the biggest increase is in "derived" words. (Source: Anglin, 1993, adapted from Figure 1, p. 65.

adverbs, (happy and happily, sad and sadly) or between adjectives and nouns (happy and happiness), and the like. Having understood these relationships, the child can now understand and create a whole class of new words, and his vocabulary thus increases rapidly. As a personal aside, I found this result especially intriguing because it matched so closely my own experience of learning vocabulary during my recent year in Germany. At first, I added words laboriously, one at a time. But sometime during the year, I suddenly understood something about the prefix structure of the language and was able to add words by the handful.

Cognitive Changes

Piaget's observations of cognitive change during these years of middle childhood point to a similar conclusion: that the school-age child is now seeing and understanding underlying patterns, basic relationships, and rules. Piaget argued that this quality of children's learning and understanding became apparent at about age 6. For Piaget, the cognitive changes at that age were as striking and as significant as the acquisition of symbol usage at age 2.

Piaget's View of Concrete Operations

The new skills we see at age 5, 6, or 7 build on all the small changes we have already seen in the preschooler, but from Piaget's perspective there is a great leap forward that occurs when the child discovers or develops a set of immensely powerful and abstract general "rules" or "strategies" for examining and interacting with the world. Piaget calls this new set of skills **concrete operations.**

By an "operation," Piaget means any of a set of abstract, internal schemes such as reversibility, addition, subtraction, multiplication, division, and serial ordering. Each of these is a kind of internal rule about objects and their relationships. The child now understands the *rule* that adding something makes it more and subtracting makes it less; she understands that objects can belong to more than one category at once and that categories have logical relationships, which is a great advance over the simple classifications of the preoperational period. The 7-year-old not only can group critters into classes of cats and dogs, she also understands that both cats and dogs are *included in* the class of animals.

Of all the operations, Piaget thought the most critical was *reversibility*—the understanding that both physical actions and mental operations can be reversed. The clay sausage in the conservation experiment can be made back into a ball, the water can be poured back into the shorter, fatter glass. This understanding of the basic reversibility of actions lies behind many of the gains made during this period. For example, if you possess the operation of reversibility, then knowing that A is larger than B also tells you that B is smaller than A. The ability to understand hierarchies of classes, such as Fido, spaniel, dog, and animal also rests on this ability to go backward as well as forward in thinking about relationships.

Piaget also proposed that during this third stage the child develops the ability to use **inductive logic.** He can go from his own experience to a general principle. For example, he can move from the observation that when you add another toy to a set and then count the set, it has one more than it did before, to a general principle that adding always makes it more.

Elementary school children are pretty good observational scientists and will enjoy cataloging, counting species of trees or birds, or figuring out the nesting habits of guinea pigs. But they are not yet good at **deductive logic,** which requires starting with a general principle and then predicting some outcome or observation, like going from a theory to a hypothesis. Suppose, for example, that I asked you to think of all the ways human relationships would be different if women were physically as strong as men. Coming up with answers requires deductive and not inductive logic, and it is hard because you must imagine things that you have not experienced. The concrete operations-child is good at dealing with things he knows or can see and manipulate; he does not do well with manipulating ideas or possibilities. Piaget thought that deductive reasoning did not develop until the period of formal operations in junior high or high school.

When researchers have attempted to test these ideas, they have often found quite clear support for Piaget's hypothesized sequences. But newer research also raises a whole host of questions about just what is going on in the development of the child's thinking.

Direct Tests of Piaget's Ideas

Unlike researchers who have studied the first two of Piaget's stages, those who have followed up on Piaget's descriptions of the concrete operational period have generally found that Piaget was right about the ages at which children first show various skills or understandings. Studies of conservation, for example, consistently show that children grasp conservation of amount by about age 6 and con-

Try thinking about this question, and watch yourself as you are thinking about it. Can you see how your deductive logic works? Can you think of everyday situations in which you use inductive or deductive logic?

Because elementary-school-age children are good at observational science, field trips like this one to hunt fossils are a particularly effective way of teaching.

servation of weight at about 7 or 8. And studies of classification skills show that only at about age 7 or 8 does the child grasp the principle of **class inclusion,** that subordinate classes are *included in* larger, superordinate classes. Collies are included in the class of dogs, and dogs are included in the class of animals, and so forth. Preschool children understand that dogs are *also* animals, but they do not yet fully understand the nature of the relationship.

A good illustration of these changes comes from a longitudinal study of concrete operations tasks by Carol Tomlinson-Keasey and her colleagues (Tomlinson-Keasey et al., 1979). They followed a group of 38 children from kindergarten through third grade, testing them with five traditional concrete-operations tasks each year: conservation of mass, weight, and volume, class inclusion, and hierarchical classification. You can see from Figure 9.3 that the children got better at all five tasks over the three-year period—with two spurts—one between the end of kindergarten and the start of first grade (about the age that Piaget thought that concrete operations really began) and another during second grade. You can also see that the different tasks were not equally easy, even though all of them appear to require similar levels of concrete operational thought. Conservation of mass was easier than conservation of weight, with conservation of volume the hardest of the three. Class inclusion was also generally harder than conservation of mass. In fact, the researchers found that conservation of mass seemed to be a necessary precursor for the development of class inclusion.

Tomlinson-Keasey also found that a child's skill on these tasks, relative to the other children, stayed approximately the same throughout the three years of testing. A 6-year-old who had developed conservation of mass early continued to be ahead of other children later on; a late-developing child went through the same sequence about two years later.

New Themes: Memory and Strategy Development

Some researchers, rather than simply repeating Piaget's tasks, have tried to devise other ways to test the proposition that school-age children, compared to younger children, approach tasks in ways that are more general, based on

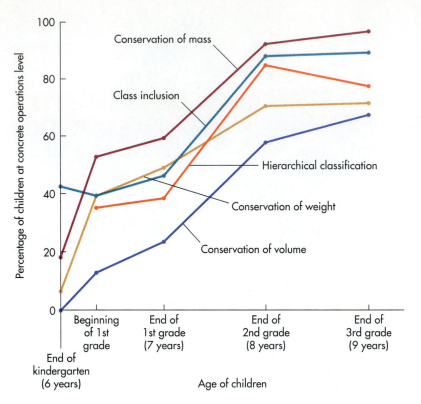

FIGURE 9.3

These results are from a longitudinal study in which the same children were given a set of concrete operations tasks five different times, beginning in kindergarten and ending in the third grade. (Source: Tomlinson-Keasy et al., 1979, adapted from Table 2, p. 1158.)

broader principles. In particular, the notion that older children consciously use strategies for solving problems or for remembering things has been the basis for a whole new look at cognitive development. Work on memory and memory strategies is a particularly good example.

Rehearsal Strategies.   Suppose you're about to go out the door to run some errands. You need to stop at the cleaners, buy some stamps, copy your IRS forms, and buy milk, bread, orange juice, carrots, lettuce, spaghetti, and spaghetti sauce at the grocery store. How do you remember all those things? There are many possible strategies, some of which I have listed (with examples) in Table 9.1. You could rehearse the list, you could organize the route in your mind, you could remember your menu for dinner when you get to the grocery store.

Do children do these things when they try to remember? One classic, early study (Keeney, Cannizzo, & Flavell, 1967) indicated that school-age children did, but younger children did not. Keeney showed children a row of seven cards with pictures on them and told them to try to remember all the pictures in the same order they were laid out. A space helmet, then placed over the child's head, kept the child from seeing the cards but allowed the experimenter to see if the child seemed to be rehearsing the list by muttering under his breath. Children under 5

TABLE 9.1
Some Common Strategies Involved in Remembering

- **Rehearsal.** Perhaps the most common strategy, involving either mental or vocal repetition or repetition of movement (as in learning to dance). May occur in children as young as 2 years under some conditions.
- **Clustering.** Grouping ideas or objects or words into clusters to help you remember them, such as "all animals," or "all the ingredients in the lasagna recipe," or "the chess pieces involved in the move called castling." This is one strategy that clearly benefits from experience with a particular subject or activity, because one learns possible categories or discovers them in the process of exploring or manipulating a set of material. Primitive clustering occurs in 2-year-olds.
- **Elaboration.** Finding shared meaning or a common referent for two or more things that one needs to remember. The helpful mnemonic for recalling the notes for the lines on the musical staff ("Every Good Boy Does Fine") is a kind of elaboration, as is associating the name of a person you have just met with some object or other word. This form of memory aid is not used spontaneously by all individuals, and it is not one they use skillfully until fairly late in development, if then.
- **Systematic searching**. When you try to remember something, you can "scan" your memory for the whole domain in which it might be found. Three- and 4-year-old children can begin to do this to search for actual objects in the real world, but are not good at doing this in memory. So search strategies may be first learned in the external world and then applied to inner searches.

Source: Flavell, 1985.

almost never showed any rehearsal, while 8- to 10-year-old children usually did. Interestingly, when 5-year-olds were *taught* to rehearse, they were able to do so and their memory scores improved. But when these same 5-year-olds were then given a new problem without being reminded to rehearse, they stopped rehearsing. That is, they could use the strategy if they were reminded, but they did not produce it spontaneously—a pattern described as a *production deficiency*.

More recent work suggests that preschool age children can show some kinds of strategies in their remembering if the task is quite simple, such as the game of hide-and-seek (DeLoache, 1989). In one of DeLoache's research techniques, the child watches the experimenter hide an attractive toy in some obvious place (e.g., behind a couch), and is then told that when a buzzer goes off, she can go and find the toy. While playing with other toys during the four-minute delay interval, 2-year-olds often talked about the toy's hiding place or pointed to or looked at the hiding place—all of which seem clearly to be early forms of mnemonic strategies.

These results and others like them tell us that there is no magic shift at age 5 or 6 or 7 from nonstrategic to strategic behavior. Primitive strategies are used by children as young as 2, perhaps younger. At the same time, it does appear to be the case that school-age children use strategies far more flexibly and efficiently, and this becomes more and more true as one moves through the school years. For example, when learning a list of words, 8-year-olds are more likely to practice the words one at a time ("cat, cat, cat") while still older children practice them in groups ("desk, lawn, sky, shirt, cat"). When we test the 8-year-olds again a year later, they show signs of a shift toward the more efficient strategy (Guttentag, Ornstein, & Siemens, 1987).

Other Memory Strategies.   Other strategies that help improve memory involve putting the items to be learned or remember into some meaningful organization. When you organize your grocery shopping list in your mind so that all the fruits and vegetables are in one group and all the canned food in another, you are using this principle, called clustering or chunking. George Miller showed years ago (1956) that in active short-term memory, most of us can deal with only 7 bits of information at a time, such as a 7-digit phone number. But if each "bit" contains not just a single piece of information but a "chunk," such as "vegetables" or "things I need for the macaroni and cheese recipe," then the amount of information you can deal with increases considerably.

Studies of clustering often involve having children or adults learn lists of words that have potential categories built into them. For example, I might ask you to remember a list of words that includes a mixture of names for furniture, animals, and foods. I let you learn the list any way you wish, but when you then name off the items later, I can check for the kind of organization you used by seeing whether you name the same-category words together.

School-age children do show this kind of internal organization when they recall things, while preschoolers do not. And within the school years, older children use this strategy more and more efficiently, using a few large categories rather than many smaller ones (Bjorklund & Muir, 1988).

In sum, we can see some primitive signs of memory strategies under optimum conditions as early as age 2 or 3 but with increasing age children use more and more powerful ways of helping themselves remember things. In the use of each strategy children also appear to shift from a period in which they don't use it at all to a period in which they will use it if reminded or taught to one in which they use it spontaneously. Finally, they use these strategies more and more skillfully and generalize them to more and more situations. These are obviously changes in the *quality* of the child's strategies as well as the quantity.

Expertise

However, . . . and this is a big however . . . all of these apparent developmental changes may well turn out to be as much a function of expertise as they are of age. Piaget obviously thought that children apply broad forms of logic to all their experiences in any given stage. If that's true, then the amount of specific experience a child has had with some set of material shouldn't make a lot of difference. A child who understands hierarchical classification but who has never seen a picture of a dinosaur ought to be able to create classifications of dinosaurs about as well as could a child who had played a lot with dinosaur models. A child who understands the principle of transitivity (that if A is greater than B, and B is greater than C, then A is greater than C) ought to be able to demonstrate this ability with sets of strange figures as well as she could with a set of toys familiar to her. But in fact that seems not to be the case.

There is now a great deal of research that shows specific knowledge makes a huge difference. Children and adults who know a lot about some subject or some set of materials (dinosaurs, baseball cards, mathematics, or whatever) not only categorize information in that topic area in more complex and hierarchical

Memory and the Child as Witness

In England, a 7-year-old was able to provide the police with details of her experience after a sexual assault and later able to identify her attacker in a line up (Davies, 1993). In several famous cases in the United States, children as young as 3- to 5-year-olds have testified in court about physical or sexual abuse by nursery school teachers, testimony that has sometimes led to convictions. Testimony by children has been increasing in frequency, as courts have relaxed their rules about child witnesses (Penrod, 1993), but it continues to raise a storm of controversy, centering on two main issues: (1) Can young children accurately remember faces or events, and report on their experiences? (2) Are children more suggestible than adults about what they might have seen or experienced? Will they report what they have been told to say, or what they actually saw or felt?

A few answers have begun to emerge from a growing body of research addressing these questions, although in many areas we are a long way from definitive answers. Among other things, there is still a good deal of controversy about whether stress has the effect of improving or worsening children's memory for events—a highly relevant issue, given the fact that most of the events children would testify about in a court are likely to have been highly stressful. Nonetheless, there are a few things that seem fairly clear.

1. Recall of specific events or of the faces of people seen at a previous time, does improve with age, but even preschoolers can recall action-related events with considerable accuracy. When experimenters have staged various crises or happenings and later asked children about them or asked children to identify someone who had been involved in a witnessed event, preschoolers and school age children can describe what happened and pick out a photo of the "culprit" almost as well as adults can. They report less detail than adults do, but they rarely report something that didn't actually occur (Baker-Ward et al., 1993; Ceci & Bruck, 1993; Davies, 1993). In one real-life study, Steward (1993) asked preschool children to describe their experiences on a recent visit to a medical clinic—visits that had been videotaped at the time. They reported only a quarter of the actual occasions when they had been touched on some part of their body by a medical person, but virtually all of the reports they did give (94 percent) were accurate.

2. Younger children, particularly preschoolers, *are* more suggestible than older children or adults. This has usually been studied by showing a film, or telling a story to children and adults. The researchers then ask questions about what the subject saw and inject some misleading question into the set—a question that assumes something that didn't really happen—(e.g., "He was carrying a pipe wrench when he came into the room, wasn't he?"). Some days or weeks later, the subjects are again asked to describe what happened in the film or story. In this way you can check to see whether the inaccurate or misleading suggestion has been absorbed into the story. Such misleading suggestions affect young children more than older children or adults. Of particular importance is the finding that it is possible to mislead young children enough in this way so that they will report inaccurately about physical events, such as having been kissed while being bathed or having been spanked (Ceci & Bruck, 1993). This is much more true of preschoolers than of school age children, although no one is quite sure just what mechanism is involved in this age difference.

Thus it *is* possible for an interviewer—psychologist, social worker, attorney or whomever—to nudge a child's testimony in one direction or another. Adult witnesses are *also* susceptible to suggestions of various kinds. So the difference here is one of degree and not of kind. From the legal point of view, this does not mean that children should not testify; it speaks only to the weight one might give their recollections and the care that should be used in the framing of questions.

ways, they are also better at remembering new information on that topic and better at applying more advanced forms of logic to material in that area. Expertise not only fosters greater speed in performing some well-practiced task, it also changes the way we think about that material and the way we go about solving problems in that domain. Furthermore, such expertise seems to generalize very little to other tasks (Ericsson & Crutcher, 1990).

These school-age chess players, unless they are rank novices, would remember a series of chess moves or the arrangement of chess boards far better than I could, since they have expertise and I do not.

Think about your own areas of expertise and the areas about which you have little knowledge. Can you see any differences in the *way* you think about these different areas, in the form of logic you use or the way you go about remembering?

Much of the most interesting work has been done by Michelene Chi and her various colleagues (Bedard & Chi, 1992; Chi & Ceci, 1987; Chi, Hutchinson, & Robin, 1989). In her most famous study (1978) she showed that expert chess players can remember the placement of chess pieces on a board much more quickly and accurately than can novice chess players, *even when the expert chess players are children and the novices are adults*. To paraphrase Flavell (1985), expertise makes any of us look very smart, very cognitively advanced; lack of expertise makes us look very dumb.

Since young children are novices at almost everything, while older children are more expert at many things, perhaps the apparent age difference in the use of cognitive strategies, such as memory strategies, is just the effect of more specific knowledge, more experience, and *not* the result of stagelike changes in fundamental cognitive structures.

Overview of the Thinking of the School Child

When we look at what we know about the thinking of children between 6 and 12, we find a sort of paradox. On the one hand, Piaget seems to have been more accurate in his descriptions of this period than any other. He did not underestimate the school child's abilities as he had the abilities of infants and preschoolers. Nor did he overestimate them, as he did the skills of the teenager, as you'll see in Chapter 11. What we see in this age period is the emergence, or perhaps the more consistent use, of more complex sorts of analysis and strategy. Children this age, much more than younger children, also know what they know and can reflect on the ways they learn or remember things.

All of this sounds very like Piaget's description of this period. Yet it looks very much as if these cognitive skills do not arise at all from the mechanism

Piaget suggested, which was some kind of general *equilibration*—a broad reorganization of schemes—at about age 6. The developmental process now appears to be far more gradual and is affected heavily by the amount of experience the child has in a particular domain. At the same time, it *is* true that the 8-year-old approaches new tasks differently. He is more likely to attempt a more complex strategy, and if that strategy fails, he is more likely to try another one. So although the process may be gradual, there still appears to be genuine qualitative change. But if the change is not in some basic structures, as Piaget thought, just what might those differences consist of? The third major approach to cognitive development, known as *information processing*, may offer some answers.

Information Processing: Another View of Cognitive Development

Theorists like Piaget, who study cognitive structure, ask what overall structure of logic the child uses in solving problems and how those structures change with age. The information processing theorists ask what the child is *doing* intellectually when faced with a task, what intellectual *processes* she brings to bear, and how those processes might change with age. The information processing approach is not really a theory of cognitive development; it is an approach to studying thinking and remembering—a set of questions and some methods of analysis.

The basic metaphor underlying this approach has been that of the human mind as computer. Like a computer, we can think of the "hardware" of cognition, such as the physiology of the brain, the nerves and connective tissue, and the "software" of cognition, which would be the set of strategies or "programs" using the basic hardware. To understand thinking in general, we need to understand the processing capacity of the hardware and just what programs have to "run" to perform any given task. What inputs (facts or data) are needed, what coding, decoding, remembering or analyzing are required? To understand cognitive *development*, we need to discover whether there are any changes with age in the basic processing capacity of the system and/or in the nature of the programs used. Do children develop new types of processing (new programs)? Or do they simply learn to use basic programs on new material?

Changes in Processing Capacity. One obvious place to look for an explanation of developmental changes in cognitive skills is in the hardware itself. Any computer has physical limits to the number of different operations it can perform at one time or in a given space of time. As the brain and nervous system develop in the early years of life, with synapses formed and then pruned to remove the redundant ones, perhaps the capacity, the speed, or the efficiency of the system increases.

One type of evidence that is often mentioned to support the possibility of an age change in processing capacity is the finding that young children are able to remember fewer items in lists of numbers, letters, or words than are older children. You can see the results of one typical study in Figure 9.4.

Such results are consistent with the hypothesis that there is an increase in basic memory capacity with age. But there are a number of plausible competing explanations. For example, younger children clearly have less *experience* with

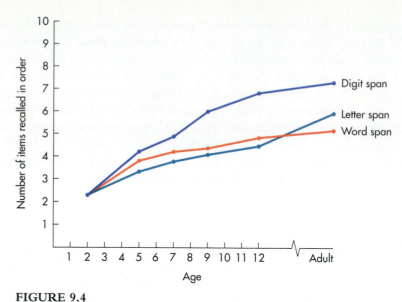

FIGURE 9.4

Psychologists have tried to measure basic memory capacity by asking subjects to listen to a list of numbers, letters, or words and then to repeat back the list in order. This figure shows the number of such items that children of various ages are able to remember and report accurately. (Source: Dempster, 1981, from Figures 1, 2, and 3, pp. 66, 67, 68.)

numbers, letters, and words. Perhaps their poorer performance on tests that measure memory span is simply another example of the fact that experts can do things better than novices. In fact, when the degree of experience is better matched, such as by having older children try to remember new letterlike figures, much of the age difference in memory span disappears. Most experts in this area of research now believe that there is probably no basic increase in underlying capacity, but that there may well be improvements in efficiency, which in turn frees up more "memory space" for storage (Schneider & Pressley, 1989).

Processing Efficiency.   The best evidence that cognitive processing becomes more efficient is that it gets steadily faster with age. Robert Kail (1991a; 1991b; Kail & Park, 1992) has found virtually the same exponential increase with age in processing speed for a wide variety of tasks, including such perceptual-motor tasks as tapping, simple response time to a stimulus (like pressing a button when you hear a buzzer), and cognitive tasks such as mental addition. Furthermore, Kail finds virtually identical patterns of speed increases in studies in Korea and in the United States, which adds a useful bit of cross-cultural validity to the argument.

The most plausible explanation for this common pattern is that there is some fundamental change in the physical system itself that allows greater and greater speed of both response and mental processing. The most likely candidate for such a basic change is the "pruning" of synapses—a process I talked about in Chapter 4 (Hale, Fry, & Jessie, 1993). If pruning begins at about 18 months and then continues steadily throughout childhood, one effect could be to make the "wiring diagram" steadily more efficient and thus faster.

Most developmentalists now accept these increases in the basic efficiency of the processing system as the base upon which cognitive development occurs (Kuhn, 1992).

Rules for Problem Solving.   Another area in which information processing researchers have found qualitative progressions is in problem solving. Some of the best known work in this area has been Robert Siegler's study of the development of *rules* (Siegler, 1976; 1978; 1981). Siegler's approach is a kind of cross between Piagetian theory and information processing. He argues that cognitive development consists in acquiring a set of basic rules, which are then applied to a broader and broader range of problems on the basis of experience. There are no stages, only sequences.

In one test of this approach, Siegler uses a balance scale with a series of pegs on either side of the center, like the one in Figure 9.5. Discs can be placed on these pegs, and the child is asked to predict which way the balance will fall, depending on the location and number of discs. A complete solution requires the child to take into account both the number of discs on each size and the specific location of the discs.

Children do not develop such a complete solution immediately. Instead, Siegler predicts that four rules will develop, in order: Rule I, which is basically a "preoperational" rule, takes into account only one dimension, the number of weights. Children using this rule will predict that the side with more discs will go down, no matter which peg they are placed on. Rule II is a transitional rule. The child still judges on the basis of number, except when there are the same number of weights on both sides; in that case he takes distance from the fulcrum into account. Rule III is basically a concrete operational rule, since the child tries to take both distance and weight into account simultaneously, except that when the information is conflicting (such as when the side with weights closer to the fulcrum has more weights), the child simply guesses. Rule IV involves the understanding of the actual formula for calculating the combined effect of weight and distance (distance $\times$ weight for each side).

Siegler has found that virtually all children perform on this and similar tasks as if they were following one or another of these rules, and that the rules seem to develop in the given order. Very young children behave as if they don't have a rule (they guess or behave randomly so far as Siegler can determine); when a rule develops, it is always Rule I that comes first. But progression from one rule to the next is heavily dependent on experience. If the experimenter allows the children to practice with the balance scale so that they can make predictions and then check which way the balance actually falls, many children show rapid shifts upward in the sequence of rules.

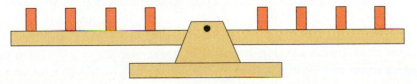

FIGURE 9.5
This balance scale is similar to what Siegler used in his experiments.

Experience with a teeter-totter may be one source of knowledge about how balance scales work.

Write down four good ways to study. In choosing one of these methods, does it matter what subject you are studying? How do you know all this? Do you think about it consciously when you are starting to study? The fact that you know these things and can think about them is evidence that you have metacognition, that you know what you know and how to think.

Thus Siegler is attempting to describe a logical sequence children follow, not unlike the basic sequence of stages that Piaget describes, but Siegler shows that the specific step in this sequence that we see in a particular child is dependent not so much on age as on the child's specific experience with a given set of material. In Piaget's terminology, this is rather like saying that when accommodation of some scheme occurs, it always occurs in a particular sequence, but the rate with which the child moves through that sequence depends on experience.

Metacognition and Executive Processes.   A third area in which information processing researchers have been active is in studying how children come to know what they know. If I gave you a list of things to remember and then asked you later to tell me how you had gone about trying to remember it, you would have little difficulty explaining your mental process. You may even have consciously considered the various alternative strategies and then selected the best one. You could also tell me good ways to study, or which kinds of tasks will be hardest, and why. These are all examples of metamemory or metacognition— knowing about remembering or knowing about knowing. Such skills are a part of a larger category that information processing theorists refer to as **executive processes,** planning what to do, considering alternative strategies—all similar to what an executive may do.

These skills are of particular interest because there is some suggestion that it may be precisely such metacognitive or executive skills that emerge (gradually) with age. Performance on a whole range of tasks will be better if the child can monitor her own performance or recognize when a particular strategy is called for and when it is not. I pointed out in Chapter 7 that 4- and 5-year-old children do show some such monitoring, but it is rarely found earlier than that and it clearly improves fairly rapidly after school age. Such executive skills may well form the foundation of some of the age changes Piaget described.

A Summary of Developmental Changes in Information Processing

If I add up all the bits and pieces of evidence about information processing capacity and skills, I arrive at a set of tentative generalizations:

1. There is probably *not* any increase in the basic processing capacity of the system, but there does seem to be an increase in the efficiency with which the "hardware" is used, which results in steadily greater processing speed.
2. The sheer amount of specific knowledge the child has about any given task increases as the child experiments, explores, and studies things. This leads to more and more "expert" approaches to remembering and solving problems.
3. The child acquires genuinely new strategies, probably in some kind of order. In particular, a school-age child seems to develop some "executive" or "metacognitive" abilities—she knows that she knows and can *plan* a strategy for the first time.
4. The child applies existing strategies to more and more different domains with more and more flexibility. If a child learned to rehearse on one kind of memory problem, the older child is more likely to try it on a new memory task; the younger child (particularly younger than 5 or 6) is not

likely to generalize the strategy to the new task—although once again it is true that we see some transfer in children as young as 2 when the conditions are carefully constructed (Crisafi & Brown, 1986).

5. With increasing age, the child can apply a wider range of different strategies to the same problem, so that if the first doesn't work, the child can use a back-up or alternative strategy. If you can't find your misplaced keys by retracing your steps, you try a back-up, such as looking in your other purse or the pocket of your jacket, or searching each room of the house in turn. Young children do not do this; school-age children and adolescents do.

Thus some of the changes that Piaget observed and chronicled with such detail and richness seem to be the result simply of increased experience with tasks and problems (a quantitative change, if you will). But there also seems to be a qualitative change in the complexity, generalizability, and flexibility of strategies the child uses.

Schooling and its Impact

Although I started this chapter by pointing out that children all over the world begin school at age 6 or 7, thus far I have been talking about cognitive development as if it were entirely separate from the experience of schooling. But surely schooling itself must have some impact—on the child's thinking, on the child's skills, on the child's beliefs about his own skills.

Schooling and Cognitive Development

One question is whether some kind of school experience is itself necessary for the child to develop the full range of strategic skills that we commonly see in children this age. Perhaps schooling itself helps to stimulate or trigger the transition to more abstract forms of thinking. If this is true, then we ought to find that children who do not attend school are delayed in acquiring concrete operational skills.

Researchers have attempted to test this hypothesis by studying children in societies or cultures in which schooling is not compulsory or not universally available. By comparing similar groups of children, some of them in school and some of them not, it may be possible to discover the role that schooling plays in cognitive development.

A wide variety of such studies—in Mexico, Peru, Colombia, Liberia, Zambia, Nigeria, Uganda, Hong Kong, and many other countries—has led to the conclusion that school experiences are indeed *causally* linked to the emergence of advanced cognitive skills. Children who do not attend schools not only do not learn many complex concepts and strategies, they are also not as good at generalizing a learned concept or principle to some new setting. So attending school helps children learn to think—precisely what it is intended to do.

A good example of recent research on schooling is Harold Stevenson's study of the Quechua Indian children of Peru (Stevenson & Chen, 1989; Stevenson et al., 1991). He and his associates tested 6- to 8-year-old children in rural areas as well as in city barrios, and in each setting they tested some who had been in school for about 6 months and some who had not yet started school or who were living in an area where a school was not available. Stevenson found that in both rural and urban areas, schooled children performed better on virtually all tasks, including a measure of seriation (putting things in serial order, such as by size or length) and a measure of concept formation. These differences remained even if the parents' level of education, the nutritional status of the child, and the amount of educational enrichment at home, were taken into account. Only on measures of memory, such as the ability to repeat back a set of numbers that had been read to the child, were there no differences.

This does not mean that schooling is the only way for children to acquire complex forms of thinking. Specific experience in some area can also promote expertise. But schooling exposes children to many specific skills and classes of knowledge, and it appears to stimulate the development of more abstract, flexible, generalized strategies for remembering and solving problems.

Adjusting to School

In the early years of schooling, the child faces a whole host of tasks. He must adapt to the rules of the classroom, he must get along with several dozen other children, and he must learn to read.

Learning to Read.   What do we know about the process of learning to read and about individual differences in the speed or ease with which children learn this skill? Somewhat to my surprise, IQ turns out not to be a good predictor of reading ability in the early years of school. What matters far more is the child's specific understanding of the structure and sound of language. Especially significant are two very specific bits of knowledge: the child's ability to recognize individual letters, and the child's awareness that spoken and written words are made up of individual sounds (Adams, 1990).

I already mentioned in Chapter 5 that very young babies pay attention to individual sounds, which linguists call *phonemes*. But the understanding that words are made up of strings of such sounds—an understanding referred to as *phonemic awareness*—seems to be a more advanced understanding, one that is essential to reading.

Suppose you say to a child, "Tell a word which starts the same as tap." (Maclean, Bryant, & Bradley, 1987). To do this, the child has to be able to identify which sound in the string of sounds that makes that word comes first. He must also be able to recognize this same sound in other words. You can get at this same skill in other ways, such as by asking children to recognize or produce rhyming words or to say the first sound in a syllable. There is now abundant evidence that children who are more skilled at such tasks at age 3 or 4 or 5 later learn to read much more easily (Adams, 1990; Bryant et al., 1990; Wagner, Torgesen, & Rashotte, 1994).

Letter recognition and phonemic awareness also interact with more basic cognitive skills. For instance, Tunmer and his colleagues (Tunmer, Herriman, & Nesdale, 1988) have found that the best predictor of reading skill at the end of first grade is the child's letter recognition at the beginning of the year. But

CULTURES & CONTEXTS

How Asian Teachers Teach Math and Science So Effectively

The *way* school subjects are taught may also make a major difference—a possibility that emerges especially clearly from comparisons of mathematics and science teaching in Asia and America. James Stigler and Harold Stevenson (1991) have observed in 120 classrooms in Japan, Taiwan, and the United States, and are convinced that Asian teachers have devised a particularly effective mode of teaching these subjects.

Japanese and Chinese teachers approach mathematics and science by crafting a series of "master lessons," each organized around a single theme or idea. These lessons are like good stories, with a beginning, a middle, and an end. They frequently begin with a problem posed for the students. Here is one example from a fifth grade class in Japan:

> The teacher walks in carrying a large paper bag full of clinking glass. . . . She begins to pull items out of the bag, placing them, one-by-one, on her desk. She removes a pitcher and a vase. A beer bottle evokes laughter and surprise. She soon has six containers lined up on her desk. . . . The teacher, looking thoughtfully at the containers, poses a question: "I wonder which one would hold the most water?" . . . the teacher calls on different students to give their guesses: "the pitcher," . . . "the teapot." The teacher stands aside and ponders: "Some of you said one thing, others said something different. . . . How can we know who is correct?" (Stigler & Stevenson, 1991, p. 14)

The lesson continues as the students agree on a plan for determining which will hold the most. Frequently, in such lessons, students are divided into small groups, each with a task, which they then report back to the class as a whole. At the end of the lesson, the teacher reviews the original problem and what they have learned. In this particular case, the children have not only learned something about measurement but about the process of hypothesis testing.

In United States classrooms, in contrast, it is extremely uncommon for a teacher to spend 30 or 60 minutes on a single coherent math or science lesson involving the whole class of children and a single topic. Instead, they shift often from one topic to another during a single math or science "lesson." They might do a brief bit on addition, then talk about measurement, then about telling time, and back to addition. Asian teachers shift *activities* in order to provide variety, such as shifting from lecture format to small-group discussions; American teachers shift *topics* for the same apparent purpose.

Stigler and Stevenson also found striking differences in the amount of time teachers actually spend leading instruction for the whole class. In the United States classrooms they observed, this occurred only 49 percent of the time; group instruction occurred 74 percent of the time in Japan and 91 percent in Taiwan.

Stigler and Stevenson point out that there is nothing in the Asian type of teaching that is new to Western teachers. American educators frequently recommend precisely such techniques. "What the Japanese and Chinese examples demonstrate so compellingly is that when widely implemented, such practices can produce extraordinary outcomes" (p. 45).

among those children who began first grade with poor phonemic awareness or letter recognition, those with good concrete operational knowledge caught up much more quickly in reading than did children who lagged behind in these basic cognitive skills. Thus good skills in either area—language awareness or logical abilities—can form the foundation for reading, but of the two, language awareness seems to be the more central.

Where does such early language awareness come from? How does it happen that some 5- and 6-year-olds have extensive understanding of the way words are put together, while others have little? The answer seems to be quite simple: exposure and expertise. For a child to learn about letters and sounds, he has to have had a great deal of exposure to language, both written and spoken. Such children are talked to a lot as infants, read to regularly, may have toy letters to play with, are told the sounds that go with each letter, or may be quite specifically taught the alphabet at an early age.

Nursery rhymes are also frequently a significant part of the early experience of good readers. In one study, researchers found that among a sample of children in England, those who knew more nursery rhymes at age 3½ later had greater phonemic awareness and learned to read more readily than did those who knew fewer rhymes (Maclean et al., 1987). Because nursery rhyme knowledge was *not* predictive of the child's later mathematical ability in this study, it looks very much as if we are dealing here with a quite specific body of expertise.

Of all the types of early experience that may contribute to such expertise, the most crucial seems to be the experience of being read to, regularly and in a fashion that invites the child's attention and response—a point I made in a *Research Report* in Chapter 7. Families that do not engage in such reading, or do not encourage other pre-reading experiences, have children who have far more difficulty learning to read once they begin school.

For those lacking such expertise at the start of school, the only solution is to try to build a parallel base of knowledge through many of the same kinds of experiences that more expert readers have had at home. This means that poor readers need a great deal of exposure to sound/letter combinations. But they also need to learn how to recognize patterns of letters in words. One need not—indeed must not—choose between those two hotly contesting educational systems, phonics and "whole word" training. Both are needed, along with instruction in syntax, so that the child will understand better what words *could* appear in certain places in sentences.

Marilyn Adams, who has analyzed all the evidence, also makes a persuasive case that the poor reader must have maximum possible success in oral reading, preferably with texts that are full of the sort of rhyme and repetition that will help to foster phonemic awareness and learning of language regularities. Programs with this emphasis have been highly successful with poor readers while more drill-like phonics programs have not (Hatcher, Hulme, & Ellis, 1994). In other words, poor readers seem to learn to read most easily through programs that to some degree mimic the naturally occurring home experiences of good readers: a great deal of reading, "play" with words, active questioning, and experimentation.

Chances are that this boy will have an easier time learning to read later because his Dad has read to him regularly.

Fitting In and Adapting.   Whether a child comes to school ready to learn to read is clearly one of the key factors influencing the child's overall adjustment to school. But it is not the only factor. Parent involvement in the school also matters, as do some aspects of the child's temperament.

When parents, from the beginning of first grade, come to parent-teacher conferences and open houses, attend school events, and get involved in supervising the child's homework, children are more strongly motivated, feel more competent, and adapt better to school. They learn to read more readily and get better grades through elementary school (Grolnick & Slowiaczek, 1994; Reynolds & Bezruczko, 1993). This effect of parent involvement has been found within groups of poor children as well as among the middle class, which tells us that the effect is not just a social class difference in disguise. For example, in a large study of poor, Black, inner-city children, Arthur Reynolds (Reynolds &

Bezruczko, 1993) finds that the parents' involvement with the child's school when the child was in second grade correlated about .30 with the child's reading achievement two years later, in fourth grade.

But it also matters whether the child's own personality or temperament matches the qualities valued and rewarded within the school setting. For example, Karl Alexander and his colleagues (Alexander & Entwisle, 1993) have found that children who are enthusiastic, interested in new things, cheerful, easy-going, and not restless do better in the early years of school than those who are more withdrawn, moody, or high-strung.

What all of this research indicates is that how a child starts out in the first few years of school has a highly significant effect on the rest of her school experience and success. To a considerable degree, the "rich get richer." Children who come to school with good skills clearly have an easier time. They then acquire more new skills and can thus adapt to later school demands more easily. Children who enter school with poor skills and with less optimal temperamental qualities learn less in the early years. The trajectory is not inevitable. Parent involvement can make a difference; a particularly skillful first grade teacher can make a difference. But the child does not enter school with a blank slate; she brings her history, her qualities with her.

Self-Judgments in School.   The child's success at the various school tasks, in turn, affects his view of himself and his own abilities. Kindergarten and first grade children seem to judge themselves and their abilities mostly on direct information of their own success or failure. They pay relatively little attention to how well others do at a particular task; in fact the great majority will confidently tell you that they are the smartest in their class. But by third grade or so, children begin to compare themselves with others and judge themselves accordingly. They notice whether their classmates finish a test sooner than they did or whether someone else got a better grade or more corrections on his spelling paper.

Teachers' behavior shows a similar change: In the first few grades, teachers emphasize effort and work habits. But over succeeding years, they gradually begin to use more comparative judgments. By junior high, children are being compared not only to each other but to fixed standards, other schools, or national norms (Stipek, 1992).

The beliefs about their own abilities that students develop through this process are usually quite accurate. Students who consistently do well in comparison to others come to believe that they are academically competent. Further, and perhaps more important, they come to believe that they are in control of academic outcomes. Interestingly, this seems to be less true of girls than of boys, at least in American culture. On average, girls get better school grades than boys do, but they have lower perceptions of their own ability. When they do well, they are more likely to attribute it to hard work rather than ability; when they do poorly, they see it as their own fault (Stipek & Gralinski, 1991).

Collectively, these experiences of success and failure mean that by seventh or eighth grade, most students have very well-established ideas about their own academic skills and their ability to control the events around themselves.

Assessing Students' Progress: IQ and Achievement Tests in the Schools

One of the sources of information children have about how well they are doing in school is the results from tests of various kinds given in the schools. There are two basic types, IQ tests—which you read about in Chapter 7—and **achievement tests.**

IQ Tests in the Schools.   You already know that IQ test scores are good predictors of school performance. It is for this reason that such tests are most often used within school systems as a method of selecting or identifying children who might need or benefit from special programs. Children whose speed of learning seems to be much faster or slower than normal may be given an IQ test to see if they might be retarded or gifted. Similarly, a child who is having difficulty learning to read but is otherwise doing okay may be given a test like the WISC-III or other special tests designed to diagnose specific learning disabilities or brain damage. In each case, the pattern of scores on the test as a whole, or on individual subtests, is then used along with other data to decide if the child should be in a special class.

Such uses of IQ tests are very close to what Binet envisioned nearly 100 years ago. Nonetheless, such diagnostic functions for IQ tests have been the subject of a good deal of debate, much of it heated.

Everyone agrees that schools must often diagnose or sort children into groups. Clearly, some children do require additional assistance and many benefit from special programs. The arguments center on whether IQ tests ought to be used as the central basis for such sorting. There are several strong reasons why they should not:

First, as I pointed out in Chapter 7, IQ tests do not measure all the facets of a child's functioning that may be relevant. For example, clinicians have found that some children with IQs below 70, who would be considered retarded if the score alone were used for classification, nonetheless have sufficient social skills to enable them to function well in a regular classroom. If we use only the IQ score, some retarded children would be incorrectly placed in special classes. Second, there is the problem of the self-fulfilling prophecy of an IQ test score. Because many parents and teachers still believe that IQ scores are a permanent, unchanging feature of a child, once a child is labeled as "having" a particular IQ, that label tends to be difficult to remove later.

The most important negative argument is that tests may simply be biased in such a way that some subgroups of children are more likely to score high or low, even though their underlying ability is the same. For example, the tests may contain items that are not equally accessible to minorities and Whites; taking such tests and doing well may also require certain test-taking skills, motivations, or attitudes less common among some minority children, especially African-American children (Kaplan, 1985; Reynolds & Brown, 1984).

In response to these arguments, most major tests have been revised to eliminate all obvious types of bias. Yet a troubling fact remains: When IQ tests are used for diagnosis in schools, proportionately more minority than White chil-

There is little controversy over assigning children to special classes like this one for the hearing impaired. But there is a great deal of controversy about the best way to assign children to classes for the learning impaired or for the retarded.

dren continue to be diagnosed as retarded or slow. This fact has led to a number of lawsuits, including *Larry P. v. Riles*, a case in which a group of parents of Black children sued the California school system for bias. The parents argued that there was no underlying difference in basic ability between Black and White children, so if differences in test scores led to larger numbers of Black children being assigned to special classes, the tests must clearly be biased.

The school system argued that IQ tests don't measure underlying capacity or ability, but only a child's existing repertoire of basic intellectual skills. In the terms I used in Chapter 7, this is like saying that an IQ test cannot tell you what the upper limit of some child's intellectual "reaction range" may be; all it can tell you is where the child is now functioning within that range. By school age, the child's level of functioning has already been affected by such environmental factors as prenatal care, diet, health, and family stability—all of which tend to be less optimal among African-Americans. Thus the test may accurately reflect a child's current abilities and be a proper basis for assigning the child to a special program, even though that child might have a greater underlying capacity or competence that could have been expressed under more ideal life circumstances.

In this particular case, the judge ruled in favor of the parents and prohibited the use of standardized IQ test scores for placement in special classes in California. Other legal decisions have gone the other way (Elliott, 1988), so the legal question is not settled, although there are now many places in the United States in which the use of IQ tests for diagnosis and placement of African-American or other minority children is forbidden. One unintended consequence of this is that since placement decisions must still be made, they are now being made based on evidence that may be even more culturally biased, such as less-standardized tests or teacher evaluations.

I have no quick or easy solution to this dilemma. It is certainly true that schools in the United States reflect the dominant middle-class White culture, with all its values and assumptions. But it is also true that succeeding in these schools is essential if the child is to acquire the basic skills needed to cope with the complexities of life in an industrialized country. For a host of reasons, including poorer prenatal care, greater poverty, and different familial patterns, more African-American children appear to *need* special classes in order to acquire the skills they lack. Yet I am well aware that there is a self-fulfilling prophecy about placing a child in a special class. Expectations are typically lower in such classes, so the children—who were already learning more slowly—are challenged still less and so proceed even more slowly. Yet to offer no special help to children who come to school lacking the skills they need to succeed there seems equally unacceptable to me. In the end, I conclude that IQ tests are more reliable and valid than the alternatives. I would not want a single IQ test used as the sole basis for a placement decision, especially early in elementary school when IQ test scores are still relatively variable. I would want to take into account the level of stress in the child's life at the time the test was given. But it seems foolish to me to throw out the tests altogether.

Do you agree with me? Why or why not?

Achievement Tests.   The second major type of test that schools use is an **achievement test,** a type of exam with which nearly all of you have doubtless had personal experience. Achievement tests are designed to assess *specific* information learned in school, using items like those in Table 9.2. The child taking an achievement test doesn't end up with an IQ score, but his performance is still compared to that of other children in the same grade across the country.

TABLE 9.2
Some Sample Items from a Fourth-Grade Achievement Test

Vocabulary	Language Expression	Mathematics
jolly old man	Who wants ____ books?	What does the "3" in 13 stand for?
1. angry	1. that	1. 3 ones
2. fat	2. these	2. 13 ones
3. merry	3. them	3. 3 tens
4. sorry	4. this	4. 13 tens

Reference Skills	Spelling	Mathematics Computation		
Which of these words would be first in ABC order?	Jason took the *cleanest* glass.	79	149	62
1. pair	right _____	+14	− 87	× 3
2. point	wrong _____			
3. paint				
4. polish				

Source: From Comprehensive Tests of Basic Skills, Form S. Reprinted by permission of the publisher, CTB/McGraw-Hill, Del Monte Research Park, Monterey, CA 93940. Copyright © 1973 by McGraw-Hill, Inc. All rights reserved. Printed in the USA.

In the United States, virtually all fourth graders—like these in Austin, Texas—are given achievement tests, so as to allow schools to compare their students' performance against national norms.

How are these tests different from an IQ test? IQ tests are intended to tell us something about how well a child *can* think and learn, while an achievement test tells us something about what a child *has* learned. Or, to put it another way, the designers of IQ tests thought they were measuring the child's basic capacity, her underlying **competence,** while an achievement test is intended to measure what the child has actually learned (her **performance**). This is an important distinction. Each of us presumably has some upper limit of ability—what we could do under ideal conditions, when we are maximally motivated, well, and rested. But since everyday conditions are rarely ideal we typically perform below our hypothetical ability.

In fact, it is not possible to measure competence. We can never be sure that we are assessing any ability under the best of all possible circumstances. We *always* measure performance. The authors of the famous IQ tests believed that standardizing the procedures for administering and scoring the tests would allow them to come close to measuring competence. Certainly it is good practice to design the best possible test and to administer it carefully. But it is important to understand that no test really measures "underlying" competence, only performance when the test is taken.

If you follow this logic to the end, you realize that all IQ tests are really achievement tests. The difference between tests we call IQ tests and those we call achievement tests is really a matter of degree. IQ tests include items that tap fairly fundamental intellectual processes like comparison or analysis; the achievement tests call for specific information the child has learned in school or elsewhere. College entrance tests, like the Scholastic Aptitude Tests (SATs, which many of you have taken recently) fall somewhere in between. They are designed to measure basic "developed abilities," such as the ability to reason with words, rather than just specific knowledge. All three types of tests, though, measure aspects of a child or young person's performance and not competence.

The use of achievement tests in schools has been almost as controversial as the use of IQ tests. The major argument in favor of such tests is that they provide parents and taxpayers with a way of assessing the quality of their schools and provide teachers with important information about the strengths and weaknesses of their class or individual students. But do such tests actually serve any of these purposes well? Maybe not. For one thing, when schools know that they are being evaluated based on test scores, there is a strong incentive to "teach to the test" (Corbett & Wilson, 1989). For another, teachers report that even when they do not spend time teaching specific material that is likely to be tested, they do spend more time on the general subject matter covered by the tests, and therefore have less time for skills that are not included in most achievement tests, such as discussing ideas, solving problems inductively, or creative activities (Darling-Hammond & Wise, 1985). Furthermore, teachers also say that they rarely use test scores as a basis for diagnosing a specific child's strengths and weaknesses. Most feel that a child's day-to-day classroom performance yields better diagnostic information than a one-shot test under high stress conditions. The failure of most standardized tests to tap the child's ability to draw inferences, apply information, or ask good questions seems especially troublesome, because these are all problem solving skills that appear to have long-range significance for adult success.

In recent years, a number of variations of a new form of test—**performance tests**—have been designed to get around some of these difficulties. You can read about them in *The Real World* box on page 288.

School Quality

A very different set of questions about school experience has to do with variations in the quality of the schools themselves. Real estate agents have always touted a "good school district" as a reason for settling in one town or neighborhood rather than another. Now we have research to show that the real estate agents were right: Specific characteristics of schools and teachers do affect children's development.

Researchers interested in possible effects of good and poor schools have most often approached the problem by identifying unusually "effective" or "successful" schools (Good & Weinstein, 1986; Rutter, 1983). In this research, an effective school is defined as one in which pupils show one or more of the following characteristics at higher rates than you would predict, knowing the kind of families or neighborhoods the pupils come from: high scores on standardized tests, good school attendance, low rates of disruptive classroom behavior or delinquency, a high rate of later college attendance, or high self-esteem. Some schools seem to achieve such good outcomes consistently, year after year, so the effect is not just chance variation. When these successful schools are compared to others in similar neighborhoods that have less impressive track records, certain common themes emerge, summarized in Table 9.3.

What strikes me when I read this list is how much the effective schools sound like authoritative parenting. There are clear goals and rules, good control, good communication, and high nurturance. The same seems to be true of effective teachers. It is the "authoritative" teachers whose pupils do best academically. Such teachers have clear goals, clear rules, effective management strategies, and personal and warm relationships with their pupils (Linney & Seidman, 1989). In such classrooms or in such schools pupils make significantly more rapid progress in basic skills, including reading and mathematics, than they do in less optimal schools (Sylva, 1994).

TABLE 9.3
Characteristics of Unusually Effective Schools

- **Qualities of pupils**. A *mixture* of backgrounds or abilities but with a reasonably large concentration of pupils who come to school with good academic skills. When too many children have poor skills this makes it more difficult for the rest of the things on this list to occur.
- **Goals of the school**. Effective schools have a strong emphasis on academic excellence, with high standards and high expectations, clearly stated by the administration and shared by the staff.
- **Organization of classrooms**. Classes are focused on specific academic learning. Daily activities are structured, with a high percentage of time in actual group instruction.
- **Homework**. Homework is assigned regularly, and graded quickly.
- **Discipline**. Most discipline is handled within the classroom, with relatively little fallback to "sending the child to the principal." In really effective schools, not much class time is actually spent in discipline, because these teachers have very good control of the class. They intervene early in potentially difficult situations rather than imposing heavy discipline after the fact.
- **Praise**. Pupils receive high doses of praise for good performance or for meeting stated expectation.
- **Teacher experience**. Teacher *education* is not related to effectiveness of schools, but teacher *experience* is, presumably because it takes time to learn effective class management and instruction strategies.
- **Building surroundings.** Age or general appearance of the school building is not critical, but maintenance of good order, cleanliness, and attractiveness do have an effect.
- **School leadership**. Effective schools have strong leaders, and those leaders state their goals clearly and often.
- **Responsibilities for children**. In effective schools, children are more likely to be given real responsibilities—in individual classrooms and in the school as a whole.
- **Size.** As a general rule, smaller schools are more effective, in part because in such schools children feel more involved and teachers can give them more responsibility. This effect is particularly clear in studies of high schools.

Sources: Rutter, 1983; Linney & Seidman, 1989; Sylva, 1994.

But as with any system, the quality of the whole is more than the sum of the quality of the teachers or classrooms. Each school also has an overall climate or ethos that makes a difference for the youngsters. The most positive school climate occurs when the principal provides clear and strong leadership, when there are widely shared goals, dedication to effective teaching, and concrete assistance provided for such teaching. In such schools, pupils and parents are respected, and there is usually a high rate of parent participation in school activities.

Individual Differences in Cognitive Functioning in Middle Childhood

In talking about several facets of schooling, I have already raised a number of issues of individual differences—differences in children's early reading ability, the use of IQ tests to identify students for special classes, and the like. But let me explore two other individual difference questions, both of which may have considerable practical relevance.

Traditional achievement tests, like IQ tests, are designed to show how well a given child, or a classroomful of children, performs against some average or norm. Hence both achievement and IQ tests are sometimes referred to as *norm-referenced*. In both cases the norm is the performance of the average child of a given age. An alternative way to think about testing is to define some criterion, some absolute standard that you think all children should meet, and compare each child's performance to that criterion. Many educators today are advocating exactly such *criterion-referenced* tests, especially the performance test form of criterion-referenced test.

For example, suppose that one of the goals of an educational system is that each student be able to write clearly and persuasively, using complete sentences and correct grammar. Such a skill can only be assessed with a test that actually asks the students to write something. Then each student's writing can be evaluated against some absolute standard as acceptable or not acceptable. Similarly, a performance test in science or mathematics might involve an actual science experiment. Children would complete the experiment on their own, describe and explain the results in writing.

An example would probably help. In one reading/writing test devised as part of the Maryland School Performance Assessment Program, eighth graders are asked to read and write about the intense cold of the winter in the Yukon Territory of Canada. They read a Jack London story "To Build a Fire," about a man who dies of the cold. Later they also read a brief excerpt about "Hypothermia: Causes, Effects, Prevention." Over several days, the students answer questions in test booklets about these readings, discuss some of the material in class, and at the end must write a piece giving advice to a group of friends about what they would need to do to stay safe on a winter hiking trip, or they must write a story or play or poem expressing their feelings about extreme states, or write a speech intended to persuade people not to travel in the Yukon (Mitchell, 1992).

The Real World
Performance Tests:
A New Way to Measure
School Achievement

Here's another example, this time from a mathematics performance test for junior high school students:

> Five students have test scores of 62, 75, 80, 86, and 92. Find the average score. How much is the average score increased if each student's score is increased by 1, 5, 8, or X points? Write a statement about how much the average score is increased if each individual score is increased X points, and *write an argument to convince another student that the statement is true* (Mitchell, 1992, p. 67)

The students' performance on both the writing and mathematics tests are normally scored (by experts, usually on a statewide basis) on a 4-point or 6-point scale, with the top one or two points reserved for those performances that meet the criterion, and lower scores for unacceptably poor responses. Thus the issue is not whether the students in some class or school do better or worse than other children, but whether each one individually meets some absolute standard.

Tests like these are now in use in a number of states in the United States, as well as in England and Wales, where many of the performance tests of science and mathematics were first devised. They are more complicated (and more expensive) to administer and score than are norm-referenced achievement tests, but they are growing in popularity not only because they assess the actual behaviors or skills educators are interested in, but also because the very existence of such tests shapes the way in which reading, writing, science, and mathematics are taught in the classroom. Just as teachers who know their students will be tested with standard achievement tests inevitably "teach to the test," so teachers who know their students will be tested with performance tests of reading, writing, math or science, must change the way they teach these subjects to be sure that their students acquire the needed reasoning and communication skills. Since these are precisely the skills that most educators believe teachers should teach in schools, performance tests may prove to be a vehicle for educational reform.

Individual Differences in Information Processing

In my earlier discussion of information processing, I focused on the *developmental* aspects—those changes in processing capacity or efficiency or strategies that appear to be common across children. But information-processing researchers have also turned their attention to questions of individual differences, asking what fundamental processes lie behind an individual's performance on an IQ test or other measure of cognitive skill. Generally the strategy has been to look at the relationship between IQ scores on standard tests and measures of specific information processing. This strategy has yielded a few preliminary connections.

Speed of Information Processing.   If increases in speed of processing are one of the underpinnings of age changes in cognitive skills, then it makes sense to hypothesize that differences in speed may also underlie individual differences in IQ. A number of different investigators have found just such a link: Subjects with faster reaction times or speed of performance on a variety of simple tasks also have higher IQ scores on standard tests (Vernon, 1987). Some have taken this argument a step further and proposed that a score on an intelligence test reflects nothing more than the basic efficiency of the neural system in any given individual (Vernon, 1993).

Most of this research has been done with adults, but a link between speed of reaction time and IQ has also been found in a few studies with children (Keating, List, & Merriman, 1985). Furthermore, there are some pretty clear suggestions that such speed-of-processing differences may be built in at birth. The fact that measures of the speed of infant habituation are correlated so strongly with later IQ—a finding I talked about in Chapter 5—certainly points to such a conclusion.

One of the synonyms for "intelligent" is "quick." Do you think this reflects some basic assumption that speed of processing is a central ingredient of what we think of as intelligent behavior? Can one be very intelligent and slow?

Other IQ-Processing Links.   Another research approach has been to compare the information processing strategies that normal-IQ and retarded children use. For example, Judy DeLoache (DeLoache & Brown, 1987) has compared the searching strategies of groups of 2-year-olds who were either developing normally or showed delayed development. When the search task was very simple, such as searching for a toy hidden in some distinctive location in a room, the two groups did not differ in search strategies or skill. But when the experimenter surreptitiously moved the toy before the child was allowed to search, normally developing children were able to search in alternative, plausible places, such as in nearby locations; developmentally delayed children simply persisted in looking in the place where they had seen the toy hidden. They either could not change strategies or did not have alternative, more complex strategies in their repertoires.

Research with older children confirms this difference in the flexibility of strategy use. Retarded children can learn fairly complex tasks, but they have much more trouble generalizing or transferring their learning to slightly different problems or tasks (Campione & Brown, 1984; Campione et al., 1985). Thus one aspect of "intelligence" is just this ability to transfer, to generalize from one task to another. Older children generalize more readily, as do those with higher IQ.

Sex Differences in Cognitive Skills

Comparisons of total IQ test scores for boys and girls do *not* reveal consistent differences. It is only when we break down the total score into several separate skills that some patterns of sex differences emerge. On average, studies in the U.S. show girls are slightly better on verbal tasks and at arithmetic computation, and that boys are slightly better at numerical reasoning. For example, on the math

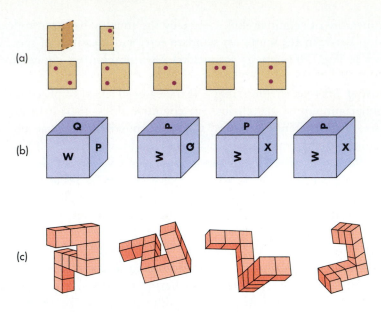

FIGURE 9.6
Three illustrations of spatial ability tests: (a) *Spatial visualization*: The figure at the top represents a square piece of paper being folded. A hole is punched through all the thicknesses of the folded paper. Which figure shows what the paper looks like when it is unfolded? (b) *Spatial orientation*: Compare the three cubes on the right with the one on the left. No letter appears on more than one face of a given cube. Which of the three cubes on the right could be a different view of the cube on the left? (c) *Mental rotation*: In each pair, can the three-dimensional objects be made congruent by rotation? (Source: Halpern, 1986, Figure 3.1, p. 50, & Figure 3.2, p. 52.)

portion of the Scholastic Aptitude Tests (SATs), the average score for boys is consistently higher than the average score for girls. Many of these differences have been getting smaller in recent years, although this is not true for the SAT mathematics score difference, which has persisted over the past 3 decades among students in the U.S. (Brody, 1992; Byrnes & Takahira, 1993; Jacklin, 1989).

Two other differences are also found regularly. More boys than girls are found among children who test as gifted in mathematics (Benbow, 1988; Lubinski & Benbow, 1992). And on tests of spatial visualization, like the ones illustrated in Figure 9.6, boys have higher average scores. On measures of mental rotation (illustrated by item *c* in the figure) the sex difference is quite large.

I want to point out that even on tests of mental rotation, the two distributions overlap. That is, there are many girls and women who are good at this type of task, and many boys and men who are not. But this sex difference may have real consequences for some aspects of advanced mathematics and science, where the ability to do mental, spatial manipulations is often important. The fact that girls score lower on such tests does not mean that no women are qualified for occupations that demand such skill; it does mean that fewer girls or young women will be able to pass the entrance requirements for such jobs.

Where might such differences come from? The explanatory options should be familiar by now. Biological influences have been most often argued in the case of sex differences in spatial abilities, where there may be both genetic differences and—more speculatively—differences in brain functioning resulting from pre-natal variations in hormones (Newcombe & Baenninger, 1989).

In contrast, environmental explanations have been prominent in discussions of the sex differences in mathematical or verbal reasoning. Especially in the case of mathematics there is considerable evidence that girls' and boys' skills are sys-tematically shaped by a series of environmental factors:

- Boys take more math courses than girls do. When the amount of math exposure is held constant, the sex difference becomes much smaller.
- Parental attitudes about mathematics are markedly different for boys and girls. Parents are more likely to attribute a daughter's success in mathematics to effort or good teaching; poor performance by a girl is attributed to lack of ability. In contrast, parents attribute a boy's success to ability and his failure to lack of application (Holloway & Hess, 1985; Parsons, Adler, & Daczala, 1982).
- Girls and boys have different experiences in math classes. In elementary school, teachers pay more attention to boys during math instruction (and more attention to girls during reading instruction), and in high school, math teachers direct more of their questions and comments to boys, even when girls are outspoken in class.

The cumulative effect of these differences in expectation and treatment show up in high school, when sex differences on standardized math tests usually become evident. In part, then, the sex differences in math achievement test scores appear to be perpetuated by subtle family and school influences on chil-dren's attitudes. Whether these differences can explain the greater percentage of boys than girls who show real giftedness in mathematics is not so clear—it is an issue that continues to be debated rather heatedly.

> As you can see, a lot of effort has been spent trying to discover or explain possible sex differences in mathematical ability. What are the practical implications either way?

S U M M A R Y

1. Researchers have studied the period of middle childhood less than other age periods, but it is nonetheless highly significant for the child's development.

2. Physical development from 6 to 12 is steady and slow. The onset of puberty brings a whole host of hormonal changes.

3. Illnesses are less common during this period than at earlier ages, but con-tinue to be fairly regular. Other health problems include accidents and obesity.

4. Obesity, increasing in frequency in Western countries, appears to be caused by hereditary tendencies plus some combination of too little energy expenditure or too many calories taken in.

5. During the school years, children learn a great deal about the conversational customs of language; they also add many thousands of new words to their vocabularies.

6. Piaget proposed a major change in the child's thinking at about age 6, when powerful "operations," such as reversibility, addition, or multiple classification were understood. The child also learns to use inductive logic, but does not yet use deductive logic.

7. Recent research on this period confirms many of Piaget's descriptions of sequences of development but calls into question Piaget's basic concept of stages.

8. Studies of expertise also point to a more important role of specific task experience in the sophistication of the child's thinking than Piaget believed.

9. Information processing theorists have searched for the basic building blocks of cognition, both the "hardware" and the "software."

10. Most theorists conclude that there are no age-related changes in the capacity of the hardware, but there are clearly improvements in speed and efficiency.

11. One form of increased efficiency is the greater and greater use of various types of processing strategies with age, including strategies for remembering. Preschoolers use some strategies, but school-age children use them far more and more flexibly.

12. At school age, most children also develop some "executive skills," the ability to monitor their own cognitive processes and thus to plan their mental activity.

13. School has a significant effect in fostering this shift to a more abstract or strategic form of thinking. Children who lack school experience show fewer such skills.

14. The best single predictor of the child's ease of learning to read in first and second grade is the child's "phonemic awareness," an awareness fostered by being read to, by rhyming, by extensive exposure to language.

15. The child's adaptation to the school setting is affected by cognitive readiness, by parental involvement, and by the child's temperament.

16. One of the main effects of school experience is to shape a child's sense of self-efficacy. By adolescence, children have a clearly developed idea of their comparative skills and abilities.

17. Children's intellectual or school performance is assessed with both IQ tests and achievement tests. Both must be understood as measures of performance, not competence. Both are controversial.

18. In recent years, a new form of test, the "performance test," has also become more widespread.

19. Children's intellectual and social development is affected by the quality of the schools they attend. Successful or effective schools have many of the same qualities we see in "authoritative" families: clear rules, good control, good communication, and high warmth.

20. Studies of individual differences in information processing suggest that variations in IQ are linked both to speed of basic neural processing and to flexibility and generality of strategy use.

21. There are no sex differences in overall IQ, but boys are typically better at tasks involving spatial visualization, and on tests of advanced mathematical ability. Girls are somewhat better on verbal tasks. There is still dispute about how to explain such differences.

KEY TERMS

achievement tests	deductive logic	performance tests
class inclusion	executive processes	
competence	inductive logic	
concrete operations	performance	

SUGGESTED READINGS

Adams, M. J. (1990). *Beginning to read: Thinking and learning about print.* Cambridge, MA: The MIT Press. This is a wonderful book about reading. It is easy to read, complete, thoughtful, and up-to-date. If you are planning a career as a teacher, especially if you expect to teach early elementary school grades, you should go right out and buy a copy.

Collins, W. A. (Ed.) (1984). *Development during middle childhood. The years from six to twelve.* Washington, D.C.: National Academy Press. Although it is no longer totally current, this book is useful because it covers the exact age range I'm discussing in this chapter and the next. It includes chapters on most aspects of the child's functioning, including physical development, health, and cognitive change.

Chapter Ten

Social and Personality Development from 6 to 12

t age 8, Roger was prone to emotional outbursts, insisted on his own way when he played with other children, and bullied weaker children on the playground. At 13 he was arrested for shoplifting, and he dropped out of school at 17. As an adult, he had a hard time finding and keeping a job, and his marriage lasted only a few years. His wife claimed that she couldn't deal with his temper.

David, in contrast, was very shy at age 8. He rarely entered other groups of children when they were playing, although he would join in if asked or urged. He had a few friends in school, but was mostly a loner. He went to college, but had a very hard time settling on a career, and changed jobs frequently until his late twenties. His marriage has been stable, but he has been disappointed at his rate of progress in his job. His job supervisors say that David has a habit of withdrawing whenever they press him for something or when the stress level at work gets high, so they are reluctant to promote him.

Both cases are fictitious, but the links between these types of childhood social behavior and adult outcomes are not. Certainly the cognitive changes I described in the last chapter play a central role in preparing the child for the demands of adolescence and adulthood. But it is probably in relationships, more than in cognition, that middle childhood has its greatest impact on the life course.

Let me build a bridge between cognition and social relationships by beginning with a look at how children in this age range *understand* themselves and their relationships. Such understandings form part of the basis of the relationships themselves.

Children's Understanding of Self and Relationships

The Self-Concept at School Age

In Chapter 8, I pointed out that by age 5 or 6, most children define themselves along a whole range of dimensions. But these early self-descriptions are highly concrete, often quite situation-specific. Over the elementary school years we see a shift toward a more abstract, more comparative, and more generalized self-definition. A 6-year-old might describe herself as "smart" or "dumb;" a 10-year-old is more likely to give a comparative description, such as "smarter than most other kids," or "not as good at baseball as my friends" (Ruble, 1987). At the same time, the child's self-concept also becomes gradually less focused on external characteristics and more on stable, internal qualities. The school-age child also begins to see her own (and other people's) characteristics as relatively stable, and for the first time she develops a global sense of her own self-worth (Harter, 1987).

A number of these themes are illustrated nicely in an older study by Montemayor and Eisen (1977) of self-concepts in 9- to 18-year-olds. Each child was asked to give 20 answers to the question "Who am I?" They found that the younger children in this study were still using mostly surface qualities to describe themselves, such as in this description by a 9-year-old:

Before you go on and read any of the examples, take a moment and write down 20 answers to the "Who am I?" question yourself. Then after you have read the children's answers, go back and look at your own answers to the question again. What types of descriptions did you include?

> My name is Bruce C. I have brown eyes. I have brown hair. I have brown eyebrows. I am nine years old. I LOVE! Sports. I have seven people in my family. I have great! eye site. I have lots! of friends. I live on 1923 Pinecrest Dr. I am going on 10 in September. I'm a boy. I have a uncle that is almost 7 feet tall. My school is Pinecrest. My teacher is Mrs. V. I play Hockey! I'm almost the smartest boy in the class. I LOVE! food. I love fresh air. I LOVE school. (Montemayor & Eisen, 1977, pp. 317–318)

In contrast, look at the self-description of this 11-year-old girl in the sixth grade:

> My name is A. I'm a human being. I'm a girl. I'm a truthful person. I'm not very pretty. I do so-so in my studies. I'm a very good cellist. I'm a very good pianist. I'm a little bit tall for my age. I like several boys. I like several girls. I'm old-fashioned. I play tennis. I am a *very* good swimmer. I try to be helpful. I'm always ready to be friends with anybody. Mostly I'm good, but I lose my temper. I'm not well-liked by some girls and boys. I don't know if I'm liked by boys or not." (Montemayor & Eisen, 1977, p. 317–318)

This girl, like the other youngsters of this age in the Montemayor and Eisen study, not only describes her external qualities, she also emphasizes her beliefs, the quality of her relationships, and general personality traits. Thus as the child moves through the years of middle childhood, her self-scheme becomes more complex, less tied to external features, more centered on feelings, on ideas.

Describing Other People

Children's descriptions of others move through highly similar changes, from the concrete to the abstract, from the ephemeral to the stable. If you ask 6- to 8-year-olds (or preschoolers) to describe others, they focus almost exclusively on external features—what the person looks like, where he lives, what he does. This description by a 7-year-old boy in England is typical:

> He is very tall. He has dark brown hair, he goes to our school. I don't think he has any brothers or sisters. He is in our class. Today he has a dark orange [sweater] and gray trousers and brown shoes. (Livesley & Bromley, 1973, p. 213)

When young children do use internal or evaluative terms to describe people, they are likely to use quite global terms, such as "nice" or "mean" or "good" or "bad." Further, young children do not seem to see these qualities as lasting or general traits of the individual, applicable in all situations or over time (Rholes & Ruble, 1984). In other words, the 6- or 7-year-old has not yet developed a concept we might think of as "conservation of personality."

Beginning at about age 7 or 8, though, at just about the same time that children begin to describe themselves using more psychological terms and develop a global sense of self-worth, we see the emergence of similar ideas of global or enduring personality in others. The child focuses more on the inner traits or qualities of another person and assumes that those traits will be visible in many situations (Gnepp & Chilamkurti, 1988). You can see the change in this description by a nearly-10-year-old:

> He smells very much and is very nasty. He has no sense of humour and is very dull. He is always fighting and he is cruel. He does silly things and is very stupid. He has brown hair and cruel eyes. He is sulky and 11 years old and has lots of sisters. I think he is the most horrible boy in the class. He has a croaky voice and always chews his pencil and picks his teeth and I think he is disgusting. (Livesley & Bromley, 1973, p. 217)

If you asked 4-year-olds and 8-year-olds to describe this boy, their descriptions would probably be quite different. The younger children would probably describe his physical characteristics; the older children might focus more on his feelings or on general qualities.

This description still includes many external, physical features, but goes beyond such concrete, surface qualities to the level of personality traits, such as lack of humor or cruelty.

Less anecdotal evidence for some of these changes comes from a study by Carl Barenboim (1981). Using a *sequential* research design of a type I described in Chapter 1, he asked 6-, 8-, and 10-year-olds to describe three people, and then a year later asked them to do the same thing again. Thus he has both longitudinal and cross-sectional information. Figure 10.1 shows age changes in two of the categories Barenboim used in his analysis. A *behavioral comparison* was any description that involved comparing a child's behaviors or physical features with another child or with a norm. Examples would be "Billy runs a lot faster than Jason" or "She draws the best in our whole class." Statements that involved some internal personality construct he called *psychological constructs*, such as "Sarah is so kind," or "He's a real stubborn idiot!" You can see that behavioral comparisons peaked at around age 8 or 9, but that psychological statements rose steadily throughout middle childhood. Other research by Barenboim (1977) indicates that psychological constructs peak at 13 or 14, at which point they make up more than half of teenagers' descriptions of others.

> Write down a description of your best friend. How does your description compare with the ones the children gave? Can you define the difference in precise terms?

Concepts of Relationships

A very similar developmental progression emerges when we ask children to describe or define various kinds of relationships. Let me use descriptions of friendships as an illustration.

Among preschool children, friendships seem to be understood mostly in terms of physical characteristics. If you ask a young child how people make friends, the answer is usually that they "play together" or spend time physically near each other (Damon, 1977; 1983; Selman, 1980). Friendship is understood to involve sharing toys or giving of goods to one another.

FIGURE 10.1
These data from Barenboim's study show the change in children's descriptions of their peers during the years of middle childhood. The colored lines represent longitudinal data, the dashed lines cross-sectional comparisons. (Source: Barenboim, 1981, Figure 1, p. 134.)

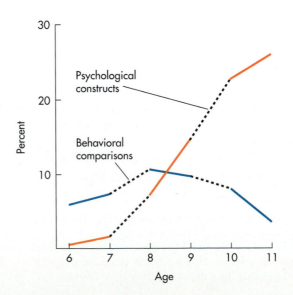

Robert Selman's research (1980) and extensive studies by Thomas Berndt (1983; 1986), show that in elementary school this early view of friendship gives way to one in which the key concept seems to be *reciprocal trust*. Friends are now people who help and trust one another. Because this is also the age at which children's understanding of others becomes less external, more psychological, we shouldn't be surprised that friends are now seen as special people, with particular desired qualities other than mere proximity. In particular, the qualities of generosity and helpfulness become important parts of the definition of friendship for many children in this age range. Children this age also understand friendship to have a temporal dimension: friends are people with whom one has a history of connection and interaction, rather than someone one has just met or played with once.

Linking Cognition and Social Behavior

The picture that emerges from putting all these jigsaw pieces together is of a child whose attention shifts from externals to internals. Just as the school child can understand conservation in part because he can set aside the *appearance* of change and focus on the underlying continuity, so the child of this same age looks beyond (or behind) physical appearance and searches for deeper consistencies that will help her to interpret both her own and other people's behavior.

Selman suggests another link between thinking and relationships in these years. The preschool child may have a theory of others' minds, but he does not yet understand that other people also read *his* mind. Put another way, the 4-year-old may understand the statement "I know that you know." But he does not yet understand the next step in this potentially infinite regress: "I know that you know that I know." This reciprocal aspect of perspective taking seems to be grasped some time in the early elementary school years. Selman's point is that only when the child understands reciprocality of perspective do we see really reciprocal relationships between friends. Only then do qualities like fairness and trust become central to children's ideas of friendship.

Just what is cause and what is effect is not so obvious. We should not necessarily assume that the cognitive horse is pulling the relationship cart, although that is one possibility. It is also plausible that the child learns important lessons about the distinction between appearance and reality, external and internal qualities, in play with peers and interactions with parents and teachers. Whichever way the causality runs, the central point is that children's relationships with others both reflect and shape their *understanding* of themselves and of relationships. With that in mind, let's look at the relationships themselves.

Relationships in Middle Childhood

Relationships with Parents

Among elementary school children, as among preschoolers, visible attachment behaviors such as clinging or crying appear only in stressful situations, such as perhaps the first day of school, illness or upheaval in the family, or the death of

What factors other than the generally lower level of novelty or stress might account for the elementary-school child's rather sharp drop in overt affection displayed toward parents?

a pet. Because fewer experiences are new and potentially stressful to the 7- or 8-year-old than to the preschooler, we see much less obvious safe-base behavior and less open affection from child to parent (Maccoby, 1984).

But it would be a great mistake to assume that the attachment itself has weakened. School children continue to use their parents as a safe base, continue to rely on their presence and support, continue to be strongly influenced by their parents' judgments. What does change is the agenda of issues between parent and child. With preschoolers, parents are most concerned with teaching the child some level of physical independence and controlling the child's behavior. They worry about toilet training, temper tantrums, defiance, and fights with siblings. Occasions requiring discipline are common. When the child reaches elementary school, disciplinary encounters decline. The agenda now includes such issues as whether the child will do regular chores, the standards for the child's school performance, and the level of independence that the parents will permit (Maccoby, 1984). Can Joe stop off at his friend's house after school without asking ahead of time? How far from home may Diana ride her bike? In many nonwestern cultures, parents must also now begin to teach children quite specific tasks, such as agricultural work and care of younger children or animals, which may be necessary for the survival of the family.

When we look at the various ways parents try to accomplish all these tasks, we see the same parental styles as were evident among parents of preschoolers: authoritarian, authoritative, permissive, and neglecting. And in this age range, as at the earlier ages, it is clear that the authoritative style is by far the best for fostering and supporting the child's emerging competence.

Baumrind (1991) has provided illustrative data in a recent analysis of her small longitudinal sample. She classified each parent's style of interaction on the basis of extensive interviews and direct observation when the children were preschoolers. When the children were 9, she measured their level of social competence. Those rated "optimally competent" were seen both as assertive and as responsible in their relationships; those rated "partially competent" typically lacked one of these skills, and those rated as incompetent showed neither. You can see in Table 10.1 that the children from authoritative families were nearly all rated as fully competent, while those from neglecting families were most often rated as incompetent.

TABLE 10.1
Social Competence in 9-Year-Olds as a Function of Parental Style

Parental Style	Percentage of Children Rated		
	Competent	Partially Competent	Incompetent
Authoritative	85	15	0
Authoritarian	30	57	13
Permissive	8	67	25
Neglecting	0	47	53

Source: Baumrind, 1991, adapted from Table 5.1, p. 129.

Relationships with Peers

The biggest shift in relationships in the years of middle childhood is the increasing centrality of the peer group. The vertical relationships with parents or teachers obviously don't disappear, but playing with other kids is what 7-, 8-, 9-, or 10-year-old children prefer. Such activities—along with watching TV—take up virtually all children's time when they are not in school, eating, or sleeping (Timmer, Eccles, & O'Brien, 1985).

Shared play interests continue to form the major basis of these school-age peer relationships. Furthermore, kids this age *define* play groups in terms of common activities, rather than in terms of common attitudes or values. You can see this pattern in Figure 10.2, which shows the results of a study by Susan O'Brien and Karen Bierman (1988). They asked fifth, eighth, and eleventh grade subjects to tell them about the different groups of kids that hang around together at their school and then to say how they could tell that a particular bunch of kids was "a group." For the fifth graders, the single best criterion of "a group" was that the kids did things together. For eighth graders, shared attitudes and common appearance became much more important.

Beyond the centrality of shared activities, the most striking thing about peer group interactions in the elementary school years is how sex segregated they are, a pattern that appears to exist in every culture in the world (Harkness & Super, 1985). Boys play with boys, girls play with girls, each in their own areas and at their own kinds of games. There are some ritualized "boundary violations" between these separate territories, such as chasing games (e.g., "You can't catch me, nyah nyah," followed by chasing accompanied by the girls screaming. (Thorne, 1986)). But on the whole, girls and boys actively avoid interacting with one another. Given a forced choice between playing with a child of the opposite gender or a child of a different race, researchers have found that elementary-school-age children will make the cross-race choice rather than the cross-gender choice (Maccoby & Jacklin, 1987).

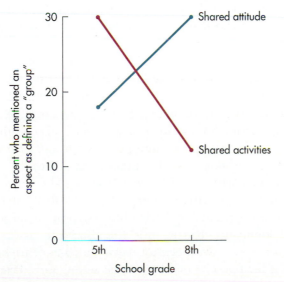

FIGURE 10.2
O'Brien and Bierman's results illustrate the change between elementary and high school in children's ideas about what defines a "group" of peers. (Source: O'Brien & Bierman, 1988, Table 1, p. 1363.)

In this age range, boys play with boys, girls with girls. It is also typical for boys this age to do something physical together, like these skateboarders.

Friendships.   This pattern is even more pronounced when we look at friendships. By age 7, sex segregation in friendships is almost total. In one study, parents reported that about a quarter of the friendships of their 5- or 6-year-olds but *none* of the friendships of their 7- and 8-year-olds were cross-sex (Gottman, 1986).

School-age children spend more time with their friends than do preschoolers, and they gradually develop a larger collection of individual friendships. Second graders name about four friends each, while seventh graders name about seven (Reisman & Shorr, 1978). Many of these friendships are remarkably stable. Thomas Berndt, who has studied children's friendships extensively, finds that between half and three-quarters of close friendships in the elementary school years persist as long as a full school year; many last much longer (Berndt, Hawkins, & Hoyle, 1986; Berndt & Hoyle, 1985) and such stability is as common among first graders as among eighth graders.

Children's behavior within these friendship relationships is quite different than what they display with strangers, but I suspect the differences are not quite what you would predict. Children are more polite to strangers or nonfriends. They are more open with pals, which means not only that they exchange supportive comments, but also that they are more critical toward one another than toward strangers.

There are also intriguing differences in the quality of relationship in boys' and girls' friendships in these years. Waldrop and Halverson (1975) refer to boys' relationships as *extensive* and to girls' relationships as *intensive*; boys' friendship groups are larger and are more accepting of newcomers than are girls'. They play more outdoors and roam over a larger area in their play. Girlfriends are more likely to play in pairs or in smaller, more exclusive groups, and they spend more play time indoors or near home or school (Gottman, 1986).

At the level of actual interaction we also see sex differences, generally consistent with the distinction between restrictive and enabling styles I described in Chapter 8. Boys' groups and boys' friendships appear to be focused more on competition and dominance than are girls' friendships. In fact, among school-age boys, we see *higher* levels of competition between pairs of friends than between strangers, which is the opposite of what we see among girls. Friendships between

Do you still have any friends from your elementary school years? If not, why do you think those early friendships did not survive? If yes, what do you think differentiates an early friendship that survives from one that does not?

CULTURES & CONTEXTS

Gender Segregation in Other Cultures

Many of the statements I make about "children's development" are based exclusively on research done in the United States or other western industrialized countries. It is always appropriate to ask whether the same developmental changes or the same behavioral patterns would appear in children reared in very different environments. In the case of gender segregation, the answer seems quite clear: What we observe on United States school playgrounds is true all over the world.

A good example is an observational study of children in a Kipsigis settlement in rural Kenya (Harkness & Super, 1985). This particular settlement consists of 54 households engaged in traditional hoe agriculture and cattle raising. Women care for the children, cook, and carry firewood and water. Men are in charge of the cows, plow the fields when needed, maintain the dwellings, and participate in the political business of the community.

For this study, observers went to the settlement at different times of day to record the gender of each child's companions. They found little sex segregation among children younger than 6, but clear separation for children between 6 and 9. In this age group, two-thirds of boys' and three-quarters of girls' companions were of the same gender. The differences were even larger when they looked at the sex of the child to which each youngster addressed his or her specific bids for attention: 72 percent of boys' and 84 percent of girls' bids were made to another child of the same gender.

These numbers reflect somewhat less sex segregation than we commonly observe in the United States. But what impresses me is that there is even this much in a culture in which children spend a good deal of their time in their own compound, with only siblings and half-siblings available as playmates.

This is not to say that context or culture have no effect. They clearly do. The Kipsigis encourage certain kinds of sex segregation by assigning somewhat different tasks to boys and girls. And in Western countries, children attending "progressive" schools in which equality of sex roles is a specific philosophy show less sex segregation in their play than is true in more traditional schools (Maccoby & Jacklin, 1987). But even in progressive schools, the majority of contacts are still with children of the same gender. All in all, it seems to be the case universally that when children this age are free to choose their playmates, they strongly prefer playmates of the same sex.

girls also include more agreement, more compliance, and more self-disclosure than is true for boys.

Leaper's study, which I described in Chapter 8 (Table 8.2, page 234), illustrates the difference. He finds that "controlling" speech—a category that includes rejecting comments, ordering, manipulating or challenging, defiance or refutation, or resisting the other's attempt to control—is twice as common in 7- and 8-year-old male friend pairs as among female pairs. Among the 4- and 5-year-olds in this study there were no sex differences in controlling speech.

None of this should obscure the fact that there are great similarities in the interactions of male and female friendship pairs. As one example, collaborative and cooperative exchanges are the most common forms of communication within both boys' and girls' friendships. Neither should we necessarily conclude that boys' friendships are less important to them than are girls'. Nonetheless, it seems clear that there are differences in form and style that have enduring implications for the patterns of friendship over the full life span.

Aggression and Other Less Friendly Patterns. I pointed out in Chapter 8 that physical aggression declines over the preschool years, while verbal aggression increases. In the elementary school years, physical aggression becomes still less common, and children learn the cultural rules about when and how much it is

Why do you think it is that among boys, competition is such a strong feature of friendship interactions? Do you think this is true in every culture?

acceptable to display anger or aggression. In most cultures, this means that anger is more and more disguised, and aggression more and more controlled with increasing age (Underwood, Coie, & Herbsman, 1992).

One interesting exception to this general pattern is that in all-boy pairs or groups, at least in United States studies, physical aggression seems to remain both relatively high and constant over the years of childhood (Cairns et al., 1989). Indeed, at every age, boys show more aggression and more assertiveness than do girls, both within friendship pairs and in general. You already know from Chapter 1 that boys are more likely to be diagnosed as having a "conduct disorder." But the same sex difference exists when we look at more every-day types of aggression. Table 10.2 gives some highly representative data from Offord's large, careful survey in Canada (Offord, Boyle, & Racine, 1991) in which both parents and teachers completed checklists describing each child's behavior. In the

TABLE 10.2

Percentage of Boys and Girls Aged 4 to 11 Rated by Their Teachers as Displaying Each Type of Aggressive Behavior

Behavior	Boys	Girls
Mean to others	21.8	9.6
Physically attacks people	18.1	4.4
Gets in many fights	30.9	9.8
Destroys own things	10.7	2.1
Destroys others' things	10.6	4.4
Threatens to hurt people	13.1	4.0

Source: Offord, Boyle, & Racine, 1991, from Table 2.3, p. 39.

table I've listed only the information provided by teachers, but parent ratings yielded parallel findings. It is clear that boys are described as far more aggressive on nearly any measure.

It seems inescapable that there is at least some biological basis for this sex difference. Similar sex differences occur in all human societies and in all primates, and there appears to be at least some hormonal link to levels of testosterone (Maccoby & Jacklin, 1974). So boys are doubtless more inclined toward aggression from the beginning. But nurture as well as nature is surely involved. You will remember from Chapter 8, for example, that fathers and mothers begin to reinforce sex-stereotyped toy choice and behavior in their children at very early ages, and that this is particularly true of sons.

At the same time, it is also true that the same family forces appear to foster high levels of aggression in both boys and girls. Highly aggressive children—male or female—are most likely to come from families that display inconsistent discipline, rejection of the child, harsh punishment, and lack of parental supervision (Eron, Huesmann, & Zelli, 1991). Thus while the *rate* of aggression differs between the sexes, the family dynamic that contributes to it does not.

Individual Differences

The shared developmental patterns I've been talking about so far tell us a good deal about the nature of children's self-concepts and relationships in this age period. But if we are to understand development, we must understand the individual pathways as well as the common ones. Two of the most important individual variations in this age range are in self-esteem and popularity.

Self-Esteem

So far, I have mostly talked about the self-concept as if there were no values attached to the categories by which we define ourselves. But that's clearly not the case. There is also an evaluative aspect to the self-concept, an aspect you probably noticed in the answers to the "Who am I" question I have already quoted. The 9-year-old clearly makes a lot of positive statements about himself, while the 11-year-old offers a more mixed evaluation.

By early elementary school age, these evaluative judgments coalesce into a *global* self-evaluation. Children at this age readily answer questions about how well they like themselves as people, or how happy they are, or how well they like the way they are leading their lives. This global evaluation of one's own worth is usually referred to as **self-esteem.**

Susan Harter's extremely interesting research on self-esteem suggests that each child's level of self-esteem is a product of two internal assessments or judgments (Harter, 1987; 1990). First, each child experiences some degree of discrepancy between what he would like to be (or thinks he *ought* to be) and what he thinks he is. When that discrepancy is low, the child's self-esteem is generally high. When the discrepancy is high—when the child sees himself as failing to live up to his own goals or values—self-esteem will be much lower.

Whether these girls' self-esteem will be affected by their soccer performance will depend as much on whether they value sports prowess as on how successful or unsuccessful they actually are.

Think about the following somewhat paradoxical proposition: If Harter's model of self-esteem is correct, then our self-esteem is most vulnerable in the area in which we may appear (and feel) the most competent. Does this fit with your experience?

The standards are not the same for every child. Some value academic skills highly, others value sports skills, or having good friends. The key to self-esteem, Harter proposes, is the amount of discrepancy between what the child desires and what the child thinks he has achieved. Thus a child who values sports prowess, but who isn't big enough or coordinated enough to be good at sports, will have lower self-esteem than will an equally small or uncoordinated child who does not value sports skill so highly. Similarly, being good at something, like singing, playing chess, or being able to talk to your mother, won't raise a child's self-esteem unless the child values that particular skill.

The second major influence on a child's self-esteem, according to Harter, is the overall sense of support the child feels from the important people around her, particularly parents and peers. Children who feel that other people generally like them the way they are have higher self-esteem scores than do children who report less overall support.

Both these factors are clear in the results of Harter's own research. She asked third, fourth, fifth, and sixth graders how important it was to them to do well in each of five domains and how well they thought they actually did in each. The total discrepancy between these sets of judgments comprised the discrepancy score. Remember that a high discrepancy score indicates that the child reported that he was *not* doing well in areas that mattered to him. The social support score was based on children's replies to a set of questions about whether they thought others (parents and peers) liked them as they were, treated them as a person, or felt that they were important. Figure 10.3 shows the results for the third and fourth graders; the findings for the fifth and sixth graders are virtually identical, and both sets of results strongly support Harter's hypothesis. Note that a low discrepancy score alone does not protect the child completely from low self-esteem if she lacks sufficient social support. And a loving and accepting family and peer group does not guarantee high self-esteem if the youngster does not feel she is living up to her own standards.

A particularly deadly combination occurs when the child perceives that the parents' support is *contingent* on good performance in some area—getting good grades, making the first-string football team, being popular with other kids. If the

FIGURE 10.3

For these children in Harter's studies, self-esteem was about equally influenced by the amount of support the child saw herself as receiving from parents and peers and by the degree of discrepancy between the value the child places on various domains and the skill she sees herself having in each of those domains. (Source: Harter, 1987, Figure 9.2, p. 227.)

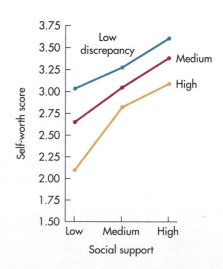

child does not measure up to the standard, he experiences both an increased discrepancy between ideal and achievement and a loss of support from the parents.

Consistency of Self-Esteem Over Time.   How stable are these self-judgments? Is a third grader with low self-esteem doomed to feel less than worthy for the rest of his life? A number of longitudinal studies of elementary-school-age children and teenagers show that global self-esteem is quite stable in the short term, but somewhat less so over periods of several years. The correlation between two self-esteem scores obtained a few months apart is generally about .60. Over several years, this correlation drops to something more like .40 (Alsaker & Olweus, 1992), a level of consistency that has even been found over periods as long as a decade, from early adolescence into early adulthood (Block & Robins, 1993). So it is true that a child with high self-esteem at age 8 or 9 is more likely to have a high self-esteem at age 10 or 11. But it is also true that there is a good deal of variation around that stability. Self-esteem seems to be particularly unstable in the years of early adolescence, around age 11 and 12. This makes sense in Harter's terms, since these are years when the standards children may set for themselves are likely to change, as they move from elementary to junior high and from prepubescent to pubescent (Harter, 1990). In later adolescence, self-esteem appears to become more stable again, although still not totally fixed.

Consequences of Variations in Self-Esteem.   When we look at the consequences of variations in self-esteem, the clearest research finding is that self-esteem is *strongly* negatively correlated with depression in both middle childhood and adolescence. That is, the lower the self-esteem score, the more depressed the child describes himself to be. The correlations in several of Harter's studies range from −.67 to −.80—numbers that are quite astonishingly high for research of this type (Harter, 1987; Renouf & Harter, 1990). Bear in mind, though, that this is still correlational evidence. These findings don't prove that there is a causal connection between low self-esteem and depression. They only tell us that the two tend to go together. More persuasive is Harter's finding from her longitudinal studies that when the self-esteem score rises or falls, the depression score drops or rises accordingly.

Origins of Differences in Self-Esteem.   Where do differences in self-esteem come from? There are at least three sources. First, of course, a child's own direct experience with success or failure in various arenas plays an obvious role. If I take ballet lessons, it will not take me long to figure out whether I am any good at it or not. Comparative information is also involved here, of course. If I see that all the other kids can do things that I cannot do so easily, or that I find something easy that others struggle with, that adds substantially to my self-knowledge. The child's experience of success or difficulty in school, which I talked about in the last chapter, is clearly one source of such information.

Second, the value a child attaches to some skill or quality is obviously affected fairly directly by peers' and parents' attitudes and values. For example, peer (and general cultural) standards for appearance establish benchmarks for all children and teens. (Which is why the present Western cultural emphasis on

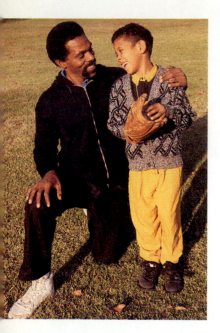

Playing catch with Dad is a classic father-son activity in American culture. One of the side effects is likely to be that the son comes to believe that skill in sports is something that his Dad values highly.

One reasonable hypothesis might be that neglected children would be more likely to have had insecure attachments as infants. Can you think of refinements of this hypothesis? And how could you test it?

extreme thinness in girls has led to so many eating disorders). Similarly, the degree of emphasis parents place on the child performing well in school is an important element in the child's internal expectations in that area.

Finally, labels and judgments from others play a highly significant role. To a very considerable extent, we come to think of ourselves as others think of us (Cole, 1991). Children who are repeatedly told that they are "pretty" or "smart" or "a good athlete" are likely to have higher self-esteem than are children who are told that they are "dumb," or "clumsy," or a "late bloomer." A child who brings home a report card with Cs and Bs on it and hears the parent say, "That's fine, honey. We don't expect you to get all As," draws conclusions both about the parents expectations and about their judgments of his abilities. From all these sources, the child fashions his ideas (his internal model) about what he should be and what he is.

Once again, then, we see the power of both the internal working model the child creates and the family and peer interactions that are the crucible in which the child forges this model. Like the child's internal model of attachment, a child's self-scheme is not fixed in stone. It is responsive to changes in others' judgments as well as to changes in the child's own experience of success or failure. But once created, the model does tend to persist, both because the child will tend to choose experiences that will confirm and support his self-scheme and because the social environment—including the parents' evaluations of the child—tends to be at least moderately consistent.

Popularity and Rejection

In a similar way, a child's degree of rejection by peers tends to be consistent over the years of middle childhood and into adolescence. Rejected children tend to stay rejected; if they move out of this category, it is rare for them to move all the way to a high level of acceptance (Asher, 1990).

Psychologists who study popularity (and unpopularity) in children have recently concluded that it is important to make a distinction between several subgroups of unpopular children. The most frequently studied are those children who are overtly *rejected* by peers. If you ask children to list peers they would *not* like to play with, or if you observe which children are avoided on the playground, you can get a measure of rejection of this type. A second type has come to be called *neglected*. Children in this category are reasonably well liked, but lack individual friends and are rarely chosen as most preferred by their peers. Neglected children have been studied far less than have the rejected, but the preliminary evidence suggests that while neglect is much less stable over time than is rejection, neglected children are nonetheless more prone to depression and loneliness than are accepted children (Cillessen et al., 1992; Rubin et al., 1991).

Where might such differences in popularity or peer acceptance come from?

Qualities of Rejected and Popular Children. Some of the characteristics that differentiate popular and unpopular children are things outside a child's control. In particular, attractive children and physically larger children are more likely to be popular—perhaps merely a continuation of the preference for attractive faces that Langlois detected in young infants and that I described in Chapter 5. The most crucial ingredients, though, are not how the child looks but how the child behaves.

Popular children behave in positive, supporting, nonpunitive and non-aggressive ways toward most other children. They explain things and take their playmates' wishes into consideration. Rejected children are aggressive, disruptive, and uncooperative. To be sure, not all aggressive children are rejected. It is when they *also* lack compensating positive social skills that they are most likely to be overtly rejected by their peers (Black, 1992; Coie & Cillessen, 1993; Denham & Holt, 1993; Newcomb, Bukowski, & Pattee, 1993).

This conclusion emerges from a variety of types of research, including at least a few cross-cultural studies. Aggression and disruptive behavior is linked to rejection and unpopularity among Chinese children as well as American children, for example (Chen, Rubin, & Sun, 1992). Among the best sources of evidence are studies in which groups of previously unacquainted children are brought together to play for some number of hours, over several weeks. At the end of these sessions, the children pick their favorite and least favorite playmates from among the group. Since the researchers have observed the actual behavior of the children throughout the sessions, they can link the child's behavior with his or her later popularity. In these studies, children who are most consistently positive and supportive are those who end up being chosen as leaders or as friends. Those who consistently participate in conflicts are more often rejected.

Rejected children also seem to have quite different internal working models of relationships and of aggression from those of popular children. In a whole series of studies, Kenneth Dodge has shown that aggressive/rejected children are much more likely to see aggression as a useful way to solve problems. They are also much more likely to interpret someone else's behavior as hostile or attacking than is true for less-aggressive or more popular children. For example, in one study Dodge showed kindergarten, second, and fourth grade children videotapes, each of which showed an interaction in which one child destroyed the toy of a second child (Dodge, Murphy, & Buchsbaum, 1984). These videos were carefully created so that the destroying child's intent was varied. In some vignettes, the intent was clearly hostile, in others it was accidental, in some it was ambiguous, and in others it was prosocial, such as knocking down the playmate's block tower in order to help clean up the room. Dodge found that in each age group, the popular children were better at detecting the actor's intent, with neglected and rejected children least accurate. In particular, neglected and rejected children were more likely to see hostile intent when it was not present, a pattern that has been found in other studies, especially among rejected children (Dodge & Feldman, 1990). Furthermore, when rejected or aggressive children perceive such hostile intent, they are more likely to retaliate. In turn, such retaliation is likely to elicit hostility from others, further confirming their expectation that other people are hostile to them (Dodge et al., 1990; Dodge & Frame, 1982; Quiggle et al., 1992).

This body of research can also be linked to Gerald Patterson's work, whose model I described in Chapters 1 and 2 (Figure 1.2, page 9). Patterson is persuaded

R E S E A R C H   R E P O R T

Long-term Consequences of Childhood Aggression and Peer Rejection

The seriousness of unpopularity in childhood is amply demonstrated in a growing body of research showing that rejection by one's peers in elementary school—especially rejection related to excess aggressiveness—is one of the very few aspects of childhood functioning that consistently predicts behavior problems or emotional disturbances in adolescence and adulthood. Let me give you a sampling of the findings.

- Leonard Eron, in a 22-year longitudinal study, has found that a high level of aggressiveness toward peers at age 8 was related to various forms of aggressiveness at age 30, including "criminal behavior, number of moving traffic violations, convictions for driving while intoxicated, aggressiveness toward spouses, and how severely the subjects punished their own children" (Eron, 1987, p. 439).

- In the Concordia Project in French Canada, Lisa Serbin (Serbin, 1991) has studied several thousand children who were initially identified by their peers in Grade 1, 4 or 7 as either highly aggressive, withdrawn, or both. A large comparison group of nonaggressive and nonwithdrawn children was also studied. Both aggressive girls and aggressive boys later showed poorer school achievement in high school. In adulthood, 45.5 percent of the aggressive but only 10.8 percent of the nonaggressive men had appeared in court. For women, the ratio was about two to one (3.8 percent vs. 1.8 percent).

- Farrington (1991) has studied a group of 400 working-class boys in England, beginning when they were 8 and continuing into their thirties. Those who were rated by their teachers as most aggressive at age 8, 10, and 12 were more likely to describe themselves at 32 as getting into fights, carrying a weapon, or fighting police officers. They were also

twice as likely as were less aggressive children to commit a violent offense (20.4 percent vs. 9.8 percent), twice as likely to be unemployed, more likely to hit their wives, and half again as likely to have a drunk driving conviction.

- Kupersmidt and Coie (1990), in a study of a small group of fifth graders who were followed to the end of high school, report that negative outcomes in high school—including poor school performance, regular truancy, dropping out of school, or juvenile court appearance— were considerably more common among rejected children than among the popular. This effect was particularly evident for subjects who were highly aggressive as children and for those who were both aggressive and rejected.

There are obviously several ways we could explain such a link between early aggression or unpopularity and later behavior problems. The simplest explanation is that problems with peers arise out of high levels of aggression and that such aggression simply persists as the individual's primary mode of interaction. It is also possible that a failure to develop friendships itself causes problems that later become more general. Or it could signify a seriously warped internal working model of relationships or all of the above.

Whatever the explanation, the point to remember is that such deviant behavior does tend to persist and may have profound effects on an individual's entire life pattern. None of these studies shows perfect continuity; all speak only of increased risks or increased probabilities. But it would be foolish to think that life begins all over again at age 20, with entirely new choices and a clean slate. Instead, we carry the traces of our childhood forward with us through our lives, in the form of established behavior patterns and powerful internal working models.

that a child's excess aggressiveness can be traced originally to ineffective parental control. But once the child's aggressiveness is well established, the child displays this same behavior with peers, is rejected by those peers, and is then driven more and more toward the only set of peers who will accept him, usually other aggressive or delinquent youngsters.

Happily, not all rejected children remain rejected or develop serious behavior problems or delinquency. And not all aggressive children are rejected. Recent research gives us a few hints about what may differentiate between these different subgroups. For example, among aggressive children, some also show fairly high levels of altruistic or prosocial behavior, and this mixture of qualities carries a much more positive prognosis than does aggression unleavened by help-fulness (Tremblay, 1991). Differences in the type of aggression a child shows may also prove to be predictive of later outcomes. Dodge (1991) suggests that children who show what he calls *proactive* aggression, who aggress in order to get their way or to obtain some desired end, may be more amenable to intervention or treatment than are children displaying *reactive* aggression, who aggress to retaliate against perceived wrong. The latter group seems intent on injuring the other person whereas the proactively aggressive child backs off as soon as he achieves his goal. Distinctions like these may help us not only to refine our predictions, but to design better intervention programs for rejected/aggressive children.

The Role of the Larger Culture

As at earlier ages, the daily life of the school-age child is shaped not just by the hours she spends in school or playing with pals. She is also affected by her family's economic circumstances, the neighborhood she lives in, the arrangements for her after-school care, and the television programs she watches. Within the family, the pattern of interaction between parent and child is also affected by many of these same forces, as well as by the quality of the parent's job, the amount of emotional support the parent(s) have from family or friends, and many other factors I've talked about in earlier chapters. Let me talk about two of these components of the larger culture that seem especially important in middle childhood: the effects of poverty, and the effects of television.

The Effects of Poverty

Every society is made up of social layers, usually called **social classes,** with each layer having a different degree of access to goods or status. In Western societies, the social class of a given family is most often defined in terms of the income and education of the adults in that family. In the United States, three social classes are usually identified: middle-class, working-class, and poverty-level families. Members of each of these groups or social layers tend to share certain values or styles of interaction (Luster, Rhoades, & Haas, 1989), with the largest differences found between families living in poverty and those in higher social class groups. For children, it is clear that the disadvantages of poverty are enormous.

Figure 10.4 shows the percentages of children under 16, from different ethnic groups in the United States, who were living below the poverty line in 1991—defined as an income for a family of four of $13,924 per year or less. *More children in the United States live in poverty than in any other industrialized country in the world.* And in this country, poverty is a far more common experience for minority children and youth, especially if they live with a single mother. Roughly 70 percent of Black and Hispanic children reared by single mothers live in poverty.

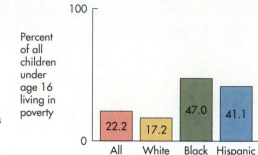

FIGURE 10.4

The percentage of children under age 16 living in poverty in the United States in 1991. (Source: U.S. Bureau of the Census, 1993, Table 738, p. 470.)

Furthermore, when minority families are poor, they stay poor longer. Vonnie McLloyd (1993) notes that two-fifths of Black children, but only 6 percent of Whites, grow up in families that are poor for as long as 5 to 6 years. Half of White children grow up in families that are never poor and never live in a poor neighborhood, while this is true for only 5 percent of Blacks. Thus even those Black families that do not fall below the poverty line at any one moment are likely to have fallen below it at some time, and/or spend some time living in a poor neighborhood.

The Effects of Poverty on Families and Children.   Among many other things, poverty reduces options for parents. They cannot afford prenatal care, so their children are more likely to be born with some sort of disability. When the mother works, she has fewer choices of affordable child care. Such children spend more time in poor-quality care, and they shift more from one care arrangement to another. Poor families are also larger (Broman, Nichols, & Kennedy, 1975), with children more closely spaced, and they live in smaller and less adequate housing. The total environment is more chaotic, more highly stressed, with fewer resources.

Mothers and fathers living in poverty also treat their children quite differently than do mothers and fathers in working-class or middle-class families in the United States. They talk to them less, provide fewer age-appropriate toys, spend less time with them in intellectually stimulating activities, are stricter and more physical in their discipline, explaining things less often and less fully (Farran, Haskins, & Gallagher, 1980). They are more likely to be either neglecting or authoritarian, and less likely to be authoritative (Dornbusch et al., 1987).

Some of this pattern of parental behavior is undoubtedly a response to the extraordinary stresses and special demands of the poverty environment (among other things, obedience may be quite simply more necessary in some poverty environments); some of the pattern may also be straightforward modeling of the way these same parents were brought up in their own childhood; some may be a product of ignorance of children's needs. Poor parents with relatively more education, for example, typically talk to their children more, are more responsive, and provide more intellectual stimulation than do equally poor parents with lower levels of education (Kelley, Sanches-Hucles, & Walker, 1993). But what-

The Real World
Latchkey Children

Many parents find themselves unable to afford or unable to arrange after-school care for their elementary school children. This leaves the child to care for herself in the hours between the end of school and the parent(s)'s return from work. Such children are referred to as *latchkey children*.

It has been very difficult to discover just how many latchkey children there are, in part because such a practice has had a lot of bad press, so parents are not always willing to acknowledge that their children care for themselves part of the time. Most current estimates are that between 5 and 10 percent of children between age 6 and 13 in the United States spend at least some part of their days in "self-care" (Cain & Hofferth, 1989; U.S. Bureau of the Census, 1990). In families in which all the parental figures are working, the rate is about twice that (Cain & Hofferth, 1989).

Self-care is most likely for children 10 and over and for only a short time each day, most often after school. Contrary to what you may assume, such care arrangements are *not* found primarily among families in poverty environments. On the contrary, they are more common among middle- and upper-class White families in suburban or rural areas.

There is very little decent research to tell us what effect such self-care may have on children. The bulk of the evidence suggests that latchkey children do not differ from other kids in their school performance, self-concept, or susceptibility to peer pressure (Cole & Rodman, 1987) if the child has a clear routine, is in daily contact with the parent(s) by phone during the self-care hours, and has neighbors or others to turn to in case of need. When these conditions cannot be met—as may be the case for children living in public housing developments or in other environments without good support—self-care may simply exacerbate existing problems.

Among adolescents who lack supervision for parts of each day, those who stay in their own homes for the unsupervised hours seem to do better than those who spend the time "hanging out" or at a friend's house. The latter groups seem to be especially susceptible to peer pressure during the peer-sensitive years of early adolescence (Steinberg, 1986).

Overall, the relatively scant research literature suggests that self-care by children is not the unmitigated disaster that many popular press reports would have us believe. But there are enough red flags to suggest that we need to know a good deal more about the specific conditions needed to support children who must care for themselves for part of each day.

ever the cause, children reared in poverty not only experience different physical conditions but quite different interactions with their parents.

Not surprisingly, such children turn out differently, as I have pointed out repeatedly in earlier chapters. Children from poverty environments have higher rates of birth defects and early disabilities; they recover less well from early problems; they are more often ill and malnourished throughout their childhood years. Typically, they also have lower IQs and move more slowly through the sequences of cognitive development that Piaget described. The more years they have lived in poverty, the larger the observed IQ decrement, even when family structure and the mother's level of education is taken into account (Duncan, 1993). They do less well in school and are less likely to go on to college (Patterson, Kupersmidt, & Vaden, 1990). Such children, in turn, are more likely to be poor as adults, thus continuing the cycle through another generation.

The Special Case of Inner-City Poverty. All of these effects are probably much worse for children growing up in poverty-ravaged urban areas. They are exposed to street gangs and street violence, to drug pushers, to overcrowded homes and abuse. Whole communities have become like war zones.

In the United States, almost 13 million children live in such urban poverty (Garbarino, Kostelny, & Dubrow, 1991). More than one and a half million of them live in public housing developments, including some with the highest crime rates in the country. A recent survey in Chicago (Kotulak, 1990) revealed that nearly 40 percent of elementary and high school students in the inner city had witnessed a shooting, a third had seen a stabbing. Guns are common in schools as well as on the streets. I was stunned to read that in a study in Seattle, Washington (a city with a rate of urban poverty well below that of Chicago, New York, or Los Angeles), investigators found that 11.4 percent of the teen males reported owning a handgun. A third of these gun owners had fired at someone (Callahan & Rivara, 1992).

In the early years of childhood, when youngsters spend most of their time with a parent, other caregiver, or with siblings, it may be possible for parents to protect them from some of the dangers inherent in such poverty environments. But in middle childhood, when children pass through the streets to travel to and from school and to play with their peers, they experience the impact of urban poverty and decay far more keenly. Many show all the symptoms of post-traumatic stress disorder (Garbarino et al., 1992), including sleep disturbances, irritability, inability to concentrate, angry outbursts, and hypervigilance. Many experience flashbacks or intrusive memories of traumatic events. And because they are likely to have missed out on many of the forms of intellectual stimulation and consistent family support that would allow them to succeed in school, they have high rates of problems and academic failures. Less than half of urban poor children graduate from high school (Garbarino et al., 1991). The reasons for such school failures are obviously complex, but there is little doubt that the chronic stress poor children experience is one highly significant component.

The Role of Stress and Protective Factors.   Arnold Sameroff and his colleagues have argued that the effects of various kinds of stresses accumulate. A child may be able to handle one or two, but as the stresses and risks add up, the probability that a child will thrive intellectually, emotionally, or socially declines steadily (Sameroff et al., 1987). For a child growing up in poverty, perhaps espe-

> Are you also shocked by such statistics? What do you think we ought to do about it?

When you look at scenes of urban poverty like this, you can see why some refer to them as "war zones."

Children in Danger

I cannot leave the subject of urban poverty—so common now in America—without getting up on my soap box one more time. This time, I will let James Garbarino speak for me:

> What is truly needed in America's urban war zones is restoration of a safe environment where children can have a childhood, and where parents can exert less energy on

protecting children from random gunfire and more on helping children to grow. No one can eliminate all risk from the lives of families. But America does have the resources to make a real childhood a real possibility even for the children of the urban poor. But sometimes the war close to home is the most difficult to see (Garbarino et al., 1991, p. 148).

---

cially urban poverty, the chances of experiencing multiple separate types of stress are very high indeed.

At the same time, studies of resilient and vulnerable children (Easterbrooks, Davidson, & Chazan, 1993; Garmezy & Masten, 1991; Masten, Best, & Garmezy, 1990) suggest that there are certain characteristics or circumstances that may help to protect some children from the detrimental effects of repeated stresses and upheavals, including the following:

- high IQ in the child
- competent adult parenting, such as an authoritative style
- effective schools
- a secure initial attachment of the child to the parent

For example, in a major longitudinal study in Kauai, Hawaii, Emmy Werner (1994; Werner & Smith, 1982) has found that a subset of those children reared in poverty nonetheless became competent, able, autonomous adults. The families of these resilient children were clearly more authoritative, more cohesive, more loving than were the equivalently poor families whose children had less good outcomes. Similarly, studies of boys reared in high-crime inner-city neighborhoods show that high intelligence and at least a minimum level of family cohesion are key ingredients affecting a boy's chance of creating a successful adult life pattern (Long & Vaillant, 1984; McCord, 1982). Boys reared in poverty-level families in which there was alcoholism, parents with strong antisocial tendencies, or low IQ were simply much less likely to develop the competence needed to bootstrap themselves out of their difficult circumstances.

Thus the outcome depends on some joint effect of the number of stresses the child must cope with and the range of competencies or advantages the child brings to the situation. Poverty does not guarantee bad outcomes, but it stacks the deck against most children.

Television and Its Effects

Another major influence on children, particularly in industrialized countries, is television. Ninety-eight percent of American homes have a television set. Children between the ages of 2 and 11 spend an average of 28 hours a week watching TV, a number that is only slightly lower in adolescence (about 23 hours a week) (American Psychological Association, 1993). Indeed, "By the time American children are 18 years old, they have spent more time watching television than in any other activity except sleep" (Huston et al., 1990). High levels of viewing are more common among African-American children than among Whites or Hispanics, and more common in families in which the parents are less-well educated (Anderson et al., 1986)

Viewing rates are not as high in most other countries, but TV ownership is above 50 percent of households in Latin America and in most of Eastern and Western Europe, so this is not an exclusively American phenomenon (Comstock, 1991).

Just what are children seeing during all of those hours? Preschoolers see many programs designed specifically to be educational or informative, such as Sesame Street or Mr. Rogers' Neighborhood. As they get older, however, children increasingly watch cartoons, comedies, and adult-entertainment programs (Huston et al., 1990).

I can give you only a few tidbits from the vast amount of research designed to detect the effects of such viewing on children. Still, a taste is better than no meal at all.

Positive Educational Effects of TV. Programs specifically designed to be educational, or to teach children positive values, do indeed have demonstrable effects. This is particularly clear among preschoolers, for whom most such programming is designed. Children who watch Sesame Street more regularly, for example, develop larger vocabularies than do children who do not watch or watch less often (Rice et al., 1990), and those who watch programs that emphasize sharing, kindness, and helpfulness, such as Mr. Rogers' Neighborhood, Sesame Street, or even Lassie, show more kind and helpful behavior (Murray, 1980). These studies show that, as Huston and Wright say, "television can be an ally, not an enemy, for parents. Parents can use television programs for their children's benefit just as they use books and toys" (1994, p. 80).

Negative Effects of TV on Cognitive Skills. On the other side of the argument, however, is evidence that in elementary school and high school, higher levels of TV viewing are associated with *lower* scores on achievement tests, including measures of such basic skills as reading, arithmetic, and writing. This is particularly clear in the results of an enormous study in California that included over 500,000 sixth and twelfth graders (California Assessment Program, 1980). In this very large sample, the more hours the students watched TV, the lower their scores on standardized tests. This relationship was actually *stronger* among children from well-educated families, so this result is not an artifact of the fact that working-class or low-education families watch more TV. However, among children with limited English fluency, high levels of viewing were associated with somewhat higher school achievement. Thus television can help to teach children things they did not already know, just as Sesame Street helps to teach vocabulary to preschoolers. But among children with basic skills at the start of school, a high level of TV viewing time appears to have a negative effect on school performance.

In the United States, children the age of these two watch an average of 4 hours of TV every day. Amazing.

How many different explanations can you think of for the relationship between amount of TV watching and school performance? What kind of data would you need to check the plausibility of each of your explanations?

Family Viewing Patterns

Statements about the average number of hours of children's viewing disguise very large variations among families not only in viewing patterns but also in attitudes about television. To a considerable extent, parents control their children's TV through explicit rules and through attitudes—an example of the way in which broad cultural forces interact with individual family styles. Nearly half of families have consistent rules about what type or which specific programs a child may view; about 40 percent restrict the number of hours a child can watch, while another 40 percent encourage the child's viewing at least some of the time (Comstock, 1991).

Michelle St. Peters (St. Peters et al., 1991), in one recent study, found that she could classify families into one of four types, based on the degree of regulation and degree of encouragement of TV viewing parents imposed. *Laissez-Faire* parents had few regulations but did not specifically encourage viewing. *Restrictive* parents had high regulations and little encouragement, while *promotive* parents had few regulations and high levels of encouragement for TV viewing. *Selective* parents had high regulations but encouraged some specific types of viewing.

In a two-year longitudinal study of 5-year-olds and their parents, St. Peters found that children in restrictive families watched the least TV (11.9 hours per week). When they watched, it was most likely to be entertainment or educational programs aimed specifically at children (such as Sesame Street, Mr. Rogers' Neighborhood, or Walt Disney). The heaviest viewers were children with parents classed as promotive, who watched an average of 21.1 hours per week. They watched not only children's programs but also adult comedy, drama, game shows, and action adventure. In laissez-faire families, children watched an intermediate number of hours (16.7), mostly devoted to child entertainment and comedy, a pattern similar to what appeared in the selective families, although the latter group watched more informative programs directed at children than did laissez-faire children.

The key point here is that families create the conditions for children's viewing and thus for what children learn from TV. Not only do parents establish a degree of regulation, they may also watch with the child and interpret what the child sees. A family that wishes to do so can take advantage of the beneficial things TV has to offer and minimize exposure to programs with aggressive, violent, or sexist content. The difficulty for many families, however, is that such a planned approach to TV may mean that the parents will have to give up their own favorite programs. . . .

Television and Aggression.   By far the largest body of research has focused on the potential impact of TV on children's aggressiveness. On American television, the level of violence has remained high over the past two decades, despite many Congressional investigations and cries of alarm. In prime time programs, a violent act occurs 5 or 6 times per hour; on Saturday morning cartoons, the rate is 20 to 25 times per hour. MTV, available in roughly 60 percent of homes in the U.S., has far higher rates of violence than one finds in prime time commercial shows.

Observers also agree that the "good guys" are just as likely to be violent as the "bad guys," and that violence on most TV programs is rewarded; people who are violent get what they want. In fact, violence is usually portrayed as a successful way of solving problems. Furthermore, the consequences of violence—pain, blood, and damage—are seldom shown, so the child is protected from seeing the painful and negative consequences of aggression and thus receives an unrealistic portrayal of those consequences.

Does the viewing of such a barrage of violence *cause* higher rates of aggression or violence in children? Demonstrating such a causal link is rather like demonstrating a causal link between smoking and lung cancer. Unequivocal findings would require an experimental design—a strategy ruled out for obvious ethical reasons. One cannot assign some people randomly to smoke for 30 years, nor assign some children to watch years of violent TV while others watch none. But we now have three types of research evidence that all point strongly toward the existence of a causal link.

Researchers have conducted some short-term experiments in which one group of children is exposed to a few episodes of moderately aggressive TV, while others watch neutral programs. These studies generally show a short-term increase in aggression among those who watched the aggressive programs. A second type of research relies on correlational evidence, which, as always, leaves us with a problem of interpretation. For example, children who already behave aggressively may *choose* to watch more TV and more violent TV. And families that watch TV a great deal may also be more likely to use patterns of discipline that will foster aggressiveness in the child. Nonetheless, good correlational studies, especially those with longitudinal designs, can strongly indicate a causal connection. One research example will make the point clear.

In his 22-year longitudinal study of aggressiveness from age 8 to 30, Leonard Eron (1987) has found that the best predictor of a young man's aggressiveness at age 19 was the violence of television programs he watched when he was 8. Twelve years later, when the men were 30, Eron found that the seriousness of criminal behavior was strongly related to the frequency of TV viewing at age 8, as you can see in Figure 10.5. The pattern is the same for women, by the way, but the level of criminal offenses is far lower, just as the level of aggression is lower among girls in childhood.

Eron also found that at age 8, boys who watched a lot of violent television were already more highly aggressive with their peers, indicating that aggressive boys choose to watch more violent TV. However, among the already aggressive 8-year-olds, those who watched the most TV were more delinquent or aggressive as teenagers and as adults (Eron, 1987; Huesmann, Lagerspetz, & Eron, 1984). Shorter-term longitudinal studies in Poland, Finland, Israel, and Australia show similar links between TV viewing and aggression among children in each case (Eron et al., 1991), which further strengthens the point. Evidence like this

FIGURE 10.5
These data from Leonard Eron's 22-year longitudinal study show the relationships between the amount of TV a group of boys watched when they were 8 and the average severity of criminal offenses they had committed by the age of 30. (Source: Eron, 1987, Figure 3, p. 440.)

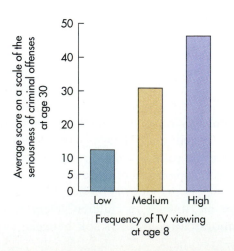

suggests that the causality runs both ways: "aggressive children prefer violent television, and the violence on television causes them to be more aggressive" (Eron, 1987, p. 438).

The newest type of evidence, perhaps the most persuasive of all, comes from epidemiology. Brandon Centerwall (1989; 1992) proposed that if we think of societal violence as an epidemic disease, we could use exactly the same strategy to study it that an epidemiologist would use in trying to trace the causal factors in any other epidemic. In his study, Centerwall looked at the homicide rate in Canada and among Whites in both the United States and South Africa, as a function of the time since television was introduced into each country.

TV was introduced in both the United States and Canada in about 1950, in South Africa about 25 years later. In each of these three countries, the homicide rate began to rise *rapidly* 10 to 15 years after TV viewing became widespread. That is, as soon as the first generation of children who had grown up watching TV became young adults, homicide rates soared. Figure 10.6 shows the results for both Canada and the United States.

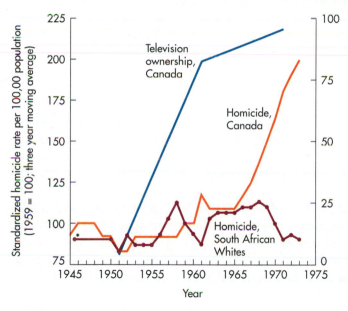

FIGURE 10.6
Centerwall looked at societal violence as if it were a disease and asked what relationship the introduction of TV in each culture had to the rate of such violence. (Source: Centerwall, 1989, Figure 1, p. 6, and Figure 2, p. 7.)

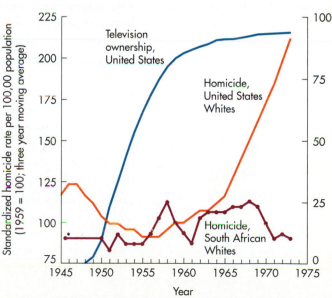

Taking all three types of evidence together, the conclusion seems inescapable that "viewing violence increases violence" (American Psychological Association, 1993 p. 33). It also leads to emotional desensitization toward violence and to a belief that aggression is a good way to solve problems. Violent television is clearly not the only nor even the major cause of aggressiveness among children or adults. But it is a significant influence, both individually and at the broader cultural level.

For parents, the clear message from all the research is that television is an educational medium. Children learn from what they watch—vocabulary words, helpful behaviors, and aggressive behaviors and attitudes. The overall content of television—violence and all—may indeed reflect general cultural values. But an individual family can pick and choose among the various cultural messages by controlling what the child watches on TV.

> Given what you have just read, would you restrict your child's TV watching, and if so, in what way? Would you be willing to give up having a television altogether if you thought that were necessary for your child's optimum development?

SUMMARY

1. Patterns of relationships established in elementary school may have greater impact on adolescent and adult life patterns than do cognitive changes in these same years.

2. In middle childhood, the self-concept becomes more abstract, more comparative, more generalized.

3. Similar changes occur in children's descriptions of others, and in their understanding of relationships such as friendships. Friendships are increasingly seen as reciprocal relationships in which generosity and trust are important elements.

4. These changes parallel the cognitive changes we see in the same years, particularly the child's reduced reliance on appearances.

5. Relationships with parents become less overtly affectionate, with fewer attachment behaviors, in middle childhood. The strength of the attachment, however, appears to remain strong.

6. Peer relationships become increasingly central. Gender segregation of peer-group activities is at its peak in these years and appears in every culture.

7. Individual friendships also become more common and more enduring; they are almost entirely sex segregated. Boys' and girls' friendships appear to differ in quite specific ways. Boys' relationships are more extensive and more "restrictive," with higher levels of competition and aggression; girls' relationships are more intensive and enabling, with more compliance and agreement.

8. Physical aggression declines, while verbal insults and taunts increase. Boys show markedly higher levels of aggression, a difference that doubtless has both biological and social origins.

9. Self-esteem appears to be shaped by two factors: the degree of discrepancy a child experiences between goals and achievements and the degree of perceived social support from peers and parents.

10. Low self-esteem is strongly associated with depression in children this age.

11. Socially rejected children are most strongly characterized by high levels of aggression or bullying and low levels of agreement and helpfulness. Aggressive/rejected children are much more likely to show behavior problems in adolescence and a variety of disturbances in adulthood.

12. Rejected children are more likely to interpret others' behavior as threatening or hostile. Thus they have different internal models of relationship.

13. A large fraction of children, including the majority of Black children, grow up in poverty and experience heightened danger and violence. The stress associated with this environment is one factor in poorer school performance.

14. Although it is difficult to establish causal relationships, most evidence points to a link between high levels of TV viewing and both current and later aggression.

15. TV may have some beneficial educational effects in teaching specific knowledge or attitudes; but heavy viewing is associated with lower levels of school achievement in nearly all groups.

KEY TERMS

self-esteem
social class

SUGGESTED READINGS

Asher, S. R., & Coie, J. D. (Eds.) (1990). *Peer rejection in childhood*. Cambridge: Cambridge University Press. This edited volume contains papers by all the leading researchers on this important subject. The papers are aimed at an audience of fellow psychologists, so the technical level is fairly high. Still, it is a wonderful next source if you are interested in this subject.

Comstock, G. (1991). *Television and the American child*. San Diego: Academic Press. This is about as complete and current a book as you will find on this subject. The author, who is a respected professor of communications, not only analyzes an enormous array of research, he provides a great deal of actual data, so that you can see research results for yourself.

Garbarino, J., Dubrow, N., Kostelny, K., & Pardo, C. (1992). *Children in danger. Coping with the consequences of community violence*. San Francisco: Jossey-Bass. A striking, frightening book about children growing up in "war zones," including urban poverty in the United States, as well as in literal war zones in other countries.

Summing Up Development in Middle Childhood

BASIC CHARACTERISTICS OF MIDDLE CHILDHOOD

The Figure summarizes the changes and continuities of middle childhood. There are obviously many gradual changes: greater and greater physical skill, less and less reliance on appearance and more and more attention to underlying qualities and attributes, greater and greater significance of peers. The one period in which there seems to be a more rapid change is right at the beginning of middle childhood, at the point of transition from the preschooler to the school child. And of course at the other end of this age range, puberty causes another set of rapid changes.

The Transition Between 5 and 7. Some kind of a transition into middle childhood has been noted in a great many cultures. There seems to be widespread recognition that a 6-year-old is somehow qualitatively different from a 5-year-old: more responsible, more able to understand complex ideas. Among the Kipsigis of Kenya, for example, the age of 6 is said to be the first point at which the child has *ng'omnotet*, translated as *intelligence* (Harkness & Super, 1985). The fact that schooling begins at this age seems to reflect an implicit or explicit recognition of this fundamental shift.

Psychologists who have studied development across this transition have pointed to a whole series of changes.

- Cognitively, there is a shift to what Piaget calls concrete operational thinking. The child now understands conservation problems, seriation, and class inclusion. More generally, the child seems to pay less attention to surface properties of objects and more to underlying continuities and patterns. We see this not only in children's understanding of physical objects but in their understanding of others, of relationships, and of themselves. In studies of information processing, we see a parallel rapid increase in the child's use of executive strategies.

- In the self-concept, we first see a global judgment of self-worth at about age 7 or 8.

- In peer relationships, gender segregation becomes virtually complete by age 6 or 7, especially in individual friendships.

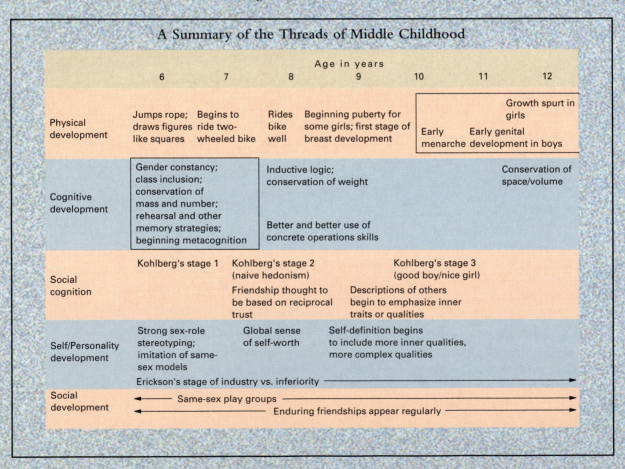

A Summary of the Threads of Middle Childhood

	Age in years						
	6	7	8	9	10	11	12
Physical development	Jumps rope; draws figures like squares	Begins to ride two-wheeled bike	Rides bike well	Beginning puberty for some girls; first stage of breast development	Early menarche	Early genital development in boys	Growth spurt in girls
Cognitive development	Gender constancy; class inclusion; conservation of mass and number; rehearsal and other memory strategies; beginning metacognition		Inductive logic; conservation of weight				Conservation of space/volume
			Better and better use of concrete operations skills				
Social cognition	Kohlberg's stage 1	Kohlberg's stage 2 (naive hedonism)		Kohlberg's stage 3 (good boy/nice girl)			
		Friendship thought to be based on reciprocal trust		Descriptions of others begin to emphasize inner traits or qualities			
Self/Personality development	Strong sex-role stereotyping; imitation of same-sex models		Global sense of self-worth	Self-definition begins to include more inner qualities, more complex qualities			
	Erickson's stage of industry vs. inferiority ⟶						
Social development	⟵ Same-sex play groups ⟶						
	⟵ Enduring friendships appear regularly ⟶						

The apparent confluence of these changes is impressive and seems to provide some support for the existence of a Piagetlike stage. On the surface, at least, there seems to be some kind of change in the basic structure of the child's thinking that is reflected in all aspects of the child's functioning. But impressive as these changes are, it is not so clear that what is going on here is a rapid, pervasive, structural change to a whole new way of thinking and relating. Children don't make this shift all at once in every area of their thinking or relationships. For example, while the shift from a concrete to a more abstract self-concept may become noticeable at 6 or 7, it occurs quite gradually and is still going on at age 11 and 12. Similarly, a child may grasp conservation of quantity at age 5 or 6, but typically does not understand conservation of weight until several years later.

Furthermore, expertise, or the lack of it, strongly affects the pattern of the child's cognitive progress. Thus while I think most psychologists would agree that there is a set of important changes that normally emerge together at about this age, most would also agree that there is no rapid or abrupt reorganization of the child's whole mode of operating.

CENTRAL PROCESSES

In trying to account for the developmental shifts we see during middle childhood, my bias has been to see the cognitive changes as most central, the necessary but not sufficient condition for the alterations in relationships and in the self-scheme during this period. A good illustration is the emergence of a global sense of self-worth, which seems to require not only a tendency to look beyond or behind surface characteristics, but also the use of inductive logic. The child appears to arrive at a global sense of self-worth by some summative, inductive process.

Similarly, the quality of the child's relationships with peers and parents seems to rest, in part, on basic cognitive understanding of reciprocity and perspective taking. The child now understands that others read him as much as he reads them. Children of 7 or 8 will now say of their friends that they "trust each other," something you would be very unlikely to hear from a 5-year-old.

Such a cognitive bias dominated theories and research on middle childhood for many decades, largely as a result of the powerful influence of Piaget's theory. This imbalance has begun to be redressed in recent years, as the central importance of the peer group and the child's social experience have been better understood. There are two aspects to this revision of thinking. First, we have reawakened to the (obvious) fact that a great deal of the experience on which the child's cognitive progress is based occurs in social interactions, particularly in play with other children. Second, we have realized that social relationships make a unique set of demands, both cognitive and interactive.

People, as objects of thought, are simply not the same as rocks, beakers of water, or balls of clay. Among many other things, people behave *intentionally*, and they can reveal or conceal information about themselves. Further, unlike relationships with objects, relationships with people are mutual and reciprocal. Other people talk back, respond to your distress, offer things, get angry.

Children also have to learn social scripts, those special rules that apply to social interactions, such as politeness rules, rules about when you can and cannot speak, or about power or dominance hierarchies. Such scripts change with age, so at each new age the child must learn a new set of roles, a new set of rules about what she may and may not do. To be sure, these changes in the scripts are partly in *response* to the child's growing cognitive sophistication. But they also reflect changes in the child's role in the social system. One obvious example is the set of changes when children start school. The script associated with the role of "student" is simply quite different from the one connected with the role of "little kid." School classrooms are more tightly organized than are preschools or day-care centers, expectations for obedience are higher, and there are more drills and routines to be learned. These changes are bound to affect the child's pattern of thinking.

Just what role physical change plays in this collection of developments I do not know. Clearly there *are* physical changes going on. Girls, in particular, begin the early steps of puberty during elementary school. But we simply don't know whether the rate of physical development in these years is connected in any way to the rate of the child's progress through the sequence of cognitive or social understandings. The one thing we know is that bigger, more coordinated, early developing children are likely to have slightly faster cognitive development and be somewhat more popular with peers. Obviously this is an area in which we need far more knowledge.

INFLUENCES ON THE BASIC PROCESSES: THE ROLE OF CULTURE

Most of what I have said about middle childhood—and about other ages as well—is almost entirely based on research on children growing up in Western cultures. I've tried to balance the scales a bit as I've gone along, but we must still ask, again and again, whether the patterns we see are specific to particular cultures or whether they reflect underlying developmental processes common to all children everywhere.

In the case of middle childhood, there are some obvious differences in the experiences of children in Western cultures versus those growing up in villages in Africa, in Polynesia, or in other parts of the world where families live by subsistence agriculture and schooling is not a dominant force in children's lives (Weisner, 1984). In many such cultures, children of 6 or 7 are thought of as "intelligent" and responsible and are given almost adult-like roles. They are highly likely to be given the task of caring for younger siblings and begin their apprenticeships in the skills they will need as adults, such as water carrying, agricultural skills, or animal husbandry, learning alongside the adult. In some west African and Polynesian cultures, it is also common for children this age to be sent out to foster care, either with relatives or to apprentice with a skilled tradesperson.

Such children obviously have a very different set of social tasks to learn in the middle childhood years than do children growing up in industrialized countries. They do not need to learn how to relate to or make friends with strangers in a new school environment. Instead, from an early age they need to learn their place in an existing network of roles and relationships. For the Western child, the roles are less prescribed, the choices for adult life are far more varied.

Yet the differences in the lives of Western and non-Western children should not obscure the very real similarities. In all cultures, children this age develop individual friendships, segregate their play groups by gender, develop the cognitive underpinnings of reciprocity, learn the beginnings of what Piaget calls concrete operations, and acquire some of the basic skills that they will require for adult life. These are not trivial similarities. They speak to the power of the common process of development, even in the midst of obvious variation in experience.

Chapter Eleven

Physical Development in Adolescence

ost of us use the word "adolescence" as if the term applied to a fairly precise set of years, such as the teenage years, or the time that starts with junior high school, or the years from 12 to 20. But in fact, the relevant age range is fairly fuzzy on the edges. If we mean to include the physical process of puberty within the years of adolescence, then we need to think of adolescence as beginning before age 12, especially for girls, some of whom begin puberty at 8 or 9. And on the other end, it is not clear that it is still appropriate to refer to a young man of 18 with a job and a wife and child as an adolescent.

It makes more sense to think of adolescence as the period that lies psychologically and culturally between childhood and adulthood rather than as a specific age range. It is the period of transition in which the child changes physically, mentally, and emotionally into an adult. The timing of this transition differs from one society to another and from one individual to another within a culture. But every child must cross through such a transitional period to achieve adult status. In many cultures, this highly significant change in status is marked by rituals and rites of various kinds; in most industrialized cultures, such initiation rites have disappeared, perhaps because the transitional stage is often quite lengthy, lasting from perhaps 12 to 18—even later for those who go to college and thus postpone some aspects of full adult status.

Because the physical and emotional changes that are part of this transition are so striking, the period of adolescence has acquired a reputation as being full of *sturm und drang* (storm and stress). Such a description considerably exaggerates the degree of emotional upheaval most adolescents experience. But the *importance* of the process is difficult to exaggerate, beginning with the remarkable physical changes of **puberty.**

Physical Changes at Adolescence

The many body changes associated with puberty are largely controlled by hormones, which play a central role in the physical drama of adolescence.

Hormones

Hormones, which are secretions of the various **endocrine glands** in the body, govern pubertal growth and physical changes in several ways, summarized in Table 11.1. Of all the endocrine glands, the most critical is the **pituitary;** it provides the trigger for release of hormones from other glands. For example, the thyroid gland only secretes thyroxine when it has received a signal to do so in the form of a specific thyroid-stimulating hormone secreted by the pituitary.

Of course hormones play a central role in growth and development at earlier ages as well. Thyroid hormone (thyroxine) is present from about the fourth month of gestation and appears to be involved in stimulating normal brain development prenatally. Growth hormone is also produced by the pituitary beginning as early as 10 weeks after conception. Presumably it helps to stimulate the very rapid growth of cells and organs of the body. And as I mentioned in Chapter 3, testosterone is produced prenatally in the testes of the developing

In the initiation rite of the Kota tribe of the Congo, boys' faces are painted blue to make them appear ghostlike, which symbolizes the phantom of their now-departed childhood.

CULTURES & CONTEXTS

Adolescent Initiation Rituals

So important is the change in status from child to adult that many societies have both promoted and marked this passage with some kind of rite or ritual. There is an enormous amount of variability in the content of such rituals, but certain practices are especially common (Cohen, 1964).

One such practice, more common for boys than for girls, is the separation of the child from the family, which anthropologists refer to as *extrusion*. The child may spend the day with his family, but sleep elsewhere, or may live in a separate dwelling with other boys or with relatives. Such a separation typically occurs quite early in adolescence, some time before the actual initiation ritual. In traditional Hopi and Navaho cultures, for example, boys typically sleep apart from the family beginning at age 8 or 10; in the Kurtatchi of Melanesia, boys go through an extrusion ceremony at about age 9 or 10, after which they sleep in a special hut for boys and unmarried men (Cohen, 1964). This practice obviously symbolizes the separation of the child from the birth family, marking a coming-of-age. But it also emphasizes that the child "belongs" not just to the family but to the larger group of kin or societal/tribal members.

A related theme is the accentuation of differences between females and males. In many cultures, for example, nudity taboos begin only at adolescence. Before that age, it is quite o.k. for boys and girls to see one another naked; after that age it is not. In some cultures, adolescents are forbidden to speak to any opposite-sex siblings, a taboo that may extend until one of the siblings marries (Cohen, 1964). This practice seems to have at least two purposes. First and most obviously, it strengthens the incest taboo that is so important to avoid inbreeding. Second, it signifies the beginning of the time in life when males and females have quite different life patterns. Girls and boys have begun to learn gender-appropriate tasks long before adolescence, but at adolescence they take up those roles far more completely.

These two patterns may form the backdrop for the initiation ritual itself, which is usually briefer and more intense. During this time—usually in groups and separately for each sex—adolescents are indoctrinated by the elders into the customary practices of their tribe or society. They may learn special religious rituals or practices, such as the learning of Hebrew as preparation for the *bar mitzva* or *bas mitzva* in the Jewish tradition. They may learn the history and songs of their tribe or people. Often, there is drama and pageantry as part of the entire process.

Very frequently, physical mutilation or trials also play a part in the initiation. Boys may be circumcised, cut so as to create certain patterns of scars, or sent out into the wilderness to undergo spiritual purification or to prove their manhood by achieving some feat. This is less common in girls' initiation rituals, but physical trials or mutilation do occur, such as the removal of the clitoris, whipping, or scarification.

Among the Hopi, for example, both boys and girls go through specific rituals in which they are taught the religious ceremonies of the Katchina cult and are whipped. After these ceremonies, they may participate fully in the adult religious practices. Among the Malekula of New Hebrides, boys are circumcised and secluded. Girls in this culture go through a kind of initiation just before they are married, rather than at puberty: they must have their two upper incisor teeth ceremonially knocked out and be secluded for 10 days.

In modern United States culture, as in most other Western cultures, there are no universally shared initiation rites, but there are still many changes of status and a few experiences that have some properties in common with traditional adolescent *rites de passage*. We do not deliberately separate adolescents from family or from adults, but we do send adolescents to a new level of school, thus effectively segregating them from all but their peers. Boot camp, for those who enter the military, is a more obvious parallel, because the recruits are sent to a separate location and undergo various physical trials before they are accepted.

Until relatively recent times, it was also common for adolescent boys and girls in our culture to attend separate schools. Even within coeducational schools, physical education classes were sex-segregated until very recently, as were such traditional gender-stereotyped classes as home economics and shop.

Other changes in legal standing also mark the passage to adult status in modern Western cultures. Young people can have a driver's license at 16 and can see R-rated movies at 17. At 18, they can vote, marry, enter the military without parental consent, and be tried in adult rather than juvenile court for any legal offense—although legal access to alcohol is typically withheld until age 21.

These various remnants of ancient initiation patterns are considerably less condensed in modern society than is true in many cultures around the world. One result of this is that the passage into adult status is much less clear for young people in most industrialized countries. Perhaps this is one reason why adolescents in our society often create their own separation and distinctness, such as wearing unusual or even outlandish clothing or hair styles.

TABLE 11.1
Major Hormones Involved in Physical Growth and Development

Gland	Hormone(s) Secreted	Aspects of Growth Influenced
Thyroid	Thyroxine	Affects normal brain development and overall rate of growth.
Adrenal	Adrenal androgen	Involved in some changes at puberty, particularly the development of secondary sex characteristics in girls.
Testes (boys)	Testosterone	Crucial in the formation of male genitals prenatally; also triggers the sequence of primary and secondary sex characteristic changes at puberty in the male.
Ovaries (girls)	Estradiol	Affects development of the menstrual cycle and breasts in girls but has less to do with other secondary sex characteristics than testosterone does for boys.
Pituitary	Growth hormone; Activating hormones	Affects rate of physical maturation. Signals other glands to secrete.

male and influences both the development of male genitals and some aspects of brain development.

After birth, the rate of growth is governed largely by thyroid hormone and pituitary growth hormone. Thyroid hormone is secreted in greater quantities for the first two years of life and then falls to a lower level and remains steady until adolescence (Tanner, 1978).

Secretions from the testes and ovaries, as well as adrenal androgen, remain at extremely low levels until about age 7 or 8, when adrenal androgen begins to be secreted—the first signal of the changes of puberty (Shonkoff, 1984). Following this first step there is a complex sequence of hormonal changes, laid out in a simplified schematic in Figure 11.1.

The timing of these changes varies a lot from one child to the next, but the sequence remains the same. At a signal from the hypothalamus, the pituitary gland begins secreting increased levels of **gonadotrophic hormones** (2 in males, 3 in females). These in turn stimulate the development of the glands in the testes and ovaries, which then begin to secrete more hormones, testosterone in boys and a form of **estrogen** called *estradiol*, in girls. Over the course of puberty, the levels of testosterone increase 18-fold in boys, while levels of estradiol increase 8-fold in girls (Nottelmann et al., 1987).

At the same time, the pituitary also secretes three other hormones that interact with the specific sex hormones and affect growth, although as you can see in Figure 11.1, the interaction is a little different for boys and girls. In particular, the growth spurt and pubic hair development are more influenced by adrenal androgen in girls than in boys. Adrenal androgen is chemically very similar to testosterone, so it takes a "male" hormone to produce the growth spurt in girls.

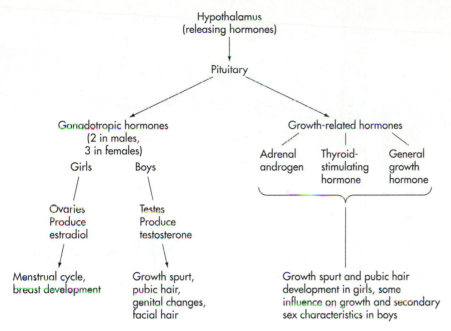

FIGURE 11.1

The action of the various hormones at puberty is exceedingly complex. This figure oversimplifies the process but gives you some sense of the sequence and the differences between the patterns for boys and girls.

Having said that, I need to add a caution: it is somewhat misleading to talk about "male" and "female" hormones. Both males and females have at least some of each. The difference is essentially in the relative proportion of the two. Within any one gender, these proportions differ as well, so some males have relatively more testosterone or less estrogen, while in others the two may be more balanced. Similarly, some girls may have a pattern of hormones that includes relatively more androgen, while others may have relatively little.

All these hormonal changes are reflected in two sets of body changes: the well-known changes in sex organs and a much broader set of changes, in muscles, fat, bones, and body organs.

Height, Shape, Muscles, and Fat

Height. One of the most dramatic changes is in height. You'll remember from earlier chapters that in infancy, the baby gains in height very rapidly, adding 10 to 12 inches in length in the first year. The toddler and school child grows much more slowly. The third phase begins with the dramatic adolescent growth spurt, triggered by the big increases in growth hormones. During this phase, the child may add 3 to 6 inches a year for several years. After the growth spurt, in the fourth phase, the teenager again adds height and weight slowly until reaching final adult size. You can see the shape of the growth curve in Figure 11.2.

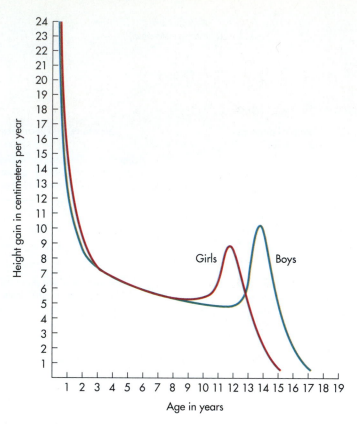

FIGURE 11.2

These curves show the **gain** in height for each year from birth through adolescence. You can see the several clear phases: very rapid growth in infancy, slower growth in the preschool and elementary school years, a growth spurt at adolescence, and the cessation of growth at adulthood. (Sources: Tanner, 1978, p. 14; Malina, 1990.)

Shape.   At the same time, because the different parts of the child's body do not grow to full adult size at the same pace, the shape and proportions of the adolescent's body go through a series of changes. A teenager's hands and feet grow to full adult size earliest, followed by the arms and legs, with the trunk usually the slowest part to grow. So kids first outgrow their shoes, then their pants and long-sleeved shirts. But a bathing suit may continue to fit fine for quite some time, even when the rest of the body has changed. Because of this asymmetry in the body parts, we often think of an adolescent as "awkward" or uncoordinated. Interestingly, research does not bear that out. Robert Malina, who has done extensive research on physical development, has found no point in the adolescent growth process at which teenagers become consistently less coordinated or less skillful at physical tasks (Malina, 1990).

Children's heads and faces also change in childhood and adolescence. During the elementary school years, the size and shape of a child's jaw change when the permanent teeth come in. In adolescence both jaws grow forward and the forehead becomes more prominent. This set of changes often gives teenagers' faces (especially boys') an angular, bony appearance, quite unlike their earlier look—as you can see in the pictures in Figure 11.3.

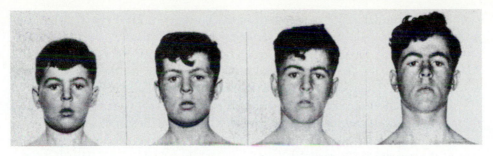

FIGURE 11.3
These photos of the same boy before, during, and after puberty show the striking changes in the jaws and forehead that dramatically alter appearance in many teenage boys. The same changes occur in girls' faces but are not as dramatic. (Source: Tanner, 1962, Plate 1, p. 17.)

Muscles.   Muscle fibers, like bone tissues, go through a growth spurt at adolescence, becoming thicker and denser. As a result, adolescents become quite a lot stronger in just a few years. Both boys and girls show this increase in muscle tissue and strength, but as you can see in Figure 11.4, the increase is much greater in boys. Among adult men, about 40 percent of total body mass is muscle, compared to only about 24 percent in adult women.

Differences in hormone patterns at adolescence appear to be major contributors to the sex differences in muscle growth. But there are also some hints that sex differences in exercise patterns or activity may also be involved. For example, boys have comparatively much greater arm strength, but the two sexes are more equal in leg strength (Tanner, Hughes, & Whitehouse, 1981). Such a pattern makes sense if we assume that all teenagers walk and use their legs a similar amount, but that boys use their arm muscles more in various sports activities than girls do. Still, there does seem to be a basic hormonal difference as well, because we know that very fit girls and women are still not as strong as very fit boys and men.

What kind of research study could you design that would test the hypothesis that the difference in muscle tissue between teenage boys and girls is primarily the result of differences in exercise or activity levels?

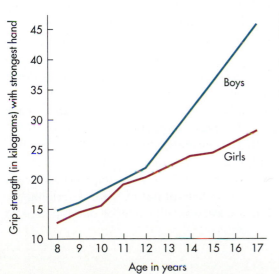

FIGURE 11.4
Both boys and girls get stronger over the years of adolescence, but boys gain much more. (Source: Adapted from Montpetit, Montoye, & Laeding, 1967, from Tables 1 and 2, p. 233.)

Fat.   Another major component of the body is fat, most of which is stored immediately under the skin. This *subcutaneous fat* is first laid down beginning at about 34 weeks prenatally and has an early peak at about 9 months after birth (the so-called "baby fat.") The thickness of this layer of fat then declines until about age 6 or 7, after which it rises until adolescence.

Once again there is a sex difference in these patterns. From birth, girls have slightly more fat tissue than boys do, and this difference becomes gradually more marked during childhood. At adolescence, the difference grows still further. The size of the change is illustrated nicely in the results of a large study of Canadian teenagers (Smoll & Schutz, 1990). Between seventh and twelfth grades, the percentage of body weight made up of fat rose from 21.8 to 24 percent among girls in this group, but dropped from 16.1 to 14.0 percent among boys. So during and after puberty, proportions of fat rise among girls and decline among boys, while the proportion of weight that is muscle rises in boys and declines in girls.

Of course, as with muscle tissue, this sex difference in fat may be partially a life-style or activity-level effect; girls and women who are extremely athletic, such as long-distance runners or ballet dancers, typically have body fat levels that approximate those of the average boy. But if we compare equally fit boys and girls, boys still have lower fat levels.

Other Body Changes.   Puberty also brings important changes in other body organs. In particular, the heart and lungs increase considerably in size and the heart rate drops. Both of these changes are more marked for boys than for girls—another of the factors that increases the capacity for sustained effort by boys relative to girls. Before about age 12, boys and girls have similar physical strength, speed, and endurance, although even at these earlier ages, when there is a difference it favors the boys because of their lower levels of body fat. After puberty, boys have a clear advantage in all three (Smoll & Schutz, 1990).

Development of Sexual Maturity

The physical result of the hormonal changes that take place during puberty is not only a spurt in height but, more importantly, a set of physical changes that bring about full sexual maturity. This includes changes in the reproductive systems themselves—*primary sex characteristics*—such as the testes and penis in the male and the ovaries, uterus, and vagina in the female, and all those changes in *secondary sex characteristics* that are the more visible signs of puberty, such as breast development, body and facial hair, and lowered voice pitch in boys.

Each of these physical developments occurs in a defined sequence. Each sequence is customarily divided into 5 stages, originally suggested by J. M. Tanner (1978). Stage 1 always describes the preadolescent stage, Stage 2 the first signs of pubertal change, Stages 3 and 4 the intermediate steps, and Stage 5 the final adult characteristic. Table 11.2 gives an example of these sequences for each sex. These stages have proven to be extremely helpful not only for describing the normal progress through puberty, but for assessing the rate of development of individual youngsters.

Suppose you were a member of a local school board, faced with a decision about whether to have teenage boys and girls play on the same competitive teams, such as volleyball, soccer, or baseball. Given what I have said about sex differences in physical characteristics at puberty, how would you decide? Why?

TABLE 11.2
Examples of Tanner's Stages of Pubertal Development

Breast Development	Stage	Male Genital Development
No change except for some elevation of the nipple	1	Testes, scrotum, and penis are all about the same size and shape as in early childhood
Breast bud stage: Elevation of the breast and the nipple as a small mound. Areolar diameter is enlarged over Stage 1	2	Scrotum and testes slightly enlarged. Skin of the scrotum is reddened and changed in texture but but little or no enlargement of the penis
Breast and areola both enlarged and elevated more than in Stage 2 but no separation of their contours	3	Penis slightly enlarged, at first mainly in length. Testes and scrotum are further enlarged
Areola and nipple form a secondary mound projecting above the contour of the breast	4	Penis further enlarged, with growth in breadth and development of glans. Testes and scrotum further enlarged and scrotum skin still darker
Mature stage. Only the nipple projects with the areola recessed to the general contour of the breast	5	Genitalia are adult in size and shape

Source: Petersen & Taylor, 1980, p. 127.

Sexual Development in Girls. Studies of preteens and teens in both Europe and North America (Malina, 1990) reveal that for girls, the various sequential changes are interlocked in a particular pattern, shown schematically in Figure 11.5. The first steps are typically the early changes in breasts and pubic hair, followed by the peak of the growth spurt. Only then does first menstruation occur, an event called **menarche** (pronounced men-are-kee). Menarche typically occurs two years after the beginning of other visible changes and is succeeded only by the final stages of breast and pubic hair development. Among girls in industrialized countries today, menarche occurs, on average, between age 12½ and 13½, with 95 percent of all girls experiencing this event between the ages of 11 and 15 (Malina, 1990).

Menarche does not signal full sexual maturity. Although it is possible to conceive shortly after menarche, irregularity is the norm for some time. In as many as three-quarters of the cycles in the first year, and half the cycles in the second and third years after menarche, no ovum is produced (Vihko & Apter, 1980). Full adult fertility thus develops over a period of years.

Sexual Development in Boys. In boys, as in girls, the peak of the growth spurt typically comes fairly late in the sequence, as you can see in Figure 11.6. Malina's data suggest that on average a boy completes stages 2, 3 and 4 of genital development, and stages 2 and 3 of pubic hair development before he reaches the growth peak (Malina, 1990), with facial hair and the lowering of the voice coming only quite near the end of the sequence. Precisely when in this

FIGURE 11.5

The figure shows the normal sequence and timing of pubertal changes for girls. The box on each black line represents the average attainment of that change, while the line indicates the range of normal times. Note the *wide* range of normality for all of these changes. Also note how relatively late in the sequence the growth spurt and menarche occur. (Sources: Chumlea, 1982; Garn, 1980; Malina, 1990; Tanner, 1978.)

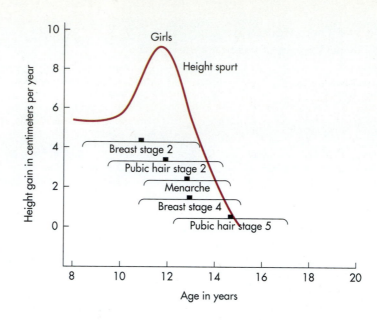

FIGURE 11.6

The sequence of pubertal changes for boys begins about two years later than does the girls' sequence, but as with girls, the height spurt occurs relatively late in the sequence. (Sources: Chumlea, 1982; Malina, 1990; Tanner, 1978.)

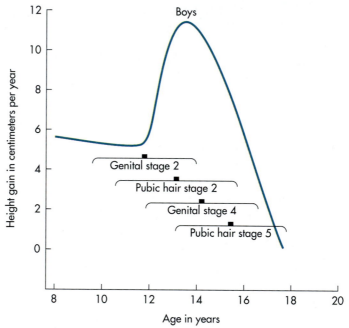

sequence the boy begins to produce viable sperm is very difficult to determine, although current evidence places this event some time between ages 12 and 14, usually *before* the boy has reached the peak of the growth spurt (Brooks-Gunn & Reiter, 1990).

Two things are particularly interesting about these sequences. First, if you compare Figures 11.5 and 11.6, you will see that although boys begin the early stages of pubertal change only a bit later than girls, girls are about two years ahead of boys in the growth spurt. Most of you remember that period in late elementary school or junior high when all the girls were suddenly taller than the boys. (Do I remember that time! I *towered* over everyone.)

A second intriguing thing is that while the order of development seems to be highly consistent *within* each sequence (such as breast development, or pubic hair development), there is quite a lot of variability *across* sequences. I've given you the normative or average pattern, but individual teenagers often do not follow that normative pattern. For instance, a boy may be in stage 2 of genital development but already in stage 5 of pubic hair development; a girl might move through several stages of pubic hair development before the first clear breast changes or experience menarche much earlier in the sequence than normal. So far physiologists have not figured out why this variation exists or what it might mean, but it is an important point to keep in mind if you are trying to make a prediction about an individual teenager.

Early versus Late Pubertal Development

Yet another form of variation in the pattern of puberty—one that is arguably far more important psychologically—is the *timing* of the entire process. Among adolescents, children of the same age may range from Stage 1 to Stage 5 in the steps of sexual maturation. These variations are not trivial, especially for a child who is unusually early or unusually late in development. What happens to a girl who begins to menstruate at 10 or a boy who does not go through a growth spurt until age 16? Do they turn out differently?

Early developing girls, like the one on the right, report much less positive adolescent experiences and more depression than on-time or later-developing girls.

A recent burst of research on this question has led to an interesting and complex hypothesis that once again points to the importance of internal models. The general idea is that each young child or teenager has an internal model about the "normal" or "right" timing for puberty (Faust, 1983; Lerner, 1985; 1987; Petersen, 1987). Each girl has an internal model about the "right age" to develop breasts or begin menstruation; each boy has an internal model or image about when it is right to begin to grow a beard or for his voice to get lower. According to this hypothesis, it is the discrepancy between an adolescent's expectation and what actually happens that determines the psychological effect, just as it is the discrepancy between goals and achievements that determines self-esteem. Those whose development occurs outside the desired or expected range are likely to think less well of themselves, to be less happy with their bodies and with the process of puberty, perhaps have fewer friends, or experience other signs of distress.

In American culture today, most young people seem to share the expectation that pubertal changes will happen sometime between age 12 and 14; anything earlier is seen as "too soon," anything later is thought of as late. If you compare these expectations to the actual average timing of pubertal changes, you'll see that such a norm includes girls who are average in development and boys who are *early*. So we should expect that these two groups—normal developing girls and early developing boys—should have the best psychological functioning. Early maturing boys may have an added advantage because they are more likely to be of the *mesomorphic* body type, with wide shoulders and a large amount of muscle. This body type is consistently preferred at all ages, and because boys with this body type tend to be good at sports, the early developing boy should be particularly advantaged.

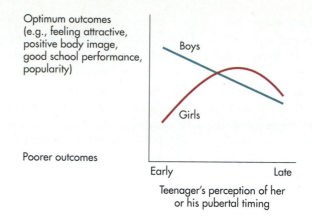

FIGURE 11.7

According to this model of the effects of early and late puberty, the best position for girls is to be "on time," while for boys the best position is to be "early." For both sexes, however, it is the *perception* of earliness or lateness, not the actual timing, that is thought to be critical. (Source: Adapted from Tobin-Richards et al., 1983, p. 137.)

Figure 11.7 shows the specific predictions graphically. Because of the twin advantages of having puberty fall within the "normative" time and having a more mesomorphic body type, early boys should be best-off, followed by average boys and girls. The least well-off should be late developing boys and early developing girls, both of whom are "off time."

Research generally confirms these predictions. Girls who are early developers (before 11 or 12 for major body changes) show consistently more negative body images, such as thinking themselves too fat (Petersen, 1987; Simmons, Blyth, & McKinney, 1983; Tobin-Richards, Boxer, & Petersen, 1983). Such girls are also more likely to get into trouble in school and at home (Magnusson, Stattin, & Allen, 1986) and are more likely to be depressed (Rierdan & Koff, 1991; Rierdan & Koff, 1993). There are also hints that very late development in girls is also somewhat negative, but the effect of lateness is not so striking for girls as it is for boys.

Among boys, as Figure 11.7 predicts, the relationship is essentially linear. The earlier the boy's development, the more positive his body image, the better he does in school, the less trouble he gets into, and the more friends he has (Duke et al., 1982).

In nearly all of these studies, earliness or lateness has been defined in terms of the actual physical changes. The results are even clearer when researchers have instead asked teenagers about their internal model of earliness or lateness. For example, Rierdan, Koff, and Stubbs (1989) have found that the negativeness of a girl's menarcheal experience was predicted by her *subjective* sense of earliness; those who perceived themselves as early reported a more negative experience. But such a negative experience was *un*related to the actual age of her menarche.

This link between the internal model and the outcome is especially vivid in a study of ballet dancers by Jeanne Brooks-Gunn (Brooks-Gunn, 1987; Brooks-Gunn & Warren, 1985). She studied 14- to 18-year-old girls, some of whom were serious ballet dancers studying at a national ballet company school.

> Do you remember your own puberty as very early, early, on time, or late? Do you think that perception had any effect on your overall experience of adolescence?

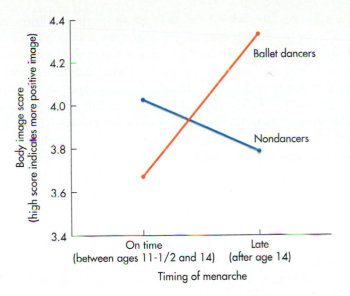

FIGURE 11.8
Serious ballet dancers clearly prefer to have a very late puberty. In this study, those dancers whose menarche was "on time" by ordinary standards actually had poorer body images than did those who were objectively quite late, while the reverse was true for nondancers. Thus it is perception of timing, not actual timing that is critical. (Source: Brooks-Gunn & Warren, 1985, from Table 1, p. 291.)

In this group, a very lean, almost prepubescent body is highly desirable. Given this, we would expect that among dancers, those who were very late in pubertal development would actually have a better image of themselves than those who were on time. And that is exactly what Brooks-Gunn found, as you can see in Figure 11.8. Among nondancers the same age, normal-time menarche was associated with a better body image than late menarche, but exactly the reverse was true for the dancers.

Thus it seems to be the discrepancy or mismatch between the desired or expected pattern and a youngster's actual pattern that is critical, not the absolute age of pubertal development. Because the majority of young people share similar expectations, we can see common effects of early or late development. But to predict the effect of early or late development in any individual teenager, we would need to know more about her or his internal model or the culturally defined models that may be operating.

Adolescent Sexuality

The many physical changes of puberty not only mean that the young person is stronger and faster and better coordinated than before, they also obviously make mature sexual behavior possible. But unlike early motor development, which proceeds in pretty much the same way for all children, sexual behavior involves clear choices for the teenager. Should I or shouldn't I? What do we know about the choices teenagers make about their sexual activity?

As is usually the case, what I can tell you about this is almost entirely specific to the U.S. or to other industrialized countries. It is good to keep in mind that the whole question of adolescent sexuality is a central issue for those of us in such cultures in large part because we have created such a long delay between physical sexual maturity and social maturity. Young people are physically mature at 13 or 14, but are not financially independent or fully trained until age 20 or later. In cultures in which 12- or 14-year-olds are considered adults, ready to take on adult tasks and responsibilities, to marry and to bear children, adolescent sexuality is handled very differently. In the U.S., where adolescent pregnancy has become extremely common, it is perceived as a significant problem.

Adolescent sexual activity has increased fairly dramatically in the U.S. since the late 1950s (Miller, Christopherson, & King, 1993). In the 1980s—the latest period for which we have good data—about half of boys and about a quarter of the girls aged 15 to 17 were sexually active. By age 19, over 80 percent of males and roughly 60 percent of girls say they have had at least one experience of intercourse (Hofferth, Kahn, & Baldwin, 1987; Sonenstein, Pleck, & Ku, 1989).

At every age, there are consistent ethnic differences: Hispanic-American youth are least likely to be sexually active and African-American youth are most likely, with Anglos somewhere in between (Fennelly, 1993). Black adolescents in the U.S. become sexually active about two years earlier than their Anglo or Hispanic peers (Hayes, 1987). For example, among young men included in the 1988 National Survey of Adolescent Males, a nationally representative sample of nearly 2000 young men between the ages of 15 and 19, 80.6 percent of Blacks were sexually active, compared to 56.8 percent of Whites and 59.7 percent of Hispanics (Sonenstein et al., 1989). Similar discrepancies are found among girls (Hofferth, 1987a).

The form and pattern of sexual activity also shows ethnic differences in U.S. groups. Among both Anglos and Hispanics, sexual activity appears to move through a fairly typical sequence over time and within any one dating relationship, from hand-holding to kissing to stroking of breasts or genitals to intercourse. So intercourse is considerably more likely in couples who are "going steady" and quite unlikely on a first date. Among Blacks, at least in the U.S., this sequence does not appear to hold: they are more likely to move directly to intercourse (Miller et al., 1993).

In boys, the likelihood of sexual activity is correlated with the amount of testosterone in the blood. Among girls hormones appear to play a smaller role. Girls' *interest* in sexuality is somewhat related to hormones, but the likelihood of intercourse is not (Dyk, 1993). For girls, social influences are far more important ingredients in their decisions about sexuality.

Despite these heightened levels of sexual activity, it is remarkable how little teenagers know about physiology and reproduction. At best, only about half of White and a quarter of Black teenagers can describe the time of greatest fertility in the menstrual cycle (Freeman & Rickels, 1993; Morrison, 1985). Many are convinced they cannot get pregnant because they are "too young." Perhaps in part because of such ignorance, contraceptive use in the U.S. is still comparatively low—especially in comparison to most European countries, where teenage sexual behavior is as common but contraceptive information is far more widespread. Both Sweden and the Netherlands, for example, have very low teenage birth rates. In both, contraceptive information is widely available and contraceptive use is culturally acceptable (Jones et al., 1986). In the U.S., despite increases in contraceptive use in recent years, less than half of teenage girls use any type of contraceptives the first time they have intercourse, and fewer still use effective methods, such as condoms or the pill, on a regular basis (Jorgensen, 1993). Contraceptive use is even less likely among Hispanics than among Anglos (Fennelly, 1993).

How many different reasons can you think of why teenagers would *not* use contraceptives? Which of those explanations might account for the lower use of contraception among Hispanic-American teens?

Teenage Pregnancy

Given these facts, we shouldn't be surprised that the rate of teenage pregnancy is high in the U.S.—far higher than in most other industrialized countries (Jones et al., 1986). In the Netherlands, for example, the pregnancy rate for girls between the ages of 15 and 19 is 14 per 1,000 girls per year. In the United States it is 96 pregnancies per 1,000 girls per year. Sandra Hofferth estimates (1987a) that fully 44 percent of all teenage girls in the U.S. will be pregnant at least once before the age of 20. Most of these pregnancies occur outside of marriage, and most are unintended (Miller & Jorgensen, 1993). About half of these pregnancies are carried to term.

Let me try to put these fairly astonishing numbers into some kind of context. Birth rates have actually dropped among the entire U.S. population in the past decades, *including among teenagers.* Indeed, the proportion of all births in the United States that were to teenagers has declined steadily in the past decades. In 1970, for example, half of all births were to women/girls age 19 and younger, compared to only 31 percent in 1990 (U.S. Bureau of the Census, 1993). What has increased steadily since the 1960s is the rate of births to *nonmarried* teens. In 1988, 78 percent of all girls under 18 who gave birth were unmarried; among Black girls, the rate was 95 percent (Furstenberg, 1991). Thus it is not that more and more teenagers are bearing children, but that more and more pregnant teenage girls are choosing to rear their children without marrying.

Whether one sees this as a worrisome trend or not depends not only on one's religious or moral beliefs, but also in part on evidence about the long-term consequences of adolescent childbearing for the adult lives of women. The bulk of that evidence points to negative consequences, although it has been difficult to sort out just what effects are due to early childbearing itself and which might be due to self-selection or the impact of poverty. Most studies indicate that teenage childbearing—whether married or unmarried—is associated with more children who are more closely spaced, fewer years of total education throughout adult life, lower levels of occupational success, lower income in adulthood, and higher likelihood of divorce in adult life. These relationships are found among African-American, Hispanic, and Anglo teens, so these negative outcomes are not just ethnic differences in disguise (Astone, 1993; Freeman & Rickels, 1993; Hofferth, 1987b; Moore et al., 1993).

However, there are some mitigating facts. First of all, more than half of girls who become pregnant before age 18 nonetheless manage to complete high school by the time they are in their early twenties—a fact that runs counter to

Teenage sexual activity is not more common in the U.S. than in most Western industrialized countries, but teen pregnancy is. Girls like this one who give birth during their teens are more likely to have problems in adulthood, including lower income, less education, and higher risk of divorce, although many teenage Moms manage to surmount these problems.

Whether a girl becomes pregnant during her teenage years depends on a host of factors, including family background, educational aspirations, timing of sexual activity, and subcultural attitudes. Here are a few of the findings (Hayes, 1987):

- The younger a girl is when she becomes sexually active, the more likely she is to have at least one teen pregnancy.
- Girls who come from poor families, single-parent families, or those whose parents are relatively uneducated, are more likely to become pregnant.
- Girls whose mothers became sexually active early and who bore their first child early, are more likely to become pregnant as teens.
- Black and Hispanic teenagers are more likely than are Anglos to become pregnant, in part because Blacks are more likely to be sexually active. Hispanics

The Real World
Which Teenage Girls
Get Pregnant?

are less likely to be sexually active, but also less likely to use contraception than are Anglos.

- The better a girl does in school and the stronger her educational aspirations, the more likely she is to use birth control consistently and the less likely she is to get pregnant.
- The more stable and committed the relationship between a teenage girl and her sexual partner, the *less* likely she is to become pregnant.
- Girls who have good communication about contraception with their mothers and whose mothers support the use of contraception are less likely to become pregnant.

The riskiest time for pregnancy is in the first year or so after a girl has become sexually active. It is during these early months that girls are least likely to seek out contraceptive information or to use contraception consistently.

Is it possible that these apparent consequences of teen childbearing are really caused by self-selection? That is, teenage mothers may simply be a different group to start with—less interested in school, from different kinds of homes. How could you figure out if that were the explanation?

prevailing stereotypes (Upchurch, 1993). And many of those who struggle economically in their early adult years manage to recover in their thirties and forties, especially if they are able to complete at least high school (Upchurch, 1993; Werner & Smith, 1992). Despite these findings, though, teenage mothers as a group are still disadvantaged. For Black inner-city girls in particular, the chances of moving out of poverty in adulthood seem to be far better for those who delay childbearing into their twenties (Freeman & Rickels, 1993). To avoid some of these negative consequences, we may need to take a page or two from the pregnancy-prevention expertise developed in many other industrialized countries, especially about appropriate timing and content of sex and/or contraceptive education in the schools.

Health in Adolescence

Adolescents have fewer acute illnesses than do infants, toddlers, or school-age children, but teenagers engage in many forms of risky behavior, often described as sensation-seeking, which lead to markedly increased rates of accidents, injuries, and illnesses in this age range. Jeffrey Arnett (1992) makes the sweeping assertion that "Adolescence bears a heightened potential for recklessness compared to other developmental periods in every culture and in every time" (p. 339). What form this recklessness will take, or even whether it is allowed expression at all, depends on the particular culture and historical time. In the United States, at this time, we see adolescents engaging in unprotected sex, driving faster, tailgating more often, and using seat belts less than older adults (Arnett, 1992). Rates of driving while intoxicated are also high among adolescents, although arrests for driving while intoxicated are actually at their peak among those in their middle twenties (U.S. Bureau of the Census, 1993).

Such high-risk behaviors, not surprisingly, lead to a variety of problems, especially for teenage males, in whom the tendency toward sensation seeking or risk-taking is especially marked. The three leading causes of death for males between the ages of 15 and 24 are auto accidents, homicide, and suicide (U.S. Bureau of the Census, 1993). And 80 out of every 1,000 teenage males in the U.S. were on the receiving end of some kind of violent crime, a rate nearly double that for teenage girls (Hammond & Yung, 1993). These figures are still higher among minority teens, including Hispanic, African-American, and Native-American.

Furthermore, about 2.5 million adolescents contract a sexually transmitted disease each year, a rate that has been rising in the past decade, especially for syphilis (1993). Unprotected sex among adolescents has also led to a marked rise in the risk of AIDS—a disease that is the fastest growing cause of death among adolescents and young adults. Those teens at greatest risk for infection with HIV are runaways, those with homosexual experiences, those engaged in prostitution, and intravenous drug users. But the disease has begun to spread beyond these risk groups within the adolescent population in the United States.

Many psychologists, sociologists, and epidemiologists have become extremely concerned about the level of problem behavior among teenagers. In a recent editorial in a major professional journal on adolescents, Richard Lerner and his colleagues (Lerner, Entwisle, & Hauser, 1994) conclude that

> There is nothing short of a 'generational time bomb' involving today's American adolescents: Approximately half of American adolescents are at moderate or greater risk for engaging in unsafe sexual behaviors, teenage pregnancy, and teenage child bearing; in drug and alcohol use and abuse; in school underachievement, failure, and dropout; and in delinquency and crimes, often of a violent nature. . . In fact, 50% of today's 10- to 17-year-olds engage in two or more of these risk behaviors, and 10% of in this age-range engage in all of these risks. (p. 1)

Not a pretty picture.

In other cultures, the level of problems is not as high, but risk-taking behaviors are still at a peak in adolescence, albeit in different forms. In Denmark, for example, where a driver's license cannot be obtained until age 18, teenagers drive mopeds or ride bicycles while intoxicated instead of driving cars (Arnett & Balle-Jensen, 1993). One result is that the rate of deaths in auto accidents among teenagers is roughly half as high in Denmark as in the United States, where teens can drive at 16.

Alcohol and Drug Use in Adolescence

National data suggest that many types of teenage drug use have been declining in the United States over the past several decades. For example, 23 percent of teenagers in 1974 reported that they had used marijuana, compared to only 13 percent in 1991. In the same years, the percentage of teenagers who had ever

During adolescence we see a rise in a whole range of high-risk behaviors, particularly those that involve sensation-seeking, such as smoking, drinking, and driving fast.

used cocaine also declined slightly, from 3.6 to 2.4 percent (U.S. Bureau of the Census, 1993).

The figures for alcohol are not so comforting. In 1985, 92 percent of high school seniors said they had tried alcohol at least once, two-thirds had done so in the past month, and 15 percent were heavy users. These teenagers said they had five or more drinks in a row, three or more times in the most recent two-week period (Dryfoos, 1990). There are also distressing indications that alcohol use is on the increase among preteens. One large recent study of first, fourth, and seventh grade boys in Pittsburgh showed that 7.8 percent of *first graders* had tried beer at least once. Among fourth graders the comparable figure was 12 percent, rising to 56.5 percent among seventh graders (Van Kammen, Loeber, & Stouthamer-Loeber, 1991)—results similar to what has been found in Canada (Porter-Serviss, Opheim, & Hindmarsh, 1994). And a study of Oklahoma students revealed that 4.5 percent of middle school and 19.2 percent of high school students used alcohol weekly.

In the Oklahoma study, the most frequent reason teenagers gave for using drugs was because they were depressed (Novacek, Raskin, & Hogan, 1991), followed by a desire to escape from their problems, to relax, and to have a good time. Those who used drugs regularly did *not* seem to do so to enhance their sense of group belonging; rather they did so to help them cope with the stresses of their lives or to feel good.

Risky Behavior in Context.   This finding raises a more general point, one that Richard Jessor (1992) makes particularly clearly. He points out that:

> . . . adolescent risk behaviors are functional, purposive, instrumental, and goal-directed and that the goals involved are often those that are central in normal adolescent development. (p. 378)

The goals involved are peer acceptance or respect, establishing autonomy from parents and from other authority figures, coping with anxiety or fear of failure,

One third of all teenagers try smoking at least once; nearly a third of those—10 percent of all high school seniors in 1993—become regular smokers, smoking at least a half a pack of cigarettes a day. The likelihood of smoking is roughly the same among males and females, but White students are three times as likely as are Blacks to adopt this habit.

The Real World
How To Get Your
Teenager to Stop
Smoking or Not to Start

How could such numbers be turned around? If you had a teenager, how could you prevent her or him from starting to smoke? One obvious thought is to make clear to the adolescent just what the long term risks of smoking are. Many teens have the mistaken belief that there is no great risk to smoking a pack or two of cigarettes a day. Besides, teenagers (like many adults) feel invulnerable and immortal. They engage in many kinds of risky behaviors for the thrill of it, and because they genuinely feel that nothing can happen to them. So it simply doesn't help very much to tell them about possible future problems. Several other strategies are much more successful.

Emphasize the Bad Breath. Tell them about all the negative *social* consequences of smoking. Their breath will smell bad, their teeth will turn yellow, their hair and clothes will smell like smoke all the time, and their ability to do well in athletics may be impaired. Tell them that teenagers themselves say that they find smokers less attractive. And tell teenage girls that smoking will not help them lose weight—a major reason for smoking for nearly all teenage girls—at least not enough to counterbalance the social costs.

Focus on the Manipulation. Remind your child that the cigarette companies are trying to manipulate them through their advertising. You may want to get them to look at specific ads and talk about the particular forms of manipulation involved. Because teenagers hate to be manipulated (by you or anyone else), this may be a successful argument.

Lobby The Schools. If the school your child attends has a designated smoking area, try to persuade them to abolish it and simply forbid smoking in any part of the school. In schools that allow smoking 25 percent more of the students become smokers than is true in schools that forbid it on the school grounds.

Pay Attention to Your Child's Friends. Teenagers whose friends smoke are more likely to take up the habit. You need to start paying attention to this *very* early—certainly by junior high school, when you may still have enough influence over the child's choice of friends to help steer the child toward a different crowd of kids.

Do not Call Smoking an "Adult Choice". Many tobacco company programs ostensibly aimed at reducing teenage smoking tell teenagers that they are too young to smoke. But because teenagers want to do anything defined as "adult," this message may encourage smoking rather than the reverse. Instead, tell teenagers that they are old enough to know better; they are old enough to decide *not* to smoke.

and affirming maturity. Jessor argues that these are absolutely normal, central goals of adolescence. To the extent that risky behavior, such as smoking, drinking, or early sexual activity, helps individual teenagers to meet those goals, such behaviors will be hard to change, *unless* alternative ways of meeting these same goals are available and encouraged. It is not an accident that those teens who are most likely to engage in all these risky behaviors are those who have shown behavior problems at earlier ages, have had poor school records, early rejection by peers, neglect at home, or a combination of these early problems (Robins & McEvoy, 1990). By default, such children or teens are drawn to peers who share their patterns and their internal models of the world, and for these adolescents, risky behaviors of various kinds provide an avenue for meeting some of the goals Jessor mentions.

Suicide

Another increasing risk among teenagers is suicide. Suicide is very uncommon in children before adolescence. Even among children between 10 and 14, less than one child in 100,000 in the United States commits suicide each year. But among those between 15 and 19, the rate is considerably higher and rising. Rates have tripled since 1960, and now represent about 12 percent of teen deaths.

The likelihood of suicide is about four times as high among adolescent boys as among girls, and nearly twice as high among Whites as among non-Whites *except* for Native-American, who attempt and commit suicide at higher rates than any other group (Blum et al., 1992). The rate among Native-Americans is 26.3 per 100,000 per year, compared to about 20 per 100,000 among White teen males.

In contrast, suicide *attempts* are estimated to be three times more common in girls than in boys (Garland & Zigler, 1993). Girls, more often than boys, use less "successful" methods, such as self-poisoning. In one study in England, for example, the rate of hospital admissions for self-poisoning among girls rose from 4 per 10,000 among 12-year-olds to over 50 per 10,000 at age 16. Among boys, the rate at age 16 was one-fifth that level (Hawton & Goldacre, 1982).

It is obviously very difficult to uncover the contributing factors in successful or completed suicides, because the crucial individual is no longer available to be interviewed. Researchers and clinicians are forced to rely on second hand reports from parents or others about the mental state of the suicide before the act—reports that are bound to be at least partially invalid, because in many cases parents or friends had no suspicion that a suicide attempt was imminent. Nonetheless, it does seem clear that some kind of significant emotional disturbance is virtually a universal ingredient, including but not restricted to depression. Behavior problems such as aggression are also common in the histories of completed suicides, as is a family history of psychiatric disorder or suicide (Garland & Zigler, 1993). Suicide is also considerably more common among those teenagers who are heavy alcohol or drug users and high in other forms of risk-taking behavior (Windle, Miller-Tutzauer, & Domenico, 1992).

But these factors alone are not enough to explain suicidal behavior. After all, many teenagers (and adults) display one or more of these risk factors, and very few actually commit suicide. David Shaffer and his colleagues, in their analysis of the problem of suicide prevention (Shaffer et al., 1988), suggest at least three other elements that seem to be involved: (1) some triggering stressful event. Studies of suicides suggest that among adolescents, this triggering event is often a disciplinary crisis with the parents, some rejection or humiliation, such as breaking up with a girlfriend or boyfriend, or failure in some valued activity—which could trigger a major loss of self-esteem. (2) Some altered mental state, which might be an attitude of hopelessness, reduced inhibitions from alcohol consumption, or rage (Swedo et al., 1991). Among girls, in particular, the sense of hopelessness seems to be common: a feeling that the world is against them *and they can't do anything about it*. (3) There must be an opportunity—a loaded gun available in the house, a bottle of sleeping pills in the parents' medicine cabinet, or the like.

Attempts to prevent teen suicide have not been notably successful. Despite the fact that most suicides and suicide attempters have displayed significantly deviant behavior for some period of time before the event, most do not find their way to mental health clinics or other professionals, and increasing the availability of such clinics has not proven effective in reducing suicide rates.

Other prevention efforts have focused on education, such as providing information to all high school students about risk factors in the hope that students might recognize a problem in a friend. Special training in coping abilities has also been offered, so that teenagers might be able to find some nonlethal solution to their problems. Unfortunately, most such programs appear to be ineffective in changing student attitudes or knowledge (Shaffer et al., 1991).

These discouraging results are not likely to change until we know a great deal more about the developmental pathways that lead to this particular form of psychopathology. What makes one teenager particularly vulnerable and another able to resist the temptation? What combination of stressful circumstances is most likely to trigger a suicide attempt, and how do those stressful circumstances interact with the teenager's personal resources? Only when we can answer questions of this kind will we be on the road to understanding and preventing teenage suicide.

Bulimia and Anorexia

Also on the rise are two eating disorders—bulimia and anorexia nervosa—that have become remarkably common among teenage girls in many Western countries. I want to talk about these disorders at some length, not only because they have become disturbingly frequent, but because what we are learning about the causes underlines both the impact of cultural values and the importance of the child's internal working models.

Bulimia (sometimes called *bulimia nervosa*) involves an intense concern about weight, combined with binge eating followed by purging, either through self-induced vomiting, excessive use of laxatives, or excessive exercise (Attie, Brooks-Gunn, & Petersen, 1990). Alternating periods of restrained and binge eating are common among individuals in all weight groups. Only when binge eating occurs as often as twice a week and is combined with repeated episodes of some kind of purging is the syndrome properly called bulimia. Bulimics are ordinarily not exceptionally thin, but they are obsessed with their weight and feel intense shame about their abnormal behavior. Often, they experience significant depression.

The incidence of bulimia appears to have been increasing in recent decades, particularly among White teenage and young adult women, but just how common it is has been hard to establish. Studies in the U.S. and in other industrialized countries indicate that when teenagers report on their eating or dieting behavior via questionnaires, about 10 percent report some kind of binge eating combined with purging. When researchers use stricter criteria, especially when individual interviews rather than questionnaires are involved, the rate appears to be more like 1 to 2 percent (Fairburn & Beglin, 1990). Thus while a relatively small number of girls and young women have persistent and severe forms of this

FIGURE 11.9
When this anorexic 15-year-old looks at herself in the mirror, chances are she sees herself as "too fat," despite her obvious emaciation.

disorder, many more describe milder eating disorders. The rate among teenage and college-age boys appears to be considerably lower (Attie et al., 1990; Howat & Saxton, 1988; Johnson et al., 1984; Pyle et al., 1983).

Anorexia nervosa is less common but potentially more deadly. It is characterized by extreme dieting, intense fear of gaining weight, and obsessive exercise. In girls or women, who are by far the most common sufferers, the weight loss eventually produces a cessation of menstruation. Hormone balance is so disturbed that anorexics typically develop thick, soft hair over their bodies. And their body image is so distorted that they can look in the mirror at a skeletally thin body and remain convinced that they are "too fat"—a point that is vividly clear in the photo in Figure 11.9. Ten to 15 percent of anorexics literally starve themselves to death.

The incidence of anorexia has been hard to establish; the best current estimate is that it affects between 0.5 and 1.0 percent of girls or young women in the U.S. (Millstein & Litt, 1990; Rolls, Fedoroff, & Guthrie, 1991), but is considerably more common among subgroups who are under pressure to maintain extreme thinness, such as ballet dancers and high-performance athletes in sports in which thinness is highly valued, such as gymnastics (Stoutjesdyk & Jevne, 1993).

Causes of Eating Disorders. The causes of both disorders are unknown. Some theorists have proposed biological causes, such as some kind of brain dysfunction in the case of bulimics, who often show abnormal brainwaves. Others argue for a psychoanalytic explanation, such as a fear of growing up in the case of anorexic patients. My own view is that the most promising explanation lies in the discrepancy between the young person's internal image of what kind or shape of body she desires, and her (or his) perception of her own body. Both syndromes seem to be increasing in frequency because of the currently intense emphasis in many Western countries on a very slender, almost prepubescent body shape as the ideal. From very early in life, girls, much more than boys, are taught both explicitly and implicitly that it matters if they are pretty or attractive, and that thinness is one of the critical variables in attractiveness. Current research, for example, shows that roughly three-quarters of teenage girls have dieted or are dieting. If you look only at chronic dieters (those who have dieted at least 10 times in the past year), the figures are lower, but still striking, as you can see in Figure 11.10. These numbers come from a questionnaire study of all

FIGURE 11.10
Percentage of junior high and high school students in Minnesota in 1987–88 who reported having dieted at least 10 times in the previous year. (Source: Storey et al., 1991, from Table 3, p. 995.)

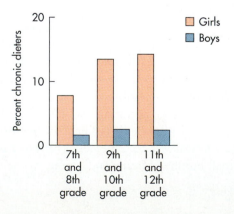

RESEARCH REPORT

An Australian Study Illustrating Sex Differences in Body Image among Adolescents

Susan Paxton and her colleagues (Paxton et al., 1991) have recently reported on a study of Australian high school students that illustrates that the preoccupation with thinness among teenage girls is not restricted to the United States, and shows what that preoccupation can do to girls' body images.

A total of 562 teenagers, in grades 7 through 11, reported on their current weight and height and their judgment of that weight as underweight, a good weight, or overweight. They also responded to questions about the effect being thinner might have on their lives and described their weight control behaviors, including dieting and exercise.

Paxton reports a number of particularly interesting results. First of all, among teenagers who were actually normal weight for their height, 30.1 percent of the girls but only 6.8 percent of the boys described themselves as overweight. Thus the girls *perceive* themselves as too fat when they are actually normal. Furthermore, the majority of girls thought that being thinner would make them happier; a few even thought that being thinner would make them more intelligent. Boys, in contrast, thought that being thinner would actually have some negative effects.

Not surprisingly, these differences in the perception of thinness were reflected in dieting behavior in this sample. Twenty-three percent of the girls reported that they went on a crash diet at least occasionally, 4 percent said they did so once or twice a week. The comparable percentages for boys were 9 percent and 1 percent respectively. More girls than boys also reported using diet pills, laxatives, and vomiting, although the rates were low for both sexes. Once again, we see internal models at work.

junior high and high school students in Minnesota in 1987–1988—a total of more than 36,000 teenagers (Story et al., 1991). You can see that such dieting is far less common among boys than among girls. Such dieting was also more common among Hispanic and White girls than among Blacks.

Those girls who most fully accept and internalize this model of beauty are most prone to develop bulimia or anorexia. For example, Ruth Striegel-Moore and her colleagues (Striegel-Moore, Silberstein, & Rodin, 1986) have found that bulimic girls and women are more likely than are nonbulimics to agree with statements like "attractiveness increases the likelihood of professional success."

Both bulimia and anorexia seem to develop in adolescence, and not before that, precisely because one of the effects of puberty is to increase the amount of fat in the girl's body. This is particularly true of early developing girls, who characteristically acquire and retain higher fat levels than do later-maturing girls. Indeed, early developing girls are nearly twice as likely to have an eating disorder as are normal or late developing girls (Killen et al., 1992). Thus an early developing girl who deeply believes that thinness is essential for beauty, and that beauty is essential for happiness, especially if she sees her own body as failing to meet her internalized standard, seems at particularly high risk for developing bulimia or anorexia (Attie & Brooks-Gunn, 1989; Rolls et al., 1991; Striegel-Moore et al., 1986).

> How deeply entrenched are the societal patterns that contribute to these eating disorders, in your opinion? If you wanted to change our society in such a way that the incidence of bulimia and anorexia would go down, what changes would you make?

A Final Word

The facts and figures I have been talking about in this chapter are a nice illustration of the way in which physical development interacts with culture and internal models. The physical changes of puberty are one of the most obviously maturationally controlled aspects of development. Yet the way in which each youngster experiences the adolescent period, including puberty, is just as obviously shaped by cultural expectations and definitions and by each young person's own internal model of self. Similarly, the striving for autonomy and acceptance that may be part of the motivation for risky behaviors may be a normal part of the adolescent tradition in every culture, but the specific risky behaviors we see are obviously affected by culture, just as each adolescent's own internal models affect the likelihood that he or she will choose risky behaviors as a way to express independence. Thus we cannot understand development, in general or in particular, without looking simultaneously at all three of these elements.

SUMMARY

1. Adolescence is defined not only as a time of pubertal change, but as the transitional period between childhood and full adult role adoption.

2. Because of the importance of this transition, it is marked by rites and rituals in many cultures—although not in most modern Western countries.

3. The physical changes of adolescence are triggered by a complex set of hormonal changes, beginning at about age 8 or 9. Very large increases in gonadotrophic hormones, including estrogen and testosterone, are central to the process.

4. These hormonal changes result in a rapid growth spurt in height and an increase in muscle mass and in fat. Boys add more muscle, and girls more fat.

5. In girls, mature sexuality occurs through a set of changes beginning as early as age 8 or 9. Menarche occurs relatively late in the sequence.

6. Sexual maturity is later in boys, with the growth spurt occurring a year or more after the start of genital changes.

7. Variations in the rate of pubertal development have some psychological effects. In general, the larger the discrepancy between a teenager's concept of what is normal or desirable timing for puberty and his perception of his own timing, the more negative the effects. In United States culture today, girls who develop very early and boys who develop very late are most likely to report negative experiences.

8. At adolescence, pubertal changes make mature sexual behavior possible. Sexual activity among teens has increased in recent decades. Perhaps half of teenage boys and a quarter of teenage girls in the U.S. are sexually active, and 1 in 10 teenage girls becomes pregnant each year.

9. Long-term consequences for girls who bear children during adolescence are generally negative, although a minority of such girls are able to overcome their early disadvantages.

10. Adolescents have fewer acute illnesses than younger children, but more deaths from accidents, particularly automobile accidents. In general, they show higher rates of various kinds of risky behaviors.

11. Drug usage among teenagers has been declining in recent decades, but regular alcohol use may be on the rise. Those most likely to use or abuse drugs are

those who also show other forms of deviant or problem behavior, including poor school success.

12. Suicide rates also rise in adolescence, especially among White and Native-American males. Suicide attempts are more common in girls.

13. Two eating disorders, bulimia and anorexia, are also far more common among teenage girls. Both appear to be a response to the cultural emphasis on thinness and to a young person's judgment of the discrepancy between her ideal and her actual body.

14. While maturational changes are clearly at the heart of the adolescent transition, the teenager's experience of puberty and adolescence is strongly shaped by culture and internal models and expectations.

KEY TERMS

anorexia nervosa
bulimia
endocrine glands

estrogen
gonadotrophic
hormones

menarche
pituitary gland
puberty

SUGGESTED READINGS

Gullotta, T. P., Adams, G. R., & Montemayor, R. (Eds.) (1993). *Adolescent sexuality*. Newbury Park, CA: Sage. A first-rate volume of papers on all aspects of this important subject. Of particular interest are papers by Dyk—reviewing information on physical changes at adolescence—and Miller et al., on sexual behavior in adolescents.

Hayes, C. D. (1987). *Risking the future. Vol. 1. Adolescent sexuality, pregnancy, and childbearing*. Washington, D. C.: National Academy Press. This book summarizes the results of an extensive study for the Committee on Child Development Research and Public Policy of the National Research Council. The chapter on "trends in adolescent sexuality and fertility" is especially thorough and informative.

Malina, R. M. (1990). Physical growth and performance during the transitional years (9–16). In R. Montemayor, G. R. Adams, & T. P. Gullotta (Eds.), *From childhood to adolescence: A transitional period?* (p. 41–62). Newbury Park, CA: Sage. To some extent Malina has picked up where Tanner has left off, providing us with updated information on normal physical growth. This particular paper focuses on puberty, but it contains references to much of Malina's work on other ages as well.

Tanner, J. M. (1978). *Fetus into man. Physical growth from conception to maturity*. Cambridge, MA: Harvard University Press. A detailed but very thorough and remarkably understandable small book that covers all but the most current information about physical growth.

Chapter Twelve

Cognitive Development in Adolescence

A sk an 8-year-old what she wants to be when she grows up and she is likely to say, "a fireman" or "a nurse" or "a mommy." Ask a 15-year-old the same question and you are likely to get a quite different answer, such as: "Well, I'm thinking about several things. I know I want to go to college, but I don't know where, and I'm not sure what I want to study. Maybe science." The teenager's response is typically more future oriented, more thoughtful, more questioning, with options explored. Such a change might merely reflect the fact that the adolescent is much closer to significant life decisions and so is more aware of their complexity. But it could also reflect an underlying change in the kind of thinking that has become possible. Piaget proposes just such a major shift at adolescence, a move to what he calls *formal operations*.

Piaget's View of Formal Operational Thought

Piaget's observations led him to conclude that this new level of thinking emerged fairly rapidly in early adolescence, between roughly 12 and 16. It has a number of key elements.

From the Actual to the Possible. One of the first steps in the process is for the child to extend her concrete operational reasoning abilities to objects and situations that she has not seen or experienced first hand or that she cannot see or manipulate directly. Instead of thinking only about real things and actual occurrences, as the younger child can do, she must start to think about possible occurrences. The preschool child plays "dress up" by putting on real clothes. The teenager *thinks* about options and possibilities, imagining herself in different roles, going to college or not going to college, marrying or not marrying, having children or not. She can imagine future consequences of actions she might take now, so that some kind of long-term planning becomes possible.

Systematic Problem Solving. Another important feature of formal operations is the ability to search systematically and methodically for the answer to a problem. To study this, Piaget and his colleague Barbel Inhelder (Inhelder & Piaget, 1958) presented adolescents with complex tasks, mostly drawn from the physical sciences. In one of these tasks, subjects were given varying lengths of string and a set of objects of various weights which can be tied to the strings to make a swinging pendulum. They were shown how to start the pendulum by pushing the weight with differing amounts of force and by holding the weight at different heights. The subject's task was to figure out which one or combination of length of string, weight of object, force of push, or height of push determines the "period" of the pendulum, that is, the amount of time for one swing. (In case you have forgotten your high school physics, the answer is that only the length of the string affects the period of the pendulum.)

If you give this task to a concrete-operational child, she will usually try out many different combinations of length, weight, force, and height in an inefficient way. She might try a heavy weight on a long string and then a light weight on a

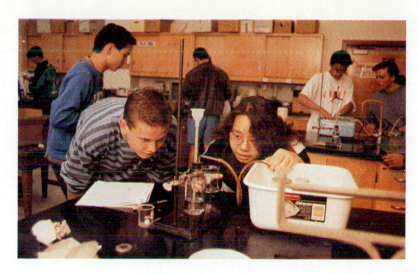

Most students do not encounter a demand for deductive logic until high school science classes, like this chemistry class.

short string. Because both string length and weight have changed, there is no way to draw a clear conclusion about either factor.

In contrast, an adolescent using a formal operations approach is likely to be more organized, attempting to vary just one of the four factors at a time. She may try a heavy object with a short string, then with a medium string, then with a long one. After that, she might try a light object with the three lengths of string. Of course not all adolescents (or all adults, for that matter) are quite this methodical in their approach. But there is a very dramatic difference in the overall strategy used by 10-year-olds and 15-year-olds that marks the shift from concrete to formal operations.

Logic.   Another facet of this shift is the appearance of deductive logic in the child's repertoire of skills. I mentioned in Chapter 9 that the concrete operational child is able to use inductive reasoning, which involves arriving at a conclusion or a rule based on a lot of individual experiences. The more difficult kind of reasoning, deductive reasoning, involves "if–then" relationships: "If all people are equal, then you and I must be equal." Children as young as 4 or 5 years can understand some such relationships if the premises given are factually true. But only at adolescence are young people able to understand and use the basic *logical* relationship (Ward & Overton, 1990).

A great deal of the logic of science is of this deductive type. We begin with a theory and propose, "If this theory is correct, then I should observe such and such." In doing this, we are going well beyond our observations. We are conceiving things that we have never seen that *ought* to be true or observable. We can think of this change as part of a general decentering process that began much earlier in cognitive development. The preoperational child gradually moves away from his egocentrism and comes to be able to take the physical or emotional perspective of others. During formal operations, the child takes another step by freeing himself even from his reliance upon specific experiences.

Can you think of any real life examples of tasks that demand this sort of systematic problem solving?

Post-Piagetian Work on Adolescent Thought

Early research, following Piaget's ideas, did indeed indicate that, as Edith Neimark put it: (1982, p. 493)

> An enormous amount of evidence from an assortment of tasks shows that adolescents and adults are capable of feats of reasoning not attained under normal circumstances by [younger] children, and that these abilities develop fairly rapidly during the ages of about 11 to 15.

Furthermore, many of the qualities of adolescent thought Piaget identified do seem to emerge during this period. Adolescents, much more than school-age children, operate with possibilities in addition to reality, and they are more likely to use deductive logic. As Flavell puts it (1985, p. 98), the thinking of the school-age child "hugs the ground of . . . empirical reality," while the teenager is more likely to soar into the realm of speculation and possibility. An 8-year-old thinks that "knowing" something is a simple matter of finding out the facts; a teenager is more likely to see knowledge as relative, as less certain (Bartsch, 1993).

Some additional illustrations would probably make the change clearer. In an early cross-sectional study, Susan Martorano (1977) tested 20 girls at each of four grades (sixth, eighth, tenth, and twelfth) on ten different tasks that require one or more of what Piaget called formal operations skills. Indeed, many of the tasks she used were those Piaget himself had devised. Results from two of these tasks are in Figure 12.1. The pendulum problem is the same one I described earlier; the "balance" problem requires a youngster to predict whether or not two varying weights, hung at varying distances on either side of a scale, will balance—a problem very like the one that Siegler has used in the research I described in Chapter 9. To solve this problem using formal operations, the teenager must consider both weight and distance simultaneously—what Siegler calls Rule IV. You can see in the figure that older students generally did better, with the biggest improvement in scores between eighth and tenth grades (between ages 13 and 15).

In a more practical vein, Catherine Lewis (1981) has shown that these new cognitive abilities alter the ways teenagers go about making decisions. Older teenagers are more focused on the future, on possibilities, and on options, when they consider decisions. Lewis asked eighth-, tenth-, and twelfth-grade students

FIGURE 12.1

These are the results from two of the ten different formal operational tasks used in Martorano's cross-sectional study. (Source: Martorano, 1977, p. 670. Copyright by the American Psychological Association.)

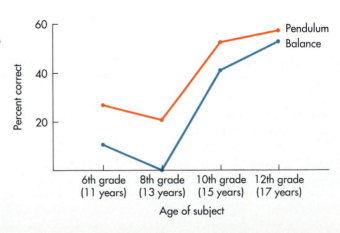

to respond to a set of dilemmas, each of which involved a person facing a difficult decision, such as whether or not to have an operation to remove a facial disfigurement, or how to decide which doctor to trust when the doctors give differing advice. Forty-two percent of the twelfth graders, but only 11 percent of the eighth graders, mentioned future possibilities in their answers to these dilemmas.

In answer to the cosmetic surgery dilemma, for example, a twelfth grader said:

> Well, you have to look into the different things. . . that might be more important later on in your life. You should think about, will it have any effect on your future and with, maybe, the people you meet. . . (p. 541)

An eighth grader, in response to the same dilemma, said:

> The different things I would think about in getting the operation is like if the girls turn you down on a date, or the money, or the kids teasing you at school. . . (p. 542)

The eighth grader, as is characteristic of the school-age child, is focused on the here and now, on concrete things. The teenager is considering things that *might* happen in the future.

But note that even among the twelfth graders in Lewis's study nearly three-fifths did not show this type of future orientation. And take another look at Figure 12.1; only about 50 to 60 percent of twelfth graders solved the two formal operations problems. In Martorano's study, in fact, only 2 of the 20 twelfth-grade subjects used formal operations logic on all ten problems.

These findings reflect a common pattern in research on adolescent thinking: by no means all teenagers (or adults) use these more abstract forms of logic and thought. Keating (1980) estimates that only about 50 to 60 percent of 18- to 20-year-olds in Western countries seem to use formal operations at all, let alone consistently. In non-Western countries the rates are even lower.

Why Doesn't Every Teenager Use Formal Logic?

Why? There are several possibilities. One is that the usual methods of measuring formal operations are simply extremely difficult or unclear. When the instructions are clearer or the researchers give subjects hints or rules, teenagers can demonstrate some aspects of formal operations (Danner & Day, 1977)—just as preschoolers can display some "concrete operations" skills when tasks are made simpler or clearer.

A related possibility is that expertise is once again the crucial element. That is, most of us have some formal operational ability, but we can only apply it to topics or tasks with which we are familiar. For example, I use formal operations reasoning about psychology because it is an area I know well. But I am a lot less skillful at applying the same kind of reasoning to fixing my car—about which I know next to nothing. Willis Overton and his colleagues (Overton et al., 1987) have found considerable support for this possibility in their research. They found that as many as 90 percent of adolescents could solve quite complex logic problems if the problems were stated using familiar content, while only half could solve the identical logical problem when it was stated in abstract language.

What was the last major decision you had to make? Think for a minute about how you went about it. What factors did you consider? Did you think about future consequences or only about the here and now?

Still a third possibility is that most of our everyday experiences and tasks do not require formal operations. Inductive reasoning or other simpler forms of logic are quite sufficient most of the time. So we get into a cognitive rut, applying our most usual mode of thinking to new problems as well. We can kick our thinking up a notch under some circumstances, especially if someone reminds us that it would be useful to do so, but we simply don't rehearse formal operations very much.

The fact that formal operations thinking is found more often among young people or adults in Western cultures than among those in nonindustrialized cultures may be interpreted in the same way. Because of the high technology and the complexity of life in industrialized countries, there is simply more demand for formal operational thought. By this argument, all nonretarded teenagers and adults are assumed to have the *capacity* for formal logic, but only those of us whose lives demand its development will actually acquire it.

Notice that all these explanations undermine the very notion that there is a universal "stage" of thinking in adolescence. Yes, there are more abstract forms of thinking that may develop in adolescence, but they are neither universal nor broadly used by individual teenagers or adults. Whether one develops or uses these forms of logic depends heavily on experience, expertise, and environmental demand.

Which of these explanations of the relative lack of formal operations among adolescents and adults do you find most persuasive? Think about your own experience. Do you use this type of thinking consistently or only in certain situations? What sort of circumstances are most likely to trigger its use?

An Evaluation of Piaget's Theory

Each time I have talked about cognitive development I have raised some issues about Piaget's theory or about the general notion of underlying stages, so the issues are not new to you. But let me pull the threads together for one last look.

Clearly, the child comes a long way in only about 15 years. He moves from very rudimentary abilities to represent things to himself with images and words, to classifications, to conservation, to abstract, deductive logic. In broad outline, Piaget's observations about this sequence have been frequently confirmed. Children do clearly change not only in what they know but in the way they approach problems.

But it now seems quite unlikely that this developmental progression involves coherent, general stages of the kind Piaget envisioned. Nor do new cognitive skills emerge full-blown. Rather, they are preceded by more rudimentary or partial versions of the same skills at earlier ages. For example, virtually all the achievements of the concrete operational period are present in at least rudimentary or fragmentary form in the preschool years. This observation undermines the basic notion of a stage as Piaget proposed it.

Most of those who study cognitive development today would thus describe a much more gradual process, characterized by sequences but not by broad stages. This leaves us with a number of major disputes that are far from resolved. The most central of these is the question of whether knowledge or cognitive skill is totally *domain-specific* or at least partially *domain-general*? If a child learns a new type of logic or a new memory strategy when playing with his favorite dinosaur collection, does this new skill generalize to other tasks, other situations (which would make it domain-general), or does he use this new skill only in the very specific situation in which he first learned it (domain-specific)? Piaget appears to have been wrong about broad general stages, but that still leaves a wide range of possibilities. Development might be *totally* situation (domain)-specific, or it might have at least some generality, with some basic skills or understandings changing with age and being applied across several different domains or tasks. We see some sign of just such a semigeneral, almost stagelike shift in children's theory of mind at about age 4. On the other side of the coin, the research on expertise makes thinking look highly domain-specific. This issue is at the center of most current research on children's thinking.

A second key issue with its roots in Piagetian theory is the question of why particular, new intellectual skills emerge at the time that they do. Why does vocabulary explode at about 18 months? Why does the ability to understand conservation appear only at about age 5 or 6? Piaget's theory obviously offered one answer to this question. But if he is wrong about broad stages, we are still left with the task of explaining the overall timing of cognitive development (Siegler, 1992). Another alternative, common among information processing theorists, is to propose some kind of built-in constraints, such as systematic improvements in the efficiency of the neural wiring at particular age points. Such models may help us understand *change* in children's thinking, but whether they will help us understand *qualitative* changes in children's thinking, such as from nonsystematic to systematic, or from attention to appearances to attention to underlying principles, is not yet clear.

The theoretical issues are obviously highly complex and well beyond the scope of this book. I raise them here not only so that you can see the direction of our current struggles, but also so that you understand why Piaget's theory remains so central in our discussions. Piaget was clearly wrong in several important respects. But as yet we have no alternative that handles all the facts any better.

The Development of Moral Reasoning

Another aspect of cognitive development that interested Piaget and has continued to fascinate researchers, is the child's reasoning about moral questions. How does a child decide what is good or bad, right or wrong, in his own and other people's behavior? When you serve on a jury, you must make such a judgment, as you do in everyday life: Should you give the store clerk back the excess change she handed you? Should you turn in a classmate you see cheating on an exam? What about someone who lies in a job interview? Does your judgment change if you know that the person desperately needs the job to support his handicapped child?

These questions do not become relevant only at adolescence. Children younger than adolescents clearly make such judgments as well. But because several key changes in moral reasoning appear to coincide with adolescence or with the emergence of formal operations reasoning, this is a good place to introduce you to this very intriguing body of theory and research.

Kohlberg's Theory

Piaget was the first to offer a description of the development of moral reasoning (Piaget, 1932), but Lawrence Kohlberg's work has had the most powerful impact (Colby et al., 1983; Kohlberg, 1964; 1976; 1980; 1981). Building on and revising Piaget's ideas, Kohlberg pioneered the practice of assessing moral reasoning by presenting a subject with a series of hypothetical dilemmas in story form, each of which highlighted a specific moral issue, such as the value of human life. One of the most famous is the dilemma of Heinz:

> In Europe, a woman was near death from a special kind of cancer. There was one drug that the doctors thought might save her. It was a form of radium that a druggist in the same town had recently discovered. The drug was expensive to make, but the druggist was charging ten times what the drug cost him to make. He paid $200 for the radium and charged $2000 for a small dose of the drug. The sick woman's husband, Heinz, went to everyone he knew to borrow the money, but he could only get together about $1000 which is half of what it cost. He told the druggist that his wife was dying, and asked him to sell it cheaper or let him pay later. But the druggist said, "No, I discovered the drug and I'm going to make money from it." So Heinz got desperate and broke into the man's store to steal the drug for his wife. (Kohlberg & Elfenbein, 1975, p. 621).

After hearing this story, the child or young person is asked a series of questions, such as whether Heinz should have stolen the drug. What if Heinz didn't love his wife? Would that change anything? What if the person dying was a stranger? Should Heinz steal the drug anyway?

On the basis of answers to dilemmas like this one, Kohlberg concluded that there were three main levels of moral reasoning, with two stages within each level. These are summarized briefly in Table 12.1.

At Level I, **preconventional morality,** the child's judgments are based on sources of authority who are close by and physically superior to himself—usually the parents. Just as his descriptions of others at this same stage are largely external, so the standards the child uses to judge rightness or wrongness are external rather than internal. In particular, it is the outcome or consequences of his actions that determine the rightness or wrongness of those actions.

In stage 1 of this level—the *punishment and obedience orientation*—the child relies on the physical consequences of some action to decide if it is right or wrong. If he is punished, the behavior was wrong; if he is not punished, it was right. He is obedient to adults because they are bigger and stronger.

In stage 2—*individualism, instrumental purpose, and exchange*—the child begins to do things that are rewarded and avoid things that are punished. (For this reason, the stage is sometimes called a position of "naive hedonism.") If it feels good, or brings pleasant results, it is good. There is some beginning of concern for other people during this phase, but only if that concern can be expressed as something that benefits the child himself as well. So he can enter into agreements like "If you help me, I'll help you."

As illustration, here are some responses to variations of the Heinz dilemma, drawn from studies of children and teenagers in a number of different cultures, all of which would be rated as Stage 2:

> **TABLE 12.1**
> **Kohlberg's Stages of Moral Development**
>
> **Level 1: Preconventional Morality**
> - **Stage 1: Punishment and obedience orientation.** The child decides what is wrong on the basis of what is punished. Obedience is valued for its own sake, but the child obeys because the adults have superior power.
> - **Stage 2: Individualism, instrumental purpose, and exchange.** The child follows rules when it is in his immediate interest. What is good is what brings pleasant results.
>
> **Level 2: Conventional Morality**
> - **Stage 3: Mutual interpersonal expectations, relationships, and interpersonal conformity.** Moral actions are those that live up to the expectations of the family or other significant group. "Being good" becomes important for its own sake.
> - **Stage 4: Social system and conscience (law and order).** Moral actions are those so-defined by larger social groups or the society as a whole. One should fulfill duties one has agreed to and uphold laws except in extreme cases.
>
> **Level 3: Principled or Postconventional Morality**
> - **Stage 5: Social contract or utility and individual rights.** Acting so as to achieve the "greatest good for the greatest number." The teenager or adult is aware that most values are relative and laws are changeable, although rules should be upheld in order to preserve the social order. Still, there are some basic nonrelative values, such as the importance of each person's life and liberty.
> - **Stage 6: Universal ethical principles.** The adult develops and follows self-chosen ethical principles in determining what is right. These ethical principles are part of an articulated, integrated, carefully thought out, and consistently followed system of values and principles.
>
> Sources: After Kohlberg, 1976, and Lickona, 1978.

Taiwan: "He should steal the food for his wife because if she dies he'll have to pay for the funeral, and that costs a lot."

Puerto Rico: He should steal the drug because "he should protect the life of his wife so he doesn't have to stay alone in life."

Turkey: [*Suppose it wasn't his wife who was starving but his best friend. Should he steal the food for his friend?*] "Yes, because one day when he is hungry his friend would help."

—from Snarey, 1985, p. 221

At the next major level, **conventional morality,** there is a shift from judgments based on external consequences and personal gain to judgments based on rules or norms of a group to which the child belongs, whether that group is the family, the peer group, a church, or the nation. What the chosen reference group defines as right or good *is* right or good in the child's view, and the child internalizes these norms to a considerable extent.

Stage 3 (the first stage of level 2) is the stage of *mutual interpersonal expectations, relationships, and interpersonal conformity* (sometimes also called the *Good Boy/Nice Girl* stage). Children at this stage believe that good behavior is what pleases other people. They value trust, loyalty, respect, gratitude, and maintenance of mutual relationships. Andy, a boy Kohlberg interviewed who was at Stage 3, said:

These students, participating in the Hispanic Youth Legislature, are most likely reasoning at Stage 3 of Kohlberg's stages of moral reasoning: What is good is what family or peers define as good and right.

> I try to do things for my parents, they've always done things for you. I try to do everything my mother says, I try to please her. Like she wants me to be a doctor and I want to, too, and she's helping me get up there. (Kohlberg, 1964, p. 401).

Another mark of this third stage is that the child begins to make judgments based on intentions as well as on outward behavior. If someone "means well" or "didn't mean to do it," their wrongdoing is seen as less serious than if they did it "on purpose."

Stage 4, the second stage of the conventional level, shows the child turning to larger social groups for her norms. Kohlberg labeled this the stage of *social system and conscience*. It is also sometimes called the *law and order orientation*. People reasoning at this stage focus on doing their duty, respecting authority, following rules and laws. The emphasis is less on what is pleasing to particular people (as in Stage 3) and more on adhering to a complex set of regulations. The child doesn't question the regulations themselves.

The transition to level 3, **principled morality,** (*post-conventional morality*) is marked by several changes, the most important of which is a shift in the source of authority. At level 1 children see authority as totally outside themselves; at level 2, the judgments or rules of external authority are internalized, but they are not questioned or analyzed; at level 3, a new kind of personal authority emerges in which individual choices are made, with individual judgments based on self-chosen principles.

In stage 5 at this level—which Kohlberg calls the *social contract* orientation—we see the beginning of such self-chosen principles. Rules, laws, and regulations are still seen as important because they insure fairness. But people operating at this level also see times when the rules, laws, and regulations need to be ignored or changed. Our American system of government is based on moral reasoning of this kind, since we have provisions for changing laws and for allowing personal

Imagine a society in which everyone handled moral issues at Kohlberg's Stage 3. Now think about one in which everyone operated at Stage 5. How would those two societies be likely to differ?

protests against a given law, such as during the Civil Rights protests of the 1960s, the Vietnam War protests of the 1960s and 1970s, or the protests against apartheid in the 1980s.

In his original writing about moral development, Kohlberg also included a sixth stage, the *universal ethical principles* orientation. People who reason in this way assume personal responsibility for their own actions, based upon fundamental and universal principles, such as justice and basic respect for persons. Kohlberg later waffled a good bit on whether such a stage was the logical and necessary end point of the sequence and on whether people reasoning at such a level actually existed (Kohlberg, 1978; Kohlberg, 1984; Kohlberg, Levine, & Hewer, 1983). If they exist at all, it seems likely that such universal ethical principles guide the moral reasoning of only a few very unusual individuals—perhaps those who devote their lives to humanitarian causes, such as Mother Theresa or Gandhi.

In all of this, it is *very* important to understand that what defines the stage or level of a person's moral judgment is not the specific moral choice but the *form of reasoning* used to justify that choice. For example, either the choice that Heinz should steal the drug or that he should not, could be justified with logic at any given stage. I've already given you some examples of a stage 2 justification for Heinz's stealing the drug; here's a Stage 5 justification of the same choice, drawn from a study in India:

Kohlberg thought that there were at least a few people, perhaps like Mother Theresa, whose moral reasoning was based on universal ethical principles.

> [What if Heinz was stealing to save the life of his pet animal instead of his wife?] If Heinz saves an animal's life his action will be commendable. The right use of the drug is to administer it to the needy. There is some difference, of course—human life is more evolved and hence of greater importance in the scheme of nature—but an animal's life is not altogether bereft of importance. . . (Snarey, 1985, p. 223, drawn originally from Vasudev, 1983, p. 7).

If you compare this answer to the ones I quoted before, you can clearly see the difference in the form of reasoning the subject used, even though the action being justified is precisely the same.

Kohlberg argued that this sequence of reasoning is both universal and hierarchically organized, just as Piaget thought his proposed stages of cognitive development were universal and hierarchical. That is, each stage follows and grows from the preceding one and has some internal consistency. Individuals should not move "down" the sequence, but only "upward" along the stages, if they move at all. Kohlberg did *not* suggest that all individuals eventually progress through all six stages, nor even that each stage is tied to specific ages. But he insisted that the order is invariant and universal. Let me take a critical look at these claims.

Age and Moral Reasoning

Kohlberg's own findings, confirmed by many other researchers (Rest, 1983; Walker, de Vries, & Trevethan, 1987), show that preconventional reasoning (Stages 1 and 2) is dominant in elementary school, and Stage 2 reasoning is still evident among many early adolescents. Conventional reasoning (stages 3 and 4) emerges as important in middle adolescence and remains the most common form of moral reasoning in adulthood. Post-conventional reasoning (stages 5 and

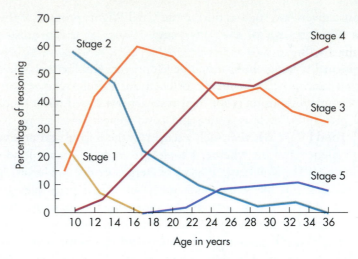

FIGURE 12.2

These findings are from Colby & Kohlberg's long-term longitudinal study of a group of boys who were asked about Kohlberg's moral dilemmas every few years from age 10 through early adulthood. Note that postconventional or principled reasoning was quite uncommon, even in adulthood. (Source: Colby et al., 1983, Figure 1, p. 46. © The Society for Research in Child Development.)

6) is relatively rare, even in adulthood. For example, in one study of men in their 40s and 50s, only 13 percent were rated as using Stage 5 moral reasoning (Gibson, 1990).

Let me give you two examples illustrating these overall age trends. The first, shown in Figure 12.2, comes from Kohlberg's own longitudinal study of 58 boys, first interviewed when they were ten, and subsequently followed for more than 20 years (Colby et al., 1983). Table 12.2 shows cross-sectional data from a study by Lawrence Walker and his colleagues (Walker et al., 1987). They studied 10 boys and 10 girls at each of 4 ages and interviewed the parents of each child as well. Note that Walker scored each response on a 9-point scale rather than just

TABLE 12.2

Percentage of Children and Their Parents Who Show Moral Reasoning at Each of Kohlberg's Stages

| Age | Stage | | | | | | | | |
	1	1–2	2	2–3	3	3–4	4	4–5	5
6 (1st grade)	10%	70%	15%	5%	—	—	—	—	—
9 (4th grade)	—	25	40	35	—	—	—	—	—
12 (7th grade)	—	—	15	60	25%	—	—	—	—
15 (10th grade)	—	—	—	40	55	5%	—	—	—
Adult (avg age about 40)	—	—	—	1	15	70	11%	3%	—

Source: Walker, de Vries, & Trevethan, 1987, Table 1, p. 849.

scoring the five main stages. This system, which has become quite common, allows for the fact that many people's reasoning falls between two specific stages.

The results of these two studies are not identical, but there is nonetheless remarkable agreement on the order of emergence of the various stages and on the approximate ages at which they predominate. In both studies, Stage 2 reasoning dominates at age 10, and Stage 3 reasoning is most common at about age 16.

Sequence of Stages

The evidence also seems fairly strong that the stages follow one another in the sequence Kohlberg proposed. There have been a number of long-term longitudinal studies of teenagers and young adults, in the United States (Colby et al., 1983), in Israel (Snarey, Reimer, & Kohlberg, 1985) and in Turkey. In each, the changes in subjects' reasoning nearly always occurred in the hypothesized order. Subjects did not skip stages and only about 5–7 percent of the time was there any indication of regression (movement down the sequence rather than up). Similarly, when Walker retested the subjects in his study two years later, he found only 6 percent had moved down, mostly only half a stage, while 22 percent had moved up and none had skipped a stage (Walker, 1989). Such a rate of regression is about what you would expect to find, given the fact that the measurements of stage reasoning are not perfect. On the whole, I agree with James Rest (1983) that the evidence is "fairly compelling" that moral judgment changes over time in the sequence Kohlberg describes.

Universality of Stages of Moral Reasoning

But is this sequence of stages only a phenomenon of Western culture? Or has Kohlberg uncovered a genuinely universal process? Thus far, variations of Kohlberg's dilemmas have been presented to children or adults in 27 different cultural areas, including both Western and non-Western, industrialized and non-industrialized (Snarey, 1985).

John Snarey, who has reviewed and analyzed these many studies, notes several things in support of Kohlberg's position: (1) In studies of children, an increase with age in the stage of reasoning used is found consistently in every culture; (2) The few longitudinal studies report "strikingly similar findings" (1985, p. 215), with subjects moving upward in the stage sequence with few reversals; (3) Cultures differ in the highest level of reasoning observed. In complex urban societies (both Western and non-Western), Stage 5 is typically the highest stage observed, while in those cultures Snarey calls "folk" societies, Stage 4 is typically the highest. Collectively, this evidence seems to provide quite strong support for the universality of Kohlberg's stage sequence.

Moral Development: A Critique

Kohlberg's theory about the development of moral reasoning has been one of the most provocative theories in all of developmental psychology. Over 1,000 studies have explored or tested aspects of the theory, and several competing theories have been proposed. The remarkable thing is how well the theory has stood the test of this barrage of research and commentary. There does appear to be a clear set of stages in the development of moral reasoning, and these stages seem to be universal.

Still, the theory has not emerged unscathed. Some psychologists are less impressed than Snarey with the data on universality (Shweder, Mahapatra, & Miller, 1987). Also troubling is the fact that so few teenagers or adults seem to reason at the post-conventional level (stages 5 or 6). Shweder points out that the effective range of variation is really only from stage 2 to stage 4, which is not nearly so interesting or impressive as is the full range of stages.

But by far the most vocal critics have been those who have pointed out that Kohlberg is really not talking about all aspects of "moral reasoning." Instead, as Kohlberg himself acknowledged in his later writings (Kohlberg et al., 1983), he is talking about the development of reasoning about *justice and fairness*. We might also want to know about other ethical bases than justice, such as an ethic based on concern for others or for relationships. In this category, the best-known critic has been Carol Gilligan.

Gilligan's Ethic of Caring.   Carol Gilligan (1982a; 1982b; 1987; Gilligan & Wiggins, 1987) is fundamentally dissatisfied with Kohlberg's focus on justice and fairness as the defining features of moral reasoning. Gilligan argues that there are, in fact, at least two distinct "moral orientations," justice and care. Each has its own central injunction: not to treat others unfairly (justice) and not to turn away from someone in need (caring). Boys and girls learn both of these injunctions, but Gilligan has hypothesized that girls are more likely to operate from an orientation of caring or connection, while boys are more likely to operate from an orientation of justice or fairness. Because of these differences, they tend to perceive moral dilemmas quite differently.

Given the emerging evidence on sex differences in styles of interaction and in friendship patterns, which I have talked about in several earlier chapters, Gilligan's hypothesis makes some sense. Perhaps girls, focused more on intimacy

Gilligan argues that these young women are much more likely to be using an "ethic of caring" than an "ethic of justice" as a basis for their moral judgments. This *may* be true among adult women; it appears not to be true among children or adolescents.

in their relationships, judge moral dilemmas by different criteria. But in fact, research on moral dilemmas has *not* shown that boys are more likely to use justice reasoning or that girls more often use care reasoning. Several studies of adults do show such a pattern (Lyons, 1983), but studies of children generally have not (Smetana, Killen, & Turiel, 1991; Walker et al., 1987).

For example, Lawrence Walker (Walker et al., 1987) scored children's answers to moral dilemmas using both Kohlberg's fairness scheme and Gilligan's criteria for a care orientation. He found no sex difference for either hypothetical dilemmas like the Heinz dilemma, or for the real-life dilemmas suggested by the children themselves. Only among adults did Walker find a difference, in the direction that Gilligan would expect.

Gilligan's arguments have often been quoted in the popular press as if they were already proven, when in fact the empirical base is really quite weak. Gilligan herself has done no systematic studies of children's (or adult's) care reasoning. Yet despite these weaknesses, I am not ready to discard all of her underlying points, primarily because the questions she is asking seem to me to fit with the newer research on sex differences in styles of relationship. This seems to me to be clearly an area in which we need to learn a great deal more.

Moral Judgment and Behavior.   Kohlberg's theory has sometimes been criticized on the grounds that children's or adults' moral behavior does not always match their reasoning. But Kohlberg never said that there should be a one-to-one correspondence between the two. Reasoning at Stage 4 (conventional reasoning) does not mean that you will never cheat or always be kind to your mother. Still, the form of reasoning a young person typically applies to moral problems should have at least *some* connection with real-life choices. One connection that Kohlberg proposed is that the higher the level of reasoning a young person shows, the stronger the link to behavior ought to become. Thus young people reasoning at Stage 4 or Stage 5 should be more likely to follow their own rules or reasoning than should children reasoning at lower levels.

For example, Kohlberg and Candee (1984) studied students involved in the early "Free Speech" movement at Berkeley in the late 1960s (a precursor to the Vietnam War protests). They interviewed and tested the moral judgment levels of a group that had participated in a sit-in at the university administration building, plus a group randomly chosen from the campus population. Of those who thought it was morally right to sit in, nearly three-quarters of those reasoning at stages 4 or 5 actually did sit in, compared to only about a quarter of those reasoning at Stage 3. Thus the higher the stage of reasoning, the more consistent the behavior was with the reasoning.

In other research, Kohlberg and others approached the question simply by asking whether there is a link between stage of moral reasoning and the probability of making some "moral choice," such as not cheating. In one study, Kohlberg (1975) found that only 15 percent of students reasoning at the principled level (stage 5) cheated when they were given an opportunity, while 55 percent of conventional level and 70 percent of preconventional students cheated. In addition, there is now strong evidence that delinquents have lower levels of moral reasoning than do nondelinquents (Chandler & Moran, 1990; Smetana, 1990),

Suppose Gilligan were right, and adult women typically reason with an ethic of care while men reason with an ethic of justice. What do you think would be the implications of such a difference—for male/female relationships, for men and women as political leaders, or in other ways?

Do you think that a person's stage or level of moral reasoning has any impact on political behavior, such as voting or political party affiliation? Can you generate a hypothesis about such a link and figure out how you might test that hypothesis?

even when the two groups are carefully matched for educational and social class levels. Thus those who actually do break the law also reason at lower levels about moral issues.

Yet despite this abundance of evidence for a link between moral reasoning and behavior, no one has found the correspondence to be perfect. After all, in Kohlberg's studies, 15 percent of the principled moral reasoners did cheat, and a quarter of Stage 4 and Stage 5 reasoners who thought it morally right to participate in a sit-in did not do so. As Kohlberg says, "One can reason in terms of principles and not live up to those principles." (Kohlberg, 1975, p. 672).

What else besides level of reasoning might matter? We don't have all the answers to that question yet, but some influences are clear. First, simple habits are involved. Every day each of us faces small moral situations that we have learned to handle in a completely automatic way. Sometimes these automatic choices may be at a lower level of reasoning than we would use if we sat down and thought about it. For example, I may make the same donation to a particular charity every year without stopping to consider whether I could now afford more or whether that particular charity is really the place where my money could best be used.

Second, in any given situation, even though you might think it morally right to take some action, you may not see that action as morally *necessary* or obligatory. I might be able to make a good argument for the moral acceptability of a sit-in protest, but still not see it as my *own* duty or responsibility to participate.

Third, the cost to the person of doing something helpful (or refraining from doing something morally "wrong," like cheating) may be an important factor. If helping someone else has little cost in time, money, or effort, then most children and adults will help, regardless of their overall level of social cognitive reasoning. But when there is some cost, then we find a more consistent correlation between level of reasoning and behavior. This suggests the more general principle that moral reasoning becomes a factor in moral behavior only when there is something about the situation that heightens the sense of moral conflict, such as when there is a cost involved or when the individual feels personally responsible.

Most children and adults will readily show helpful actions like this if there is little personal cost attached. But if the cost of helping goes up—such as when you're in a hurry to get somewhere else—then those with higher levels of moral reasoning are more likely to help.

Finally, there are often competing motives or ethics at work as well, such as the pressure of a peer group, or motives for self-protection, or self-reward. Gerson and Damon found this very clearly in a study in which they asked groups of four children to divide up ten candy bars. The candy was a reward for work the children had done on a project, and some of the group members had worked harder than others. When asked separately about how the candy bars ought to be divided, children usually argued for various kinds of fair arrangements, such as a model in which the child who worked the hardest should get the most. But when faced with the actual distribution of the candy bars, some children gave themselves the most; others went along with a group consensus and divided the candy equally. We might expect that in early adolescence, when the impact of the peer group is particularly strong, this group effect on moral actions might be especially strong, too.

Thus moral *behavior* results from a complex of influences, of which the level of moral reasoning is only one element. Our knowledge about these links is improving, but we badly need to know more, both about group pressure and

A lot of what I have said about Kohlberg's theory may seem pretty abstract to you. In Kohlberg's own view, though, there were many potential practical implications for education. The question that interested him was whether children or young people can be taught higher stages of moral reasoning, and if so, whether such a change in moral reasoning would change their behavior in school.

We know from early research by Elliot Turiel (1966) that at least under some conditions, exposing young people to moral arguments one step above their own level of reasoning can lead to an increase in their level of moral judgment. Young people who attend college also continue to show increases in moral stage scores, while those who quit school after high school typically show no further increase (Rest & Thoma, 1985). Because arguments about moral and philosophical issues in class and over coffee (or a few beers) in the wee small hours of the night are one of the hallmarks of the college experience for many young people, perhaps it is the discussion—the exposure to other people's ideas, other people's logic—that makes a difference.

If that's true, what would happen if high school students were given systematic opportunities to explore moral dilemmas; would that change them, too? Apparently it can.

One educational application has involved the creation of special discussion classes in which moral dilemmas similar to those Kohlberg devised are presented and argued. In the process, the teacher attempts to model higher levels of reasoning. Other programs are broader based, involving not just discussion, but also cross-age teaching (to encourage nurturance and caring), empathy training, cooperation games, volunteer service work, and the like. The dozens of studies on the effectiveness of programs of this kind show that on average, the programs succeed in shifting young people's moral reasoning upward about a half a stage (Schaefli, Rest, & Thoma, 1985). The largest effects are generally found in programs focusing exclusively on discussions of moral dilemmas, but broader-based programs work, too. Courses lasting longer than 3 or 4 weeks seem to work better than very short programs, and the effects are generally larger with older students—college students and even post-college age adults. Among high school students, there is some impact but it is not as large.

An even broader-based educational application, designed to change students' moral behavior as much as their moral reasoning, has been the development of the so-called "just community." These experimental schools, typically set up as a "school within a school," operate as a

The Real World
Application of Kohlberg's Theory to Education

kind of laboratory for moral education (Higgins, 1991; Higgins, Power, & Kohlberg, 1984; Kohlberg & Higgins, 1987; Power & Reimer, 1978).

Kohlberg insisted that the crucial feature of these just communities must be complete democracy: each teacher and student has one vote, and community issues and problems have to be discussed in open forum. Rules are typically created and discussed at weekly community-wide meetings. In this way, students become *responsible* for the rules, and for one another.

In experimental schools following this model, Kohlberg and his co-workers found that as students' level of Kohlbergian moral reasoning shifted upward, so did their reasoning about responsibility and caring. The link between moral reasoning and moral behavior was strengthened as well. For example, stealing and other petty crime virtually disappeared in one school after the students had repeatedly discussed the problem and arrived—painfully—at a solution that emphasized the fact that stealing damaged the whole community, and thus the whole community had to be responsible. For example, after one stealing episode the group agreed that if the stolen money had not been returned (anonymously) by a specified date, each community member would be assessed 15 cents to make up the victim's loss (Higgins, 1991).

This effect of just communities makes sense when you think about the factors that seem to affect moral behavior. In these schools, two elements were added that would tend to support more moral behavior: a sense of personal responsibility and a group norm of higher moral reasoning and caring.

Among teenagers, the emotional impact of the group pressure may be especially significant, in addition to whatever effect there may be from exposure to more mature arguments. If you are arguing your position about some moral dilemma, but find yourself in the minority, the "social disequilibrium" you feel may help to make you more open to other arguments and thus to change your view. Certainly in experimental schools like those Kohlberg studied, this added emotional impact is no doubt part of the process (Haan, 1985).

Classes in moral education have not proven to be the "quick fix" that many educators hoped for. The gains in moral reasoning are not huge and may not be reflected in increases in moral behavior in the school unless there is an effort to alter the overall moral atmosphere of the entire school. But these programs do show that there are provocative and helpful applications of at least some of the abstract developmental theories.

about all the other factors that lead each of us to behave in ways that are less thoughtful, considerate, or fair than we "know how" to do.

Moral Reasoning and Cognitive Development

Before I leave this subject, there is one other set of linkages I need to explore, namely the potential connection between the sequences of development in moral reasoning and the broader sequences of cognitive development I have been talking about throughout the book.

Kohlberg's own hypothesis was that the child first moves to a new level of logical thought, then applies this new kind of logic to relationships as well as objects, and only then applies this thinking to moral problems. More specifically, Kohlberg argued that at least some formal operations and at least some mutual perspective taking in relationships are necessary (but not sufficient) for the emergence of conventional moral reasoning. Full formal operations and still more abstract social understanding may be required for post-conventional reasoning.

The research examining such a sequential development is scant, but supports Kohlberg's hypothesis. Lawrence Walker (1980) found that among a group of fourth to seventh graders he tested on all three dimensions (concrete and formal operations, social understanding, and moral reasoning), half to two-thirds were reasoning at the same level across the different domains, which makes the whole thing look unexpectedly "stage-like." When a child was ahead in one progression, the sequence was always that the child developed logical thinking first, then more advanced social understanding, and then the parallel moral judgments.

This research seems to tell us that there is *some* coherence in a child's or young person's thinking or reasoning about quite different problems. Children who have not yet understood principles of conservation are not likely to understand that another person's behavior may not match his feelings. But once conservation is understood, the child begins to extend this principle to people and to relationships. Similarly, a young person still using concrete operations is unlikely to use post-conventional moral reasoning. But the coherence is not automatic. The basic cognitive understanding makes advances in social and moral reasoning *possible*, but does not guarantee them. Experience in relationships and with moral dilemmas is necessary too.

The moral of this (if you will excuse the pun) is that just because a young person or adult shows signs of formal operations does *not* necessarily mean that the teenager or young adult will show sensitive, empathetic, and forgiving attitudes toward friends or family. You may find it helpful to bear this in mind in your own relationships.

Schooling During the Adolescent Years

Just as the school experience is formative in middle childhood, school is a central force in the lives of adolescents. But the effect is different in the two cases. In middle childhood, school experience is focused on learning a whole set of basic skills and specific knowledge—how to read, how to do mathematics, how to write. While there is certainly more specific knowledge conveyed to students in junior high and high school and schooling may contribute to the development of formal operational thought, schooling serves a host of other functions in adolescence. Not only is it an arena in which teenagers can practice new heterosexual social skills, it is also the setting in which society attempts to shape young people's attitudes and behaviors to prepare them for adult life. High schools teach driver's education, "family life" education including sexuality, home economics, civics, and current affairs. Guidance counselors may also help the teenager decide about college, or about future job options, and organized sports programs also offer opportunities for nonacademic success (or failure).

Despite this very broad range of educational roles that the high school plays, most researchers have focused primarily on academic success or school completion as measures of the impact of schooling. So let me say a word or two about the two ends of the continuum, those who achieve academic success and those who drop out of school.

Those Who Achieve

The best single predictor of a student's academic performance in high school is IQ. It is true that middle-class kids are more likely to succeed in school, and that children growing up in poverty environments are less likely to do well, but social class itself is only weakly related to school achievement. Within each racial group and each social class group, it is those with higher IQ who are most likely to get good grades, complete high school, and go on to college.

Both adolescent IQ and school grades also predict adult job success to at least some degree (Barrett & Depinet, 1991). A myriad of studies of military jobs, for example, shows correlations in the range of .45 to .55 between scores on IQ-like tests and the recruits' later proficiency and success at a wide range of jobs (Hunter & Hunter, 1984; Ree & Earles, 1992). Outside of the military, the same general relationship holds, although education plays a key intervening role. Students with higher IQ or better grades in high school tend to go on to more years of additional education, and this is as true among children reared in poverty as it is among the middle class (Barrett & Depinet, 1991). Those extra years of education, in turn, have a powerful effect on the career path a young person enters in early adulthood (Featherman, 1980; Rosenbaum, 1984).

These relationships exist not just because brighter kids have an easier time with school work, but also because the cumulative effect of success over many years of schooling fosters a greater sense of self-efficacy in these intellectually more able students. Those who achieve, especially those who achieve despite poverty backgrounds or other daunting obstacles, also are more likely to have parents who have high aspirations for them (Brooks-Gunn, Guo, & Furstenberg, 1993) or an authoritative family style—a point I'll come back to in a moment. So there is—as always—an interaction between the effect of the family and the effect of the school.

The best single prediction of achieving in high school is the student's IQ or earlier school achievement. But family interactive style makes a difference too.

Those Who Drop Out

At the other end of the continuum are those who drop out of school before completing high school. According to the U.S. Education Department (New York Times, 1994), 11 percent of students who entered high school in 1988 had failed to graduate by 1993. Hispanics had the highest dropout rates in this group at 32 percent, compared to 16 percent for African-Americans, and 10 for Anglos. For both Anglos and African-Americans, these figures represent a decline in the dropout rate over the past several decades. In 1972, for example, 26 percent of African-Americans had dropped out of high school before graduating.

Despite these ethnic differences, however, social class is a far better predictor than is ethnicity. Kids growing up in poor families are considerably more likely to drop out of high school than are those from more economically advantaged families. When you hold social class constant there are few differences in drop-out rates among Blacks, Whites, and Hispanics (Entwisle, 1990). But because minority youth in the United States are so much more likely to come from poor families or from families that do not provide psychological support for academic achievement, they are also more likely to drop out of school. When a teenager's peer group also puts a low value on achievement, as is true in many Black and Hispanic teen groups in the United States, the risk of dropping out is even stronger (Takei & Dubas, 1993).

Teenagers who drop out of school list many reasons for such a decision, including not liking school, poor grades, being suspended, or needing to find work to support a family. Girls who drop out most often do so because they plan to marry, are pregnant, or feel that school is simply not for them (Center for Educational Statistics, 1987). Lists of reasons like this, though, don't begin to capture the multifaceted nature of the decision to drop out. It is too simple, for example, to say that girls drop out because they are pregnant; some get pregnant because they are not interested in school and feel that they are ready for adult

If the averages work out, one of these six students will drop out before completing high school.

Underachievers

A particularly puzzling and interesting group of students are those who achieve at consistently lower levels than you would predict, based on their IQ or other test scores: *Underachievers.* Two or three times as many boys as girls fall into this category, but underachievers come from families at every economic level and from every ethnic group.

A large and comprehensive study by Robert McCall and his colleagues (McCall, Evahn, & Kratzer, 1992) gives us a picture of this group. They studied 6,720 teenagers who had completed an extensive questionnaire when they were juniors or seniors in high school during the middle 1960s. Thirteen years later, when the subjects were between 28 and 31 years old, nearly 5,000 of them were interviewed on the phone, asking them about their adult lives.

Within this large group, McCall identified those whose school grades had been significantly lower than what would have been predicted by standardized test scores. He then compared the underachievers to several other subgroups, including some who had the same apparent ability but had achieved at a level commensurate with their ability, and others who had achieved at about the same lower level as the underachievers, but whose standardized scores were also lower.

Several results stand out from these analyses. First, the underachievers had consistently low self-esteem. In high school, they saw themselves as having less competence, less ability to do well in school. They had lower aspirations for their future as well. Such low self-esteem and low expectations were not unique to underachievers. Other students who were getting poor grades in school expressed many of the same ideas, which suggests—as I noted in Chapter 9—that students' perceptions of their abilities are strongly linked to the evaluations they are receiving in school.

What was unique about the underachievers, though, was their consistently poorer performance in adulthood—poorer even than students who had been receiving equivalent low grades in high school. The underachievers were less likely to complete college than any of the other groups, had lower status jobs with lower income at age 30, and were 50 percent more likely to have divorced in the 13 years after high school.

There were a few underachievers who "caught up" later in life. In particular, those few who, despite their relatively poor grades, nonetheless had high aspirations and saw themselves as able to complete college, did catch up to their higher-achieving peers. But this was the exception. Most did not "get their act together" later on, and this was particularly true of those whose high school performance was substantially below expectations. In the end, McCall concludes that the most striking quality of underachievers is their "lack of persistence in the face of challenge and adversity" (p. 143). They lack the "stick-to-iteveness" needed to succeed in school, on a job, or in a marriage.

McCall's study doesn't tell us where such lack of persistence may have come from. Nor does it indicate what type of intervention, if any, would be successful in altering the pattern of underachievement and nonperseverance characteristic of these young people. But it does suggest that underachievement is a recognizable syndrome, one we need to know more about.

---

life. Low self-esteem or a low sense of self-efficacy, perhaps fostered by years of low achievement, also undoubtedly plays some role, just as it does among underachievers. In recent years, during economic hard times, many teenagers have also come to the conclusion that a high school diploma won't buy them much in the job world—not a totally unreasonable view, given the poor job prospects for many high school graduates in many parts of the country (and the world) today (Rosenbaum, 1991).

Yet in the long term, teens who use such a rationale for dropping out of high school are wrong. Unemployment is higher among high school dropouts than in any other education group, and dropouts who find jobs earn lower wages than do those with a high school diploma. The difference between these two groups is not as large as it once was; a man or woman with a high school diploma can no longer count on finding good paying, skilled industrial jobs as was the case several decades ago. But a high school education still offers some distinct advantages. Those who drop out enter a very different—and far less optimal—life trajectory.

School Achievement and Family Style

I want to end this chapter by returning to a point I have made briefly several times, but that deserves considerable elaboration, namely that there is a link between school achievement and family style. The best single study is that of Sanford Dornbush and Laurence Steinberg and their colleagues, a study I mentioned briefly in Chapter 8 (Dornbusch et al., 1987; Lamborn et al., 1991; Steinberg, Elmen, & Mounts, 1989; Steinberg et al., 1992). The study involves over 8,000 high school students in California and Wisconsin. The researchers measured three of the four major parenting styles (all but the neglecting) by asking the teenagers themselves to complete a questionnaire about their relationship with their parents. Questions reflecting an authoritarian style included one about how often the parents tell the teen not to argue with adults and another about whether or not the parents say that they are correct and not to be questioned. Students were also asked how their parents would react if they got bad grades or good grades. An authoritarian response was scored if a student said that his parents would punish him if he got poor grades and tell him to do better if he got good grades.

If the student reported that hard work was not important to the parents, or that the parents don't care if the student gets bad grades, or that there are no rules about TV watching, or that the parents do not attend school functions or help the student with homework, the family was rated as high in permissiveness. Students whose families were rated as authoritative replied positively to items saying that their parents tell the teen to look at both sides of the issues, that the parents sometimes agree that the teen knows more, that they emphasize joint decision making in the family, and that they praise good grades and offer to help after bad grades, urging the student to try harder.

Steinberg and Dornbusch then looked at the relationship between these family styles and the teenager's school performance. Figure 12.3 gives one of the main results, the link between family style and school grades. The information about school grades also came from the students, who chose a broad category that best described their grades, such as "mostly A's" or "about half B's and half C's". These category scores were then converted to a scale, with 4 representing the highest category and .5 the lowest. Figure 12.3 shows this scale score.

The figure shows the average grades not only for the three pure styles, but also for several mixtures of style—a possibility in this case because of the way parental style was measured. It is clear that the pure authoritative style (high scores on authoritative items and low scores on permissive and authoritarian items) is associated with the best grades, with a mixture of authoritative and permissive styles the second best, and either permissive or authoritarian parenting or a combination of the two, associated with poorer outcomes.

Notice from Figure 12.3 that the *worst* grades were for teens from families who were inconsistent—who showed some characteristics of all three family styles. How could you explain this?

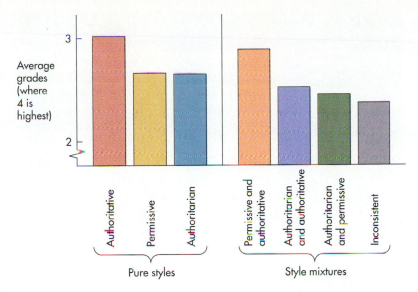

FIGURE 12.3

School grades as a function of parental style—pure styles or mixtures—in Steinberg and Dornbusch's large study of teenagers. (Source: Dornbusch et al., 1987, from Table 4, p. 1255.)

Steinberg and Dornbusch continued their contact with these teenagers over two years, which allowed them to look at possible links between the parents' style at the beginning of the study and the students' *later* school performance. In this longitudinal analysis, they found the same kinds of patterns: those students whose parents were most authoritative at the beginning of the study continued to get better grades and to be more involved in school over the succeeding two years.

But the system is more complex than this makes it sound. It is not just that authoritative parents create a good family climate and thereby support and motivate their child optimally. Authoritative parents also behave differently *toward the school*. They are much more likely to be involved with the school, attending school functions, or talking to teachers, and this involvement seems to play a crucial role in the process, just as it does during elementary school. When an otherwise authoritative parent is *not* also more involved with the school, the outcomes for the student are not so clearly positive. The reverse combination, a parent who is highly involved with the school but is not authoritative, also shows less optimal outcomes. It is the combination of authoritativeness and school involvement that is associated with the best results (Steinberg et al., 1992).

Ethnic Group Differences in Styles. Because the sample in the Steinberg and Dornbusch study is so large, it has been possible for them to look separately at subgroups of African-American, Hispanic-American, and Asian-American youth and their families (Steinberg et al., 1991). In the process, they have uncovered some very interesting patterns that point us both toward common processes and toward unique cultural variations.

Table 12.3 shows the percentages of authoritative·families from each of the four ethnic groups involved in this study, broken down further by social class and

TABLE 12.3
Ethnic Differences in Authoritative Parenting

| | Percentage of Authoritative Families | | | |
| | Working Class | | Middle Class | |
Ethnic Group	Intact*	Not Intact	Intact	Not Intact
White	17.2	11.5	25.0	17.6
Black	13.4	12.2	14.0	16.0
Hispanic	10.7	9.8	15.8	12.9
Asian	7.5	6.1	15.6	10.8

*"Intact" means the child is still living with both biological parents; "Not intact" may mean either single-parent, stepfamily, or any other family configuration other than both natural parents.

Source: Steinberg et al., 1991, from Table 1, p. 25.

the intactness of the family. The authoritative pattern was most common among White families and least common among Asian-Americans, but in each ethnic group, authoritative parenting was more common among the middle class and (with one exception) more common among intact families than in single-parent or step-parent families.

More important, Steinberg and Dornbusch found that many of the relationships between authoritative parenting and positive outcomes occurred in all ethnic groups. In all four groups, teenagers from authoritative families had more self-reliance and less delinquency than did those from nonauthoritative families.

School performance, on the other hand, was *not* linked to authoritative parenting in the same ways in all four groups: good grades were strongly linked to such a parenting style for Whites and for Hispanic-Americans, but only very weakly for Asian-Americans or African-Americans. In particular, Asian-Americans as a group do extremely well in school even though their parents are among the least authoritative. Thus styles of parenting *cannot* explain the ethnic group differences in academic achievement.

In an effort to understand these group differences, Steinberg and Dornbusch have looked at a variety of other aspects of the family and cultural systems (Steinberg, Dornbusch, & Brown, 1992). One key element seems to be the beliefs students and parents have about the importance of education for later success in life. All four groups share a belief that doing well in school will lead to better chances later. But the groups disagree on the consequences of doing poorly in school. Asian students, more than any other group, believe that a good job is unlikely to follow a bad education, while both Hispanics and Blacks are more optimistic (or more cavalier) about the risks associated with poor school performance. Perhaps as a result of their greater fear of failure, Asian students spend much more time on homework than do other groups.

Furthermore, Asian-American students (and Whites) get very good peer support for academic achievement, while African-American teens get little peer support for such an activity, which undermines the beneficial effects of authoritative parenting. Indeed, interviews with the African-American students in the

Asian-American students get good peer support for school achievement.

Steinberg and Dornbusch study suggest that academically oriented African-American youth find it very difficult to find a peer group that will support their academic goals. Other research, in fact, suggests that the more aware of racial discrimination African-American high school students are, the less important they perceive academic achievement to be. Those who believe that good jobs will not be open to them in any case see little reason to try hard in high school (Taylor et al., 1994). Those Black students who nonetheless persist in their achievement striving often resolve the issue by choosing primarily peers from other ethnic groups. Thus the dilemma for African-American students, more than any other subgroup in American culture, seems to involve a choice between doing well in school or being accepted by peers.

Taking all of this together, it appears that authoritarian parenting is associated with positive psychological outcomes such as higher self-esteem and lower levels of psychological distress in all groups. But academic achievement is a more complex process, involving a heavier dose of peer influence that may either support or override the impact of parental style.

S U M M A R Y

1. Piaget proposed a fourth major level of cognitive development in adolescence, formal operational thought. It is characterized by the ability to apply basic operations to ideas and possibilities, in addition to actual objects.
2. Deductive logic and systematic problem solving are also part of formal operational thought.
3. Researchers have found clear evidence of such advanced forms of thinking in at least some adolescents. But formal operational thinking is not universal, nor is it consistently used even by those who possess the ability.
4. Such evidence once more calls Piaget's general model into question; it is not clear that general stages of cognitive development exist. But no alternative theory can explain why certain cognitive skills emerge for the first time at particular ages.
5. Theorists are also still arguing about how general or how specific a child's knowledge or cognitive skills may be.
6. Another facet of adolescent thinking is the development of new levels of moral reasoning. Kohlberg proposes six stages of such reasoning, organized into three levels.
7. Preconventional moral reasoning includes reliance on external authority; what is punished is bad; what feels good is good.
8. Conventional morality is based on rules and norms provided by outside groups, the family, church, or society. This is the dominant form of moral reasoning among teenagers and adults.
9. Principled or post-conventional morality is based on self-chosen principles. Only about 15 percent of adults reason at this level.
10. Research evidence suggests that these levels and stages do develop in a specified order, and that they are found in this same sequence in all cultures studied so far.

11. Kohlberg's model has been criticized on the grounds that it deals only with reasoning about justice and fairness. Gilligan suggests that people may also reason based on caring and connection, and that girls are more likely to use the latter model. Research does not support Gilligan on the latter point.

12. Moral reasoning is not perfectly correlated with moral behavior. Moral behavior is also affected by habits, the degree of responsibility the individual feels, and the cost associated with behaving morally.

13. There appears to be some link between the emergence of formal operations logic and the development of conventional moral reasoning. The former may be necessary, but not sufficient, for the latter.

14. Academic success or failure in high school has long-term consequences for job success in adulthood. School achievement, in turn, is better predicted by IQ than by social class.

15. Those who drop out are more likely to be minorities, poor, or doing poorly in school.

16. School performance in high school is also promoted by an authoritative parental style, although this is far more true among Caucasian and Hispanic groups than among Asian-Americans or African-Americans. Asian teens, on average, perform well in school although their families are most often authoritarian in style. Beliefs about the importance of effort and the bad consequences of school failure are part of the explanation.

KEY TERMS

conventional morality
preconventional morality
principled morality

SUGGESTED READINGS

Kurtines, W. M., & Gewirtz, J. L. (Eds.), (1991). *Handbook of moral behavior and development.* Hillsdale, NJ: Lawrence Erlbaum Associates. This is a massive three-volume work, prepared as a commemoration of the work of Lawrence Kohlberg. Volume 1 deals with theory, Volume 2 with research, and Volume 3 with application. If this area intrigues you, there is no more complete source.

Entwisle, D. R. (1990). Schools and the adolescent. In S. S. Feldman & G. R. Elliott (Eds.), *At the threshold. The developing adolescent* (pp. 197–224). Cambridge: Harvard University Press. A good, current review of this important subject.

Chapter Thirteen

Social Behavior and Personality in Adolescence

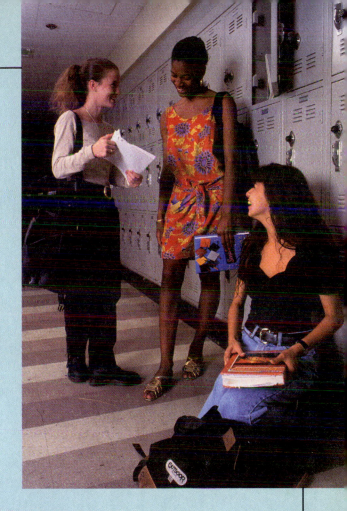

In my own memories of adolescence, the physical changes loom large. Certainly the fact that I grew 6 inches the year I was 12, towering over absolutely everyone, was a highly important event. I recall very vividly that I had little notion how long my arms and legs were during this period and regularly hit people as I was making grand gestures; I recall my mother's despair at keeping me in clothes that fit; I know that this experience colored all my relationships and deeply affected my self-concept.

Significant as these physical changes were, my memories of those years are equally colored by another set of adolescent tasks: gaining some independence from my family, figuring out who I was and what I could or should do with my life, discovering some of the mysterious secrets of relationships with that other species, *boys*. It is these tasks of independence, identity, and relationship that are the central story of this chapter.

Understanding the Self and Relationships at Adolescence

Let me begin, as I did in Chapter 10, by looking at the cognitive aspect of these tasks. How does the child's understanding of himself and his relationships change at adolescence?

The Self-Concept

In Chapter 10, I talked about the fact that the child's self-concept becomes less and less tied to outer qualities, more and more focused on enduring internal characteristics during the elementary school years. This trend continues in adolescence, when self-definitions become more and more abstract. You may remember the replies of a 9-year-old and an 11-year-old to the "Who am I?" question used in Montemayor and Eisen's study, which I quoted in Chapter 10 (page 297). Here's an answer by a 17-year-old's answer to the same question:

> I am a human being. I am a girl, I am an individual. I don't know who I am. I am a Pisces. I am a moody person. I am an indecisive person. I am an ambitious person. I am a very curious person. I am not an individual. I am a loner. I am an American (God help me). I am a Democrat. I am a liberal person. I am a radical. I am a conservative. I am a pseudoliberal. I am an atheist. I am not a classifiable person (i.e. I don't want to be). (Montemayor & Eisen, 1977, p. 318).

Clearly, this girl's self-concept is even less tied to her physical characteristics or even her abilities than are those of the younger children. She is describing abstract traits or ideology.

You can see the change very graphically in Figure 13.1, based on the answers of all 262 subjects in the Montemayor and Eisen study. Researchers placed each of the subjects' answers to the "Who am I?" question in one or more specific categories, such as references to physical properties ("I am tall," "I have blue eyes") or references to ideology ("I am a Democrat," "I believe in God," etc.). As you can see, appearance was a highly salient dimension in the preteen and early teen years, but became less dominant in late adolescence, at a

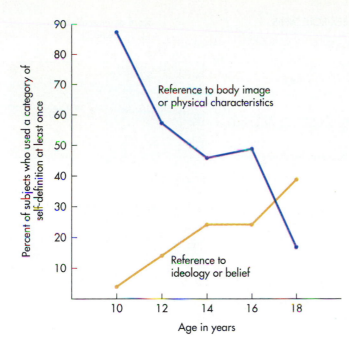

FIGURE 13.1
As they get older, children and adolescents define themselves less and less by what they look like and more and more by what they believe or feel. (Source: Montemayor & Eisen, 1977, from Table 1, p. 316.)

time when ideology and belief became more salient. By late adolescence, most teenagers think of themselves in terms of enduring traits, beliefs, personal philosophy, and moral standards (Damon & Hart, 1988).

At the same time, the adolescent's self-concept becomes more differentiated, as the teenager comes to see herself somewhat differently in each of several roles: as a student, with friends, with parents, and in romantic relationships (Harter & Monsour, 1992). Self-concepts also become more flexible in the sense that categories are held less rigidly. One example of this is the greater flexibility adolescents show in their views about what is acceptable behavior for people of their gender.

Sex-Role Concepts in Adolescence.   Seven- and 8-year-olds appear to treat gender categories as if they were fixed rules, but adolescents see that a wide range of behaviors occurs among members of each gender group (Huston-Stein & Higgens-Trenk, 1978; Urberg & Labouvie-Vief, 1976). Indeed, a significant minority of teenagers and youths begin to define themselves with both masculine and feminine traits.

In the early days of research on masculinity and femininity, psychologists conceived of these two qualities as opposite ends of a single continuum. A person could be masculine *or* feminine, but couldn't be both. Following the lead of Sandra Bem (1974), and of Janet Spence and Robert Helmreich (1978), psychologists today conceive of masculinity and femininity as two separate dimensions. Thus an individual can express both masculine and feminine sides of herself, can be both compassionate and independent, both gentle and assertive.

This conceptualization creates four basic "types," as shown in Figure 13.2. The two traditional (strongly sex-typed) sex-roles are the masculine and the

Why should it make such a difference whether we think of masculinity and femininity as two ends of a single continuum or as two separate dimensions?

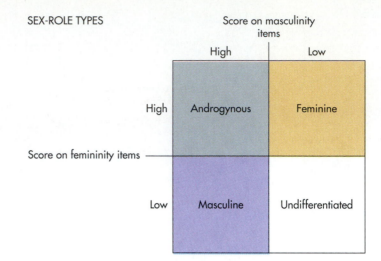

SEX-ROLE TYPES

FIGURE 13.2
In this way of conceptualizing
masculinity and femininity,
each person expresses some
level of each. When each
dimension is dichotomized,
four "types" are produced.

feminine combinations. The two new types that become evident when we think about sex-roles in this way are called *androgynous* and *undifferentiated*. Androgynous individuals think of themselves as having both masculine and feminine traits; undifferentiated individuals describe themselves as lacking both.

Several studies show that roughly 25–35 percent of United States high school students define themselves as androgynous (Lamke, 1982a; Spence & Helmreich, 1978). More girls than boys seem to show this pattern and there are more girls who define themselves with primarily masculine traits than there are boys who define themselves primarily with feminine qualities.

More striking is the finding for *both* adolescent boys and girls, that either a masculine or an androgynous sex-role self-concept is associated with higher self-esteem (Lamke, 1982a; 1982b). This makes sense if we assume that both boys and girls value many of the qualities that are stereotypically masculine, such as independence and competence. Thus a teenage boy can achieve high self-esteem and success with his peers by adopting a traditional masculine sex-role. For girls, though—at least in many Western cultures—adoption of a traditional feminine sex-role without some balancing "male" characteristics seems to carry a risk of lower self-esteem and even poorer relationships with peers (Massad, 1981).

Findings like these suggest the possibility that while the creation of rigid rules or schemas for sex-roles is a normal—even essential—process in young children, a blurring of those rules may be an important process in adolescence, particularly for girls, for whom a more androgynous self-concept is associated with positive outcomes.

Identity in Adolescence

A somewhat different way to look at adolescent self-concept is through the lens of Erikson's theory. In his model, the central task or dilemma of adolescence is that of *identity versus role confusion*. Erikson argues that the child's early sense of identity comes partly unglued in early adolescence because of the combination of rapid body growth and the sexual changes of puberty. He refers to this period as one in which the adolescent mind is in a kind of *moratorium* between childhood and adulthood. The old identity will no longer suffice; a new identity must be forged, one that must serve to place the young person among the myriad roles of adult life—occupational roles, sexual roles, religious roles. Confusion about all these role choices is inevitable. Erikson puts it this way:

> In general it is primarily the inability to settle on an occupational identity which disturbs young people. To keep themselves together they temporarily overidentify, to the point of apparent complete loss of identity, with the heroes of cliques and crowds. . . . They become remarkably clannish, intolerant, and cruel in their exclusion of others who are "different," in skin color or cultural background . . . and often in entirely petty aspects of dress and gesture arbitrarily selected as *the* signs of an in-grouper or out-grouper. It is important to understand . . . such intolerance as the necessary *defense against a sense of identity confusion*, which is unavoidable at [this] time of life. (1980, pp. 97–98)

The teenage clique or group thus forms a base of security from which the young person can move toward a unique solution of the identity process. Ultimately, each teenager must achieve an integrated view of himself including his own pattern of beliefs, occupational goals, and relationships.

Nearly all the current work on the formation of adolescent identity has been based on James Marcia's descriptions of *identity statuses* (Marcia, 1966; 1980), which are rooted in Erikson's general conceptions of the adolescent identity process. Following one of Erikson's ideas, Marcia argues that there are two key parts to any adolescent identity formation: a *crisis* and a *commitment*. By a "crisis" Marcia means a period of decision making when old values, old choices are reexamined. This may occur as a sort of upheaval—the classic notion of a crisis—or it may occur gradually. The outcome of the reevaluation is a commitment to some specific role, some particular ideology.

If you put these two elements together, as in Figure 13.3, you can see that four different "identity statuses" are possible.

- **Identity achievement:** the person has been through a crisis and reached a commitment.

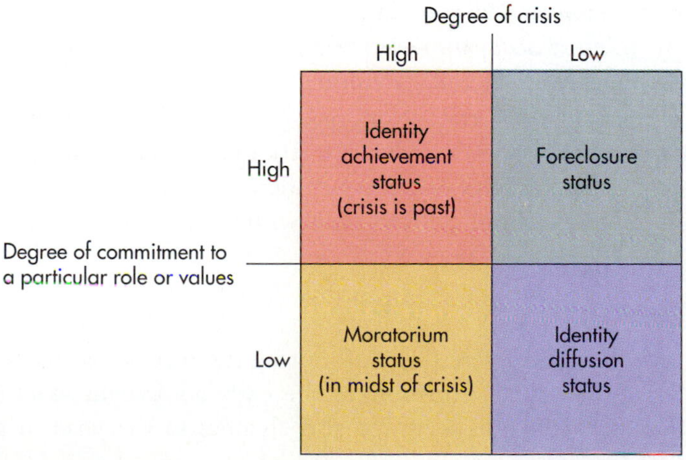

Degree of crisis

	High	Low
High	Identity achievement status (crisis is past)	Foreclosure status
Low	Moratorium status (in midst of crisis)	Identity diffusion status

Degree of commitment to a particular role or values

FIGURE 13.3

The four identity statuses proposed by Marcia, based on Erikson's theory. For a fully achieved identity, the young person must both have examined his or her values or goals and have reached a firm commitment. (Source: Marcia, 1980.)

The implication in Marcia's formulation is that the foreclosure status is less-developmentally mature—that one must go through a crisis in order to achieve a mature identity. Does this make sense to you?

- **Moratorium:** a crisis is in progress, but no commitment has yet been made.
- **Foreclosure:** a commitment has been made without having gone through a crisis. No reassessment of old positions has been made. Instead the young person has simply accepted a parentally or culturally defined commitment.
- **Identity Diffusion:** the young person is not in the midst of a crisis (although there may have been one in the past) and makes no commitment. Diffusion may thus represent either an early stage in the process (before a crisis) or a failure to reach a commitment after a crisis.

Whether every young person goes through some kind of identity crisis I cannot tell you, since there are no longitudinal studies covering all the relevant years. Cross-sectional studies of the years of adolescence and early adulthood, however, suggest that the whole process of identity formation may occur later than Erikson thought, when it occurs at all. In one combined analysis of eight separate cross-sectional studies, Alan Waterman (1985) found that the identity achievement status occurred most often in college, not during the high school years. Among these subjects, the moratorium status was relatively uncommon except in the early years of college. So if most young people are going through an identity crisis, the crisis is occurring fairly late in adolescence and not lasting terribly long. What's more, about a third of the young people at every age were in the foreclosure status, which may indicate that many young people simply do not go through a crisis at all, but follow well-defined grooves.

As a further caveat, it is important to note that all of the subjects in the studies Waterman analyzed were in college or likely to attend college. It may be that young people who go to work immediately after high school will face the need to form at least an occupational identity earlier than is true for those who go to college. The college years involve a kind of postponement of full adult status, a period in which students are actively encouraged to question, doubt, and try out alternatives. Those who go directly into the working world do not have that luxury and thus must work out some kind of personal identity sooner, a possibility supported by at least some research (Munro & Adams, 1977).

It is also worth pointing out that the whole conception of an adolescent identity crisis has been strongly influenced by current cultural assumptions in Western societies. In such cultures today, full adult status is postponed for almost a decade after puberty. In addition, young people do not normally or necessarily adopt the same roles or occupations as their parents. Indeed, they are encouraged to choose for themselves. In such a cultural system, adolescents are faced with what may be a bewildering array of options, a pattern that might well foster the sort of identity crisis Erikson described. In less-industrialized cultures, especially those with clear initiation rites of the type I described in Chapter 11, there may well be a shift in identity from child to adult without a crisis of any kind.

Self-Esteem

Self-esteem also shows an interesting shift during the teenage years. Not only are self-esteem scores particularly unstable in the early adolescent years (a fact you may recall from Chapter 10), there are also changes in the level of self-esteem

CULTURES & CONTEXTS

Ethnic Identity in Adolescence

For minority teenagers, especially those of color in a predominantly white culture, there is another aspect of creating an identity in adolescence: They must also develop an ethnic or racial identity, including self-identification as a member of some specific group and commitment to that group and its values and attitudes, as well as positive (or negative) attitudes about the group.

Jean Phinney (1990; Phinney & Rosenthal, 1992) has proposed that in adolescence, the development of a complete ethnic identity moves through three rough stages. The first stage is an "unexamined ethnic identity," equivalent to what Marcia calls a foreclosed status. For some subgroups in U.S. society, such as African-Americans and Native-Americans, this unexamined identity typically includes the negative images and stereotypes common in the wider culture. Indeed, it may be especially at adolescence, with the advent of the cognitive ability to reflect and interpret, that the young person becomes keenly aware of the way in which his own group is perceived by the majority. As Spencer and Dornbusch say (1990) "The young African-American may learn as a child that black is beautiful but conclude as an adolescent that white is powerful" (p. 131). The same is doubtless true of other minority groups in the U.S.

Many youngsters in these and other minority groups initially prefer the dominant White culture, or wish they had been born into the majority. An African-American journalist, Sylvester Monroe, who grew up in an urban housing project, clearly describes this initial negative feeling:

> If you were black, you didn't quite measure up. . . For a black kid there was a certain amount of self-doubt. It came at you indirectly. You didn't see any black people on television, you didn't see any black people doing certain things. . . You don't think it out but you say, "well, it must mean that white people are better than we are. Smarter, brighter—whatever" (Spencer & Dornbusch, 1990, pp. 131–132).

Not all minority teenagers arrive at such negative views of their own group. Individual youngsters may have very positive ethnic images if that is the content of the identity that parents or others around the child convey. Phinney's point is rather that this initial ethnic identity is not arrived at independently but comes from outside sources.

The second stage is the "ethnic identity search," parallel to the crisis in Marcia's analysis of ego identity. This search is typically triggered by some experience that makes ethnicity salient—perhaps an example of blatant prejudice or merely the widening experience of high school. At this point the young person begins to compare her own ethnic group with others, to try to arrive at her *own* judgments.

This exploration stage is eventually followed by a resolution of the conflicts and contradictions—analogous to Marcia's status of identity achievement. This is often a difficult process. For example, some African-American adolescents who wish to try to compete in and succeed in the dominant culture may experience ostracism from their Black friends, who accuse them of "acting White," and betraying their Blackness. Latinos often report similar experiences. Some resolve this by keeping their own ethnic group at arm's length; others deal with it by creating essentially two identities, as expressed by one young Chicano interviewed by Phinney:

> Being invited to someone's house, I have to change my ways of how I act at home, because of culture differences. I would have to follow what they do . . . I am used to it now, switching off between the two. It is not difficult. (Phinney & Rosenthal, 1992, p. 160).

Some resolve the dilemma by wholeheartedly choosing their own ethnic group's patterns and values, even though that may limit their access to the larger culture.

In both cross-sectional and longitudinal studies, Phinney has found that African-American teens and young adults do indeed move through these steps or stages toward a clear ethnic identity. Furthermore, there is evidence that among Black, Asian-American, and Mexican-American teens and college students, those who have reached the second or third stage in this process—those who are searching or who have reached a clear identity—have higher self-esteem and better psychological adjustment than do those who are still in the "unexamined" stage (Phinney, 1990). In contrast, among Caucasian students, ethnic identity has essentially no relationship to self-esteem or adjustment.

This stagelike model may be a decent beginning description of the process of ethnic identity formation. But let us not lose sight of the fact that the details and the content of the ethnic identity will differ markedly from one subgroup to another. Those groups that encounter more overt prejudice will have a different road to follow than will those who may be more easily assimilated; those whose own ethnic culture espouses values that are close to those of the dominant culture will have less difficulty resolving the contradictions than will those whose family culture is at greater variance with the majority. Whatever the specifics, young people of color and those from clearly defined ethnic groups have an important additional identity task in their adolescent years.

By this age, most teenagers have a much more positive view of themselves than they did at age 10 or 12.

Can you think of examples of how your own self-concept affects your choices and your behavior?

teenagers report. Average self-esteem scores tend to drop slightly at the beginning of adolescence and then rise steadily and substantially (Harter, 1990; Wigfield et al., 1991). By the end of adolescence, the average 19- or 20-year-old has a considerably more positive sense of her global self-worth than she did at age 8 or 11.

The brief drop in self-esteem at the onset of adolescence seems to be linked not so much to age as to changing schools at the same time as puberty (Harter, 1990). Researchers have noted it especially among students who shift to junior high school at seventh grade (Wigfield et al., 1991). When the transition process is more gradual, such as for children in a middle school that includes fifth through eighth grades, there is no parallel drop in self-esteem in early adolescence.

Summary of Developmental Changes in the Self-Concept

Let me combine the bits of information I have given in several chapters, and sum up this developmental progression. The infant first develops a primitive sense of her own separateness. This is followed quickly by an understanding of her own constancy and of herself as an actor or agent in the world. By 18 to 24 months, most children achieve self awareness; they grasp the fact that they are also *objects* in the world. At that point, children begin to define themselves in terms of their physical properties (age, size, gender), and their activities and skills. Over the period of concrete and formal operations (from age 6 through adolescence), the content of the child's self-concept becomes gradually more abstract, less and less tied to outward physical qualities, based more on the assumption of enduring inner qualities. During late adolescence, the whole self-concept may undergo a kind of reorganization, with the creation of a new future-oriented sexual, occupational, and ideological identity.

As a final point, I want to emphasize once again that a child's self-concept, including her level of self-esteem, appears to be a highly significant mediating concept. Once such a "theory" of the self is well established, once a global judgment of one's own self-worth is established, there are reverberations throughout the child's behavior. Among other things, she systematically chooses experiences and environments that are consistent with her beliefs about herself. The child who believes she can't play baseball behaves differently from the child who believes that she can. She is likely to denigrate the importance of sports, to avoid baseballs, bats, playing fields, and other children who play baseball. If forced to play, she may make self-deprecating remarks like "You know I can't play," or she may play self-defeating games, such as refusing to watch the ball when she swings at it or not running after the ball in right field because she knows she couldn't catch it even if she did get there on time. (If you think all this sounds autobiographical, you're right!)

A child who believes that she can't do long division will behave quite differently in the classroom from the child whose self-concept includes the idea "I am good at math" (or, even more potently, "I am better at math than other kids.") If she believes she is less competent, she may not try to work long division problems on the theory that if you don't try, you can't fail. Or she may try much harder, paying the price in anxiety about failure. At a later age, such a child is much less likely to take further math courses, thus reducing her occupational options.

These beliefs are pervasive, many develop early, and although they are somewhat responsive to changing circumstances, they also act as self-fulfilling prophecies. We need to know a good deal more about the origins of the child's self-definitions if we are to understand how to modify the inaccurate elements.

Concepts of Relationships

In parallel fashion, the teenager's understanding of others, and of relationships, becomes more and more abstract, less and less tied to externals. For example, teenagers' descriptions of other people contain more comparisons of one trait with another or one person with another, more recognition of inconsistencies and exceptions, more shadings of gray than we hear in descriptions given by younger children (Shantz, 1983). As illustration, here's a description by a 15-year-old:

> Andy is very modest. He is even shyer than I am when near strangers and yet is very talkative with people he knows and likes. He always seems good tempered and I have never seen him in a bad temper. He tends to degrade other people's achievements, and yet never praises his own. He does not seem to voice his opinions to anyone. He easily gets nervous. (Livesley & Bromley, 1973, p. 221).

We see similar changes in children's descriptions of friendships, which become more qualified, more shaded. Damon's research suggests that in late adolescence, young people understand that even very close friendships cannot fill every need and that friendships are not static: they change, grow, or dissolve, as each member of the pair changes. A really good friendship, then, is one that *adapts* to these changes. At this age, young people say things about friendship like "trust is the ability to let go as well as to hang on" (Selman, 1980, p. 141).

In an intriguing series of interviews, Robert Selman (1980) has also studied friendships by asking children and adolescents how they settle disagreements or arguments with friends. Table 13.1 lists some of the answers given by children of various ages, illustrating the kind of progression I have been describing.

Relationships at Adolescence

All these cognitive changes in the child's understanding of herself and her relationships form an important part of the foundation of the adolescent's actual relationships. Those teenagers who are most developmentally advanced in their social understanding, for example, are able to form friendships more easily (Vernberg, Ewell, Beery, & Abwender, 1994). In adolescence, the key relationships continue to be with parents and with peers.

Relationships with Parents

Adolescents have two, apparently contradictory, tasks in their relationship with their parents: to establish autonomy from the parents and to maintain their sense of relatedness with their parents. We can see both processes at work when we

TABLE 13.1
Comments by Children of Various Ages about How to Solve Disagreements or Arguments Between Friends

- "Go away from her and come back later when you're not fighting." (age 5)
- "Punch her out." (age 5)
- "Around our way the guy who started it just says he's sorry." (age 8)
- "Well if you say something and don't really mean it, then you have to mean it when you take it back." (age 8½)
- "Sometimes you got to get away for a while. Calm down a bit so you won't be so angry. Then get back and try to talk it out." (age 14)
- "If you just settle up after a fight that is no good. You gotta really feel that you'd be happy the way things went if you were in your friend's shoes. You can just settle up with someone who is not a friend, but that's not what friendship is really about." (age 15½)
- "Well, you could talk it out, but it usually fades itself out. It usually takes care of itself. You don't have to explain everything. You do certain things and each of you knows what it means. But if not, then talk it out." (age 16).

Source: Selman, 1980, pp. 107–113.

Can you recognize your own thinking in these comments? How would you describe your ways of settling arguments with your friends?

---

look at teen/parent relationships. The push for autonomy shows itself in increases in conflict between parent and adolescent; the maintenance of connection is seen in the continued strong attachment of child to parent.

Increases in Conflict.   The rise in conflict between teens and their parents has been documented by a number of researchers, most notably Laurence Steinberg (1988). In the great majority of families, it seems to consist of an increase in mild bickering or conflicts over everyday issues, such as rules and regulations, dress codes, dating, grades, or housekeeping. Teenagers and their parents interrupt each other more often, become more impatient with one another.

This increase in discord is widely found, but we need to be careful not to assume that it signifies a major disruption of the quality of the parent-child relationships. Steinberg estimates that only 5–10 percent of the families studied in the United States experience a substantial or pervasive deterioration in the quality of parent-child relationship in these years of early adolescence—a fact that flies in the face of the usual assumption that adolescence is a time of inevitable storm and stress.

But if the rise in conflict doesn't signal the relationship is falling apart, what does it mean? Steinberg and others have suggested that the temporary discord, far from being a negative event, may instead be developmentally healthy and necessary—a part of the process of individuation and separation (Hill, 1988; Steinberg, 1988; 1990). Among primates, we see the same kind of increase in conflict, especially between adult males and the newly adolescent males. The young males begin to make competitive gestures and may be driven off into a brief period of independent life before returning to the troop. Among humans, we have some evidence that the increase in family conflict is linked with the hormonal changes of puberty, rather than age, which would lend further support to the argument that this is a normal and even necessary process.

It is a myth that parents and teenagers are constantly in conflict.

For example, in a short-term longitudinal study, Steinberg (1988) followed a group of teenagers over a one-year period, assessing their stage of puberty and the quality of their relationship with their parents at the beginning and end of the year. He found that as the pubertal stages began, family closeness declined, parent-child conflict rose, and autonomy in the child went up. Other researchers (Inoff-Germain et al., 1988) have taken this a step further by measuring actual hormone levels and showing links between the rise of the various hormones of puberty and the rise in aloofness toward or conflict with parents. Among girls, conflict seems to rise after menarche (Holmbeck & Hill, 1991).

The pattern of causes is obviously complex. Hormonal changes themselves may be causally linked to increases in assertiveness, perhaps especially among boys. But parents' reactions to pubertal changes may also be highly important parts of the mix. Visible pubertal changes, including menarche, change parents' expectations for the child and increase their concern about guiding and controlling the adolescent to help her avoid the shoals of too-great a level of independence.

In fact, there is good evidence that adolescence may actually be more stressful to *parents* than to the young people themselves (Gecas & Seff, 1990). Almost two-thirds of parents perceive adolescence as the most difficult stage of parenting, because of both loss of control over the adolescent and fear that the adolescent's increased independence will mean a loss of safety.

In the midst of the increased conflict, and perhaps partially as a result of it, the overall level of the teenager's autonomy within the family increases steadily throughout the adolescent years. Parents give the youngster more and more room to make independent choices and to participate in family decision making. Steinberg argues that this "distancing" is an essential part of the adolescent development process.

Attachment to Parents.   Paradoxically, in the midst of the temporarily heightened family conflict and the "distancing," teenagers' underlying emotional attachment to their parent remains strong. Results from a recent study by Mary Levitt and her colleagues (1993) illustrate the point.

Why might parents find their children's adolescence to be so stressful? How many hypotheses can you generate to explain such a finding? Do you think this is true in every culture, or is this likely to be true only of industrialized countries?

Levitt interviewed African-American, Hispanic-American, and Anglo/European-American children aged 7, 10, and 14. Each child was shown a drawing with a set of concentric circles. They were asked to place in the middle circle the "people who are the most close and important to you—people you love the most and who love you the most." In the next circle, children were asked to place the "people who are not quite as close but who are still important—people you really love or like, but not quite as much as the people in the first circle." The outer circle was to include names of somewhat more distant members of this personal "convoy." For each person the child listed, the interviewer then asked about the kind of support that person provided.

Levitt found that for all three ethnic groups, at all three ages, parents and other close family were by far the most likely to be placed in the inner circle. Even among 14-year-olds, friends were not often placed in this position. So the parents remain central. At the same time, it is clear from Levitt's results that peers become increasingly important as providers of support, as you can see in Figure 13.4. This figure shows the total amount of support the children and adolescents described from each source. Friends clearly provided more support among the 14-year-olds than among the younger children, a pattern that is evident for all three ethnic groups. You can also see in the figure that extended family support is more significant for Hispanic-American teens than for Anglos, a pattern that matches other research on Hispanic families.

The continued centrality of the parent-child relationship is confirmed in other research, including research in other Western countries. In general, a teenager's sense of well-being or happiness is more strongly correlated with the quality of his attachment to his parents than to the quality of his attachments to his peers (Greenberg, Siegel, & Leitch, 1983; Raja, McGee, & Stanton, 1992).

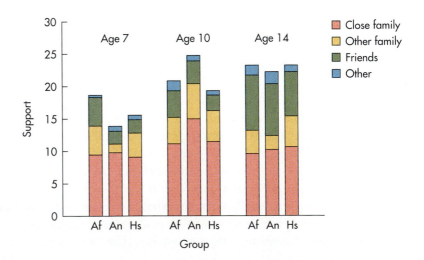

FIGURE 13.4

African-American (Af), Anglo-American (An) and Hispanic-American (Hs) children and teens were asked about the amount and type of support they received from various members of their "social convoy." Note that for teens, friends become more significant sources of support, but parents do not become *less* important. (Source: Levitt, Guacci-Franco, & Levitt, 1993, Figure 2, p. 815.)

Thus even while the teenager is becoming more autonomous, the parents seem to continue to provide a highly important psychological safe base.

Variations in Family Style.   During these adolescent years, as at all earlier times, some parents are better than others at creating such a safe base. I've already talked at some length in Chapter 12 about the link between family style and school performance. Results from the same large study by Dornbusch, Steinberg, and their colleagues show that the benefits of an authoritative style extend to many other aspects of emotional and mental health. Table 13.2 shows one set of results, from which it is clear that social and emotional outcomes were best for the young people who described their families as authoritative, and least good for those from neglectful families, with teenagers from authoritarian and permissive families falling in between. More detailed studies of subgroups of these families show that those who give their teenagers too much autonomy too soon have youngsters who have lower grades and lower levels of effort in school. Joint decision making between parents and teenagers—a hallmark of authoritative parenting—was linked to higher school performances and fewer personal problems, regardless of social class or ethnic group membership (Dornbusch et al., 1990).

Family Structure.   Family structure, too, continues to be an important factor in the teenager's life. But in adolescence we see an interesting exception to the typical pattern of effects. You'll remember that I reported in Chapter 8 that boys are usually more negatively affected than girls by parental divorce or remarriage. Among adolescents, there are some indications that it is girls who show more distress, both in families in which the girl lives with her still-single mother and in step-parent families (1991a; 1991b; Hetherington & Clingempeel, 1992). Adolescent girls, but apparently not preschool or elementary-school-age girls, have more trouble interacting with the new stepfather than do their brothers and treat him more as an intruder. They are resistant, critical, sulky, and try to avoid contact with him, despite the obvious effort of many stepfathers to be thoughtful and nonauthoritarian. Girls in this situation are also likely to become depressed and more likely than are boys in stepfamilies to get involved with drugs.

TABLE 13.2
Average Scores on Various Measures of Adolescent Behavior for Teenagers from Families with Different Styles of Discipline and Control

	Style of Parenting			
Outcome Measure	Authoritative	Authoritarian	Permissive	Neglectful
Self-Reliance	3.09_a	2.96_b	3.03_a	2.98_b
Psychological Symptoms	2.36_a	2.46_a	2.43_a	2.65_b
School Misconduct	2.16_a	2.26_b	2.38_c	2.43_c
Drug Use	1.41_a	1.38_a	1.69_b	1.68_b

Note: Numbers with different subscripts are significantly different from one another.

Source: Lamborn et al., 1991, Table 9 and Table 10, p. 1060 and p. 1961.

Why this pattern occurs is not so obvious. The daughter may feel displaced from a special or more responsible position in the family system that she held after her parents' divorce and before the mother's remarriage; she may feel disturbed by the mother's romantic and clearly sexual involvement with the stepfather. In contrast, the teenage boy may have more to gain by the addition of the stepfather. The boy acquires a male role model and may be able to discard some of the adultlike responsibilities he held in the divorced family system. Whatever the explanation, findings like these remind us once again that family systems are astonishingly complex. Simple categories like "intact" and "step-parent" families will need to give way, ultimately, to more fine-grained analyses that take into account not only the child's age and gender, but family style, the history and sequence of family structures, the presence of other relatives in the system, and so forth.

Relationships with Peers

Friendships in adolescence are more intimate and based more on mutual disclosure, than was true at earlier ages.

While the relationship with the parents remains crucial for adolescents, there is no gainsaying the fact that peer relationships become far more significant at adolescence than they have been at any earlier age, and perhaps than they will be at any later time in the life span. Teenagers spend more than half their waking hours with other teenagers and less than 5 percent of their time with either parent. Of the roughly 40 percent of their hours that can be counted as leisure time, they spend two-fifths socializing with friends, most of that time talking (Csikszentmihalyi & Larson, 1984).

These friendships are quite stable. They also become more complex and psychologically richer. Adolescent friendships are increasingly intimate, in the sense that friends more and more share their inner feelings and secrets and are more knowledgeable about each other's feelings—a pattern found in studies in Russia as well as the United States (Kon & Losenkov, 1978). Loyalty and faithfulness also become more valued characteristics of friendship in adolescence (Berndt & Perry, 1990).

This set of changes is more than just a shift in how kids spend their time. More centrally, the *function* of the peer group and peer friendships changes. In elementary school, peer groups are mostly the setting for mutual play and for all the learning about relationships and the natural world that is part of such play. But the teenager uses his friends and his peer group in another way. He is struggling to make a slow transition from the protected life of the family to the independent life of adulthood, and the peer group becomes the *vehicle* for that transition. As Erikson pointed out, the clannishness and conformity to the group is a normal—even an essential—part of the process.

Age Changes in Conformity.   Peer-group conformity seems to intensify at about age 13 or 14 and then wanes slowly as the teenager begins to arrive at a sense of identity that is more independent of the peer group (Giordano, Cernkovich, & DeMaris, 1993). For example, Thomas Berndt (1979) has found that among adolescents, the 12- to 14-year-olds are the most likely to say they would be influenced by their peers to do such mildly antisocial activities as soaping someone's windows on Halloween.

However—and this is a very important however—recent research tells us that the negative influence of the peer group has been considerably exaggerated in the popular press (Berndt, 1992; Brown, 1990). That is not to say that there is no effect. It takes only a trip to the local high school to see the conformity to specific dress or hair customs to be persuaded of the influence. But teens are more likely to follow their parents' advice about issues affecting their long-term future, and peer groups are more likely to support than oppose basic parental values. Teenagers report that when explicit peer pressure is exerted, it is more likely to be *against* misconduct than toward it (Brown, Clasen, & Eicher, 1986). The key here is to remember that to a considerable extent, adolescents *choose* their friends, their crowd. And they are likely to choose to associate with a group that shares their own family's values and attitudes. If the discrepancy between their own ideas and their friends' becomes too great, teens are more likely to move toward a more compatible group of friends than to be persuaded to shift toward the first group's values or behaviors. Those teenagers who get involved with a peer group that goes in for deviant activities of various sorts—smoking, drugs, delinquency—are not so much being pulled away from adult values by the crowd, as they are "driven to this crowd by parents' ineffective child-rearing practices" (Brown, 1990, p. 174).

Patterson's research, which I have often cited, reinforces this basic point. He finds that those kids who become involved with delinquent groups in early adolescence are those from families with ineffective parenting, poor monitoring, poor communication. Before adolescence, these young people are already lacking in the social skills that they would need to get along with most of their peers. They choose anti-social groups because that is the group that will accept them.

Other research supports the same conclusion. Andrew Fuligni, for example, (1993), finds that teenagers who perceive their parents as highly restrictive or as failing to involve the teen in family decision making are more likely to seek

R E S E A R C H   R E P O R T

Are African-American Adolescents More Susceptible to Peer Influence?

One assumption made by most adults and many social scientists is that African-American youth, more than any other group, are likely to be strongly peer oriented and to be more vulnerable to peer pressure. One typical argument is that because Black teenagers are more often living in single-parent families, they are more likely to depend on peers for affiliation and support. A recent study by Peggy Giordano and her colleagues (Giordano et al., 1993) calls this assumption into question.

Giordano studied a group of 942 teenagers, chosen as a representative sample of all adolescents living in Toledo, Ohio. Half the group was Black, the remainder mostly non-Hispanic Whites. These teens were asked a wide variety of questions about their friendships and their relationships with peers, such as:

"How important is it to you to do things your friends approve of?"

"How important is it to you to have a group of friends to hang around with."

They were also asked about family intimacy (e.g., "I'm closer to my parents than a lot of kids my age are") and about parental supervision and control.

In this sample, African-American adolescents reported significantly *more* family intimacy, *more* parental supervision and control, *less* need for peer approval, and *less* peer pressure than did White teens. This is only a single study, and there may be alternative interpretations possible. But it certainly raises questions about our common cultural assumptions.

Can you make any reasonable guesses about what qualities would characterize teenagers who are most and least susceptible to peer pressure? Personality characteristics? Intellectual skills? Family backgrounds?

advice from their peers and to be susceptible to peer influence. Similarly, Bradford Brown (Brown et al., 1993), in an analysis of data from the same large group of high school students that Dornbusch and Steinberg have studied, finds that students whose parents emphasize achievement, have good monitoring, and joint family decision making are least likely to be involved in the "druggie" crowd and most likely to be involved with peer groups labeled *populars*, or *jocks*, or *brains*.

Thus while peer influence is stronger in these adolescent years than at other times, especially at about age 13 and 14, for most teens the negative effect of peer pressure is rather small—a conclusion that probably surprises you.

Changes in Peer-Group Structure.   One point that is clear about the peer group during adolescence is that the group structure changes over time. The now classic early study is Dunphy's observation of the formation, dissolution and interaction of teenage groups in a high school in Sydney, Australia between 1958 and 1960 (Dunphy, 1963). He identified two important subvarieties of groups, using labels that have become widespread in writings on adolescence. The first type, which Dunphy called **cliques,** are made up of 4–6 young people who appear to be strongly attached to one another. Cliques have strong cohesiveness and high levels of intimate sharing. In the early years of adolescence, these cliques are almost entirely same-sex groups—a residual of the preadolescent pattern. Gradually, however, the cliques combine into larger sets Dunphy called **crowds,** made up of several cliques, some male and some female. Finally, the crowd breaks down again into heterosexual cliques and finally into loose associations of couples. In Dunphy's study, the period of the fully developed crowd was roughly between age 13 and 15—the very years when we see the greatest conformity to peer pressure.

Not all current observers of teenage peer groups agree with Dunphy that the crowd is made up simply of a collection of cliques. Bradford Brown (1990), for example, uses the term *crowd* to refer to the "reputation-based" group with which a young person is identified, either by choice or by peer designation. Groups with labels (in the United States, at least) like *jocks*, *brains*, *nerds*, *punks*, *burnouts*, *radicals*, *normals*, or *populars* are crowds in Brown's sense of the term. Cliques, in contrast, are always groups that the individual teenager chooses. But Brown would agree with Dunphy that in early adolescence, cliques are almost entirely same-sex; by late adolescence they have become mixed in gender.

Within any given school, these various cliques and reputation groups are organized into a clear, widely understood pecking order. Individual cliques often have a specific territory, such as a particular table in the lunchroom where they always sit. Among students in the seventh, eighth, and ninth grade in the United States—the years when cliques are most dominant in the social hierarchy of adolescence—the highest status cliques/crowds are usually made up of boys who play sports (often called *jocks*) and girls who are cheerleaders, although there are schools in which more scholastically oriented groups or those with other shared interests also have some social standing (Steinberg, 1993).

Whatever labels are applied, and whatever specific clique or crowd a teenager may identify with, there is agreement among theorists that the peer

What stage of teen group formation do you think this represents?

group performs the highly important function of helping the teenager make the shift from unisexual to heterosexual social relationships. The 13- or 14-year-old can begin to try out her new relationship skills in the somewhat protected environment of the crowd or clique; only after some confidence is developed do we see the beginnings of dating and later of more committed heterosexual pair relationships.

Heterosexual Relationships in Adolescence

Of all the changes in social relationships in adolescence, the most profound is the shift from the total dominance of same-sex friendships to heterosexual relationships. There is a very large cultural element in all this, of course. There are still many cultures in the world in which heterosexual contact during puberty or before marriage is tightly controlled and chaperoned; there are others in which there are no restrictions at all. Most Western cultures fall in between, with the current United States culture leaning strongly toward the no-restriction end of the continuum.

The heterosexual relationships we see in early and middle adolescence are clearly part of the preparation for assuming a full adult sexual identity. Physical sexuality is part of that role, but so are the skills of personal intimacy with the opposite sex, including flirting, communicating, and reading the form of social cues used by the other gender.

In Western societies, these skills are learned first in larger groups and then in dating pairs. Studies of adolescents in the United States in the 1980s suggest that dating begins most typically at 15 or 16, as you can see from Table 13.3, which shows results from a representative sample of Detroit teenagers (Thornton, 1990).

You'll recall from Chapter 11 that there are some ethnic differences in such heterosexual behavior. African-American teens begin dating and sexual experimentation earlier than do Anglos or Hispanics. Early dating and early sexual activity are also more common among the poor of every ethnic group and

Dating and clear heterosexual (or homosexual) coupling comes fairly late in adolescence and represents the end point of the whole sequence of peer-group structures.

TABLE 13.3
Age at First Date Among United States
Adolescents

Age	Males	Females
	(percentages)	
13 or younger	21.2	8.6
14	17.9	16.2
15	21.2	33.6
16	29.5	29.3
17–18	7.2	10.0

Source: Thornton, 1990, Table 1, pp. 246–247.

among those who experience relatively early puberty. Among girls, for example, those with early menarche are more likely to initiate sexual activity early than are same-age peers who have not yet reached menarche. Religious teachings and

The Real World
Homosexuality Among
Adolescents

I have talked about the normal sequence of peer relationships in adolescence as moving gradually toward committed heterosexual partnerships. But of course heterosexual experience is not the only kind teenagers may have. Homosexual contact is also fairly common, especially for boys and especially in childhood or early adolescence. Research on homosexuality in teenagers is not abundant, but indicates that perhaps 15 percent of boys and 10 percent of girls have at least one homosexual contact; 2 to 3 percent report continuing homosexual relationships (Dreyer, 1982). Among adults, homosexuality appears to characterize 4 to 6 percent of the population in Western countries (for which we have the best data) although estimates vary widely (Gonsiorek & Weinrich, 1991).

Recent evidence has strengthened the hypothesis that homosexuality may be built-in, either genetically or through hormone patterning in utero. Most convincing is a recent twin study by Bailey and Pillard (1991). In this sample, when one twin was homosexual the probability that the second twin was also homosexual was 52 percent among identical twins, but only 22 percent among fraternal twins. By comparison, the equivalent "concordance rate" was only 11 percent among pairs of biologically unrelated boys adopted into the same families.

Such biological evidence does not mean that there are no environmental causes of homosexuality. No behavior is entirely controlled by either nature or nurture, as I have

said many times. At the very least, we know that nearly half the identical twins in the Bailey and Pillard study did *not* share the same sexual preferences. Something beyond biology must be at work, although we do not yet know what environmental factors may be involved.

Whatever the cause, homosexual teenagers are a minority. These adolescents face high levels of prejudice and stereotyping, and are at high risk for a variety of problems. In one study, for example, four-fifths of homosexual teens interviewed in Minneapolis had deteriorating school performance, and more than a quarter dropped out of high school (Remafedi, 1987a). They must also cope with the decision about whether to "come out" about their homosexuality. Those who do come out are far more likely to tell peers than parents, although there is a risk attached to the decision to tell peers. In his Minneapolis study, Remafedi found that 41 percent of homosexual male youths had lost a friend over the issue (Remafedi, 1987b); many also experience harassment from peers. Some research suggests that as many as two-thirds of homosexual youth have not told their parents (Rotheram-Borus, Rosario, & Koopman, 1991).

There is obviously much that we do not know about homosexual adolescents. But it is a reasonable hypothesis that the years of adolescence may be particularly stressful for this subgroup. Like ethnic-minority youth, homosexual teens have an additional task facing them in forming a clear identity.

individual attitudes about the appropriate age for dating and sexual behavior also make a difference, as does family structure. Girls from divorced or remarried families, for example, report earlier dating and higher levels of sexual experience than do girls from intact families, and those with strong religious identity report less (Bingham, Miller, & Adams, 1990; Miller & Moore, 1990). But for every group, these are years of experimentation with heterosexual relationships.

Individual Differences Among Adolescents

Variations in Personality

In Chapter 2 and in Chapter 8, I talked about variations in infant and child temperament and about the impact such variations may have in a child's experience of childhood. In adolescence, equivalent discussions are normally cast in terms of **personality** rather than temperament, although the two concepts clearly overlap. Personality is the broader term, describing enduring qualities in the way each person goes about relating to the people and objects in the world around themselves. Whether we are gregarious or shy, whether we plunge into new things or hold back, whether we are independent or dependent, whether we are confident or uncertain—all of these (and many more) are usually thought of as elements of personality, presumed to persist over time. Temperament is perhaps best thought of as a *subset* of personality traits—those inherited response patterns that affect the general style of the child's reactions, such as activity versus passivity or a tendency to approach rather than withdraw. Temperament is thus one of the important building blocks of personality, the "built-in bias" in the system if you will. But personality is also clearly affected by the reinforcement patterns within the family, by the security or insecurity of the first attachment, and by many other factors.

As with theorists who study temperament, those who study personality have searched for a small set of dimensions that could adequately describe individual differences. This search has met with a good deal of recent success. Studies of adults by Robert McCrae and Paul Costa and others (McCrae, 1990; McCrae & John, 1992) have shown that personality can be well-described as varying along five main dimensions: extraversion, agreeableness, conscientiousness, neuroticism, and openness/intellect, described somewhat more fully in Table 13.4.

It now looks as if these same five dimensions may give us a good description of personality in adolescents as well. In a recent study, Oliver John and his associates (John et al., 1994) asked 350 mothers of 12- and 13-year-old boys to use a method called a *Q-sort* to describe their sons. In this method, the individual is given a set of 100 cards, each with a single descriptive term or phrase, such as "is talkative," or "has a high aspiration level," or "thin-skinned." The subject uses these cards to describe an individual by sorting them into an array of nine piles. At one end, in the "1" pile, go those descriptive terms that are least like the individual being described. At the other end, in the "9" pile, go those terms that are most characteristic of the individual, with the remaining cards falling in between. The additional restriction is that the rater must create a normal distribution of

TABLE 13.4
The "Big Five" Personality Traits Identified by McCrae and Costa

Trait	Qualities of Individual High in That Trait
Extraversion	Active, assertive, energetic, enthusiastic, outgoing, talkative
Agreeableness	Affectionate, forgiving, generous, kind, sympathetic, trusting
Conscientiousness	Efficient, organized, planful, reliable, responsible, thorough
Neuroticism	Anxious, self-pitying, tense, touchy, unstable, worrying
Openness/Intellect	Artistic, curious, imaginative, insightful, original, wide interests

Sources: McCrae & Costa, 1990; John, 1994, Table 1, p. 161.

cards: only a few cards may be placed in the "1" and "9" piles, while the largest number must go in the middle categories. This forces the rater to identify those few specific characteristics that are most like or least like the individual being described. The investigator can then look and see whether certain clusters of traits or qualities tend to go together across many individuals.

In his study of adolescents, John found that traits involved in each of the "big five" personality dimensions did indeed tend to cluster together in the ratings made by mothers of their teenage sons. Furthermore, the scores obtained by each boy on each of the five personality traits predicted other behavior in ways that you'd expect. For example, boys who reported relatively high rates of delinquent acts were described by their mothers as lower in agreeableness and conscientiousness, and higher in extraversion than were nondelinquent boys. Those who performed well in school were described by their mothers as somewhat higher in conscientiousness and openness. Those who were described by their teachers as more depressed were high in neuroticism and low in conscientiousness.

This one study is not the final word on personality variations among adolescents. Among other things, no such study has been done with teenage girls, so we do not know if the same five dimensions would adequately describe them. And of course such a study does not tell us where such personality variations may come from—how much they may be genetically determined and how much a product of experience. But it is very interesting to find that the structure or pattern of personality evident in adults is already visible in adolescence.

Deviant Behavior: Delinquency

A second dimension on which teenagers differ is the extent to which they engage in delinquent behavior. I'll have a lot more to say about many types of deviant behavior in the next chapter, when I talk about atypical development. But because delinquency is primarily a problem of the adolescent years, I need to say a word here as well.

Delinquency belongs in the general category of *conduct disorders* I described in Chapter 1. Those children labeled as delinquent show not only the high levels of the bullying, argumentativeness, or disobedience that are common to all conduct disorders, but also some deliberate violation of the law, including such things as shoplifting, auto theft, breaking and entering, smoking marijuana or using hard drugs, fighting, using weapons, attacks on others, and the like.

Some antisocial or delinquent behaviors, such as fighting, threatening others, cheating, lying, or stealing, are just as common in 4- and 5-year-olds as they are in adolescents (Achenbach & Edelbrock, 1981). In adolescence, however, the number of youngsters who display such behaviors increases considerably, and the behaviors often become more serious, more lethal, and more consistently a pattern.

It is extremely difficult to estimate how many teenagers engage in such behavior. One window on the problem is to look at the number of arrests—although arrest rates are arguably only the tip of the iceberg. Over one million juveniles in the U.S. are arrested each year, which is 3 to 4 percent of all youngsters between ages 10 and 17. Among those 15 to 17, the arrest rate is roughly 11 percent (Dryfoos, 1990). In fact, the rate of arrests among these older teens is higher than in any other age group across the entire lifespan. Many of these arrests are for relatively minor infractions: shoplifting, vandalism, liquor law violations, or the like. But about a third of these arrests are for serious crimes, including murder, burglary, rape and arson.

Self-reports of delinquency by adolescents suggest even higher rates. Data from the National Youth Survey, conducted between 1976 and 1980, indicate that four-fifths of youngsters between age 11 and age 17 say that they have been delinquent at some time or another. One-third admitted truancy and disorderly conduct, and a fifth said they had committed criminal acts, most often physical assaults or thefts (Dryfoos, 1990). More recent, smaller studies suggest similar rates today among American youth.

Just as conduct disorders are much more common among preschool and elementary school-age boys than girls, delinquent acts and arrests are far more common among teenage males than females. Among those actually arrested, the ratio is more than four to one; in self-reports the ratios vary, but the more physically violent the act, the larger the discrepancy.

Types of Delinquents.   All delinquents seem to share certain characteristics. In particular, like unpopular children at earlier ages, delinquent teenagers have deficits in *social* understanding. They are less skilled in reading others and in learning the social rules (Schonfeld et al., 1988). Delinquents are also likely to have parents (especially fathers) who are antisocial or criminal. But within this basic set of similarities, there are variations. The most frequently used category system includes two distinct subgroups: (1) *Socialized-subcultural delinquents*, who hang around with bad companions, stay out late, have a strong allegiance to their peer group or gang, and may commit various crimes as part of their peer activities. (2) *Unsocialized-psychopathic delinquents*, who are more often loners and seem to lack conscience or guilt. These are young people who appear to enjoy conflict and to have little trust in anyone.

Socialized delinquents most often come from poor neighborhoods and grow up in families with erratic discipline and little affection—a style that would be classed as ignoring or rejecting in the category system I have been describing. As I mentioned in Chapter 10, families in the same kind of poor neighborhoods

Teenage gangs or delinquent groups may strengthen tendencies toward illegal or high-risk behaviors. But young people drawn to such groups are likely to have a history of misbehavior or peer rejection, and/or to have ineffective parents.

R E S E A R C H   R E P O R T

Delinquency Among Girls

When we use the term "delinquent," most of us think immediately of teenage boys. But although the incidence of delinquency or criminality in girls is much lower, it is not zero. Girls are much less likely to be involved in forms of delinquency that involve violence, just as girls are consistently less aggressive at every age. But girls do get involved in delinquent behaviors, such as shoplifting or the use of illegal drugs (Zoccolillo, 1993).

An interesting study in New Zealand by Avshalom Caspi and his colleagues (Caspi et al., 1993) provides some interesting insights into the possible origins of such delinquent behavior. The sample of students involved in this study included all the children born in one year (1972–1973) in one town, a group of more than 1,000. The children were tested and assessed repeatedly, at age 3, 5, 7, 9, 11, 13, and 15. In this particular analysis, Caspi looked at rates of delinquency among the girls, as a function of the earliness or lateness of their menarche and whether they went to an all-girl or a mixed-sex high school. Caspi's hypothesis was that girls who attended a mixed-sex secondary school would be more likely to be involved in delinquent activities because they would have more rule-breaking models (delinquent boys) among their peers. He also expected to find that girls with early puberty would be more likely to become delinquent, especially in mixed-sex schools.

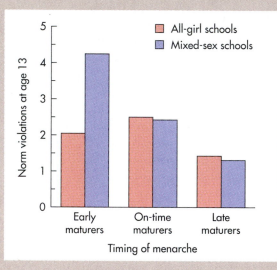

These hypotheses were generally confirmed, although there are some interesting wrinkles. At age 13, the girls were asked to report on "norm violations," which included a variety of mildly delinquent acts, such as breaking windows, stealing from pupils at school, getting drunk, swearing loudly in public, or making prank telephone calls. As you can see in Figure 13.5, such norm violations were most common among early maturing girls attending coed schools. Further analysis shows that this difference is almost entirely contributed by a small group of girls who had had a history high levels of aggression earlier in childhood *and* who had early puberty. Early maturing girls in coed schools who had no such history showed no heightened rate of delinquency.

To make it still more complicated, Caspi found that at age 15, early developing girls in coed schools continued to have high rates of delinquency, but at this age the highest rate of delinquency was found among *on-time-puberty* girls attending coed schools. Puberty, whether early or on-time, thus seems to increase the likelihood that vulnerable girls will get involved with antisocial peers. But this is only true of girls in coed schools.

I find this study fascinating not only because it points to the complex relationships between physical maturation and social relationships, but also because it offers an interesting argument in favor of all-girl schools. . .

whose children do *not* become delinquent are distinguished most by a single ingredient: high levels of maternal love. Young people whose mothers are loving and affectionate toward them are simply far less likely to show delinquency, regardless of poverty conditions (Glueck & Glueck, 1972; McCord, McCord, & Zola, 1959).

Psychopathic delinquency, in contrast, may be found equally often among teenagers from every social class level and as often in intact families as in broken homes (Achenbach, 1982). It is characterized by high rates of a variety of different types of criminal acts, often beginning quite early in childhood, and has a high rate of persistence into adulthood.

Patterson's theoretical model (recall Figure 1.3, page 11), and a great deal of confirming evidence, points to a complex of factors causing either type of delinquency. A significant early experience is failure in early parental discipline and/or direct reinforcement for aggressive behavior within the family (Patterson, Capaldi, & Bank, 1991). Other influences on the system are the child's temperament, protective factors like maternal loving affection and the sustaining conditions, such as lack of social skills or poor peer acceptance (Bates et al., 1991). These rejected/antisocial youngsters then tend to band together, further supporting one another's antisocial behavior. Such teenagers typically show high levels of many other types of deviant behavior as well, including high levels of drug and alcohol use, truancy or dropping out of school, and other high-risk behaviors. For example, in one longitudinal study of a sample of high school students from Colorado, Donovan and Jessor (1985) found correlations among boys of .54 between delinquent behavior and marijuana usage, .41 between delinquent behavior and drunken episodes, and .36 between delinquent acts and frequency of sexual experience. The correlations were similar for girls, but somewhat lower.

At each step along this deviant pathway there are diversion possibilities, but the further along one goes, the more difficult it becomes to deflect and the more persistent the deviant behavior becomes. Many teens who commit only occasional delinquent acts show no further problem in adulthood. For them, mild delinquent behavior is merely a phase. But those who show a syndrome of delinquent and high risk behavior, who come from families with low warmth and ineffective control, are quite likely to show criminality in their adult lives.

At the risk of repeating myself, one other point deserves emphasis: Many adults, observing the high rate of delinquent behavior or substance abuse among teenagers, attribute the problem to the "bad influence" of the peer group. Somehow, we think, the kids would be o.k. if they hadn't somehow fallen in with "bad companions." But the evidence provides little support for such a belief. Certainly, teenage peer groups sometimes do seduce youngsters into riskier, less-approved behavior than they might otherwise engage in. But the crucial factor seems to be the fact that a young person is drawn to such a group of peers in the first place, rather than any subsequent behavioral contamination by the group. Delinquency, drug and alcohol use or abuse, risky sexual behavior—all these are symptoms of deeper forms of deviance, many of which have their roots in earlier developmental periods.

How might we go about sorting out the causality here? What kind of study would we need to do in order to tell whether it is the peer group that lures young people into delinquent acts or the young people inclined toward such activities who are drawn to like-minded peers?

The Impact of Culture and Context

The larger culture in which the teenager is embedded naturally continues to have a significant effect on the adolescent's development. Adolescents in most Western countries continue to watch several hours of television a day, although viewing does drop somewhat in the teenage years (Comstock, 1991). Cultural values, specific habits, and attitudes are all communicated through this medium. The broad economic climate also affects families profoundly, in turn affecting teenagers.

I talked at some length about the impact of poverty in Chapter 10, and need not repeat myself here except to note that the effects may be especially severe on adolescents. Adolescents living in inner city poverty, especially, are likely to attend schools with fewer economic resources and with higher levels of crime and violence. They also face bleak job prospects in early adulthood. Girls in such settings are more likely to bear children early, most often out of wedlock (Panel on High Risk Youth, 1993). These are extremely difficult handicaps to overcome. Thus far, clearly effective intervention programs to surmount these problems have not been devised. There is only agreement that intervention efforts need to involve all the different groups and institutions in the system: the school, the neighborhood, the family, the children. Focusing on the school alone is not enough.

Joining the Work World: The Impact of Jobs on Teenagers

For many youngsters in the United States, a new point of contact with the larger culture is added during adolescence: a job.

In earlier historical eras, (and in many cultures around the world today), teenagers were already considered adults and fulfilled normal adult work responsibilities. They worked in the mines, in the fields, herding animals, and fishing. Child labor laws changed this picture drastically in the nineteenth century in most industrialized countries. Today, adolescents are in school for many hours each day and are not available for adult work—although the typical school year, with a long summer vacation, was intended quite explicitly to allow young people to join in the labor of farming and harvest during the growing season.

Yet, despite their hours in school, and despite the relative lack of importance of agricultural work, increasingly today, adolescents have jobs. Beginning in about 1950 in the United States, teenage employment rates have risen quite steadily. Today, roughly three-fifths of all high school juniors have some kind of formal part-time job during at least part of the school year, and the great majority of students have had at least some work experience before they graduate (Bachman & Schulenberg, 1993; Greenberger & Steinberg, 1986).

For some, such work is an economic necessity. Others work in order to support their favorite hobbies or habits—to earn the money to buy a stereo, perhaps a car, or to go out for pizza with their friends. Parents are frequently very supportive of such work on the grounds that it "builds character" and teaches young people about "real life." Here's one parental voice:

Most part-time teen jobs are low-skill and low-paying, like this one. Such jobs do not appear to build character, but rather to have negative effects.

> Let's face it. . . some time in life, someone is going to tell you what to do. . . . I think work is the only place to learn to deal with it. . . . Parents can give you a little discipline, but it isn't accepted. . . . You can't learn that in school, because there is another so-called tyrant, the teacher. But then they get . . . a boss, and you get out there and learn it. (Greenberger & Steinberg, 1986, p. 39).

But are parents right about such beneficial effects of work? Does it really teach responsibility and reliability? Quite the contrary. Results of several decades of research—at least for teenagers in the United States, for whom we have data—suggest that the more hours adolescents work, the more *negative* the consequences are.

In the largest single study, Jerald Bachman and John Schulenberg (1993) accumulated information from over 70,000 seniors in the graduating classes of

1985 through 1989. Subjects were drawn each year from both private and public schools in every state in the country. Roughly four-fifths of the students—both males and females—worked at least a few hours per week, most of them for pay. Nearly half of the boys (46.5 percent) and more than a third of the girls (38.4 percent) worked more than 20 hours per week.

Bachman and Schulenberg found that for both males and females, the more hours a student worked, the more he or she used drugs (alcohol, cigarettes, marijuana, cocaine), the more aggression he or she showed toward peers, the more arguments he or she had with parents, the less sleep he or she got, the less often he or she ate breakfast, the less exercise he or she had, and the less satisfied he or she was with life. An impressive list of negatives, isn't it?

Bachman and Schulenberg do not report on a link between school grades and outside employment, but that information can be gleaned from the same Steinberg and Dornbusch study of Wisconsin and California teens I have talked about several times (Steinberg & Dornbusch, 1991; Steinberg, Fegley, & Dornbusch, 1993). In this case, they have employment information from 5,300 ninth to twelfth graders, data collected in 1987 and 1988.

To give you some sense of the magnitude of the effects, Figure 13.6 shows one result from each of these two studies: the relationship between work and school grades from the Steinberg and Dornbusch study and the link between heavy alcohol use and work from the Bachman and Schulenberg study. I should note, by the way, that Steinberg and Dornbusch found essentially the same pattern of results for all the ethnic groups in their study and for students from every economic level. So this is a widespread and significant effect.

Causal Effects, or Self-Selection?   At this point, some of you are undoubtedly thinking that results like those in Figure 13.6 may not mean that working during the high school years causes bad effects. Instead, they may reflect self-selection: those students who are least interested in school, who already hang out with others who smoke or drink more, may be the same ones who choose to work more. Steinberg and his colleagues (Steinberg et al., 1993) were able to check this by looking at a subset of their sample over time. They found that those who later worked 20 hours a week had indeed been less involved with or committed to school in earlier years, which illustrates the effect of self-selection. But after they began working, these same students became even more withdrawn from school and showed increases in both drug use and delinquency, and lower self-reliance than they had shown before they began work.

These are not comforting findings. It is difficult to escape the conclusion that teenage employment distracts young people from academic tasks. What is more, there appear to be few, if any, compensations: teens with jobs do not show higher self-reliance or self-esteem, as many theorists and policy planners had supposed. They also seem to learn some less-than-ideal lessons about the "real world," because they typically work in low-paying, repetitive, often meaningless jobs in which authority is arbitrary and unethical practices, such as stealing from your employer, are common (Greenberger & Steinberg, 1986).

The one area in which we do see some positive benefit from adolescent employment is in prospects for future jobs and in later wages. For example, high

What was your own work experience as a teenager? What lessons, if any, do you think you learned from that work? In light of your own experience and the data from this study, would you want your own children to work when they are teenagers?

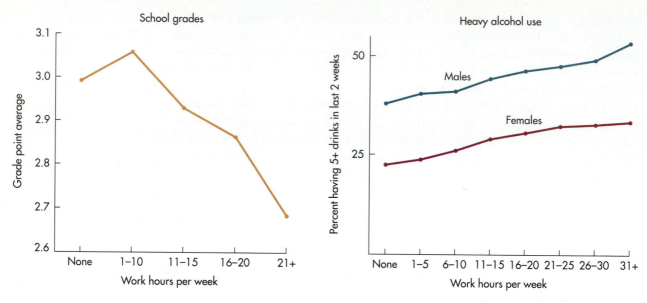

FIGURE 13.6

Evidence for the negative effect of teenage employment: data on the left come from Steinberg and Dornbusch's study; the data on the right come from Bachman and Schulenberg. (Sources: Steinberg & Dornbusch, 1991, upper section of Figure 1, p. 308; Bachman & Schulenberg, 1993, upper right section of Figure 1, p. 226.)

school seniors who have had part-time jobs are more likely to report that they have full-time work lined up after their graduation. And those who see their jobs as providing skills that will be useful in the future seem to get some benefits and to be troubled by fewer negative side effects (Mortimer et al., 1992). But this benefit was seen primarily for those whose teenage employment was in skilled areas, such as skilled trades, factories, or health care. Students who have worked only in fast food restaurants, in retail sales, babysitting, or the like do not seem to have any leg up on future employment.

All of this does not mean that no teenager should ever work. There are obviously situations that will demand such employment, and certain types of skill training that may offer an important counterweight to the potential negative effects. But findings like these certainly should make parents pause before they (we) encourage teenagers to work on the grounds that it will build character.

SUMMARY

1. Self-definitions become still more abstract at adolescence, with more emphasis on enduring, internal qualities and ideology.
2. Teenagers also increasingly define themselves in terms that include both masculine and feminine traits. When both are high, the individual is described as

androgynous. High levels of androgyny are associated with higher self-esteem in both male and female adolescents.

3. Erikson emphasized that adolescents must go through a crisis and a redefinition of the self, an idea also emphasized in Marcia's model of identity formation. Many adolescents clearly do go through such a process, but we do not know whether all do or what the timing of such a reexamination may be.

4. Self-esteem drops somewhat at the beginning of adolescence, (especially for those who enter junior high school at the start of puberty) and then rises steadily through the teen years.

5. Concepts of relationships also undergo change, becoming more flexible, more shaded. Friendships are increasingly seen as adaptive and changeable.

6. Adolescent-parent interactions typically become somewhat more conflicting in early adolescence, possibly linked to the physical changes of puberty. But the attachment to parents remains strong.

7. Authoritative family interactions continue to be the optimal pattern at adolescence. Teenagers in such families are more self-reliant, use fewer drugs, and have higher self-esteem than do those in neglecting or authoritarian families.

8. Peer relationships become increasingly important, both quantitatively and qualitatively. Theorists emphasize that peers serve an important function as a bridge between the dependence of childhood and the independence of adulthood.

9. Teenagers are most vulnerable to the pressure of their peers in fairly early adolescence, at about age 13 or 14. But the effect of peer pressure appears to be far more benign than most psychologists had previously believed.

10. At this same time, peer groups shift from same-sex cliques to mixed-sex crowds.

11. Dating normally begins slightly later, although there is wide variability.

12. Recent evidence indicates that adolescent personality, like adult personality, can be described as varying along five dimensions: extraversion, agreeableness, conscientiousness, neuroticism, and openness/intellect.

13. Delinquent acts also increase at adolescence, especially among boys, but not all teenagers show such behavior. Several types of delinquents have been identified, with different developmental pathways.

14. Delinquent behavior is correlated with high levels of other risk-taking, including both drug and alcohol use.

15. Part-time employment by teenagers has become very common. There is no indication that employment "builds character." Instead it is associated with lower school performance and higher rates of delinquent behavior.

KEY TERMS

androgyny

cliques

crowds

foreclosure

identity achievement

identity diffusion

moratorium

personality

SUGGESTED READINGS

Feldman, S. S., & Elliott, G. R. (Eds.), (1990). *At the threshold. The developing adolescent*. Cambridge, MA: Harvard University Press. Once again I recommend this first-rate edited volume. It includes many excellent chapters addressing issues I have touched on in this chapter.

Greenberger, E., & Steinberg, L. (1986). *When teenagers work. The psychological and social costs of adolescent employment*. New York: Basic Books. A persuasive, clearly written, surprising book about the effects of teenage employment.

Panel on High Risk Youth (1993). *Losing generations. Adolescents in high risk settings*. Commission on Behavioral and Social Sciences and Education, National Research Council. Washington, DC: National Academy Press. If you are looking for a single source that will review all of what we currently know about the impact of poverty on adolescents, this is the place to look.

Steinberg, L. & Levine, A. (1990). *You and your adolescent. A parent's guide for ages 10 to 20*. New York: Harper & Row. This absolutely first class book is clearly intended for parents, so it is not overly technical. But because it is written by one of the most innovative researchers studying adolescence, it is strongly based on research.

Summing Up Adolescence

BASIC CHARACTERISTICS OF ADOLESCENCE

A number of experts on adolescence argue that it makes sense to divide the period of years from 12 to about 20 into two sub-periods, one beginning at 11 or 12, the other perhaps at 16 or 17. Some label these as *adolescence* and *youth* (Keniston, 1970), others as *early* and *late* adolescence (Brooks-Gunn, 1988) However we label them, there are distinct differences.

Early adolescence is, almost by definition, a time of transition, a time in which there is significant change in virtually every aspect of the child's functioning. Late adolescence is more a time of consolidation,

when the young person establishes a cohesive new identity, with clearer goals and role commitments. Norma Haan (1981) offered a helpful way of thinking about this difference, based on Piaget's concepts of assimilation and accommodation. Early adolescence, she said, is a time dominated by assimilation, while late adolescence is primarily a time of accommodation.

The 12- or 13-year-old is assimilating an enormous amount of new physical, social, and intellectual experiences. While all this absorption is going on, but before she digests it, the young person is in a more or less perpetual state of disequilibrium. Old patterns, old schemes, no longer work very well, but new ones have not been

established. It is during this early period that the peer group is maximally important. Ultimately, the 16- or 17- or 18-year-old begins to make the needed accommodations, pulls the threads together and establishes a new identity, new patterns of social relationships, new goals, and new roles.

I've summarized the various aspects of development in these two periods in the Summary Table, but let me say a bit more about each.

Early Adolescence

In some ways the early years of adolescence have a lot in common with the early years of toddlerhood. Two-year-olds are famous for their negativism and for their constant

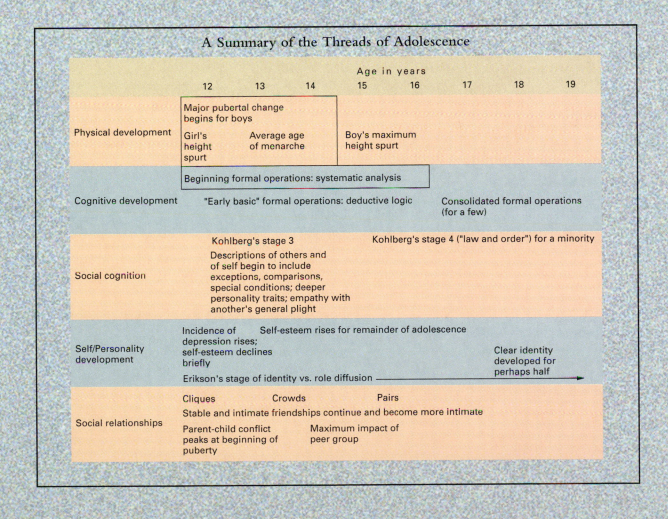

A Summary of the Threads of Adolescence

	Age in years							
	12	13	14	15	16	17	18	19
Physical development	Major pubertal change begins for boys Girl's height spurt	Average age of menarche		Boy's maximum height spurt				
Cognitive development	Beginning formal operations: systematic analysis "Early basic" formal operations: deductive logic					Consolidated formal operations (for a few)		
Social cognition	Kohlberg's stage 3 Descriptions of others and of self begin to include exceptions, comparisons, special conditions; deeper personality traits; empathy with another's general plight			Kohlberg's stage 4 ("law and order") for a minority				
Self/Personality development	Incidence of depression rises; self-esteem declines briefly Erikson's stage of identity vs. role diffusion ———	Self-esteem rises for remainder of adolescence					Clear identity developed for perhaps half	
Social relationships	Cliques	Crowds		Pairs				
	Stable and intimate friendships continue and become more intimate							
	Parent-child conflict peaks at beginning of puberty		Maximum impact of peer group					

push for more independence. At the same time they are struggling to learn a vast array of new skills. Teenagers show many of these same qualities, albeit at much more abstract levels. We see a parallel rise in conflict or negativism with parents, much of which centers around issues of independence—they want to come and go when they please, listen to the music they prefer at maximum volume, and wear the clothing and hair styles that are currently "in."

Like the negativism of the 2-year-old, it is easy to overstate the depth or breadth of the conflict between young teenagers and their parents. It is important to keep in mind that we are not talking here about major turmoil, but only a temporary increase in disagreements or disputes. The depiction of adolescence as full of *storm and stress* is as much an exaggeration as is the phrase "terrible twos." But both ages are characterized by more confrontations with parents over limits than we see at other periods.

While this push for independence is going on, the young adolescent is also facing a whole new set of demands and skills to be learned—new social skills, new levels of cognitive complexity found in formal operations tasks. The drop in self-esteem we see at the beginning of adolescence seem to be linked to this surplus of new demands and changes, as is a rapid rise in the rate of depression—a pattern I'll talk about in the next chapter. A number of investigators have found that those adolescents who have the greatest number of simultaneous changes at the beginning of puberty—changing to junior high school, moving to a new town or new house, perhaps a parental separation or divorce—also show the greatest loss in self-esteem, the largest rise in problem behavior, and the biggest drop in grade point average (Eccles & Midgley, 1990; Simmons, Burgeson, & Reef, 1988). Young adolescents who can cope with these changes one at a time show fewer symptoms of stress.

Facing major stressful demands, the 2-year-old uses Mom (or some other central attachment figure) as a safe base for exploring the world, returning for reassurance when fearful. Young adolescents seem

to do the same with the family, using it as a safe base from which to explore the rest of the world, including the world or peer relationships. Parents of young adolescents must try to find a difficult balance between providing the needed security, often in the form of clear rules and limits, and still allowing independence—just as the parent of a 2-year-old must walk the fine line between allowing exploration and keeping the child safe. Among teenagers, as among toddlers, the most confident and successful are those whose families manage this balancing act well.

Still a third way in which theorists have likened the young teenager to the 2-year-old is in egocentrism. David Elkind (1967) suggested some years ago that there is a rise in egocentrism in adolescence. This new egocentrism, according to Elkind, has two facets: (1) the belief that "others in our immediate vicinity are as concerned with our thoughts and behavior as we ourselves are" (Elkind & Bowen, 1979, p. 38), which Elkind describes as having an *imaginary audience*, and (2) the possession of a *personal fable*, a tendency to consider their own ideas and feelings unique and singularly important. This is typically accompanied by a sense of invulnerability—a feeling that may lie behind the adolescent's apparent attraction to high-risk behaviors.

Elkind's own research (Elkind & Bowen, 1979) shows that preoccupation with others' views of the self—what he calls imaginary audience behavior—peaks at about age 13 to 14. Teenagers this age are most likely to say that if they went to a party where they did not know most of the kids, they would wonder *a lot* about what the other kids were thinking of them. They also report that they worry a lot when someone is watching them work and feel desperately embarrassed if they discover a grease spot on their clothes or have newly erupted pimples. Of course younger children and adults may also worry about these things, but seem to be much less disturbed or immobilized by these worries than are 13- and 14-year-olds. You'll recall that this is the same age at which teens seem to be most susceptible to peer pressure and the peak age for the type of peer group Dunphy calls the crowd.

Drawing a parallel between the early adolescent and the toddler also makes sense in that both age groups face the task of establishing a separate identity. The toddler must separate herself from the symbiotic relationship with Mom or central care giver. She must figure out not only that she is separate but that she has abilities and qualities. Physical maturation also allows her new levels of independent exploration. The young adolescent must separate himself from his family and from his identity as a child, and begin to form a new identity as an adult. This, too, is accompanied by major maturational changes that make new levels and kinds of independence possible. In both cases, these changes are accompanied by a kind of self-preoccupation and by increases in confrontations with care givers.

Late Adolescence

To carry the basic analogy further, late adolescence is more like the preschool years. Major changes have been weathered, and a new balance has been achieved. The physical upheavals of puberty are mostly complete, the family system has changed to allow more independence and freedom, and the beginnings of a new identity have been created. This period is not without its strains. For most young people, a clear identity is not achieved until college age, if then, so the identity process continues. And the task of forming emotionally intimate sexual or presexual partnerships is a key task of late adolescence. Nonetheless, I think Haan is correct that this later period is more one of accommodation than assimilation. At the very least we know that it is accompanied by rising levels of self-esteem and declining levels of family confrontation or conflict.

CENTRAL PROCESSES AND THEIR CONNECTIONS

In others of these summaries, I have suggested that changes in one or another of the facets of development may be central to the constellation of transformations we see at a given age. In infancy, underlying physiological change along with the creation of a first central attachment appear to have such key causal roles; in the preschool years, cognitive changes seem especially dominant, while among school-age children, both cognitive and social changes appear to be formative. In adolescence, there is significant change in *every* domain. At this point, we simply do not have the research data that clarify the basic causal connections among the transformations in these various areas. Still, we have *some* information about linkages.

The Role of Puberty

The most obvious place to begin is with puberty itself. Puberty not only defines the beginning of early adolescence, it clearly affects all other facets of the young person's development, either directly or indirectly.

Direct effects might be seen in several ways. Most clearly, the surges of pubertal hormones stimulate sexual interest while they also trigger body changes that make adult sexuality and fertility possible. These changes seem inescapably causally linked to the gradual shift from same-sex peer groupings to heterosexual crowds and finally to heterosexual pair relationships.

Hormones and Family Relationships. Hormone changes may also be directly implicated in the increases in confrontation or conflict between parents and children and the rise in various kinds of aggressive or delinquent behavior. Steinberg's research suggests such a direct link because he finds pubertal stage and not age to be the critical variable in predicting the level of adolescent-parent conflict. Other investigators have found that in girls, the rise in estradiol at the beginning of puberty is associated with increases in verbal aggression and a loss of impulse control, while in boys, increases in testosterone are correlated with increases in irritability and impatience (Paikoff & Brooks-Gunn, 1990). But there are also many studies in which no such connection is found, which has led most theorists to conclude that the connections between pubertal hormones and changes in adolescent social behavior are considerably more complicated than we had first imagined.

One of the complications is that the physical changes of puberty have highly significant indirect effects as well. When the child's body grows and becomes more like that of an adult, the parents begin to treat the child differently and the child begins to see himself as a soon-to-be-adult. Both of these changes may be linked to the brief rise in parent-adolescent confrontation and may help to trigger some of the searching self-examinations that are part of this period of life.

The adolescent's pubertal changes also require other adaptations from the parents that change the family dynamics. It can be very confusing to parents to deal with a young teenager who seems, simultaneously, to demand both more independence, authority, and power, and more nurturance and guidance. What is more, the presence of a sexually charged pubescent teen may reawaken the parents' own unresolved adolescent issues, just when they are themselves facing a sense of physical decline in their forties or fifties. Then, too, teenagers may stay up late, severely restricting private time for parents. Perhaps, then, it is not surprising that many parents (particularly fathers) report that marital satisfaction is at its lowest ebb during their children's adolescence (Rollins & Galligan, 1978). Taking all this together, you can see why it is so difficult to sort out the direct and the indirect effects of pubertal hormone changes on social behavior.

Puberty and Cognitive Change. Equally difficult to demonstrate is the possible link between the physical changes of puberty and cognitive changes, particularly the shift to formal operations. That there may be *some* connection between the two seems plausible. As J. M. Tanner says:

> There is clearly no reason to suppose that the link between maturation of [brain] structure and appearance of [cognitive] function suddenly ceases at age 6 or 10 or 13. On the contrary, there is every reason to believe that the higher intellectual abilities also appear only when maturation of certain structures is complete (Tanner, 1970, p. 123).

But if there is a connection, it is clearly not an invariable one because we know that not all adolescents (or adults) ever develop formal operational thinking. So brain

changes at puberty cannot be the sole cause of the development of these most abstract forms of thinking. Neurological or hormonal changes at adolescence may be *necessary* for further cognitive gains—although even that has not been clearly established—but they cannot be *sufficient* conditions for such developments.

The Role of Cognitive Changes at Adolescence

An equally attractive possibility to many theorists has been the proposition that it is the cognitive changes that are central. No one is arguing that the cognitive shift from concrete to formal operations is causing pubertal changes. But many have argued that cognitive development is central to many of the other changes we see at adolescence, including changes in the self-concept, the process of identity formation, increases in level of moral reasoning, and changes in peer relationships.

There is ample evidence, for example, that the greater abstractness of the child's self-concept and his descriptions of others are intimately connected to the broader changes in cognitive functioning (Harter, 1990). The emergence of concrete operations at 7 or 8 is reflected in the child's use of trait labels to describe himself and others; the emergence of formal operations is reflected in self-descriptions that focus more and more on interior states and descriptions of others that are both flexible and based on subtle inferences from behavior. Similarly, you know from Chapter 12 that the emergence of higher stages of moral reasoning seems to require the ability to use formal operations logic.

Some ability to use formal operations may also be necessary but not sufficient for the formation of a clear identity. One of the characteristics of formal operations thinking is the ability to imagine possibilities that you have never experienced and to manipulate ideas in your head. These new skills may help to foster the broad questioning of old ways, old values, old patterns that are a central part of the identity-formation process. Several studies show that among high school and college students, those in Marcia's identity achievement or moratorium statuses are also much more likely to be using formal operations reasoning than are those in the diffusion or foreclosure statuses (Leadbeater & Dionne, 1981; Rowe & Marcia, 1980). In Rowe and Marcia's study, the *only* individuals who showed full identity achievement were those who were also using full formal operations. But the converse was not true. That is, there were a number of subjects who used formal operations who had not yet established a clear identity. Thus formal operations thinking may *enable* the young person to rethink many aspects of his life, but it does not guarantee that he will do so.

Overall, we are left with the impression that both the physical changes of puberty and the potential cognitive changes of formal operations are central to the phenomena of adolescence, but the connections between them and their impact on social behavior are still largely a mystery. I know it is frustrating to have me keep saying that we don't know, but that's an accurate statement of our current situation.

INFLUENCES ON THE BASIC PROCESSES

There is not space enough or time to detail all the many factors that can influence the teenager's experience of adolescence. Many I have already mentioned, including such cultural variations as the presence or absence of initiation rites, the timing of the child's pubertal development, and the degree of personal or familial stress. But one more general point is worth making:

Adolescence, like every other developmental period, does not begin with a clean slate. The individual youngster's own temperamental qualities, behavioral habits, and internal models of interaction that he established in earlier years of childhood obviously have a profound effect on the experience of adolescence. Examples are easy to find.

- Sroufe's longitudinal study, which I described in Chapter 6, (Sroufe, Carlson, & Schulman, 1993; Urban et al., 1991) shows that those who had been rated as having a secure attachment in infancy were more self-confident and more socially competent with peers at the beginning of adolescence.

- Delinquency and heightened aggressiveness in adolescence rarely appear afresh; they are nearly always presaged by earlier behavior problems and by inadequate family control as early as the years of toddlerhood (Dishion et al., 1991; Robins & McEvoy, 1990).

- Depression in adolescents is more likely among those who enter adolescence with lower self-esteem (Harter, 1987).

Avshalom Caspi and Terrie Moffitt (1991) make the more general point that *any* major life crisis or transition, including adolescence, has the effect of *accentuating* earlier personality or behavioral patterns rather than creating new ones. This is not unlike the observation that the child's attachment to the parent is only revealed when the child is under stress. Similarly, Caspi & Moffitt are arguing that in times of stress, old patterns—particularly old problems—are exacerbated. For example, you'll recall from the box in Chapter 11 that girls with very early puberty, on average, have higher rates of psychological problems than do those with normal-time puberty. But closer analysis reveals that it is only the early puberty girls who already had social problems before puberty began whose pubertal experience and adolescence is more negative. Very early puberty does not increase psychological problems for girls who were psychologically healthier to begin with.

I think this is an important point for understanding all the various transitions of adult life as well as adolescence. Not only do we carry ourselves with us as we move through the roles and demands of adult life, but those existing patterns may be most highly visible when we are under stress. This does not mean that we never change or learn new and more effective ways of responding. Many do. But we must never lose sight of the fact that by adolescence, and certainly by adulthood, our internal working models and our repertoire of coping behaviors are already established, creating a bias in the system. Another way of putting it is that while change is possible, continuity is the default option.

Chapter Fourteen

Atypical Development

hen Jeffrey was 4, he couldn't walk or talk and spent most of his time in a crib. His parents fed him pureed baby food through a bottle. After six years with a loving foster family, at age 10 Jeffrey is now in a special class in a regular elementary school and is learning to print and read.

Nine-year-old Archie seemed "different from other children even when he started school." Often he was "disoriented" or "distractible." Although he scored in the normal range on an IQ test, he had great difficulty learning to read. Even after several years of special tutoring he could read only by sounding out the words each time; he didn't recognize even familiar words by sight (Cole & Traupmann, 1981).

Janice's parents are worried about her. Right about the time that she turned 13 she seemed to change in quite disturbing ways. She's lost weight, even though she's growing fast; she doesn't seem to call up her friends anymore and is listless and gloomy. This has been going on for about 6 months now, and her parents think this is just not normal; they're going to talk to the school counselor about her and will consider family therapy if it will help.

Each of these children is "atypical" in some way. In each, the developmental processes I have been describing in the past 13 chapters haven't quite worked in the normal way. Jeffrey is a Down's syndrome child and is mentally retarded. Archie has some kind of learning disability, while Janice shows many signs of a clinical depression.

How Common are Such Problems?

How common are such problems? Given the critical practical relevance of this question, you'd think that psychologists and epidemiologists would long ago have come to some agreement. But we haven't, in large part because the line between typical and atypical is very much a matter of degree rather than of kind. *Most* children show at least some kinds of "problem behavior" at one time or another. For example, parents in the United States report that 10–20 percent of 7-year-olds still wet their beds at least occasionally; 30 percent have nightmares; 20 percent bite their fingernails, 10 percent suck their thumbs, and 10 percent swear enough for it to be considered a problem. Another 30 percent or so have temper tantrums (Achenbach & Edelbrock, 1981). Problems like these, especially if they last only a few months, should more properly be considered part of "normal" development. Usually we label a child's development "atypical" or deviant only if a problem persists for 6 months or longer or if the problem is at the extreme end of the continuum for that behavior.

When we count only such extreme or persisting problems, the incidence is much lower—although nonetheless higher than most of you will have guessed. Table 14.1 gives some current estimates for each of a series of deviant patterns. Some of these numbers are based on extensive data and are widely accepted, such as the 3.5 percent rate of mental retardation. Others are still in some dispute, such as the rate of depression in adolescence. Where the findings are not in agreement, I have given the range of current estimates.

TABLE 14.1

Estimated Incidence of Various Types of Atypical Development in the United States and Other Developed Countries

Type of Problem	Percentage of Children 0–18 With That Problem
Psychopathologies	
Externalizing Problems:	
(1) Attention Deficit Disorder (hyperactivity)	3 to 5%
(2) Conduct Disorders	5 to 7%
(3) Arrested by police (delinquency)	3%
Internalizing Problems:	
(1) Significant Anxiety and Fear	2.5%
(2) Serious or Severe Depression	
Elementary School Age children:	0.015%
Adolescents	3 to 8%
Psychoses (the most severe pathologies)	0.08%
Intellectually Atypical Development	
IQ below 70 (mentally retarded)	3.5%
Speech and Language Problems, including delayed language, articulation problems, and stuttering	3.5%
Serious Learning Disability	4.0%
Physical Problems	
Autism	0.04%
Significant Hearing Impairment	0.5%
All Other Problems, including blindness, cerebral palsy, epilepsy, etc.	0.2%

Sources: Barkley, 1990; Broman et al., 1987; Brandenburg et al, 1990; Cantwell, 1990; Chalfant, 1989; Kopp & Kaler, 1989; Rutter & Garmezy, 1983; Rutter, 1989; Tuna, 1989.

We might also want to combine all these individual rates in some way, to give us some idea of the total percentage of children with one kind or problem or another. Unfortunately this is not a simple matter of addition, since there is a good deal of overlap in the various categories. For example, many children with serious learning disabilities also show an attention deficit disorder or conduct disorders. Still, even if we allow for some overlap, the totals are astonishing: Between 14 and 20 percent of children and teenagers show at least *some* form of significant psychopathology (Achenbach et al., 1991; Brandenburg et al., 1990). If we add in cognitive disorders, the total is at least 20 percent. That is, at least one in five, and maybe as many as one in four children will show at least one form of deviant or abnormal behavior, *at some time in their early years*. The majority of these children will require some type of special help in school, in a child guidance clinic, or equivalent. When you think of these figures in terms of the demands on the school system and on other social agencies, the prospect is somewhat staggering.

If we are going to meet those needs, we must obviously understand the origins of such atypical patterns. In this chapter I can give you only a glimpse of our current knowledge, but I can at least alert you to the issues and remaining questions about the most common forms of deviance.

Do you think that such high rates of problems would be found in every culture? Why or why not?

CULTURES & CONTEXTS

Problem Behaviors Among Children in Kenya and Thailand

There is now a growing body of information showing links between particular cultural values and the type of emotional or behavioral problem children may show. In one recent study, John Weisz and his colleagues (1993) compared the incidence of externalizing and internalizing problems among teenagers in a rural Kenyan group, the Embu, and a rural Thailand group, with the rates among rural Black and White youth in the United States. Both the Thai and Embu cultures place great emphasis on obedience and politeness, a pattern of cultural values that appears to be linked to higher rates of "overcontrolled," or internalizing problems, such as shyness, fearfulness, or depression. In contrast, the United States culture, with its greater emphasis on individual freedom, appears to foster higher rates of "undercontrolled," or externalizing problems, such as fighting, showing off, or hyperactivity.

In each of the three cultures, parents were asked a series of questions about specific behaviors or symptoms their child showed. Weisz found that the Embu teens had the highest rates of internalizing and the lowest rate of externalizing problems, while American White teens had the highest rates of undercontrol, followed by African-American teens. Interestingly, the Thai group showed low rates of both types of problems, although other studies in Thailand have shown high levels of overcontrol problems in this culture.

The fact that the Embu and Thai patterns are not the same certainly reminds us yet again that cultural effects are not going to be so simple as a difference between an emphasis on obedience or on personal freedom. But the results also remind us that the pattern of frequencies of various types of problems that we note in U.S. populations is at least in part a product of our culture.

Developmental Psychopathology: A New Approach

Our knowledge about the dynamics of deviant development in general, and psychopathology in particular, has been enormously enhanced in the past few years by the emergence of a new theoretical and empirical approach, called **developmental psychopathology,** pioneered by such researchers as Norman Garmezy, Michael Rutter, Dante Cicchetti, Alan Sroufe, and others (Cicchetti, 1989, 1993; Rutter & Garmezy, 1983). These theorists have emphasized several key points:

First, normal and abnormal development both emerge from the same basic processes. To understand either we must understand both and how they interact with one another. The task of a developmental psychopathologist is to uncover those basic processes—to see both how they work "correctly" in the case of normal development and to identify the *developmental deviations* and their causes (Sroufe, 1989). Alan Sroufe's studies of the consequences of secure or insecure attachment, which I talked about in Chapter 6, are good examples of research based on such assumptions.

Second, the approach is *developmental.* Theorists in this new tradition are interested in the *pathways* leading to both deviant and normal development, from earliest infancy through childhood and into adult life. What are the sequences of experiences that lead to increased risk of depression in adolescence? What is the pathway leading to antisocial behavior or to peer rejection? And what are the factors that may inhibit or exacerbate an early deviation or may turn an initially normal developmental trajectory into a deviant pattern?

One of the potentially exacerbating factors may be the underlying developmental pathway itself. Each age has special tasks, special stresses that interact with the child's ongoing patterns and internal models to produce either normal or deviant behavior. For example, there is growing evidence that rates of depression among young people rise markedly at adolescence. A developmental psychopathologist would ask what is unique about adolescence that would contribute to such heightened depression rates.

He or she would also want to know what special qualities or early experiences a child may bring to the experience of puberty that might increase or decrease her risk of developing a pathological pattern such as depression. One of the unexpected results of many recent studies of children thought to be "at risk" for particular kinds of problems, such as children reared by depressed parents, or children in divorcing families, or abused children, has been that some children seem to be unexpectedly resilient in the face of what appear to be disturbing circumstances. The obverse has also been found repeatedly: some children seem to be unexpectedly vulnerable, despite what appear to be supportive life circumstances. Developmental psychopathologists, such as Rutter and Garmezy, have not only taken the lead in studying resilient children, they have insisted that these "exceptions" to the general rules offer us crucial information about the basic processes of both normal and abnormal development.

There is now a growing body of research cast in this framework that can help us examine the origins and manifestations of the array of psychopathologies.

The Psychopathologies of Childhood

The most helpful way to organize the many types of psychopathologies, in my view, is to divide the set into two large categories: **externalizing problems,** (also described as *disturbances of conduct*) such as hyperactivity, excessive aggressiveness or defiance, and delinquency, in which the deviance is directed outward, and **internalizing problems** (also called *emotional disturbances*) such as depression, anxiety, or eating disorders, in which the deviance is largely internal to the individual.

Externalizing Problems

Conduct Disorders.   One of the most obvious types of externalizing problems is what we might call in layman's terms *delinquency* or *antisocial behavior*. I've already talked about delinquency in Chapter 13, but the category of **conduct disorders** is actually broader than merely law-breaking behavior. In the most recent revision of the American Psychiatric Association's *Diagnostic and Statistical Manual of Mental Disorders* (called DSM-III-R), the category includes high levels of aggression, argumentativeness, bullying, disobedience, high levels of irritability, and threatening and loud behavior.

It has been clear for a long while that there are a number of subvarieties of conduct problems. The two types of delinquency I talked about in the last chapter (socialized-subcultural, and unsocialized-psychopathic) represent one

We can't tell from one picture whether these preschool boys are consistently aggressive or defiant. But we know that those who do show high levels of such behavior at this early age are far more likely to have long-term problems than are those who only develop conduct disorders/delinquency at later ages.

category system. In the last few years, developmental psychopathologists have found themselves somewhat unsatisfied with this traditional dichotomy and have struggled to find better ways to characterize the variations. Achenbach (1993) argues for two subtypes: *aggressive behavior*, which includes arguing, being mean to others, destruction of objects, fighting, attacking, showing off, sudden mood changes, temper tantrums, and loudness; and *delinquent behavior*, which includes specific law-breaking such as setting fires and stealing, but also a lack of guilt, lying, running away from home, swearing and obscenity, alcohol and drugs.

In contrast, Hinshaw (1993) argues that the crucial issue is when the deviant behavior began. *Childhood-onset conduct disorders* are more serious, with high levels of aggression, and are far more likely to persist to adult criminality; *adolescent-onset* problems appear to be milder, more transitory, more a function of hanging about with bad companions than a deeply ingrained behavior problem.

These two category systems overlap a good deal. The cluster of problems Achenbach calls aggressive behavior typically begins early and is much more persistent and thus fits within Hinshaw's childhood-onset group, while delinquent behavior most often begins in adolescence and is less persisting and serious. But the fit between the two taxonomies is not perfect. In particular, many children with early onset conduct problems show both aggressive and delinquent behaviors. But both of these category systems may turn out to be helpful in aiming researchers toward clearer questions about the origins of the various types of conduct disorders.

Why does it matter what kind (or how good) of a category system we use?

The developmental pathway for early onset conduct disorders is one you are familiar with by now from all I have said about Patterson's research on aggressive children and all I have said about delinquency. In early life, these are children who throw tantrums and defy parents; indeed they may well have insecure attachments as well (Greenberg et al., 1993). Once the defiance appears, if the parents are not up to the task of controlling the child, the child's behavior worsens to overt aggression toward others, who then reject the child, which aggravates the problem, pushing the seriously aggressive child in the direction of other children with similar problems, who become the child's only supportive peer group. By adolescence, these youngsters are firmly established in antisocial behavior, and in adulthood they are highly likely to continue with aggression, crime, or—at the least—a chaotic life.

The degree of continuity of this form of deviant behavior is quite striking, as you'll recall from the box in Chapter 10. The correlation between aggression in childhood and in adulthood averages .60 to .70—very high correlations for data of this kind and replicated in studies in both England and the United States (Farrington, 1991).

There is also some indication that the early onset/aggressive syndrome has a much stronger genetic component than is true for the later-onset/delinquent pattern (Achenbach, 1993). Thus the preschooler who already shows defiant and oppositional behavior as well as aggressiveness may have strong inborn propensities for such behavior. But if Patterson is correct—and I think he is—then whether that propensity will develop into a full-fledged, persisting conduct disorder will depend on the unfolding sequence of events, including the parents' ability to handle the child's early defiance.

Attention Deficit Hyperactivity Disorder.   A second important category of externalizing psychopathology has a rather long-winded name in DSM-III: **attention deficit hyperactivity disorder.** The briefer and more common name is simply **hyperactivity.** A glance at the diagnostic criteria, which I've listed in Table 14.2, will tell you quickly that the hallmarks of this disorder are physical restlessness and problems with attention—precisely as the label implies (Barkley, 1990).

> What kind of social policy implications (if any) do you see in the fact that early onset conduct disorders are most likely to persist to adult criminality or violence?

TABLE 14.2
Diagnostic Criteria for Attention Deficit Hyperactivity Disorder

The onset of the problem must be before age 7, and the disturbance must last at least 6 months, during which at least 8 of the following are present:

1. Often fidgets with hands or feet or squirms in seat (in adolescents, this may be limited to subjective feelings of restlessness)
2. Has difficulty remaining seated when required to do so
3. Is easily distracted by extraneous stimuli
4. Has difficulty awaiting turn in game or group situations
5. Often blurts out answers to questions before they have been completed
6. Has difficulty following through on instructions from others (not due to oppositional behavior or failure of comprehension), for example, failing to finish chores
7. Has difficulty sustaining attention in tasks or play activities
8. Often shifts from one uncompleted activity to another
9. Has difficulty playing quietly
10. Often talks excessively
11. Often interrupts or intrudes on others, for example, butts into other children's games
12. Often does not seem to listen to what is being said to him or her
13. Often loses things necessary for tasks or activities at school or at home (e.g., toys, pencils, books, assignments)
14. Often engages in physically dangerous activities without considering possible consequences (not for purpose of thrill-seeking), for example, runs into street without looking

Source: *Diagnostic and Statistical Manual for Mental Disorders* (3rd ed., rev.), 1987. Washington, D. C.: American Psychiatric Association, pp. 53–54. Copyright 1987 by the American Psychiatric Association.

But the list in Table 14.2 cannot really convey the quality of behavior of such children. Their interactions with their peers are so distinctively different that novice observers need to watch videotapes for only a few minutes before they can reliably distinguish between a child diagnosed as hyperactive and a normally behaving child—even when the hyperactive child displays no aggression and the sound is turned off (Henker & Whalen, 1989). The body language is different, the level of activity is different, and the child's social behavior is often inappropriate. About half such children also show conduct disorders, and most do poorly in school.

By definition, this is an early developing disorder. It is also a persistent problem in the majority of cases, lasting well into adulthood for at least half of those diagnosed as having this disorder (Henker & Whalen, 1989). But the severity of the long-term problem seems to be strongly influenced by whether or not the child also develops a conduct disorder. It is the combination of hyperactivity and aggressiveness or delinquency that is especially deadly (Barkley et al., 1990). You can see one facet of this effect in the results of Terrie Moffitt's (1990) recent longitudinal study of a group of 434 boys in New Zealand, including all boys born in a particular town over a one-year period. When the boys were 13 they were classed in one of four groups based on the presence or absence of two factors: attention deficit disorder and delinquency. Moffitt then traced backwards for each of these groups, looking at scores at earlier ages on measures of antisocial behavior, intelligence, and family adversity. You can see the results for antisocial behavior in Figure 14.1.

It is clear that the boys who, as adolescents, showed *both* hyperactivity and delinquency had been the most antisocial at every earlier age. Hyperactivity that was not accompanied by antisocial behavior at early ages was also not linked to delinquency at 13. Other research tells us that this same group of hyperactive *and*

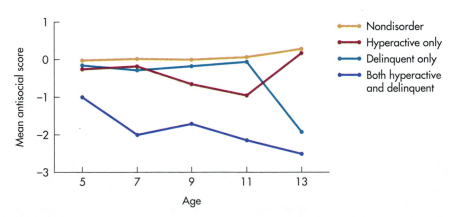

FIGURE 14.1

The boys in Moffitt's study had been studied every two years from the time they were 5. When they were 13, they were assigned to one of four hyperactivity/delinquency categories, then Moffitt backtracked from that age. You can see that those who were *both* delinquent and hyperactive at 13 had shown markedly higher rates of antisocial behavior from the time they were 5, while those who were only hyperactive at 13 had been much less socially deviant at earlier ages. (Source: Moffitt, 1990, Figure 1, p. 899.)

delinquent boys is also the most likely to have continued serious problems in adulthood, including criminal behavior.

Where might hyperactivity come from? Because the pattern begins so early and has such a strong physical component, most clinicians have assumed that this problem has some kind of biological origin. Surprisingly, early research failed to confirm such a biological hypothesis. There was no sign of any overt brain damage, and typical neurological tests did not reveal any underlying physical problem. But in the past few years, three converging lines of evidence have provided new support for the biological hypothesis.

First, physicians and psychologists have known for some time that a *biological treatment* is very often effective in reducing or eliminating the deviant behavior. Many (but not all) hyperactive children treated with a stimulant medication (most commonly Ritalin) show decreases in demanding, disruptive, and noncompliant behaviors, and more attentiveness in the classroom (Henker & Whalen, 1989). Second, there is accumulating evidence that a pattern of hyperactivity is inherited, at least in certain families. About a quarter of the parents of hyperactive children themselves have a history of hyperactivity (Biederman et al., 1990). Studies of twins also show a genetic contribution. Among identical twins, if one is diagnosed as hyperactive the other is highly likely to have the same diagnosis; among fraternal twins this "concordance rate" is much lower (Deutsch & Kinsbourne, 1990).

Finally, newer methods of assessing brain function have begun to reveal differences between the brains of hyperactive and nonhyperactive individuals. In one widely publicized study, Alan Zametkin and his colleagues (1990) used Positron-Emission Tomography (PET) scans to examine the glucose (sugar) metabolism in the brains of hyperactive and normal adults. All the hyperactive adults reported that they had also been hyperactive as children, and all had at least one offspring with the same diagnosis. Each subject was injected with a concentrated dose of glucose, and then repeated PET scans were done to look at how the brain metabolized the sugar. Zametkin found that the hyperactive adults had significantly slower brain metabolism of the glucose, and this was especially so in the portions of the brain that are known to be involved in attentiveness and the ability to inhibit inappropriate responses. Results like this may represent a real breakthrough, not only in helping us to understand the origins of hyperactivity, but conceivably in devising better treatments. At the very least, they greatly strengthen the argument that this disorder has biological origins.

But being more sure about the origins does not settle all the important questions. From the point of view of developmental psychopathology we also need to understand how such an initially deviant biological pattern affects the child's interactions with parents and peers to produce the common combination of hyperactivity and antisocial behavior. For many hyperactive children, the pathway is very like the one Patterson has described for defiant or aggressive children. These kids are just plain hard to raise. And those parents whose child-management skills are not up to the task of dealing with the hyperactive toddler's typically higher rates of noncompliance or those who face major family stresses that prevent them from maintaining good child care routines may find that the child's behavior becomes more and more disruptive, which in turn affects the child's emerging social skills adversely. By school age, parent-child conflict is high, as is child-peer conflict. Poor school performance makes it worse by lowering the child's self-esteem. Such children are then on a pathway that is highly likely to lead to continued problems at adolescence and adulthood (Campbell, 1990). In Moffitt's New Zealand study, for example, those boys who eventually showed the combination of hyperactivity and delinquency came from families with much higher than average levels of stress and fewer resources. The hyperactive boys who did not develop the accompanying antisocial behavior came from families with lower than average levels of stress and more resources.

Internalizing Problems: The Example of Depression

A different set of antecedents and a different pathway is found among children who show internalizing forms of disturbance. The particular form of deviance that has been most often addressed within the framework of developmental psychopathology has been **depression;** so let me use that as an example.

For many years, psychiatrists took the position that significant depression could not occur in children or adolescents. But there is now abundant evidence that depression is actually quite common in adolescence and occurs at least occasionally among younger children. Both Thomas Achenbach and Michael Rutter, in separate large studies, have found that approximately 10 percent of preadolescent children and 40 percent of adolescents are described by parents or teachers as appearing miserable, unhappy, sad, or depressed (Achenbach & Edelbrock, 1981; Rutter et al., 1981). When researchers asked teenagers about their state of mind, a third describe at least moderate levels of depressed mood (Petersen et al., 1993).

When depressive episodes last 6 months or longer and are accompanied by other symptoms such as disturbances of sleeping and eating and difficulty concentrating, they are usually referred to as *clinical depression* or a *depressive disorder*. Recent epidemiological studies tell us that such severe forms of depression are relatively rare in preadolescents, but are quite surprisingly common among adolescents. Estimates range fairly widely, as you have already seen in Table 14.1, but the most comprehensive studies suggest that at least 3 percent and perhaps as many as 8 percent of teenagers can be diagnosed as clinically depressed at any one time. And perhaps twice that many will experience a serious depression at some time in their adolescent years (Compas et al., 1993; Petersen et al., 1993; Reinherz et al., 1993).

Interestingly, among preadolescents, boys are about as likely as girls to be unhappy or depressed; among teenagers (as among adults) girls more often report high or chronic levels of depression, a sex difference that has been found in a number of industrialized countries and among African-Americans, Hispanic-Americans, and Anglo-Americans (Petersen et al., 1993; Roberts & Sobhan, 1992).

Although teenagers and preadolescents who describe themselves as depressed do not invariably display all the symptoms of a full-blown clinical depression as seen in adulthood, depressed youngsters do show the same kind of hormonal and other endocrine changes during their depressed episodes as psychologists observe in depressed adults, so we know that depression in children is a real and potentially serious clinical state, not just a "normal" or transitory

We can't know for sure what has caused this teenager's dejected look, but we do know that depressed mood and significant clinical depressions are considerably more common in the adolescent years than most psychiatrists or psychologists once thought.

unhappiness—a conclusion further buttressed by the fact that a significant portion of depressed teens say they think about suicide. In one longitudinal study of youth growing up in a working class neighborhood in the U.S., a fifth of those who had had a serious depression by age 18 had also attempted suicide (Reinherz et al., 1993).

The search for the developmental pathways leading to later depression begins with the clear finding that children growing up with depressed parents are much more likely than are those growing up with nondepressed parents to develop depression themselves (Downey & Coyne, 1990). Of course this could indicate a genetic factor at work here, a possibility supported by at least a few studies of twins and adopted children (Petersen et al., 1993). Or we could understand this link between parental and child depression in terms of the changes in the parent–child interaction that are caused by the parent's depression.

I mentioned in Chapter 6 that depressed mothers are much more likely than are nondepressed mothers to have children who are insecurely attached. In particular, their behavior with their child is often so nonresponsive that it seems to foster in the child a kind of helpless resignation. Such a sense of helplessness has been found to be strongly related to depression in both adults and adolescents (Dodge, 1990).

Of course not all children of depressed parents are themselves depressed. About 60 percent show no abnormality at all. Whether a child moves along a pathway toward depression or not seems to be a function of a whole series of protective or disruptive factors (Billings & Moos, 1985):

- If the parent's depression is short-lived or is medically treated so that the symptoms are less severe, the child has a much better chance of avoiding depression herself.
- The more other forms of stress the family experiences in addition to one parent's depression, such as an illness, family arguments, work stress, loss of income, job loss, or marital separation, the more likely the child is to show depressive symptoms.
- The more emotional and logistical support the family receives from others, the less likely the child is to show depressive symptoms.

Thus the family system can buffer the child from the effects of a parent's depression far more effectively if there are adequate social supports and not too many other stresses. But when stresses accumulate, the effect is magnified.

In fact, this detrimental role of stress is just as clear among children whose parent or parents are not depressed. Any combination of stresses has a similar effect, such as the parents' divorce, or the death of a parent or another loved person, or the father's loss of job, or a move, or changing schools, or whatever (Compas et al., 1993). Indeed the role of such individual life stresses may help to explain the sex differences in depression among adolescents. Anne Petersen (Petersen et al., 1991) has proposed that girls typically experience more challenges or stresses during adolescence than do boys. In particular, she argues that girls are more likely to encounter simultaneous stressful experiences in adolescence, such as pubertal changes combined with a shift in schools. In her own longitudinal study, Peterson finds that when such synchronous stresses are taken into account, the sex difference in adolescent depression disappears. That is, in

Can you think of any other reasons why girls (in Western cultures at least) would have higher rates of depression than boys?

this study, depression was *not* more common among girls than among boys when both groups had encountered equal levels of life stress or simultaneous stressful experiences.

Yet another possible causal factor in adolescent depression is social isolation from peers in early elementary school (Hymel et al., 1990). You'll remember from Chapter 10 that peer *rejection* is associated with externalizing problems (aggression); but *isolation* from peers is linked with depression. Yet another possible pathway is through lowered self-esteem. Susan Harter's studies tell us that a young person who feels she (or he) does not measure up to her own standards is much more likely to show symptoms of a clinical depression. The fact that depression increases markedly in adolescence makes good sense from this point of view. We know that in adolescence, children are much more likely to define themselves and others in *comparative* terms—to judge against some standard or to see themselves as "less than" or "more than" some other person. We also know that at adolescence, appearance becomes highly salient, and that a great many teenagers are convinced that they do not live up to the culturally defined appearance standards. Self-esteem thus drops in early adolescence, and depression rises.

Do you recall having been significantly depressed during adolescence? If so, do any of these explanations or causal factors fit your own experience?

Harter's work is certainly helpful here, but it does not answer all our questions about why depression rises so markedly at adolescence. Nor does it tell us why some teenagers are likely to see themselves as inadequate or to respond to such a sense of inadequacy with depression, while others do not. We obviously need to know a good deal more about the pathways that lead a child to be vulnerable to such stresses at puberty or at any other point in life.

Vulnerability and Resilience

This question of vulnerability or resilience has been a persistent theme among developmental psychopathologists. The research findings suggest that the same kinds of protective factors I listed in Chapter 10, when I talked about children growing up in poverty, play a role for children experiencing other kinds of stresses as well. Children who are securely attached to someone (whether it be a parent or someone else), who have good cognitive skills, and who have sufficient social skills to make connections with peers are better able to weather the stresses they encounter.

For example, in her studies of resilience among school-age children, Ann Masten (1989) has found that when children have experienced a year with high levels of life stresses, those with higher IQ are much less likely to respond to that stress by becoming disruptive. Masten speculates that this may be due to the fact that such children, who have a history of successful problem solving, have a stronger sense of self-efficacy, which may help to make them more resistant to frustration.

On the other side of the coin are the vulnerable children, who are far more likely to show some kind of significant psychopathology in the face of stress. Some kinds of vulnerabilities are inborn, such as physical abnormalities, prenatal trauma or preterm birth, malnutrition prenatally, or exposure to disease in utero. A tendency toward "difficult" temperament, which also seems to be inborn, is another significant vulnerability, not only because by definition such children have greater difficulty adapting to new experiences, but because their difficult temperament can easily affect the relationships they develop with their parents or other caregivers. Horowitz's model (Figure 1.4), which I have referred to repeatedly, suggests that such initial vulnerabilities greatly increase the likelihood that the child will develop some later problem. Only optimal rearing conditions can protect such children adequately.

Other vulnerabilities emerge during infancy or early childhood. An insecure early attachment and the internal working model that accompanies it seems to make a child more vulnerable to stress at later ages, particularly to stresses that involve losses or severe strains on key relationships. And any combination of circumstances that results in a high rate of aggressive or disruptive behavior with peers makes a child more vulnerable to a whole variety of stresses in the elementary and high school years (Masten, 1989).

Overall, it seems very helpful to think of each child as possessing some inborn *vulnerabilities*, some *protective factors*, such as a secure attachment or a middle-class family, and some *resources*, such as higher IQ, an array of friends, or good peer interaction skills. How any given child will react to stressful life circumstances or to normal developmental passages like school entry or adolescence will depend on the relative weight of these three elements—*and* on how many separate stresses the child must face at the same time. Any child, no matter how basically resilient, is more likely to show at least a short-term behavior problem when multiple stresses pile up at the same moment.

Whether a child will show a behavior problem at a stressful time like moving will depend in part on whether he faces several other stresses or life changes at the same time—such as perhaps his parents' divorce.

How would you describe your own vulnerabilities, protective factors, and resources?

Developmental Psychopathology: A Reprise

I think that even this brief foray into research on psychopathology makes clear that a developmental framework is the only one that is going to yield real understanding of the emergence of deviant behavior. Even for a disorder such as hyperactivity, which appears to be rooted in an inborn biological dysfunction, the severity and persistence of the disorder can be best understood in terms of the child's cumulative patterns of interaction and the child's own internal models of relationships. Ultimately, studies within this emerging tradition of developmental psychopathology may end up telling us as much about normal development as about the emergence of pathology.

Intellectually Atypical Development

If you go back and look at Table 14.1 you'll see that the various forms of intellectually atypical development rank right up there with the various psychopathologies in frequency of occurrence among children. Roughly one in ten children shows at least some form of intellectual abnormality.

Mental Retardation

Definitions and Labels. Of all the atypical children listed in Table 14.1, probably those studied most thoroughly are those labeled **mentally retarded.** Not too many decades ago, when mental ability was thought of as a fixed trait, mental subnormality was considered a kind of incurable disease. Labels like "idiot" or "feeble-minded" were used. But this older view has changed a great deal. Not only have the old negative labels been changed, but the basic assumptions about the nature of retardation have changed, too.

Mental retardation is now (correctly, I think) viewed as a *symptom* rather than as a disease. And like any symptom, it can change. A child's life circumstances or his health may change, and his IQ score may go up or down as a result. Remember from Chapter 8 that it is not uncommon for a child's IQ test scores to vary as much as 30 points over the childhood years. Of course many children with low IQ scores will continue to function at a low level throughout life. But it is important for educators and parents to understand that a single low IQ score need not invariably mean that the child will function at that level forever. For many children, improvement is possible.

The Assessment of Retardation.   A child is normally designated as retarded if he tests below an IQ of 70, *and* has significant problems in **adaptive behavior**—such as an inability to dress or eat alone, or a problem getting along with others, or adjusting to the demands of a regular school classroom. As Thomas Achenbach (1982) says, "Children doing well in school are unlikely to be considered retarded no matter what their IQ scores" (p. 214).

Low IQ scores are customarily divided up into several ranges, with different labels attached to each, as you can see in Table 14.3. I've given both the labels that psychologists use and those that may be more common in the school system. (There are no school system labels for children with IQs below about 35 because schools very rarely deal with children functioning at this level.)

The farther down the IQ scale you go, the fewer children there are. More than 80 percent of all children with IQs below 70 are in the "mild" range; only about 2 percent of the low-IQ youngsters (perhaps 3,500 children in the U.S.) are profoundly retarded (Broman et al., 1987).

Cognitive Functioning in Retarded Children.   In recent years there has been a great deal of fascinating research on thinking in retarded children, much of it by Ann Brown, Joseph Campione and their colleagues (Campione et al., 1982; DeLoache & Brown, 1987). As you may recall from Chapter 9, this research has been a significant ingredient in the emerging information processing approach to

TABLE 14.3
IQ Scores and Labels for Children Classed as Retarded

Approximate IQ Score Range	Label Used by Psychologists	Label Used in Schools
68–83	Borderline retarded	(No special label)
52–67	Mildly retarded	Educable mentally retarded (EMR)
36–51	Moderately retarded	Trainable mentally retarded
19–35	Severely retarded	(No special label)
Below 19	Profoundly retarded	(No special label)

studying cognitive development in children. Brown and Campione find that retarded children:

1. Think and react more slowly.
2. Require much more complete and repeated instruction to learn new information or a new strategy (compared to normal-IQ children, who may discover a strategy for themselves or profit from incomplete instruction).
3. Do not generalize or transfer something they have learned in one situation to a new problem or task. They thus appear to lack those "executive" functions that enable older, higher-IQ children (or adults) to compare a new problem to familiar ones or to scan through a repertoire of strategies until they find one that works.

On simple tasks, retarded children learn in ways and at rates that are similar to younger, normal-IQ children. The more significant deficit lies in higher-order processing. These children *can* learn, but they do so more slowly and require far more exhaustive and task-specific instruction.

Causes of Retardation.   About 15 to 25 percent of mentally retarded children have some identifiable physical problem (Broman et al., 1987). **Chromosomal anomalies,** such as Down syndrome or the Fragile X syndrome, are one major culprit. As Scarr and Kidd put it, "having too much or too little [genetic material] will affect intelligence, always for the worse" (1983, p. 380). A child may also inherit a specific disease or **inborn error of metabolism** that can cause retardation if not treated. The best known such inherited metabolism error is phenylketonuria (PKU), which I described in Chapter 3 (Table 3.2).

Still a third physical cause of retardation is **brain damage,** which can result from a large number of causes, including prenatal maternal diseases like syphilis or cytomegalovirus, malnutrition, or alcoholism. Brain damage may also occur during birth or by some accident after birth (e.g., auto accidents or falling out of a treehouse on your head).

The remaining three-quarters of retarded children show no signs of any brain damage or other physical disorder. In almost all such cases, these children come from families in which the parents have low IQs, where there is serious family disorganization, mental illness in the parents, or emotional or cognitive deprivation in the home. Often both genetic and environmental influences operate simultaneously.

Large scale studies have now shown quite conclusively that these several causes of retardation are not distributed evenly across the range of low IQ scores. The lower the IQ, the higher the likelihood that there is some physical cause. This is especially clear from the results of the Collaborative Perinatal Project, which involved nearly 40,000 American children studied from before birth to age 7. In this sample, 71.7 percent of White and 53.9 percent of Black children with IQs *below* 50 had some kind of major disorder of the central nervous system. In contrast, among those with IQs between 50 and 70, only 13.9 percent of Whites and 6.3 percent of Blacks had any identifiable physical abnormality (Broman et al., 1987).

About 15 percent of mentally retarded children have clear physical abnormalities, such as Down syndrome.

You can see this difference even more vividly in another set of data from the same study. It happened that in a fair number of cases the sample included several children from the same family. So Broman and her colleagues were able to look at the IQs of the *siblings* of retarded children. The results for White children are in Figure 14.2.

The siblings of those with IQs below 50 had normal IQs; none was retarded. But the siblings of the mildly retarded were themselves fairly likely to be mildly retarded as well, a pattern that suggests quite different causes in the two groups. Among Black children, whose family circumstances are more likely to be impoverished, the results are less clear. Siblings in both groups are about equally likely to be retarded themselves. But the findings as a whole strongly support the conclusion that there are really two distinct types of retardation, each with its own set of causes.

One implication of this conclusion is that interventions like the enriched day care and preschool Ramey devised (recall Figure 7.3) are more likely to be effective in preventing or ameliorating milder retardation that has familial-cultural causes. This is not to say that we should ignore environmental enrichment or specific early training for children with physically caused retardation. Greater breadth of experience would enrich their lives and may help to bring their level of functioning closer to the top end of their "reaction range." But even massive early interventions are not going to make most brain damaged or genetically anomalous children intellectually normal, although they can help the child to function much more independently (Spiker, 1990).

Learning Disorders

Definitions and Labels.   Some children with normal IQs and essentially good adaptive functioning nonetheless have difficulty learning to read, write, or do arithmetic. The typical label for this problem is **learning disability,**

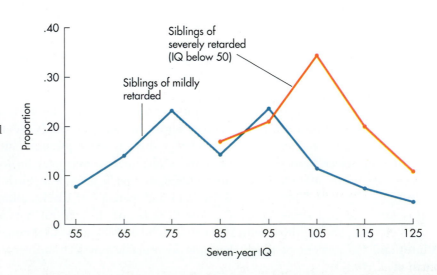

FIGURE 14.2
These data suggest that there are really two quite different kinds of retarded individuals: those whose retardation is caused by physical abnormalities, usually with IQs below 50 and who have normal IQ siblings and those whose retardation is cultural–familial in origin, usually with IQs in the mildly retarded range. The siblings of the latter group are *also* more likely to be retarded. (Source: Broman et al., 1987, Figure 10-1, p. 269.)

although you will also hear terms like *dyslexia* (literally "nonreading") or *minimal brain damage*. The official definition of this problem includes the presumption that the difficulty arises from some kind of central nervous system dysfunction or damage.

How *many* such children there are, and how they should be characterized, is still a matter of considerable dispute. Sylvia Farnham-Diggory (1992), one of the leading experts in the field, argues that up to 80 percent of all children classified by school systems as learning disabled are misclassified. She claims that only about 5 out of every 1,000 children is genuinely learning disabled. The remainder who are so classified are more appropriately called slow learners, or they suffer from some other difficulty, perhaps a temporary emotional distress, poor teaching, or whatever.

Practically speaking, however, the term learning disability is used very broadly within school systems (at least within the United States) to label a grab bag of children who have unexpected or otherwise unexplainable difficulty with school work, particularly reading. In 1985–86, 4.7 percent of all children in the U.S. were so labeled (Farnham-Diggory, 1992).

There are good reasons why schools identify so many children as learning disabled. For one thing, the diagnostic problem is extremely difficult. The designation of a learning disability is basically a *residual* diagnosis. It is the label normally applied to a child who does not learn some school task, who is *not* generally retarded, and does *not* show persistent or obvious emotional disturbance or a hearing or vision problem. Thus we can say what learning disability is *not*; what we cannot say is what it *is*.

The identification problem is complicated still further by the fact that among children identified as LD, the specific form of the problem varies widely, with some displaying difficulties in reading only, some having trouble with reading and spelling (such as the boy whose writing sample is shown in Figure 14.3) and others having more difficulty with arithmetic.

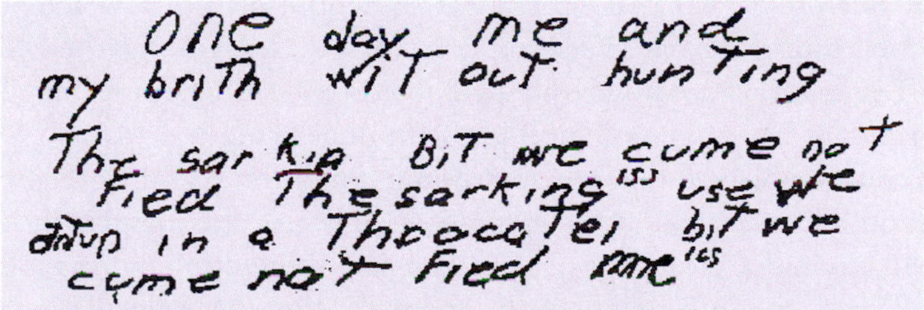

FIGURE 14.3
This story, written by 13-year-old Luke, diagnosed as learning disabled, translates as follows: "One day me and my brother went out hunting the Sark. But we could not find the Sark. So we went up in a helicopter but we could not find him." The little numbers next to some of the word's are Luke's word-counts. They show that despite his severe writing handicap, his counting abilities were intact. (Source: Farnham-Diggory, 1978, p. 61.)

Can you think of any way out of this dilemma? Should schools be given additional funds for those labeled as "slow learners" too? What might be the effects of such a policy?

Furthermore, school districts receive federal funds to pay for special education for children they identify as learning disabled, but they do *not* receive such funds for education of children labeled as "slow learners." Thus there is a strong financial incentive to label almost any kind of delayed or slow learning a "learning disability."

For all of these reasons, I cannot give you any kind of precise estimate of the frequency of the problem, although I am inclined to believe Farnham-Diggory's 5 out of 1,000.

The Nature of the Problem.   Given such problems with definition, we shouldn't be surprised that the search for causes has been fraught with difficulties. As Farnham-Diggory says, "We are trying to find out what's wrong with children whom we won't be able to accurately identify until after we know what's wrong with them" (1986, p. 153).

The most central problem has been with the basic assumption that learning disability has a neurological basis. The difficulty is that children so labeled (like hyperactive children) rarely show any signs of major brain damage on any standard tests—perhaps because many children are mislabeled, or perhaps because the brain dysfunction is more subtle than what can be measured with standard tests.

The most promising current view is that a large number of small abnormalities develop in the brain during prenatal life, such as some irregularity of neuron arrangement, or clumps of immature brain cells, or scars or congenital tumors. The growing brain compensates for these problems by "rewiring" around the problem areas. These rewirings, in turn, may slightly scramble normal information processing procedures, just enough to make reading or calculation or some other specific task very difficult (Farnham-Diggory, 1992).

Another explanation of the problem, one you may recall from Chapter 9, is that reading disability may reflect a more general problem with language. The research findings supporting this conclusion have been very helpful in pointing educators toward possible remedial programs for children with reading difficulties. But they do not tell us why a child might have such language deficits in the first place. The problem may lie in brain dysfunction, or it may well be that children whose reading problem has such an origin are among the 80 percent Farnham-Diggory says are misclassified. They do indeed have a reading problem, but they may not have a neurological problem underlying it.

I want to emphasize that the continuing confusion and disagreement about identification and explanation of learning disability occurs despite thousands of research studies and a great deal of theorizing by thoughtful and capable people. Not surprisingly, the uncertainty at the theoretical level is reflected in confusion at the practical level. Children are labeled "learning disabled" and assigned to special classes, but whether the child will be helped by a particular type of intervention program will depend on whether that specific program is (a) any good, and (b) happens to match his or her type of disability or problem. Remediation does seem to be possible, but it is *not* simple, and a program that works well for one child may not work at all for another. Of course this is not good news for parents whose child may be having difficulty with some aspect of schooling, whose only recourse is trial and error and eternal vigilance. But it reflects the disordered state of our knowledge.

School can surely be a discouraging and frustrating place for a child with a learning disability.

Giftedness

For parents whose children lie at the other end of the intellectual continuum, the gifted, the problem is almost as tough. Finding good programs for such children is a continuing dilemma. Let me give you an extreme example, a child named Michael described by Halbert Robinson (1981):

> When Michael was 2 years and 3 months old, the family visited our laboratory. At that time, they described a youngster who had begun speaking at age 5 months and by 6 months had exhibited a vocabulary of more than 50 words. He started to read English when he was 13 months old. In our laboratory he spoke five languages and could read in three of them. He understood addition, subtraction, multiplication, division, and square root, and he was fascinated by a broad range of scientific constructs. He loved to make puns, frequently bilingual ones." (p. 63)

Michael's IQ on the Stanford Binet was in excess of 180 at age 2; two years later, when Michael was 4½, he performed on the test like a 12-year-old and was listed as having an IQ beyond 220.

Definitions and Labels. We can certainly all agree that Michael should be labeled as **gifted.** But defining the term precisely is more difficult (Sternberg & Davidson, 1986). Giftedness includes those with exceptional specific talents, such as musical or artistic skills, or specific mathematical or spatial ability, as well as those with very high IQs. This broadening of the definition of giftedness is widely accepted among theorists, who agree that there are many kinds of exceptional ability, each of which may reflect unusual speed or efficiency with one or another type of cognitive function.

Within school systems, however, giftedness is still typically defined entirely by IQ tests scores, such as all scores above 130 or 140. Robinson suggested that it may be useful to divide the group of high IQ children into two sets, the "garden variety gifted," with high IQs (perhaps 130 to 150) but without extraordinary ability in any one area, and the "highly gifted" (like Michael) with extremely high IQ scores and/or remarkable skill in one or more areas. These two groups of children may have quite different experiences at home and in school.

Cognitive and Social Functioning in Gifted Children. Just as retarded children show slower and less efficient information processing, the gifted show speedy and efficient processing on simple tasks and flexible use of strategies on more complex tasks. They learn quickly and transfer that learning broadly (Sternberg & Davidson, 1985). Further, they seem to have unusually good *metacognitive* skills: they know what they know and what they don't know, and they spend *more* time than do average IQ children in planning how to go about solving some problem (Dark & Benbow, 1993).

Whether such advanced intellectual abilities transfer to *social* situations is not so well established. Many parents are concerned about placing their gifted child in a higher grade because of fears that the child will not be able to cope socially; others have assumed that rapid development in one area should be linked to rapid development in all areas.

One famous and remarkable early study of gifted children, by Lewis Terman, pointed to the latter conclusion. Terman selected about 1,500 children with high IQs from the California school system in the 1920s. These children—now adults in their seventies and eighties—have been followed regularly throughout their lives (Sears & Barbee, 1977; Terman, 1925; Terman & Oden, 1947; 1959). Terman found that the gifted children he studied were better off than their less gifted classmates in many ways other than school performance. They were healthier; they were interested in many things such as hobbies and games; they were successful in later life. Both the boys and the girls in this study went on to complete many more years of education than was typical of children of their era and had successful careers as adults.

More recent research has painted a somewhat less uniformly rosy picture. On the plus side are studies that show that the self-esteem of gifted children is as high or higher than that of less-bright children, and that they have essentially the same risks of depression or other psychopathology as do those with average IQ. Furthermore, good social development seems to be just as likely for gifted children who have been accelerated through school as for those who have been kept with their age mates but provided with "enrichment" programs (Janos & Robinson, 1985; Robinson & Janos, 1986).

Such optimism about the social robustness of gifted children may have to be tempered somewhat, however, in the case of the highly gifted subgroup, such as those with IQs above 180. These children are *so* different from their peers that they are likely to be seen as strange or disturbing. And these highly gifted children do show higher rates of emotional problems than do nongifted children (Janos & Robinson, 1985).

Also on the negative side of the ledger is the fact that many gifted children are so bored by school that they drop out, often because their school district does not allow acceleration in grade or has no special programs for the gifted. Given the fact that there is little sign of social maladjustment associated with grade-skipping, it seems to make very good sense to encourage accelerated schooling, if only to help ward off terminal boredom for the gifted child.

Are you persuaded by my arguments in favor of encouraging grade-skipping by gifted children? If you were a parent of a gifted child, what kind of data would you want to have to help make a decision on this question?

Elizabeth Lovance of Hartland, Wisconsin, on the right, skipped several grades and graduated from high school at age 14. She said of her experience of being accelerated through school: "I would have had a mental breakdown if I had remained where I was."

Physically Atypical Development

The last group of children I want to talk about, albeit briefly, are those with some clear physical problems, such as blindness or deafness. Such children experience very substantial difficulties in everyday living; most require special schooling or special facilities in school.

The Deaf Child

Most children with hearing loss can function adequately with the assistance of a hearing aid. In fact, many physicians are now fitting **hearing-impaired** children with hearing aids during infancy rather than waiting until the child is of preschool age. The situation is quite different, though, for the profoundly deaf—the child whose hearing loss is so severe that even with mechanical assistance his comprehension of sound, especially language, is significantly reduced. Here are a few facts about this group:

This hearing mother has learned to use sign language so that she can communicate with her deaf child.

1. The vast majority of deaf children (about 90 percent) are born to *hearing* parents and thus grow up in a world dominated by spoken language.
2. Most profoundly deaf children have major deficits in both spoken and written language. They have difficulty speaking, most do not lip-read well, and most read at only the most basic level (Schlesinger & Meadow, 1972).
3. Among the deaf, those with deaf parents usually do as well or *better* on measures of written and spoken language than do those with hearing parents (Liben, 1978).

It is this last fact that is the most surprising and which raises key practical and theoretical questions. Why would children raised by deaf parents have a better prognosis? Schlesinger and Meadow argue that the major reason is that these children are learning a language—in this case sign language—at the normal time. Deaf parents use sign language with each other and with their children, so the children learn that language. But a deaf child of hearing parents, unless the parents learn to sign, will learn no language. Such children do develop their own gestures, even stringing two gestures together into a kind of simple sentence. But beyond this level, the child needs language input. If the emphasis is placed exclusively on *oral* language, the deaf child has much more difficulty developing either speech or reading than if the child is taught sign language, lip reading, and oral language at the same time (Greenberg et al., 1984; Moores, 1985). Some children with good combined training can function in a normal school environment, but even with good early training, most deaf children require special schooling.

The Blind Child

If I had asked you, before you read this chapter, to tell me which would be worse, to have been blind or deaf from birth, most of you would have said it would be far worse to be blind. Yet from the point of view of the child's ability to function in most normal settings, including school, blindness is a smaller

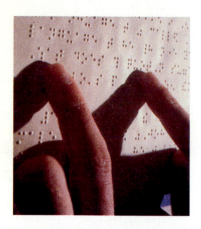

With the advent of small audiotape machines and books-on-tape, Braille is not taught or learned by the blind as often as before. But signs in Braille are still used in a variety of public places, such as elevators.

handicap. The blind child can learn to read (with Braille), can talk with others, can listen to tapes and to a teacher, and so on. Because of this greater academic potential, and because of the enormous role of language in forming and maintaining social relationships, there are more options open to the blind child or adult than to the deaf.

Still, there are obviously important limitations for the blind and important potential pitfalls. One of these lies in the earliest relationship with the parent, which I've discussed in the *Research Report* below. Later relationships may be impaired for the same reasons.

The long-term consequences of either deafness or blindness seem to depend in part on how early some kind of intervention is begun. Early intervention that involves the family seems especially helpful, which is precisely what we should expect from the perspective of developmental psychopathology. If family interventions, such as Fraiberg's (described in the *Research Report*), can help families to form secure attachments and to establish more optimum patterns of interaction, then some of the second- and third-order effects of the child's physical problem may be avoided.

R E S E A R C H   R E P O R T

Basic Attachments between Blind Babies and Their Mothers

In Chapter 6, I briefly mentioned Selma Fraiberg's work with blind infants as part of the discussion of the parent's attachment to the child. Because Fraiberg's work is so fascinating, I want to expand on the point.

Fraiberg (1974; 1975; 1977) found that blind babies begin to smile at about the same age as sighted babies (about 4 weeks) but that they smile less often. And at about 2 months, when the sighted baby begins to smile regularly at the sight of the parent's face, the blind baby's smiles become less and less frequent. The blind infant's smile is also less intense, more fleeting.

The other thing blind babies don't do is enter into mutual gaze. They don't look right at their parents, and everything we know about parents' responses to their babies underlines the importance of mutual gaze for the parents' feeling of attachment to the baby. Furthermore, the facial expressions of the blind infant are muted and sober. Many observers, including parents, conclude that the baby is depressed or indifferent. The combination of these circumstances often leaves the parents feeling as if the baby had rejected them.

Fraiberg found that most of the mothers of the blind babies in her studies gradually withdrew from their infants. They provided the needed physical care, but they stopped playing with the baby, and gave up trying to elicit

smiles or other social interactions. They often said they didn't "love" this baby.

Fortunately, it's possible to solve this particular problem. Fraiberg found that these mothers could be helped to form a strong bond with their infant if they could be shown how to "read" the baby's other signals. The blind child's face may be sober and relatively expressionless, but her hands and body move a lot and express a great deal. When the child *stops* moving when you come into the room, this means she is listening to your footsteps. Or she may move her hands when she hears your voice rather than smiling as a sighted child would do.

When parents of blind children learn to respond to these alternative "attachment behaviors" in their babies, then the mutuality of the relationship can be reestablished. And when this happens, and the parents are able to provide more varied stimulation, blind children develop more normal behavior in other ways. In particular, they don't show the "blindisms" so often observed in blind youngsters, such as rocking, sucking, head banging, and other repetitive actions.

Here, then, is a clear example of how psychological research can lead to very practical applications with families.

Sex Differences in Atypical Development

One of the most fascinating facts about atypical development is that virtually all forms of disorder are more common in boys than in girls—the major exception obviously being depression, which as I've already mentioned, is more common among adolescent girls and among adult women. I've put some of the comparisons in Table 14.4, but even this list does not convey the extent of the difference. With very few exceptions, studies of the impact of environmental stresses show that boys are more adversely affected. This is true in studies of divorce, parental discord, parental mental illness, parental job loss, and many others. In these situations boys are more likely to show disturbed behavior, a decline in school performance, or some other indication of problem (Zaslow & Hayes, 1986).

How are we to explain differences like this? One possibility is that the double X chromosome gives the girl protection from any form of inherited disorder or anomaly. Girls are obviously less likely to inherit any recessive disease that is carried on the sex chromosomes. We also have some hints that there may be a gene on the X chromosome that affects the individual's ability to respond effectively to stress. Since girls have two X chromosomes they are less likely to suffer from any disorder in that gene. If this explanation is valid, then the appropriate conclusion is not that *all* boys are more vulnerable, but that *more* boys than girls have some minor neurological dysfunction or high vulnerability to stressors of various kinds.

Two other physiological factors may also be important, each potentially explaining one or two of the differences listed in Table 14.4. First, hormonal differences may be important contributors. Since it is possible to construct a persuasive argument for the role of male hormones in aggressive behavior (as I did in

TABLE 14.4
Sex Differences in the Incidence of Atypical Development

Type of Problem	Approximate Ratio of Males to Females
Psychopathologies:	
Attention deficit hyperactivity disorder	2:1
Conduct disorders including delinquency	5:1
Anxiety and depression: preadolescence	1:1
Anxiety and depression: adolescence	1:2
Estimated number of all children with all diagnoses seen in psychiatric clinics	2:1
Intellectual atypical development:	
Mental Retardation	3:2
Learning Disabilities	3:2
Physical Problems:	
Blindness or significant visual problems	1:1
Hearing impairment	5:4
Autism	3:1

Sources: Achenbach, 1982; Anthony, 1980; Eme, 1979; Rutter & Garmezy, 1983; Rutter, 1989; Zoccolillo, 1993.

Chapter 10), it is not a very great leap to the hypothesis that the higher incidence of conduct disorders among boys may also be related in some way to hormone variations.

A second possible physiological contributor is the comparative level of physical maturity of boys and girls. Because girls of any age are more physically mature than are boys of the same age, they may have more resources with which to meet various problems. For example, researchers have frequently observed that infant boys are more irritable and less able to achieve physical or emotional equilibrium after being upset than are infant girls (Haviland & Malatesta, 1981). Since such fussiness is also common in *younger* babies, the problem may not be maleness, but immaturity.

Experiences after birth may also contribute to the differing rates of deviance. One hypothesis is that adults are simply more tolerant of disruptive or difficult behavior in boys than in girls. By this argument, boys and girls initially respond similarly to stressful situations, but boys learn early that various forms of acting out, tantrums, or defiance are tolerated or not punished severely. Girls learn to inhibit these responses—perhaps even to internalize them—because adults respond quite differently to them. There is not a great deal of research that tests such a hypothesis, but there are at least fragments of support (Eme, 1979). Studies of cultures in which *both* boys and girls are discouraged from behaving aggressively or assertively would provide very useful data to test such an explanation.

Whatever the explanation—and none of the existing explanations seems very satisfactory to me—it is nonetheless extremely interesting that girls do seem to be less vulnerable, less likely to show virtually any type of atypical development.

Can you think of any other explanations?

The Impact of an Atypical Child on the Family

How does a family deal with an atypical child? In some instances, of course, deficiencies or inadequacies in the family are part of the *cause* of the child's atypical development. But whether the original cause lies in the family or not, once a child does show some form of deviant development the family is inevitably affected, often adversely.

Grief.   One of the first reactions is often a form of grief, almost as if the child had died. This reaction makes sense if you think about the fact that the *fantasy* "perfect child" did die or was never born. The parents grieve for the child-that-never-will-be, expressed poignantly by one parent:

> I wept for the perfect baby I had lost, for the sunsets he would never see, for the 4-year-old who would never be able to play outside unsupervised. (Featherstone, 1980, p. 26)

As with other forms of grief, denial, depression, and anger are all natural elements. For many parents, there is also some guilt (e.g., "If only I hadn't had those drinks at that party while I was pregnant").

In some cases this process may result in an emotional rejection of the infant, aggravated by the difficulty many atypical infants have in entering fully into the mutually adaptive parent-child process. Such rejection seems to be particularly common when the marital relationship is conflicted, or when the family lacks adequate social support (Howard, 1978).

Adaptation by the Family. Once the initial shock and grief is dealt with as well as it can be, the family must work toward an ongoing adaptive system with the atypical child. There are often massive financial burdens; there are problems of finding appropriate schooling; there are endless daily adjustments to the child's special needs.

> I look at the people down the street. Their kids are 15 and 18 and now they can just get in the car and take off when they want to . . . and then I think, "When will that happen for us? We'll always have to be thinking of Christopher. . . . We'll never have that freedom." (Featherstone, 1980, p. 17)

The system that evolves most often leaves the mother primarily in charge of the atypical child; with physically handicapped children, fathers seem quite often to withdraw from interaction with or care of the child (Bristol et al., 1988). This is not a general withdrawal of the father from the family system, since such fathers continue to be involved with their other children. But the father's selective withdrawal leaves the mother with added burdens. One predictable response, among both mothers and fathers, is depression. Parents of atypical children are also more likely to have low self-esteem and to have lower feelings of personal competence (Howard, 1978). Where the marital relationship was poor before the birth of the atypical child, the presence of the handicapped child in the family system seems to increase the likelihood of further discord. However there is no consistent indication that having an atypical child results in an average increase in marital disharmony or risk of divorce (Longo & Bond, 1984).

The fact that many (even most) parents manage to adapt effectively to the presence of an atypical child is testimony to the devotion and immense effort expended. But there is no evading the fact that rearing such a child is very hard work, and that it strains the family system in ways that rearing a normal child does not.

A Final Point

As a final point, I think it is crucial for me to state clearly what has been only implicit throughout this chapter: children whose development is atypical in some respect are much more *like* normally developing children in other respects than they are unlike them. Blind and deaf and retarded children all form attachments in much the same way that physically and mentally normal children do (Lederberg & Mobley, 1990); children with conduct disorders go through the same sequences of cognitive development that more adjusted children show. It is very easy, when dealing with an atypical child, to be overwhelmed by the sense of differentness. But as Sroufe and Rutter and all the other developmental psychopathologists are beginning to say so persuasively, the same basic processes are involved.

S U M M A R Y

1. Approximately 20 percent of all children in the United States will need some form of special assistance because of atypical development at some time in childhood or adolescence.

2. Studies of psychopathology are more and more being cast in a *developmental* framework, with emphasis on the complex pathways that lead to deviance or normality. Such a framework also emphasizes the importance of the child's own resilience or vulnerability to stresses.

3. Psychopathologies can be divided into two broad groups: externalizing and internalizing.

4. One type of externalizing problem is conduct disorders, including both patterns of excess aggressiveness and delinquency. Conduct disorders can also be divided into early and late-onset problems. The former are more serious and persistent.

5. Early onset conduct disorders appear to have a genetic component and to be exacerbated by poor family interactions and subsequent poor peer relations.

6. Attention Deficit Hyperactivity Disorder is another type of externalizing problem, beginning in early childhood and typically persisting. The problems encountered by such children are much more acute if they also display conduct disorders.

7. Hyperactivity appears to have an initial biological cause, but deviant patterns are aggravated or ameliorated by subsequent experience.

8. Depression is one form of internalizing problem, relatively uncommon in childhood but common in adolescence. Depressed youngsters are more likely to have a family history of parental depression or to have developed low self-esteem or have a history of being ignored by peers.

9. Family stress or stress experienced directly by the child, especially multiple simultaneous stresses, exacerbate any existing or underlying tendency toward pathology.

10. Children with inborn vulnerabilities (difficult temperament or physical problems), few protective factors, and few resources are more likely to respond to stressful circumstances with pathology.

11. Children with mental retardation, normally defined as IQ below 70, combined with significant problems of adaptation, show slower development and more immature or less efficient forms of information processing strategies.

12. Two groups of retarded can be identified: those with clear physical abnormalities, overrepresented among the severely retarded, and those without physical abnormalities but with low IQ parents and/or deprived environments, who are overrepresented among the mildly retarded.

13. Roughly 4 percent of the school population in the United States are labeled as learning disabled. There is still considerable dispute about how to identify genuine learning disability, and many may be misclassified.

14. Learning disability may be caused by small anomalies in brain function; alternatively, they may reflect broader language or cognitive deficits, or both.

15. Gifted is a term applied to children with very high IQ or to those with unusual creativity or special skill. Their information processing is unusually flexible and generalized. Socially they appear to be well adjusted, except for the small group of unusually highly gifted students.

16. Deaf children do best when they can develop a language (in this case signing) at the normal language-learning age.

17. Blind children may have difficulty with early relationships because their interpersonal signals are quite different. However, they adapt much more readily to school than do the deaf.

18. Boys show almost all forms of atypical development more often than girls do. This may reflect genetic differences, hormone differences, or differences in cultural expectations.

19. Families with atypical children experience chronically heightened stress and demands for adaptation. This is frequently accompanied by depression or other disturbance in the parents.

K E Y   T E R M S

adaptive behavior
attention deficit
   hyperactivity disorder
   (ADD)
brain damage
chromosomal anomalies
conduct disorder

depression
developmental
   psychopathology
externalizing problems
gifted
hearing-impaired
hyperactivity

inborn errors of
   metabolism
internalizing problems
learning disability
mentally retarded

S U G G E S T E D   R E A D I N G S

Farnham-Diggory, S. (1992). *The learning-disabled child*. Cambridge, MA: Harvard University Press. This revision of an excellent book will give you an up-to-date source, pitched at the level of the lay reader.

Lewis, M., & Miller, S. M. (Eds.) (1990). *Handbook of developmental psychopathology*. New York: Plenum. This book is definitely written for fellow professionals, so it is often very dense and technical. But if you are interested in any aspect of psychopathology, this is a current and valuable source.

Petersen, A. C., Compas, B. C., Brooks-Gunn, J., Stemmler, M., Ey, S., & Grant, K. E. (1993). Depression in adolescence. *American Psychologist, 48*, pp. 155–168. A brief, fairly dense, review of the most current information on this important subject.

GLOSSARY

accommodation   That part of the adaptation process by which a person modifies existing schemes as a result of new experiences or creates new schemes when old ones no longer handle the data.

achievement test   A test usually given in schools, designed to assess a child's learning of specific material taught in school, such as spelling or arithmetic computation.

acuity   Sharpness of perceptual ability—how well or clearly one can see or hear or use other senses.

adaptive behavior   An aspect of a child's functioning often considered in diagnosing mental retardation. Can the child adapt to the tasks of everyday life?

affectional bond   A relatively long-enduring tie in which the partner is important as a unique individual and is interchangeable with none other.

aggression   Behavior with the apparent intent to injure some other person or object.

alpha-fetoprotein test   A prenatal diagnostic test frequently used to screen for the risk of neural tube defects.

altruism   Giving or sharing objects, time, or goods with others, with no obvious self-gain.

amniocentesis   A medical test for genetic abnormalities in the embryo/fetus that may be done at about 15 weeks of gestation.

amnion   The sac or bag, filled with liquid, in which the embryo and fetus floats during prenatal life.

androgyny   A self-concept including behavior and expressing high levels of both masculine and feminine qualities.

anorexia nervosa   A disorder characterized by extreme dieting, intense fear of gaining weight, and distorted body image.

anoxia   A shortage of oxygen. If it is prolonged, it can result in brain damage. This is one of the potential risks at birth.

Apgar score   An assessment of the newborn completed by the physician or midwife at one minute and again at five minutes after birth, assessing five characteristics: heart rate, respiratory rate, muscle tone, response to stimulation, and color.

assimilation   That part of the adaptation process that involves the "taking in" of new experiences or information into existing schemes. Experience is not taken in "as is," however, but is modified (or interpreted) somewhat so as to fit the preexisting schemes.

attachment   An especially intense and central subtype of affectional bond in which the presence of the partner adds a special sense of security, a "safe base," for the individual. Characteristic of the child's bond with the parent.

attachment behavior   The collection of (probably) instinctive behaviors of one person toward another that bring about or maintain proximity and caregiving, such as the smile of the young infant; behaviors that reflect an attachment.

attention deficit hyperactivity disorder (ADD)   The technical term for what is more normally called hyperactivity, characterized by short attention span, distractibility, and heightened levels of physical activity.

authoritarian parental style   One of the three styles that Baumrind described. It is characterized by high levels of control and maturity demands and low levels of nurturance and communication.

authoritative parental style   One of the three styles that Baumrind described. It is characterized by high levels of control, nurturance, maturity demands, and communication.

autosomes   The 22 pairs of chromosomes in which both members of the pair are the same shape and carry parallel information.

axon   The long appendage-like part of a neuron; the terminal fibers of the axon serve as transmitters in the synaptic connection with the dendrites of other neurons.

babbling   The vocalizing, often repetitively, of consonant-vowel combinations by an infant, typically beginning at about 6 months of age.

Bayley Scales of Infant Development   The best known and most widely used test of infant "intelligence."

behavior genetics   The study of the genetic basis of behavior, such as intelligence or personality.

brain damage   Some injury to the brain, either during prenatal development or later, that results in improper functioning of the brain.

bulimia   A pattern of intense concern about weight, combined with binge eating followed by purging, either through self-induced vomiting, excessive use of laxatives, or excessive exercise.

canalization   Term used to describe the degree to which development may be shaped by underlying maturational forces (as opposed to environment) during some period in the life span.

cephalocaudal   From the head downward. Describes one recurrent pattern of physical development in infancy.

cesarean section   Delivery of the child through an incision in the mother's abdomen.

chorionic villus sampling   A technique for prenatal genetic diagnosis involving taking a sample of cells from the placenta. Can be performed earlier in the pregnancy than amniocentesis.

chromosomal anomalies   Variations in the normal set of 23 pairs of chromosomes, almost always resulting in physical or mental abnormalities in the affected child. Down syndrome is an example of a chromosomal anomaly.

chromosomes   The structures, arrayed in 23 pairs, contained in each cell in the body that contains genetic information. Each chromosome is made up of many segments, called genes.

classical conditioning   One of three major types of learning. An automatic unconditioned response such as an emotion or a reflex comes to be triggered by a new cue, called the conditioned stimulus (CS), after the CS has been paired several times with the original unconditioned stimulus.

class inclusion   The relationship between classes of objects, such that a subordinate class is included in a superordinate class, as bananas are part of the class "fruit," and the class fruit is included in the class "food."

clique   A group of 6–8 friends with strong affectional bonds and high levels of group solidarity and loyalty.

cohort   A group of persons of approximately the same age who have shared similar major life experiences, such as cultural training, economic conditions, or type of education.

color constancy   The ability to see the color of an object as remaining the same despite changes in illumination or shadow. One of the basic perceptual constancies that make up "object constancy."

competence   The behavior of a person as it would be under ideal or perfect circumstances. It is not possible to measure competence directly.

componential intelligence   One of three types of intelligence in Sternberg's triarchic theory of intelligence; that type of intelligence typically measured on IQ tests, including analytic thinking, remembering facts, organizing information.

concrete operations stage   The stage of development proposed by Piaget between ages 6 and 12, in which the child acquires mental operations such as subtraction, reversibility, and multiple classification.

conditioned stimulus   In classical conditioning, the stimulus that, after being paired a number of times with an unconditioned stimulus, comes to trigger the unconditioned response.

conduct disorder   Diagnostic term for an individual showing high levels of aggressive, antisocial, or delinquent behavior.

conservation   The concept that objects remain the same in fundamental ways, such as weight or number, even when there are external changes in shape or arrangement. Typically understood by children after age 5.

contextual intelligence   One of three types of intelligence in Sternberg's triarchic theory of intelligence; often also called "street smarts," this type of intelligence includes skills in adapting to an environment and in adapting an environment to one's own needs.

control group   The group of subjects in an experiment that receives either no special treatment or some neutral treatment.

conventional morality   Kohlberg's second level of moral judgment, in which the person's judgments are dominated by considerations of group values and laws.

cooing   An early stage during the prelinguistic period, from about 1–4 months of age, when vowel sounds are repeated, particularly the *uuu* sound.

correlation   A statistic used to describe the degree or strength of a relationship between two variables. It can range from + 1.00 to −1.00. The closer it is to 1.00 the stronger the relationship being described.

cortex   The convoluted gray portion of the brain that governs most complex thought, language, and memory.

critical period   A period of time during development when the organism is especially ready to respond to and learn from a specific type of stimulation. The same stimulation at other points in development has little or no effect.

cross-cultural research   Research involving comparisons of several cultures or subcultures.

cross-modal transfer   The ability to coordinate information from two senses or to transfer information gained through one sense to another sense at a later time, such as identifying visually something you had previously explored only tactually.

cross-sectional study   A study in which researchers study different groups of individuals of different ages all at the same time.

crowd   A larger and looser group of friends than a clique, normally made up of several cliques joined together.

culture   A system of meanings and customs, shared by some identifiable group or subgroup and transmitted from one generation of that group to the next.

cumulative deficit   Any difference between groups in IQ (or achievement test) scores that becomes larger over time.

deductive logic   Reasoning from the general to the particular, from a rule to an expected instance or from a theory to a hypothesis. Characteristic of formal operational thought.

dendrites   The branchlike parts of a neuron that serve as the receptors in synaptic connections with the axons of other neurons.

deoxyribonucleic acid   Called DNA for short, this is the chemical of which genes are composed.

dependent variable   The variable in an experiment that is expected to show the impact of manipulations of the independent variable.

depression   A combination of sad mood, sleep and eating disturbances, and difficulty concentrating. When all these symptoms are present it is usually called *clinical depression*.

developmental psychopathology   A relatively new approach to the study of deviance that emphasizes that normal and abnormal development have common roots, and that pathology can arise from many different pathways or systems.

dilation   The first stage of childbirth when the cervix opens sufficiently to allow the infant's head to pass into the birth canal.

dominance   The ability of one person consistently to "win" competitive encounters with other individuals.

dominance hierarchy   A set of dominance relationships in a group describing the rank order of "winners" and "losers" in competitive encounters.

Down syndrome   A genetic anomaly in which every cell contains three copies of chromosome 21 rather than two. Children born with this genetic pattern are usually mentally retarded and have characteristic physical features.

effacement   The flattening of the cervix which, along with dilation, allows the delivery of the infant.

ego   In Freudian theory, that portion of the personality that organizes, plans, and keeps the person in touch with reality. Language and thought are both ego functions.

egocentrism   A cognitive state in which the individual (typically a child) sees the world only from his own perspective, without awareness that there are other perspectives.

embryo   The name given to the organism during the period of prenatal development from about 2 to 8 weeks after conception, beginning with implantation of the blastocyst into the uterine wall.

empathy   As defined by Hoffman, it is "a vicarious affective response that does not necessarily match another's affective state but is more appropriate to the other's situation than to one's own." (Hoffman, 1984, p. 285.)

empiricism   Opposite of "nativism." The theoretical point of view that all perceptual skill arises from experience.

endocrine glands   These glands, including the adrenals, the thyroid, the pituitary, the testes, and the ovaries, secrete hormones governing overall physical growth and sexual maturing.

equilibration   The third part of the adaptation process, as proposed by Piaget, involving a periodic restructuring of schemes into new structures.

estrogen   The female sex hormone that the ovaries secrete.

ethnic group   "A subgroup whose members are perceived by themselves and others to have a common origin and culture, and shared activities in which the common origin or culture is an essential ingredient." (Porter & Washington, 1993, p. 140.)

ethnography   A detailed description of a single culture or context, based on extensive observation, often provided by a person who lived within that culture for a period of time.

executive processes   Proposed subset of information processes involving organizing and planning strategies. Similar in meaning to metacognition.

experiential intelligence   One of three types of intelligence that Sternberg described in his triarchic theory of intelligence; includes creativity, insight, seeing new relationships among experiences.

experiment   A research strategy in which researchers randomly assign subjects to groups which are then provided with experiences that vary along some key dimension.

experimental group   The group (or groups) of subjects in an experiment that is given some special treatment intended to produce some specific consequence.

expressive language   The term used to describe the child's skill in speaking and communicating orally.

expressive style   One of two styles of early language proposed by Nelson, characterized by low rates of nounlike terms and high use of personal-social words and phrases.

externalizing problems   Category of psychopathologies that includes any deviant behavior primarily directed away from the individual, such as conduct disorders or hyperactivity.

extinction   A decrease in the strength of some response after nonreinforcement.

fallopian tube   The tube down which the ovum travels to the uterus and in which conception usually occurs.

family day care   Nonparental care in which the child is cared for in someone else's home, usually with a small group of other children.

fetal alcohol syndrome (FAS)   A pattern of physical and mental abnormalities, including mental retardation and minor physical anomalies, found often in children born to alcoholic mothers.

fetus   The name given to the developing organism from about 8 weeks after conception until birth.

fontanels   The "soft spots" in the skull present at birth. These disappear when the several bones of the skull grow together.

foreclosure   One of four identity statuses that Marcia proposed, involving an ideological or occupational commitment without having gone through a reevaluation.

formal operations stage   Piaget's name for the fourth and final major stage of cognitive development, occurring during adolescence, when the child becomes able to manipulate and organize ideas as well as objects.

gametes   Sperm and ova. These cells, unlike all other cells of the body, contain only 23 chromosomes rather than 23 pairs.

gender concept   The understanding of one's own gender, including the permanence and constancy of gender.

gender constancy   The final step in developing a gender concept, in which the child understands that gender doesn't change even though there are external changes like clothing or hair length.

gender identity   The first step in gender concept development, in which the child labels herself correctly and categorizes others correctly as male or female.

gender schema   A fundamental schema created by children beginning at age 18 months or younger by which the child categorizes people, objects, activities, and qualities by gender.

gender stability   The second step in gender concept development, in which the child understands that a person's gender continues to be stable throughout the lifetime.

gene   A uniquely coded segment of DNA in a chromosome that affects one or more specific body processes or developments.

genotype   The pattern of characteristics and developmental sequences mapped in the genes of any specific individual. Will be modified by individual experience into the phenotype.

gifted   Normally defined in terms of very high IQ (above 140 or 150), but may also be defined in terms of remarkable skill in one or more specific areas, such as mathematics or memory.

glial cells   One of two major classes of cells making up the nervous system, glial cells provide the firmness and structure, the "glue" to hold the system together.

gonadotropic hormone   Hormones produced in the pituitary gland stimulating the sex organs to develop.

goodness-of-fit   A hypothesis about the interaction of nature and nurture suggesting that negative outcomes occur when the child's characteristics do not fit with the demands of a particular family or school environment.

habituation   An automatic decrease in the intensity of a response to a repeated stimulus, which enables the child or adult to ignore the familiar and focus attention on the novel.

hearing-impaired   The phrase currently used in place of "hard of hearing" to describe children or adults with significant hearing loss.

holophrases   The expression of a whole idea in a single word. Characteristic of the child's language from about 12–18 months.

hyperactivity   The common term for attention deficit hyperactivity disorder.

id   In Freudian theory, the first, primitive portion of the personality; the storehouse of basic energy, continually pushing for immediate gratification.

identification   The process of taking into oneself ("incorporating") the qualities and ideas of another person, which Freud thought was the result of the Oedipal crisis at age 3–5. The child attempts to make himself like his parent of the same sex.

identity achievement   One of four identity statuses Marcia proposed, involving the successful resolution of an identity "crisis" that results in a new commitment.

identity diffusion   One of four identity statuses Marcia proposed, involving neither a current reevaluation nor a firm personal commitment.

inborn errors of metabolism   Inherited patterns of physical dysfunction in which the infant or child fails to metabolize one or more amino acids in the normal fashion. Phenylketonuria is the best known such error.

independent variable   A condition or event that an experimenter varies in some systematic way in order to observe the impact of that variation on the subjects' behavior.

inductive logic   Reasoning from the particular to the general, from experience to broad rules. Characteristic of concrete operational thinking.

inflections   The grammatical "markers" such as plurals, possessives, past tenses, and equivalent.

information processing   Phrase used to refer to a new, third approach to the study of intellectual development that focuses on changes with age and individual differences in fundamental intellectual skills.

insecure attachment   Includes both ambivalent and avoidant patterns of attachment in children; the child does not use the parent as a safe base and is not readily consoled by the parent if upset.

internalizing problems   A category of psychopathologies in which the deviant behavior is directed inward, including anxiety and depression.

internal working model of social relationships   Cognitive construction, for which the earliest relationships may form the template, of the workings of relationships, such as expectations of support, affection, or trustworthiness.

intrinsic reinforcements   Those inner sources of pleasure, pride, or satisfaction that serve to increase the likelihood that an individual will repeat the behavior that led to the feeling.

intelligence quotient (IQ)   Originally defined in terms of a child's mental age and chronological age, IQs are now computed by comparing a child's performance with that of other children of the same chronological age.

learning disability (LD)   Term broadly used to describe any child with an unexpected or unexplained problem in learning to read, spell, or calculate. More precisely used to refer to a subgroup of such children who have some neurological dysfunction.

libido   The term used by Freud to describe the pool of sexual energy in each individual.

longitudinal study   A research design in which researchers observe or assess the same subjects repeatedly over a period of months or years.

low birth-weight (LBW)   The phrase now used (in place of the word *premature*) to describe infants whose weight is below the optimum range at birth. Includes infants born too early (preterm or short gestation infants) and those who are "small-for-date."

maturation   The sequential unfolding of physical characteristics, governed by instructions contained in the genetic code and shared by all members of the species.

mean length of utterance   Usually abbreviated MLU; the average number of meaningful units in a sentence. Each basic word is one meaningful unit, as is each inflection, such as the *s* for plural or the *ed* for a past tense.

medulla   A portion of the brain that lies immediately above the spinal cord; largely developed at birth.

menarche   Onset of menstruation in girls.

mentally retarded   Those children who show a pattern of low IQ, poor adaptive behavior, and poor information processing skill.

metacognition   General and rather loosely used term describing an individual's knowledge of his own thinking processes. Knowing what you know and how you go about learning or remembering.

metamemory   A subcategory of metacognition; knowledge about your own memory processes.

midbrain   A section of the brain lying above the medulla and below the cortex that regulates attention, sleeping, waking, and other "automatic" functions. Largely developed at birth.

modeling   A term that Bandura and others use to describe observational learning.

moratorium   One of four identity statuses Marcia proposed, involving an ongoing reexamination but without a new commitment as yet.

motherese   The word linguists often use to describe the particular pattern of speech by adults to young children. The sentences are shorter, simpler, repetitive, and higher pitched.

motor development   Growth and change in ability to do physical activities, such as walking, running, or riding a bike.

myelin   Material making up a sheath that develops around most axons. This sheath is not completely developed at birth.

myelinization   The process by which myelin is added.

nativism   *See* "empiricism" above. The view that perceptual skills are inborn and do not require experience to develop.

nature/nurture controversy   A common label for the classic dispute about the relative roles of heredity versus environment.

negative reinforcement   The strengthening of a behavior that occurs because of the removal or cessation of an unpleasant stimulus.

neglecting parental style   Fourth type suggested by Maccoby and Martin, including low levels of control, low acceptance or even outright rejection, and low levels of warmth.

neurons   The second major class of cells in the nervous system, neurons are responsible for transmission and reception of nerve impulses.

object constancy   The general phrase describing the ability to see objects as remaining the same despite changes in retinal image.

objective self   Second step in the development of the self-concept; awareness of the self as an object with properties.

object permanence   Part of the object concept. The recognition that an object continues to exist even when it is temporarily out of sight.

observational learning   Learning of motor skills, attitudes, or other behaviors through observing someone else perform them.

Oedipus conflict   The pattern of events Freud believed occurred between age 3 and 5 when the child experiences a "sexual" desire for the parent of the opposite sex; the resulting fear of possible reprisal from the parent of the same sex is resolved when the child "identifies" with the parent of the same sex.

operant conditioning   One of the three major types of learning in which the probability of a person performing some behavior is affected by positive or negative reinforcements.

operation   Term Piaget uses for complex, internal, abstract, or reversible schemes, first seen at about age 6.

ossification   The process of hardening by which soft tissue becomes bone.

overregularization   The tendency on the part of children to make the language regular, such as using past tenses like "beated" or "goed."

ovum   The gamete produced by a woman, which, if fertilized by a sperm from the male, forms the basis for the developing organism.

partial reinforcement   Reinforcement of behavior on some schedule less frequent than every occasion.

perceptual constancies   A collection of constancies, including shape, size, and color constancy.

performance   The behavior a person shows under actual circumstances. Even when we are interested in competence, all we can ever measure is performance.

performance tests   A new category of criterion-referenced tests used in some school systems today, in which students are required to demonstrate some actual skills, such as writing, performing experiments, or mathematical reasoning.

permissive parental style   One of the three styles described by Baumrind, characterized by high levels of nurturance and low levels of control, maturity demands, and communication.

personality   The collection of individual, relatively enduring patterns of reacting to and interacting with others that distinguishes each child or adult.

phenotype   The expression of a particular set of genetic information in a specific environment; the observable result of the joint operation of genetic and environmental influences.

pituitary gland   One of the endocrine glands that plays a central role in controlling the rate of physical maturation and sexual maturing.

placenta   An organ that develops during gestation between the fetus and the wall of the uterus. The placenta filters nutrients from the mother's blood, acting as liver, lungs, and kidneys for the fetus.

positive reinforcement   Strengthening of a behavior by the presentation of some pleasurable or positive stimulus.

pragmatics   The rules for the use of language in communicative interaction, such as the rules for taking turns, the style of speech appropriate for varying listeners, and equivalent.

preconventional morality   Kohlberg's first level of morality, in which moral judgments are dominated by consideration of what will be punished and what feels good.

prelinguistic phase   The period before the child speaks his first words.

preterm infant   Descriptive phrase now widely used to label infants born before 37 weeks gestational age.

principled morality   Kohlberg's third level of morality, in which considerations of justice, individual rights, and contracts dominate moral judgment.

postpartum depression   A severe form of the common experience of postpartum blues. Affecting perhaps 10 percent of women, this form of clinical depression typically lasts 6 to 8 weeks.

preoperational period   Piaget's term for the second major stage of cognitive development, from age 2 to 6, marked at the beginning by the ability to use symbols and by the development of basic classification and logical abilities.

prosocial behavior   *See* altruism.

proximodistal   From the center outward. With cephalocaudal, describes the pattern of physical changes in infancy.

psychosexual stages   The stages of personality development suggested by Freud, including the oral, anal, phallic, latency, and genital stages.

psychosocial stages   The stages of personality development suggested by Erikson, including trust, autonomy, initiative, industry, identity, intimacy, generativity, and ego integrity.

puberty   The collection of hormonal and physical changes at adolescence that brings about sexual maturity.

punishment   Unpleasant consequences, administered after some undesired behavior by a child or adult, with the intent of extinguishing the behavior.

rapid eye movement (REM) sleep   One of the characteristics of sleep during dreaming, which occurs during the sleep of newborns as well as adults.

receptive language   Term used to describe the child's ability to understand (receive) language, as contrasted to his ability to express language.

referential style   Second style of early language proposed by Nelson, characterized by emphasis on objects and their naming and description.

reflexes   Automatic body reactions to specific stimulation, such as the knee jerk or the Moro reflex. Many reflexes remain among adults, but the newborn also has some "primitive" reflexes that disappear as the cortex is fully developed.

responsiveness   An aspect of parent-child interaction. A responsive parent is sensitive to the child's cues and reacts appropriately, following the child's lead.

restrictiveness   Term used to describe a particular pattern of parental control, involving limitation of the child's movements or options, such as the use of playpens or harnesses in a young child or strict rules about play areas or free choices in an older child.

rubella   A form of measles that, if contracted during the first three months of a pregnancy, may have severe effects on the developing baby.

saccadic movements   The rapid adjustments of the aim of the eye toward some object, such as when you scan an object to identify it or learn its properties, or to locate some new object in your visual field.

scheme   Piaget's word for the basic actions of knowing, including both physical actions (sensorimotor schemes, such as looking or reaching) and mental actions, such as classifying or comparing, or reversing. An experience is assimilated to a scheme, and the scheme is modified or created through accommodation.

secular trends   Patterns of change over several cohorts in such things as the timing of menarche or height or weight.

secure attachment   Demonstrated by the child's ability to use the parent as a safe base and to be consoled after separation, when fearful, or when otherwise stressed.

self-concept   The broad idea of "who I am," including the subjective self and the objective self.

self-esteem   A global judgment of self-worth; how well you like who you perceive yourself to be.

semantics   The rules for conveying meaning in language.

sensitive period   Similar to a critical period except broader and less specific. A time in development when a particular type of stimulation is particularly important or effective.

sensorimotor period   Piaget's term for the first major stage of cognitive development, from birth to about 18 months, when the child moves from reflexive to voluntary action.

sequential designs   A family of research designs that involves multiple cross-sectional or multiple longitudinal studies or a combination of the two.

sex chromosomes   The X and Y chromosomes, which determine the sex of the child. In humans, XX is the female pattern, XY the male pattern.

sex-role behavior   The performance of behavior that matches the culturally-defined sex-role, such as choosing "sex-appropriate" toys, or playing with same-sex children.

sex-role stereotypes   The overextension, or too-rigid definition of sex-roles or sex-role behavior.

sex-roles   the set of behaviors, attitudes, rights, duties, and obligations that are part of the "role" of being a boy or a girl, or a male or a female in any given culture.

sex-typing   *See* sex-role behavior.

shape constancy   The ability to see an object's shape as remaining the same despite changes in the shape of the retinal image. A basic perceptual constancy.

size constancy   The ability to see an object's size as remaining the same despite changes in size of the retinal image. A key element in this constancy is the ability to judge depth.

small-for-date infant   An infant who weighs less than is normal for the number of weeks of gestation completed.

social class   Widely used term to describe broad variations in economic and social positions within any given society. Four broad groups are most often described: upper class, middle class, working class, and lower class (also called poverty level). For an individual family, the designation is based on the income, occupation, and education of the adults in the household.

social cognition   Term used to describe an area of research and theory focused on the child's *understanding* of social relationships.

social referencing   Using another person's reaction to some situation as a basis for deciding one's own reaction. A baby does this when she checks her parent's facial expression or body language before responding positively or negatively to something new.

Stanford-Binet   The best-known American intelligence test. It was written by Louis Terman and his associates based upon the first tests by Binet and Simon.

states of consciousness   Five main sleep/awake states have been identified in infants, from deep sleep to active awake states.

Strange Situation   A series of episodes that Mary Ainsworth and others used in studies of attachment. The child is observed with the mother, with a stranger, left alone, and when reunited with stranger and mother.

subjective self   The first step in the development of the self-concept; the initial awareness that "I exist" separate from others.

sudden infant death syndrome (SIDS)   Unexpected death of an infant who otherwise appears healthy. Also called crib death. Cause is unknown.

superego   In Freudian theory, the "conscience" part of personality, which develops as a result of the identification process. The superego contains the parental and societal values and attitudes incorporated by the child.

synapse   The point of communication between the axon of one neuron and the dendrites of another, where nerve impulses are passed from one neuron to another, or from a neuron to some other type of cell, such as a muscle cell.

syntax   The rules for forming sentences; also called grammar.

telegraphic speech   A characteristic of early child sentences in which everything but the crucial words is omitted, as if for a telegram.

temperament   An individual's typical style of response to experiences, such as emotionality, activity, and sociability. Temperament differences may be genetic in origin and are somewhat stable over time.

teratogen   Any outside agent, such as a disease or a chemical, whose presence significantly increases the risk of deviations or abnormalities in prenatal development.

theory of mind   The idea that a child or adult has about the way their own and other people's minds work and how others are affected by their beliefs and feelings. By 4 or 5, children have a well-developed theory of mind.

tracking   Also called smooth pursuit. The smooth movements of the eye used to follow the track of some moving object.

triarchic theory of intelligence   Sternberg's theory proposing the existence of three types of intelligence—the componential, the contextual, and the experiential.

ultrasound A form of prenatal diagnosis in which high frequency sound waves are used to provide a picture of the moving fetus. Can detect many physical deformities, such as neural tube defects, as well as multiple pregnancies and gestational age.

unconditioned response In classical conditioning this is the basic unlearned response that is triggered by the unconditioned stimulus.

unconditioned stimulus In classical conditioning this is the cue or signal that automatically triggers (without learning) the unconditioned response.

uterus The female organ in which the blastocyst implants itself and within which the embryo/fetus develops. (Popularly referred to as the womb.)

very low birth-weight-infants Phrase now commonly used to describe infants who weigh 1500 grams (3⅓ lbs.) or less at birth.

warmth versus hostility The key dimension of emotional tone used to describe family interactions.

WISC The Wechsler Intelligence Scale for Children. Another well-known American IQ test that includes both verbal and performance (nonverbal) subtests. The most current version is the WISC-III.

REFERENCES

Abramovitch, R., Pepler, D., & Corter, C. (1982). Patterns of sibling interaction among preschool-age children. In M. E. Lamb & B. Sutton-Smith (Eds.), *Sibling relationships: Their nature and significance across the lifespan* (pp. 61–86). Hillsdale, NJ: Erlbaum.

Abrams, B., Newman, V., Key, T., & Parker, J. (1989). Maternal weight gain and preterm delivery. *Obstetrics and Gynecology, 74*, 577–584.

Achenbach, T. M. (1982). *Developmental psychopathology* (2nd ed.). New York: Wiley.

Achenbach, T. M. (1993). Taxonomy and comorbidity of conduct problems: Evidence from empirically based approaches. *Development and Psychopathology, 5*, 51–64.

Achenbach, T. M., & Edelbrock, C. S. (1981). Behavioral problems and competencies reported by parents of normal and disturbed children aged 4 through 16. Monographs of the Society for Research in Child Development, 46 (Serial No. 188).

Achenbach, T. M., Howell, C. T., Quay, H. C., & Conners, C. K. (1991). National survey of problems and competencies among four- to sixteen-year-olds. *Monographs of the Society for Research in Child Development, 56* (Serial No. 225).

Adair, L. S., Popkin, B. M., & Guilkey, D. K. (1993). The duration of breast-feeding: How is it affected by biological, sociodemographic, health sector, and food industry factors? *Demography, 30*, 63–80.

Adams, M. J. (1990). *Beginning to read: Thinking and learning about print.* Cambridge, MA: The MIT Press.

Adler, A. (1948). *Studies in analytical psychology.* New York: Norton.

Ainsworth, M. D. S. (1967). *Infancy in Uganda: Infant care and the growth of love.* Baltimore: Johns Hopkins University Press.

Ainsworth, M. D. S. (1972). Attachment and dependency: A comparison. In J. L. Gewirtz (Ed.), *Attachment and dependency* (pp. 97–138). Washington, DC: V. H. Winston.

Ainsworth, M. D. S. (1982). Attachment: Retrospect and prospect. In C. M. Parkes & J. Stevenson-Hinde (Eds.), *The place of attachment in human behavior* (pp. 3–30). New York: Basic Books.

Ainsworth, M. D. S. (1989). Attachments beyond infancy. *American Psychologist, 44,* 709–716.

Ainsworth, M. D. S., Blehar, M., Waters, E., & Wall, S. (1978). *Patterns of attachment.* Hillsdale, NJ: Erlbaum.

Ainsworth, M. D. S., & Wittig, B. A. (1969). Attachment and exploratory behavior of one-year-olds in a strange situation. In B. M. Foss (Ed.), *Determinants of infant behavior* (Vol. 4) (pp. 113–136). London: Methuen.

Aksu-Koc, A. A., & Slobin, D. I. (1985). The acquisition of Turkish. In D. I. Slobin (Ed.), *The crosslinguistic study of language acquisition.* Vol. 1, *The data* (pp. 839–878). Hillsdale, NJ: Erlbaum.

Al Awad, A. M. E. L., & Sonuga-Barke, E. J. S. (1992). Childhood problems in a Sudanese city: A comparison of extended and nuclear families. *Child Development, 63,* 906–914.

Alexander, K. L., & Entwisle, D. R., & Dauber, S. L. (1993). First-grade classroom behavior: Its short and long-term consequences for school performance. *Child Development, 64,* 801–814.

Allen, M. C., Donohue, P. K., & Dusman, A. E. (1993). The limit of viability—neonatal outcome of infants born at 22 to 25 weeks' gestation. *The New England Journal of Medicine, 329,* 1597–1601.

Alsaker, F. D., & Olweus, D. (1992). Stability of global self-evaluations in early adolescence: A cohort longitudinal study. *Journal of Research on Adolescence, 2,* 123–145.

Amato, P. R. (1993). Children's adjustment to divorce: Theories, hypotheses, and empirical support. *Journal of Marriage and the Family, 55,* 23–38.

American Psychological Association (1993). *Violence and youth: Psychology's response.* Vol. 1, *Summary report of the American Psychological Association Commission on Violence and Youth.* Washington, DC: American Psychological Association.

Anderson, D. R., Lorch, E. P., Field, D. E., Collins, P. A., & Nathan, J. G. (1986). Television viewing at home: Age trends in visual attention and time with TV. *Child Development, 57,* 1024–1033.

Andersson, B. (1989). Effects of public day-care: A longitudinal study. *Child Development, 60*, 857–886.

Andersson, B. (1992). Effects of day-care on cognitive and socioemotional competence of thirteen-year-old Swedish school children. *Child Development, 63*, 20–36.

Anglin, J. M. (1993). Vocabulary development: A morophological analysis. *Monographs of the Society for Research in Child Development, 58* (Serial No. 238).

Anisfeld, E., Casper, V., Nozyce, M., & Cunningham, N. (1990). Does infant carrying promote attachment? An experimental study of the effects of increased physical contact on the development of attachment. *Child Development, 61*, 1617–1627.

Anisfeld, M. (1991). Neonatal imitation. *Developmental Review, 11*, 60–97.

Anthony, E. J. (1970). The behavior disorders of childhood. In P. H. Mussen (Ed.), *Carmichael's manual of child psychology* (Vol. 2) (3rd ed.) (pp. 667–764). New York: Wiley.

Apgar, V. A. (1953). A proposal for a new method of evaluation of the newborn infant. *Current Research in Anesthesia and Analgesia, 32*, 260–267.

Arnett, J. (1992). Reckless behavior in adolescence: A developmental perspective. *Developmental Review, 12*, 339–373.

Arnett, J., & Balle-Jensen, L. (1993). Cultural bases of risk behavior: Danish adolescents. *Child Development, 64*, 1842–1855.

Asher, S. R. (1990). Recent advances in the study of peer rejection. In S. R. Asher & J. D. Coie (Eds.), *Peer rejection in childhood* (pp. 3–16). Cambridge, England: Cambridge University Press.

Asher, S. R., & Coie, J. D. (Eds.) (1990). *Peer rejection in childhood*. Cambridge, England: Cambridge University Press.

Aslin, R. N. (1981a). Experiential influences and sensitive periods in perceptual development: A unified model. In R. N. Aslin, J. R. Alberts, & M. R. Petersen (Eds.), *Development of perception. Psychobiological perspectives.* Vol. 2, *The visual system* (pp. 45–93). New York: Academic Press.

Aslin, R. N. (1987b). Visual and auditory development in infancy. In J. D. Osofsky (Ed.), *Handbook of infant development* (2nd ed.) (pp. 5–97). New York: Wiley-Interscience.

Astbury, J., Orgill, A. A., Bajuk, B., & Yu, V. Y. H. (1990). Neurodevelopmental outcome, growth and health of extremely low-birthweight survivors: How soon can we tell? *Developmental Medicine and Child Neurology, 32*, 582–589.

Astington, J. W., & Gopnik, A. (1991). Theoretical explanations of children's understanding of the mind. In G. E. Butterworth, P. L. Harris, A. M. Leslie, & H. M. Wellman (Eds.), *Perspectives on the child's theory of mind* (pp. 7–31). New York: Oxford University Press.

Astone, N. M. (1993). Are adolescent mothers just single mothers? *Journal of Research on Adolescence, 3*, 353–371.

Attie, I., & Brooks-Gunn, J. (1989). Development of eating problems in adolescent girls: A longitudinal study. *Developmental Psychology, 25*, 70–79.

Attie, I., Brooks-Gunn, J., & Petersen, A. (1990). A developmental perspective on eating disorders and eating problems. In M. Lewis & S. M. Miller (Eds.), *Handbook of developmental psychopathology* (pp. 409–420). New York: Plenum.

Avis, J., & Harris, P. L. (1991). Belief-desire reasoning among Baka children: Evidence for a universal conception of mind. *Child Development, 62*, 460–467.

Bachman, J. G., & Schulenberg, J. (1993). How part-time work intensity relates to drug use, problem behavior, time use, and satisfaction among high school seniors: Are these consequences or merely correlates? *Developmental Psychology, 29*, 220–235.

Baer, D. M. (1970). An age-irrelevant concept of development. *Merrill-Palmer Quarterly, 16*, 238–245.

Bailey, J. M., & Pillard, R. C. (1991). A genetic study of male sexual orientation. *Archives of General Psychiatry, 48*, 1089–1096.

Baillargeon, R. (1987). Object permanence in very young infants. *Developmental Psychology, 23*, 655–664.

Baillargeon, R., & DeVos, J. (1991). Object permanence in young infants: Further evidence. *Child Development, 62*, 1227–1246.

Baillargeon, R., Spelke, E. S., & Wasserman, S. (1985). Object permanence in five-month-old infants. *Cognition, 20*, 191–208.

Baird, P. A., Sadovnick, A. D., & Yee, I. M. L. (1991). Maternal age and birth defects: A population study. *The Lancet, 337*, 527–530.

Baker-Ward, L., Gordon, B. N., Ornstein, P. A., Larus, D. M., & Clubb, P. A. (1993). Young children's long-term retention of a pediatric examination. *Child Development, 64*, 1519–1533.

Baldwin, D. A. (1993). Early referential understanding: Infants' ability to recognize referential acts for what they are. *Developmental Psychology, 29*, 832–843.

Bamford, F. N., Bannister, R. P., Benjamin, C. M., Hillier, V. F., Ward, B. S., & Moore, W. M. O. (1990). Sleep in the first year of life. *Developmental Medicine and Child Neurology, 32*, 718–724.

Bandini, L. G., & Dietz, W. H. (1992). Myths about childhood obesity. *Pediatric Annals, 21*, 647–652.

Bandura, A. (1973). *Aggression: A social learning analysis.* Englewood Cliffs, NJ: Prentice-Hall.

Bandura, A. (1977). *Social learning theory.* Englewood Cliffs, NJ: Prentice-Hall.

Bandura, A. (1982). The self and mechanisms of agency. In J. Suls (Ed.), *Psychological perspectives on the self* (Vol. 1) (pp. 3–40). Hillsdale, NJ: Erlbaum.

Bandura, A. (1986). *Social foundations of thought and action: A social cognitive theory*. Englewood Cliffs, NJ: Prentice-Hall.

Bandura, A. (1989). Social cognitive theory. *Annals of Child Development, 6*, 1–60.

Barenboim, C. (1977). Developmental changes in the interpersonal cognitive system from middle childhood to adolescence. *Child Development, 48*, 1467–1474.

Barenboim, C. (1981). The development of person perception in childhood and adolescence: From behavioral comparisons to psychological constructs to psychological comparisons. *Child Development, 52*, 129–144.

Barkley, R. A. (1990). Attention deficit disorders: History, definition, and diagnosis. In M. Lewis & S. M. Miller (Eds.), *Handbook of developmental psychopathology* (pp. 65–76). New York: Plenum.

Barkley, R. A., Fischer, M., Edelbrock, C. S., & Smallish, L. (1990). The adolescent outcome of hyperactive children diagnosed by research criteria: I. An 8-year prospective follow-up study. *Journal of the American Academy of Child and Adolescent Psychiatry, 29*, 546–557.

Barnard, K. E., & Bee, H. L. (1983). The impact of temporally patterned stimulation on the development of preterm infants. *Child Development, 54*, 1156–1167.

Barnard, K. E., Bee, H. L., & Hammond, M. A. (1984). Developmental changes in maternal interactions with term and preterm infants. *Infant Behavior and Development, 7*, 101–113.

Barnard, K. E., & Eyres, S. J. (1979). *Child health assessment. Part 2: The first year of life*. (DHEW Publication No. HRA 79–25) Washington, DC: U. S. Government Printing Office.

Barnard, K. E., Hammond, M. A., Booth, C. L., Bee, H. L., Mitchell, S. K., & Spieker, S. J. (1989). Measurement and meaning of parent-child interaction. In J. J. Morrison, C. Lord, & D. P. Keating (Eds.), *Applied developmental psychology* (Vol. 3) (pp. 40–81). San Diego: Academic Press.

Barrett, G. V., & Depinet, R. L. (1991). A reconsideration of testing for competence rather than for intelligence. *American Psychologist, 46*, 1012–1024.

Bartsch, K. (1993). Adolescents' theoretical thinking. In R. M. Lerner (Ed.), *Early adolescence. Perspectives on research, policy, and intervention* (pp. 143–157). Hillsdale, NJ: Erlbaum.

Bates, E. (1993). Commentary: Comprehension and production in early language development. *Monographs of the Society for Research in Child Development, 58* (3–4, Serial No. 233), 222–242.

Bates, E., Bretherton, I., Beeghly-Smith, M., & McNew, S. (1982). Social bases of language development: A reassessment. In H. W. Reese & L. P. Lipsitt (Eds.), *Advances in child development and behavior* (Vol. 16) (pp. 8–68). New York: Academic Press.

Bates, E., Bretherton, I., & Snyder, L. (1988). *From first words to grammar. Individual differences and dissociable mechanisms*. Cambridge, England: Cambridge University Press.

Bates, E., Camaioni, L., & Volterra, V. (1975). The acquisition of performatives prior to speech. *Merrill-Palmer Quarterly, 21*, 205–226.

Bates, E., O'Connell, B., & Shore, C. (1987). Language and communication in infancy. In J. D. Osofsky (Ed.), *Handbook of infant development* (2nd ed.) (pp. 149–203). New York: Wiley.

Bates, J. E. (1989). Applications of temperament concepts. In G. A. Kohnstamm, J. E. Bates, & M. K. Rothbart (Eds.), *Temperament in childhood* (pp. 321–356). Chichester, England: Wiley.

Bates, J. E., Bales, K., Bennett, D. S., Ridge, B., & Brown, M. M. (1991). Origins of externalizing behavior problems at eight years of age. In D. J. Pepler & K. H. Rubin (Eds.), *The development and treatment of childhood aggression* (pp. 93–120). Hillsdale, NJ: Erlbaum.

Bates, J. E., Maslin, C. A., & Frankel, K. A. (1985). Attachment security, mother-child interaction, and temperament as predictors of behavior problem ratings at age three years. In I. Bretherton & E. Waters (Eds.), Growing points of attachment theory and research. *Monographs of the Society for Research in Child Development, 50* (1–2, Serial No. 209), 167–193.

Baumrind, D. (1971). Current patterns of parental authority. *Developmental Psychology Monograph, 4* (1, Part 2).

Baumrind, D. (1972). Socialization and instrumental competence in young children. In W. W. Hartup (Ed.), *The young child: Reviews of research* (Vol. 2) (pp. 202–224). Washington, DC: National Association for the Education of Young Children.

Baumrind, D. (1973). The development of instrumental competence through socialization. In A. D. Pick (Ed.), *Minnesota Symposium on child psychology* (Vol 7) (pp. 3–46). Minneapolis: University of Minnesota Press.

Baumrind, D. (1991). Effective parenting during the early adolescent transition. In P. A. Cowan & M. Hetherington (Eds.), *Family transitions* (pp. 111–163). Hillsdale, NJ: Erlbaum.

Baydar, N., & Brooks-Gunn, J. (1991). Effects of maternal employment and child-care arrangements on preschoolers' cognitive and behavioral outcomes: Evidence from the children of the National Longitudinal Survey of Youth. *Developmental Psychology, 27*, 932–945.

Bayley, N. (1969). *Bayley scales of infant development*. New York: Psychological Corporation.

Bearison, D. J., Magzamen, S., & Filardo, E. K. (1986). Socio-cognitive conflict and cognitive growth in young children. *Merrill-Palmer Quarterly, 32*, 51–72.

Becker, J. A. (1982). Children's strategic use of requests to mark and manipulate social status. In S. A. Kuczaj, II (Ed.), *Language development*. Vol. 2, *Language, thought, and culture* (pp. 1–36). Hillsdale, NJ: Erlbaum.

Beckwith, L., & Rodning, C. (1991). Intellectual functioning in children born preterm: Recent research. In L. Okagaki & R. J. Sternberg (Eds.), *Directors of development* (pp. 25–58). Hillsdale, NJ: Erlbaum.

Bedard, J., & Chi, M. T. H. (1992). Expertise. *Current Directions in Psychological Science, 1*, 135–139.

Bee, H. L., Barnard, K. E., Eyres, S. J., Gray, C. A., Hammond, M. A., Spietz, A. L., Snyder, C., & Clark, B. (1982). Prediction of IQ and language skill from perinatal status, child performance, family characteristics, and mother-infant interaction. *Child Development, 53*, 1135–1156.

Bell, L. G., & Bell, D. C. (1982). Family climate and the role of the female adolescent: Determinants of adolescent functioning. *Family Relations, 31*, 519–527.

Bellinger, D., Sloman, J., Leviton, A., Rabinowitz, M., Needleman, H. L., & Waternaux, C. (1991). Low-level lead exposure and children's cognitive function in the preschool years. *Pediatrics, 87*, 219–227.

Bellinger, D. C., Stiles, K. M., & Needleman, H. L. (1992). Low-level lead exposure, intelligence and academic achievement: A long-term follow-up study. *Pediatrics, 90* (855–861).

Belsky, J. (1985). Prepared statement on the effects of day care. In Select Committee on Children, Youth, and Families, House of Representatives, 98th Congress, Second Session, *Improving child care services: What can be done?* Washington, DC: U.S. Government Printing Office.

Belsky, J. (1987). *Science, social policy and day care: A personal odyssey.* Paper presented at the biennial meetings of the Society for Research in Child Development, Baltimore, April.

Belsky, J. (1990). The "Effects" of infant day care reconsidered. In N. Fox & G. G. Fein (Eds.), *Infant day care: The current debate* (pp. 3–40). Norwood, NJ: Ablex.

Belsky, J. (1992). Consequences of child care for children's development: A deconstructionist view. In A. Booth (Ed.), *Child care in the 1990s. Trends and consequences* (pp. 83–94). Hillsdale, NJ: Erlbaum.

Belsky, J. (1993). Etiology of child maltreatment: A developmental-ecological analysis. *Psychological Bulletin, 114*, 413–434.

Belsky, J., & Eggebeen, D. (1991). Early and extensive maternal employment and young children's socioemotional development: Children of the National Longitudinal Survey of Youth. *Journal of Marriage and the Family, 53*, 1083–1110.

Belsky, J., Lang, M. E., & Rovine, M. (1985). Stability and change in marriage across the transition to parenthood: A second study. *Journal of Marriage and the Family, 47*, 855–865.

Belsky, J., & Rovine, M. (1988). Nonmaternal care in the first year of life and the security of infant-parent attachment. *Child Development, 59*, 157–167.

Bem, S. L. (1974). The measurement of psychological androgyny. *Journal of Consulting and Clinical Psychology, 42*, 155–162.

Benbow, C. P. (1988). Sex differences in mathematical reasoning ability in intellectually talented preadolescents: Their nature, effects, and possible causes. *Behavioral and Brain Sciences, 11*, 169–232.

Berberian, K. E., & Snyder, S. S. (1982). The relationship of temperament and stranger reaction for younger and older infants. *Merrill-Palmer Quarterly, 28*, 79–94.

Berch, D. B., & Bender, B. G. (1987). Margins of sexuality. *Psychology Today, 21* (December), 54–57.

Berg, J. M. (1974). Aetiological aspects of mental subnormality. In A. M. Clarke & A. D. B. Clarke (Eds.), *Mental deficiency: The changing outlook* (3rd ed.) (pp. 82–117). New York: Free Press.

Berg, W. K., & Berg, K. M. (1987). Psychophysiological development in infancy: State, startle, and attention. In J. D. Osofsky (Ed.), *Handbook of infant development* (2nd ed.) (pp. 238–317). New York: Wiley-Interscience.

Berkowitz, G. S., Skovron, M. L., Lapinski, R. H., & Berkowitz, R. L. (1990). Delayed childbearing and the outcome of pregnancy. *New England Journal of Medicine, 322*, 659–664.

Berndt, T. J. (1979). Developmental changes in conformity to peers and parents. *Developmental Psychology, 15*, 608–616.

Berndt, T. J. (1983). Social cognition, social behavior, and children's friendships. In E. T. Higgins, D. N. Ruble, & W. W. Hartup (Eds.), *Social cognition and social development. A sociocultural perspective* (pp. 158–192). Cambridge, England: Cambridge University Press.

Berndt, T. J. (1986). Children's comments about their friendships. In M. Perlmutter (Ed.), *Minnesota symposia on child psychology* (Vol. 18) (pp. 189–212). Hillsdale, NJ: Erlbaum.

Berndt, T. J. (1992). Friendship and friends' influence in adolescence. *Current Directions in Psychological Science, 1*, 156–159.

Berndt, T. J., Hawkins, J. A., & Hoyle, S. G. (1986). Changes in friendship during a school year: Effects on children's and adolescents' impressions of friendship and sharing with friends. *Child Development, 57*, 1284–1297.

Berndt, T. J., & Hoyle, S. G. (1985). Stability and change in childhood and adolescent friendships. *Developmental Psychology, 21*, 1007–1015.

Berndt, T. J., & Perry, T. B. (1990). Distinctive features and effects of early adolescent friendships. In R. Montemayor, G. R. Adams, & T. P. Gullotta (Eds.), *From childhood to adolescence. A transitional period?* (pp. 269–287).

Bertenthal, B. I., & Campos, J. J. (1987). New directions in the study of early experience. *Child Development, 58*, 560–567.

Betancourt, H., & Lopez, S. R. (1993). The study of culture, ethnicity, and race in American psychology. *American Psychologist, 48*, 629–637.

Bettes, B. A. (1988). Maternal depression and motherese: Temporal and intonational features. *Child Development, 59*, 1089–1096.

Biederman, J., Faraone, S., Keenan, K., Knee, D., & Tsuang, M. (1990). Family-genetic and psychosocial risk factors in DSM-III attention deficit disorder. *Journal of the American Academy of Child and Adolescent Psychiatry, 29*, 526–533.

Billings, A. G., & Moos, R. H. (1985). Children of parents with unipolar depression: A controlled 1-year follow-up. *Journal of Abnormal Child Psychology, 14*, 149–166.

Bingham, C. R., Miller, B. C., & Adams, G. R. (1990). Correlates of age at first sexual intercourse in a national sample of young women. *Journal of Adolescent Research, 5*, 18–33.

Bivens, J. A., & Berk, L. E. (1990). A longitudinal study of the development of elementary school children's private speech. *Merrill-Palmer Quarterly, 36*, 443–463.

Bjorklund, D. F., & Muir, J. E. (1988). Remembering on their own: Children's development of free recall memory. In R. Vasta (Ed.), *Annals of child development* (Vol. 5) (pp. 79–124). Greenwich, CT: JAI Press.

Black, B. (1992). Negotiating social pretend play: communication differences related to social status and sex. *Merrill-Palmer Quarterly, 38*, 212–232.

Blackman, J. A. (1990). Update on AIDS, CMV, and herpes in young children: Health, developmental, and educational issues. In M. Wolraich & D. K. Routh (Eds.), *Advances in developmental and behavioral pediatrics* (Vol. 9) (pp. 33–58). London: Jessica Kingsley Publishers.

Block, J. (1971). *Lives through time.* Berkeley, CA: Bancroft.

Block, J. (1987). *Longitudinal antecedents of ego-control and ego-resiliency in late adolescence.* Paper presented at the biennial meetings of the Society for Research in Child Development, Baltimore, April.

Block, J., & Robins, R. W. (1993). A longitudinal study of consistency and change in self-esteem from early adolescence to early adulthood. *Child Development, 64*, 909–923.

Bloom, L. (1973). *One word at a time.* The Hague: Mouton.

Bloom, L. (1991). *Language development from two to three.* Cambridge, England: Cambridge University Press.

Blum, R. W., Harmon, B., Harris, L., Bergeisen, L., & Resnick, M. D. (1992). American Indian-Alaska Native youth health. *Journal of the American Medical Association, 267*, 1637–1644.

Boer, F., & Dunn, J. (Eds.). (1992). *Children's sibling relationships. Developmental and clinical issues.* Hillsdale, NJ: Erlbaum.

Booth, A. (Ed.) (1992). *Child care in the 1990s. Trends and consequences.* Hillsdale, NJ: Erlbaum.

Bornstein, M. H. (1987). Sensitive periods in development: Definition, existence, utility, and meaning. In M. H. Bornstein (Ed.), *Sensitive periods in development: Interdisciplinary perspectives* (pp. 3–18). Hillsdale, NJ: Erlbaum.

Bornstein, M. H. (Ed.) (1991). *Cultural approaches to parenting.* Hillsdale, NJ: Erlbaum.

Bornstein, M. H., Tal, J., & Tamis-LeMonda, C. S. (1991). Parenting in cross-cultural perspective: The United States, France, and Japan. In M. H. Bornstein (Ed.), *Cultural approaches to parenting* (pp. 69–90). Hillsdale, NJ: Erlbaum.

Bornstein, M. H., Tamis-LeMonda, C. S., Tal, J., Ludemann, P., Toda, S., Rahn, C. W., Pecheux, M., Azuma, H., & Vardi, D. (1992). Maternal responsiveness to infants in three societies: The United States, France, and Japan. *Child Development, 63*, 808–821.

The Boston Women's Health Collective (1992). *The new our bodies, ourselves: A book by and for women.* New York: Simon & Schuster.

Bouchard, T. J., Jr., & McGue, M. (1981). Familial studies of intelligence: A review. *Science, 212*, 1055–1059.

Boukydis, C. F. Z., & Burgess, R. L. (1982). Adult physiological response to infant cries: Effects of temperament, parental status, and gender. *Child Development, 53*, 1291–1298.

Bower, T. G. R. (1989). *The rational infant.* New York: Freeman.

Bowerman, M. (1985). Beyond communicative adequacy: From piecemeal knowledge to an integrated system in the child's acquisition of language. In K. E. Nelson (Ed.), *Children's language* (Vol. 5) (pp. 369–398). Hillsdale, NJ: Erlbaum.

Bowlby, J. (1969). *Attachment and loss* (Vol. 1), *Attachment.* New York: Basic Books.

Bowlby, J. (1973). *Attachment and loss* (Vol. 2), *Separation, anxiety, and anger.* New York: Basic Books.

Bowlby, J. (1980). *Attachment and loss* (Vol. 3), *Loss, sadness, and depression.* New York: Basic Books.

Bowlby, J. (1988a). Developmental psychiatry comes of age. *The American Journal of Psychiatry, 145*, 1–10.

Bowlby, J. (1988b). *A secure base.* New York: Basic Books.

Boyes, M. C., & Allen, S. G. (1993). Styles of parent-child interactions and moral reasoning in adolescence. *Merrill-Palmer Quarterly, 39*, 551–570.

Brackbill, Y., McManus, K., & Woodward, L. (1985). *Medication in maternity.* Ann Arbor: University of Michigan Press.

Bradbard, M. R., Martin, C. L., Endsley, R. C., & Halverson, C. F. (1986). Influence of sex stereotypes on children's exploration and memory: A competence versus performance distinction. *Developmental Psychology, 22*, 481–486.

Bradley, R. H., & Caldwell, B. M. (1984). 174 children: A study of the relationship between home environment and cognitive development during the first 5 years . In A. W. Gottfried (Ed.), *Home environment and early cognitive development: Longitudinal research* (pp. 5–56). New York: Academic Press.

Bradley, R. H., Caldwell, B. M., Rock, S. L., Barnard, K. E., Gray, C., Hammond, M. A., Mitchell, S., Siegel, L., Ramey, C. D., Gottfried, A. W., & Johnson, D. L. (1989). Home environment and cognitive development in the first 3 years of life: A collaborative study involving six sites and three ethnic groups in North America. *Developmental Psychology, 25,* 217–235.

Brandenburg, N. A., Friedman, R. M., & Silver, S. E. (1990). The epidemiology of childhood psychiatric disorders: Prevalence findings from recent studies. *Journal of the American Academy of Child and Adolescent Psychiatry, 29,* 76–83.

Breitmayer, B. J., & Ramey, C. T. (1986). Biological nonoptimality and quality of postnatal environment as codeterminants of intellectual development. *Child Development, 57,* 1151–1165.

Bretherton, I. (1991). Pouring new wine into old bottles: The social self as internal working model. In M. R. Gunnar & L. A. Sroufe (Eds.), *Minnesota symposia on child development* (Vol. 23) (pp. 1–42). Hillsdale, NJ: Erlbaum.

Bretherton, I. (1992a). The origins of attachment theory: John Bowlby and Mary Ainsworth. *Developmental Psychology, 28,* 759–775.

Bretherton, I. (1992b). Attachment and bonding. In V. B. Van Hasselt & M. Hersen (Ed.), *Handbook of social development. A lifespan perspective* (pp. 133–155). New York: Plenum Press.

Bristol, M. M., Gallagher, J. J., & Schopler, E. (1988). Mothers and fathers of young developmentally disabled and nondisabled boys: Adaptation and spousal support. *Developmental Psychology, 24,* 441–451.

Brody, G. H., Stoneman, Z., McCoy, J. K., & Forehand, R. (1992). Contemporaneous and longitudinal associations of sibling conflict with family relationship assessments and family discussions about sibling problems. *Child Development, 63,* 391–400.

Brody, N. (1992). *Intelligence* (2nd ed.). San Diego, CA: Academic Press.

Broman, S., Nichols, P. L., Shaughnessy, P., & Kennedy, W. (1987). *Retardation in young children.* Hillsdale, NJ: Erlbaum.

Broman, S. H., Nichols, P. L., & Kennedy, W. A. (1975). *Preschool IQ: Prenatal and early developmental correlates.* Hillsdale, NJ: Erlbaum.

Bronfenbrenner, U. (1979). *The ecology of human development.* Cambridge, MA: Harvard University Press.

Bronfenbrenner, U. (1989). Ecological systems theory. *Annals of Child Development, 6,* 187–249.

Brooks-Gunn, J. (1987). Pubertal processes and girls' psychological adaptation. In R. M. Lerner & T. T. Foch (Eds.), *Biological-psychosocial interactions in early adolescence* (pp. 123–154). Hillsdale, NJ: Erlbaum.

Brooks-Gunn, J. (1988). Commentary: Developmental issues in the transition to early adolescence. In M. R. Gunnar & W. A. Collins (Eds.), *Minnesota symposia on child psychology* (Vol. 21) (pp. 189–208). Hillsdale, NJ: Erlbaum.

Brooks-Gunn, J., Guo, G., & Furstenberg, F. F., Jr. (1993a). Who drops out of and who continues beyond high school? A 20-year follow-up of black urban youth. *Journal of Research on Adolescence, 3,* 271–294.

Brooks-Gunn, J., Klebanov, P. K., Liaw, F., & Spiker, D. (1993b). Enhancing the development of low-birthweight, premature infants: Changes in cognition and behavior over the first three years. *Child Development, 64,* 736–753.

Brooks-Gunn, J., & Matthews, W. S. (1979). *He and she: How children develop their sex-role identity.* Englewood Cliffs, NJ: Prentice-Hall.

Brooks-Gunn, J., & Reiter, E. O. (1990). The role of pubertal processes. In S. S. Feldman & G. R. Elliott (Eds.), *At the threshold. The developing adolescent* (pp. 16–53). Cambridge, MA: Harvard University Press.

Brooks-Gunn, J., & Warren, M. P. (1985). The effects of delayed menarche in different contexts: Dance and nondance students. *Journal of Youth and Adolescence, 13,* 285–300.

Broverman, I. K., Vogel, S. R., Broverman, D. M., Clarkson, F. E., & Rosenkrantz, P. S. (1972). Sex role stereotypes: A current appraisal. *Journal of Social Issues, 28* (2), 59–79.

Brown, B. B. (1990). Peer groups and peer cultures. In S. S. Feldman & G. R. Elliott (Eds.), *At the threshold. The developing adolescent* (pp. 171–196). Cambridge, MA: Harvard University Press.

Brown, B. B., Clasen, D. R., & Eicher, S. A. (1986). Perceptions of peer pressure, peer conformity dispositions, and self-reported behavior among adolescents. *Developmental Psychology, 22,* 521–530.

Brown, B. B., Mounts, N., Lamborn, S. D., & Steinberg, L. (1993). Parenting practices and peer group affiliation in adolescence. *Child Development, 64,* 467–482.

Brown, R. (1973). *A first language: The early stages.* Cambridge, MA: Harvard University Press.

Brown, R., & Hanlon, C. (1970). Derivational complexity and order of acquisition. In J. R. Hayes (Ed.), *Cognition and the development of language* (pp. 155–207). New York: Wiley.

Brownell, C. A. (1988). Combinatorial skills: Converging developments over the second year. *Child Development, 59,* 675–685.

Brownell, C. A. (1990). Peer social skills in toddlers: Competencies and constraints illustrated by same-age and mixed-age interaction. *Child Development, 61,* 836–848.

Brownell, C. A., & Brown, E. (1992). Peers and play in infants and toddlers. In V. B. Van Hasselt & M. Hersen (Eds.), *Handbook of social development. A lifespan perspective* (pp. 183–200). New York: Plenum Press.

Bryant, P. E., MacLean, M., Bradley, L. L., & Crossland, J. (1990). Rhyme and alliteration, phoneme detection, and learning to read. *Developmental Psychology, 26,* 429–438.

Buchanan, C. M., Maccoby, E. E., & Dornbusch, S. M. (1991). Caught between parents: Adolescents' experience in divorced homes. *Child Development, 62,* 1008–1029.

Buehler, J. W., Kaunitz, A. M., Hogue, C. J. R., Hughes, J. M., Smith, J. C., & Rochat, R. W. (1986). Maternal mortality in women aged 35 years or older: United States. *Journal of the American Medical Association, 255,* 53–57.

Bullock, M., & Lütkenhaus, P. (1990). Who am I? Self-understanding in toddlers. *Merrill-Palmer Quarterly, 36,* 217–238.

Bumpass, L. (1984). Children and marital disruption: A replication and update. *Demography, 41,* 71–82.

Burns, A. (1992). Mother-headed families: An international perspective and the case of Australia. *Social Policy Report, Society for Research in Child Development, 6* (1), 1–22.

Buss, A. H., & Plomin, R. (1984). *Temperament: Early developing personality traits.* Hillsdale, NJ: Erlbaum.

Buss, A. H., & Plomin, R. (1986). The EAS approach to temperament. In R. Plomin & J. Dunn (Eds.), *The study of temperament: Changes, continuities and challenges* (pp. 67–80). Hillsdale, NJ: Erlbaum.

Byrnes, J. P., & Takahira, S. (1993). Explaining gender differences on SAT-Math items. *Developmental Psychology, 29,* 805–810.

Cain, V. S., & Hofferth, S. L. (1989). Parental choice of self-care for school-age children. *Journal of Marriage and the Family, 51,* 65–77.

Cairns, R. B., Cairns, B. D., Necherman, H. J., Ferguson, L. L., & Gariepy, J. (1989). Growth and aggression. 1. Childhood to early adolescence. *Developmental Psychology, 25,* 320–330.

California Assessment Program (1980). *Student achievement in California schools. 1979–1980 annual report: Television and student achievement.* Sacramento: California State Department of Education.

Callahan, C. M., & Rivara, F. P. (1992). Urban high school youth and handguns. A school-based survey. *Journal of the American Medical Association, 267,* 3038–3042.

Campbell, R. L., & Bickhard, M. H. (1992). Types of constraints on development: An interactivist approach. *Developmental Review, 12,* 311–338.

Campbell, S. B. (1990). The socialization and social development of hyperactive children. In M. Lewis & S. M. Miller (Eds.), *Handbook of developmental psychopathology* (pp. 77–92). New York: Plenum.

Campbell, S. B., Cohn, J. F., Flanagan, C., Popper, S., & Meyers, T. (1992). Course and correlates of postpartum depression during the transition to parenthood. *Development and Psychopathology, 4,* 29–47.

Campbell, S. B., & Ewing, L. J. (1990). Follow-up of hard-to-manage preschoolers: Adjustment at age 9 and predictors of continuing symptoms. *Journal of Child Psychology and Psychiatry, 31,* 871–889.

Campbell, S. B., Ewing, L. J., Breaux, A. M., & Szumowski, E. K. (1986). Parent-referred problem three-year-olds: Follow-up at school entry. *Journal of Child Psychology and Psychiatry, 27,* 473–488.

Campbell, S. B., Pierce, E. W., March, C. L., & Ewing, L. J. (1991). Noncompliant behavior, overactivity, and family stress as predictors of negative maternal control with preschool children. *Development and Psychopathology, 3,* 175–190.

Campbell, S. B., & Taylor, P. M. (1980). Bonding and attachment: Theoretical issues. In P. M. Taylor (Ed.), *Parent-infant relationships* (pp. 3–24). New York: Grune & Stratton.

Campione, J. C., & Brown, A. L. (1984). Learning ability and transfer propensity as sources of individual differences in intelligence. In P. H. Brooks, C. McCauley, & R. Sperber (Eds.), *Learning and cognition in the mentally retarded.* Hillsdale, NJ: Erlbaum.

Campione, J. C., Brown, A. L., & Ferrara, R. A. (1982). Mental retardation and intelligence. In J. R. Sternberg (Ed.), *Handbook of human intelligence* (pp. 392–492). Cambridge, England: Cambridge University Press.

Campione, J. C., Brown, A. L., Ferrara, R. A., Jones, R. S., & Steinberg, E. (1985). Breakdowns in flexible use of information: Intelligence-related differences in transfer following equivalent learning performance. *Intelligence, 9,* 297–315.

Campos, J. J., & Bertenthal, B. I. (1989). Locomotion and psychological development in infancy. In F. J. Morrison, C. Lord, & D. P. Keating (Eds.), *Applied developmental psychology* (Vol. 3) (pp. 229–258). San Diego: Academic Press.

Cantwell, D. P. (1990). Depression across the early life span. In M. Lewis & S. M. Miller (Eds.), *Handbook of developmental psychopathology* (pp. 293–310). New York: Plenum.

Capron, C., & Duyme, M. (1989). Assessment of effects of socio-economic status on IQ in a full cross-fostering study. *Nature, 340,* 552–554.

Capute, A. J., Palmer, F. B., Shapiro, B. K., Wachtel, R. C., Ross, A., & Accardo, P. J. (1984). Primitive reflex profile: A quantification of primitive reflexes in infancy. *Developmental Medicine and Child Neurology, 26,* 375–383.

Capute, A. J., Palmer, F. B., Shapiro, B. K., Wachtel, R. C., Schmidt, S., & Ross, A. (1986). Clinical linguistic and auditory milestone scale: Prediction of cognition in infancy. *Developmental Medicine & Child Neurology, 28,* 762–771.

Cardon, L. R., & Fulker, D. W. (1993). Genetics of specific cognitive abilities. In R. Plomin & G. E. McClearn (Eds.), *Nature, nurture & psychology* (pp. 99–120). Washington, DC: American Psychological Association.

Carey, S., & Bartlett, E. (1978). Acquiring a single new word. *Papers and Reports on Child Language Development, 15,* 17–29.

Carlson, V., Cicchetti, D., Barnett, D., & Braunwald, K. (1989). Disorganized/disoriented attachment relationships in maltreated infants. *Developmental Psychology, 25,* 525–531.

Caron, A. J., & Caron, R. F. (1981). Processing of relational information as an index of infant risk. In S. Friedman & M. Sigman (Eds.), *Preterm birth and psychological development* (pp. 219–240). New York: Academic Press.

Carter, C. S. (1988). Patterns of infant feeding, the mother-infant interaction and stress management. In T. M. Field, P. M. McCabe, & N. Schneiderman (Eds.), *Stress and coping across development* (pp. 27–46). Hillsdale, NJ: Erlbaum.

Carver, R. P. (1990). Intelligence and reading ability in grades 2–12. *Intelligence, 14,* 449–455.

Case, R. (1991). Stages in the development of the young child's first sense of self. *Developmental Review, 11,* 210–230.

Caspi, A., Lynam, D., Moffitt, T. E., & Silva, P. A. (1993). Unraveling girls' delinquency: Biological, dispositional, and contextual contributions to adolescent misbehavior. *Developmental Psychology, 29,* 19–30.

Caspi, A., & Moffitt, T. E. (1991). Individual differences are accentuated during periods of social change: The sample case of girls at puberty. *Journal of Personality and Social Psychology, 61,* 157–168.

Ceci, S. J., & Bruck, M. (1993). Suggestibility of the child witness: A historical review and synthesis. *Psychological Bulletin, 113,* 403–439.

Center for Educational Statistics (1987). *Who drops out of high school? From high school and beyond.* Washington, DC: Office of Educational Research and Improvement, U.S. Department of Education.

Centers for Disease Control (1993). Rates of cesarean delivery—United States, 1991. *Journal of the American Medical Association, 269* (18), 2360.

Centerwall, B. S. (1989). Exposure to television as a cause of violence. In G. Comstock (Ed.), *Public communication and behavior* (pp. 1–58). San Diego, CA: Academic Press.

Centerwall, B. S. (1992). Television and violence. The scale of the problem and where to go from here. *Journal of the American Medical Association, 267* (22), 3059–3063.

Cernoch, J. M., & Porter, R. H. (1985). Recognition of maternal axillary odors by infants. *Child Development, 56,* 1593–1598.

Chalfant, J. C. (1989). Learning disabilities: Policy issues and promising approaches. *American Psychologist, 44,* 392–398.

Chandler, M., & Moran, T. (1990). Psychopathology and moral development: A comparative study of delinquent and non-delinquent youth. *Development and Psychopathology, 2,* 227–246.

Chen, X., Rubin, K. H., & Sun, Y. (1992). Social reputation and peer relationships in Chinese and Canadian children: A cross-cultural study. *Child Development, 63,* 1336–1343.

Cherlin, A. J. (1992a). Infant care and full-time employment. In A. Booth (Ed.), *Child care in the 1990s. Trends and consequences* (pp. 209–214). Hillsdale, NJ: Erlbaum.

Cherlin, A. J. (1992b). *Marriage, divorce, remarriage.* Cambridge, MA: Harvard University Press.

Chess, S., & Thomas, A. (1982). Infant bonding: Mystique and reality. *American Journal of Orthopsychiatry, 52,* 213–222.

Chess, S., & Thomas, A. (1984). *Origins and evolution of behavior disorders: Infancy to early adult life.* New York: Brunner/Mazel.

Chi, M. T. (1978). Knowledge structure and memory development. In R. S. Siegler (Ed.), *Children's thinking: What develops?* (pp. 73–96). Hillsdale, NJ: Erlbaum.

Chi, M. T. H., & Ceci, S. J. (1987). Content knowledge: Its role, representation, and restructuring in memory development. In H. W. Reese (Ed.), *Advances in child development and behavior* (Vol. 20) (pp. 91–142). Orlando, FL: Academic Press.

Chi, M. T. H., Hutchinson, J. E., & Robin, A. F. (1989). How inferences about novel domain-related concepts can be constrained by structured knowledge. *Merrill-Palmer Quarterly, 35,* 27–62.

Chomsky, N. (1965). *Aspects of a theory of syntax.* Cambridge, MA: MIT Press.

Chomsky, N. (1975). *Reflections on language.* New York: Pantheon Books.

Chomsky, N. (1986). *Knowledge of language: Its nature, origin, and use.* New York: Praeger.

Chomsky, N. (1988). *Language and problems of knowledge.* Cambridge, MA: MIT Press.

Christophersen, E. R. (1989). Injury control. *American Psychologist, 44,* 237–241.

Chumlea, W. C. (1982). Physical growth in adolescence. In B. B. Wolman (Ed.), *Handbook of developmental psychology* (pp. 471–485). Englewood Cliffs, NJ: Prentice-Hall.

Cicchetti, D. (1989). Developmental psychopathology: Past, present, and future. In D. Cicchetti (Ed.), *The emergence of a discipline: Rochester symposium on developmental psychopathology* (Vol. 1) (pp. 1–12). Hillsdale, NJ: Erlbaum.

Cicchetti, D., & Barnett, D. (1991). Attachment organization in maltreated preschoolers. *Development and Psychopathology, 3,* 397–411.

Cillessen, A. H. N., van IJzendoorn, H. W., van Lieshout, C. F. M., & Hartup, W. W. (1992). Heterogeneity among peer-rejected boys: Subtypes and stabilities. *Child Development, 63,* 893–905.

Clark, E. V. (1975). Knowledge, context, and strategy in the acquisition of meaning. In D. P. Date (Ed.), *Georgetown University round table on language and linguistics.* Washington, DC: Georgetown University Press.

Clark, E. V. (1977). Strategies and the mapping problem in first language acquisition. In J. Macnamara (Ed.), *Language learning and thought* (pp. 147–168). New York: Academic Press, 1977.

Clark, E. V. (1983). Meanings and concepts. In J. H. Flavell & E. M. Markman (Eds.), *Handbook of child psychology.* Vol 3, *Cognitive development* (pp. 787–840). New York: Wiley.

Clark, E. V. (1987). The principle of contrast: A constraint on language acquisition. In B. MacWhinney (Ed.), *Mechanisms of language acquisition* (pp. 1–34). Hillsdale, NJ: Erlbaum.

Clark, E. V. (1990). On the pragmatics of contrast. *Journal of Child Language, 41,* 417–431.

Clarke-Stewart, A. (1987). The social ecology of early childhood. In N. Eisenberg (Ed.), *Contemporary topics in developmental psychology* (pp. 292–318). New York: Wiley-Interscience.

Clarke-Stewart, A. (1990). "The 'effects' of infant day care reconsidered" reconsidered: Risks for parents, children, and researchers. In N. Fox & G. G. Fein (Eds.), *Infant day care: The current debate* (pp. 61–86). Norwood, NJ: Ablex.

Clarke-Stewart, A. (1992). Consequences of child care for children's development. In A. Booth (Ed.), *Child care in the 1990s. Trends and consequences* (pp. 63–82). Hillsdale, NJ: Erlbaum.

Cnattingius, S., Berendes, H. W., & Forman, M. R. (1993). Do delayed childbearers face increased risks of adverse pregnancy outcomes after the first birth? *Obstetrics and Gynecology, 81,* 512–516.

Cohen, Y. A. (1964). *The transition from childhood to adolescence.* Chicago: Aldine.

Coie, J. D., & Cillessen, A. H. N. (1993). Peer rejection: Origins and effects on children's development. *Current Directions in Psychological Science, 2,* 89–92.

Colby, A., Kohlberg, L., Gibbs, J., & Lieberman, M. (1983). A longitudinal study of moral judgment. *Monographs of the Society for Research in Child Development, 48* (1–2, Serial No. 200).

Cole, D. A. (1991). Change in self-perceived competence as a function of peer and teacher evaluation. *Developmental Psychology, 27,* 682–688.

Cole, D. A., & Rodman, H. (1987). When school-age children care for themselves: Issues for family life educators and parents. *Family Relations, 36,* 92–96.

Cole, M. (1992). Culture in development. In M. H. Bornstein & M. E. Lamb (Eds.), *Developmental psychology: An advanced textbook* (3rd ed.) (pp. 731–789). Hillsdale, NJ: Erlbaum.

Cole, M., & Traupmann, K. (1981). Comparative cognitive research: Learning from a learning disabled child. In W. A. Collins (Ed.), *Minnesota symposia on child psychology* (Vol. 14) (pp. 125–154). Hillsdale, NJ: Erlbaum.

Collin, M. F., Halsey, C. L., & Anderson, C. L. (1991). Emerging developmental sequelae in the "normal" extremely low birth weight infant. *Pediatrics, 88,* 115–120.

Collins, W. A. (Ed.) (1984). *Development during middle childhood. The years from six to twelve.* Washington, DC: National Academy Press.

Colombo, J. (1993). *Infant cognition. Predicting later intellectual functioning.* Newbury Park, CA: Sage.

Compas, B. E., Ey, S., & Grant, K. E. (1993). Taxonomy, assessment, and diagnosis of depression during adolescence. *Psychological Bulletin, 114,* 323–344.

Comstock, G. (1991). *Television and the american child.* San Diego, CA: Academic Press.

Connolly, K., & Dalgleish, M. (1989). The emergence of a tool-using skill in infancy. *Developmental Psychology, 25,* 894–912.

Conrad, M., & Hammen, C. (1989). Role of maternal depression in perceptions of child maladjustment. *Journal of Consulting and Clinical Psychology, 57,* 663–667.

Cooper, R. P., & Aslin, R. N. (1990). Preference for infant-directed speech in the first month after birth. *Child Development, 61,* 1584–1595.

Corbett, H. D., & Wilson, B. (1989). Two state minimum competency testing programs and their effects on curriculum and instruction. In R. Stake (Ed.), *Effects of changes in assessment policy.* Vol. 1, *Advances in program evaluation.* Greenwich, CT: JAI Press.

Cossette, L., Malcuit, G., & Pomerleau, A. (1991). Sex differences in motor activity during early infancy. *Infant Behavior and Development, 14,* 175–186.

Cratty, B. (1979). *Perceptual and motor development in infants and children* (2nd ed.). Englewood Cliffs, NJ: Prentice-Hall.

Crick, N. R., & Dodge, K. A. (1994). A review and reformulation of social information-processing mechanisms in children's social adjustment. *Psychological Bulletin, 115,* 74–101.

Crisafi, M. A., & Brown, A. L. (1986). Analogical transfer in very young children: Combining two separately learned solutions to reach a goal. *Child Development, 57,* 953–968.

Crittenden, P. M., Partridge, M. F., & Claussen, A. H. (1991). Family patterns of relationship in normative and dysfunctional families. *Development and Psychopathology, 3,* 491–512.

Crockenberg, S., & Litman, C. (1990). Autonomy as competence in 2-year-olds: Maternal correlates of child defiance, compliance, and self-assertion. *Developmental Psychology, 26,* 961–971.

Crockenberg, S. B. (1981). Infant irritability, mother responsiveness, and social support influences on the security of infant–mother attachment. *Child Development, 52,* 857–865.

Crockenberg, S. B. (1986). Are temperamental differences in babies associated with predictable differences in caregiving? *New Directions for Child Development, 31,* 53–74.

Cromer, R. F. (1991). *Language and thought in normal and handicapped children.* Oxford, England: Basil Blackwell.

Crowell, J. A., & Feldman, S. S. (1991). Mothers' working models of attachment relationships and mother and child behavior during separation and reunion. *Developmental Psychology, 27,* 597–605.

Csikszentmihalyi, M., & Larson, R. (1984). *Being adolescent: Conflict and growth in the teenage years.* New York: Basic Books.

Cummings, E. M., & Davies, P. T. (1994). Maternal depression and child development. *Journal of Child Psychology and Psychiatry, 35,* 73–112.

Cummings, E. M., Hollenbeck, B., Iannotti, R., Radke-Yarrow, M., & Zahn-Waxler, C. (1986). Early organization of altruism and aggression: Developmental patterns and individual differences. In C. Zahn-Waxler, E. M. Cummings, & R. Iannotti (Eds.), *Altruism and Aggression* (pp. 165–188). Cambridge, England: Cambridge University Press.

Cunningham, A. S., Jelliffe, D. B., & Jelliffe, E. F. P. (1991). Breast-feeding and health in the 1980s: A global epidemiologic review. *The Journal of Pediatrics, 118,* 659–666.

D'Alton, M. E., & DeCherney, A. H. (1993). Prenatal diagnosis. *The New England Journal of Medicine, 328,* 114–118.

Damon, W. (1977). *The social world of the child.* San Francisco: Jossey-Bass.

Damon, W. (1983). The nature of social-cognitive change in the developing child. In W. F. Overton (Ed.), *The relationship between social and cognitive development* (pp. 103–142). Hillsdale, NJ: Erlbaum.

Damon, W., & Hart, D. (1988). *Self understanding in childhood and adolescence.* New York: Cambridge University Press.

Danner, F. W., & Day, M. C. (1977). Eliciting formal operations. *Child Development, 48,* 1600–1606.

Dark, V. J., & Benbow, C. P. (1993). Cognitive differences among the gifted: A review and new data. In D. K. Detterman (Ed.), *Current topics in human intelligence.* Vol. 3, *Individual differences and cognition* (pp. 85–120). Horwood, NJ: Ablex.

Darling-Hammond, L., & Wise, A. E. (1985). Beyond standardization: State standards and school improvement. *Elementary School Journal* (January), 315–336.

Darlington, R. B. (1991). The long-term effects of model preschool programs. In L. Okagaki & R. J. Sternberg (Eds.), *Directors of development* (pp. 203–215). Hillsdale, NJ: Erlbaum.

Davies, G. M. (1993). Children's memory for other people: An integrative review. In C. A. Nelson (Ed.), *Minnesota symposia on child psychology* (pp. 123–157). Hillsdale, NJ: Erlbaum.

Dawson, D. A. (1991). Family structure and children's health and well-being: Data from the 1988 National Health Interview Survey on child health. *Journal of Marriage and the Family, 53,* 573–584.

de Chateau, P. (1980). Effects of hospital practices on synchrony in the development of the infant-parent relationship. In P. M. Taylor (Ed.), *Parent-infant relationships* (pp. 137–168). New York: Grune & Stratton.

de Villiers, P. A., & de Villiers, J. G. (1992). Language development. In M. H. Bornstein & M. E. Lamb (Eds.), *Developmental psychology: An advanced textbook* (3rd ed.) (pp. 337–418). Hillsdale, NJ: Erlbaum.

DeCasper, A. J., & Fifer, W. P. (1980). Of human bonding: Newborns prefer their mothers' voices. *Science, 208,* 1174–1176.

DeCasper, A. J., & Sigafoos, A. D. (1983). The intrauterine heartbeat: A potent reinforcer for newborns. *Infant Behavior and Development, 6,* 19–25.

DeCasper, A. J., & Spence, M. J. (1986). Prenatal maternal speech influences newborns' perception of speech sounds. *Infant Behavior and Development, 9,* 133–150.

Declercq, E. R. (1993). Where babies are born and who attends their births: Findings from the revised 1989 United States Standard Certificate of Live Birth. *Obstetrics & Gynecology, 81,* 997–1004.

DeLoache, J. S. (1989). The development of representation in young children. In H. W. Reese (Ed.), *Advances in child development and behavior* (Vol. 22) (pp. 2–37). San Diego, CA: Academic Press.

DeLoache, J. S., & Brown, A. L. (1987). Differences in the memory-based searching of delayed and normally developing young children. *Intelligence, 11,* 277–289.

Dempster, F. N. (1981). Memory span: Sources of individual and developmental differences. *Psychological Bulletin, 89,* 63–100.

Den Ouden, L., Rijken, M., Brand, R., Verloove-Vanhorick, S. P., & Ruys, J. H. (1991). Is it correct to correct? Developmental milestones in 555 "normal" preterm infants compared with term infants. *Journal of Pediatrics, 118,* 399–404.

Denham, S. A., & Holt, R. W. (1993). Preschoolers' likeability as cause or consequence of their social behavior. *Developmental Psychology, 29,* 271–275.

Dennis, W. (1960). Causes of retardation among institutional children: Iran. *Journal of Genetic Psychology, 96,* 47–59.

Deutsch, C. K., & Kinsbourne, M. (1990). Genetics and biochemistry in attention deficit disorder. In M. Lewis & S. M. Miller (Eds.), *Handbook of developmental psychopathology* (pp. 93–108). New York: Plenum.

The Diagram Group (1977). *Child's body.* New York: Paddington.

Diamond, A. (1991). Neuropsychological insight into the meaning of object concept development. In S. Carey & R. Gelman (Eds.), *The Epigenesis of mind. Essays on biology and cognition* (pp. 67–110). Hillsdale, NJ: Erlbaum.

Dietrich, K. N., Krafft, K. M., Bornschein, R. L., Hammond, P. B., Berger, O., Succop, P. A., & Bier, M. (1987). Low-level fetal lead exposure effect on neurobehavioral development in early infancy. *Pediatrics, 80,* 721–730.

Dietz, W. H., & Gortmaker, S. L. (1985). Do we fatten our children at the television set? Obesity and television viewing in children and adolescents. *Pediatrics, 75,* 807–812.

Dishion, T. J., Patterson, G. R., Stoolmiller, M., & Skinner, M. L. (1991). Family, school, and behavioral antecedents to early adolescent involvement with antisocial peers. *Developmental Psychology, 27,* 172–180.

Dodge, K. A. (1990). Developmental psychopathology in children of depressed mothers. *Developmental Psychology, 26,* 3–6.

Dodge, K. A. (1991). The structure and function of reactive and proactive aggression. In D. J. Pepler & K. H. Rubin (Eds.), *The development and treatment of childhood aggression* (pp. 201–218). Hillsdale, NJ: Erlbaum.

Dodge, K. A., Coie, J. D., Pettit, G. S., & Price, J. M. (1990). Peer status and aggression in boys groups: Developmental and contextual analysis. *Child Development, 61,* 1289–1309.

Dodge, K. A., & Feldman, E. (1990). Issues in social cognition and sociometric status. In S. R. Asher & J. D. Coie (Eds.), *Peer rejection in childhood* (pp. 119–155). Cambridge, England: Cambridge University Press.

Dodge, K. A., & Frame, C. L. (1982). Social cognitive biases and deficits in aggressive boys. *Child Development, 53,* 620–635.

Dodge, K. A., Murphy, R. R., & Buchsbaum, K. (1984). The assessment of intention-cue detection skills in children: Implications for developmental psychopathology. *Child Development, 55,* 163–173.

Donovan, & Jessor, R. (1985). Structure of problem behavior in adolescence and young adulthood. *Journal of Consulting and Clinical Psychology, 53,* 890–904.

Dornbusch, S. M., Carlsmith, J. M., Bushwall, S. J., Ritter, P. L., Leiderman, H., Hastorf, A. H., & Goss, R. T. (1985). Single parents, extended households, and the control of adolescents. *Child Development, 56,* 326–341.

Dornbusch, S. M., Ritter, P. L., Liederman, P. H., Roberts, D. F., & Fraleigh, M. J. (1987). The relation of parenting style to adolescent school performance. *Child Development, 58,* 1244–1257.

Dornbusch, S. M., Ritter, P. L., Mont-Reynaud, R., & Chen, Z. (1990). Family decision making and academic performance in a diverse high school population. *Journal of Adolescent Research, 5,* 143–160.

Downey, G., & Coyne, J. C. (1990). Children of depressed parents: An integrative review. *Psychological Bulletin, 108,* 50–76.

Dreyer, P. H. (1982). Sexuality during adolescence. In B. B. Wolman (Ed.), *Handbook of developmental psychology* (pp. 559–601). Englewood Cliffs, NJ: Prentice-Hall.

Dryfoos, J. (1990). *Adolescents at risk. Prevalence and prevention.* New York: Oxford University Press.

Duke, P. M., Carlsmith, J. M., Jennings, D., Martin, J. A., Dornbusch, S. M., Gross, R. T., & Siegel-Gorelick, B. (1982). Educational correlates of early and late sexual maturation in adolescence. *Journal of Pediatrics, 100,* 633–637.

Duncan, G. (1993). *Economic deprivation and childhood development.* Paper presented at the biennial meetings of the Society for Research in Child Development, New Orleans.

Dunham, P. J., Dunham, F., & Curwin, A. (1993). Joint-attentional states and lexical acquisition at 18 months. *Developmental Psychology, 29,* 827–831.

Dunn, J. (1992). Siblings and development. *Current Directions in Psychological Science, 1,* 6–9.

Dunn, J., & Brown, J. (1994). Affect expression in the family, children's understanding of emotions, and their interactions with others. *Merrill-Palmer Quarterly, 40,* 120–137.

Dunn, J., & Kendrick, C. (1982). Siblings and their mothers: Developing relationships within the family. In M. E. Lamb & B. Sutton-Smith (Eds.), *Sibling relationships: Their nature and significance across the lifespan* (pp. 39–60). Hillsdale, NJ: Erlbaum.

Dunn, J., & McGuire, S. (1994). Young children's nonshared experiences: A summary of studies in Cambridge and Colorado. In E. M. Hetherington, D. Reiss, & R. Plomin (Eds.), *Separate social worlds of siblings. The impact of nonshared environment on development* (pp. 111–128). Hillsdale, NJ: Erlbaum.

Dunphy, D. C. (1963). The social structure of urban adolescent peer groups. *Sociometry, 26,* 230–246.

Dwyer, T., & Ponsonby, A. (1992). Sudden infant death syndrome—insights from epidemiological research. *Journal of Epidemiology and Community Health, 46,* 98–102.

Dyk, P. H. (1993). Anatomy, physiology, and gender issues in adolescence. In T. P. Gullotta, G. R. Adams, & R. Montemayor (Eds.), *Adolescent sexuality* (pp. 35–56). Newbury Park, CA: Sage.

Dykens, E. M., Hodapp, R. M., & Leckman, J. F. (1994). *Behavior and development in Fragile X syndrome*. Thousand Oaks, CA: Sage.

Easterbrooks, M. A., Davidson, C. E., & Chazan, R. (1993). Psychosocial risk, attachment, and behavior problems among school-aged children. *Development and Psychopathology, 5*, 389–402.

Eaton, W. O., & Enns, L. R. (1986). Sex differences in human motor activity level. *Psychological Bulletin, 100*, 19–28.

Eccles, J. S., & Midgley, C. (1990). Changes in academic motivation and self-perception during early adolescence. In R. Montemayor, G. R. Adams, & T. P. Gullotta (Eds.), *From childhood to adolescence: A transitional period?* (pp. 134–155). Newbury Park, CA: Sage.

Egeland, B., & Farber, E. A. (1984). Infant-mother attachment: Factors related to its development and changes over time. *Child Development, 55*, 753–771.

Eisenberg, N. (1988). The development of prosocial and aggressive behavior. In M. H. Bornstein & M. E. Lamb (Eds.), *Developmental psychology: An advanced textbook* (2nd ed.) (pp. 461–496). Hillsdale, NJ: Erlbaum.

Eisenberg, N. (1990). Prosocial development in early and mid-adolescence. In R. Montemayor, G. R. Adams, & T. P. Gullotta (Eds.), *From childhood to adolescence: A transitional period?* (pp. 240–268). Newbury Park, CA: Sage.

Eisenberg, N. (1992). *The caring child*. Cambridge, MA: Harvard University Press.

Eisenberg, N., Shell, R., Pasternack, J., Lennon, R., Beller, R., & Mathy, R. M. (1987). Prosocial development in middle childhood: A longitudinal study. *Developmental Psychology, 23*, 712–718.

Ekman, P. (1972). Universals and cultural differences in facial expressions of emotion. In J. Cole (Ed.), *Nebraska symposium on motivation, 1971* (pp. 207–282). Lincoln: University of Nebraska Press.

Ekman, P. (1973). Cross-cultural studies of facial expression. In P. Ekman (Ed.), *Darwin and facial expression* (pp. 169–222). New York: Academic Press.

Ekman, P. (1989). The argument and evidence about universals in facial expressions of emotion. In H. Wagner and A. Manstead (Eds.), *Handbook of social psychophysiology* (pp. 143–164). Chichester, England: Wiley.

Elkind, D. (1967). Egocentrism in adolescence. *Child Development, 38*, 1025–1034.

Elkind, D., & Bowen, R. (1979). Imaginary audience behavior in children and adolescents. *Developmental Psychology, 15*, 38–44.

Elliott, R. (1988). Tests, abilities, race, and conflict. *Intelligence, 12*, 333–350.

Eme, R. F. (1979). Sex differences in childhood psychopathology: A review. *Psychological Bulletin, 86*, 374–395.

Emery, R. E. (1988). *Marriage, divorce, and children's adjustment*. Newbury Park, CA: Sage.

Entwisle, D. R. (1990). Schools and the adolescent. In S. S. Feldman & G. R. Elliott (Eds.), *At the threshold. The developing adolescent* (pp. 197–224). Cambridge, MA: Harvard University Press.

Entwisle, D. R., & Alexander, K. L. (1990). Beginning school math competence: Minority and majority comparisons. *Child Development, 61*, 454–471.

Entwisle, D. R., & Doering, S. G. (1981). *The first birth*. Baltimore: Johns Hopkins University Press.

Epstein, S. (1991). Cognitive-experiential self theory: Implications for developmental psychology. In M. R. Gunnar & L. A. Sroufe (Eds.), *Minnesota symposia on child development* (Vol. 23) (pp. 79–123). Hillsdale, NJ: Erlbaum.

Ericsson, K. A., & Crutcher, R. J. (1990). The nature of exceptional performance. In P. B. Baltes, D. L., Featherman, & R. M. Lerner (Eds.), *Life-span development and behavior* (Vol. 10) (pp. 188–218). Hillsdale, NJ: Erlbaum.

Erikson, E. H. (1963). *Childhood and society* (2nd ed.). New York: Norton.

Erikson, E. H. (1964). *Insight and responsibility*. New York: Norton.

Erikson, E. H. (1974). *Dimensions of a new identity: The 1973 Jefferson lectures in the humanities*. New York: Norton.

Erikson, E. H. (1980). *Identity and the life cycle* (reissued edition). New York: W. W. Norton.

Eron, L. D. (1987). The development of aggressive behavior from the perspective of a developing behaviorism. *American Psychologist, 42*, 435–442.

Eron, L. D., Huesmann, L. R., & Zelli, A. (1991). The role of parental variables in the learning of aggression. In D. J. Pepler & K. H. Rubin (Eds.), *The development and treatment of childhood aggression* (pp. 169–188). Hillsdale, NJ: Erlbaum.

Escalona, K. S. (1981). The reciprocal role of social and emotional developmental advances and cognitive development during the second and third years of life . In E. K. Shapiro & E. Weber (Eds.), *Cognitive and affective growth: Developmental interaction* (pp. 87–108). Hillsdale, NJ: Erlbaum.

Espinosa, M. P., Sigman, M. D., Neumann, C. G., Bwibo, N. O., & McDonald, M. A. (1992). Playground behaviors of school-age children in relation to nutrition, schooling, and family characteristics. *Developmental Psychology, 28*, 1188–1195.

European Collaborative Study (1991). Children born to women with HIV-1 infection: Natural history and risk of transmission. *The Lancet, 337*, 253–260.

Fagan, J. F., III (1992). Intelligence: A theoretical viewpoint. *Current Directions in Psychological Science*, *1*, 82–86.

Fagan, J. F., III, & Shepherd, P. A. (1986). *The Fagan Test of Infant Intelligence: Training manual*. Cleveland, OH: Infantest Corporation.

Fagan, J. F., III, & Singer, L. T. (1983). Infant recognition memory as a measure of intelligence. In L. P. Lipsett (Ed.), *Advances in infancy research* (Vol. 2) (pp. 31–78). Norwood, NJ: Ablex.

Fagan, J. F., III, & McGrath, S. K. (1981). Infant recognition memory and later intelligence. *Intelligence*, *5*, 121–130.

Fagard, J., & Jacquet, A. (1989). Onset of bimanual coordination and symmetry versus asymmetry of movement. *Infant Behavior and Development*, *12*, 229–235.

Fagot, B. I., & Hagan, R. (1991). Observations of parent reactions to sex-stereotyped behaviors: Age and sex effects. *Child Development*, *62*, 617–628.

Fagot, B. I., & Leinbach, M. D. (1989). The young child's gender schema: Environmental input, internal organization. *Child Development*, *60*, 663–672.

Fagot, B. I., & Leinbach, M. D. (1993). Gender-role development in young children: From discrimination to labeling. *Developmental Review*, *13*, 205–224.

Fagot, B. I., Leinbach, M. D., & O'Boyle, C. (1992). Gender labeling, gender stereotyping, and parenting behaviors. *Developmental Psychology*, *28*, 225–230.

Fairburn, C. G., & Beglin, S. J. (1990). Studies of the epidemiology of bulimia nervosa. *The American Journal of Psychiatry*, *147*, 401–408.

Famularo, R., Stone, K., Barnum, R., & Whatron, R. (1986). Alcoholism and severe child maltreatment. *American Journal of Orthopsychiatry*, *56*, 481–485.

Farnham-Diggory, S. (1986). Time, now, for a little serious complexity. In S. J. Ceci (Ed.), *Handbook of cognitive, social, and neuropsychological aspects of learning disability* (Vol. 1). Hillsdale, NJ: Erlbaum.

Farnham-Diggory, S. (1992). *The learning-disabled child*. Cambridge, MA: Harvard University Press.

Farran, D. C., Haskins, R., & Gallagher, J. J. (1980). Poverty and mental retardation: A search for explanations. *New Directions for Exceptional Children*, *1*, 47–66.

Farrar, M. J. (1992). Negative evidence and grammatical morpheme acquisition. *Developmental Psychology*, *28*, 90–98.

Farrington, D. P. (1991). Childhood aggression and adult violence: Early precursors and later life outcomes. In D. J. Pepler & K. H. Rubin (Eds.), *The development and treatment of childhood aggression* (pp. 5–30). Hillsdale, NJ: Erlbaum.

Faust, M. S. (1983). Alternative constructions of adolescent growth. In J. Brooks-Gunn & A. C. Petersen (Eds.), *Girls at puberty. Biological and psychosocial perspectives* (pp. 105–126). New York: Plenum Press.

Featherman, D. L. (1980). Schooling and occupational careers: Constancy and change in worldly success. In O. G. Brim, Jr. & J. Kagan (Eds.), *Constancy and change in human development* (pp. 675–738). Cambridge, MA: Harvard University Press.

Featherstone, H. (1980). *A difference in the family*. New York: Basic Books.

Feldman, S. S. (1987). Predicting strain in mothers and fathers of 6-month-old infants: A short-term longitudinal study. In P. W. Berman & F. A. Pedersen (Eds.), *Men's transitions to parenthood* (pp. 13–36). Hillsdale, NJ: Erlbaum.

Feldman, S. S., & Elliott, G. R. (1990). *At the threshold. The developing adolescent*. Cambridge, MA: Harvard University Press.

Fennelly, K. (1993). Sexual activity and childbearing among Hispanic adolescents in the United States. In R. M. Lerner (Ed.), *Early adolescence. Perspectives on research, policy, and intervention* (pp. 335–352). Hillsdale, NJ: Erlbaum.

Fergusson, D. M., Horwood, L. J., & Lynskey, M. T. (1993). Maternal smoking before and after pregnancy: Effects on behavioral outcomes in middle childhood. *Pediatrics*, *92*, 815–822.

Fernald, A., & Kuhl, P. (1987). Acoustic determinants of infant preference for motherese speech. *Infant Behavior and Development*, *10*, 279–293.

Feshbach, S. (1970). Aggression. In P. H. Mussen (Ed.), *Carmichael's manual of child psychology* (Vol. 2, 3rd ed.) (pp. 159–260). New York: Wiley.

Field, T. (1990). *Infancy*. Cambridge, MA: Harvard University Press.

Field, T., Healy, B., Goldstein, S., Perry, S., Bendell, D., Schanberg, S., Zimmerman, E. A., & Duhn, C. (1988). Infants of depressed mothers show "depressed" behavior even with nondepressed adults. *Child Development*, *59*, 1569–1579.

Field, T. M. (1977). Effects of early separation, interactive deficits, and experimental manipulations on infant-mother face-to-face interaction. *Child Development*, *48*, 763–771.

Field, T. M. (1978). Interaction behaviors of primary versus secondary caretaker fathers. *Developmental Psychology*, *14*, 183–185.

Field, T. M. (1991). Quality infant day-care and grade school behavior and performance. *Child Development*, *62*, 863–870.

Field, T. M., De Stefano, L., & Koewler, J. H. I. (1982). Fantasy play of toddlers and preschoolers. *Developmental Psychology*, *18*, 503–508.

Field, T. M., Healy, B., Goldstein, S., & Guthertz, M. (1990). Behavior-state matching and synchrony in mother-infant interactions of nondepressed versus depressed dyads. *Developmental Psychology*, *26*, 7–14.

Field, T. M., Woodson, R., Greenberg, R., & Cohen, D. (1982). Discrimination and imitation of facial expressions by neonates. *Science, 218,* 179–181.

Finkelstein, N. W. (1982). Aggression: Is it stimulated by day care? *Young Children, 37,* 3–9.

Fischer, K. W., & Bidell, T. (1991). Constraining nativist inferences about cognitive capacities. In S. Carey & R. Gelman (Eds.), *The epigenesis of mind: Essays on biology and cognition* (pp. 199–236). Hillsdale, NJ: Erlbaum.

Fish, M., Stifter, C. A., & Belsky, J. (1991). Conditions of continuity and discontinuity in infant negative emotionality: Newborn to five months. *Child Development, 62,* 1525–1537.

Flavell, J. H. (1982). Structures, stages, and sequences in cognitive development. In W. A. Collins (Ed.), *Minnesota symposia on child psychology* (Vol. 15) (pp. 1–28). Hillsdale, NJ: Erlbaum.

Flavell, J. H. (1985). *Cognitive development* (2nd ed.). Englewood Cliffs, NJ: Prentice-Hall.

Flavell, J. H. (1986). The development of children's knowledge about the appearance-reality distinction. *American Psychologist, 41,* 418–425.

Flavell, J. H. (1992). Cognitive development: Past, present, and future. *Developmental Psychology, 28,* 998–1005.

Flavell, J. H. (1993). Young children's understanding of thinking and consciousness. *Current Directions in Psychological Science, 2,* 40–43.

Flavell, J. H., Everett, B. A., Croft, K., & Flavell, E. R. (1981). Young children's knowledge about visual perception: Further evidence for the Level 1-Level 2 distinction. *Developmental Psychology, 17,* 99–103.

Flavell, J. H., Green, F. L., & Flavell, E. R. (1989). Young children's ability to differentiate appearance-reality and level 2 perspectives in the tactile modality. *Child Development, 60,* 201–213.

Flavell, J. H., Green, F. L., & Flavell, E. R. (1990). Developmental changes in young children's knowledge about the mind. *Cognitive Development, 5,* 1–27.

Flavell, J. H., Green, F. L., Wahl, K. E., & Flavell, E. R. (1987). The effects of question clarification and memory aids on young children's performance on appearance-reality tasks. *Cognitive Development, 2,* 127–144.

Flavell, J. H., Zhang, X. D., Zou, H., Dong, Q., & Qi, S. (1983). A comparison of the appearance-reality distinction in the People's Republic of China and the United States. *Cognitive Psychology, 15,* 459–466.

Fleming, A. S., Ruble, D. L., Flett, G. L., & Schaul, D. L. (1988). Postpartum adjustment in first-time mothers: Relations between mood, maternal attitudes, and mother-infant interactions. *Developmental Psychology, 24,* 71–81.

Floyd, R. L., Rimer, B. K., Giovino, G. A., Mullen, P. D., & Sullivan, S. E. (1993). A review of smoking in pregnancy: Effects on pregnancy outcomes and cessation efforts. *Annual Review of Public Health, 14,* 379–411.

Folven, R. J., & Bonvillian, J. D. (1991). The transition from nonreferential to referential language in children acquiring American Sign Language. *Developmental Psychology, 27,* 806–816.

Fonagy, P., Steele, H., & Steele, M. (1991). Maternal representations of attachment during pregnancy predict the organization of infant-mother attachment at one year of age. *Child Development, 62,* 891–905.

Fox, N. A., Kimmerly, N. L., & Schafer, W. D. (1991). Attachment to mother/attachment to father: A meta-analysis. *Child Development, 62,* 210–225.

Fraiberg, S. (1974). Blind infants and their mothers: An examination of the sign system. In M. Lewis & L. A. Rosenblum (Eds.), *The effect of the infant on its caregiver* (pp. 215–232). New York: Wiley.

Fraiberg, S. (1975). The development of human attachments in infants blind from birth. *Merrill-Palmer Quarterly, 21,* 315–334.

Fraiberg, S. (1977). *Insights from the blind.* New York: New American Library (Meridian Books).

Frankel, K. A., & Bates, J. E. (1990). Mother-toddler problem solving: Antecedents in attachment, home behavior, and temperament. *Child Development, 61,* 810–819.

Frankenberg, W. K., Dodds, J. B., Fandal, A. W., Kazuk, E., & Cohrs, M. (1975). *Denver developmental screening test: Reference manual.* Denver: University of Colorado Medical Center.

Freedman, D. G. (1979). Ethnic differences in babies. *Human Nature, 2,* 36–43.

Freeman, E. W., & Rickels, K. (1993). *Early childbearing. Perspectives of black adolescents on pregnancy, abortion, and contraception.* Newbury Park, CA: Sage.

Freud, S. (1905). *The basic writings of Sigmund Freud* (Brill, A. A., Trans.). New York: Random House.

Freud, S. (1920). *A general introduction to psychoanalysis* (Riviere, J., Trans.). New York: Washington Square Press.

Frey, K. S., & Ruble, D. N. (1992). Gender constancy and the "cost" of sex-typed behavior: A test of the conflict hypothesis. *Developmental Psychology, 28,* 714–721.

Fu, Y., Pizzuti, A., Fenwick, R. G., Jr., King, J., Rajnarayan, S., Dune, P. W., Dubel, J., Nasser, G. A., Ashizawa, T., de Jong, P., Wieringa, B., Korneluk, R., Perryman, M. B., Epstein, H. F., & Caskey, C. T. (1992). An unstable triplet repeat in a gene related to Myotonic muscular dystrophy. *Science, 225,* 1256–1258.

Fuligni, A. J., & Eccles, J. S. (1993). Perceived parent-child relationships and early adolescents' orientation toward peers. *Developmental Psychology, 29,* 622–632.

Furrow, D. (1984). Social and private speech at two years. *Child Development, 55,* 355–362.

Furstenberg, F. F., Jr. (1991). As the pendulum swings: Teenage childbearing and social concern. *Family Relations, 40,* 127–138.

Furstenberg, F. F., Jr., & Cherlin, A. J. (1991). *Divided families: What happens to children when parents part.* Cambridge, MA: Harvard University Press.

Garbarino, J., Dubrow, N., Kostelny, K., & Pardo, C. (1992). *Children in danger. Coping with the consequences of community violence.* San Francisco: Jossey-Bass.

Garbarino, J., Kostelny, K., & Dubrow, N. (1991). *No place to be a child. Growing up in a war zone.* Lexington, MA: Lexington Books.

Garbarino, J., & Sherman, D. (1980). High-risk neighborhoods and high-risk families: The human ecology of child maltreatment. *Child Development, 51,* 188–198.

Gardner, D., Harris, P. L., Ohmoto, M., & Hamasaki, T. (1988). Japanese children's understanding of the distinction between real and apparent emotion. *International Journal of Behavioral Development, 11,* 203–218.

Gardner, H. (1983). *Frames of mind: The theory of multiple intelligence.* New York: Basic Books.

Garland, A. F., & Zigler, E. (1993). Adolescent suicide prevention. Current research and social policy implications. *American Psychologist, 48,* 169–182.

Garmezy, N. (1993). Vulnerability and resilience. In D. C. Funder, R. D. Parke, C. Tomlinson-Keasey, & K. Widaman (Eds.), *Studying lives through time. Personality and development* (pp. 377–398). Washington, DC: American Psychological Association.

Garmezy, N., & Masten, A. S. (1991). The protective role of competence indicators in children at risk. In E. M. Cummings, A. L. Green, & K. H. Karraker (Eds.), *Lifespan developmental psychology. Perspectives on stress and coping* (pp. 151–174). Hillsdale, NJ: Erlbaum.

Garmezy, N., & Rutter, M. (Eds.). (1983). *Stress, coping, and development in children.* New York: McGraw-Hill.

Garn, S. M. (1980). Continuities and change in maturational timing. In O. G. Brim, Jr. & J. Kagan (Eds.), *Constancy and change in human development* (pp. 113–162). Cambridge, MA: Harvard University Press.

Gesell, A. (1925). *The mental growth of the preschool child.* New York: Macmillan.

Gazzaniga, J. M. (1993). Relationship between diet composition and body fatness, with adjustment for resting energy expenditure and physical activity, in preadolescent children. *American Journal of Clinical Nutrition, 58,* 21–28.

Gecas, V., & Seff, M. A. (1990). Families and adolescents: A review of the 1980s. *Journal of Marriage and the Family, 52,* 941–958.

Gelman, R. (1972). Logical capacity of very young children: Number invariance rules. *Child Development, 43,* 75–90.

Genesee, F. (1993). Bilingual language development in preschool children. In D. Bishop & K. Mogford (Eds.), *Language development in exceptional circumstances* (pp. 62–79). Hove, UK: Erlbaum.

Gentner, D. (1982). Why nouns are learned before verbs: Linguistic relativity versus natural partitioning. In S. A. Kuczaj, II (Ed.), *Language development.* Vol. 2, *Language, thought, and culture* (pp. 301–334). Hillsdale, NJ: Erlbaum.

Gibson, D. R. (1990). Relation of socioeconomic status to logical and sociomoral judgment of middle-aged men. *Psychology and Aging, 5,* 510–513.

Gilbert, T. J., Percy, C. A., Sugarman, J. R., Benson, L., & Percy, C. (1992). Obesity among Navajo adolescents. Relationship to dietary intake and blood pressure. *American Journal of Diseases of Children, 146,* 289–295.

Gilligan, C. (1982a). New maps of development: new visions of maturity. *American Journal of Orthopsychiatry, 52,* 199–212.

Gilligan, C. (1982b). *In a different voice: psychological theory and women's development.* Cambridge, MA: Harvard University Press.

Gilligan, C. (1987). Adolescent development reconsidered. *New Directions for Child Development, 37,* 63–92.

Gilligan, C., & Wiggins, G. (1987). The origins of morality in early childhood relationships. In J. Kagan & S. Lamb (Eds.), *The emergence of morality in young children* (pp. 277–307). Chicago: The University of Chicago Press.

Giordano, P. C., Cernkovich, S. A., & DeMaris, A. (1993). The family and peer relations of black adolescents. *Journal of Marriage and the Family, 55,* 277–287.

Gleitman, L. R., & Gleitman, H. (1992). A picture is worth a thousand words, but that's the problem: The role of syntax in vocabulary acquisition. *Current Directions in Psychological Science, 1,* 31–35.

Glueck, S., & Glueck, E. (1972). *Identification of pre-delinquents: Validation studies and some suggested uses of Glueck Table.* New York: Intercontinental Medical Book Corp.

Gnepp, J., & Chilamkurti, C. (1988). Children's use of personality attributions to predict other people's emotional and behavioral reactions. *Child Development, 50,* 743–754.

Goldberg, S. (1972). Infant care and growth in urban Zambia. *Human Development, 15,* 77–89.

Goldberg, W. A. (1990). Marital quality, parental personality, and spousal agreement about perceptions and expectations for children. *Merrill-Palmer Quarterly, 36,* 531–556.

Goldfield, B. A., & Reznick, J. S. (1990). Early lexical acquisition: Rate, content, and the vocabulary spurt. *Journal of Child Language, 17,* 171–183.

Gonsiorek, J. C., & Weinrich, J. D. (1991). The definition and scope of sexual orientation. In J. C. Gonsiorek & J. D. Weinrich (Eds.), *Homosexuality. Research implications for public policy* (pp. 1–12). Newbury Park, CA: Sage Publications.

Good, T. L., & Weinstein, R. S. (1986). Schools make a difference. Evidence, criticisms, and new directions. *American Psychologist, 41*, 1090–1097.

Goodenough, F. L. (1931). *Anger in young children.* Minneapolis: University of Minnesota Press.

Goodsitt, J. V., Morse, P. A., Ver Hoeve, J. N., & Cowan, N. (1984). Infant speech recognition in multisyllabic contexts. *Child Development, 55*, 903–910.

Gopnik, A., & Astington, J. W. (1988). Children's understanding of representational change and its relation to the understanding of false belief and the appearance-reality distinction. *Child Development, 59*, 26–37.

Gopnik, A., & Meltzoff, A. (1987). The development of categorization in the second year and its relation to other cognitive and linguistic developments. *Child Development, 58*, 1523–1531.

Gopnik, A., & Meltzoff, A. N. (1992). Categorization and naming: Basic-level sorting in eighteen-month-olds and its relation to language. *Child Development, 63*, 1091–1103.

Gortmaker, S. L., Dietz, W. H., Sobol, A. M., & Welher, C. A. (1987). Increasing pediatric obesity in the United States. *American Journal of the Diseases of Children, 141*, 535–540.

Gottman, J. M. (1986). The world of coordinated play: Same- and cross-sex friendship in young children. In J. M. Gottman & J. G. Parker (Eds.), *Conversations of friends. Speculations on affective development* (pp. 139–191). Cambridge, England: Cambridge University Press.

Gralinski, J. H., & Kopp, C. B. (1993). Everyday rules for behavior: Mothers' requests to young children. *Developmental Psychology, 29*, 573–584.

Greenberg, J., & Kuczaj, S. A., II (1982). Towards a theory of substantive word-meaning acquisition. In S. A. Kuczaj, II (Ed.), *Language development. Vol. l, Syntax and semantics* (pp. 275–312). Hillsdale, NJ: Erlbaum.

Greenberg, M. T., Calderon, R., & Kusche, C. (1984). Early intervention using simultaneous communication with deaf infants: The effect on communication development. *Child Development, 55*, 607–616.

Greenberg, M. T., Siegel, J. M., & Leitch, C. J. (1983). The nature and importance of attachment relationships to parents and peers during adolescence. *Journal of Youth and Adolescence, 12*, 373–386.

Greenberg, M. T., Speltz, M. L., & DeKlyen, M. (1993). The role of attachment in the early development of disruptive behavior problems. *Development and Psychopathology, 5*, 191–213.

Greenberger, E., & Steinberg, L. (1986). *When teenagers work. The psychological and social costs of adolescent employment.* New York: Basic Books.

Greenough, W. T. (1991). Experience as a component of normal development: Evolutionary considerations. *Developmental Psychology, 27*, 11–27.

Greenough, W. T., Black, J. E., & Wallace, C. S. (1987). Experience and brain development. *Child Development, 58*, 539–559.

Griffith, D. R., Azuma, S. D., & Chasnoff, I. J. (1994). Three-year outcome of children exposed prenatally to drugs. *Journal of the American Academy of Child and Adolescent Psychiatry, 33*, 20–27.

Grolnick, W. S., & Slowiaczek, M. L. (1994). Parents' involvement in children's schooling: A multidimensional conceptualization and motivational model. *Child Development, 65*, 237–252.

Grossmann, K., Grossmann, K. E., Spangler, G., Suess, G., & Unzner, L. (1985). Maternal sensitivity and newborns' orientation responses as related to quality of attachment in northern Germany. *Monographs of the Society of Research in Child Development, 50* (1–2, Serial No. 209), 233–256.

Grusec, J. E. (1992). Social learning theory and developmental psychology: The legacies of Robert Sears and Albert Bandura. *Developmental Psychology, 28*, 776–786.

Grusec, J. E., & Lytton, H. (1988). *Social development. History, theory, and research.* New York: Springer-Verlag.

Grusec, J. E., Saas-Kortsaak, P., & Simutis, Z. M. (1978). The role of example and moral exhortation in the training of altruism. *Child Development, 49*, 920–923.

Gullotta, T. P., Adams, G. R., & Montemayor, R. (Eds.). (1993). *Adolescent sexuality.* Newbury Park, CA: Sage.

Gunnar, M. R. (1990). The psychobiology of infant temperament. In J. Colombo & J. Fagen (Eds.), *Individual differences in infancy: Reliability, stability, prediction* (pp. 387–410). Hillsdale, NJ: Erlbaum.

Gunnar, M. R., Larson, M. C., Hertsgaard, L., Harris, M. L., & Brodersen, L. (1992). The stressfulness of separation among nine-month-old infants: Effects of social context variables and infant temperament. *Child Development, 63*, 290–303.

Guralnick, M. J., & Paul-Brown, D. (1984). Communicative adjustments during behavior-request episodes among children at different developmental levels. *Child Development, 55*, 911–919.

Guttentag, R. E., Ornstein, P. A., & Siemens, L. (1987). Children's spontaneous rehearsal: Transitions in strategy acquisition. *Cognitive Development, 2*, 307–326.

Gzesh, S. M., & Surber, C. F. (1985). Visual perspective-taking skills in children. *Child Development, 56*, 1204–1213.

Haan, N. (1981). Adolescents and young adults as producers of their own development. In R. M. Lerner & N. A. Busch-Rossnagel (Eds.), *Individuals as producers of their own development* (pp. 155–182). New York: Academic Press.

Haan, N. (1985). Processes of moral development: Cognitive or social disequilibrium? *Developmental Psychology, 21,* 996–1006.

Hack, M., Breslau, N., Weissman, B., Aram, D., Klein, N., & Borawski, E. (1991). Effect of very low birth weight and subnormal head size on cognitive abilities at school age. *New England Journal of Medicine, 325,* 231–237.

Haddow, J. E., Palomaki, G. E., Knight, G. J., Cunningham, G. C., Lustig, L. S., & Boyd, P. A. (1994). Reducing the need for amniocentesis in women 35 years of age or older with serum markers for screening. *New England Journal of Medicine, 330,* 1114–1118.

Haith, M. M. (1980). *Rules that babies look by.* Hillsdale, NJ: Erlbaum.

Hakuta, K., & Garcia, E. E. (1989). Bilingualism and education. *American Psychologist, 44,* 374–379.

Hale, S., Fry, A. F., & Jessie, K. A. (1993). Effects of practice on speed of information processing in children and adults: Age sensitivity and age invariance. *Developmental Psychology, 29,* 880–892.

Halpern, D. F. (1986). *Sex differences in cognitive abilities.* Hillsdale, NJ: Erlbaum.

Hammond, W. R., & Yung, B. (1993). Psychology's role in the public health response to assaultive violence among young African-American men. *American Psychologist, 48,* 142–154.

Hanna, E., & Meltzoff, A. N. (1993). Peer imitation by toddlers in laboratory, home, and day-care contexts: Implications for social learning and memory. *Developmental Psychology, 29,* 701–710.

Harkness, S., & Super, C. M. (1985). The cultural context of gender segregation in children's peer groups. *Child Development, 56,* 219–224.

Harris, M. (1992). *Language experience and early language development: From input to uptake.* Hove, England: Erlbaum.

Harris, P. L. (1989). *Children and emotion. The development of psychological understanding.* Oxford: Basil Blackwell.

Harter, S. (1987). The determinations and mediational role of global self-worth in children. In N. Eisenberg (Ed.), *Contemporary topics in developmental psychology* (pp. 219–242). New York: Wiley-Interscience.

Harter, S. (1990). Processes underlying adolescent self-concept formation. In R. Montemayor, G. R. Adams, & T. P. Gullotta (Eds.), *From childhood to adolescence: A transitional period?* (pp. 205–239). Newbury Park, CA: Sage.

Harter, S., & Monsour, A. (1992). Developmental analysis of conflict caused by opposing attributes in the adolescent self-portrait. *Developmental Psychology, 28,* 251–260.

Harter, S., & Pike, R. (1984). The Pictorial Perceived Competence Scale for Young Children. *Child Development, 55,* 1969–1982.

Harter, S., & Whitesell, N. R. (1989). Developmental changes in children's understanding of single, multiple, and blended emotion concepts. In C. Saarni & P. L. Harris (Eds.), *Children's understanding of emotion* (pp. 81–116). Cambridge, England: Cambridge University Press.

Hartup, W. W. (1974). Aggression in childhood: Developmental perspectives. *American Psychologist, 29,* 336–341.

Hartup, W. W. (1989). Social relationships and their developmental significance. *American Psychologist, 44,* 120–126.

Hartup, W. W. (1992). Peer relations in early and middle childhood. In V. B. Van Hasselt & M. Hersen (Eds.), *Handbook of social development. A lifespan perspective* (pp. 257–281). New York: Plenum Press.

The Harvard Education Letter (1992, July/August). *Youth sports: Kids are the losers.* p. 1–3.

Haskins, R. (1985). Public school aggression among children with varying day-care experience. *Child Development, 56,* 689–703.

Haskins, R. (1989). Beyond metaphor: The efficacy of early childhood education. *American Psychologist, 44,* 274–282.

Hatcher, P. J., Hulme, C., & Ellis, A. W. (1994). Ameliorating early reading failure by integrating the teaching of reading and phonological skills: The phonological linkage hypothesis. *Child Development, 65,* 41–57.

Haviland, J. J., & Malatesta, C. Z. (1981). The development of sex differences in nonverbal signals: Fallacies, facts, and fantasies. In C. Mayo & N. M. Henley (Eds.), *Gender and nonverbal behavior* (pp. 183–208). New York: Springer-Verlag.

Haviland, J. M., & Lelwicka, M. (1987). The induced affect response: 10-week-old infants' responses to three emotional expressions. *Developmental Psychology, 23,* 97–104.

Hawley, T. L., & Disney, E. R. (1992). Crack's children: The consequences of maternal cocaine abuse. *Social Policy Report. Society for Research in Child Development, VI* (4), 1–22.

Hawton, K., & Goldacre, M. (1982). Hospital admissions for adverse effects of medicinal agents (mainly self-poisoning) among adolescents in the Oxford region. *British Journal of Psychiatry, 141,* 166–170.

Hayes, C. D. (1987). *Risking the future.* Vol. 1, *Adolescent sexuality, pregnancy, and childbearing.* Washington, DC : National Academy Press.

Hayes, C. D., Palmer, J. L., & Zaslow, M. J. (1990). *Who cares for America's children?* Washington, DC: National Academy Press.

Heagarty, M. C. (1991). America's lost children: Whose responsibility? *The Journal of Pediatrics, 118,* 8–10.

Helms, J. E. (1992). Why is there no study of cultural equivalence in standardized cognitive ability testing? *American Psychologist, 47,* 1083–1101.

Henker, B., & Whalen, C. K. (1989). Hyperactivity and attention deficits. *American Psychologist, 44,* 216–223.

Henneborn, W. J., & Cogan, R. (1975). The effect of husband participation on reported pain and the probability of medication during labour and birth. *Journal of Psychosomatic Research, 19,* 215–222.

Hess, E. H. (1972). "Imprinting" in a natural laboratory. *Scientific American, 227,* 24–31.

Hetherington, E. M. (1989). Coping with family transitions: Winners, losers, and survivors. *Child Development, 60,* 1–14.

Hetherington, E. M. (1991a). The role of individual differences and family relationships in children's coping with divorce and remarriage. In P. A. Cowen & M. Hetherington (Eds.), *Family transitions* (pp. 165–194). Hillsdale: Erlbaum.

Hetherington, E. M. (1991b). Presidential address: Families, lies, and videotapes. *Journal of Research on Adolescence, 1,* 323–348.

Hetherington, E. M., & Camera, K. A. (1984). Families in transition: The process of dissolution and reconstitution. In R. D. Parke, R. N. Emde, H. P. McAdoo, & G. P. Sackett (Eds.), *Review of child development research.* Vol. 7, *The family* (pp. 398–440). Chicago: University of Chicago Press.

Hetherington, E. M., & Clingempeel, W. G. (1992). Coping with marital transitions: A family systems perspective. *Monographs of the Society for Research in Child Development, 57* (2–3, Serial No. 227).

Hicks, T., Fowler, K., Richardson, M., Dahle, A., Adams, L., & Pass, R. (1993). Congenital cytomegalovirus infection and neonatal auditory screening. *Journal of Pediatrics, 123,* 779–782.

Higgins, A. (1991). The just community approach to moral education: Evolution of the idea and recent findings. In W. M. Kurtines & J. L. Gewirtz (Eds.), *Handbook of moral behavior and development.* Vol. 3, *Application* (pp. 111–141). Hillsdale, NJ: Erlbaum.

Higgins, A., Power, C., & Kohlberg, L. (1984). The relationship of moral atmosphere to judgments of responsibility. In W. M. Kurtines & J. L. Gewirtz (Eds.), *Morality, moral behavior, and moral development* (pp. 74–108). New York: Wiley-Interscience.

Hill, J. P. (1988). Adapting to menarche: Familial control and conflict. In M. R. Gunnar & W. A. Collins (Eds.), *Minnesota symposia on child psychology* (Vol. 21) (pp. 43–78). Hillsdale, NJ: Erlbaum.

Hinde, R. A., Titmus, G., Easton, D., & Tamplin, A. (1985). Incidence of "friendship" and behavior toward strong associates versus nonassociates in preschoolers. *Child Development, 56,* 234–245.

Hinshaw, S. P., Lahey, B. B., & Hart, E. L. (1993). Issues of taxonomy and comorbidity in the development of conduct disorder. *Development and Psychopathology, 5,* 31–49.

Hirsch, H. V. B., & Tieman, S. B. (1987). Perceptual development and experience-dependent changes in cat visual cortex. In M. H. Bornstein (Ed.), *Sensitive periods in development: Interdisciplinary perspectives* (pp. 39–80). Hillsdale, NJ: Erlbaum.

Hirsh-Pasek, K., Trieman, R., & Schneiderman, M. (1984). Brown and Hanlon revisited: Mothers' sensitivity to ungrammatical forms. *Journal of Child Language, 11,* 81–88.

Hirshberg, L. M., & Svejda, M. (1990). When infants look to their parents: I. Infants' social referencing of mothers compared to fathers. *Child Development, 61,* 1175–1186.

Hofferth, S. L. (1985). Updating children's life course. *Journal of Marriage and the Family, 47,* 93–115.

Hofferth, S. L. (1987a). Teenage pregnancy and its resolution. In S. L. Hofferth & C. D. Hayes (Eds.), *Risking the future. Adolescent sexuality, pregnancy, and childbearing. Working papers* (pp. 78–92). Washington, DC: National Academy Press.

Hofferth, S. L. (1987b). Social and economic consequences of teenage childbearing. In S. L. Hofferth & C. D. Hayes (Eds.), *Risking the future. Adolescent sexuality, pregnancy, and childbearing. Working papers* (pp. 123–144). Washington, DC: National Academy Press.

Hofferth, S. L., Kahn, J. R., & Baldwin, W. (1987). Premarital sexual activity among U.S. teenage women over the past three decades. *Family Planning Perspectives, 19,* 46–53.

Hoffman, H. J., & Hillman, L. S. (1992). Epidemiology of the sudden infant death syndrome: Maternal, neonatal, and postneonatal risk factors. *Clinics in Perinatology, 19* (4), 717–737.

Hoffman, L. W., & Manis, J. D. (1978). Influences of children on marital interaction and parental satisfactions and dissatisfactions. In R. M. Lerner & G. B. Spanier (Eds.), *Child influences on marital and family interaction.* New York: Academic Press.

Holloway, S. D., & Hess, R. D. (1985). Mothers' and teachers' attributions about children's mathematics performance. In I. E. Sigel (Ed.), *Parental belief systems. The psychological consequences for children* (pp. 177–200). Hillsdale, NJ: Erlbaum.

Holmbeck, G. N., & Hill, J. P. (1991). Conflictive engagement, positive affect, and menarche in families with seventh-grade girls. *Child Development, 62,* 1030–1048.

Honigfeld, L. S., & Kaplan, D. W. (1987). Native-American post-neonatal mortality. *Pediatrics, 80,* 575–578.

Honzik, M. P. (1986). The role of the famiy in the development of mental abilities: A 50-year study. In N. Datan, A. L. Greene, & H. W. Reese (Eds.), *Life-span developmental psychology. Intergenerational relations* (pp. 185–210). Hillsdale, NJ: Erlbaum.

Hopkins, J., Marcus, M., & Campbell, S. B. (1984). Postpartum depression: A critical review. *Psychological Bulletin, 95,* 498–515.

Horowitz, F. D. (1987). *Exploring developmental theories: Toward a structural/behavioral model of development.* Hillsdale, NJ: Erlbaum.

Horowitz, F. D. (1990). Developmental models of individual differences. In J. Colombo & J. Fagen (Eds.), *Individual differences in infancy: Reliability, stability, prediction* (pp. 3–18). Hillsdale, NJ: Erlbaum.

Howard, J. (1978). The influence of children's developmental dysfunctions on marital quality and family interaction. In R. M. Lerner & G. B. Spanier (Eds.), *Child influences on marital and family interaction. A life-span perspective* (pp. 275–298). New York: Academic Press.

Howat, P. M., & Saxton, A. M. (1988). The incidence of bulimic behavior in a secondary and university school population. *Journal of Youth and Adolescence, 17,* 221–321.

Howes, C. (1983). Patterns of friendship. *Child Development, 54,* 1041–1053.

Howes, C. (1987). Social competence with peers in young children: Developmental sequences. *Developmental Review, 7,* 252–272.

Howes, C. (1990). Can the age of entry into child care and the quality of child care predict adjustment in kindergarten? *Developmental Psychology, 26,* 292–303.

Howes, C., & Matheson, C. C. (1992). Sequences in the development of competent play with peers: Social and pretend play. *Developmental Psychology, 28,* 961–974.

Howes, C., Phillips, D. A., & Whitebook, M. (1992). Thresholds of quality: Implications for the social development of children in center-based child care. *Child Development, 63,* 449–460.

Hubbard, F. O. A., & van IJzendoorn, M. H. (1987). Maternal unresponsiveness and infant crying. A critical replication of the Bell & Ainsworth study. In L. W. C. Tavecchio & M. H. van IJzendoorn (Eds.), *Attachment in social networks* (pp. 339–378). Amsterdam: Elsevier Science Publishers B. V. North-Holland.

Hubbard, J. A., & Coie, J. D. (1994). Emotional correlates of social competence in children's peer relationships. *Merrill-Palmer Quarterly, 40,* 1–20.

Huesmann, L. R., Lagerspetz, K., & Eron, L. D. (1984). Intervening variables in the television violence-aggression relation: Evidence from two countries. *Developmental Psychology, 20,* 746–775.

Hunter, A. G., & Ensminger, M. E. (1992). Diversity and fluidity in children's living arrangements: Family transitions in an urban Afro-American community. *Journal of Marriage and the Family, 54,* 418–426.

Hunter, J. E., & Hunter, R. F. (1984). Validity and utility of alternative predictors of job performance. *Psychological Bulletin, 86,* 721–735.

Huntington, L., Hans, S. L., & Zeskind, P. S. (1990). The relations among cry characteristics, demographic variables, and developmental test scores in infants prenatally exposed to methadone. *Infant Behavior and Development, 13,* 533–538.

Hurwitz, E., Gunn, W. J., Pinsky, P. F., & Schonberger, L. B. (1991). Risk of respiratory illness associated with day-care attendance: A nationwide study. *Pediatrics, 87,* 62–69.

Huston, A. C., & Wright, J. C. (1994). Educating children with television: The forms of the medium. In D. Zillmann, J. Bryant, & A. C. Huston (Eds.), *Media, children, and the family. Social scientific, psychodynamic, and clinical perspectives* (pp. 73–84). Hillsdale, NJ: Erlbaum.

Huston, A. C., Wright, J. C., Rice, M. L., Kerkman, D., & St. Peters, M. (1990). Development of television viewing patterns in early childhood: A longitudinal investigation. *Developmental Psychology, 2,* 409–420.

Huston-Stein, A., & Higgens-Trenk, A. (1978). Development of females from childhood through adulthood: Career and feminine role orientations. In P. B. Baltes (Ed.), *Life-span development and behavior* (Vol. 1) (pp. 258–297). New York: Academic Press.

Hutt, S. J., Lenard, H. G., & Prechtl, H. F. R. (1969). Psychophysiological studies in newborn infants. In L. P. Lipsitt & H. W. Reese (Eds.), *Advances in child development and behavior* (Vol. 4) (pp. 128–173). New York: Academic Press.

Hutto, C., Parks, W. P., Lai, S., Mastrucci, M. T., Mitchell, C., Munoz, J., Trapido, E., Master, I. M., & Scott, G. B. (1991). A hospital-based prospective study of perinatal infection with human immunodeficiency virus type 1. *Journal of Pediatrics, 118,* 347–353.

Hymel, S., Rubin, K. H., Rowden, L., & LeMare, L. (1990). Children's peer relationships: Longitudinal prediction of internalizing and externalizing problems from middle to late childhood. *Child Development, 61,* 2004–2021.

Ingram, D. (1981). Early patterns of grammatical development. In R. E. Stark (Ed.), *Language behavior in infancy and early childhood* (pp. 327–358). New York: Elsevier/North-Holland.

Inhelder, B., & Piaget, J. (1958). *The growth of logical thinking from childhood to adolescence.* New York: Basic Books.

Inoff-Germain, G., Arnold, G. S., Nottelmann, E. D., Susman, E. J., Cutler, G. B., Jr., & Chrousos, G. P. (1988). Relations between hormone levels and observational measures of aggressive behavior of young adolescents in family interactions. *Developmental Psychology, 24,* 129–139.

Isabella, R. A., Belsky, J., & von Eye, A. (1989). Origins of infant-mother attachment: An examination of interactional synchrony during the infant's first year. *Developmental Psychology, 25,* 12–21.

Istvan, J. (1986). Stress, anxiety, and birth outcomes. A critical review of the evidence. *Psychological Bulletin, 100,* 331–348.

Izard, C. E., Haynes, O. M., Chisholm, G., & Baak, K. (1991). Emotional determinants of infant-mother attachment. *Child Development, 62,* 906–917.

Izard, C. E., Huebner, R. R., Risser, D., McGinnes, G. C., & Dougherty, L. M. (1980). The young infant's ability to produce discrete emotional expressions. *Developmental Psychology, 16,* 132–140.

Jacklin, C. N. (1989). Female and male: Issues of gender. *American Psychologist, 44,* 127–133.

Jacobson, S. W., & Frye, K. F. (1991). Effect of maternal social support on attachment: Experimental evidence. *Child Development, 62,* 572–582.

Janos, P. M., & Robinson, N. M. (1985). Psychosocial development in intellectually gifted children. In F. D. Horowitz & M. O'Brien (Eds.), *The gifted and talented. Developmental perspectives* (pp. 149–196). Washington, DC: American Psychological Association.

Jensen, A. R. (1980). *Bias in mental testing.* New York: The Free Press.

Jessor, R. (1992). Risk behavior in adolescence: A psychosocial framework for understanding and action. *Developmental Review, 12,* 374–390.

John, O. P., Caspi, A., Robins, R. W., Moffitt, T. E., & Stouthamer-Loeber, M. (1994). The "little five": Exploring the nomological network of the five-factor model of personality in adolescent boys. *Child Development, 65,* 160–178.

Johnson, C., Lewis, C., Love, S., Lewis, L., & Stuckey, M. (1984). Incidence and correlates of bulimic behavior in a female high school population. *Journal of Youth and Adolescence, 13,* 15–26.

Jones, E. F., Forrest, J. D., Goldman, N., Henshaw, S. K., Lincoln, R., Rosoff, J. L., Westoff, C. F., & Wulf, D. (1986). *Teenage pregnancy in industrialized countries.* New Haven, CT: Yale University Press.

Jones, K. L., Smith, D. W., Ulleland, C. N., & Streissguth, A. (1973). Pattern of malformation in offspring of chronic alcoholic mothers. *Lancet, 1,* 1267–1271.

Jorgensen, S. R. (1993). Adolescent pregnancy and parenting. In T. P. Gullotta, G. R. Adams, & R. Montemayor (Eds.), *Adolescent sexuality* (pp. 103–140). Newbury Park, CA: Sage.

Jung, C. G. (1916). *Analytical psychology.* New York: Moffat, Yard.

Jung, C. G. (1939). *The integration of personality.* New York: Holt, Rinehart and Winston.

Kagan, J., Kearsley, R., & Zelazo, P. (1978). *Infancy: Its place in human development.* Cambridge, MA: Harvard University Press.

Kagan, J., Reznick, J. S., & Snidman, N. (1990). The temperamental qualities of inhibition and lack of inhibition. In M. Lewis & S. M. Miller (Eds.), *Handbook of developmental psychopathology* (pp. 219–226). New York: Plenum Press.

Kagan, J., Snidman, N., & Arcus, D. (1993). On the temperamental categories of inhibited and uninhibited children. In K. H. Rubin & J. B. Asendorpf (Eds.), *Social withdrawal, inhibition, and shyness in childhood* (pp. 19–28). Hillsdale, NJ: Erlbaum.

Kail, R. (1991a). Developmental change in speed of processing during childhood and adolescence. *Psychological Bulletin, 109,* 490–501.

Kail, R. (1991b). Processing time declines exponentially during childhood and adolescence. *Developmental Psychology, 27,* 259–266.

Kail, R., & Park, Y. (1992). Global developmental change in processing time. *Merrill-Palmer Quarterly, 38,* 525–541.

Kandel, E. R. (1985). Nerve cells and behavior. In E. R. Kandel & J. H. Schwartz (Eds.), *Principles of neural science* (2nd ed.) (pp. 13–24). New York: Elsevier.

Kaplan, R. M. (1985). The controversy related to the use of psychological tests. In B. B. Wolman (Ed.), *Handbook of intelligence. Theories, measurements, and applications* (pp. 465–504). New York: Wiley.

Karmiloff-Smith, A. (1991). Beyond modularity: Innate constraints and developmental change. In S. Carey & R. Gelman (Eds.), *The epigenesis of mind. Essays on biology and cognition* (pp. 171–197). Hillsdale, NJ: Erlbaum.

Kataria, S., Frutiger, A. D., Lanford, B., & Swanson, M. S. (1988). Anterior fontanel closure in healthy term infants. *Infant Behavior and Development, 11,* 229–233.

Keating, D. P. (1980). Thinking processes in adolescence. In J. Adelson (Ed.), *Handbook of adolescent psychology* (pp. 211–246). New York: Wiley.

Keating, D. P., List, J. A., & Merriman, W. E. (1985). Cognitive processing and cognitive ability: multivariate validity investigation. *Intelligence, 9,* 149–170.

Keeney, T. J., Cannizzo, S. R., & Flavell, J. H. (1967). Spontaneous and induced verbal rehearsal in a recall task. *Child Development, 38,* 935–966.

Kellam, S. G., Ensminger, M. E., & Turner, R. J. (1977). Family structure and the mental health of children: Concurrent and longitudinal community-wide studies. *Archives of General Psychiatry, 34,* 1012–1022.

Kelley, M. L., Sanches-Hucles, J., & Walker, R. R. (1993). Correlates of disciplinary practices in working- to middle-class African-American mothers. *Merrill-Palmer Quarterly, 39,* 252–264.

Kempe, A., Wise, P. H., Barkan, S. E., Sappenfield, W. M., Sachs, B., Gortmaker, S. L., Sobol, A. M., First, L. R., Pursley, D., Reinhart, H., Kotelchuck, M., Cole, F. S., Gunter, N., & Stockbauer, J. W. (1992). Clinical determinants of the racial disparity in very low birth weight. *The New England Journal of Medicine, 327,* 969–973.

Kendall-Tackett, K. A., Williams, L. M., & Finkelhor, D. (1993). Impact of sexual abuse on children: A review and synthesis of recent empirical studies. *Psychological Bulletin, 113*, 164–180.

Keniston, K. (1970). Youth: A "new" stage in life. *American Scholar, 8* (Autumn), 631–654.

Kerr, M., Lambert, W. W., Stattin, H., & Klackenberg-Larsson, I. (1994). Stability of inhibition in a Swedish longitudinal sample. *Child Development, 65*, 138–146.

Killen, J. D., Hayward, C., Litt, I., Hammer, L. D., Wilson, D. M., Miner, B., Taylor, B., Varady, A., & Shisslak, C. (1992). Is puberty a risk factor for eating disorders? *American Journal of Diseases of Childhood, 146*, 323–325.

Kilpatrick, S. J., & Laros, R. K. (1989). Characteristics of normal labor. *Obstetrics and Gynecology, 74*, 85–87.

Kitchen, W. H., Doyle, L. W., Ford, G. W., Murton, L. J., Keith, C. G., Rickards, A. L., Kelly, E., & Callanan, C. (1991). Changing two-year outcome of infants weighing 500 to 999 grams at birth: A hospital study. *Journal of Pediatrics, 118*, 938–943.

Klaus, H. M., & Kennell, J. H. (1976). *Maternal-infant bonding.* St. Louis, MO: Mosby.

Klesges, R. C., Shelton, M. L., & Klesges, L. M. (1993). Effects of television on metabolic rate: Potential implications for childhood obesity. *Pediatrics, 91*, 281–286.

Kline, M., Tschann, J. M., Johnston, J. R., & Wallerstein, J. S. (1989). Children's adjustment in joint and sole physical custody families. *Developmental Psychology, 25*, 430–438.

Kohlberg, L. (1964). Development of moral character and moral ideology. In M. L. Hoffman & L. W. Hoffman (Eds.), *Review of child development research* (Vol. 1) (pp. 283–332). New York: Russell Sage Foundation.

Kohlberg, L. (1966). A cognitive-developmental analysis of children's sex-role concepts and attitudes. In E. E. Maccoby (Ed.), *The development of sex differences* (pp. 82–172). Stanford, CA: Stanford University Press.

Kohlberg, L. (1975). The cognitive-developmental approach to moral education. *Phi Delta Kappan,* pp. 670–677.

Kohlberg, L. (1976). Moral stages and moralization: The cognitive-developmental approach. In T. Lickona (Ed.), *Moral development and behavior: Theory, research, and social issues* (pp. 31–53). New York: Holt.

Kohlberg, L. (1978). Revisions in the theory and practice of moral development. *New Directions for Child Development, 2*, 83–88.

Kohlberg, L. (1980). *The meaning and measurement of moral development.* Worcester, MA: Clark University Press.

Kohlberg, L. (1981). *Essays on moral development.* Vol. 1, *The philosophy of moral development.* New York: Harper & Row.

Kohlberg, L. (1984). *Essays on moral development.* Vol. 2, *The psychology of moral development.* San Francisco: Harper & Row.

Kohlberg, L., & Candee, D. (1984). The relationship of moral judgment to moral action. In W. M. Kurtines & J. L. Gewirtz (Eds.), *Morality, moral behavior, and moral development* (pp. 52–73). New York: Wiley.

Kohlberg, L., & Elfenbein, D. (1975). The development of moral judgments concerning capital punishment. *American Journal of Orthopsychiatry, 54*, 614–640.

Kohlberg, L., & Higgins, A. (1987). School democracy and social interaction. In W. M. Kurtines & J. L. Gewirtz (Eds.), *Moral development through social interaction* (pp. 102–130). New York: Wiley-Interscience.

Kohlberg, L., Levine, C., & Hewer, A. (1983). *Moral stages: A current formulation and a response to critics. Contributions to human development, 10.* Basel: S. Karger.

Kohlberg, L., & Ullian, D. Z. (1974). Stages in the development of psychosexual concepts and attitudes. In R. C. Friedman, R. M. Richart, & R. L. Vande Wiele (Eds.), *Sex differences in behavior* (pp. 209–222). New York: Wiley.

Kolata, G. (1992, April 26). A parents' guide to kids' sports. *The New York Times Magazine,* pp. 12–15, 40, 44, 46.

Kon, I. S., & Losenkov, V. A. (1978). Friendship in adolescence: Values and behavior. *Journal of Marriage and the Family, 40*, 143–155.

Kopp, C. B. (1983). Risk factors in development. In M. M. Haith & J. J. Campos (Eds.), *Handbook of child psychology: Infancy and developmental psychobiology* (Vol. 2) (pp. 1081–1188). New York: Wiley.

Kopp, C. B. (1990). Risks in infancy: appraising the research. *Merrill Palmer Quarterly, 36*, 117–140.

Kopp, C. B., & Kaler, S. R. (1989). Risk in infancy: Origins and implications. *American Psychologist, 44*, 224–230.

Korner, A. F., Hutchinson, C. A., Koperski, J. A., Kraemer, H. C., & Schneider, P. A. (1981). Stability of individual differences of neonatal motor and crying patterns. *Child Development, 52*, 83–90.

Kotulak, R. (1990, September 28). *Chicago Tribune,* p. 1, 16.

Kuczaj, S. A., II (1977). The acquisition of regular and irregular past tense forms. *Journal of Verbal Learning and Verbal Behavior, 49*, 319–326.

Kuczaj, S. A., II (1978). Children's judgments of grammatical and ungrammatical irregular past tense verbs. *Child Development, 49*, 319–326.

Kuczynski, L., Kochanska, G., Radke-Yarrow, M., & Girnius-Brown, O. (1987). A developmental interpretation of young children's noncompliance. *Developmental Psychology, 23*, 799–806.

Kuhl, P. K., & Meltzoff, A. N. (1984). The intermodal representation of speech in infants. *Infant Behavior and Development, 7*, 361–381.

Kuhn, D. (1992). Cognitive development. In M. H. Bornstein & M. E. Lamb (Eds.), *Developmental psychology. An advanced textbook* (3rd ed.) (pp. 211–272). Hillsdale, NJ: Erlbaum.

Kupersmidt, J. B., & Coie, J. D. (1990). Preadolescent peer status, aggression, and school adjustment as predictors of externalizing problems in adolescence. *Child Development, 61*, 1350–1362.

Kurtines, W. M., & Gewirtz, J. L. (Eds.). (1991). *Handbook of moral behavior and development*. Vol. 1, *Theory*. Vol. 2, *Research*. Vol. 3, *Application*. Hillsdale, NJ: Erlbaum.

La Freniere, P., Strayer, F. F., & Gauthier, R. (1984). The emergence of same-sex affiliative preferences among preschool peers: A developmental/ethological perspective. *Child Development, 55*, 1958–1965.

Lamb, M. E. (1981). The development of father-infant relationships. In M. E. Lamb (Ed.), *The role of the father in child development* (2nd ed.) (pp. 459–488). New York: Wiley.

Lamb, M. E., Frodi, A. M., Hwang, C., Frodi, M., & Steinberg, J. (1982). Mother- and father-infant interaction involving play and holding in traditional and nontraditional Swedish families. *Developmental Psychology, 18*, 215–221.

Lamb, M. E., Frodi, M., Hwang, C., & Frodi, A. M. (1983). Effects of paternal involvement on infant preferences for mothers and fathers. *Child Development, 54*, 450–458.

Lamb, M. E., Sternberg, K. J., & Prodromidis, M. (1992). Nonmaternal care and the security of infant-mother attachment: A reanalysis of the data. *Infant Behavior and Development, 15*, 71–83.

Lambert, C. (1993, March/April). The demand side of the health care crisis. *Harvard Magazine*, pp. 30–33.

Lamborn, S. D., Mounts, N. S., Steinberg, L., & Dornbusch, S. M. (1991). Patterns of competence and adjustment among adolescents from authoritative, authoritarian, indulgent, and neglectful families. *Child Development, 62*, 1049–1065.

Lamke, L. K. (1982a). Adjustment and sex-role orientation. *Journal of Youth and Adolescence, 11*, 247–259.

Lamke, L. K. (1982b). The impact of sex-role orientation on self-esteem in early adolescence. *Child Development, 53*, 1530–1535.

Langlois, J. H., Ritter, J. M., Roggman, L. A., & Vaughn, L. S. (1991). Facial diversity and infant preferences for attractive faces. *Developmental Psychology, 27*, 79–84.

Langlois, J. H., Roggman, L. A., Casey, R. J., Ritter, J. M., Rieser-Danner, L. A., & Jenkins, V. Y. (1987). Infant preferences for attractive faces: Rudiments of a stereotype? *Developmental Psychology, 23*, 263–369.

Langlois, J. H., Roggman, L. A., & Rieser-Danner, L. A. (1990). Infants' differential social responses to attractive and unattractive faces. *Developmental Psychology, 26*, 153–159.

Leadbeater, B. J., & Dionne, J. (1981). The adolescent's use of formal operational thinking in solving problems related to identity resolution. *Adolescence, 16*, 111–121.

Leaper, C. (1991). Influence and involvement in children's discourse: Age, gender, and partner effects. *Child Development, 62*, 797–811.

Lederberg, A. R., & Mobley, C. E. (1990). The effect of hearing impairment on the quality of attachment and mother-toddler interaction. *Child Development, 61*, 1596–1604.

Lee, V. E., Brooks-Gunn, J., Schnur, E., & Liaw, F. (1990). Are Head Start effects sustained? A longitudinal follow-up comparison of disadvantaged children attending Head Start, no preschool, and other preschool programs. *Child Development, 61*, 495–507.

Lerner, R. M. (1985). Adolescent maturational changes and psychosocial development: A dynamic interactional perspective. *Journal of Youth and Adolescence, 14*, 355–372.

Lerner, R. M. (1986). *Concepts and theories of human development* (2nd ed.). New York: Random House.

Lerner, R. M. (1987). A life-span perspective for early adolescence. In R. M. Lerner & T. T. Foch (Eds.), *Biological-psychosocial interactions in early adolescence* (pp. 9–34). Hillsdale, NJ: Erlbaum.

Lerner, R. M., Entwisle, D. R., & Hauser, S. T. (1994). The crisis among contemporary American adolescents: A call for the integration of research, policies, and programs. *Journal of Research on Adolescence, 4*, 1–4.

Lester, B. M. (1987). Prediction of developmental outcome from acoustic cry analysis in term and preterm infants. *Pediatrics, 80*, 529–534.

Lester, B. M., Boukydis, C. F. Z., Garcia-Coll, C. T., Hole, W., & Peucker, M. (1992). Infantile colic: Acoustic cry characteristics, maternal perception of cry, and temperament. *Infant Behavior and Development, 15*, 15–26.

Lester, B. M., & Dreher, M. (1989). Effects of marijuana use during pregnancy on newborn cry. *Child Development, 60*, 765–771.

Levano, K. J., Cunningham, G., Nelson, S., Roark, M., Williams, M. L., Guzick, D., Dowling, S., Rosenfeld, C. R., & Buckley, A. (1986). A prospective comparison of selective and universal electronic fetal monitoring in 34,995 pregnancies. *New England Journal of Medicine, 315*, 615–619.

Levitt, M. J., Guacci-Franco, N., & Levitt, J. L. (1993). Convoys of social support in childhood and early adolescence: Structure and function. *Developmental Psychology, 29*, 811–818.

Lewis, C. C. (1981). How adolescents approach decisions: Changes over grades seven to twelve and policy implications. *Child Development, 52*, 538–544.

Lewis, M. (1990). Social knowledge and social development. *Merrill-Palmer Quarterly, 36*, 93–116.

Lewis, M. (1991). Ways of knowing: Objective self-awareness of consciousness. *Developmental Review, 11*, 231–243.

Lewis, M., Allesandri, S. M., & Sullivan, M. W. (1992). Differences in shame and pride as a function of children's gender and task difficulty. *Child Development, 63*, 630–638.

Lewis, M., & Brooks, J. (1978). Self-knowledge and emotional development. In M. Lewis & L. A. Rosenblum (Eds.), *The development of affect* (pp. 205–226). New York: Plenum.

Lewis, M., & Brooks-Gunn, J. (1979). *Social cognition and the acquisition of self.* New York: Plenum.

Lewis, M., & Brooks-Gunn, J. (1981). Visual attention at three months as a predictor of cognitive functioning at two years of age. *Intelligence, 5,* 131–140.

Lewis, M., & Miller, S. M. (Eds.). (1990). *Handbook of developmental psychopathology.* New York: Plenum Press.

Lewis, M., Ramsay, D. S., & Kawakami, K. (1993). Differences between Japanese infants and caucasian american infants in behavioral and cortisol response to innoculation. *Child Development, 64,* 1722–1731.

Lewis, M., & Sullivan, M. W. (1985). Infant intelligence and its assessment. In B. B. Wolman (Ed.), *Handbook of intelligence* (pp. 505–599). New York: Wiley-Interscience.

Lewis, M. D. (1993). Early socioemotional predictors of cognitive competence at 4 years. *Developmental Psychology, 29,* 1036–1045.

Liben, L. S. (1978). The development of deaf children: An overview of issues. In L. S. Liben (Ed.), *Deaf children: Developmental perspectives* (pp. 3–20). New York: Academic Press.

Lickona, T. (1983). *Raising good children.* Toronto: Bantam Books.

Lieberman, A. F. (1993). *The emotional life of the toddler.* New York: The Free Press.

Lillard, A. S., & Flavell, J. H. (1992). Young children's understanding of different mental states. *Developmental Psychology, 28,* 626–634.

Linney, J. A., & Seidman, E. (1989). The future of schooling. *American Psychologist, 44,* 336–340.

Lipsitt, L. P. (1982). Infant learning. In T. M. Field, A. Houston, H. C. Quay, L. Troll, & G. E. Finley (Eds.), *Review of human development* (pp. 62–78). New York: Wiley.

Livesley, W. J., & Bromley, D. B. (1973). *Person perception in childhood and adolescence.* London: Wiley.

Lockman, J. J., & Thelen, E. (1993). Developmental biodynamics: Brain, body, behavior connections. *Child Development, 64,* 953–959.

Long, J. V. F., & Vaillant, G. E. (1984). Natural history of male psychological health: Escape from the underclass. *The American Journal of Psychiatry, 141,* 341–346.

Longo, D. C., & Bond, L. (1984). Families of the handicapped child: Research and practice. *Family Relations, 33,* 57–65.

Lore, R. K., & Schultz, L. A. (1993). Control of human aggression: A comparative perspective. *American Psychologist, 48,* 16–25.

Lubinski, D., & Benbow, C. P. (1992). Gender differences in abilities and preferences among the gifted: Implications for the math-science pipeline. *Current Directions in Psychological Science, 1,* 61–66.

Luster, T., Rhoades, K., & Haas, B. (1989). The relation between parental values and parenting behavior: A test of the Kohn hypothesis. *Journal of Marriage and the Family, 51,* 139–147.

Lyons, N. P. (1983). Two perspectives: On self, relationships, and morality. *Harvard Educational Review, 53,* 125–145.

Lyons-Ruth, K., Alpern, L., & Repacholi, B. (1993). Disorganized infant attachment classification and maternal psychosocial problems as predictors of hostile-aggressive behavior in the preschool classroom. *Child Development, 64,* 572–585.

Lyons-Ruth, K., Repacholi, B., McLeod, S., & Silva, E. (1991). Disorganized attachment behavior in infancy: Short-term stability, maternal and infant correlates, and risk-related subtypes. *Development and Psychopathology, 3,* 388–396.

Lytton, H., & Romney, D. M. (1991). Parents' differential socialization of boys and girls: A meta-analysis. *Psychological Bulletin, 109,* 267–296.

Maccoby, E. E. (1980). *Social development. Psychological growth and the parent-child relationships.* New York: Harcourt Brace Jovanovich.

Maccoby, E. E. (1984). Middle childhood in the context of the family. In W. A. Collins (Ed.), *Development during middle childhood. The years from six to twelve* (pp. 184–239). Washington, DC: National Academy Press.

Maccoby, E. E. (1988). Gender as a social category. *Developmental Psychology, 24,* 755–765.

Maccoby, E. E. (1990). Gender and relationships. A developmental account. *American Psychologist, 45,* 513–520.

Maccoby, E. E., & Jacklin, C. N. (1974). *The psychology of sex differences.* Stanford, CA: Stanford University Press.

Maccoby, E. E., & Jacklin, C. N. (1987). Gender segregation in childhood. In H. W. Reese (Ed.), *Advances in child development and behavior* (Vol. 20) (pp. 239–288). Orlando, FL: Academic Press.

Maccoby, E. E., & Martin, J. A. (1983). Socialization in the context of the family: Parent-child interaction . In E. M. Hetherington (Ed.), *Handbook of child psychology: Socialization, personality, and social development* (Vol. 4) (pp. 1–102). New York: Wiley.

MacDonald, K. (1992). Warmth as a developmental construct: An evolutionary analysis. *Child Development, 63,* 753–773.

MacGowan, R. J., MacGowan, C. A., Serdula, M. K., Lane, J. M., Joesoef, R. M., & Cook, F. H. (1991). Breast-feeding among women attending Women, Infants, and Children clinics in Georgia, 1987. *Pediatrics, 87,* 361–366.

Maclean, M., Bryant, P., & Bradley, L. (1987). Rhymes, nursery rhymes, and reading in early childhood. *Merrill-Palmer Quarterly, 33*, 255–281.

Maffeis, C., Schutz, Y., Piccoli, R., Gonfiantini, E., & Pinelli, L. (1993). Prevalence of obesity in children in north-east Italy. *International Journal of Obesity, 14*, 287–294.

Magnusson, D., Stattin, H., & Allen, V. L. (1986). Differential maturation among girls and its relation to social adjustment: A longitudinal perspective. In P. B. Baltes, D. L. Featherman, & R. M. Lerner (Eds.), *Life-span development and behavior* (Vol. 7) (pp. 136–173). Hillsdale, NJ: Erlbaum.

Main, M., & Cassidy, J. (1988). Categories of response to reunion with the parent at age 6: Predictable from infant attachment classifications and stable over a 1-month period. *Developmental Psychology, 24*, 415–426.

Main, M., & Hesse, E. (1990). Parents' unresolved traumatic experiences are related to infant disorganized attachment status: Is frightened and/or frightening parental behavior the linking mechanism? In M. T. Greenberg, D. Cicchetti, & E. M. Cummings (Eds.), *Attachment in the preschool years. Theory, research, and intervention* (pp. 161–182). Chicago: University of Chicago Press.

Main, M., Kaplan, N., & Cassidy, J. (1985). Security in infancy, childhood, and adulthood: A move to the level of representation. *Monographs of the Society for Research in Child Development, 50* (Serial No. 209), 66–104.

Main, M., & Solomon, J. (1990). Procedures for identifying infants as disorganized/disoriented during the Ainsworth Strange Situation. In M. T. Greenberg, D. Cicchetti, & E. M. Cummings (Eds.), *Attachment in the preschool years. Theory, research, and intervention* (pp. 121–160). Chicago: University of Chicago Press.

Malina, R. M. (1982). Motor development in the early years. In S. G. Moore & C. R. Cooper (Eds.), *The young child. Reviews of research* (Vol. 3) (pp. 211–232). Washington, DC: National Association for the Education of Young Children.

Malina, R. M. (1990). Physical growth and performance during the transition years. In R. Montemayor, G. R. Adams, & T. P. Gullotta (Eds.), *From childhood to adolescence: A transitional period?* (pp. 41–62). Newbury Park, CA: Sage.

Malinosky-Rummell, R., & Hansen, D. J. (1993). Long-term consequences of childhood physical abuse. *Psychological Bulletin, 114*, 68–79.

Mangelsdorf, S. C. (1992). Developmental changes in infant-stranger interaction. *Infant Behavior and Development, 15*, 191–208.

Maratsos, M. (1992). Constraints, modules, and domain specificity: An introduction. In M. R. Gunnar & M. Maratsos (Eds.), *Minnesota symposia on child psychology* (Vol. 25) (pp. 1–24). Hillsdale, NJ: Erlbaum.

Marcia, J. E. (1966). Development and validation of ego identity status. *Journal of Personality and Social Psychology, 3*, 551–558.

Marcia, J. E. (1980). Identity in adolescence. In J. Adelson (Ed.), *Handbook of adolescent psychology* (pp. 159–187). New York: Wiley.

Marcus, G. F., Pinker, S., Ullman, M., Hollander, M., Rosen, T. J., & Fei, X. (1992). Overregularization in language acquisition. *Monographs of the Society for Research in Child Development, 57* (4, Serial No. 228).

Marcus, R. F. (1986). Naturalistic observation of cooperation, helping, and sharing and their association with empathy and affect . In C. Zahn-Waxler, E. M. Cummings, & R. Iannotti (Eds.), *Altruism and aggression. Biological and social origins* (pp. 256–279). Cambridge, England: Cambridge University Press.

Marean, G. C., Werner, L. A., & Kuhl, P. K. (1992). Vowel categorization by very young infants. *Developmental Psychology, 28*, 396–405.

Markman, E. M. (1989). *Categorization and naming in children; Problems of induction.* Cambridge, MA: MIT Press, Bradford Books.

Markman, E. M. (1992). Constraints on word learning: Speculations about their nature, origins, and domain specificity. In M. R. Gunnar & M. Maratsos (Eds.), *Minnesota symposia on child psychology* (Vol. 25) (pp. 59–101). Hillsdale, NJ: Erlbaum.

Martin, C. L. (1991). The role of cognition in understanding gender effects. In H. W. Reese (Ed.), *Advances in child development and behavior* (Vol. 23) (pp. 113–150). San Diego, CA: Academic Press.

Martin, C. L. (1993). New directions for investigating children's gender knowledge. *Developmental Review, 13*, 184–204.

Martin, C. L., & Halverson, C. F., Jr. (1981). A schematic processing model of sex typing and stereotyping in children. *Child Development, 52*, 1119–1134.

Martin, C. L., & Halverson, C. F., Jr. (1983). The effects of sex-typing schemas on young children's memory. *Child Development, 54*, 563–574.

Martin, C. L., & Little, J. K. (1990). The relation of gender understanding to children's sex-typed preferences and gender stereotypes. *Child Development, 61*, 1427–1439.

Martin, C. L., Wood, C. H., & Little, J. K. (1990). The development of gender stereotype components. *Child Development, 61*, 1891–1904.

Martorano, S. C. (1977). A developmental analysis of performance on Piaget's formal operations tasks. *Developmental Psychology, 13*, 666–672.

Marvin, R. S., & Greenberg, M. T. (1982). Preschoolers' changing conceptions of their mothers: A social-cognitive study of mother-child attachment. *New Directions for Child Development, 18*, 47–60.

Massad, C. M. (1981). Sex role identity and adjustment during adolescence. *Child Development, 52*, 1290–1298.

Masten, A. S. (1989). Resilience in development: Implications of the study of successful adaptation for developmental psychopathology. In D. Cicchetti (Ed.), *The emergence of a discipline: Rochester symposium on developmental psychopathology* (Vol. 1) (pp. 261–294). Hillsdale, NJ: Erlbaum.

Masten, A. S., Best, K. M., & Garmezy, N. (1990). Resilience and development: Contributions from the study of children who overcome adversity. *Development and Psychopathology, 2,* 425–444.

Matas, L., Arend, R. A., & Sroufe, L. A. (1978). Continuity of adaptation in the second year: The relationship between quality of attachment and latter competence. *Child Development, 49,* 547–556.

Mather, P. L., & Black, K. N. (1984). Heredity and environmental influences on preschool twins' language skills. *Developmental Psychology, 20,* 303–308.

Mathew, A., & Cook, M. (1990). The control of reaching movements by young infants. *Child Development, 61,* 1238–1257.

Maurer, D., & Maurer, C. (1988). *The world of the newborn.* New York: Basic Books.

McBride, G. (1991). Nontraditional inheritance—II. The clinical implications. *Mosaic, 22* (Fall), 12–25.

McCall, R. B. (1993). Developmental functions for general mental performance. In D. K. Detterman (Ed.), *Current topics in human intelligence.* Vol. 3, *Individual differences and cognition* (pp. 3–30). Norwood, NJ: Ablex.

McCall, R. B., & Carriger, M. S. (1993). A meta-analysis of infant habituation and recognition memory performance as predictors of later IQ. *Child Development, 64,* 57–79.

McCall, R. B., Evahn, C., & Kratzer, L. (1992). *High school underachievers.* Newbury Park, CA: Sage.

McCarthy, J., & Hardy, J. (1993). Age at first birth and birth outcomes. *Journal of Research on Adolescence, 3,* 374–392.

McCord, J. (1982). A longitudinal view of the relationship between parental absence and crime. In J. Gunn & D. P. Farrington (Eds.), *Abnormal offenders, delinquency, and the criminal justice system* (pp. 113–128). London: Wiley.

McCord, W., McCord, J., & Zola, I. K. (1959). *Origins of crime.* New York: Columbia University Press.

McCormick, K. F. (1992). Attitudes of primary care physicians toward corporal punishment. *Journal of the American Medical Association, 267,* 3161–3165.

McCrae, R. R., & Costa, P. T., Jr. (1990). *Personality in adulthood.* New York: The Guilford Press.

McCrae, R. R., & John, O. P. (1992). An introduction to the Five-Factor Model and its applications. *Journal of Personality, 60,* 175–215.

McFalls, J. A., Jr. (1990). The risks of reproductive impairment in the later years of childbearing. *Annual Review of Sociology, 16,* 491–519.

McGue, M., Bouchard, T. J., Jr., Iacono, W. G., & Lykken, D. T. (1993). Behavioral genetics of cognitive ability: A life-span perspective. In R. Plomin & G. E. McClearn (Eds.), *Nature, nurture, & psychology* (pp. 59–76). Washington, DC: American Psychological Association.

McHale, S. M., & Lerner, R. M. (1990). Stages of human development. In R. M. Thomas (Ed.), *The encyclopedia of human development and education* (pp. 163–166). Oxford: Pergamon Press.

McKey, R. H., Condelli, L., Granson, H., Barrett, B., McConkey, C., & Plantz, M. (1985). *The impact of Head Start on children, families and communities (final report of the Head Start Evaluation, Synthesis and Utilization Project).* Washington, DC: CSR.

McLaughlin, B. (1984). *Second-language acquisition in childhood: Preschool children* (2nd ed.). Hillsdale, NJ: Erlbaum.

McLloyd, V. (1993). *Research on childhood poverty: Exploring its relevance to current policy debates.* Paper presented at the biennial meetings of the Society for Research in Child Development, New Orleans.

Mellin, L. M., Irwin, C. E., & Scully, S. (1992). Prevalence of disorded eating in girls: A survey of middle-class children. *Journal of the American Dietetic Association, 92,* 851–853.

Meltzoff, A. N. (1988). Infant imitation and memory: Nine-month-olds in immediate and deferred tasks. *Child Development, 59,* 217–225.

Meltzoff, A. N., & Borton, R. W. (1979). Intermodal matching by human neonates. *Nature, 282,* 403–404.

Meltzoff, A. N., & Moore, M. K. (1983). Newborn infants imitate adult facial gestures. *Child Development, 54,* 702–709.

Mervis, C. B., & Mervis, C. A. (1982). Leopards are kitty-cats: Object labeling by mothers for their thirteen-month-olds. *Child Development, 53,* 267–273.

Miller, B. C., Christopherson, C. R., & King, P. K. (1993). Sexual behavior in adolescence. In T. P. Gullotta, G. R. Adams, & R. Montemayor (Eds.), *Adolescent sexuality* (pp. 57–76). Newbury Park, CA: Sage.

Miller, B. C., & Jorgensen, S. R. (1993). Adolescent fertility-related behavior and its family linkages. In D. M. Klein & J. Aldous (Eds.), *Social stress and family development* (pp. 210–233). New York: Guilford Press.

Miller, B. C., & Moore, K. A. (1990). Adolescent sexual behavior, pregnancy, and parenting: Research through the 1980s. *Journal of Marriage and the Family, 52,* 1025–1044.

Miller, G. A. (1956). The magical number seven, plus or minus two: Some limits on our capacity for processing information. *Psychological Review, 63,* 81–96.

Millstein, S. G., & Litt, I. R. (1990). Adolescent health. In S. S. Feldman & G. R. Elliott (Eds.), *At the threshold. The developing adolescent* (pp. 431–456). Cambridge, MA: Harvard University Press.

Miranda, S. B., & Fantz, R. L. (1974). Recognition memory in Down's Syndrome and normal infants. *Child Development, 45,* 651–660.

Mischel, W. (1966). A social learning view of sex differences in behavior. In E. E. Maccoby (Ed.), *The development of sex differences* (pp. 56–81). Stanford, CA: Stanford University Press.

Mischel, W. (1970). Sex typing and socialization. In P. H. Mussen (Ed.), *Carmichael's manual of child psychology* (Vol. 2) (pp. 3–72). New York: Wiley.

Mitchell, E. A., Ford, R. P. K., Steward, A. W., Taylor, B. J., Becroft, D. M. O., Thompson, J. M. D., Scragg, R., Hassall, I. B., Barry, D. M. J., Allen, E. M., & Roberts, A. P. (1993). Smoking and sudden infant death syndrome. *Pediatrics, 91,* 893–896.

Mitchell, P. R., & Kent, R. D. (1990). Phonetic variation in multisyllable babbling. *Journal of Child Language, 17,* 247–265.

Mitchell, R. (1992). *Testing for learning. How new approaches to evaluation can improve American schools.* New York: The Free Press.

Moffitt, T. E. (1990). Juvenile delinquency and attention deficit disorder: Boys' developmental trajectories from age 3 to age 15. *Child Development, 61,* 893–910.

Montemayor, R., & Eisen, M. (1977). The development of self-conceptions from childhood to adolescence. *Developmental Psychology, 13,* 314–319.

Montpetit, R. R., Montoye, H. J., & Laeding, L. (1967). Grip strength of school children, Saginaw, Michigan–1964. *Research Quarterly, 38,* 231–240.

Moon, C., Cooper, R. P., & Fifer, W. P. (1993). Two-day-olds prefer their native language. *Infant Behavior and Development, 16,* 495–500.

Moon, C., & Fifer, W. P. (1990). Syllables as signals for 2-day-old infants. *Infant Behavior and Development, 13,* 377–390.

Moore, E. G. J. (1986). Family socialization and the IQ test performance of traditionally and transracially adopted black children. *Developmental Psychology, 22,* 317–326.

Moore, K. A., Myers, D. E., Morrison, D. R., Nord, C. W., Brown, B., & Edmonston, B. (1993). Age at first childbirth and later poverty. *Journal of Research on Adolescence, 3,* 393–422.

Moore, K. L. (1988). *The developing human. Clinically oriented embryology* (4th ed.). Philadelphia: W. B. Saunders.

Moores, D. F. (1985). Early intervention programs for hearing impaired children: A longitudinal assessment. In K. E. Nelson (Ed.), *Children's language* (Vol. 5) (pp. 159–196). Hillsdale, NJ: Erlbaum.

Morisset, C. E., Barnard, K. E., Greenberg, M. T., Booth, C. L., & Spieker, S. J. (1990). Environmental influences on early language development: The context of social risk. *Development and Psychopathology, 2,* 127–149.

Morrison, D. M. (1985). Adolescent contraceptive behavior: A review. *Psychological Bulletin, 98,* 538–568.

Morse, P. A., & Cowan, N. (1982). Infant auditory and speech perception. In T. M. Field, A. Houston, H. C. Quay, L. Troll, & G. E. Finley (Eds.), *Review of human development* (pp. 32–61). New York: Wiley.

Mortimer, J. T., Finch, M., Shanahan, M., & Ryu, S. (1992). Work experience, mental health, and behavioral adjustment in adolescence. *Journal of Research on Adolescence, 2,* 25–57.

Munro, G., & Adams, G. R. (1977). Ego-identity formation in college students and working youth. *Developmental Psychology, 13,* 523–524.

Munroe, R. H., Shimmin, H. S., & Munroe, R. L. (1984). Gender understanding and sex role preference in four cultures. *Developmental Psychology, 20,* 673–682.

Murray, J. L., & Bernfield, M. (1988). The differential effect of prenatal care on the incidence of low birth weight among blacks and whites in a prepaid health care plan. *New England Journal of Medicine, 319,* 1385–1391.

Murray, J. P. (1980). *Television & youth. 25 years of research and controversy.* Stanford, CA: The Boys Town Center for the Study of Youth Development.

Myers, B. J. (1987). Mother-infant bonding as a critical period. In M. H. Bornstein (Ed.), *Sensitive periods in development: Interdisciplinary perspectives* (pp. 223–246). Hillsdale, NJ: Erlbaum.

Naeye, R. L., & Peters, E. C. (1984). Mental development of children whose mothers smoked during pregnancy. *Obstetrics & Gynecology, 64,* 601–607.

National Center for Health Statistics (1984). Advance report on final natality statistics, 1982. *Monthly Vital Statistics Report, 33* (No. 6), Supplement, Sept. 28, 1984.

National Research Council (1993). *Understanding child abuse and neglect; Panel on research on child abuse and neglect, Commission on Behavioral and Social Sciences and Education.* Washington, DC: National Academy Press.

Neimark, E. D. (1982). Adolescent thought: Transition to formal operations. In B. B. Wolman (Ed.), *Handbook of developmental psychology* (pp. 486–502). Englewood Cliffs, NJ: Prentice-Hall.

Nelson, C. A. (1987). The recognition of facial expression in the first two years of life: Mechanisms of development. *Child Development, 58,* 889–909.

Nelson, K. (1973). Structure and strategy in learning to talk. *Monographs of the Society for Research in Child Development, 38* (Serial No. 149).

Nelson, K. (1977). Facilitating children's syntax acquisition. *Developmental Psychology, 13,* 101–107.

Nelson, K. (1985). *Making sense: The acquisition of shared meaning.* New York: Academic Press.

Nelson, K. (1988). Constraints on word learning. *Cognitive Development, 3*, 221–246.

Newcomb, A. F., Bukowski, W. M., & Pattee, L. (1993). Children's peer relations: A meta-analytic review of popular, rejected, neglected, controversial, and average sociometric status. *Psychological Bulletin, 113*, 99–128.

Newcombe, N. S., & Baenninger, M. (1989). Biological change and cognitive ability in adolescence. In G. R. Adams, R. Montemayor, & T. P. Gullotta (Eds.), *Biology of adolescent behavior and development* (pp. 168–194). Newbury Park, CA: Sage.

Nightingale, E. O., & Goodman, M. (1990). *Before birth. Prenatal testing for genetic disease.* Cambridge, MA: Harvard University Press.

Nilsson, L. (1990). *A child is born.* New York: Delacorte Press.

Norton, A. J., & Glick, P. C. (1986). One parent families: A social and economic profile. *Family Relations, 35*, 9–18.

Nottelmann, E. D., Susman, E. J., Blue, J. H., Inoff-Germain, G., Dorn, L. D., Loriaux, D. L., Cutler, G. B., Jr., & Chrousos, G. P. (1987). Gonadal and adrenal hormone correlates of adjustment in early adolescence. In R. M. Lerner & T. T. Foch (Eds.), *Biological-psychosocial interactions in early adolescence* (pp. 303–324). Hillsdale, NJ: Erlbaum.

Novacek, J., Raskin, R., & Hogan, R. (1991). Why do adolescents use drugs? Age, sex, and user differences. *Journal of Youth and Adolescence, 20*, 475–492.

Nowakowski, R. S. (1987). Basic concepts of CNS development. *Child Development, 58*, 568–595.

O'Brien, M. (1992). Gender identity and sex roles. In V. B. Van Hasselt & M. Hersen (Eds.), *Handbook of social development. A lifespan perspective* (pp. 325–345). New York: Plenum Press.

O'Brien, S. F., & Bierman, K. L. (1988). Conceptions and perceived influence of peer groups: Interviews with preadolescents and adolescents. *Child Development, 59*, 1360–1365.

O'Connor, S., Vietze, P. M., Sandler, H. M., Sherrod, K. B., & Altemeier, W. A. (1980). Quality of parenting and the mother–infant relationships following rooming-in. In P. M. Taylor (Ed.), *Parent-infant relationships* (pp. 349–368). New York: Grune & Stratton.

O'Hara, M. W., Schlechte, J. A., Lewis, D. A., & Varner, M. W. (1992). Controlled prospective study of postpartum mood disorders: Psychological, environmental, and hormonal variables. *Journal of Abnormal Psychology, 100*, 63–73.

O'Neill, D. K., Astington, J. W., & Flavell, J. H. (1992). Young children's understanding of the role that sensory experiences play in knowledge acquisition. *Child Development, 63*, 474–490.

Offord, D. R., Boyle, M. H., & Racine, Y. A. (1991). The epidemiology of antisocial behavior in childhood and adolescence. In D. J. Pepler & K. H. Rubin (Eds.), *The development and treatment of childhood aggression* (pp. 31–54). Hillsdale, NJ: Erlbaum.

Okamoto, E., Davidson, L. L., & Conner, D. R. (1993). High prevalence of overweight in inner-city schoolchildren. *American Journal of Diseases of Children, 147*, 155–159.

Oller, D. K. (1981). Infant vocalizations: Exploration and reflectivity. In R. E. Stark (Ed.), *Language behavior in infancy and early childhood* (pp. 85–104). New York: Elsevier/North-Holland.

Olshan, A. F., Baird, P. A., & Teschke, K. (1989). Paternal occupational exposures and the risk of Down syndrome. *American Journal of Human Genetics, 44*, 646–651.

Olson, H. C., Sampson, P. D., Barr, H., Streissguth, A. P., & Bookstein, F. L. (1992a). Prenatal exposure to alcohol and school problems in late childhood: A longitudinal prospective study. *Development and Psychopathology, 4*, 341–359.

Olson, S. L., Bates, J. E., & Kaskie, B. (1992b). Caregiver-infant interaction antecedents of children's school-age cognitive ability. *Merrill-Palmer Quarterly, 38*, 309–330.

Overton, W. F., Ward, S. L., Noveck, I. A., Black, J., & O'Brien, D. P. (1987). Form and content in the development of deductive reasoning. *Developmental Psychology, 23*, 22–30.

Padilla, A. M., Lindholm, K. J., Chen, A., Duran, R., Hakuta, K., Lambert, W., & Tucker, G. R. (1991). The English-only movement: Myths, reality, and implications for psychology. *American Psychologist, 46*, 120–130.

Page, D. C., Mosher, R., Simpson, E. M., Fisher, E. M. C., Mardon, G., Pollack, J., McGillivray, B., de la Chapelle, A., & Brown, L. G. (1987). The sex-determining region of the human Y chromosome encodes a finger protein. *Cell, 51*, 1091–1104.

Paikoff, R. L., & Brooks-Gunn, J. (1990). Physiological processes: What role do they play during the transition to adolescence? In R. Montemayor, G. R. Adams, & T. P. Gullotta (Eds.), *From childhood to adolescence. A transitional period?* (pp. 63–81). Newbury Park, CA: Sage.

Palkovitz, R. (1985). Fathers' birth attendance, early contact, and extended contact with their newborns: A critical review. *Child Development, 56*, 392–406.

Panel on High Risk Youth (1993). *Losing generations. Adolescents in high risk settings. Commission on Behavioral and Social Sciences and Education, National Research Council.* Washington, DC: National Academy Press.

Papousek, H., & Papousek, M. (1991). Innate and cultural guidance of infants' integrative competencies: China, the United States, and Germany. In M. H. Bornstein (Ed.), *Cultural approaches to parenting* (pp. 23–44). Hillsdale, NJ: Erlbaum.

Parke, R. D., & Tinsley, B. R. (1981). The father's role in infancy: Determinants of involvement in caregiving and play. In M. E. Lamb (Ed.), *The role of the father in child development* (2nd ed.) (pp. 429–458). New York: Wiley.

Parke, R. D., & Tinsley, B. R. (1984). Fatherhood: Historical and contemporary perspectives. In K. A. McCluskey & H. W. Reese (Eds.), *Life-span developmental psychology. Historical and generational effects* (pp. 203–248). Orlando, FL: Academic Press.

Parmelee, A. H., Jr. (1986). Children's illnesses: Their beneficial effects on behavioral development. *Child Development, 57,* 1–10.

Parmelee, A. H., Jr. , & Sigman, M. D. (1983). Perinatal brain development and behavior. In M. M. Haith & J. J. Campos (Eds.), *Handbook of child psychology: Infancy and developmental psychobiology* (Vol. 2) (pp. 95–156). New York: Wiley.

Parmelee, A. H., Jr., Wenner, W. H., & Schulz, H. R. (1964). Infant sleep patterns from birth to 16 weeks of age. *Journal of Pediatrics, 65,* 576–582.

Parsons, J. E., Adler, T. F., & Daczala, C. M. (1982). Socialization of achievement attitudes and beliefs: Parental influences. *Child Development, 53,* 310–321.

Passman, R. H., & Longeway, K. P. (1982). The role of vision in maternal attachment: Giving 2-year-olds a photograph of their mother during separation. *Developmental Psychology, 18,* 530–533.

Patterson, C. J., Kupersmidt, J. B., & Vaden, N. A. (1990). Income level, gender, ethnicity, and household composition as predictors of children's school-based competence. *Child Development, 61,* 484–494.

Patterson, G. R. (1980). Mothers: The unacknowledged victims. *Monographs of the Society for Research in Child Development, 45* (Serial No. 186).

Patterson, G. R., & Bank, L. (1989). Some amplifying mechanisms for pathological processes in families. In M. R. Gunnar & E. Thelen (Eds.), *Minnesota symposia on child psychology* (Vol. 22) (pp. 167–209). Hillsdale, NJ: Erlbaum.

Patterson, G. R., Capaldi, D., & Bank, L. (1991). An early starter model for predicting delinquency. In D. J. Pepler & K. H. Rubin (Eds.), *The development and treatment of childhood aggression* (pp. 139–168). Hillsdale, NJ: Erlbaum.

Patterson, G. R., DeBarsyshe, B. D., & Ramsey, E. (1989). A developmental perspective on antisocial behavior. *American Psychologist, 44,* 329–335.

Paxton, S. J., Wertheim, E. H., Gibbons, K., Szmukler, G. I., Hillier, L., & Petrovich, J. L. (1991). Body image satisfaction, dieting beliefs, and weight loss behaviors in adolescent girls and boys. *Journal of Youth and Adolescence, 20,* 361–379.

Pederson, D. R., Moran, G., Sitko, C., Campbell, K., Ghesquire, K., & Acton, H. (1990). Maternal sensitivity and the security of infant-mother attachment: A Q-sort study. *Child Development, 61,* 1974–1983.

Pedlow, R., Sanson, A., Prior, M., & Oberklaid, F. (1993). Stability of maternally reported temperament from infancy to 8 years. *Developmental Psychology, 29,* 998–1007.

Pegg, J. E., Werker, J. F., & McLoed, P. J. (1992). Preference for infant-directed over adult-directed speech: Evidence from 7-week-old infants. *Infant Behavior and Development, 15,* 325–345.

Penrod, S. (1993). The child witness, the courts, and psychological research. In C. A. Nelson (Ed.), *Minnesota symposia on child psychology* (Vol. 26) (pp. 159–170). Hillsdale, NJ: Erlbaum.

Perner, J. (1991). On representing that: The asymmetry between belief and desire in children's theory of mind. In D. Frye & C. Moore (Eds.), *Children's theories of mind: Mental states and social understanding* (pp. 139–156). Hillsdale, NJ: Erlbaum.

Petersen, A. C. (1987). The nature of biological-psychosocial interactions: The sample case of early adolescence. In R. M. Lerner & T. T. Foch (Eds.), *Biological-psychosocial interactions in early adolescence* (pp. 35–62). Hillsdale, NJ: Erlbaum.

Petersen, A. C., Compas, B. E., Brooks-Gunn, J., Stemmler, M., Ey, S., & Grant, K. E. (1993). Depression in adolescence. *American Psychologist, 48,* 155–168.

Petersen, A. C., Sarigiani, P. A., & Kennedy, R. E. (1991). Adolescent depression: Why more girls? *Journal of Youth and Adolescence, 20,* 247–272.

Petersen, A. C., & Taylor, B. (1980). The biological approach to adolescence. In J. Adelson (Ed.), *Handbook of adolescent psychology* (pp. 117–158). New York: Wiley.

Peterson, A. C., Compas, B. C., Brooks-Gunn, J., Stemmler, M., Ey, S., & Grant, K. E. (1993). Depression in adolescence. *American Psychologist, 48,* 155–168.

Petitto, L. A. (1988). "Language" in the prelinguistic child. In F. S. Kessell (Ed.), *The development of language and language researchers: Essays in honor of Roger Brown* (pp. 187–222). Hillsdale, NJ: Erlbaum.

Petitto, L. A. (1992). Modularity and constraints in early lexical acquisition: Evidence from children's early language and gesture. In M. R. Gunnar & M. Maratsos (Eds.), *Modularity and constraints in language and cognition* (pp. 25–58). Hillsdale, NJ: Erlbaum.

Pettit, G. S., Bakshi, A., Dodge, K. A., & Coie, J. D. (1990). The emergence of social dominance in young boys' play groups: Developmental differences and behavioral correlates. *Developmental Psychology, 26,* 1017–1025.

Phinney, J. S. (1990). Ethnic identity in adolescents and adults: Review of research. *Psychological Bulletin, 108,* 499–514.

Phinney, J. S., & Rosenthal, D. A. (1992). Ethnic identity in adolescence: Process, context, and outcome. In G. R. Adams, T. P. Gullotta, & R. Montemayor (Eds.), *Adolescent identity formation* (pp. 145–172). Newbury Park, CA: Sage.

Piaget, J. (1932). *The moral judgment of the child.* New York: Macmillan.

Piaget, J. (1952). *The origins of intelligence in children.* New York: International Universities Press.

Piaget, J. (1954). *The construction of reality in the child.* New York: Basic Books. (Original work published 1937).

Piaget, J. (1970). Piaget's theory. In P. H. Mussen (Ed.), *Carmichael's manual of child psychology* (3rd ed., Vol. 1) (pp. 703–732). New York: Wiley.

Piaget, J. (1977). *The development of thought. Equilibration of cognitive structures.* New York: The Viking Press.

Piaget, J., & Inhelder, B. (1959). *La gènese des structures logiques élémentaires: Classifications et sériations* [*The origin of elementary logical structures: Classification and seriation*]. Neuchâtel: Delachaux et Niestlé.

Piaget, J., & Inhelder, B. (1969). *The psychology of the child.* New York: Basic Books.

Pianta, R., Egeland, B., & Erickson, M. F. (1989). The antecedents of maltreatment: Results of the Mother-Child Interaction Research Project. In D. Cicchetti & V. Carlson (Eds.), *Child maltreatment* (pp. 203–253). Cambridge, England: Cambridge University Press.

Pickens, J., & Field, T. (1993). Facial expressivity in infants of depressed mothers. *Developmental Psychology, 29,* 986–988.

Pinker, S. (1987). The bootstrapping problem in language acquisition. In B. MacWhinney (Ed.), *Mechanisms of language acquisition* (pp. 399–442). Hillsdale, NJ: Erlbaum.

Pinker, S. (1994). *The language instinct. How the mind creates language.* New York: William Morrow.

Pitkin, R. M. (1977). Nutrition during pregnancy: The clinical approach. In M. Winick (Ed.), *Nutritional disorders of American women.* New York: Wiley.

Plomin, R. (1989). Environment and genes: Determinants of behavior. *American Psychologist, 44,* 105–111.

Plomin, R., & DeFries, J. C. (1985a). A parent-offspring adoption study of cognitive abilities in early childhood. *Intelligence, 9,* 341–356.

Plomin, R., & DeFries, J. C. (1985b). *Origins of individual differences in infancy. The Colorado Adoption Project.* Orlando, FL: Academic Press.

Plomin, R., Loehlin, J. C., & DeFries, J. C. (1985). Genetic and environmental components of "environmental" influences. *Developmental Psychology, 21,* 391–402.

Plomin, R., Reiss, D., Hetherington, E. M., & Howe, G. W. (1994). Nature and nurture: Genetic contributions to measures of the family environment. *Developmental Psychology, 30,* 32–43.

Plomin, R., & Rende, R. (1991). Human behavioral genetics. *Annual Review of Psychology, 42,* 161–190.

Plomin, R., Rende, R., & Rutter, M. (1991). Quantitative genetics and developmental psychopathology. In D. Cicchetti & S. L. Toth (Eds.), *Internalizing and externalizing expressions of dysfunction: Rochester symposium on developmental psychopathology* (pp. 155–202). Hillsdale, NJ: Erlbaum.

Ponsonby, A., Dwyer, T., Gibbons, L. E., Cochrane, J. A., & Wang, Y. (1993). Factors potentiating the risk of sudden infant death syndrome associatead with the prone position. *The New England Journal of Medicine, 329,* 377–382.

Porter, J. R., & Washington, R. E. (1993). Minority identity and self-esteem. *Annual Review of Sociology, 19,* 139–161.

Porter-Serviss, S., Opheim, E. E., & Hindmarsh, K. W. (1994). Perceptions and attitudes with respect to drug use among grades 4 to 6 students: 1992. *The International Journal of the Addictions, 29,* 225–233.

Poulson, C. L., Nunes, L. R. D., & Warren, S. F. (1989). Imitation in infancy: A critical review. In H. W. Reese (Ed.), *Advances in child development and behavior* (Vol. 22) (pp. 272–298). San Diego, CA: Academic Press.

Power, C., & Reimer, J. (1978). Moral atmosphere: An educational bridge between moral judgment and action. *New Directions for Child Development, 2,* 105–116.

Prechtl, H. F. R., & Beintema, D. J. (1964). *The neurological examination of the full-term newborn infant. Clinics in Developmental Medicine, 12.* London: Hinemann.

Pulkkinen, L. (1982). Self-control and continuity from childhood to late adolescence. In P. Baltes & O. G. Brim, Jr. (Eds.), *Life span development and behavior* (Vol. 4) (pp. 64–107). New York: Academic Press.

Pye, C. (1986). Quiche Mayan speech to children. *Journal of Child Language, 13,* 85–100.

Pyle, R., Mitchell, J., Eckert, E., Halverson, P., Neuman, P., & Goff, G. (1983). The incidence of bulimia in freshman college students. *International Journal of Eating Disorders, 2,* 75–85.

Quiggle, N. L., Garber, J., Panak, W. F., & Dodge, K. A. (1992). Social information processing in aggressive and depressed children. *Child Development, 63,* 1305–1320.

Raja, S. N., McGee, R., & Stanton, W. R. (1992). Perceived attachments to parents and peers and psychological well-being in adolescence. *Journal of Youth and Adolescence, 21,* 471–485.

Ramey, C. T. (1992). High-risk children and IQ: Altering intergenerational patterns. *Intelligence, 16,* 239–256.

Ramey, C. T. (1993). A rejoinder to Spitz's critique of the Abecedarian experiment. *Intelligence, 17,* 25–30.

Ramey, C. T., & Campbell, F. A. (1987). The Carolina Abecedarian Project. An educational experiment concerning human malleability. In J. J. Gallagher & C. T. Ramey (Eds.), *The malleability of children* (pp. 127–140). Baltimore: Paul H. Brookes.

Ramey, C. T., & Haskins, R. (1981a). The modification of intelligence through early experience. *Intelligence*, *5*, 5–19.

Ramey, C. T., & Haskins, R. (1981b). Early education, intellectual development, and school performance: A reply to Arthur Jensen and J. McVicker Hunt. *Intelligence*, *5*, 41–48.

Ramey, C. T., Lee, M. W., & Burchinal, M. R. (1989). Developmental plasticity and predictability: Consequences of ecological change. In M. H. Bornstein & N. A. Krasnegor (Eds.), *Stability and continuity in mental development* (pp. 217–234). Hillsdale, NJ: Erlbaum.

Ramey, C. T., Yeates, K. W., & Short, E. J. (1984). The plasticity of intellectual development: Insights from inventive intervention. *Child Development*, *55*, 1913–1925.

Rappoport, L. (1972). *Personality development: The chronology of experience*. Glenview, IL: Scott, Foresman.

Rawlings, J. S., & Weir, M. R. (1992). Race- and rank-specific mortality in a US military population. *American Journal of Diseases of Childhood*, *146*, 313–316.

Razel, M. (1985). A reanalysis of the evidence for the genetic nature of early motor development. In I. E. Sigel (Ed.), *Advances in applied developmental psychology* (Vol. 1) (pp. 171–212). Norwood, NJ: Ablex.

Reading, R., Raybould, S., & Jarvis, S. (1993). Deprivation, low birth weight, and children's height: A comparison between rural and urban areas. *British Medical Journal*, *307*, 1458–1462.

Ree, M. J., & Earles, J. A. (1992). Intelligence is the best predictor of job performance. *Current Directions in Psychological Science*, *1*, 86–89.

Reinherz, H. Z., Giaconia, R. M., Pakiz, B., Silverman, A. B., Frost, A. K., & Lefkowitz, E. S. (1993). Psychosocial risks for major depression in late adolescence: A longitudinal community study. *Journal of the American Academy of Child and Adolescent Psychiatry*, *32*, 1155–1163.

Reisman, J. M., & Shorr, S. I. (1978). Friendship claims and expectations among children and adults. *Child Development*, *49*, 913–916.

Reiss, D., Plomin, R., Hetherington, E. M., Howe, G. W., Rovine, M., Tryon, A., & Hagan, M. S. (1994). The separate worlds of teenage siblings: An introduction to the study of nonshared environment and adolescent development. In E. M. Hetherington, D. Reiss, & R. Plomin (Eds.), *Separate social worlds of siblings. The impact of nonshared environment on development* (pp. 63–109). Hillsdale, NJ: Erlbaum.

Remafedi, G. (1987a). Adolescent homosexuality: Psychosocial and medical implications. *Pediatrics*, *79*, 331–337.

Remafedi, G. (1987b). Male homosexuality: The adolescent's perspective. *Pediatrics*, *79*, 326–330.

Renouf, A. G., & Harter, S. (1990). Low self-worth and anger as components of the depressive experience in young adolescents. *Development and psychopathology*, *2*, 293–310.

Report of the National Institute (1993). Report of National Institute of Child Health and Human Development workshop on Chorionic Villus Sampling and limb and other defects, October 20, 1992. *Teratology*, *48*, 7–13.

Rest, J. R. (1983). Morality. In J. H. Flavell & E. M. Markman (Eds.), *Handbook of child psychology: Cognitive development* (Vol. 3) (pp. 556–629). New York: Wiley.

Rest, J. R., & Thoma, S. J. (1985). Relation of moral judgment development to formal education. *Developmental Psychology*, *21*, 709–714.

Reynolds, A. J., & Bezruczko, N. (1993). School adjustment of children at risk through fourth grade. *Merrill-Palmer Quarterly*, *39*, 457–480.

Reynolds, C. R., & Brown, R. T. (Eds.). (1984). *Perspectives on bias in mental testing*. New York: Plenum.

Rhoades, E. R., Brenneman, G., Lyle, J., & Handler, A. (1992). Mortality of American Indian and Alaska Native Infants. *Annual Review of Public Health*, *13*, 269–285.

Rholes, W. S., & Ruble, D. N. (1984). Children's understanding of dispositional characteristics of others. *Child Development*, *55*, 550–560.

Ricciuti, H. N. (1993). Nutrition and mental development. *Current Directions in Psychological Science*, *2*, 43–46.

Rice, M. L., Huston, A. C., Truglio, R., & Wright, J. (1990). Words from "Sesame Street": Learning vocabulary while viewing. *Developmental Psychology*, *26*, 421–428.

Richardson, G. A., & Day, N. L. (1994). Detrimental effects of prenatal cocaine exposure: Illusion or reality? *Journal of the American Academy of Child and Adolescent Psychiatry*, *33*, 28–34.

Ridenour, M. V. (1982). Infant walkers: Developmental tool or inherent danger. *Perceptual and Motor Skills*, *55*, 1201–1202.

Rierdan, J., & Koff, E. (1991). Depressive symptomatology among very early maturing girls. *Journal of Youth and Adolescence*, *20*, 415–425.

Rierdan, J., & Koff, E. (1993). Developmental variables in relation to depressive symptoms in adolescent girls. *Development and Psychopathology*, *5*, 485–496.

Rierdan, J., Koff, E., & Stubbs, M. L. (1989). Timing of menarche, preparation, and initial menstrual experience: Replication and further analysis in a prospective study. *Journal of Youth and Adolescence*, *18*, 413–426.

Roberts, R. E., & Sobhan, M. (1992). Symptoms of depression in adolescence: A comparison of Anglo, African, and Hispanic americans. *Journal of Youth and Adolescence*, *21*, 639–651.

Robins, L. N., & McEvoy, L. (1990). Conduct problems as predictors of substance abuse. In L. N. Robins & M. Rutter (Eds.), *Straight and devious pathways from childhood to adulthood* (pp. 182–204). Cambridge, England: Cambridge University Press.

Robinson, H. B. (1981). The uncommonly bright child. In M. Lewis & L. A. Rosenblum (Eds.), *The uncommon child* (pp. 57–82). New York: Plenum.

Robinson, J. L., Kagan, J., Reznick, J. S., & Corley, R. (1992). The heritability of inhibited and uninhibited behavior: A twin study. *Developmental Psychology, 28,* 1030–1037.

Robinson, N. M. (1978). Perinatal life for mother and baby. Common problems of the perinatal period. In D. W. Smith, E. L. Bierman, & N. M. Robinson (Eds.), *The biologic ages of man* (2nd ed.) (pp. 97–106). Philadelphia: Saunders.

Robinson, N. M., & Janos, P. M. (1986). Psychological adjustment in a college-level program of marked academic acceleration. *Journal of Youth and Adolescence, 15,* 51–60.

Rogers, J. (1991). Nontraditional inheritance—I. Mechanisms Mendel never knew. *Mosaic, 22* (Fall), 3–11.

Rohner, R. P., Kean, K. J., & Cournoyer, D. E. (1991). Effects of corporal punishment, perceived caretaker warmth, and cultural beliefs on the psychological adjustment of children in St. Kitts, West Indies. *Journal of Marriage and the Family, 53,* 681–693.

Rollins, B. C., & Feldman, H. (1970). Marital satisfaction over the family life cycle. *Journal of Marriage and the Family, 32,* 20–27.

Rollins, B. C., & Galligan, R. (1978). The developing child and marital satisfaction of parents. In R. M. Lerner & G. M. Spanier (Eds.), *Child influences on marital and family interaction. A life-span perspective* (pp. 71–106). New York: Academic Press.

Rolls, B. J., Fedoroff, I. C., & Guthrie, J. F. (1991). Gender differences in eating behavior and body weight regulation. *Health Psychology, 20,* 133–142.

Rooks, J. P., Weatherby, N. L., Ernst, E. K. M., Stapleton, S., Rosen, D., & Rosenfield, A. (1989). Outcomes of care in birth centers. The national birth center study. *The New England Journal of Medicine, 321,* 1804–1811.

Rose, S. A. (1993). Infant information processing and later intelligence. In D. K. Detterman (Ed.), *Current topics in human intelligence* (Vol. 3) (pp. 31–54). Norwood, NJ: Ablex.

Rose, S. A., & Ruff, H. A. (1987). Cross-modal abilities in human infants. In J. D. Osofsky (Ed.), *Handbook of infant development* (2nd ed.) (pp. 318–362). New York: Wiley-Interscience.

Rosenbaum, J. E. (1984). *Career mobility in a corporate hierarchy.* New York: Academic Press.

Rosenbaum, J. E. (1991). Are adolescent problems caused by school or society? *Journal of Research on Adolescence, 1,* 301–322.

Rosenblith, J. F., & Sims-Knight, J. E. (1989). *In the beginning. Development in the first two years of life.* Newbury Park, CA: Sage.

Ross, G., Kagan, J., Zelazo, P., & Kotelchuck, M. (1975). Separation protest in infants in home and laboratory. *Developmental Psychology, 11,* 256–257.

Rotheram-Borus, M. J., Rosario, M., & Koopman, C. (1991). Minority youths at high risk: Gay males and runaways. In M. E. Colten & S. Gore (Eds.), *Adolescent stress. Causes and consequences* (pp. 181–200). New York: Aldine de Gruyter.

Rovee-Collier, C. (1986). The rise and fall of infant classical conditioning research: Its promise for the study of early development. In L. P. Lipsitt & C. Rovee-Collier (Eds.), *Advances in infancy research* (Vol. 4) (pp. 139–162). Norwood, NJ: Ablex.

Rovee-Collier, C. (1993). The capacity for long-term memory in infancy. *Current Directions in Psychological Science, 2,* 130–135.

Rovet, J., & Netley, C. (1983). The triple X chromosome syndrome in childhood: Recent empirical findings. *Child Development, 54,* 831–845.

Rowe, D. C. (1994). *The limits of family influence: Genes, experience, and behavior.* New York: Guilford Press.

Rowe, I., & Marcia, J. E. (1980). Ego identity status, formal operations, and moral development. *Journal of Youth and Adolescence, 9,* 87–99.

Rubin, K. H., Fein, G. G., & Vandenberg, B. (1983). Play. In E. M. Hetherington (Ed.), *Handbook of child psychology: Socialization, personality, and social development* (Vol. 4) (pp. 693–774). New York: Wiley.

Rubin, K. H., Hymel, S., Mills, R. S. L., & Rose-Krasnor, L. (1991). Conceptualizing different developmental pathways to and from social isolation in childhood. In D. Cicchetti & S. L. Toth (Eds.), *Internalizing and externalizing expressions of dysfunction: Rochester symposium on developmental psychopathology* (Vol. 2) (pp. 91–122). Hillsdale, NJ: Erlbaum.

Ruble, D. N. (1987). The acquisition of self-knowledge: A self-socialization perspective. In N. Eisenberg (Ed.), *Contemporary topics in developmental psychology* (pp. 243–270). New York: Wiley-Interscience.

Ruble, D. N., Balaban, T., & Cooper, J. (1981). Gender constancy and the effects of sex-typed televised toy commercials. *Child Development, 52,* 667–673.

Ruble, T. L. (1983). Sex stereotypes: Issues of change in the 1970's. *Sex Roles, 9,* 397–402.

Russell, G. (1982). Shared-caregiving families: An Australian study. In M. E. Lamb (Ed.), *Nontraditional families* (pp. 139–172). Hillsdale, NJ: Erlbaum.

Russell, J. A. (1989). Culture, scripts, and children's understanding of emotion. In C. Saarni & P. L. Harris (Eds.), *Children's understanding of emotion* (pp. 293–318). Cambridge, England: Cambridge University Press.

Rutter, D. R., & Durkin, K. (1987). Turn-taking in mother-infant interaction: An examination of vocalizations and gaze. *Developmental Psychology, 23,* 54–61.

Rutter, M. (1978). Early sources of security and competence. In J. S. Bruner & A. Garton (Eds.), *Human growth and development*. London: Oxford University Press.

Rutter, M. (1983). School effects on pupil progress: Research findings and policy implications. *Child Development, 54*, 1–29.

Rutter, M. (1987). Continuities and discontinuities from infancy. In J. D. Osofsky (Ed.), *Handbook of infant development* (2nd ed.) (pp. 1256–1296). New York: Wiley-Interscience.

Rutter, M. (1989). Isle of Wight revisited: Twenty-five years of child psychiatric epidemiology. *Journal of the American Academy of Child and Adolescent Psychiatry, 28*, 633–653.

Rutter, M. (1990). Commentary: Some focus and process considerations regarding effects of parental depression on children. *Developmental Psychology, 26*, 60–67.

Rutter, M., & Garmezy, N. (1983). Developmental psychopathology. In E. M. Hetherington (Ed.), *Handbook of child psychology*. Vol. 4, *Socialization, personality, and social development* (pp. 775–912). New York: Wiley.

Rutter, M., Tizard, J., & Whitmore, K. (1981). *Education, health and behaviour*. Huntington, NY: Krieger. (Originally published 1970).

Ryan, A. S., Rush, D., Krieger, F. W., & Lewandowski, G. E. (1991). Recent declines in breast-feeding in the United States, 1984 through 1989. *Pediatrics, 88*, 719–727.

Sack, W. H., Mason, R., & Higgins, J. E. (1985). The single parent family and abusive child punishment. *American Journal of Orthopsychiatry, 55*, 252–259.

Sagi, A. (1990). Attachment theory and research from a cross-cultural perspective. *Human Development, 33*, 10–22.

Sagi, A., van IJzendoorn, M. H., & Koren-Karie, N. (1991). Primary appraisal of the strange situation: A cross-cultural analysis of preseparation episodes. *Developmental Psychology, 27*, 587–596.

Saigal, S., Szatmari, P., Rosenbaum, P., Campbell, D., & King, S. (1991). Cognitive abilities and school performance of extremely low birth weight children and matched term control children at age 8 years: A regional study. *Journal of Pediatrics, 118*, 751–760.

Sameroff, A., Seifer, R., Barocas, R., Zax, M., & Greenspan, S. (1987). Intelligence quotient scores of 4-year-old children: Social-environmental risk factors. *Pediatrics, 79*, 343–350.

Sapir, E. (1929). The status of linguistics as a science. *Language, 5*, 207–214.

Scafidi, F. A., Field, T. M., Schanberg, S. M., Bauer, C. R., Tucci, K., Roberts, J., Morrow, C., & Kuhn, C. M. (1990). Massage stimulates growth in preterm infants: A replication. *Infant Behavior and Development, 13*, 167–188.

Scarr, S., & Eisenberg, M. (1993). Child care research: Issues, perspectives, and results. *Annual Review of Psychology, 44*, 613–644.

Scarr, S., & Kidd, K. K. (1983). Developmental behavior genetics. In M. M. Haith & J. J. Campos (Eds.), *Handbook of child psychology*. Vol. 2, *Infancy and developmental psychobiology* (pp. 345–434). New York: Wiley.

Scarr, S., & Weinberg, R. A. (1983). The Minnesota adoption studies: Genetic differences and malleability. *Child Development, 54*, 260–267.

Schaefer, E. S. (1989). Dimensions of mother-infant interaction: Measurement, stability, and predictive validity. *Infant Behavior and Development, 12*, 379–393.

Schaefli, A., Rest, J. R., & Thoma, S. J. (1985). Does moral education improve moral judgment? A meta-analysis of intervention studies using the Defining Issues Test. *Review of Educational Research, 55*, 319–352.

Schaffer, H. R. (1990). *Making decisions about children. Psychological questions and answers*. Oxford, England: Basil Blackwell.

Schaie, K. W. (1983a). What can we learn from the longitudinal study of adult psychological development? In K. W. Schaie (Ed.), *Longitudinal studies of adult psychological development* (pp. 1–19). New York: Guilford Press.

Schlesinger, H. S., & Meadow, K. P. (1972). *Sound and sign*. Berkeley, CA: University of California Press.

Schneider, M. L. (1992). The effect of mild stress during pregnancy on birthweight and neuromotor maturation in rhesus monkey infants (Macaca mulatta). *Infant Behavior and Development, 15*, 389–403.

Schneider, W., & Pressley, M. (1989). *Memory development between 2 and 20*. New York: Springer-Verlag.

Schoendorf, K. C., Hogue, C. J. R., Kleinman, J. C., & Rowley, D. (1992). Mortality among infants of black as compared with white college-educated parents. *New England Journal of Medicine, 326*, 1522–1526.

Schoendorf, K. C., & Kiely, J. L. (1992). Relationship of Sudden Infant Death Syndrome to maternal smoking during and after pregnancy. *Pediatrics, 90*, 905–908.

Schonfeld, I. S., Shaffer, D., O'Connor, P., & Portny, S. (1988). Conduct disorder and cognitive functioning: Testing three causal hypotheses. *Child Development, 59*, 993–1007.

Schor, E. L. (1987). Unintentional injuries: Patterns within families. *American Journal of the Diseases of Children, 141*, 1280.

Schramm, W. F., Barnes, D. E., & Bakewell, J. M. (1987). Neonatal mortality in Missouri home births, 1978–84. *American Journal of Public Health, 77*, 930–935.

Scollon, R. (1976). *Conversations with a one-year-old*. Honolulu: University of Hawaii Press.

Sears, P. S., & Barbee, A. H. (1977). Career and life satisfactions among Terman's gifted women. In J. C. Stanley, W. C. George, & C. H. Solano (Eds.), *The gifted and the creative* (pp. 28–66). Baltimore: Johns Hopkins University Press.

Seidman, D. S., Ever-Hadani, P., & Gale, R. (1989). The effect of maternal weight gain in pregnancy on birth weight. *Obstetrics and Gynecology, 74,* 240–246.

Seitz, V. (1988). Methodology. In M. H. Bornstein & M. E. Lamb (Eds.), *Developmental psychology: An advanced textbook* (2nd ed.) (pp. 51–84). Hillsdale, NJ: Erlbaum.

Selman, R. L. (1980). *The growth of interpersonal understanding.* New York: Academic Press.

Sepkoski, C. (1987). *A longitudinal study of the effects of obstetric medication.* Paper presented at the biennial meetings of the Society for Research in Child Development, Baltimore.

Serbin, L. A., Powlishta, K. K., & Gulko, J. (1993). The development of sex typing in middle childhood. *Monographs of the Society for Research in Child Development, 58* (2, Serial No. 232).

Serdula, M. K., Ivery, D., Coates, R. J., Freedman, D. S., Williamson, D. F., & Byers, T. (1993). Do obese children become obese adults? A review of the literature. *Preventive Medicine, 22,* 167–177.

Shaffer, D., Garland, A., Gould, M., Fisher, P., & Trautman, P. (1988). Preventing teenage suicide: A critical review. *Journal of the American Academy of Child and Adolescent Psychiatry, 27,* 675–687.

Shaffer, D., Garland, A., Vieland, V., Underwood, M., & Busner, C. (1991). The impact of curriculum-based suicide prevention programs for teenagers. *Journal of the American Academy of Child and Adolescent Psychiatry, 30,* 588–596.

Shantz, C. U. (1983). Social cognition. In J. H. Flavell & E. M. Markman (Eds.), *Handbook of child psychology.* Vol. 3, *Cognitive development* (pp. 495–555). New York: Wiley.

Sherrod, K. B., O'Connor, S., Vietze, P. M., & Altemeier, W. A. I. (1984). Child health and maltreatment. *Child Development, 55,* 1174–1183.

Sherry, B., Springer, D. A., Connell, F. A., & Garrett, S. M. (1992). Short, thin, or obese? Comparing growth indexes of children from high- and low-poverty areas. *Journal of the American Dietetic Association, 92,* 1092–1095.

Shonkoff, J. P. (1984). The biological substrate and physical health in middle childhood. In W. A. Collins (Ed.), *Development during middle childhood. The years from six to twelve* (pp. 24–69). Washington, DC: National Academy Press.

Shore, C. (1986). Combinatorial play, conceptual development, and early multiword speech. *Developmental Psychology, 22,* 184–190.

Shweder, R. A., Mahapatra, M., & Miller, J. G. (1987). Culture and moral development. In J. Kagan & S. Lamb (Eds.), *The emergence of morality in young children* (pp. 1–82). Chicago: The University of Chicago Press.

Siegal, M. (1987). Are sons and daughters treated more differently by fathers than by mothers? *Developmental Review, 7,* 183–209.

Siegler, R. S. (1976). Three aspects of cognitive development. *Cognitive Psychology, 8,* 431–520.

Siegler, R. S. (1978). The origins of scientific reasoning. In R. S. Siegler (Ed.), *Children's thinking: What develops?* (pp. 109–150). Hillsdale, NJ: Erlbaum.

Siegler, R. S. (1981). Developmental sequences within and between concepts. *Monographs of the Society for Research in Child Development, 46* (2, Serial No. 189).

Siegler, R. S. (1992). What do developmental psychologists really want? In M. R. Gunnar & M. Maratsos (Eds.), *Minnesota symposia on child psychology* (Vol. 25) (pp. 221–232). Hillsdale, NJ: Lawrence Erlbaum Associates.

Sigman, M., Neumann, C., Carter, E., Cattle, D. J., D'Souza, S., & Bwibo, N. (1988). Home interactions and the development of Embu toddlers in Kenya. *Child Development, 59,* 1251–1261.

Silverstein, L. B. (1991). Transforming the debate about child care and maternal employment. *American Psychologist, 46,* 1025–1032.

Simmons, R. G., Blyth, D. A., & McKinney, K. L. (1983). The social and psychological effects of puberty on white females. In J. Brooks-Gunn & A. C. Petersen (Eds.), *Girls at puberty. Biological and psychosocial perspectives* (pp. 229–272). New York: Plenum.

Simmons, R. G., Burgeson, R., & Reef, M. J. (1988). Cumulative change at entry to adolescence. In M. R. Gunnar & W. A. Collins (Eds.), *Minnesota symposia on child psychology* (Vol. 21) (pp. 123–150). Hillsdale, NJ: Erlbaum.

Simons, R. L., Robertson, J. F., & Downs, W. R. (1989). The nature of the association between parental rejection and delinquent behavior. *Journal of Youth and Adolescence, 18,* 297–309.

Skinner, B. F. (1957). *Verbal behavior.* New York: Prentice-Hall.

Slaby, R. G., & Frey, K. S. (1975). Development of gender constancy and selective attention to same-sex models. *Child Development, 46,* 849–856.

Slater, A. M., & Bremner, J. G. (Eds.) (1989). *Infant development.* Hillsdale, NJ: Erlbaum.

Slobin, D. I. (1985a). Introduction: Why study acquisition crosslinguistically? In D. I. Slobin (Ed.), *The crosslinguistic study of language acquisition.* Vol. 1, *The data* (pp. 3–24). Hillsdale, NJ: Erlbaum.

Slobin, D. I. (1985b). Crosslinguistic evidence for the language-making capacity. In D. I. Slobin (Ed.), *The crosslinguistic study of language acquisition.* Vol. 2, *Theoretical issues* (pp. 1157–1256). Hillsdale, NJ: Erlbaum.

Smetana, J. G. (1990). Morality and conduct disorders. In M. Lewis & S. M. Miller (Eds.), *Handbook of developmental psychopathology* (pp. 157–180). New York: Plenum.

Smetana, J. G., Killen, M., & Turiel, E. (1991). Children's reasoning about interpersonal and moral conflicts. *Child Development, 62,* 629–644.

Smith, D. W. (1978). Prenatal life. In D. W. Smith, E. L. Bierman, & N. M. Robinson (Eds.), *The biologic ages of man* (2nd. ed.) (pp. 42–62). Philadelphia, PA: W. B. Saunders.

Smoll, F. L., & Schutz, R. W. (1990). Quantifying gender differences in physical performance: A developmental perspective. *Developmental Psychology, 26,* 360–369.

Snarey, J. R. (1985). Cross-cultural universality of social-moral development: A critical review of Kohlbergian research. *Psychological Bulletin, 97,* 202–232.

Snarey, J. R., Reimer, J., & Kohlberg, L. (1985). Development of social-moral reasoning among kibbutz adolescents: A longitudinal cross-sectional study. *Developmental Psychology, 21,* 3–17.

Snyder, L. (1978). Communicative and cognitive abilities and disabilities in the sensorimotor period. *Merrill-Palmer Quarterly, 24,* 161–180.

Soken, N. H., & Pick, A. D. (1992). Intermodal perception of happy and angry expressive behaviors by seven-month-old infants. *Child Development, 63,* 787–795.

Sonenstein, F. L., Pleck, J. H., & Ku, L. C. (1989). Sexual activity, condom use and AIDS awareness among adolescent males. *Family Planning Perspectives, 21,* 152–158.

Sosa, R., Kennell, J. H., Klaus, M. H., Robertson, S., & Urrutia, J. (1980). The effect of a supportive companion on perinatal problems, length of labor and mother-infant interaction. *New England Journal of Medicine, 303,* 597–600.

Spelke, E. S. (1979). Exploring audible and visible events in infancy. In A. D. Pick (Ed.), *Perception and its development: A tribute to Eleanor J. Gibson* (pp. 221–236). Hillsdale, NJ: Erlbaum.

Spelke, E. S. (1991). Physical knowledge in infancy: Reflections on Piaget's theory. In S. Carey & R. Gelman (Eds.), *The epigenesis of mind. Essays on biology and cognition* (pp. 133–169). Hillsdale, NJ: Erlbaum.

Spelke, E. S., & Owsley, C. J. (1979). Intermodal exploration and knowledge in infancy. *Infant Behavior and Development, 2,* 13–27.

Spence, J. T., & Helmreich, R. L. (1978). *Masculinity and femininity.* Austin, TX: University of Texas Press.

Spencer, M. B., & Dornbusch, S. M. (1990). Challenges in studying minority youth. In S. S. Feldman & G. R. Elliott (Eds.), *At the threshold. The developing adolescent* (pp. 123–146). Cambridge, MA: Harvard University Press.

Spieker, S. J., & Booth, C. L. (1988). Maternal antecedents of attachment quality. In J. Belsky & T. Nezworski (Eds.), *Clinical implications of attachment* (pp. 95–135). Hillsdale, NJ: Erlbaum.

Spiers, P. S., & Guntheroth, W. G. (1994). Recommendations to avoid the prone sleeping position and recent statistics for Sudden Infant Death Syndrome in the United States. *Archives of Pediatric and Adolescent Medicine, 148,* 141–146.

Spiker, D. (1990). Early intervention from a developmental perspective. In D. Cicchetti & M. Beeghly (Eds.), *Children with Down syndrome. A developmental perspective* (pp. 424–448). Cambridge, England: Cambridge University Press.

Spiker, D., Ferguson, J., & Brooks-Gunn, J. (1993). Enhancing maternal interactive behavior and child social competence in low birth weight, premature infants. *Child Development, 64,* 754–768.

Sroufe, L. A. (1988). The role of infant-caregiver attachment in development. In J. Belsky & T. Nezworski (Eds.), *Clinical implications of attachment* (pp. 18–40). Hillsdale, NJ: Erlbaum.

Sroufe, L. A. (1989). Pathways to adaptation and maladaptation: Psychopathology as developmental deviation. In D. Cicchetti (Ed.), *The emergence of a discipline: Rochester symposium on developmental psychopathology* (pp. 13–40). Hillsdale, NJ: Erlbaum.

Sroufe, L. A. (1990). A developmental perspective on day care. In N. Fox & G. G. Fein (Eds.), *Infant day care: The current debate* (pp. 51–60). Norwood, NJ: Ablex.

Sroufe, L. A., Carlson, E., & Schulman, S. (1993). Individuals in relationships: Development from infancy through adolescence. In D. C. Funder, R. D. Parke, C. Tomlinson-Keasey, & K. Widaman (Eds.), *Studying lives through time. Personality and development* (pp. 315–342). Washington, DC: American Psychological Association.

Sroufe, L. A., Egeland, B., & Kreutzer, T. (1990). The fate of early experience following developmental change: Longitudinal approaches to individual adaptation in childhood. *Child Development, 61,* 1363–1373.

St. Peters, M., Fitch, M., Huston, A. C., Wright, J. C., & Eakins, D. J. (1991). Television and families: What do young children watch with their parents? *Child Development, 62,* 1409–1423.

Starfield, B. (1991). Childhood morbidity: Comparisons, clusters, and trends. *Pediatrics, 88,* 519–526.

Starfield, B., & Pless, I. B. (1980). Physical health. In O. G. Brim, Jr. & J. Kagan (Eds.), *Constancy and change in human development* (pp. 272–324). Cambridge, MA: Harvard University Press.

Stein, Z., Susser, M., Saenger, G., & Morolla, F. (1975). *Famine and human development: The Dutch hunger winter of 1944–1945.* New York: Oxford University Press.

Steinberg, A. (1993). Hallways, lunchrooms, and football games: How schools help create jocks and burnouts. *The Harvard Education Letter, IX* (May/June), 1–4.

Steinberg, L. (1986). Latchkey children and susceptibility to peer pressure: An ecological analysis. *Developmental Psychology, 22,* 433–439.

Steinberg, L. (1988). Reciprocal relation between parent-child distance and pubertal maturation. *Developmental Psychology, 24,* 122–128.

Steinberg, L. (1990). Autonomy, conflict and harmony in the parent-adolescent relationship. In S. S. Feldman & G. R. Elliott (Eds.), *At the threshold: The developing adolescent* (pp. 255–276). Cambridge, MA: Harvard University Press.

Steinberg, L., & Dornbusch, S. M. (1991). Negative correlates of part-time employment during adolescence: Replication and elaboration. *Developmental Psychology, 27,* 304–313.

Steinberg, L., Dornbusch, S. M., & Brown, B. B. (1992). Ethnic differences in adolescent achievement: An ecological perspective. *American Psychologist, 47,* 723–729.

Steinberg, L., Elmen, J. D., & Mounts, N. S. (1989). Authoritative parenting, psychosocial maturity, and academic success among adolescents. *Child Development, 60,* 1424–1436.

Steinberg, L., Fegley, S., & Dornbusch, S. M. (1993). Negative impact of part-time work on adolescent adjustment: Evidence from a longitudinal study. *Developmental Psychology, 29,* 171–180.

Steinberg, L., Lamborn, S. D., Dornbusch, S. M., & Darling, N. (1992). Impact of parenting practices on adolescent achievement: Authoritative parenting, school involvement, and encouragement to succeed. *Child Development, 63,* 1266–1281.

Steinberg, L., & Levine, A. (1990). *You and your adolescent. A parent's guide for ages 10 to 20.* New York: Harper & Row.

Steinberg, L., Mounts, N. S., Lamborn, S. D., & Dornbusch, S. D. (1991). Authoritative parenting and adolescent adjustment across varied ecological niches. *Journal of Research on Adolescence, 1,* 19–36.

Sternberg, R. J. (1979). The nature of mental abilities. *American Psychologist, 34,* 214–230.

Sternberg, R. J., & Davidson, J. E. (1985). Cognitive development in the gifted and talented. In F. D. Horowitz & M. O'Brien (Eds.), *The gifted and talented. Developmental perspectives* (pp. 37–74). Washington, DC: American Psychological Association.

Sternberg, R. J., & Davidson, J. E. (Eds.). (1986). *Conceptions of giftedness.* Cambridge, England: Cambridge University Press.

Sternberg, R. J., & Wagner, R. K. (1993). The g-ocentric view of intelligence and job performance is wrong. *Current Directions in Psychological Science, 2,* 1–5.

Stevenson, H. W., & Chen, C. (1989). Schooling and achievement: A study of Peruvian children. *International Journal of Educational Research, 13,* 883–894.

Stevenson, H. W., Chen, C., Lee, S., & Fuligni, A. J. (1991). Schooling, culture, and cognitive development. In L. Okagaki & R. J. Sternberg (Eds.), *Directors of development* (pp. 243–268). Hillsdale, NJ: Erlbaum.

Stevenson, H. W., & Lee, S. (1990). Contexts of achievement: A study of American, Chinese, and Japanese children. *Monographs of the Society for Research in Child Development, 55* (1–2, Serial No. 221).

Stevenson, H. W., Lee, S., Chen, C., Lummis, M., Stigler, J., Fan, L., & Ge, F. (1990). Mathematics achievement of children in China and the United States. *Child Development, 61,* 1053–1066.

Steward, M. S. (1993). Understanding children's memories of medical procedures: "He didn't touch me and it didn't hurt!" In C. A. Nelson (Ed.), *Minnesota symposia on child psychology* (Vol. 26) (pp. 171–225). Hillsdale, NJ: Erlbaum.

Stewart, J. F., Popkin, B. M., Guilkey, D. K., Akin, J. S., Adair, L., & Flieger, W. (1991). Influences on the extent of breast-feeding: A prospective study in the Philippines. *Demography, 28,* 181–199.

Stewart, R. B., Cluff, L. E., & Philp, R. (1977). *Drug monitoring: A requirement for responsible drug use.* Baltimore: Williams & Wilkins.

Stigler, J. W., Lee, S., & Stevenson, H. W. (1987). Mathematics classrooms in Japan, Taiwan, and the United States. *Child Development, 58,* 1272–1285.

Stigler, J. W., & Stevenson, H. W. (1991). How Asian teachers polish each lesson to perfection. *American Educator* (Spring), 12–20, 43–47.

Stipek, D. (1992). The child at school. In M. H. Bornstein & M. E. Lamb (Eds.), *Developmental psychology: An advanced textbook* (3rd ed.) (pp. 579–625). Hillsdale, NJ: Erlbaum.

Stipek, D., & Gralinski, H. (1991). Gender differences in children's achievement-related beliefs and emotional responses to success and failure in math. *Journal of Educational Psychology, 83,* 361–371.

Story, M., Rosenwinkel, K., Himes, J. H., Resnick, M., Harris, L. J., & Blum, R. W. (1991). Demographic and risk factors associated with chronic dieting in adolescents. *American Journal of Diseases of Childhood, 145,* 994–998.

Stoutjesdyk, D., & Jevne, R. (1993). Eating disorders among high performance athletes. *Journal of Youth and Adolescence, 22,* 271–282.

Strayer, F. F. (1980). Social ecology of the preschool peer group. In A. Collins (Ed.), *Minnesota symposia on child psychology* (Vol. 13) (pp. 165–196). Hillsdale, NJ: Erlbaum.

Streissguth, A. P., Aase, J. M., Clarren, S. K., Randels, S. P., LaDue, R. A., & Smith, D. F. (1991b). Fetal alcohol syndrome in adolescents and adults. *Journal of the American Medical Association, 265,* 1961–1967.

Streissguth, A. P., Barr, H. M., & Sampson, P. D. (1990). Moderate prenatal alcohol exposure: Effects on child IQ and learning problems at age 7½ years. Alcoholism. *Clinical and Experimental Research, 14,* 662–669.

Streissguth, A. P., Barr, H. M., Sampson, P. D., Darby, B. L., & Martin, D. C. (1989). IQ at age 4 in relation to maternal alcohol use and smoking during pregnancy. *Developmental Psychology, 25,* 3–11.

Streissguth, A. P., Landesman-Dwyer, S., Martin, J. C., & Smith, D. W. (1980). Teratogenic effects of alcohol in humans and laboratory animals. *Science, 209,* 353–361.

Streissguth, A. P., Martin, D. C., Barr, H. M., Sandman, B. M., Kirchner, G. L., & Darby, B. L. (1984). Intrauterine alcohol and nicotine exposure: Attention and reaction time in 4-year-old children. *Developmental Psychology, 20,* 533–541.

Streissguth, A. P., Martin, D. C., Martin, J. C., & Barr, H. M. (1981). The Seattle longitudinal prospective study on alcohol and pregnancy. *Neurobehavioral Toxicology and Teratology, 3,* 223–233.

Striegel-Moore, R. H., Silberstein, L. R., & Rodin, J. (1986). Toward an understanding of risk factors for bulimia. *American Psychologist, 41,* 246–263.

Strobino, D. M. (1987). The health and medical consequences of adolescent sexuality and pregnancy: A review of the literature. In S. L. Hofferth & C. D. Hayes (Eds.), *Risking the future. Adolescent sexuality, pregnancy, and childbearing. Working papers* (pp. 93–122). Washington, DC: National Academy Press.

Stunkard, A. J., Harris, J. R., Pedersen, N. L., & McClearn, G. E. (1990). The body-mass index of twins who have been reared apart. *New England Journal of Medicine, 322,* 1483–1487.

Stunkard, A. J., Sorensen, T. I. A., Hanis, C., Teasdale, T. W., Chakraborty, R., Schull, W. J., & Schulsinger, F. (1986). An adoption study of human obesity. *New England Journal of Medicine, 314,* 193–198.

Sue, S., & Okazaki, S. (1990). Asian-American educational achievements: A phenomenon in search of an explanation. *American Psychologist, 45,* 913–920.

Super, C. M., & Harkness, S. (1982). The infant's niche in rural Kenya and metropolitan America. In L. Adler (Ed.), *Issues in cross-cultural research* (pp. 47–56). New York: Academic Press.

Swedo, S. E., Rettew, D. C., Kuppenheimer, M., Lum, D., Dolan, S., & Goldberger, E. (1991). Can adolescent suicide attempters be distinguished from at-risk adolescents? *Pediatrics, 88,* 620–629.

Sylva, K. (1994). School influences on children's development. *Journal of Child Psychology and Psychiatry, 35,* 135–170.

Taffel, S. M., Placek, P. J., & Liss, T. (1987). Trends in the United States cesarean section rate and reasons for the 1980–85 rise. *American Journal of Public Health, 77,* 955–959.

Takei, Y., & Dubas, J. S. (1993). Academic achievement among early adolescents: Social and cultural diversity. In R. M. Lerner (Ed.), *Early adolescence. Perspectives on research, policy, and intervention* (pp. 175–190). Hillsdale, NJ: Erlbaum.

Tamis-LeMonda, C., & Bornstein, M. H. (1987). Is there a "sensitive period" in human mental development? In M. H. Bornstein (Ed.), *Sensitive periods in development: Interdisciplinary perspectives* (pp. 163–182). Hillsdale, NJ: Erlbaum.

Tanner, J. M. (1962). *Growth at adolescence* (2nd ed.). Oxford: Blackwell Scientific Publications.

Tanner, J. M. (1970). Physical growth. In P. H. Mussen (Ed.), *Carmichael's manual of child psychology* (Vol. 1, 3rd ed.) (pp. 77–156). New York: Wiley.

Tanner, J. M. (1978). *Fetus into man. Physical growth from conception to maturity.* Cambridge, MA: Harvard University Press.

Tanner, J. M., Hughes, P. C. R., & Whitehouse, R. H. (1981). Radiographically determined widths of bone, muscle and fat in the upper arm and calf from 3–18 years. *Annals of Human Biology, 8,* 495–517.

Taylor, M., Cartwright, B. S., & Carlson, S. M. (1993). A developmental investigation of children's imaginary companions. *Developmental Psychology, 29,* 276–285.

Taylor, R. D., Casten, R., Flickinger, S. M., Roberts, D., & Fulmore, C. D. (1994). Explaining the school performance of African-American adolescents. *Journal of Research on Adolescence, 4,* 21–44.

Terman, L. (1916). *The measurement of intelligence.* Boston: Houghton Mifflin.

Terman, L. (1925). *Mental and physical traits of a thousand gifted children* (Vol. 1). *Genetic studies of genius.* Stanford, CA: Stanford University Press.

Terman, L., & Merrill, M. A. (1937). *Measuring intelligence: A guide to the administration of the new revised Stanford-Binet tests.* Boston: Houghton Mifflin.

Terman, L., & Oden, M. (1947). *Genetic studies of genius* (Vol. 4), *The gifted child grows up.* Stanford, CA: Stanford University Press.

Terman, L., & Oden, M. (1959). *Genetic studies of genius* (Vol. 5), *The gifted group at mid-life.* Stanford, CA: Stanford University Press.

Teti, D. M., Gelfand, D. M., & Pompa, J. (1990). Depressed mothers' behavioral competence with their infants: Demographic and psychosocial correlates. *Development and Psychopathology, 2,* 259–270.

Tew, M. (1985). Place of birth and perinatal mortality. *Journal of the Royal College of General Practitioners, 35,* 390–394.

Thal, D., & Bates, E. (1990). Continuity and variation in early language development. In J. Colombo & J. Fagen (Eds.), *Individual differences in infancy: Reliability, stability, prediction* (pp. 359–385). Hillsdale, NJ: Erlbaum.

Thelen, E. (1981). Rhythmical behavior in infancy: An ethological perspective. *Developmental Psychology, 17,* 237–257.

Thelen, E. (1984). Learning to walk: Ecological demands and phylogenetic constraints. In L. P. Lipsitt & C. Rovee-Collier (Eds.), *Advances in infancy research* (Vol. 3) (pp. 213–260). Norwood, NJ: Ablex.

Thelen, E. (1989). The (re)discovery of motor development: Learning new things from an old field. *Developmental Psychology, 25,* 946–949.

Thelen, E. (1992). Development as a dynamic system. *Current Directions in Psychological Science, 1*, 189–193.

Thelen, E., & Adolph, K. E. (1992). Arnold L. Gesell: The paradox of nature and nurture. *Developmental Psychology, 28*, 368–380.

Thomas, A., & Chess, S. (1977). *Temperament and development.* New York: Brunner/Mazel.

Thomas, R. M. (Ed.). (1990). *The encyclopedia of human development and education. Theory, research, and studies.* Oxford: Pergamon Press.

Thomas, R. M. (1990a). Motor development. In R. M. Thomas (Ed.), *The encyclopedia of human development and education. Theory, research, and studies* (pp. 326–330). Oxford: Pergamon Press.

Thompson, S. K. (1975). Gender labels and early sex role development. *Child Development, 46*, 339–347.

Thorne, B. (1986). Girls and boys together . . . but mostly apart: Gender arrangements in elementary schools. In W. W. Hartup & Z. Rubin (Eds.), *Relationships and development* (pp. 167–184). Hillsdale, NJ: Erlbaum.

Thornton, A. (1990). The courtship process and adolescent sexuality. *Journal of Family Issues, 11*, 239–273.

Timmer, S. G., Eccles, J., & O'Brien, K. (1985). How children use time. In F. T. Juster & F. P. Stafford (Eds.), *Time, goods, and well being* (pp. 353–369). Ann Arbor: Institute for Social Research, The University of Michigan.

Tobin-Richards, M. H., Boxer, A. M., & Petersen, A. C. (1983). The psychological significance of pubertal change: Sex differences in perceptions of self during early adolescence. In J. Brooks-Gunn & A. C. Petersen (Eds.), *Girls at puberty. Biological and psychosocial perspectives* (pp. 127–154). New York: Plenum.

Tomasello, M., & Mannle, S. (1985). Pragmatics of sibling speech to one-year-olds. *Child Development, 56*, 911–917.

Tomlinson-Keasey, C., Eisert, D. C., Kahle, L. R., Hardy-Brown, K., & Keasey, B. (1979). The structure of concrete operational thought. *Child Development, 50*, 1153–1163.

Trehub, S. E., Bull, D., & Thorpe, L. A. (1984). Infants' perception of melodies: The role of melodic contour. *Child Development, 55*, 821–830.

Trehub, S. E., & Rabinovitch, M. S. (1972). Auditory-linguistic sensitivity in early infancy. *Developmental Psychology, 6*, 74–77.

Trehub, S. E., Thorpe, L. A., & Morrongiello, B. A. (1985). Infants' perception of melodies: Changes in a single tone. *Infant Behavior and Development, 8*, 213–223.

Tremblay, R. E. (1991). Commentary. Aggression, prosocial behavior, and gender: Three magic words, but no magic wand. In D. J. Pepler & K. H. Rubin (Eds.), *The development and treatment of aggression* (pp. 71–78). Hillsdale, NJ: Erlbaum.

Tronick, E. Z., Morelli, G. A., & Ivey, P. K. (1992). The Efe forager infant and toddler's pattern of social relationships: Multiple and simultaneous. *Developmental Psychology, 28*, 568–577.

Tuna, J. M. (1989). Mental health services for children: The state of the art. *American Psychologist, 44*, 188–199.

Tunmer, W. E., Herriman, M. L., & Nesdale, A. R. (1988). Metalinguistic abilities and beginning reading. *Reading Research Quarterly, 23*, 134–158.

Turiel, E. (1966). An experimental test of the sequentiality of developmental stages in the child's moral judgment. *Journal of Personality and Social Psychology, 3*, 611–618.

Umberson, D., & Gove, W. R. (1989). Parenthood and psychological well-being. Theory, measurement, and stage in the family life course. *Journal of Family Issues, 10*, 440–462.

Underwood, M. K., Coie, J. D., & Herbsman, C. R. (1992). Display rules for anger and aggression in school-age children. *Child Development, 63*, 366–380.

Ungerer, J. A., & Sigman, M. (1984). The relation of play and sensorimotor behavior to language in the second year. *Child Development, 55*, 1448–1455.

United States Bureau of the Census (1990). *Statistical abstract of the United States, 1990* (110th ed.). Washington, DC: U.S. Government Printing Office.

United States Bureau of the Census (1993). *Statistical Abstract of the United States, 1993* (113th ed.). Washington, DC: U.S. Government Printing Office.

Upchurch, D. M. (1993). Early schooling and childbearing experiences: Implications for post-secondary school attendance. *Journal of Research on Adolescence, 3*, 423–443.

Urban, J., Carlson, E., Egeland, B., & Sroufe, L. A. (1991). Patterns of individual adaptation across childhood. *Development and Psychopathology, 3*, 445–460.

Urberg, K. A., & Labouvie-Vief, G. (1976). Conceptualizations of sex roles: A life-span developmental study. *Developmental Psychology, 12*, 15–23.

Valdez-Menchaca, M. C., & Whitehurst, G. J. (1992). Accelerating language development through picture book reading: A systematic extension to Mexican day care. *Developmental Psychology, 28*, 1106–1114.

Van de Perre, P., Simonen, A., Msellati, P., Hitimana, D., Vaira, D., Bazebagira, A., Van Goethem, C., Stevens, A., Karita, E., Sondag-Thull, D., Dabis, F., & Lepage, P. (1991). Postnatal transmission of human immunodeficiency virus type 1 from mother to infant. *New England Journal of Medicine, 325*, 593–598.

van IJzendoorn, M. H., Goldberg, S., Kroonenberg, P. M., & Frenkel, O. J. (1992). The relative effects of maternal and child problems on the quality of attachment: A meta-analysis of attachment in clinical samples. *Child Development, 63*, 840–858.

van IJzendoorn, M. H., & Kroonenberg, P. M. (1988). Cross-cultural patterns of attachment: A meta-analysis of the Strange Situation. *Child Development, 59,* 147–156.

Van Kammen, W. B., Loeber, R., & Stouthamer-Loeber, M. (1991). Substance use and its relationship to conduct problems and delinquency in young boys. *Journal of Youth and Adolescence, 20,* 399–413.

Vernberg, E. M., Ewell, K. K., Beery, S. H., & Abwender, D. A. (1994). Sophistication of adolescents' interpersonal negotiation strategies and friendship formation after relocation: A naturally occurring experiment. *Journal of Research on Adolescence, 4,* 5–19.

Vernon, P. A. (Ed.). (1987). *Speed of information-processing and intelligence.* Norwood, NJ: Ablex.

Vernon, P. A. (1993). Intelligence and neural efficiency. In D. K. Detterman (Ed.), *Current topics in human intelligence.* Vol. 3, *Individual differences and cognition* (pp. 171–187). Horwood, NJ: Ablex.

Victoria Infant Collaborative Study Group (1991). Eight-year outcome in infants with birth weight of 500–999 grams: Continuing regional study of 1979 and 1980 births. *Journal of Pediatrics, 118,* 761–767.

Vihko, R., & Apter, D. (1980). The role of androgens in adolescent cycles. *Journal of Steroid Biochemistry, 12,* 369–373.

Vorhees, C. F., & Mollnow, E. (1987). Behavioral teratogenesis: Long-term influences on behavior from early exposure to environmental agents. In J. D. Osofsky (Ed.), *Handbook of infant development* (2nd ed.) (pp. 913–971). New York: Wiley-Interscience.

Vuchinich, S., Bank, L., & Patterson, G. R. (1992). Parenting, peers, and the stability of antisocial behavior in preadolescent boys. *Developmental Psychology, 28,* 510–521.

Vygotsky, L. S. (1962). *Thought and language.* New York: Wiley.

Wachs, T. D., Bishry, Z., Sobhy, A., McCabe, G., Galal, O., & Shaheen, F. (1993). Relation of rearing environment to adaptive behavior of Egyptian toddlers. *Child Development, 64,* 586–604.

Wagner, R. K., Torgesen, J. K., & Rashotte, C. A. (1994). Development of reading-related phonological processing abilities: New evidence of bidirectional causality from a latent variable longitudinal study. *Developmental Psychology, 30,* 73–87.

Wahlström, J. (1990). Gene map of mental retardation. *Journal of Mental Deficiency Research, 34,* 11–27.

Wald, E. R., Guerra, N., & Byers, C. (1991). Frequency and severity of infections in day care: Three-year follow-up. *Journal of Pediatrics, 118,* 509–514.

Walden, T. A. (1991). Infant social referencing. In J. Garber & K. A. Dodge (Eds.), *The development of emotion regulation and dysregulation* (pp. 69–88). Cambridge, England: Cambridge University Press.

Waldrop, M. F., & Halverson, C. F. (1975). Intensive and extensive peer behavior: Longitudinal and cross-sectional analysis. *Child Development, 46,* 19–26.

Walker, H., Messinger, D., Fogel, A., & Karns, J. (1992). Social and communicative development in infancy. In V. B. Van Hasselt & M. Hersen (Eds.), *Handbook of social development. A lifespan perspective* (pp. 157–181). New York: Plenum Press.

Walker, L. J. (1980). Cognitive and perspective-taking prerequisites for moral development. *Child Development, 51,* 131–139.

Walker, L. J. (1989). A longitudinal study of moral reasoning. *Child Development, 60,* 157–160.

Walker, L. J., de Vries, B., & Trevethan, S. D. (1987). Moral stages and moral orientations in real-life and hypothetical dilemmas. *Child Development, 58,* 842–858.

Walker-Andrews, A. S., & Lennon, E. (1991). Infants' discrimination of vocal expressions: Contributions of auditory and visual information. *Infant Behavior and Development, 14,* 131–142.

Wallerstein, J. (1989, January 22). Children after divorce. Wounds that don't heal. *The New York Times Magazine,* p. 19–21, 41–44.

Wallerstein, J. S. (1984). Children of divorce: Preliminary report of a ten-year follow-up of young children. *American Journal of Orthopsychiatry, 54,* 444–458.

Walton, G. E., Bower, N. J. A., & Bower, T. G. R. (1992). Recognition of familiar faces by newborns. *Infant Behavior and Development, 15,* 265–269.

Walton, G. E., & Bower, T. G. R. (1993). Amodal representation of speech in infants. *Infant Behavior and Development, 16,* 233–253.

Ward, S. L., & Overton, W. F. (1990). Semantic familiarity, relevance, and the development of deductive reasoning. *Developmental Psychology, 26,* 488–493.

Waterman, A. S. (1985). Identity in the context of adolescent psychology. *New Directions for Child Development, 30,* 5–24.

Watson, J. D., & Crick, F. H. C. (1953). Molecular structure of nucleic acid. A structure for deoxyribose nucleic acid. *Nature, 171,* 737–738.

Watson, M. W., & Getz, K. (1990a). Developmental shifts in Oedipal behaviors related to family role understanding. *New Directions for Child Development, 48,* 5–28.

Watson, M. W., & Getz, K. (1990b). The relationship between Oedipal behaviors and children's family role concepts. *Merrill-Palmer Quarterly, 36,* 487–506.

Waxman, S., & Gelman, R. (1986). Preschoolers' use of superordinate relations in classification and language. *Cognitive Development, 1,* 139–156.

Waxman, S. R., & Hall, D. G. (1993). The development of a linkage between count nouns and object categories:

Evidence from fifteen- to twenty-one-month-old infants. *Child Development, 64,* 1224–1241.

Waxman, S. R., & Kosowski, T. D. (1990). Nouns mark category relations: Toddlers' and preschoolers' word-learning biases. *Child Development, 61,* 1461–1473.

Webster-Stratton, C. (1988). Mothers' and fathers' perceptions of child deviance: Roles of parent and child adjustment and child deviance. *Journal of Consulting and Clinical Psychology, 56,* 909–915.

Wechsler, D. (1974). *Manual for the Wechsler Intelligence Scale for Children—Revised.* New York: Psychological Corp.

Wegman, M. E. (1992). Annual summary of vital statistics—1991. *Pediatrics, 90,* 835–845.

Wegman, M. E. (1993). Annual summary of vital statistics—1992. *Pediatrics, 82,* 743–754.

Weinberg, R. A. (1989). Intelligence and IQ: Landmark issues and great debates. *American Psychologist, 44,* 98–104.

Weinberg, R. A., Scarr, S., & Waldman, I. D. (1992). The Minnesota transracial adoption study: A follow-up of IQ test performance. *Intelligence, 16,* 117–135.

Weisner, T. S. (1984). Ecocultural niches of middle childhood: A cross-cultural perspective. In W. A. Collins (Ed.), *Development during middle childhood. The years from six to twelve* (pp. 335–369). Washington, D. C.: National Academy Press.

Weisz, J. R., Sigman, M., Weiss, B., & Mosk, J. (1993). Parent reports of behavioral and emotional problems among children in Kenya, Thailand, and the United States. *Child Development, 64,* 98–109.

Wellman, H. M. (1982). The foundations of knowledge: concept development in the young child. In S. G. Moore & C. C. Cooper (Eds.), *The young child. Reviews of research* (Vol. 3) (pp. 115–134). Washington, DC: National Association for the Education of Young Children.

Wellman, H. M. (1988). First steps in the child's theorizing about the mind. In J. W. Astington, P. L. Harris, & D. R. Olson (Eds.), *Developing theories of mind* (pp. 64–92). New York: Cambridge University Press.

Wen, S. W., Goldenberg, R. L., Cutter, G. R., Hoffman, H. J., Cliver, S. P., Davis, R. O., & DuBard, M. D. (1990). Smoking, maternal age, fetal growth, and gestational age at delivery. *American Journal of Obstetrics and Gynecology, 162,* 53–58.

Werker, J. F., & Tees, R. C. (1984). Cross-language speech perception: Evidence for perceptual reorganization during the first year of life. *Infant Behavior and Development, 7,* 49–63.

Werner, E. E. (1986). A longitudinal study of perinatal risk. In D. C. Farran & J. D. McKinney (Eds.), *Risk in intellectual and psychosocial development* (pp. 3–28). Orlando, FL: Academic Press.

Werner, E. E. (1994). Risk, resilience, and recovery: Perspectives from the Kauai Longitudinal Study. *Development and Psychopathology, 5,* 503–515.

Werner, E. E., & Smith, R. S. (1982). *Vulnerable but invincible: A study of resilient children.* New York: McGraw-Hill.

Werner, E. E., & Smith, R. S. (1992). *Overcoming the odds. High risk children from birth to adulthood.* Ithaca, NY: Cornell University Press.

Werner, H. (1948). *Comparative psychology of mental development.* Chicago: Follett.

Whitehurst, G. J., Falco, F. L., Lonigan, C. J., Fischel, J. E., DeBaryshe, B. D., Valdez-Menchaca, M. C., & Caulfield, M. (1988). Accelerating language development through picture book reading. *Developmental Psychology, 24,* 552–559.

Whiting, B. B., & Edwards, C. P. (1988). *Children of different worlds: The formation of social behavior.* Cambridge, MA: Harvard University Press.

Wiesenfeld, A. R., Malatesta, C. Z., & DeLoach, L. L. (1981). Differential parental response to familiar and unfamiliar infant distress signals. *Infant Behavior and Development, 4,* 281–296.

Wigfield, A., Eccles, J. S., MacIver, D., Reuman, D. A., & Midgley, C. (1991). Transitions during early adolescence: Changes in children's domain-specific self-perceptions and general self-esteem across the transition to junior high school. *Developmental Psychology, 27,* 552–565.

Wilcox, A. J., Weinberg, C. R., O'Connor, J. F., Baird, D. D., Schlatterer, J. P., Canfield, R. E., Armstrong, E. G., & Nisula, B. C. (1988). Incidence of early loss of pregnancy. *New England Journal of Medicine, 319,* 189–194.

Williams, J. E., & Best, D. L. (1990). *Measuring sex stereotypes. A multination study* (rev. ed.). Newbury Park, CA: Sage.

Willig, A. (1985). Meta-analysis of studies on bilingual education. *Review of Educational Research, 55,* 269–317.

Windle, M., Miller-Tutzauer, C., & Domenico, D. (1992). Alcohol use, suicidal behavior, and risky activities among adolescents. *Journal of Research on Adolescents, 2,* 317–330.

Winick, M. (1980). *Nutrition in health and disease.* New York: Wiley.

Woodward, A. L., & Markman, E. M. (1991). Constraints on learning as default assumptions: Comments on Merriman & Bowman's "The mutual exclusivity bias in children's word learning". *Developmental Review, 11,* 137–163.

World Health Organization (1981). *Contemporary patterns of breast-feeding. Report on the WHO collaborative study on breast-feeding.* Geneva: World Health Organization.

Youngblade, L. M., & Belsky, J. (1992). Parent-child antecedents of 5-year-olds' close friendships: A longitudinal analysis. *Developmental Psychology, 28,* 700–713.

Zahn-Waxler, C., & Radke-Yarrow, M. (1982). The development of altruism: Alternative research strategies. In N. Eisenberg (Ed.), *The development of prosocial behavior* (pp. 109–138). New York: Academic Press.

Zametkin, A. J., Nordahl, T. E., Gross, M., King, A. C., Semple, W. E., Rumsey, J., Hamburger, S., & Cohen, R. M. (1990). Cerebral glucose metabolism in adults with hyperactivity of childhood onset. *New England Journal of Medicine, 323,* 1361–1366.

Zaslow, M. J., & Hayes, C. D. (1986). Sex differences in children's responses to psychosocial stress: Toward a cross-context analysis. In M. E. Lamb, A. L. Brown, & B. Rogoff (Eds.), *Advances in developmental psychology* (Vol. 4) (pp. 285–238). Hillsdale, NJ: Erlbaum.

Zelazo, N. A., Zelazo, P. R., Cohen, K. M., & Zelazo, P. D. (1993). Specificity of practice effects on elementary neuromotor patterns. *Developmental Psychology, 29,* 686–691.

Zeskind, P. S., & Lester, B. M. (1978). Acoustic features and auditory perceptions of the cries of newborns with prenatal and perinatal complications. *Child Development, 49,* 580–589.

Zeskind, P. S., & Ramey, C. T. (1981). Preventing intellectual and interactional sequelae of fetal malnutrition: A longitudinal, transactional, and synergistic approach to development. *Child Development, 52,* 213–218.

Zigler, E., & Hall, N. W. (1989). Physical child abuse in America: Past, present, and future. In D. Cicchetti & V. Carlson (Eds.), *Child maltreatment* (pp. 38–75). Cambridge, England: Cambridge University Press.

Zigler, E., & Hodapp, R. M. (1991). Behavioral functioning in individuals with mental retardation. *Annual Review of Psychology, 42,* 29–50.

Zoccolillo, M. (1993). Gender and the development of conduct disorder. *Development and Psychopathology, 5,* 65–78.

CREDITS

1: Myrleen Ferguson/PhotoEdit; 2: Paul Conklin; 7: David Young-Wolff/PhotoEdit; 13: Daemmrich/The Image Works; 16: Myrleen Ferguson/PhotoEdit; 19: Jim Whitmer; 23: Laura Dwight; 29: David Young-Wolff/Tony Stone Worldwide; 30: Robert Brenner/PhotoEdit; 36: Jerry Howard/Positive Images; 38: Myrleen Ferguson/PhotoEdit; 41: Don Smetzer; 46: Laura Dwight; 50: Michael Heron/Monkmeyer Press Photo Service; 52: Tony Freeman/PhotoEdit; 54: Laura Dwight; 61: Julie Marcotte/Stock Boston; 62: LeRoy/SPL/Photo Researchers; 72: Laura Dwight; 79: Streissguth; 82: Laura Dwight; 86: S.I.U./Peter Arnold, Inc.; 88: David Young-Wolff/PhotoEdit; 90: Hyman/Stock Boston; 97:Elizabeth Crews/The Image Works; 100 (all): *From The Neurological Examination of the Full Term Newborn Infant*, by Heinz F. R. Prechtl, Second Edition; *A Manual for Clinical Use* from the Department of Developmental Neurology, University of Groningen; *Clinics in Developmental Medicine*, No. 63, 1977. Spastics International Medical Publications, now MacKeith Press; London: William Heinemann Medical Books Ltd.; Philadelphia: J. B. Lippincott Co. Printed in England by The Lavenham Press Ltd., Lavenham, Suffolk; 101: Photo Researchers, Inc.; 107: Laura Dwight; 112 (all): Laura Dwight; 114: Laura Dwight; 121: Laura Dwight; 123 (all): Laura Dwight; 124: Laura Dwight; 128: Laura Dwight; 129: From Carolyn Rovee-Collier, *Current Directions in Psychological Science*, 2(4), 130–135. 1993; 131: Laura Dwight; 135: Laura Dwight; 136 (all): Zimbel/Monkmeyer Press Photo Service; 140: Tiffany Field; 144: Laura Dwight; 148: Laura Dwight; 153: Laura Dwight; 154: Myrleen Ferguson/PhotoEdit; 158 (all): Laura Dwight; 159: Laura Dwight; 164: Laura Dwight; 171: PhotoEdit; 173: Laura Dwight; 175: Jim Harrison/Stock Boston; 178: Bob Daemmrich/Stock Boston; 189: Laura Dwight; 191: Brent Jones; 196: Laura Dwight; 197: Miro Vintoniv/Stock Boston; 199: Laura Dwight; 205 (all): Laura Dwight; 207 (all): Laura Dwight; 213: Laura Dwight; 214: Bob Daemmrich; 217: Elizabeth Crews/The Image Works; 223: Myrleen Ferguson/PhotoEdit; 224: Laura Dwight; 226: Martin Rogers/Stock Boston; 229: Elizabeth Crews/The Image Works; 231: Laura Dwight; 236: Laura Dwight; 238: Willie Hill/The Image Works; 239: Laura Dwight; 242 (all): Photos from *Unmasking the Face* by Paul Ekman and Wallace V.

Friesen, Prentice Hall, 1975; 244: Laura Dwight; 252: Phil Borden/PhotoEdit; 259: Laura Dwight; 260 (right): Paul Conklin; 260 (left): Robert Frerck; 263: PhotoEdit; 267: Daemmrich/The Image Works; 272: R. Sidney/The Image Works; 276: Tony Freeman/PhotoEdit; 280: Tony Freeman/PhotoEdit; 283: David Young-Wolff/PhotoEdit; 285: Bob Daemmrich/Stock Boston; 295: Daemmrich Photos; 297: Freeman/Grishaber/PhotoEdit; 302: Tony Freeman/PhotoEdit; 304: Tony Freeman/PhotoEdit; 306: Daemmrich/The Image Works; 308: Michael Newman/PhotoEdit; 314: Burt Glinn/Magnum Photos; 316: Hache/Photo Researchers; 325: Daemmrich/Stock Boston; 326: Daniel Laine/Actuel; 331: Tanner, 1962; 335: David Young-Wolff; 339: Gale Zucker/Stock Boston; 342 (right): Robert Brenner/PhotoEdit; 342 (left): Michael Newman/PhotoEdit; 346: William Thompson; 351: John Warner/St. Labre Indian School, Ashland, Montana; 353: Elizabeth Crews/The Image Works; 360: Bob Daemmrich/The Image Works; 361: J. C. Francolon/Gamma-Liaison; 364: Willie Hill, Jr./The Image Works; 366: D&I MacDonald/PhotoEdit; 369: Billy E. Barnes/Stock Boston; 370: Bob Daemmrich Photos/Stock Boston; 374: W. Hill, Jr./The Image Works; 377: Michael Newman/PhotoEdit; 384: Mary Kate Denny/PhotoEdit; 387: Winter/The Image Works; 390: Willie L. Hill/The Image Works; 393: Jerry Howard/Positive Images; 393: Laura Dwight; 397: J. P. Laffont/Sygma; 400: Daemmrich Photos; 409: David Ximeno Tejada/Tony Stone Worldwide; 414: Laura Dwight; 418: Myrleen Ferguson/PhotoEdit; 421: Tom & Deeann McCarthy/The Stock Market; 423: Jerry Howard/Positive Images; 426: Stephen Shames/Matrix; 428: Dal Bayles/NYT Pictures; 429: Gaye Hilsenrath/The Picture Cube; 430: Tony Freeman/PhotoEdit

Name Index

Subject Index

Abstract modeling, 40–41
Abuse, child:
  consequences of, *245*
  and failure of bonding, *160*
  spanking and, *246*
Accidents:
  in adolescence, 340–347
  automobile, 192, 341
  in middle childhood, 262
  in preschool years, 191–192
Accommodation, 54
Achievement:
  adolescents and, 369
  parenting and, 372–373
Achievement tests, 282, 284–286, *288*
Acute illnesses, 191
Adaptation:
  by babies, 124
  by family of atypical child, 433
  by humans, 53
Adaptive behavior, 422
Adaptive reflexes, 99–100
ADD (attention deficit hyperactivity disorder), 415–418
Adolescence:
  basic characteristics of, 405–406
  body image and, *347*
  central processes in, 406–408
  cognitive development in, 351–376
  culture and, *327*, *383*, 399–402
  depression in, 418–420
  deviant behavior in, 396–399
  health in, 340–347
  height, shape, muscles, and fat in, 329–332, *347*
  heterosexual relationships in, 393–395
  homosexuality in, *394*
  hormones and, 326, 328–329
  identity in, 380–382, *383*
  individual differences in, 395–399
  initiation rituals of, *327*
  jobs in, 400–402
  moral reasoning in, 357–368
  parents and, 385–390
  peer relationships in, 390–395
  personality differences in, 395–396
  physical development in, 325–349
  pregnancy in, 339–340
  pubertal development in, *333*, 335–337
  relationships in, 378–395
  risky behavior in, 340–343
  schooling and, 368–375

  self-concept in, 378–385
  self-esteem in, 382, 384
  sexuality in, 337–340
  sexual maturity in, 332–335
  social behavior and personality in, 377–404
  suicide in, 344–345
Adopted children:
  and heredity vs. environment, 32
  IQ of, *32*, 215
  temperament and, 34
Adrenal androgen, 328
Affectional bonds, defined, 154, 155
AFP (alpha-feloprotein test), *75*
African-Americans:
  adolescent sexuality of, 338–340, 393
  breast-feeding by, *106*
  cultural values of, *12*
  early physical development of, *118*
  as ethnic and racial category, 10
  ethnic identity in adolescence of, *383*
  family structure of, 249–250
  infant mortality of, 11, 93, 116
  inherited diseases of, *74*
  IQ tests and, 219–220, 282–284
  low-birth-weight babies of, 90
  mental retardation and, 423
  obesity and, 263
  parenting styles and, 373–375
  peer influence of, *391*
  poverty and, 311–312, 340
  school dropout rates of, 370
  social relationships of, 388
  teenage pregnancy and, 339–340
Afterbirth, 86
Age:
  cohorts and, 18
  conformity and, 390–392
  learning and, 39, 41
  moral reasoning and, 361–363
  pregnancy and, 81–83
Agency, 170
Aggression:
  abuse and, *245*
  as conduct disorder, 414
  continuity of, 415
  day care and, 177–178
  defined, 230
  in middle childhood, 303–305
  of preschoolers, 230–231
  rejection and, 309–311, *310*